# THE NEW ILLUSTRATED

NEW & REVISED

# FAMILY MEDICAL & HEALTH GUIDE

## BY THE EDITORS OF
## CONSUMER GUIDE®

## WITH IRA J. CHASNOFF, M.D., JEFFREY W. ELLIS, M.D., AND ZACHARY S. FAINMAN, M.D.

PUBLICATIONS INTERNATIONAL, LTD.

# TABLE OF CONTENTS

**Notice:**
In this book, the authors and editors have done their best to outline the symptoms and general treatment for various conditions, injuries, and diseases. Also, recommendations are made regarding certain drugs, medications, and preparations; and descriptions of certain medical tests and procedures are offered.

Different people react to the same treatment, medication, preparation, test, or procedure in different ways. This book does not attempt to answer all questions about all situations that you may encounter.

Neither the Editors of CONSUMER GUIDE® and Publications International, Ltd., nor the consultants, authors, or publisher take responsibility for any possible consequences from any treatment, procedure, test, action, or application of medication or preparation by any person reading or following the information in this book. The publication of this book does not constitute the practice of medicine, and this book does not attempt to replace your physician. The authors and publisher advise the reader to check with a physician before administering any medication or undertaking any course of treatment.

Medical Consultants:
    Ira J. Chasnoff, M.D., Pediatrics
    Jeffrey W. Ellis, M.D., Obstetrics and Gynecology
    Zachary S. Fainman, M.D., Internal Medicine
Consultant for Prescription Drugs:
    Nicola Giacona, Pharm.D.

Illustrations: Teri J. McDermott, M.A., Medical Illustrator

# INTRODUCTION

The objective of *The New Illustrated Family Medical & Health Guide* is to help you take charge of your family's health care. The best way to begin is to become a knowledgeable patient and an informed consumer of health services.

Health care in America is changing rapidly. Health-care providers increasingly view patients as consumers of their services, and each person is being called on to accept the responsibility of making informed decisions about his own health. Each day brings reports of sophisticated new diagnostic techniques and methods of treatment, but this outpouring of information can be more overwhelming than it is reassuring. To take full advantage of this new era in medicine, you owe it to yourself and your family to learn all you can about safeguarding your health. *The New Illustrated Family Medical & Health Guide* provides a wealth of information about medical care and health practices that will help you make crucial decisions for your family.

This book is designed to help the one person who is ultimately responsible for your health and the health of your family—you. After all, you are the one person who can closely monitor your physical well-being and regulate your personal health habits on a daily basis. You are the one who decides what you eat, how much you exercise, and where you go when a medical problem arises. You are the one who

wishes to avoid expensive trips to the doctor while at the same time being prudent about obtaining medical advice when it is truly necessary. You are the one who is most directly concerned with preserving your good health and preventing illness. *The New Illustrated Family Medical & Health Guide*, with its wide coverage of health and medical topics, will give you the information you need to protect the health and well-being of every member of your family.

This book offers important information on making the right decisions about nutrition and lifestyle changes and on recognizing and coping with common symptoms. You will also find advice on how to select the doctor who is the most appropriate for your family's medical needs, as well as explanations of the various specialties in medicine— from anesthesiology to urology.

To help you understand disease as a departure from the normal healthy state, *The New Illustrated Family Medical & Health Guide* offers a survey of the human body and how it works in sickness and in health. There are chapters on each of the various organ systems of the body, with clear explanations of how they function in the healthy body and what has gone wrong in various abnormal conditions. In those sections that describe a disease or disorder, the cause, the risk factors, the symptoms, the treatment, and the prognosis are discussed, and preventive action is

outlined, if available. Each entry is as inclusive as possible, with language that is clear and understandable.

As you read on, you will learn about commonly administered clinical and laboratory tests and other diagnostic procedures. If you have to undergo tests, you will know what to expect, how to prepare yourself so as to experience as little discomfort as possible, and what the results may indicate.

If your doctor prescribes a medication, you will learn how to read the prescription and interpret the directions. There is also important information about saving money on prescriptions when you buy drugs and about storing your medications so as to preserve their effectiveness.

This book is intended as a home adviser about health and medical problems. However, it is not a substitute for your own doctor. If you suspect that you may need medical care, you should always consult a physician. The information in this book will help you to communicate with the doctor about your medical problems and concerns and to understand the basis for your doctor's treatment plan.

Remember that maintaining good health is a team effort between you and your doctor. With the help of *The New Illustrated Family Medical & Health Guide*, you can become a more active participant in protecting your family's health. Read it in good health!

# STAYING HEALTHY

Medicine and health care today are based on the premise that definite physical factors are responsible for diseases and disorders. The discovery in the nineteenth century that microorganisms cause many infectious diseases led to remarkable advances in medical care. So for many years, the public relied on the miracles of medicine to cure illnesses and to prolong life as much as possible.

In this century, noninfectious disorders—cancer, heart disease, hypertension, birth defects—have become the major causes of sickness and death. Modern medical research shows more and more that it is what individuals do for themselves and how they take care of their bodies that make the greatest difference in the length and quality of their lives.

Most people are born healthy, with bodies meant to last a full lifetime. Many diseases and disorders can be prevented with a healthy lifestyle. That includes eating nutritious meals, exercising regularly, controlling weight, getting adequate sleep and rest, avoiding hazardous substances and harmful habits, and having regular physical examinations.

The effects of abusing our health by such practices as smoking cigarettes, consuming a high-fat diet, and overindulging in alcohol do not usually show up for years. By then, it is often too late to reverse the ill effects.

In contrast, following the simple guidelines for a healthy lifestyle produces immediate results—a better-looking body, more energy, and less need for expensive medical care. Even those with inherited tendencies to suffer from certain disorders can decrease the risk of developing problems by taking care of themselves.

Good health in the future depends on taking care of your body today. Practicing preventive health care does not guarantee that a person will live past 100 years of age or run marathons at age 90, but neither does it mean living a life of constant denial or deprivation. It does involve changing some habits and learning new ways.

Be an active participant and take responsibility for your health. You have taken the first step by picking up this book. Read it and learn more about how the body functions. Be aware of the seven warning signs of cancer and be attuned to the changes in your body that could be symptoms of illness. Think about the quality of your life and the ways that your family can practice preventive medicine to stay healthy.

A man who was celebrating his 100th birthday was asked what advice he could give about living a long life. The man replied, "Keep breathing!" Good advice, but as you will learn in this chapter, living a long, *healthy* life is not quite that simple. Nevertheless, practicing preventive health care is well worth your efforts.

# EATING TO STAY HEALTHY: GOOD NUTRITION

Nutrition refers to the way the body uses food to maintain itself and grow. Planning good nutrition involves learning which nutrients the body needs and identifying and eating the foods that supply those nutrients.

Your body is made up of billions of cells—the basic building blocks of the body. To survive, each cell needs a continuous supply of fuel for energy, oxygen with which to burn the fuel, water, and other nutrients. The process of digestion breaks down all food into nutrients that are small enough to pass through the wall of the small intestine and be absorbed into the bloodstream. The bloodstream carries the nutrients to each cell in the body, where they are broken down and utilized. Some nutrients provide energy, others help form new tissues, and still others enable the body to grow or restore itself.

## Nutrients

There are six categories of nutrients, and all are present in many foods. In order of predominance, they are water, fats, carbohydrates, proteins, vitamins, and minerals. The body is composed of similar materials in about the same order of predominance. Thus, the body of a person who weighs 125 pounds contains about 75 pounds of water, 25 pounds of fat, and 25 pounds of protein, carbohydrates, vitamins, and minerals.

The body requires varying amounts of all six categories of nutrients to maintain body heat, to move, to build and restore bones and tissues—in short, for any function or activity.

## Calories—body energy

Fuel supplied by nutrients is measured in calories. When a person consumes more nutrients or calories than the body burns up during basic body functions or exercise, the excess is stored as fat. So good nutrition also involves consuming sufficient amounts of all the nutrients the body needs to keep growing and functioning without adding extra weight.

To obtain all the essential nutrients without consuming too many calories, a person must learn to select foods wisely. Foods that provide more nutrients than calories are said to have a high nutrient density. For example, three ounces of steak and three ounces of sardines provide the same amount of iron, but the steak contains 330 calories, while the sardines have only 175 calories; with respect to iron, therefore, the sardines have a higher nutrient density than the steak.

In contrast, 12 ounces of beer has almost no nutritional value but provides 150 calories of energy that, if not used, is converted to fat. Thus, beer is not the wisest food choice.

### Making wise choices

There is growing evidence that excessive amounts of cholesterol, animal fats, sugar, and salt are underlying factors in such major disorders as heart attack, hypertension, diabetes, cancer of the colon, and kidney and liver diseases. Yet the average American diet is laden with these substances. How can you be sure that you are getting the nutrients you need to stay healthy without eating too much of those substances that may be harmful?

The federal government periodically publishes a list of Recommended Dietary Allowances (RDAs), or suggested intakes, of certain nutrients, based on the latest scientific information available. It also sets guidelines for average caloric needs to maintain certain weights accord-

ing to an individual's height and age. The RDAs are guidelines, not requirements, for healthy persons. The needs of pregnant women, the elderly, and those with medical problems often differ from the RDA guidelines.

Labels on packaged goods usually list the nutritional values of the items and the percentages of the RDAs that they meet. In addition, many recipes now include nutritional and caloric data. All this information helps you keep tabs on, and control your intake of, calories and nutrients.

It's not necessary to count nutrients when making diet choices. Foods are grouped by their similarities in nutritional content. After learning to recognize the groups to which items belong, a person can maintain a well-balanced diet by eating from the four food groups each day: two servings of meat or fish protein; two servings of milk or dairy products; four servings of fruits or vegetables; and four servings of grains, breads, or cereals.

Those who prefer a vegetarian diet must select their nutrients from fewer food groups. The lacto-ovo-vegetarian (lacto refers to milk, and ovo refers to eggs) excludes meat, fish, and poultry but can substitute other protein-rich foods, such as milk, eggs, and legumes (beans and peas). The strict vegetarian, who also eliminates dairy products, must add other supplements to the diet.

### Keeping up-to-date about nutrition

In recent years, research has uncovered more and more information about nutrition. Although the volume of new facts may

seem to complicate the choices, the more knowledge you have access to, the more easily you can make decisions in your own best interests. To keep abreast of the most recent scientific data, read and listen to as many informed sources as possible and become aware of the differences in information.

For instance, some figures strongly suggest certain assumptions, but they do not scientifically prove them. Studies reveal that in cultures in which people consume foods containing a lot of fiber, there are virtually no colon disorders, in contrast to cultures in which people eat primarily low-fiber foods. These facts suggest, but do not prove, that a high-fiber diet has beneficial effects.

The flood of new information has also spurred much debate. A prime example is the controversy that surrounds the non-sugar sweeteners. The government banned cyclamates in 1969 because some tests indicated that they might cause cancer. But when the government tried to prohibit saccharin eight years later for the same reason, consumers protested that the benefits were greater than the potential risks. The ban has been suspended, and consumers are free to use the product if they wish. Recently, a third sweetener, aspartame, came under scrutiny because of reported side effects.

Another source of controversy is the use of food additives. Most packaged foods contain additives—many of which are natural substances—considered safe by the government. The additives retard or prevent spoilage; maintain or add vitamins, minerals, and proteins; enhance the flavor and appearance; or help in the preparation of the food.

Additives are listed on package labels—an important point for people with allergies to certain ingredients or for those who must follow strict sugar-free or salt-free diets.

Current data warns of the possible perils of excessive use of substances that are safe or even necessary to use in moderation. Two of these are salt (sodium chloride) and caffeine. The body requires small daily amounts of sodium to maintain the volume and constant flow of blood in the blood vessels. But too much sodium seems to contribute to the development of hypertension (high blood pressure), a disorder that often produces no symptoms but that can lead to kidney failure, stroke, and heart disease. Caffeine—an ingredient in coffee, tea, cocoa, many cola drinks, and many nonprescription medicines—is a great pick-me-up in small doses. However, it is also a habit-forming stimulant that, in larger doses, may lead to nervousness, insomnia, and irregular heartbeat. Studies have linked caffeine to certain birth defects and to fibrocystic breast disease (a condition characterized by noncancerous lumps in the breast).

Be wary of the many health food quacks. They promote gimmicks, worthless products, and megadoses of vitamins with claims of preventing and curing all sorts of nutritional deficiencies or problems, building muscles without exercise, and melting away pounds without dieting.

Reliable information about nutrition is available, often free of charge, from national and local health and medical associations and from the U.S. Department of Agriculture.

With so many discoveries being made in the field of nutri-tion, it often seems that what applies today may change tomorrow. However, one fact will not become outdated: it is less expensive and less time-consuming to prevent the diseases that result from nutritional deficiencies than it is to cure them.

Follow these nutritional rules to change bad eating habits.
• Eat well-balanced, nutritious meals, including breakfast.
• Limit calories sensibly to lose weight.
• Read labels to learn the ingredients of packaged foods.
• Drink plenty of water.
• Cut out or moderate intake of animal fats, caffeine, sugar, salt, alcohol, and other substances that add calories without nutritional benefit or that pose possible hazards.
• Learn as much as possible about how your body functions.
• Stay alert to new findings.

The following sections will explain in more detail some of the more important and interesting nutrition-related topics.

# Amino acids

Amino acids are the main building blocks of proteins and are found in all living cells. There are 20 or more different kinds of amino acids, each of which contains carbon, hydrogen, oxygen, and nitrogen. Each protein molecule is made up of thousands of amino acid molecules, linked to each other in chains.

### Functions

In the body, food proteins are broken down to their amino acids in the small intestine. The amino acids are then transported through the bloodstream to form, maintain, and repair body protein. Sometimes they are also used as fuel. In the cells, enzymes (special proteins that cause or speed up chemical processes in the body) break down some amino acids into simpler compounds, use some for structure, and form others into chains of new proteins.

### Types

Nutritionists divide amino acids into two groups:
• Nonessential amino acids, which can be manufactured by the body if not enough of them are supplied by the diet
• Essential amino acids, which must be included in our diets if we are to remain healthy

Rich sources of amino acids include meat, fish, fowl, eggs, milk, cheese, grains, nuts, and legumes (peas and beans). The proteins from animal sources are much more complete—that is, they contain more essential amino acids in the right proportions—than those from plant sources. Therefore, the person who avoids meat and dairy products should include substantial amounts of two or more plant proteins in each day's meals.

# Beriberi

Beriberi is a disease that is caused by an insufficiency of thiamin (vitamin $B_1$). It has been most common in those parts of the world where people's diets have been limited almost entirely to polished (white) rice. Milling removes the brown rice husks, which are rich in thiamin.

Other causes of beriberi include the following:
• Increased need for thiamin, such as occurs with fever,

pregnancy, breast-feeding, or overactivity of the thyroid gland (which causes the body to increase the rate at which it uses nutrients)

• Failure of the body to absorb enough thiamin, such as may occur with long-lasting diarrhea

• Poor use of the vitamin by the body, as in severe liver disease

A combination of these factors occurs in alcoholism, because of lowered food intake, poor vitamin absorption, increased need for thiamin, and poor use of it by the body.

### Symptoms

Because thiamin is necessary for the proper use of fats, starches, and sugars and for the normal functioning of nervous tissue and of enzymes (which modulate body processes), symptoms of beriberi usually occur in the digestive and nervous systems. In severe cases, heart muscle is damaged. Early symptoms include fatigue, irritability, poor memory, loss of appetite, constipation, abdominal discomfort, and difficulty in rising from the squatting position. There may be burning of the feet, prickling of the soles, and tenderness and cramps in the calves. Certain muscle reflexes are lost. Mental confusion, paralysis of speech and eye muscles, coma, and death can occur in untreated beriberi affecting the brain. Heart damage from beriberi produces heart failure with buildup of body fluids, seen as swelling in the abdomen and legs, and difficulty in breathing. Babies who are breast-fed by mothers deficient in thiamin may develop heart failure and loss of speech and certain muscle reflexes.

### Treatment

Treatment for beriberi consists of daily doses of thiamin, at first by injection into a muscle or vein and later by mouth. Improvement usually begins in one or two days.

### Prevention

Eating a well-balanced diet of fruits, vegetables, meat, and whole grains is the best way to prevent such B-vitamin deficiency diseases as beriberi. Beriberi itself is rare in the United States because breads, cereals, and flours are enriched with thiamin.

# Carbohydrates

Carbohydrates are organic substances made up of carbon, hydrogen, and oxygen. Carbohydrates are a basic fuel source for the body. They come in the form of sugars, starches, and glycogen (a storage form of carbohydrate). Nonfood carbohydrates are gums and cellulose (plant fiber).

Sugars such as sucrose, glucose, fructose (fruit sugar), and lactose (milk sugar) can be used very quickly by the body. Starches must be turned into sugars by digestive enzymes before they can be used. Sugars travel through the bloodstream and are stored in the liver and muscles (as glycogen) or are incorporated into fat for more permanent storage.

Potatoes, rice, and wheat are rich sources of starch; they are made up of 90 percent starch, after the water has been removed. Fruits and vegetables generally have less starch and more fiber, which aids in digestion.

Starches and sugars are essential to life, but they have a poor reputation because many of them are refined before use and stripped of some of their vitamins, minerals, and fiber. The bran and the germ of wheat and the husk of rice—all rich in vitamins, minerals, and fiber—are often removed. Highly refined carbohydrates provide calories without some other food benefits. That is one reason why whole-grain breads and cereals are recommended.

# Cholesterol

Cholesterol is a fatlike substance, found in all animal fats and oils. It is manufactured by the liver from saturated fats and is a basic ingredient in the formation of male and female hormones, vitamin D, blood, bile, cell membranes, brain tissue, the sheaths that protect nerve fibers, and other body substances. After the first six months of life, the liver can make all the cholesterol the body needs—about 1,000 milligrams a day. However, the average American consumes an additional 600 milligrams of cholesterol a day from such sources as eggs and meat.

### High cholesterol level and disease

Eating foods containing cholesterol and saturated fats (found in dairy products, animal fat, and coconut and palm oils) can raise the level of cholesterol in the blood. When the blood contains too much cholesterol, or when there is an inherited defect that interferes with the body's ability to use or process cholesterol and fats, the risk of heart attack and blood-vessel disease rises.

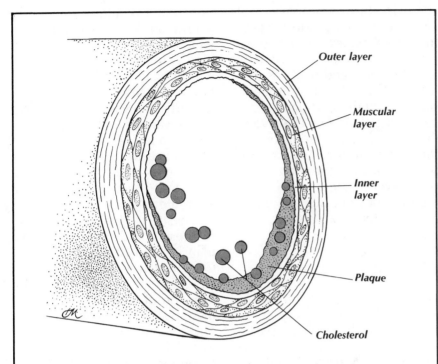

*The deposition of cholesterol particles on the inner wall of a blood vessel contributes to the formation of a plaque, which impedes blood flow.*

Labels on figure: Outer layer, Muscular layer, Inner layer, Plaque, Cholesterol

Atherosclerosis (one type of hardening of the arteries), which causes most heart attacks, probably begins with an injury to an artery wall. Normally, a blood clot would form over the injury and heal it. But when there is too much cholesterol in the blood, cholesterol is deposited at the site of the wound, which promotes the formation of a plaque. The plaque—made up of cholesterol, dead and dying cells, connective tissue, and calcium—may eventually grow to obstruct the artery. If the blockage is in one of the arteries nourishing heart muscle, it can cause a heart attack.

Normal levels of cholesterol in the blood are generally considered to be in the range of 100 to 280 milligrams per 100 milliliters. However, many dietitians and doctors recommend keeping the cholesterol level below 180, and some researchers suggest that the healthiest range is 100 to 150. Studies show that heart attack risk rises in almost direct proportion to the amount of cholesterol in the blood.

Not all people with high cholesterol levels develop heart disease or atherosclerosis, however. This seems to be due to the level of high-density lipoprotein (HDL) in their blood. HDL transports excess cholesterol to the liver, from which it is eliminated in the bile. Persons with high levels of HDL seem to have less risk of vascular (blood vessel) disease. Some people have high HDL levels because of heredity. Exercise raises HDL levels. Cigarette smoking lowers HDL levels.

**Lowering the cholesterol level**

You can reduce the cholesterol in your diet by avoiding fatty meats, cutting back on eggs, and eating more fish and poultry, which contain less cholesterol and saturated fat than meats. There is some evidence to suggest that increasing dietary fiber is also a good idea. Palm and coconut oils should be avoided. Taking off excess weight, exercising regularly, and quitting smoking also help.

# Fluoride

Fluoride is a compound of the chemical element fluorine. Fluoride is found in soil and is necessary to plant life and to the formation of teeth and bones in animals, including humans. In the human body, traces of fluoride are found in the bones, the teeth, the thyroid gland, and the skin.

**Preventing tooth disease**

It has been found that fluoride can help prevent or reduce tooth decay when taken in somewhat larger amounts than are naturally present in the teeth. The best source of fluoride for prevention of tooth decay is fluoridated drinking water. Water with a fluoride content of one part per million is considered safe and effective, especially if given to children while their teeth are developing. The maximum benefit is obtained when the child drinks fluoridated water daily until the permanent teeth are complete (between the ages of 10 and 13). However, if fluoride intake is excessive before the permanent teeth erupt (while the tooth enamel is still forming), the enamel may become stained and mottled. If the teeth have erupted, this staining and mottling cannot occur.

### Effects on other diseases

There is evidence that fluoridation prevents dental problems other than cavities, such as periodontal diseases (diseases of the gums and the bones supporting the teeth) and abnormal positioning of the teeth. Many physicians and researchers have found that fluoride also may play a significant role in the treatment and prevention of osteoporosis (abnormal thinness and brittleness of the bones, common in women after menopause and in both men and women over the age of 65). One recent study of over 1,000 persons aged 45 or older showed that osteoporosis was less frequent in those who had lived most of their lives in areas where the drinking water has a high fluoride content. There was also significantly less atherosclerosis (hardening of the arteries, often because of calcium deposits), suggesting that fluoride helps keep calcium in the hard tissues of the body and not in the soft tissues. It seems, therefore, that fluoride plays an important role in preventing osteoporosis and atherosclerosis, two of the main diseases of aging.

### The fluoridation debate

Fluoridation of drinking water has been a controversial issue. Opponents of fluoridation are concerned about the unknown long-range effects of adding fluoride to the water supply and about what they see as the infringement on freedom of choice inherent in imposing this "compulsory medication" on the population. Supporters of fluoridation counter these charges by pointing out that fluoride is not a medication but a preventive, used in the same way that chlorine is used to kill bacteria in water supplies. They also assert that fluoride is normally found in teeth and bones as well as in water and that other methods of obtaining fluoride are more costly and less effective in the long run than fluoridation of the water supply. Most health scientists today believe that a fluoride level of about one part per million does not damage either teeth or other body tissues.

# Obesity

Obesity is a term commonly applied to the condition in which the body weight is 20 percent or more above normal. It has been linked statistically to high blood pressure, diabetes, cardiovascular disease, and chronic back and joint pains, among other ailments. It is a potentially serious condition that shortens the life span.

The risk of disease and death among the obese is greater for men than for women, but for both it increases in direct proportion to the degree of overweight. For example, it has been estimated that among those who are 20 percent overweight, there are 25 percent more deaths for men and 21 percent more for women than among those of normal weight in a given age group; for those who are 30 percent overweight, there are 42 percent more deaths for men and 30 percent more for women.

### Causes

Obesity tends to occur more frequently in some families than in others. This may indicate a hereditary tendency, or it may be due to shared food consumption patterns and attitudes toward food. Women tend to gain weight after menopause, and men gain in middle age. Overweight children often grow up to be overweight adults. This is particularly true when food is used as a reward for a child or is withheld as a punishment. Food may then come to represent security and love—an attitude toward food that often continues into adult life.

Obesity is most often the direct result of taking in more food than is "burned off" in activity. Certain glandular disturbances can affect the appetite or the distribution of fat in the body, but these conditions are uncommon. The appetite for food is influenced by habit as well as by emotional factors, and it is not always prompted by hunger. The appetite control center, or feeding center, is thought to be located in the area of the brain called the hypothalamus. The term appestat (suggested by the word thermostat) has been coined to describe the mechanism of appetite control.

The connection between smoking, appetite, and weight gain is unclear. Because smoking has been said to decrease appetite, giving up smoking is often thought to be followed by increased appetite and weight gain. The gain in weight that may follow when smoking is stopped has also been attributed to the dependence of some smokers on oral satisfaction; when they stop smoking, they may be impelled to substitute the oral satisfaction of eating for that of smoking.

### Treatment

The treatment for obesity is twofold: eat less and exercise

more. A low-calorie diet that is nutritionally well balanced and that can form the basis of permanent eating habits is the first step. Combined with a regular exercise program, such a diet can eliminate obesity. Anyone embarking on such a program, however, should consult a doctor for a checkup and for guidance.

Appetite-decreasing drugs can be harmful and should be taken only under medical supervision. Even physicians who use them in selected cases recognize that these drugs are at best only a temporary prop, not an answer to the problem of obesity over a long period of time.

Crash diets and fad diets can lead to nutritional deficiencies; if they are effective at all, it is basically only because they furnish fewer calories. The quick weight loss that many such diets promise is often merely a loss of fluid from body tissues; weight lost will quickly be regained as fluid is replaced.

Massage is not effective in removing or redistributing local fat deposits. Hot baths and sweating serve only to remove water from the tissues, which will soon be replaced.

In extreme cases, surgery is sometimes performed to remove excessive layers of fatty tissue. However, the expense of the operation and the inherent dangers of any surgery make this a treatment to be used only as a last resort. The same caution should be exercised with stomach-stapling surgery or intestinal bypass surgery.

### Prevention

It is particularly important for parents to teach their children good eating habits and to control any tendency toward obesity before it becomes a serious problem. The old notions that children should have food urged on them and that a fat child is a healthy child should be recognized as not only false but harmful. Older people, too, need to take special care to avoid obesity. They tend to be less active than in their younger days, yet may continue to follow their established eating patterns. Reduced activity may make it necessary for the elderly to seek out means of regular exercise—whether it be calisthenics or sports, such as swimming, bicycling, or hiking—that are suited to their capacities and tastes.

One safeguard for those of all ages is to control weight strictly, at an early stage, by weighing daily and embarking on a program of diet and exercise as soon as the weight is three to five pounds above the norm for the individual's height and body type. It is far easier to take off a few pounds than to wait until massive obesity requires a protracted and difficult struggle. Increased life span and improved health and vigor—not to mention improved appearance—will be a satisfying reward.

# Pellagra

Pellagra is a disorder caused by a deficiency of niacin (also known as nicotinic acid), a vitamin found in many foods. Niacin is vital to many of the important chemical reactions by which energy is generated in the body, as well as to maintenance of healthy skin and normal functioning of the nervous system. Since niacin is abundant in many foods, only those who seriously neglect their diets, such as alcoholics, are likely to lack the daily requirement of between 9 and 20 milligrams of niacin. At one time, pellagra was widespread in the United States, especially in the South, but today it occurs far less frequently.

### Symptoms

Physical symptoms of pellagra include weakness; loss of appetite; sore, red, cracked skin with symmetrical spots that turn scaly and brownish; a painful scarlet mouth, tongue, and gums; a burning sensation throughout the digestive tract; diarrhea; and headaches. Psychological symptoms are anxiety, forgetfulness, insomnia (inability to sleep), irritability, and dementia (loss of intellectual abilities).

### Treatment

The deficiency can be reversed by eating a balanced diet and taking niacin supplements.

# Pica

Pica is an abnormal craving to eat substances not ordinarily considered to be foods.

### Causes

The causes of pica are not completely understood. In the case of a pregnant woman who eats laundry starch, pica may be an almost instinctive effort to make up for deficiencies in the diet. In the case of a child who eats chips of lead-based paint (a common cause of lead poisoning in children), the cause is less clear: it could be a teething impulse, or it could be the result of unconscious drives that are not fully understood.

### Common substances ingested

Although lead poisoning is the most serious pica problem with children, the effects of pica are as varied as the substances that are consumed. The substances most commonly eaten as a result of pica are those that are used as ingredients in the manufacture of such products as paints, matches, soaps, cleaners, and pesticides. Some doctors also include consumption of a variety of growing plants, such as mushrooms, century plants, and toxic (poisonous) plants (for example, poison ivy), as pica.

Some pica sufferers (especially children) eat nonfoods indiscriminately; others exhibit pica as a compulsion to consume only one or several specific inedible substances.

### Treatment

The treatment for pica is not simple, since medical science has not yet pinned down the root of the compulsion. Obviously, if the craving is induced by a deficiency of an element such as iron, the treatment is to remedy the deficiency. Medical treatment for the effects of ingested nonfoods depends on the nature of the substance consumed. If a child is the pica sufferer, the first line of defense is to remove the material from his reach and to search the immediate area for other such substances.

## Scurvy

Scurvy is a disease caused by vitamin C deficiency. It is charac-terized by anemia (deficiency of red blood cells), spongy gums, a tendency to bleed, and abnormal bone and tooth formation. The disease may be either acute (short-term) or chronic (long-term).

### Causes

Vitamin C is essential for the formation and maintenance of connective tissue, bone tissue, and teeth. It is also essential for the healing of wounds and burns.

There are two forms of scurvy, infantile and adult. Vitamin C deficiency in infants is due simply to lack of sufficient quantities of vitamin C. In adults, scurvy is usually due to improper diet. Adult scurvy may also result from being on an "ulcer diet" for gastrointestinal disorders that limits citrus fruits and juices because of their acid content. Pregnancy and breast-feeding increase the vitamin C requirement; pregnant women and nursing mothers must be sure to include adequate vitamin C in the diet. In addition, diarrhea, inflammatory disease, burns, surgery, and exposure to intense cold all increase the vitamin C requirement.

### Symptoms

Infantile scurvy usually appears between the ages of six months and one year. The earliest symptoms include irritability, loss of appetite, and failure to gain weight. Often the child screams or cries whenever he is moved and may hold his legs motionless because of the pain caused by internal bleeding of the bone surface. There may be abnormal enlargement or hard-ening of the joints or long bones (especially in the thighs) and a tendency toward gum hemorrhage as the teeth erupt. Fever, anemia, and increased pulse and respiration rates are also common signs.

Adult scurvy usually takes a long time to develop. Early symptoms include extreme fatigue, weakness, irritability, weight loss, loss of appetite, multiple splinter hemorrhages at the nails, failure of wounds to heal, loosening of teeth, and swollen, purplish, and spongy gums. Secondary infections, gangrene (death and decay of tissue, frequently due to inadequate blood supply), breaks in old scars, spontaneous hemorrhaging, muscle pain, pain in the joints, and small hemorrhagic spots on the skin of the legs are all symptoms of a more advanced stage of the disorder. In some cases there is edema (fluid retention) in the lower extremities and a form of arthritis that resembles rheumatoid arthritis. There may even be bleeding in the conjunctiva (the membrane that covers the front of the eye and lines the eyelids).

### Diagnosis

In a case of infantile scurvy, an x-ray study of the ends of the long bones of the legs will show areas of crosswise thickening and increased density, the so-called white lines. If the diagnosis is doubtful, a therapeutic dose of vitamin C given orally will stop the pain of infantile scurvy almost immediately and reduce the swelling and bleeding of the gums within 72 hours.

In adults, scurvy can mimic arthritis, hemorrhagic disease, and gingivitis (inflammation of the gums). The blood level of vitamin C is usually low, but this is not always an accurate diagnostic indication. The level of vitamin C in the urine will be low, and there may be anemia not caused by blood loss.

### Treatment

Fortunately, scurvy is easy to treat. Vitamin C given orally for one week, supplemented with orange and tomato juice, is the remedy for infantile scurvy. If diarrhea or vomiting is present, half the recommended oral dose can be given intravenously.

For adult scurvy, vitamin C is taken orally until symptoms have disappeared; the patient can then receive maintenance doses. Vitamin C is given for several months for chronic scurvy that appears in connection with gingivitis, hemorrhaging, or joint symptoms.

### Prevention

A balanced diet with plenty of vitamin C is the best preventive measure for scurvy. Fortunately, natural sources of vitamin C are plentiful: besides citrus fruits and tomatoes, many green vegetables, such as green peppers, are rich in vitamin C. In the case of patients on bland diets or ulcer diets, a physician should be consulted about how to prevent vitamin C deficiency.

# Vitamins and minerals

Vitamins and minerals are substances that are essential in small amounts to maintain good health, to promote growth, and to regulate body functions. Most

vitamins and minerals are supplied by the diet, but sometimes (as in the case of vitamins D and K) they are formed in the body as well.

A balanced and varied diet usually provides all the necessary vitamins and minerals without the need for supplements. Dark-green vegetables, yellow fruits and vegetables, citrus fruits, whole-grain products, dairy products, meats, seafood, and dried beans and peas supply adequate quantities of vitamins and minerals, as well as other nutrients.

A carefully selected diet is essential for everyone, but is especially vital for those individuals with special needs. Pregnant and nursing women, newborns and growing children, and elderly and ill persons have special nutritional requirements. Most of these needs can be met by a varied diet. It is important to remember that during periods of physical growth and change or during illness, a nutritious diet is imperative.

### Deficiency

Occasionally, a person may experience a vitamin or mineral deficiency (insufficient intake to maintain good health). There may be several reasons for such a deficiency of a vitamin or mineral:
- An unbalanced diet that features too many vitamin- or mineral-deficient foods. For example, some vegetarians omit all animal protein sources and are either careless about or unaware of the proper balance of vegetable nutrients.
- An inadequate diet that lacks the proper amounts of nutritious foods. People on strict weight-reducing programs or

those who restrict their diets for religious reasons may be susceptible to deficiencies.
- An inability of the body to absorb or utilize vitamins or minerals despite a nutritious diet.
- An unusual need for vitamins or minerals (for example, during pregnancy or illness).
- An excessive intake of one vitamin, which may adversely affect use of another vitamin, even though the second vitamin is present in normal amounts. For instance, large amounts of vitamin E may change the body's use of vitamin K to the point of causing a vitamin K deficiency.

All of these reasons point up the importance of careful attention to balance in the diet. In addition, it is necessary to understand that there are two categories of vitamins: fat-soluble (vitamins A, D, E, and K) and water-soluble (B vitamins, folic acid, niacin, and vitamin C). Fat-soluble vitamins are stored in the body, whereas water-soluble vitamins are eliminated daily. Therefore, vitamin deficiencies are more likely to involve water-soluble vitamins, which must be replenished daily.

### Toxicity

Vitamin toxicity is more likely to occur with fat-soluble vitamins, which can accumulate to toxic levels in the body tissues where they are stored. In general, water-soluble vitamins, because they are excreted daily, are considered nontoxic, although unusually large doses (especially large doses of vitamin $B_6$ and niacin) may cause side effects.

Vitamin and mineral toxicity can be as dangerous as deficiency. Again, a balanced and adequate diet is the key to preventing any toxic effects of vitamins and minerals.

The table in this section lists some of the most common vitamins and minerals, with their sources, their functions in the body, and the effects, if any, of having too little or too much of them in the body.

## VITAMINS

A vitamin is any of a large group of organic substances often identified as "enzyme components," which are found in many foods in small amounts and are necessary for normal body functioning. Many vitamins help to regulate the rate at which chemical reactions take place in the body.

### Vitamin supplementation

Vitamins are not themselves direct sources of energy. As enzyme components, they can act only in the presence of nutrients contained in food. Hence, taking massive doses of supplements without eating food is useless and may even be dangerous.

In general, vitamin megadoses (large doses far beyond daily requirements) are not needed. Many reputable nutritional guides suggest that for persons on restricted-calorie diets (containing less than 1,000 to 1,200 calories daily), a multivitamin preparation may be useful, but higher potency or "therapeutic" formulas are not generally necessary.

### Recommended daily allowances

The Food and Drug Administration has developed a system of nutrition labeling for foods, the U.S. Recommended Daily Allowances (USRDAs). The USRDAs for selected vitamins for adults and children four years and older are as follows:

| | |
|---|---|
| Vitamin A | 5,000 international units |
| Vitamin $B_1$ | 1.5 milligrams |
| Vitamin $B_2$ | 1.7 milligrams |
| Vitamin $B_6$ | 2 milligrams |
| Vitamin C | 60 milligrams |
| Vitamin D | 400 international units |
| Vitamin E | 30 international units |
| Folic acid | 0.4 milligram |
| Biotin | 0.3 milligram |
| Niacin | 20 milligrams |

### Vitamin A

Vitamin A is found in fish-liver oils, liver, butter, egg yolks, cheese, dark-green vegetables, and yellow vegetables and fruits. Deficiency of this vitamin in the diet causes inadequate production of rhodopsin (a substance important in the functioning of the eye), resulting in night blindness. Vitamin A deficiency can also result in disorders of the skin and mucous membranes and decreased resistance to infection.

### Vitamin B

The name vitamin B may refer to any member of the vitamin B complex, including thiamin, riboflavin, niacin, niacinamide, the $B_6$ group, biotin, pantothenic acid, folic acid, para-aminobenzoic acid, inositol, cyanocobalamin (vitamin $B_{12}$), and choline.

Vitamin $B_1$, or thiamin, is found in enriched and whole-grain breads and cereals, meat (especially pork and liver), fish, dried beans and peas, and nuts. A deficiency can result in beriberi, a disease characterized by abnormal heart function, swelling, and inflammation of the nerves.

Vitamin $B_2$, or riboflavin, is found in milk, meats (especially liver), eggs, dark-green vegetables, and enriched cereal products. It acts as a catalyst in bodily processes that involve oxidation (use of oxygen). Dietary deficiencies may result in stomatitis (inflammation of the mucous membranes of the mouth), cheilitis (inflammation of the lips), and eye disorders.

Vitamin $B_6$ is a group of substances (pyridoxine, pyridoxal, and pyridoxamine) that are widely distributed in animal and plant tissues. These substances are involved in the metabolism of amino acids (the building blocks of protein) and in the breakdown of glycogen (a stored sugar). Vitamin $B_6$ is found in wheat, bran, yeast, and seeds. A deficiency can result in functional disturbances of the nervous system.

Vitamin $B_{12}$, or cyanocobalamin, affects the formation of red blood cells and is found in all animal products, especially liver and other meats, fish, cheese, and eggs. When vitamin $B_{12}$ is absent from the diet or is not absorbed by the body, anemia (deficiency of red blood cells) may result.

Biotin acts as a coenzyme, or biologic catalyst, in several metabolic reactions. Some of these reactions are important for the manufacture of fatty acids; others are essential for the synthesis of glucose, a primary source of energy. Some biotin is normally produced in the intestinal tract by bacteria that live there. Because of the difficulty of measuring how much biotin these bacteria actually make, nutritionists have been unable to establish how much biotin the body needs each day. However, it has been found that ordinary mixed diets usually provide from 100 to 300 micrograms of biotin a day. This amount, plus the amount produced by intestinal bacteria, is apparently enough. Biotin deficiency is almost unheard of in humans.

Folic acid is found in dark-green vegetables, liver, and legumes. Folic acid functions as a coenzyme, or catalyst, in a number of biological reactions. One of the most important of these is the synthesis of deoxyribonucleic acid (DNA). When plants and animals grow, cells must divide and multiply. To do this, a cell has to synthesize DNA—to double its supply so that each of the two new cells has a full supply of the gene-containing material.

In adults, symptoms of folic acid deficiency—such as anemia, nerve damage, and sore, red, swollen tongue—may not appear for months because the body tends to hold on to its supply of the vitamin. In infants and children, however, symptoms may appear much more quickly. Because they are growing rapidly, infants and children need proportionally more folic acid than do adults; a deficiency slows and stunts growth.

Symptoms of deficiency may also occur rapidly in pregnant women because they need more of the vitamin. Pregnancy increases the need for folic acid because it is a time of rapid growth and manufacture of new cells. Anemia caused by folic acid deficiency is quite prevalent among pregnant women subsisting on restricted diets, such as those of low-income populations in developing countries.

## Vitamin C

Vitamin C, or ascorbic acid, is found in many vegetables and fruits, especially green peppers and most citrus fruits. It is an essential element in the human diet. A deficiency may result in a disease called scurvy, in which the victim suffers anemia, spongy gums, bleeding, and edema (fluid retention in the tissues). An overdose of vitamin C (such as may result from taking "megadoses") may cause gout, kidney stones, and decreased fertility.

## Vitamin D

Vitamin D includes any of several related antirickets compounds. These compounds are present in fish-liver oils, liver, butter, cream, egg yolks, and fortified milk, and are also produced in the body on exposure to sunlight. A vitamin D deficiency may cause rickets in children and osteomalacia (softening of the bones) or osteoporosis (decreased bone mass) in adults.

## Vitamin E

Vitamin E is necessary in human diets for normal muscular and reproductive functioning and development, normal red blood cell functioning, and other biochemical processes. Vitamin E is found in wheat germ oil, vegetable oils, whole-grain products, egg yolks, meats (especially liver), and dark-green vegetables.

## Vitamin K

Vitamin K is a group of vitamins found in their natural state in egg yolk and liver and in spinach, cabbage, and other leafy green vegetables. These vitamins play a role in clotting of the blood by increasing the production of prothrombin, the clotting agent in the blood. A deficiency can result in blood coagulation abnormalities.

## MINERALS

Minerals are natural, nonorganic substances with a specific chemical composition and characteristic crystalline structure. Minerals are essential for health and growth. They are important components of the bones and soft tissues, and they play a vital role in regulating the cardiovascular system, the internal pressure of body fluids, nerve responses, and oxygen conduction.

The body requires some minerals in relatively large amounts; these "macrominerals" are calcium, chloride, magnesium, phosphorus, potassium, sodium, and sulfur. Others are called trace minerals (or micronutrients) because they are needed only in minute quantities; these include iron, manganese, copper, iodine, zinc, chromium, cobalt, fluoride, and selenium. Still other minerals, such as lead, mercury, and cadmium, are harmful.

### Mineral supplementation

Although minerals are essential, they are required only in specific amounts and can be harmful if taken in excess. Those who use mineral supplements should take care not to surpass the daily requirement. An overload can upset the balance of other minerals and block their

(Continued on page 22)

| Vitamin | Primary Sources | Functions |
|---|---|---|
| Vitamin A | Liver, fish-liver oils, egg yolks, yellow and dark-green vegetables, butter, cream | • Aids vision, especially night vision<br>• Maintains healthy skin and mucous membranes<br>• Promotes normal growth and reproduction |
| Vitamin $B_1$ (thiamin)<br>*Can be destroyed by high temperatures and leached from foods in cooking water; foods should be prepared at lowest possible temperature in least amount of water for shortest period of time* | Whole-grain (or enriched) breads and cereals, meats (especially pork and liver), dried beans and peas, nuts, fish | • Maintains healthy nervous system<br>• Prevents irritability<br>• Promotes normal appetite and digestion<br>• Helps body metabolism<br>• Aids heart function |
| Vitamin $B_2$ (riboflavin)<br>*Can be destroyed by light; cover food and keep milk out of direct light* | Milk, milk products, meats (especially liver), eggs, dark-green vegetables, enriched cereal products | • Helps body utilize foods to produce energy<br>• Maintains healthy skin and eyes |
| Niacin | Meats, eggs, milk | • Helps body use oxygen to produce energy from foods<br>• Maintains healthy skin, mouth, tongue, and digestive tract<br>• Aids health of nervous system |
| Vitamin $B_6$ | Liver, pork, whole-grain cereals, dried beans and peas, bananas | • Helps body utilize protein<br>• Aids in manufacture of hormones and red blood cells<br>• Maintains health of nervous system |
| Folic acid | Dark-green vegetables, liver, dried beans and peas | • Promotes normal growth and development<br>• Promotes red blood cell formation and prevents macrocytic anemia |
| Vitamin $B_{12}$ (cyanocobalamin) | Eggs, fish, cheese, meats (especially liver) | • Helps in production of red blood cells and of cells lining digestive tract<br>• Prevents pernicious anemia<br>• Maintains healthy nervous system |
| Vitamin C (ascorbic acid)<br>*Can be destroyed by cooking, air contact, fine mincing of food, and use of copper utensils* | Citrus fruit, tomatoes, potatoes, cabbage, green peppers, strawberries, cantaloupe | • Promotes tooth and bone formation<br>• Strengthens walls of blood vessels<br>• Aids in connective tissue formation<br>• Helps in healing wounds and broken bones |
| Vitamin D<br>*Sunlight on skin enables body to form vitamin D* | Vitamin D-fortified milk, fish-liver oils, liver, cream, butter, egg yolks | • Helps body absorb calcium and phosphorus for growth of bones and teeth |

| Symptoms of Deficiency | Symptoms of Toxicity |
|---|---|
| • Night blindness<br>• Dry, rough skin<br>• Dryness of outer layers of eyes<br>• Decreased resistance to infections | • Excessive doses may cause headache, peeling skin, hair loss, enlarged liver and spleen, loss of appetite, vomiting, weight loss, blurred vision |
| • Beriberi (muscle weakness, muscle cramps, loss of appetite, nervous system disorders, lack of coordination, edema, abnormal heart function) | • No known toxicity |
| • Cracks at corners of mouth<br>• Inflamed and sore lips<br>• Inflamed tongue<br>• Itching and burning eyes | • No known toxicity |
| • Pellagra (rough, red skin; diarrhea; and, in advanced cases, delirium) | • Large doses may cause flushing and burning skin, dizziness, nausea, vomiting, diarrhea, and skin rash |
| • Decreased number of red blood cells (anemia)<br>• Convulsions<br>• Skin inflammation<br>• Nervous system deterioration | • No known toxicity from excessive doses, but individuals may develop temporary dependence on vitamin after taking large doses<br>• Large doses may interfere with medications used to treat Parkinson's disease |
| • Stunted growth (especially of fetus during pregnancy and of infants)<br>• Reduced production of white blood cells<br>• Sore, swollen tongue<br>• Inflamed intestines | • No known toxicity, but very high doses can interfere with drugs for treatment of epilepsy and can delay diagnosis of pernicious anemia |
| • Macrocytic anemia<br>• Pernicious anemia | • No known toxicity, but those with pernicious anemia should receive injections, not oral doses, of $B_{12}$ to avoid nerve damage |
| • Scurvy (hemorrhages under skin, muscle weakness, loose teeth, bleeding gums, fatigue)<br>• Poor or slow wound healing<br>• Greater susceptibility to infection | • No known toxicity, but patient may develop temporary dependence on vitamin after taking large doses<br>• Large doses may interfere with accuracy of some lab tests, may counteract drugs to dissolve blood clots, and may contribute to formation of kidney stones |
| • Rickets (poor bone and tooth development in children, causing bowlegs and decayed teeth)<br>• Osteomalacia (loss of calcium from bones in adults, causing weak and easily fractured bones) | • Excessive doses cause large amounts of calcium to be absorbed, resulting in possible kidney damage because of accumulation of calcium in body tissues |

(Continued on page 20)

| Vitamin or Mineral | Primary Sources | Functions |
|---|---|---|
| Vitamin E (tocopherol) | Vegetable oils, wheat germ, whole-grain products, egg yolks, liver, dark-green vegetables | • Prevents oxygen in body from combining with wastes to form toxic substances (antioxidant) |
| Vitamin K *Formed in intestinal tract in healthy persons* | Egg yolks, leafy green vegetables, liver, milk products | • Maintains normal blood clotting |
| Calcium | Milk, milk products | • Helps bone and tooth formation<br>• Aids in blood clotting<br>• Maintains healthy muscle function<br>• Helps transmission of nerve impulses |
| Phosphorus | Meats, poultry, fish, eggs, whole-grain products | • Works with calcium to ensure bone and tooth formation<br>• Aids metabolism |
| Sodium | Table salt; salt used in food processing; natural salt occurring in meats, milk, milk products, eggs, fish | • Regulates body's water and acid-base balances<br>• Helps transmission of nerve impulses<br>• Maintains healthy muscles |
| Chloride | Table salt | • Helps maintain water balance in body<br>• Helps form component of stomach acid |
| Potassium | Bananas, citrus fruits, carrots, leafy green vegetables, potatoes, tomatoes, milk, whole-grain products, meats | • Regulates acid-base balance of body<br>• Helps transmission of nerve impulses<br>• Promotes healthy muscle action |
| Magnesium | Dried beans and peas, whole-grain cereals, cocoa, dark-green vegetables, seafood, nuts | • Maintains healthy nerve and muscle functions<br>• Helps bone and tooth formation<br>• Helps regulate use of sugars for energy |
| Iron | Liver, seafood, meats, egg yolks, dried beans and peas, green vegetables | • Helps form hemoglobin, which helps carry oxygen from lungs to body cells<br>• Aids metabolism |
| Iodine | Iodized salt, seafood | • Controls energy production<br>• Regulates body heat<br>• Maintains healthy connective tissue<br>• Promotes physical and mental development |
| Fluoride | Seafood, meats, fluoridated water | • Helps bone and tooth formation and protects against tooth decay |
| Zinc | Seafood, meats, dried beans and peas, milk, cheese, egg yolks | • Promotes normal growth and sexual maturity<br>• May help wound healing<br>• Aids protein digestion |

| Symptoms of Deficiency | Symptoms of Toxicity |
|---|---|
| • Rarely occurs | • Rarely occurs, although some people taking large doses over long periods may experience nausea, fatigue, and intestinal discomfort |
| • Hemorrhage<br>• Delayed blood clotting | • Rupture of red blood cells, causing jaundice<br>• Large doses can interfere with action of drugs used to prevent blood clots |
| • Rickets (poor bone and tooth development in children, causing bowlegs and decayed teeth)<br>• Osteomalacia (loss of calcium from bones in adults, causing weak and easily fractured bones) | • Possible kidney damage because of accumulation of calcium in body tissues |
| • Weight loss<br>• Anemia<br>• Abnormal growth | • No known toxicity |
| • No known deficiency | • Confusion<br>• Coma |
| • No known deficiency | • No known toxicity |
| • Deficiency rare—usually occurs only with excessive loss of potassium due to overuse of diuretics, causing weakness, paralysis, heart disturbances | • Nausea, vomiting<br>• Heart disturbances<br>• Weakness<br>• Paralysis |
| • Weakness<br>• Muscle tremors<br>• Behavior changes | • No known toxicity |
| • Iron deficiency anemia (lack of hemoglobin, causing shortness of breath, weakness, fatigue, rapid heartbeat) | • Most potentially toxic mineral, causing nausea, abdominal cramps, liver and intestinal damage, skin discoloration |
| • Malfunction of thyroid gland<br>• Goiter (enlarged thyroid gland)<br>• Impaired physical and mental development<br>• Subnormal body temperature | • Goiter |
| • Inclination toward dental cavities | • Mottled or pitted teeth |
| • Retarded growth<br>• Sexual immaturity<br>• Slow or poor healing | • Vomiting<br>• Diarrhea<br>• Kidney damage |

(Continued from page 17)
performance, can result in decreased physical capabilities, and can contribute to such conditions as anemia, bone demineralization (mineral depletion) and brittleness, nervous system disease, and fetal abnormalities. With certain minerals, even consuming twice the daily requirement or taking one day's requirement all in one dose can lead to severe illness. Taking minerals in excessive quantities is especially risky for children, pregnant or nursing women, and the elderly.

## Calcium

Calcium is the most prevalent mineral in the body; in fact, the bones and teeth together contain an average of two to three pounds of calcium. It regulates certain body processes—normal nerve function, muscle tone, and blood clotting. The best sources of calcium are milk and milk products.

## Phosphorus

Phosphorus coexists with calcium in the bones and teeth but is also present in most body tissues. Phosphorus is present in so many foods that a deficiency is rare; it is most abundant in meat, poultry, fish, eggs, and whole-grain products.

## Sodium chloride

Sodium and chlorine combine to form sodium chloride (table salt), yet each element functions separately. Sodium maintains regular water balance both inside and outside the cells, and is found in blood plasma and fluids outside the cells. Foods rich in sodium include meat, fish, poultry, eggs, milk, and such processed foods as bacon, ham, bread, and crackers. Chlorine is a constituent of hydrochloric acid, which is concentrated in gastric (stomach) juices and is necessary for the functioning of the digestive system. People who perspire heavily may have to add salt to their diet, but most people eat too much salt because of their high consumption of processed foods and added table salt. Surplus salt increases water retention and, in predisposed individuals, has been associated with edema and high blood pressure.

## Potassium

Potassium, mainly present in the fluid in cells, regulates the balance and volume of body fluids in tandem with sodium. Because most foods (both plant and animal) are rich in potassium, a nutritional deficiency is very rare, although it may occur in conjunction with prolonged diarrhea, use of diuretics (medications that remove water from the body), or a diet that lacks protein.

## Magnesium

Magnesium is contained mostly in bones, although it is present in all body tissues. It is vital to the enzymes that help convert food into energy. Magnesium deficiencies usually occur only in postsurgical patients, alcoholics, and others who do not eat a well-balanced diet. Magnesium-rich foods include whole-grain cereals, dried peas and beans, cocoa, nuts, seafood, and dark-green vegetables.

## Sulfur

Sulfur, found in all tissues, is a part of several important amino acids and of the vitamins thiamin and biotin. It is not fully understood how it works in the body.

## Iron

Iron is found throughout the body, chiefly in the blood, liver, spleen, and bone marrow. It is an integral part of the compounds that are necessary to transport oxygen to the cells and to regulate its use there. Foods that provide significant amounts of iron include liver, seafood, meats, egg yolks, fish, green vegetables, and dried peas and beans.

An inadequate supply of iron in the diet causes iron deficiency anemia, which most often affects women in their reproductive years (especially pregnant women), infants, and teenagers (particularly during the adolescent growth spurt).

## Manganese

Manganese is fundamental for the normal building of tendons and bones and is part of some enzymes. Foods rich in this mineral include bran, coffee, tea, nuts, peas, and beans. Manganese deficiency in humans is virtually unknown.

## Copper

Copper, an element involved in the storage and release of iron to form the oxygen-carrying hemoglobin in red blood cells, is most vital in the early months of life. If a pregnant woman's intake is sufficient, her baby will be born with enough copper. It is most available in processed foods, organ meats, shellfish, nuts, and dried peas and beans.

### Iodine

Iodine is indispensable to the normal working of the thyroid gland. A shortage can result in goiter (thyroid enlargement). Before the introduction of iodized salt in the United States in 1924, iodine-deficiency goiter was common in inland areas. Foods obtained from the sea are rich in iodine.

### Zinc

Zinc is a fundamental part of the enzymes that move carbon dioxide in the red blood cells from the tissues to the lungs for exhalation. A deficiency of zinc may show up as a loss of the sense of taste or delayed healing of wounds. Associated with protein, zinc is found in meats (especially liver), cheese, dried beans and peas, seafood, egg yolks, and milk. Although it is available in whole-grain cereal, it is not likely to be absorbed because of the presence of other substances.

### Cobalt

Cobalt is not needed in the body by itself, but is part of the nutrient cyanocobalamin (vitamin $B_{12}$), which is available in meat, eggs, fish, and dairy products.

### Chromium

Chromium acts with insulin in the use of glucose (a form of sugar). A shortage produces a condition that is similar to diabetes. Chromium is present in dried brewer's yeast, whole-grain cereals, and liver.

### Selenium

Selenium appears to work in conjunction with vitamin E. Not much is known about selenium, except that it is important in the body and that it is found in animals and plants where it is accessible in the earth. A deficiency may cause muscle pain and impairment of heart function.

### Fluoride

Fluoride is important in the formation of teeth and resistance to dental caries (cavities), especially in children, and helps maintain calcium in the bones of the elderly. It is available in fluoridated water, seafood, and meats.

# AVOIDING HAZARDOUS SUBSTANCES TO STAY HEALTHY

The nation's leading recreational drugs are alcohol, tobacco, cocaine, and marijuana. All are used by both adults and minors, although only the first two are legal—and only for adults. All are powerful substances that are addictive to young and old alike and that have the capacity to injure or destroy the body.

The perspective from which to view these hazardous substances when considering changes in your lifestyle is that this is one area of your life over which you can exercise control. There are many situations that threaten our good health that we cannot prevent or avoid—for example, aging, being exposed to microorganisms and environmental pollutants, and suffering from inherited disorders. But the risks posed by the substances discussed in the following sections can be controlled by limiting or avoiding their use.

# Alcohol

In cultures around the world, drinking alcohol is generally a socially acceptable way for adults to relax and enjoy themselves. In moderation, drinking alcohol is a fairly harmless practice for most people. However, alcohol is a central nervous system depressant. The short-term effects can disrupt mental and motor skills, resulting in bad judgment, poor coordination, and a tendency to have accidents. Consumed heavily on a regular basis, alcohol damages internal organs, especially the liver and the heart.

The fact that alcohol is so prevalent and acceptable in our society makes it easier to form a dependence on it—a good reason why those who drink should examine their drinking habits from time to time. It has been estimated that one American in ten suffers from alcoholism at some time in his life.

### Alcoholism

Alcoholism is a disorder in which a person repeatedly drinks excessive amounts of alcoholic beverages, with resulting harm to health, relations with other people, and work performance. The person becomes physically and psychologically dependent on alcohol. There is a genuine craving for alcohol when it is withdrawn for one to three days, and unpleasant responses such as delirium tremens (characterized by a severe stress reaction, hallucinations, and tremors) and convulsions may be seen when alcohol is not available.

### Causes of alcoholism

Various causes of alcoholism have been suggested. These include depression, self-hatred, and having a shy, lonely, immature, or dependent personality. Some societies and groups within those societies encourage overuse of alcohol as recreation and as an escape from life's problems. There is also evidence that a tendency to alcoholism may be inherited or may be the result of a chemical defect. Whatever the cause, alcoholism is a self-damaging disease and an ineffective way to deal with life.

### Symptoms of alcoholism

The fact that a person is an alcoholic is not always obvious. Alcoholics often do not recognize their own alcoholism or try to hide symptoms from spouses, other family members, friends, and employers. Signs of alcoholism include:
• Frequent drunkenness
• Tolerance to alcohol (A great deal of liquor is required before the person shows signs of intoxication; however, this is not true in all cases, especially if alcohol has damaged the liver.)

• Physical dependence, resulting in withdrawal symptoms a day or more after stopping drinking (Symptoms may range from tremors and physical pain to seizures and visions of bugs or strange creatures.)
• Continued drinking even when it is harming the person's health and personal life
• Poor job performance
• Depression

Other signs may include an odor of liquor on the breath in the morning, stealthy drinking, suspicious work absences (to sleep off hangovers), and frequent falls, accidents, and cigarette burns on hands and body (caused by drunken carelessness).

Alcoholism can cause permanent damage to the liver, brain, heart, and nervous system. Moderate to heavy drinking by a pregnant woman can result in mental retardation in her baby, as well as low birth weight and birth defects.

If an alcoholic has been drinking as much as a gallon of beer or a pint of whiskey a day for several months, sudden withdrawal of alcohol may even result in death because of convulsions or delirium tremens.

### Treatment of alcoholism

Alcoholism is not a cause for shame or embarrassment, nor is it a sign of failure or degeneracy. It is a disease that, like any other, requires professional treatment, not only for the alcoholic's sake but also for the sake of the others—family, friends, and co-workers—whose lives he affects.

Treatment of severe alcoholism involves two stages, immediate and long-term. Both require a physician's attention.

The first step is to stop the drinking while treating the symptoms of withdrawal. The drug disulfiram is sometimes prescribed, to be taken daily by mouth; it causes vomiting if the patient drinks anything alcoholic. It stops the person from drinking, but the patient may refuse to continue taking it because of its unpleasant effects.

In a crisis situation, withdrawal is best done in a hospital alcoholic unit. Under a doctor's care, psychological support and reassurance may be enough to comfort the patient during the withdrawal stage. Frequently, however, other measures are needed. The patient may be undernourished from drinking so much and eating so little and may need replacement doses of vitamins, particularly thiamin (vitamin $B_1$). Fluids containing glucose (a form of sugar) and salt water may be added to the blood, which has been robbed of water and glucose by the effects of overuse of alcohol. Tranquilizing drugs may be given to help ease withdrawal symptoms, which may continue for days.

Long-term treatment may include psychiatric help to treat the problem that caused the alcoholism in the first place, such as depression or mental illness. For many alcoholics, the solution is to join an organization known as Alcoholics Anonymous (AA). Members help each other overcome their drinking problems and vow to stay away from alcohol completely. In helping each other, they develop confidence and positive feelings about themselves.

### Prevention of alcoholism

Alcoholism is a significant social and medical problem that

cannot be easily stopped. However, its threat may be diminished by:

• Learning about the full extent of its dangers
• Finding more healthful ways to deal with life's problems and disappointments—by facing, rather than avoiding, them
• Learning to recognize the symptoms of alcoholism
• Seeking help from a physician or a group like Alcoholics Anonymous

# Cocaine

Cocaine is prepared from the leaves of the plant *Erythroxylon coca*. The earliest known use of the coca plant dates back to approximately A.D. 600. However, it was not until 1855 that cocaine was isolated from coca leaves.

## Use

In recent years, there has been an enormous increase in cocaine use. At the present time, it is estimated that some ten million Americans have used cocaine and that about five million use it on a regular basis. Since the drug is relatively expensive, users often believe that it puts them in an elite group, and they frequently take the drug to boost their self-esteem. Multiple drug use is common among cocaine users, with most also using alcohol or marijuana.

Cocaine is usually used in one of four ways: nasal inhalation of the powdered form ("snorting"), intravenous injection, smoking the crystalline form ("crack"), or inhalation of the vapor ("free-basing"). Free-basing is an extremely dangerous technique, rapidly delivering high concentrations of cocaine to the central nervous system.

## Effects

Cocaine is best known for its effect as a central nervous system stimulant. At lower doses, cocaine produces talkativeness, euphoria (a heightened sense of well-being), excitement, enormous self-confidence, and a deceptive sense of increased concentration. At higher doses, tremors, seizures, and severe mental disorders can develop. Cocaine also impairs the appetite; with chronic (long-term) use, poor nutritional intake results.

Cocaine also acts by impairing the control of neurologic hormones at nerve endings throughout the body. This causes the heart rate to increase rapidly, the heart to beat irregularly, and the blood vessels to constrict; this combination of events results in a rapid rise in blood pressure. There have been frequent reports of healthy young adults suffering a stroke or heart attack due to the acute effects of cocaine.

According to a number of recent studies, a pregnant woman who uses cocaine endangers not only her own health but also that of her unborn child. Associated with cocaine use in pregnancy is an increased risk of miscarriage, as well as a greater incidence of premature births. Infants have been born addicted to the drug and have suffered severe neurologic and behavioral consequences as a result of their mothers' drug habits.

## Treatment

In the past, it was thought that cocaine is not addictive and does not produce dependence or a withdrawal syndrome. However, with the increasing use of cocaine (in particular, large amounts of free-base cocaine), it has become apparent that a withdrawal syndrome does exist. This syndrome usually consists of depression, irritability, sleep disturbance, gastrointestinal upset, and headaches. The onset of the syndrome begins approximately 24 to 48 hours after cessation of cocaine use and lasts seven to ten days.

Because of the diversity of reasons for cocaine use, a multifaceted approach to the treatment of patients is required. The goals of treatment include the cessation of all chemical abuse, the restoration of normal patterns of behavior, and the development of new attitudes and more positive ways of coping with life's problems. Hospitalization is required for every patient for whom outpatient attempts to cease cocaine use have repeatedly failed or for whom severe complications in physical, psychological, or social functioning exist. Cocaine addiction, like any other addiction, is a long-term problem, with remissions (periods when the disorder seems to get better) and exacerbations (periods when it gets worse). As with any chronic disease, treatment must continue on a long-term basis.

# Marijuana

Marijuana, or cannabis, is the dried flower clusters, stems, and leaves of the Indian hemp plant (*Cannabis sativa*), and looks like coarse tobacco. It is also known as "weed," "pot," "grass," "tea," and "Mary Jane," as well as a number of other slang equivalents.

Marijuana has been smoked, drunk, eaten, and sniffed throughout recorded history. When marijuana is rolled into a cigarette, it is called a "joint" or a "reefer." When it is smoked, it has a very distinctive odor.

## Immediate effects

All of the effects of smoking or ingesting marijuana are not yet known because long-term studies are still under way. It is known that marijuana raises the heart rate by as much as 50 percent and lowers sex hormone and fertility levels in both males and females.

Visible symptoms of marijuana use include reddened eyes, dilated pupils, and lack of physical coordination. Sometimes, users feel lethargic and nauseated. Reactions to marijuana differ: some users feel happy, talkative, and silly; others may become withdrawn.

Marijuana relaxes the body and the mind. It gives a feeling of exhilaration and euphoria. In addition, marijuana alters perceptions—colors seem brighter, music more intense—and gives a sense of time being extended. However, these effects are often accompanied or followed by mood swings, panic, depression, hallucinations, and fear of death, particularly if marijuana is being used in combination with other drugs.

Marijuana does not increase intellectual functioning or creative capacity, although it may produce that impression during use. Actually, marijuana affects the brain by interfering with the ability to think, to make judgments, and to solve problems. Marijuana also slows reaction time and hinders coordination and visual perception. For these

reasons, driving a car while under the influence of marijuana is dangerous.

## Long-term effects

It is believed that use of marijuana may cause long-term physical effects, including damage to the brain, heart, lungs, and reproductive system.

Users of marijuana often experience a decrease in motivation and become psychologically dependent on the drug because it represents a way to avoid facing the problems and stresses of life. Marijuana users do not, however, appear to become physically addicted to it and generally do not suffer serious withdrawal reactions when they abstain from its use. Most users of marijuana do not progress to use of hard drugs, such as heroin or cocaine, although that risk does exist.

Moderate use of marijuana does not appear to pose highly dangerous long-term effects. Nevertheless, there are several reasons for concern about the use of this substance. First, much of the marijuana used is smoked by young people in their formative years; they tend to use the drug more regularly than adults. Second, improved methods of cultivation have resulted in harvests of the plant that are increasingly more potent. Third, unlike alcohol, the mind-altering chemical in marijuana can remain in the body for a week or more. Fourth, because the substance is illegal, there are no quality controls over its content; large quantities of marijuana have been found to be contaminated with pesticides or laced with more dangerous or addictive narcotics. Fifth, because marijuana cigarettes do not have

filters, their smoke irritates lung tissue much more than the smoke of regular filtered cigarettes. Marijuana cigarettes also contain more tar and benzopyrene (a cancer-causing agent) than tobacco cigarettes.

# Tobacco

Tobacco use usually begins as a social behavior and results in significant physical consequences to the body. Cigarette smoke is much more hazardous in this regard than pipe or cigar smoke. Cigarette smoking tends to be habit-forming, and the accumulated effects increase the risks for development of life-threatening disease.

The chemical makeup of cigarette smoke is complicated and still under scientific investigation. One of the chemicals in tobacco is tar, a powerful carcinogen (cancer-causing agent). Another chemical, nicotine, produces harmful effects on the nervous system. Various chemicals in tobacco interfere with other biochemical processes and body functions.

## Links to cancer

Smoking cigarettes, pipes, and cigars and chewing smokeless tobacco have been linked to oral cancers. Oral cancers include those of the mouth, lips, salivary glands, tongue, and throat. Symptoms of oral cancers include a persistent sore, which may bleed; a thickened area; discoloration; difficulty in chewing or swallowing; and persistent sore throat. Such symptoms should be called to a physician's attention immediately.

Cigarette smoking has also been implicated in lung cancer.

Initially, cigarette smoke may destroy the tiny hairs that normally function in clearing away mucus in the respiratory tract. The bronchial lining may then undergo changes that result in cancer cell production. Early symptoms of lung cancer may include coughing, wheezing, and chest pain. Anyone with a history of smoking should be alert to these symptoms. If you have not smoked cigarettes, your chances of developing lung cancer are very greatly reduced. If you do have a history of smoking, stopping will decrease your risk of developing lung cancer.

**Links to chronic respiratory diseases**

Emphysema and chronic bronchitis are most often caused by smoking. Both conditions are considered chronic obstructive pulmonary diseases, in which there is airway blockage. Emphysema and chronic bronchitis frequently coexist. In emphysema, abnormally large amounts of air accumulate in the air sacs of the lungs, making exhalation especially difficult. In chronic bronchitis, the bronchi (large airways) undergo changes that impede the flow of air into the lungs.

The initial symptom of emphysema is shortness of breath. This may be accompanied by a persistent cough. Progression of the disease, usually occurring over a period of years, results in severe breathing difficulty and restriction of activity. In chronic bronchitis, a persistent cough develops initially and is usually accompanied by excessive production of mucus. If you experience shortness of breath or develop a persistent cough, consult your physician. Stopping smoking will generally provide the best means of slowing the course of these diseases in smokers. Fortunately, emphysema and chronic bronchitis can usually be prevented by avoiding cigarette smoking.

**Links to circulatory disorders**

Stopping smoking can also significantly reduce the incidence of atherosclerosis, in which the walls of the arteries thicken and lose elasticity. This condition is associated with heart attacks and strokes.

**Interactions with medications**

Smoking can also produce indirect adverse reactions in the body. Chemicals in smoke can interfere with the action of some medications by altering the absorption rate and duration of effect. Always mention your smoking habits to the physician when drugs are being prescribed. The physician will then be able to make the proper adjustments in dosage.

**Effects on nonsmokers**

Nonsmokers who continuously breathe the cigarette smoke of others are known as passive smokers. Research indicates that passive smokers suffer ill effects from exposure to cigarette smoke, including increased heart rates and blood pressure levels and constriction of the airways in the lungs. Children are especially vulnerable to the respiratory effects of breathing "second-hand" smoke.

**Breaking the smoking habit**

Stopping smoking is beneficial to yourself and to those around you, even if there are not yet any signs of disease. (Never starting is even better.) Unfortunately, despite the proved medical risks of tobacco use, many smokers who want to quit seem unable to break the habit. For those who cannot do it on their own, help is available from many sources, such as the American Cancer Society and the American Lung Association.

If you want to try quitting by yourself, it may help first to figure out why you smoke and then to substitute other activities or substances when you feel the urge to light up. The motivation for smoking may be addiction, habit, a response to anxiety, a need to have something to do with the mouth and hands, or a desire for stimulation or relaxation.

There is no single method for quitting smoking that is right for everyone. Ex-smokers have quit in a variety of ways. If one plan fails, try another; if you don't succeed the first time, keep trying. Remember, smoking is a learned behavior that can be changed.

# YOU AND YOUR DOCTOR

Most people never think about how to choose a doctor until they need one in a hurry. When a person is injured or suddenly becomes ill, finding a good doctor is a necessity, and there is often no time to spare in finding one.

If a person does not have a family doctor, injury or sudden illness often means a quick visit to the emergency room or outpatient section of the nearest hospital, where staff physicians who know nothing about the patient's personal medical history must treat him symptomatically and, more often than not, on an urgent basis. This is usually not a good way to establish a lasting physician-patient relationship.

A better way to assure yourself of good medical care is to have a personal physician who is familiar with you and your family's medical history and who is available (or has associates who are available) when you need care. In this way, your health needs are being met by someone who knows you and whom you know.

The best time, then, to choose a doctor is when you don't need one. You should never wait until you have no choice about the doctor you see. How do you choose a doctor? Here are some guidelines for making an informed choice.

## Choosing a family doctor

Many families want a doctor who is familiar both with family members as individuals and with the family as a group. Doctors who have specialized in family medicine are called family practitioners. Their education and training enable them not only to provide medical care but also to recognize and handle the social,

emotional, and psychological factors that affect the health and well-being of their patients and their families. Whereas a physician needs to have only one year of internship (postgraduate hospital training, usually divided among several branches of medicine) before entering general practice, today's family practitioner completes a one-year internship and a two-year residency in family practice, during which he or she receives more intensive training in general surgery, internal medicine, obstetrics/gynecology, and pediatrics, among other fields.

Family practitioners care for all the members of a family, so that there is usually no need for a different specialist for each individual. A family practitioner is well equipped to handle most aspects of medical care, such as uncomplicated pregnancies, immunizations, and routine physicals. A family practitioner can generally diagnose and treat all of the common ailments, as well as many uncommon ones, and can guide you to the right specialist when you need one.

In addition to providing comprehensive medical care for all family members, today's family practitioner is as interested in maintaining your good health as in curing or treating illness. The family practitioner's overall goal is to treat each family member as an individual with physical, emotional, and social needs, as well as medical requirements.

How can you find a family practitioner who is right for your family? You can call the county medical society or your local chapter of the American Medical Association. These organizations have uniform requirements for physicians to be admitted to their membership (for example, completion of appropriate training

and board certification). They also can tell you where you can find a specialist. However, these societies do not offer an opinion on the overall quality of a physician. This is something you must assess for yourself. The questions listed below will help you make this assessment.

You should also ask people in your neighborhood about the doctor they see. They may be able to offer suggestions based on their personal experience with local physicians. In addition, if you live in a city, you may find that there is a local organization that evaluates the medical profession on behalf of the consumer. Neighborhood consumer groups often will make medical referral information available to you at no charge and will steer you toward physicians who have a record of treating their patients with respect and concern.

In the process of selecting a family physician, you should draw up a list of basic questions to ask the doctor:

- Will the doctor treat all family members?
- Does the doctor provide care during pregnancy and perform deliveries?
- Does the doctor have staff privileges at a nearby accredited hospital?
- Does the doctor perform surgery? If so, what types?
- Does the doctor encourage preventive medicine, such as routine checkups, immunizations, and follow-up tests?
- Does the doctor make emergency house calls for bedridden family members?
- Does the doctor have office hours that are convenient for your family, especially for those who work or attend school?
- What arrangement does the doctor have for a substitute when he or she is unavailable?

• What are the fees for the various services?
• Is the doctor certified by the American Board of Family Practice (or a specialty board of another area)?

The answers to these questions, along with the recommendations of friends and neighbors, will help you select the right doctor for you and your family.

# How to choose a specialist

In approaching the problem of finding a specialist, you should remember that most specialists receive their patients through referrals from family doctors or from other specialists. Many have a policy of not accepting a patient who has not first been examined and referred by a family doctor. This is a method of making sure that those who really need specialists see them and that those who do not need them do not incur the expense that seeing a specialist entails.

Your family doctor will usually decide whether your medical complaint needs the attention of a specialist. For example, if you have a mild inflammation of the ear canal (perhaps as a result of a fungal infection from swimming in polluted water), your family doctor is quite capable of treating it. If there is chronic inflammation of the ear canal, however, or if you have suffered a partial loss of hearing, your doctor will probably refer you to an otorhinolaryngologist (ear, nose, and throat specialist).

You must also remember that difficulties in one area of the body affect other areas, so a specialist is not always needed to diagnose and treat a problem. For example, visual problems may be limited to abnormalities in the eye itself, but they may also be the result of a wide variety of causes, including diabetes, arteriosclerosis (hardening of the arteries), a stroke, or a tumor in a part of the brain that controls vision. The human body is an organic system. Changes in one part of the system affect other parts, and no part of the system functions in isolation. Consequently, the first task in treating an illness is to discover the underlying primary cause of the ailment. When the culprit is found, you may then be referred to a specialist who deals with the specific area of the body most affected by that problem.

The first line of action in selecting a specialist is to follow your family doctor's advice. He or she will know whether you need a specialist. However, you can always ask for a second opinion or seek out a specialist on your own. If for no other reason than to know that you did all you were able to do, you should always try to get as much information as possible about your own or a family member's illness. You may even find something that one of the doctors missed.

If your family doctor refers you to a specialist, or if you seek one on your own, you should know what each specialty consists of and what to expect when you see each specialist. The following section gives you a brief description of more than 30 medical and surgical specialties. As you read about each one, remember that an internship is the period immediately after graduation from medical school, during which a doctor receives supervised practical experience in a hospital setting. A residency, also supervised in a hospital setting, follows an internship; it is a period of advanced training in a doctor's chosen medical specialty. The length of a residency varies, depending on the specialty. Board certification means that a doctor has been certified as meeting the professional standards of a medical specialty organization called a board, which usually requires a residency in an accredited institution, acceptable performance on a rigorous set of examinations, and, in some fields, a year or two of clinical experience.

**Allergy and immunology**

This branch of medicine is concerned with the study, diagnosis, and treatment of disorders related to immunity (the body's ability to resist disease or threatening substances). The body's immune system fights against the intrusion of outside forces, whether they are irritating substances that cause allergic reactions or microorganisms that cause infection. This is the system that helps us fight off illness every day of our lives. Modern immunological research indicates that many infections can be as much a result of defects in a person's immune system as they are a result of exposure to viruses or bacteria.

Immunologists are also studying the role of the immune system in cancer growth. It may someday be possible to prevent cancer by modifying the immune system to reject cancerous growths in the body. Immunologists are also interested in the opposite effect of the immune system—the rejection of foreign substances that are actually beneficial (the most obvious example is an organ transplant). Immunologists are seeking ways to effect selective operation of the immune system, so that the body would reject cancer cells but accept a new heart, kidney, or liver.

The best-known branch of immunology deals with allergies, which are responses of the body's immune system to irritating substances in the environment. Doctors who practice as allergists are involved in identifying environmental irritants that cause symptoms and in formulating a plan of treatment. Allergists treat allergies by suggesting environmental modifications to eliminate the offending substance or by using drugs to relieve the symptoms. Another option is a program of desensitization, which involves injecting minute amounts of the offending agent to make the immune system less sensitive to it. Once such a program has been set up, your family doctor can often give the injections. Allergists also consult in the management of certain diseases, such as asthma.

An immunologist must complete a residency in internal medicine or pediatrics after graduating from medical school. After this residency, he or she completes a two-year fellowship program in allergy and immunology. Specialty board examinations are also required.

## Anesthesiology

With the use of anesthetics, surgery may now be done without pain during the procedure. Many minor procedures may be done with a local anesthetic (a painkiller that is usually injected into or rubbed onto the affected area), but more complex procedures require that the patient be unconscious.

An anesthesiologist is a specialist in the use of those drugs that cause a cessation of the experience of pain. The word "anesthesia" is derived from two Greek roots: *ana,* meaning the loss or lack of something, and *esthesia,* the act or process of sensing. Hence, "anesthesia" means, literally, a lack of sensation.

Anesthesiologists must complete medical school, an internship, and a residency in their specialty before starting their practice. They may also receive some training in a field other than anesthesiology, such as internal medicine, pediatrics, or obstetrics. Some of them also do tours of surgical residency, in order to broaden and deepen their knowledge of surgical techniques and needs.

## Bariatrics

Bariatrics is a relatively new field in medicine, brought into popularity by the public's keen interest in the problems of being overweight.

Bariatricians have been making advances in what is known about being overweight or underweight, by dispelling myths and substituting hard scientific evidence. Their training usually includes an internship in internal medicine, with a special residency in bariatrics. Bariatricians are certified by their specialty group, the American Society of Bariatric Physicians.

## Cardiology

Cardiology is a branch of internal medicine that deals with the diagnosis and treatment of disorders of the heart and circulatory system, including those that stem from birth abnormalities, childhood diseases, or advancing age. Cardiologists take care of a variety of heart conditions, such as rheumatic heart disease in children and congestive heart failure and heart attacks in adults.

Cardiology and cardiovascular surgery complement each other. Over the years, doctors in these fields have worked closely together in the treatment of heart diseases. For example, the cardiologist may determine that a child has been born with a hole between the chambers of the heart; the cardiovascular surgeon is the one who will repair this hole through open-heart surgery.

In the past few years, many advances in the medical and surgical treatment of heart disease have been made. A cardiologist must be acquainted not only with anatomy and physiology, but also with modern computerized diagnostic equipment. One special diagnostic procedure performed by cardiologists is cardiac catheterization, in which a catheter (a long, thin, flexible tube) is inserted into the heart and adjacent blood vessels, allowing the injection of a special dye that affords visualization of those structures. Angioplasty (the opening of a blocked artery by insertion of a balloon-tipped catheter) is a treatment procedure that is commonly performed by cardiologists.

Training in cardiology includes completion of a residency in internal medicine, followed by at least two years of specialized training in cardiology.

## Cardiovascular surgery

The cardiovascular surgeon performs many different types of surgery on the heart and blood vessels, including replacement of heart valves and bypasses of blocked coronary arteries. Open-heart surgery came into its own during the 1950s and underwent further refinement in the 1960s and 1970s. Two decades have passed since the first heart transplant. In 1982, the first implantation of an artificial heart took place.

Training in cardiovascular surgery includes the completion of a general surgery residency, followed by two or three years of specialized training.

## Dentistry

Dentistry is concerned with the prevention, diagnosis, and treatment of diseases, disorders, and malformations of the teeth, mouth, and jaws. Most people select a dentist with a general practice who can provide routine dental care and, if necessary, recommend a dental specialist for those conditions needing specialized treatment. Some of the dental specialties include:
- Orthodontia (straightening of teeth)
- Periodontia (treatment of gums and underlying bone)
- Endodontia (root canal treatment)
- Exodontia (extraction of teeth)

A dentist planning to establish a general practice will complete four years of dental school and perhaps an optional one-year general residency. Dental specialists have additional specific training in their specialty.

Finding a family dentist is much like finding a family doctor. You should ask friends and neighbors for recommendations or contact your local dental society. Your family doctor may also be able to suggest a dentist.

## Dermatology

Dermatology is the study of diseases and disorders of the skin ranging from acne to psoriasis to skin cancer.

The dermatologist must also be knowledgeable about diseases that primarily affect other parts of the body but that may have some bearing on the condition of the skin. In addition, dermatologists have training in allergies since over the years many skin conditions have been recognized as allergic reactions instead of skin diseases.

Dermatologists are required to do an internship, usually in internal medicine, followed by a three-year residency in dermatology.

## Endocrinology

When we think of "messages" being sent throughout the body, we usually think of the nervous system. But there is another communication system in the body, called the endocrine system. It is made up of the ductless glands, including the pituitary gland, the adrenal glands, the thyroid gland, the parathyroid glands, the islet cells in the pancreas, the ovaries (in women), and the testes (in men). These glands secrete hormones that travel as messengers throughout the body to direct and integrate a vast number of bodily functions. Disorders of the endocrine system include diabetes, Cushing's syndrome, and growth abnormalities.

An endocrinologist is a specialist in the diagnosis and treatment of disorders of the endocrine system. He or she must complete an internship and a residency in internal medicine, followed by two years of training in endocrinology.

## Epidemiology

Specialists in this medical field study the outbreak, frequency, distribution, and control of communicable diseases. The unofficial headquarters of this activity is the Centers for Disease Control (once the Communicable Disease Center) in Atlanta, Georgia.

Epidemiology deals not only with communication of disease in general, but also with the specific conditions under which certain diseases seem to flourish. For example, the relatively new field of urban epidemiology specifically addresses itself to those diseases and conditions peculiar to city settings. In addition, epidemiologists work to devise ways of preventing disease, such as developing vaccines.

Epidemiology is also concerned with causes of illness other than infectious diseases. For example, lead poisoning as a result of eating lead-based paint was a major cause of brain damage among children before epidemiologists discovered the connection. Epidemiologists have led the medical field in seeking environmental causes for a host of disorders once attributed to bacteria or other sources. Air and water pollution, toxic substances in foods, toxic substances used in the manufacture of a variety of products—all have come under the scrutiny of the epidemiologist.

Epidemiology attracts physicians not only from internal medicine but also from other fields, such as immunology, occupational medicine, and pediatrics. An epidemiologist will usually have completed three years of specialized training and a year of independent research or teaching.

## Gastroenterology

A gastroenterologist specializes in the diagnosis and treatment of diseases and disorders of the stomach and the intestines, as well as related organs that help in the digestive process, such as the esophagus, liver, and pancreas. The word "gastroenterology" comes from three Greek roots: *gastro,* meaning stomach; *enteron,* meaning intestine; and *logos,* meaning study. Gastritis (inflammation of the stomach), enteritis (inflammation of the intestinal tract), ulcers, inability to digest certain foods, constipation, diarrhea, hyperacidity, and heartburn are among the disorders treated by the gastroenterologist.

Gastroenterologists often use the procedure called endoscopy, in which a flexible tubelike instrument is used to directly view hollow organs, such as the esophagus, stomach, and colon. Diagnosis and treatment of many conditions, such as ulcers and polyps, may be done with this procedure. Biopsies (in which tissue samples are gathered for testing) are also carried out with endoscopy.

These specialists are trained as internists or pediatricians with an additional two-year fellowship in gastroenterology.

## Hematology

Hematology is the study of diseases and disorders of the blood and the blood-forming tissues, such as the bone marrow and the spleen. A hematologist is proficient in a wide range of diagnostic techniques in which blood and bone marrow samples are used to shed light on disease processes. Blood analyses can aid a diagnostician in developing treatment for a patient. The hematologist's primary concern, however, is the host of diseases and disorders relative to the blood itself, including inability of the red blood cells to carry sufficient oxygen, inability of the white blood cells to fight against invading microorganisms, and inability of the bone marrow to manufacture enough red blood cells. The hematologist is also an expert on cancer of the blood (leukemia) and on blood clotting problems, such as hemophilia.

The hematologist must be firmly grounded not only in internal medicine, anatomy, and physiology, but also in biochemistry. Knowledge of computerized diagnostic equipment and sophisticated biochemical analyses is also necessary.

A hematologist completes an internship and a residency in internal medicine plus two years of training in hematology. Many, if not most, hematologists are also trained as oncologists (cancer specialists).

## Internal medicine

Internal medicine is the branch of medicine that deals with the diagnosis and treatment of diseases of adults, except for those conditions that require management by a surgeon or an obstetrician. Like the family practitioner, the internist is trained to handle a wide range of illnesses; in fact, many people select an internist as their family doctor. The internist is specifically trained to deal with chronic (long-term) illnesses, such as diabetes and high blood pressure, and acute (short-term) diseases, such as infections. In addition, an internist has both the range and the depth to diagnose illnesses that might escape detection by a specialist if they lie outside his or her special field. For this reason, internists are often called diagnosticians.

After graduating from medical school, an internist completes one year of internship, followed by two years of residency in internal medicine. Internal medicine is also the basis for many other specialties, such as cardiology, endocrinology, gastroenterology, hematology, and nephrology. That is why these branches are often referred to as subspecialties and the doctors who practice them, as subspecialists. In order to become a subspecialist, an internist must complete at least two years of additional training, referred to as a fellowship, in his or her chosen subspecialty before becoming eligible for subspecialty board certification.

## Nephrology

Nephrologists treat kidney disorders. Their patients are usually referred to them by internists when kidney problems are diagnosed as needing special care. In treating kidney disorders, the nephrologist may make use of medications or dialysis (removal of wastes and other undesirable sustances from the blood by means of a special machine). Referral for surgery (for example, if a transplant is indicated) is also initiated by a nephrologist. Nephrologists also perform kidney biopsies, which are used to diagnose and follow up a number of kidney diseases.

Nephrologists are thoroughly grounded in internal medicine, with special attention to the physiological processes performed by the kidneys. Because of the complex nature of kidney function, they must be equally well grounded in biochemistry and the tools of modern biochemical analysis. A nephrologist must also be familiar with all of the latest computerized diagnostic equipment, as well as the latest in dialysis machines.

Training includes internship and a residency in internal

medicine, followed by a two-year fellowship in nephrology, after which the specialty board examinations may be taken.

## Neurology

Neurology is the field of medical science that is concerned with the nervous system—the brain, the spinal cord, and the complex network of nerves. Clinical neurology concerns itself specifically with the diagnosis and treatment of diseases of the nervous system, but the neurologist must be familiar with the total functioning of the body because disorders of other systems can affect the nervous system and vice versa.

Training in neurology includes a one-year internal medicine internship, followed by a three-year residency in neurology.

## Obstetrics/gynecology

The fields of obstetrics and gynecology are closely related, and physicians generally practice these specialties together. While gynecology encompasses the diagnosis and treatment of disorders of the female reproductive system, obstetrics deals specifically with pregnancy, childbirth, and related conditions.

Many obstetricians are members of a group practice. Most obstetric groups make sure that every doctor in the group either has seen or is familiar with each patient during her pregnancy. Thus, when it comes time for delivery, the mother will generally be taken care of by a doctor whom she knows.

After medical school, an obstetrician/gynecologist completes a five-year residency. During this time, he or she will also receive some training in internal medicine, general surgery, and care of the newborn infant.

The obstetrician/gynecologist often acts as the primary caregiver for women. He or she will also work closely with other medical specialists if specific problems occur that do not directly involve the reproductive system.

## Occupational medicine

Occupational medicine began with industrial and business clinics, which were usually staffed by a physician and an industrial nurse (one who has specialized in the care of patients within a working environment). Occupational medicine has grown to include the study, diagnosis, and treatment of a vast range of illnesses caused by the industrial environment itself. Asbestos-induced cancer, "black lung" (in which coal dust literally turns the inside of the lungs black, with accompanying damage to the lungs), allergic reactions to industrial fibers, eye damage from welding arcs, and injury to the feet from jobs that require standing are but a few of the hundreds of disorders treated by occupational medicine physicians.

Specialists in occupational medicine generally have a background in internal medicine, with special training in the causes of industry-related illnesses. Often these doctors complete a public health program before going on to their specialty residency.

## Oncology

Oncology is the study of tumors, particularly cancer. This rel-atively new field is often associated with hematology (the study of the blood). Strictly speaking, oncology deals only with solid tumors and not with cancers of the blood. Today, however, many in the field are trained as hematologist-oncologists, so that they are certified to deal with both types of cancer.

Oncology requires expertise in a large number of medical and technical disciplines, from surgery to nutrition, from immunology to biochemistry, from diagnosis of symptoms to treatment of tumors with nuclear radiation.

There are subspecialties within the field of oncology. The medical oncologist is primarily responsible for prescribing and implementing chemotherapy, along with diagnosing and treating complications unique to cancer and coordinating the total treatment plan for cancer patients. Surgical oncologists perform cancer surgery. Pediatric oncologists diagnose and treat cancer in children. Gynecologic oncologists deal with cancer that occurs in the female reproductive system.

After graduating from medical school, a medical oncologist completes an internship and residency in internal medicine, followed by an additional training program in oncology, which includes training in hematology and chemotherapy. Surgical oncologists are usually general surgeons who have completed a fellowship in cancer surgery. Pediatric and gynecologic oncologists are first certified in their respective fields and then go on to oncology fellowships.

## Ophthalmology

An ophthalmologist is a medical doctor who diagnoses and

treats diseases and injuries of the eyes. Most ophthalmologists are also eye surgeons. They perform a variety of operations, such as reattaching retinas, removing cataracts, relieving pressure caused by glaucoma, and repairing blood vessel ruptures and other injuries.

Ophthalmologists have a background in both internal medicine and surgery. This specialty requires an additional three- or four-year residency in ophthalmology after a one-year general internship before specialty board examinations may be taken.

There are allied health-care workers who are often referred to as "eye doctors," but who are not medical doctors and therefore are not permitted to treat diseases of the eyes or to prescribe drugs. An optometrist tests the eyes for the purpose of fitting a person with glasses or contact lenses. An optician makes and fits glasses according to the ophthalmologist's or the optometrist's specifications. An ocularist fits artificial eyes.

## Orthopedics

Orthopedics is the branch of surgery that is concerned with the diagnosis and treatment of disorders of the bones and joints. The orthopedist treats broken bones, disorders of the bones and joints that can be corrected surgically, and bone tumors, as well as other problems of the skeletal system. Because of his or her knowledge of the functioning of the musculoskeletal system, the orthopedist often treats sports injuries and may serve as the physician for amateur and professional athletic teams.

The orthopedist is required to complete a one-year internship

in general surgery, four years of training in orthopedic surgery, and a year of medical practice before taking specialty board examinations.

## Otorhinolaryngology

This specialty combines the study of the ear, nose, and throat into a single discipline commonly referred to as ENT. The more formal term "otorhinolaryngology" is derived from the Greek roots ot- ("ear"), rhin- ("nose"), laryng- ("voice box"), and logos ("study").

The ears and throat are connected by the eustachian tubes, which lead from the middle ear to the throat. The nose leads directly into the part of the throat referred to as the nasopharynx. Inflammations of the nose may spread to the throat, and vice versa. Inflammations of the throat often spread through the eustachian tubes to the ears. Consequently, infection in any of these areas could result in infection in all of them.

Ear, nose, and throat specialists are primarily surgeons. They perform such varied procedures as rhinoplasty (reconstructive nose surgery); removal of tumors from the oral, nasal, and neck areas; reconstructive ear surgery; and sinus surgery. They also function as diagnosticians of diseases of the head and neck, excluding the brain and eyes.

This specialty requires a one-year residency in general surgery and a four-year residency in otorhinolaryngology.

## Pathology

Pathology is the study of the changes in body tissues brought about by disease and the ways in

which these changes provide clues not only to the causes of disease and death, but also to ways in which the spread of disease may be checked.

There are a variety of sub-specialties within pathology, including the following:
• Cellular pathology, in which cells are the focus of study
• Clinical pathology, in which laboratory methods are used to aid clinical diagnosis
• Comparative pathology, in which diseases in humans are compared with those in other animals
• General pathology, which is the study of the processes that may occur in various diseases
• Forensic pathology, in which the results of pathologic examinations (such as autopsies and analyses of tissue samples) are used as evidence in legal proceedings

Much of the pathologist's work is done with the microscope, preparing and examining biopsy specimens (tissue samples). Pathologists are charged with deciding whether a tissue specimen indicates the presence of a disease. They also perform autopsies to determine the cause or causes of death. The pathologist must be knowledgeable about both the cause and the course of disease processes.

Pathologists ordinarily do work in both internal medicine and surgery during their training. A strong laboratory background is a necessity, with extensive training in modern instrumentation. Three- to four-year residencies in pathology are required, depending on the subspecialty.

## Pediatrics

Pediatricians specialize in the diagnosis and treatment of diseases of children from birth through adolescence. They administer the appropriate immunizations to prevent disease and watch for any abnormalities that may appear during the growth of the child. They also advise parents about the child's social and psychological needs.

After completion of medical school, pediatricians must have at least three years of training in general pediatrics. This is followed by an examination by the specialty board.

## Peripheral vascular diseases

While cardiovascular surgeons treat disorders that affect the heart and its blood vessels specifically, surgeons who specialize in peripheral vascular diseases treat conditions that affect the rest of the circulatory system. Among these conditions are the following:
• Arteriosclerosis, in which the artery walls become abnormally thickened or hardened (in advanced cases, the arteries may become partially or completely blocked)
• Arterial occlusion and embolism, in which undissolved material in the bloodstream (such as clumps of clotted blood, bacteria, or tissue fragments) blocks the flow of blood in the artery, causing a loss of blood to tissue beyond the blockade and sometimes necrosis (death of tissue)
• Carotid occlusive disease, in which the carotid arteries (the arteries in the neck that supply the brain with blood) become blocked
• Aortic or femoral artery occlusive disease, in which the aorta (the main artery from the heart going through the chest and abdomen) or one of the femoral

arteries (the main arteries that carry blood to the legs) becomes blocked
• Venous thrombosis, in which the veins become clogged, usually with blood clots, with resulting pain and swelling of the affected extremity (if venous thrombosis is often associated with inflammation, it is called thrombophlebitis; if the vein becomes inflamed without thrombosis, it is referred to as phlebitis)
• Pulmonary embolism, in which blood clots travel to the lungs
Specialists in this area can be internists with extensive cardiovascular training. For the most part, however, they are surgeons.

## Physical medicine and rehabilitation

The field of physical medicine and rehabilitation is concerned with the diseases and disorders of the neuromuscular system (the nerves and muscles). Specialists in this field are skilled in using heat, cold, water, electricity, massage, and exercise to help patients regain use and function of parts of the body that have been damaged by stroke, severe arthritis, or spinal or other injury.

After completion of medical school, the physical medicine and rehabilitation specialist is required to complete at least three additional years of training, followed by two years of specialty practice. Specialty board examinations are required.

## Podiatry

Podiatrists treat diseases and injuries of the feet. Only recently have all the states recognized podiatry as a legitimate healing

field. Doctors in this area have degrees in podiatric medicine, but not M.D. degrees; they have not attended medical school. Many podiatrists have joined the ranks of sports medicine practitioners, since many foot injuries result from sports activities.

Many podiatrists are qualified to perform surgery on the feet when it is indicated. They also fit a variety of orthotic devices (corrective devices inserted into shoes) to correct foot problems. The boom in jogging and running that has accompanied the fitness movement has increased the demand for podiatric services.

## Preventive medicine

Specialists in this relatively new field seek to prevent illnesses from happening. Physicians from every field have made contributions to preventive medicine. Practitioners range from immunologists (who seek to prevent illness with inoculations) to urban epidemiologists (who search out the causes of widespread illnesses, such as childhood lead poisoning, and try to alter the environment so that illnesses can be prevented).

Preventive medicine advocates often recommend regular or periodic physical examinations, prescribe certain regimens, and warn against toxic environments. Critics of the field claim that there are no safeguards against some types of illnesses. Advocates of the field point out that the same was said of infections before antibiotics.

Occupational medicine and public health specialists are important members of this field of medicine. In addition, preventive medicine is concerned with reviewing present health services and anticipating and planning to meet future medical needs.

Preventive medicine specialists complete at least three years of specialized training, one year of research or teaching, and examinations by their specialty board.

## Proctology

The proctologist specializes in diseases and disorders of the anus and rectum. The rectum is the last portion of the large intestine; the anus is the opening to the outside from the rectum. Some of the conditions a proctologist treats include hemorrhoids (enlarged blood vessels around the anus) and rectal cancer.

Proctologists complete a residency in general surgery plus one or two years of training in colon and rectal surgery.

## Psychiatry

A psychiatrist is a medical doctor, with the authority to prescribe medications and make medical decisions, who deals with mental disorders. (Psychologists do not have a medical degree and therefore cannot prescribe drugs.) Many psychiatrists use psychoanalysis as part of their therapeutic or diagnostic method, and all psychiatrists have intensive training in psychology.

There are four chief branches of psychiatry: (1) descriptive psychiatry, which is based on the observation of external factors that may be the cause of mental illness; (2) dynamic psychiatry, which is the study of the processes, origins, and mechanisms of emotional states; (3) forensic psychiatry, which deals with the legal aspects of mental illness; and (4) orthomolecular psychiatry, which is the study of the molecular bases of mental illnesses. Areas such as psychopharmacology (the study of

the effects of drugs on a person's emotional and mental state) and psychophysiology (the study of the physiology of mental illness) are offshoots of orthomolecular psychiatry.

Psychiatrists go through the usual medical sequence: medical school, internship, and residency. The psychiatrist may spend five years or more in specialized training in psychiatry and neurology.

## Pulmonary medicine

This field deals with the study, diagnosis, and treatment of diseases and disorders of the lungs and related passageways. Among the diseases included are:
- Lung cancer
- Tuberculosis
- Pneumonia (inflammation of the lungs)
- Bronchitis (inflammation of the passageways from the windpipe into the lungs)
- Tracheitis (inflammation of the windpipe)
- Black lung (in which the lungs become clogged with coal dust)
- Pleurisy (inflammation of the lining of the lungs and the chest cavity)
- Emphysema (in which lung tissue is destroyed, causing air to become trapped within the lungs, often accompanied by severe breathing problems)

These specialists also perform bronchoscopy (examination of the trachea and bronchial passages directly with a flexible, lighted, tubelike instrument) and specialize in managing ventilators (artificial breathing machines).

The pulmonary specialist's training is in internal medicine, followed by two years of specialized training in the diagnosis and treatment of pulmonary diseases and disorders.

## Radiology/radiation oncology/nuclear medicine

A radiologist is a physician who uses x-rays to diagnose and treat disorders. Radiologists have training in physics and instrumentation, as well as in biochemistry and the effects of radiation on human tissues.

Diagnostic radiology is primarily concerned with the administration of radiation to produce images of the body and the interpretation of the resultant x-ray films. Some procedures involve the injection of special dyes, called contrast media. Other procedures also performed by radiologists use sound waves or magnetic impulses, rather than radiation, to create images.

A specialist in diagnostic radiology must complete a four-year residency in that field, which is often preceded by a year of internship in another medical field. Some diagnostic radiologists then subspecialize by completing a fellowship in a branch of radiology, such as neuroradiology (imaging of the nervous system) or uroradiology (imaging of the urinary tract).

Radiation oncology is concerned with the application of radiation in the treatment of cancer. A specialist in radiation oncology must have completed a one-year internship, either rotating among specialties or in internal medicine, followed by a three-year residency in the specialty.

Nuclear medicine is the field in which radioactive substances, called isotopes, are used to diagnose and treat diseases, such as an overactive thyroid gland. A nuclear medicine specialist must have completed a three-year residency in diagnostic radiology, plus a one-year residency in nuclear radiology.

### Rheumatology

Rheumatology is the field of medicine concerned with the study, diagnosis, and medical treatment of diseases and disorders of bones, joints, and muscles. These disorders are often characterized by inflammation or degeneration and include such conditions as arthritis, gout, lupus erythematosus, and other diseases of the connective tissues.

A rheumatologist has completed an internship and residency in internal medicine, followed by two or more years of training and experience in rheumatology.

### Sports medicine

This is one of the newest fields in medicine and has come into its own largely as a result of two factors: the training and rehabilitation needs of both amateur and professional athletes and the tremendous growth in fitness- and sports-related activities among members of the public. Doctors from a variety of fields now list themselves as sports medicine practitioners. Many of them have trained as orthopedists, since that specialty field is concerned with the mechanics of muscular and skeletal function. Exercise physiology has become an integral part of medical and sports training programs, and what was once a collection of lore on how to get the most out of your body in a game has become a field of medical research and practice.

Sports medicine has made great contributions to the general public welfare by producing hard evidence of the benefits of healthful exercise. As a consequence, information about subjects such as nu-

trition, kinesiology (the study of body movement), and biomechanics (the study of lever systems and their effect on performance) has become available to the average weekend athlete. Training need no longer be haphazard or hazardous; by using information available from sports medicine practitioners, you can train for strength, power, endurance, or speed without incurring injuries. Each goal calls for a different kind of training method. Sports medicine and exercise physiology have made a science out of athletic training.

In a sense, with the advent of sports medicine as a medical field, athletics serves the same function for ordinary people that auto racing serves for the development of new ways to make the family car better: the desire for high performance calls for research and ingenuity in converting research findings into practical applications. Sports medicine converts the lessons learned on the playing field and in the laboratory into insights into the medical problems of ordinary people who want to play a little golf, tone up, and trim down.

### Surgery

Surgery is the branch of medicine that uses surgical operations to treat disease, injury, or deformity. Surgeons go into the human body by way of incisions through the skin and muscles to alter, correct, remove, or replace the offending organ or tissue. There are many surgical specialties, among them the following:
• General surgery (including surgery of the abdomen and breasts)

• Thoracic (chest) surgery
• Cardiac (heart) surgery
• Oral (mouth) surgery (usually performed by dentists with a subspecialty in oral surgery)
• Neurosurgery (surgery of the nervous system, particularly the brain and spinal cord)
• Plastic surgery (to correct damage caused by injury or to improve the appearance)
• Orthopedic surgery (to correct disorders of the bones, joints, ligaments, and tendons)

Surgeons work closely with internists, pathologists, radiologists, anesthesiologists, and other specialists. In a very real sense, everything that physicians know about diagnosing and treating illnesses is relevant in an operating room.

After the usual four years of medical school, surgeons complete a general surgery internship and a general surgery residency, followed by additional training in their specific field of surgery.

### Urology

Urology deals with diseases and disorders of the kidneys, the urinary tract, the prostate gland, and the male sex organs. The urologist's skills include knowledge of diagnostic procedures and surgical techniques, as well as the ability to treat infections of the urinary tract and the male reproductive system.

After completion of medical school, the urologist has two years of training in general surgery, followed by a three-year training period in urology and urologic surgery and an 18-month period of clinical practice before specialty board examinations may be taken.

# COPING WITH SYMPTOMS

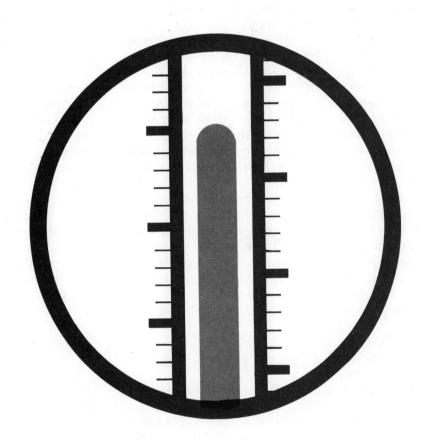

**COPING WITH SYMPTOMS**

Most of us are aware of what we need to do to promote good health; choosing a proper diet, getting appropriate exercise and adequate rest, and dealing with stress effectively are only a few of the good health habits that contribute to fitness and vigor. However, many of us forget that understanding illness is also important to maintaining health and vitality. By learning to recognize the symptoms of illness, we can better prevent and treat problems that threaten our good health.

A symptom is an abnormal physical or psychological condition that accompanies or results from a disease or disorder. It indicates a departure from the normal well-being of the body. Sometimes a symptom is a disorder in and of itself. For example, indigestion may be simply the temporary result of eating too much or too fast or of eating fatty or spicy foods. However, indigestion may be a sign of a more serious disorder, such as an ulcer, a heart attack, or cancer in the intestinal tract; if that is the case, indigestion is more than a temporary inconvenience, and you need to be able to tell the difference.

At other times, a symptom is a defensive reaction of the body—an attempt to restore the body to normal functioning. Falling into a faint in an overheated room, for instance, is the body's method of restoring adequate blood supply to the brain by lowering the head to the same level as the heart. However, fainting may be a sign of a serious illness, and you need to know when fainting should be reported to your doctor.

### Observing symptoms

Your ability to recognize and understand symptoms of illness is

important in helping your doctor diagnose and treat disorders. When you go to the doctor with a medical problem, you should be prepared to describe your symptoms exactly. You should note the time of their onset and the nature of your activity when they occur (for example, after eating, on awakening, after strenuous exercise like shoveling snow, or when lying down). Be prepared to describe the rapidity with which your symptoms appear. Sometimes the symptoms themselves provide fewer clues than does the manner in which they occur.

To do all of this well, you must learn to be observant of your body. The following descriptions of some of the more common symptoms will help you become alert to changes in your body. This section also offers some guidance on when to seek medical attention for symptoms. As an additional aid, you may want to read the introductions to the chapters in this book that discuss the various systems of the body. Those introductions explain the normal functioning of the body systems and may help you recognize when your body is not working the way it should.

## Chest pain

Chest pain is a major symptom in many disorders, including heart disease, indigestion, and pleurisy. It is important that you report to your doctor any prolonged or severe chest pain, since prompt evaluation and treatment may be lifesaving.

### Heart disease

In heart disease, chest pains may be the temporary discomfort

of angina pectoris or the similar, but more severe and long-lasting, signs of a heart attack. In both cases, the discomfort is felt as an aching or crushing sensation beneath the breastbone and may radiate to the left shoulder and arm. It may also be felt in the back, throat, jaws, and teeth, or it may spread to the abdomen. In angina, the discomfort typically is brought on by exertion and disappears in a few minutes with rest or with the taking of nitroglycerin. In a heart attack, the pain is usually much more intense and deep and is not relieved by nitroglycerin; in addition, the patient is restless, pale, and perspiring.

When the chest pains of angina or a heart attack spread to the abdomen, they are often mistaken for the discomfort of indigestion. Conversely, severe indigestion, ulcer pains, and gallbladder attacks can be mistaken for a heart attack. If there is any possibility that the symptoms might be those of a heart attack, the only recommended plan of action is to obtain emergency medical assistance immediately. The diagnosis must always be left to a physician.

### Indigestion

Indigestion is a sign of failure of proper digestion and absorption of food. Among the signs of indigestion may be discomfort in the chest, whether perceived as the burning sensation of heartburn or as sharp, dull, or gnawing pains in the chest area. If chest pain or discomfort occurs only in relation to eating, it is probably due to simple indigestion. Any change in the severity or the frequency of symptoms, however, should always be reported to a physician.

40

## Pleurisy

The chest pains of pleurisy, which may be sharp and stabbing or merely uncomfortable, may occur with every breath or only when the patient breathes deeply or coughs. The pains are caused by inflammation of the pleurae (the membranes that surround the lungs and line the chest cavity). The pains may appear only over the site of the infection or may radiate to the lower chest and abdomen.

## Other causes

Among other causes of chest pain are rib injuries, pneumonia, a blood clot in the lung, endocarditis (inflammation of the tissues surrounding the heart), inflammation of the nerves supplying the chest wall, and tenderness of the chest muscles after injury or exertion.

# Constipation

Constipation is a condition in which the stools (feces) are hard and their elimination from the bowels is infrequent and difficult. This condition is often more uncomfortable than harmful, although occasionally a change in the bowel movements, (for example, prolonged constipation or extreme discomfort when eliminating) may be a symptom of a serious illness, such as cancer, intestinal obstruction, or a nervous system or endocrine gland disorder.

It is important to remember, however, that it is not necessary to have a bowel movement every day. From three bowel movements per day to three per week is considered in the normal range.

## Causes

Common causes of constipation are physical inactivity; lack of fiber or roughage in the diet; inadequate fluid intake; emotional stress, particularly depression; drug side effects; and the habit of postponing bowel movements.

## Symptoms

Conditions that often accompany constipation are difficulty and strain in producing a bowel movement, a bloated feeling, abdominal cramps, headache, gassiness, and hemorrhoids.

## Treatment

The treatment of constipation usually depends on its cause. In mild cases that are not related to other disorders, simple methods of recommended treatment include adding more fiber-rich foods (such as bran, whole-grain breads and cereals, fruits, vegetables, and other forms of roughage) to the diet; drinking eight to ten glasses of water daily; increasing exercise; and developing good bathroom habits. This last recommendation may involve an attempt to have a bowel movement at the same time every day, usually 30 to 60 minutes after breakfast. Early morning is a good time, because the entry of food into an empty stomach activates and increases normal intestinal contractions; also, residue from the previous day's meals has moved by this time to the rectal area for elimination.

Laxatives and enemas are usually not recommended for treating simple constipation. Laxatives, in particular, should be used only when absolutely necessary; overuse can lead to irritation of the lining of the rectum, and the intestine can become so dependent on the stimulation of laxatives that it cannot function properly without them. Frequent enemas can also lead to dependence.

## Prevention

Drinking plenty of water, getting adequate exercise, eating fiber-rich foods, and recognizing the urge for a bowel movement as soon as it is felt should be beneficial in promoting regular elimination and preventing constipation.

# Cough

A cough is a normal reflex of the body to clear the airways. Coughing can result from inhaling dust, dirt, or irritating fumes; from breathing icy air; or from drawing food into the airways. It can also be caused by mucus and other secretions from such respiratory disorders as the common cold, influenza, pneumonia, and tuberculosis. Persistent coughs (those that last several weeks) without other respiratory symptoms may, on occasion, suggest diseases of other organs, such as the heart. For example, a cough may be an early sign of congestive heart failure.

## Types

The type of cough—productive or nonproductive—partially determines how it should be treated. Productive coughs (those that produce fluid or mucus) are often caused by a lung infection. When microorganisms attack the lungs, the lung tissue produces large amounts of secretions in defense. These accumulated secretions irritate the lungs, resulting in coughing that brings up fluid or mucus. A yellowish or reddish fluid in particular may indicate infection or other serious problems that require a doctor's attention.

Nonproductive coughing does not bring up fluid. It occurs when secretions from nasal passages drip into the throat or when smoke, dust, pollen, or other irritants enter the respiratory tract. Irritations and tumors may also cause a nonproductive cough, as can any inflammation of the airways or lung tissue, infectious or not. Another cause of nonproductive coughing is insufficient moisture in the air. The airways become dry and irritated, and coughing develops. This is particularly common in winter, when humidity is lowest. By adding moisture to the air, a humidifier or vaporizer may provide more relief than any cough-suppressing drug.

### Treatment

Because coughing has the vital function of clearing the airways, it should never be totally suppressed. In fact, suppressing a cough in an individual with chronic lung disease may be dangerous. Furthermore, indiscriminate use of cough suppressants may mask important symptoms. However, controlling a cough that disrupts sleep or aggravates other conditions may sometimes be necessary. This may be accomplished by using a cough suppressant or an expectorant. A suppressant helps to inhibit the cough by depressing the coughing center in the brain. An expectorant promotes the dis-

charge of mucus from the respiratory tract.

For all but the mildest coughs with obvious causes, and certainly for persistent coughs, a doctor should be consulted to determine the cause and to suggest appropriate treatment.

# Dehydration

Dehydration is a condition in which the body in general or certain body tissues in particular suffer from lack of water.

### Causes

Tissue dehydration may occur in dry climates and during the winter heating season: extremely dry air causes rapid evaporation of water from the skin and from the mucous linings of the respiratory (breathing) system. The results are discomfort and sometimes cracking of the skin, unless it is protected by lotions, and increased susceptibility of the respiratory system to infections.

Dehydration of the entire body can be life-threatening. Illnesses that produce diarrhea and vomiting are common causes of dehydration, since both of these conditions cause loss of body fluids. Cholera, which results in extreme diarrhea and vomiting, can kill through dehydration. Other causes of dehydration include diabetes, kidney disease, excessive use of diuretics (drugs that remove excess water from the blood), liver disease, and inflammation of the abdominal cavity.

Burns may also be a cause of dehydration. Tissue beneath a burn swells with body fluid. If the burn covers much of the body, the buildup of fluid in burn tissue draws considerable water from

the blood. This can decrease the blood volume so much that shock (general collapse of the circulatory system) occurs.

### Symptoms

Symptoms of dehydration include thirst; sudden weight loss; rough, dry skin; dry mucous membranes; rapid heartbeat and low blood pressure; lack of energy; and weakness. In an extreme case, the patient goes into shock, which is characterized by pale skin; bluish lips and fingertips; rapid, shallow breathing; and a weak, rapid, irregular pulse. Blood tests reveal thickening of the blood because of decreased water content.

### Treatment

The treatment of mild to moderate dehydration is to have the patient drink water with some salts added. However, if the individual has been vomiting, suffers from diarrhea, or is unconscious, it may be necessary for medical personnel to administer saline (saltwater) solution intravenously (through a vein). The intravenous method is always used in severe cases of dehydration. The goal is to replace totally the lost fluid within 48 to 72 hours, together with the valuable mineral salts that have also been lost.

# Diarrhea

Diarrhea is abnormally frequent and excessively liquid bowel movements. This is often the body's defensive attempt to rid itself of irritating or toxic substances. It is a symptom that accompanies many disorders, both mild and serious.

## Types

There are two basic types of diarrhea, acute (short-term) and chronic (long-term). Acute diarrhea, the more common form, comes on quickly and usually lasts no more than two or three days, although it can last as long as two weeks. Chronic diarrhea may also appear suddenly, but it lingers for many weeks or months, either being constantly present or alternately appearing and disappearing.

Both acute and chronic diarrhea can become a serious problem because of the danger of dehydration (excessive loss of body fluids and salts), as well as loss of nutrients. Diarrhea may also be a symptom of an inflammatory bowel disease (for example, Crohn's disease or ulcerative colitis).

## Causes

The reasons for the consistency of the stool (feces) in diarrhea are complex. In an infection, the intestine may pour out massive quantities of fluids and salts in response to a bacterial toxin (poison) or other irritant. In inflammatory bowel disease, protein, blood, and mucus are lost through the inflamed lining of the colon, taking large quantities of water with them. Other disorders speed up the normal movement of the colon, thereby not allowing time for absorption of fluids. Yet another type of diarrhea is caused by poor absorption of a type of sugar called lactose, which draws fluid out of the colon. In many cases, diarrhea is caused by a combination of these mechanisms.

Other causes of diarrhea include changes in the diet, drugs taken for other disorders (particu-larly antibiotics, which upset the bacterial balance in the intestines), stress, and food allergies.

## Symptoms

The symptoms often experienced with the characteristic loose and frequent stools are nausea, cramps or pain in the abdomen, gassiness, fatigue, and fever.

## Diagnosis

Diagnostic evaluation will include assessment of the patient's normal diet and emotional state, as well as recent changes in daily habits. In addition, a sample of the stool may be examined for color, consistency, odor, chemical content, and presence of blood. Stool cultures are often done to identify the causative microorganism if infection is suspected.

## Treatment

Treatment for diarrhea usually involves removing or correcting the cause of the condition. If diarrhea lasts for more than three days or is a recurring problem, a doctor should be consulted, as this may be a warning sign of a more serious illness. Anti-diarrheal medications can be prescribed for particularly bothersome or persistent diarrhea, but these should be used only with caution; in the case of some infections, they may actually prolong the course of the illness.

The discomfort of occasional bouts of acute diarrhea, however, is usually treated with simple remedies, such as adequate rest and increased intake of liquids to replace lost fluids. The diet should consist of light meals, perhaps soup or broth at first; as solid food is added to the diet, irritating substances, such as bran, fruits and vegetables, fried foods, coffee, and alcoholic beverages should be avoided.

# Dizziness and vertigo

Dizziness and vertigo are sensations of disorientation and distorted perception. Occasional episodes are not serious, but recurrent dizziness or vertigo can be a symptom of a variety of disorders, particularly those involving the eyes, ears, or nervous system.

Dizziness and vertigo are sometimes confused with each other. Dizziness is characterized by unsteadiness and a distorted sense of the environment; the word *dizziness* is often used to describe a sensation of light-headedness or faintness. Vertigo is a false sense of movement, often the perception that one is spinning or that one's environment is whirling around. Vertigo is often accompanied by nausea.

## Causes

Dizziness and vertigo can be caused by a malfunction in one of the parts of the body that is responsible for giving the brain information on balance, position, and movement. These parts include the eye, the inner ear, and certain areas of the brain. Thus, balance can be disturbed by any injury, impairment, or disorder involving the eyes, ears, and certain areas of the brain, as well as the nerves leading to and from these areas. A wide variety of problems, such as injury to the head, ear infections, and migraine headaches, can include dizziness or vertigo as a symptom. Also, occasional mild upsets to the body can cause dizziness (but usually not vertigo), including such harmless factors as being overheated, overtired, or tense. Standing up too quickly after reclining or sitting for some time is another harmless cause of dizziness.

### Symptoms

Dizziness is characterized by feelings of unsteadiness, swaying, light-headedness, weakness, and faintness, and may be accompanied by nausea and vomiting. Vertigo is marked by a feeling of spinning and may be associated with unsteady walking, a tendency to fall or to veer to one side while walking, paleness, sweating, nausea and vomiting, and continuous rapid eye movement.

### Prevention and treatment

Simple dizziness can easily be avoided. Getting up slowly after reclining or sitting, leaving overheated rooms to get some fresh air, eating a balanced diet, and getting adequate rest should all help to prevent common episodes of dizziness. Recurrent dizziness, however, should be brought to the attention of a physician.

True vertigo, on the other hand, may be a sign of physical disease, such as labyrinthitis (inflammation of the inner ear) or a brain disorder. Frequently, however, no cause is found, and the vertigo is treated symptomatically with drugs. In all cases, any episode of true vertigo should be reported to a physician.

# Edema

Edema is the accumulation of excessive amounts of fluid within the body's tissues. It is a symptom of many conditions, both minor and serious.

The fluid that accumulates comes from the blood. Normally, there is a constant exchange of fluid between the blood vessels and other body tissues. The blood removes any extra fluids and carries them to the kidneys, from which they are excreted via the urinary tract. Edema occurs when that exchange does not take place properly, either allowing too much liquid to leave the blood vessels or too little fluid to enter the blood vessels.

### Causes

A change in pressure within the blood vessels because of heart disease, high blood pressure, blocked or damaged vessels, or a kidney disorder can cause an imbalance in fluid exchange.

Mild edema is common before menstruation and during pregnancy, when the blood volume increases. Being overweight, wearing tight clothing, and becoming overheated can also lead to edema.

### Forms of edema

Edema can be confined to a small area of the body or can become generalized. Some forms are more noticeable than others. For example, the swelling that appears around a splinter in the skin is edema. However, generalized edema results in widespread swelling and puffiness, usually first noticed in the fingers and feet. The most serious forms of edema occur within the internal organs of the body. Heart disease, for example, may result in internal edema of the lungs, causing them to fill with fluid and thereby creating severe difficulty in breathing.

### Treatment

Simple or temporary edema can be relieved by decreasing salt intake, since the sodium in salt causes the body to retain fluid. More severe or internal edema can be treated with a diuretic (a drug that stimulates the kidneys to produce more urine and thus rid the body of excess fluid). Edema that is symptomatic of an underlying disorder will often disappear with management of that condition.

### Prevention

Controlling weight gain, eating a balanced diet low in salt, and wearing loose clothing may prevent milder forms of edema. Any prolonged edema not attributable to causes such as hot weather or menstruation should be investigated by a physician to determine the cause.

# Fainting

Fainting is a temporary loss of consciousness and is often the result when the body attempts to supply extra blood to the brain. Fainting can be a symptom of a relatively mild condition, such as hunger, or a serious disorder, such as heartbeat irregularity.

When the brain experiences a temporary reduction of its blood supply, the body reacts defensively; in effect, it causes itself to fall down, bringing the head to the level of the heart and thereby minimizing the effect of gravity, which favors pooling of blood in the legs. The net effect is an increase in the amount of blood coming back to the heart, which allows the heart to pump blood to the brain more easily.

## Causes

Fainting can be caused by interference with any one of several internal mechanisms that protect and maintain the brain's blood supply by working against gravity and its tendency to allow blood to pool in the lower parts of the body. One of these mechanisms is the "muscle pump." The muscles of the legs act to squeeze the veins in the legs, thereby forcing blood up toward the heart. If a person stands motionless for a long period of time without using these muscles, blood pools in the legs, reducing the amount available to the brain. This reduction frequently causes fainting or loss of consciousness. The ability of the heart to increase its rate and force of contraction when under stress is another built-in protective mechanism.

These protective functions are impaired by a variety of conditions, such as an overheated or crowded environment, emotional stress, hunger, extreme fatigue, various drugs (particularly some high blood pressure medications), as well as certain circulatory disorders.

## Symptoms

The symptoms that usually precede fainting are light-headedness, confusion, spots be-fore the eyes, white or grayish coloring of the face, and cold, moist skin. Nausea and vomiting may also be present.

## Treatment

Fainting is treated by taking several simple steps to make the person more comfortable. The patient should be lying down, preferably with the feet higher than the head (to help blood return to the brain), and the clothing should be loosened. The patient should have plenty of fresh air to breathe. Recovery should occur within a few seconds of fainting, but a sense of disorientation may linger for several minutes. Spirits of ammonia and smelling salts are not usually recommended for fainting, as they may be ineffective or may cause vomiting.

Recurrent fainting should be reported to a doctor.

## Prevention

Fainting can often be prevented by lying down, preferably with the legs up, as soon as any of the warning symptoms is noticed. This precaution lowers the brain to the level of the heart, increasing the blood supply to the brain.

# Fatigue

Fatigue may be physical or mental exhaustion, an overwhelming feeling of weariness, or a lack of energy and enthusiasm for even pleasant activities. It is a symptom of a vast number of diseases and disorders.

Fatigue should not be confused with weakness, which is an actual loss of physical strength.

## Causes

Feeling fatigued and tiring rapidly with minimal activity are often among the early signs of an approaching illness. Fatigue is a warning signal of a variety of diseases and disorders, among them the common cold, influenza, hepatitis, infectious mononucleosis, and other infectious diseases; heart disease; lung disorders, such as emphysema; some glandular diseases, such as diabetes; anemia and nutritional deficiencies; and some diseases of the nervous system. Overwork, either physical or mental, can also cause fatigue, as can psychological disorders or emotional stress.

## Symptoms

In addition to the general feeling of being more tired than usual, fatigue can be accompanied by nervousness, anxiety, depression, and feelings of irritability, as well as by headache, diminished sexual function, and difficulty in concentrating. When fatigue is due to psychological problems, sleep disorders, including insomnia, and a pattern of frequent nighttime and early morning awakening are often present as well.

## Treatment

Fatigue is best treated by treating the physical disorder or psychological problem that is causing it. Some types of fatigue, particularly those due to physical overexertion, can probably be prevented by getting adequate exercise and rest, as well as by eating well-balanced meals and reducing stress, tension, and overwork.

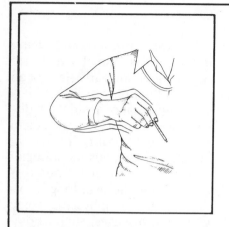  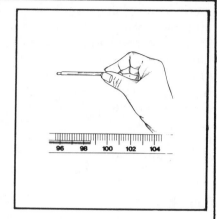

*Before taking someone's temperature, shake down the mercury in the thermometer so that the top of the column is below 96°F. Then place the thermometer under the person's tongue and have her hold it there (with her mouth closed) for three minutes. The average normal temperature taken by mouth is 98.6°F to 99.6°F. A false reading will be obtained if the person drinks a hot or cold beverage immediately before measurement.*

# Fever

Fever is an abnormally high body temperature. A fever is present when the body temperature rises above the normal range of 98.6°F to 99.6°F. Generally, if the body temperature is more than 101.5°F when measured with a rectal thermometer, 100.5°F when measured with an oral thermometer, or 99.5°F when measured under the arm, it is considered abnormal.

Fever is a symptom of illness and often appears to be an undesirable condition, but many researchers believe that fever acts as a defense mechanism for the body when it is being attacked by bacteria or viruses. There is a regulatory center in the brain that acts to maintain a constant body temperature regardless of the surrounding environment. Fever occurs when this center responds to an illness or infection, such as a common cold or influenza, by setting the body temperature higher. This mechanism is thought to work because infectious microorganisms cannot survive the higher than normal temperatures.

## Causes

Infections are the most common cause of fever, but a fever can also be a symptom of heart attack, some forms of cancer, and disorders in the portion of the brain that regulates temperature (such as stroke, brain tumor, and brain injury).

## Symptoms

The early signs of fever include chills or hot flashes, flushed skin, increased pulse and breathing rates, headache, and aching of muscles or joints. A slight fever may be accompanied by none of these symptoms, however. A high fever may result in delirium or convulsions, and a prolonged fever may cause weakness and dehydration (excessive loss of body fluids).

## Treatment

Treatment of fever depends on its severity, duration, and cause. Immediate emergency medical treatment should be sought if the temperature is more than 105°F (even though fevers tend to be high in very young children) or if convulsions have occurred. A doctor should be consulted if a high fever (103°F to 104°F) lasts for 12 to 24 hours; if a moderate fever (101°F to 102°F) lasts for several days; if the body temperature fluctuates widely; or if the fever disappears and then returns several days later, which usually signals a new infection.

The goal in treating a patient with a fever is actually to diagnose and treat the cause of the fever, rather than the fever itself. Merely lowering a mild fever may do more harm than good, because it reduces the protection that the fever may be providing in fighting off the infection; it may also mask the underlying cause or disturb the natural course that the disease would have taken, thus hindering diagnosis. Therefore, treating a fever should never be confused with treating its cause.

At times, however, fever should be lowered to keep the patient comfortable and to prevent the weakness and dehydration that can result from prolonged fever. Increasing fluid intake and taking aspirin or an aspirin substitute (such as acetaminophen) will usually lower a fever; taking tepid, not cold, baths and using comfortable, but not overly warm, clothing and blankets will help to lower the fever and also keep the patient from feeling chilled.

It should be noted that any drug treatment for fever, especially for children, should be undertaken only after consulting with a doctor. An association between the use of aspirin in children with viral illnesses (particularly chicken pox and influenza) and the often fatal Reye's syndrome (a condition characterized by severe, sudden deterioration of liver and brain function) has been demonstrated. It is therefore recommended that the use of aspirin be avoided in children with viral illnesses unless it has been prescribed by a physician.

# Heartburn

Heartburn is an uncomfortable, burning sensation felt behind the lower part of the breastbone, sometimes extending up into the upper chest or lower neck. Despite its name, it is not caused by pain in the heart or by a heart attack. In fact, heartburn is often triggered by simple digestive upsets, although occasionally a severe case may be a symptom of a more serious disorder.

### Causes

Heartburn occurs when the acidic digestive juices and partially digested food from the stomach back up into the lower esophagus (the passageway between the mouth and the stomach) and irritate its tissues.

Heartburn most often develops ten minutes to one hour after eating. It may be caused by overeating, smoking, lying down or bending over after eating (which allows the backup of stomach acids and food into the esophagus), taking aspirin, or consuming alcoholic drinks, coffee, spicy or highly seasoned foods, or acidic fruits or fruit juices. Heartburn is a common problem during pregnancy because the expanding uterus exerts pressure on the stomach and esophagus, encouraging digestive juices to move up toward the throat; this disappears after childbirth.

### Symptoms

The major symptom of heartburn is the characteristic burning sensation behind the breastbone and up toward the throat. It may be accompanied by gassiness, belching, and an uncomfortable, tight feeling in the chest.

Heartburn can usually be relieved by merely standing or sitting upright or by drinking milk or something soothing and non-acidic. Nonprescription antacids may also be helpful in more severe cases. Any case of persistent, uncontrollable, or severe heartburn should be reported to a doctor because it may be a sign of a more severe condition, such as peptic ulcer.

### Prevention

Heartburn can often be prevented by avoiding spicy, acidic, or other troublesome foods, as well as coffee and alcoholic beverages, if they seem to trigger it. Eating smaller meals more frequently and refraining from

smoking at mealtimes are also beneficial in avoiding heartburn. Sleeping with the back and head propped up on pillows may prevent the stomach contents from flowing upward and into the esophagus.

# Hypothermia

Hypothermia is a condition in which the body temperature falls well below the normal temperature of 98.6°F. The person's condition can become serious if the symptoms or signs are ignored. Among the causes of accidental hypothermia are immersion in cold water, certain drugs, and long periods of being exposed to the cold without appropriate clothing. Hypothermia can easily occur in newborns and infants, because their heat-retaining mechanisms are not fully developed. Elderly persons are also at risk, because their heat-retaining mechanisms are easily overtaxed.

### Symptoms

The signs and symptoms of hypothermia include an altered level of consciousness, slow breathing, low pulse rate, listlessness, and mental confusion. The hands, feet, and abdomen of the hypothermic person are cold to the touch.

### Treatment

Basic treatment for hypothermia is gradual rewarming of the body. The rewarming must be gradual to prevent the sudden enlargement of blood vessels at the surface of the body, which may divert too much blood from some of the body's vital internal organs.

Medical help should always be obtained for a person with hypothermia. While waiting for help to arrive, the cold person should be covered with blankets and, if alert, should be offered a warm, nonalcoholic beverage. Alcoholic drinks do not help because they tend to reduce body heat. Also, briskly rubbing hands or feet to restore warmth is *not* recommended. Any other type of treatment depends on the underlying cause of the drop in body temperature. In severe cases in which body temperature is critically reduced, warm fluids may be given intravenously. Peritoneal dialysis (a process by which warm fluids are injected into and withdrawn from the abdominal cavity) is sometimes used to restore normal temperature, as is immersion in a specially designed tank filled with warm water.

# Indigestion

Indigestion (also called dyspepsia) is the discomfort caused by difficulty in digesting food. It is an uncomfortable feeling of fullness, pressure, slight pain, or gassiness and is usually related to eating. (Constipation, diarrhea, heartburn, and nausea are *not* indigestion, although they may be related to the problem.)

## Causes

Indigestion is usually caused by an eating problem, such as eating too fast or too much; chewing insufficiently; eating in an emotionally upsetting environment; eating particularly bothersome foods, such as spicy, fatty, or oily foods, or those that may cause an allergic reaction; or smoking, especially immediately before or after a meal. Indigestion can also be caused by serious disorders, such as cancer, ulcers, and diseases involving the organs associated with digestion (the esophagus, intestines, gallbladder, liver, stomach, and pancreas). In addition, heart attack, tumors, and emotional problems may be accompanied by symptoms that are similar to those of indigestion.

Any case of indigestion that lingers for some time or that cannot be controlled in any way should be reported to a doctor for diagnosis and appropriate treatment.

## Diagnosis

The cause of indigestion is diagnosed primarily by observing the symptoms and the conditions under which they occur. A doctor will want a description of the symptoms and of the patient's dietary habits; of the time, length, and location of the discomfort, as well as the circumstances surrounding it and the foods eaten preceding it; and of the emotional environment that usually exists during meals and snacks. X-ray studies of the gastrointestinal tract or stool (feces) analysis may also be used to make a diagnosis of the cause of indigestion.

## Treatment

Antacids often relieve indigestion, but they should not be used without the advice of a physician by people who have kidney disease.

## Prevention

The best treatment consists of preventing indigestion in the first place. Eating balanced meals in a relaxed setting, eliminating foods that can cause indigestion, and refraining from smoking, especially at mealtimes, should be beneficial in the prevention of indigestion.

# Insomnia

Insomnia is the inability to sleep during normal sleeping hours when there is no apparent reason for wakefulness. Insomnia may vary from simple restlessness, to wakefulness on and off throughout the night, to total sleeplessness.

## Causes

Although the condition is most often associated with psychological or emotional problems, it can also be related to physical disorders or to conditions in the immediate environment.

Depression and anxiety are often the cause of insomnia. Among physical disorders that can lead to insomnia are urination problems, heart trouble, high blood pressure, infection, hardening of the arteries, spastic colon, and leg cramps. Less serious causes of insomnia can be found in the immediate environment—bright lights, noise, excessive heat or cold, lack of ventilation. Insomnia may also be caused by having too many or too few bedclothes, by being constipated or hungry, or by having consumed too much coffee, tea, cola, or other beverage containing caffeine, which is a stimulant.

Strangely, drugs to promote sleep can cause insomnia. The careless or inappropriate use of tranquilizers and sedatives can disrupt sleep patterns. If high doses of tranquilizers or sedatives are taken, the waking-sleeping pattern can be reversed, and sleep can become irregular. The person may doze throughout the day and then be unable to sleep at night.

## Treatment

A person who has persistent insomnia should consult a physician so that the underlying cause—emotional or physical—can be diagnosed and treated.

## Prevention

Ways of preventing or coping with simple insomnia include taking a 10- or 15-minute walk before bedtime, taking a warm bath, drinking warm milk (milk contains a substance called tryptophan, which promotes drowsiness), reading, or watching television. Taking sleep-promoting medications should be discussed with a doctor.

# Itching

Itching is an uncomfortable or irritating sensation on the surface of the skin, accompanied by an urge to scratch. It has been described as a pricking, stinging, burning, or crawling feeling.

## Causes

The biological reactions that lead to itching are not clearly understood, but it is known that this stimulation of the nerve endings in the skin can be caused by both physical and psychological factors.

Itching can be caused by insect bites; small cuts or scrapes;

hives and other allergic reactions; a fungal infection; the rash that often accompanies infectious diseases, such as chicken pox; dry skin, often stemming from bathing or showering too frequently or using harsh soaps; reactions to drugs; and psychological stress.

## Symptoms

Itching is characterized by a feeling of discomfort, the urge to scratch, and possibly redness, peeling, and other irritations of the skin as a result of scratching. Itching of just the scalp and forearms with no obvious cause may be triggered by psychological stress.

## Treatment

Treatment of itching depends on its cause. Itching from dry skin is usually treated by applying skin lotions or creams to small areas and using body lotions or bath oils for larger areas; reducing the frequency of showers and baths to only twice weekly (because water tends to dry the skin); and trying a new brand of soap or shampoo.

If itching seems to be a reaction to a drug, the doctor should be consulted before making any changes in medication. (A patient should *never* stop taking a drug without the approval of his doctor.) Generally, the doctor will either lower the dosage to relieve the itching or give advice on treatment of the itching while maintaining the original dosage.

If no outside substances seem to be triggering itching, psychological or emotional stress may be the cause. Treatment will center on removing the stress or learning how to deal with it.

If itching persists for more than a week after attempts at self-treatment, a doctor should be consulted because persistent itching with no visible cause may be a symptom of diabetes, thyroid disease, kidney failure, liver disease, or cancer.

## Prevention

Limiting bathing to twice weekly and using humidifiers to keep the air moist should help prevent the itching caused by dry skin.

# Loss of appetite

Loss of appetite (also known as anorexia) is a lack of interest in or desire for food. Simple loss of appetite should not be confused with the illness called anorexia nervosa, which occurs most often in young women. Rather, loss of appetite is a common symptom that accompanies many illnesses.

## Causes

Appetite is controlled by two areas of the brain—the "feeding" center and the "fullness" center—that work to regulate feelings of hunger depending on the body's need for food. In rare cases, appetite loss can be caused by damage to these areas of the brain. More commonly, it results from fatigue, the common cold, and psychological problems, such as anxiety and depression. Serious disorders that can lead to longer periods of appetite loss include certain types of cancer, as well as glandular and intestinal diseases.

## Symptoms

Loss of appetite is indicated by a general lack of interest in food or eating, reduced food intake, and, in severe cases, weakness and a decrease in the body's natural resistance to disease.

## Treatment

A doctor's advice should be sought if appetite loss stems from emotional or psychological problems, if it lasts for long periods, or if it seems to have no obvious cause. Counseling may be beneficial if emotional problems are connected to loss of appetite.

# Nasal congestion

Nasal congestion occurs when the blood vessels in the nose enlarge. These enlarged blood vessels leak fluid into the surrounding tissues, which fills the nasal cavity and impairs breathing.

Nasal congestion is not a serious problem in itself, although it may be bothersome enough to interfere with daily activities and sleep. Persistent cases should be reported to a doctor, as nasal congestion may be a symptom of mild infections or more serious disorders.

## Causes

The common cold, influenza, allergy, and bronchitis are the most frequent causes of nasal congestion. Persistent cases may be caused by structural abnormalities in the nose or by the daily use of certain drugs, particularly those often prescribed for high blood pressure, which act to enlarge all blood vessels, including those in the nose.

## Treatment

Occasional nasal congestion is often treated with over-the-counter (nonprescription) decongestants, such as nasal sprays, nose drops, and nasal inhalers, all of which act to shrink swollen blood vessels in the nose and stop fluid secretion. However, they can also shrink blood vessels elsewhere in the body, resulting in increased blood pressure and heart rate, as well as nervousness and insomnia. For this reason, over-the-counter decongestants should not be used without the advice of a physician by those with high blood pressure, heart disease, diabetes, or thyroid disorders.

Those who do use decongestants for nasal congestion should use them only for brief periods, perhaps three days at the most. Since they act to constrict the blood vessels, their overuse tends to tire the blood vessels, relaxing them completely and making the nose more congested than it was before decongestants were used. This is called rebound congestion.

In addition, specific medicine that is inserted in the nose may be prescribed by a doctor. Also, the use of vaporizers or humidifiers is often beneficial in relieving some of the discomfort of nasal congestion.

# Nausea and vomiting

Nausea is an extremely uncomfortable or queasy feeling in the stomach area, often accompanied by an urge to vomit.

Vomiting is the forceful ejection of the contents of the stomach through the mouth.

Both nausea and vomiting can be symptoms of relatively mild upsets in the body, such as motion sickness, or of more serious disorders, such as peptic ulcer.

The sensation of nausea and the urge to vomit originate in an area of the brain called the vomiting center. In response to certain messages from nerves in the digestive system or the inner ear (part of which controls balance) or to direct stimulation by certain drugs, the vomiting center can trigger the muscular actions that result in vomiting.

Nausea and vomiting are usually temporary conditions and may be beneficial if they result in the expulsion of something potentially harmful to the body. However, persistent or recurring vomiting can lead to a dangerous loss of fluids and salts (called dehydration) and of nutrients, and can also damage the esophagus (the passageway from the mouth to the stomach) and the upper portion of the stomach.

## Causes

Several relatively mild conditions and disorders may cause nausea and vomiting, including motion sickness, the "morning sickness" of pregnancy, excessive alcohol intake, emotional upset, and drug side effects. Eating too much, eating especially bothersome foods (such as oily or greasy foods), and eating spoiled food may also be responsible. More serious conditions that may be accompanied by nausea and vomiting are severe injury or pain, serious disorders of the digestive system (such as peptic ulcer or gastritis), heart disease, and certain glandular disorders.

Vomiting without a preceding feeling of nausea may be a symptom of brain injury or brain tumor.

### Symptoms

The symptoms that accompany nausea include a "sour" or queasy stomach, chills, perspiration, drowsiness, headache, rapid heartbeat and breathing rates, and excessive production of saliva.

### Treatment

In most cases, nausea and vomiting require little or no treatment—they will subside when the cause is removed or corrected. However, if vomiting occurs regularly or frequently without an obvious cause, or if blood or red or dark-brown spots appear in the vomitus (the material discharged during vomiting), medical treatment should be sought immediately. (The physician may want to examine a sample of the vomitus.)

Home remedies will often help to relieve the discomfort of occasional bouts of nausea and vomiting. Drinking tea, noncola beverages (especially ginger ale), and soup or broth is often suggested to replace the fluids lost due to vomiting. Solid food usually is not recommended, but when vomiting subsides, toast or crackers may be tried before returning to a normal diet.

Several medications can successfully control the urge to vomit, but they need to be prescribed by a doctor and should be used only with caution. Any woman who is pregnant or thinks she may be pregnant should consult her doctor before taking this (or any other) type of medication.

# Pain

Pain is an unpleasant or uncomfortable sensation that can range from mild irritation to excruciating agony. It is probably the most commonly reported symptom and may be associated with innumerable disorders and diseases.

### Causes

Pain occurs when specialized nerve endings are stimulated; within a fraction of a second this pain "signal" travels through a network of nerves to the brain. Pain can be a warning sign, indicating impending damage to the body, or it can be a protective mechanism, causing a person to remove the cause of the pain or to reflexively draw away from the source. Most healthy people have occasional, brief twinges of pain that have no specific cause and are usually harmless. However, bothersome, recurring, or persistent pain can be caused by thousands of factors. Most commonly, pain is a symptom of disease, injury, or abnormal changes in the body.

### Types

There are many types of pain. Pain can be dull and constant, sharp and sudden, crushing, burning, piercing, or aching. When it is felt in areas other than the location of the disorder (for example, when the pain of heart attack is felt in the arm), it is called referred pain.

### Diagnosis

Unexplainable pain should be reported promptly to a doctor for investigation and possible treatment. It is best to observe any accompanying symptoms and to be prepared to answer two questions that the doctor will almost certainly ask in trying to identify the cause of the pain: "What brings on the pain?" and "What brings relief?"

### Treatment

The ideal treatment for pain consists of finding and correcting its source. In some cases, however, such as in widespread cancer, this would be impossible, so the pain itself needs to be treated, most commonly with analgesic drugs (painkilling medications). Aspirin and acetaminophen are probably the most common painkillers that can be obtained without a prescription. More potent painkillers, such as narcotics, must be prescribed by a doctor. Other drugs, both prescription and nonprescription, are designed to treat and relieve the pain of a specific disorder (for example, antacids treat the discomfort of heartburn or ulcers).

If the pain comes from the muscles (such as that from overexertion or from a bruising injury to the soft tissues), adequate rest of the affected area may bring relief. Surface treatment of this type of pain is often very beneficial; this consists of massage or application of heat or cold (depending on the injury and the time elapsed since incurring it) to the painful area.

# Rash

A rash is an eruption on the surface of the skin, covering either small areas of the body or extensive areas, in the form of red spots, patches, or blisters. A rash often causes itching, but this is not always the case. A rash is usually a temporary condition, appearing and disappearing within a few days, if not sooner. If so, there is little need for worry; however, a rash can also be a symptom of infectious diseases or other disorders.

### Causes

Allergic rashes may be caused by exposure to the sun, heat, cold, the chemicals in household cleansers or detergents, fabrics, or certain foods. A rash may also be a symptom of certain diseases, such as measles, rubella (German measles), chicken pox, and shingles.

Rashes that appear regularly with no other symptoms may indicate the presence of an allergy; if a rash is accompanied by other symptoms, such as fever, it is more likely that the cause is an infectious disease.

### Treatment

Any rash that lasts for more than a few days should be examined by a doctor. A rash will usually disappear when its cause is treated. In the case of an allergy, the only treatment may be something to relieve itching and irritation, but allergy testing may indicate which irritant to avoid in the future.

# Sore throat

A sore throat is a painful irritation in the throat, often a symptom of the common cold. A sore throat can range from mild scratchiness to severe pain and difficulty in swallowing.

### Causes

A sore throat is most frequently seen as a symptom of the common cold, when the nasal passages are congested and the person is forced to breathe through the mouth, leaving the throat dry and irritated. Coughing may also irritate the throat, as will the secretions that drain into the throat from the back of the nose during a cold.

Irritating environmental substances, such as smoke, pollen, pollution, and dust, can cause a sore throat when inhaled; also, soreness of the throat may result when hot liquids or foods are swallowed.

A severe sore throat may be caused by a bacterial (frequently streptococcal) infection of the throat, middle ear, nose, or sinuses. Left untreated, a certain type of strep throat can lead to rheumatic fever (a disease that can affect the heart valves) or to glomerulonephritis (a disease of the kidneys).

### Symptoms

A sore throat is characterized by dryness and scratchiness in the throat and pain when swallowing. A doctor should be notified if a sore throat lasts more than several days, if it occurs without a cold, or if no obvious irritant can be found; these circumstances may indicate a serious disease, a blood disorder, or a severe infection. If a sore throat is accompanied by fever, achiness, and fatigue, or if the throat and mouth are very red or covered with yellow or white spots, a bacterial infection may be present, and appropriate cultures should be obtained. A recently developed screening test allows the physician to diagnose a strep-tococcal infection (strep throat) within minutes.

### Treatment

A simple sore throat accompanying a cold is treated by relieving the other cold symptoms. A nasal decongestant may be used if the nose is congested. A cough suppressant may be used if coughing is irritating the throat; cough suppressants are not always recommended, however, because they allow mucus to accumulate and thus may trigger further complications. Sour, hard candy can stimulate saliva production, which will moisten the throat. Frequent gargling with warm salt water soothes the irritated tissues of the throat by reducing swelling.

If a strep infection is the cause of the sore throat, antibiotics are prescribed to prevent rheumatic fever and to fight the infection, as well as aspirin or an aspirin substitute, such as acetaminophen, to relieve pain and fever.

# Vital signs

Vital signs is a term used in diagnostic medicine for four easily observed variables—temperature, pulse rate, respiratory rate, and blood pressure. Although evaluation of the vital signs is not sufficient to arrive at a clear diagnosis of a patient's condition, these four items taken together serve as important indicators of the presence of disease or injury. They are usually the first step in a diagnostic evaluation.

### Temperature

Temperature is a useful index of a patient's condition, since a fever (an abnormal rise in body temperature) is usually a significant indicator of disease. Fever is generally a sign of infection, but it can be present whenever there is tissue destruction (from a severe sunburn, for example, or when large amounts of tissue deteriorate due to lack of blood supply).

## Pulse rate

The pulse rate reflects the heart rate. The heart rate varies with a person's level of physical activity; for example, the heart beats faster during exercise and more slowly during rest. An inappropriate heart rate may indicate disease. A feverish patient will have an increased heart rate, while a weak but rapid pulse is characteristic of severe blood loss or diseases of the heart itself. An irregular pulse rate may also indicate a reaction to stress or to overconsumption of caffeine.

## Respiratory rate

The respiratory rate is the rate of breathing. Patients with fever hyperventilate (have an increased respiratory rate), which lowers body temperature. Hyperventilation is a common response to pain or stress, as well. Any condition that leads to acidosis (the presence of abnormally high acid levels in the body) drives the respiratory rate upward. Diseases of the lungs, which decrease their ability to oxygenate the blood, also increase the respiratory rate.

## Blood pressure

The blood pressure is an indicator of the amount of blood in circulation and the pumping force of the heart. A decrease in circulating blood volume, such as occurs in cases of severe bleeding, lowers blood pressure and deprives the tissues of adequate blood flow. Reflexes then are initiated that compensate, in part, for the reduced blood volume and pressure. For example, the heart rate increases in an attempt to make up for the reduction in blood volume and the blood vessels supplying the digestive organs narrow, which diverts blood to more vital areas, such as the brain. Sustained elevation of blood pressure constitutes a disorder in its own right—hypertension.

# INFECTIOUS DISEASES

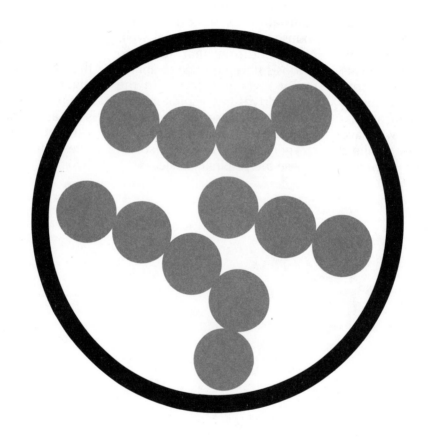

The human body is both surrounded and inhabited by billions of microorganisms (living organisms that are so small that they can be seen only with a microscope). Most microorganisms are harmless or even beneficial; for example, certain bacteria that normally live in the digestive system help digest food. Occasionally, however, a microorganism capable of causing a disease invades the body. Diseases caused by such microorganisms are called infectious diseases.

Infectious diseases are contagious; that is, they can be passed from one person to another. They can be transmitted by skin contact, in contaminated food or drink, or via airborne particles containing the microorganisms. Animal or insect bites are another means of transmission. (If an insect, for example, bites an infected person, the insect can carry the microorganism and pass the disease by biting another person.) The two most common types of infectious diseases are bacterial infections and viral infections.

Disease-causing, or pathogenic, bacteria either attack the body's tissues directly or cause damage by secreting poisonous substances called toxins. Fortunately, bacterial infections are frequently curable; certain bacteria can be killed by drugs. Other bacterial diseases can be prevented by vaccination. (Bacteria will be discussed later in this chapter.)

Viruses are the smallest known microorganisms. They are responsible for diseases as relatively harmless as the common cold and as serious as meningitis. Viruses live and reproduce only within living cells, and only certain cells are susceptible to a specific virus. You can be host to many viruses without suffering any adverse effects, but if enough cells are attacked, you will become sick.

There is no effective medical treatment for most viral infections. Because a virus lives inside a cell, any treatment designed to kill the virus is also likely to harm the cell. In addition, there are thousands of different viruses—each with different properties—and an agent effective against one virus probably will not affect the others. Although there are vaccinations for some viral diseases, therapy for most viral diseases is limited to treating the symptoms.

## The body's defenses

Despite the prevalence of disease-causing microorganisms, the body is not defenseless against these invaders. The body fights infections in three ways: by preventing these organisms from entering the body, by attacking those that do manage to enter, and by inactivating those organisms it cannot kill. Sometimes, too, the body fights disease by developing defensive symptoms. Fever is an example. During an illness, the body's temperature regulator may respond to the illness by raising the body's temperature. Some researchers believe that this is an effective response because the microorganisms causing the disease may not be able to survive the higher body temperature.

The skin is the first barrier that guards the underlying tissues of the body. Where there are natural openings in the skin, there are also defenses. For example, tear glands in the eyes secrete and bathe the eyes with fluid that contains bacteria-fighting components. The salivary glands in the mouth and the tonsils in the throat help prevent microorganisms from attacking the mouth and throat. Many openings in the body, as well as internal passages, are lined with mucous membranes. These delicate layers produce mucus, a slippery secretion that moistens and protects by repelling or trapping microorganisms. Internally, certain body organs fight infection. For instance, the liver and the spleen (a large glandlike organ located in the abdomen) filter out harmful substances from the blood flowing through them. The lining of the stomach produces acids that attack germs in food that has been eaten. The body's lymph system manufactures white blood cells, which attack and kill invading organisms.

## The lymph system

The lymph system is a network of vessels that carry lymph, a watery fluid containing white blood cells, throughout the body. Lymph drains from the blood vessels and body tissues, carrying away waste products. The waste products are filtered out of the lymph by small structures called lymph nodes (popularly known as lymph glands). Within the lymph nodes, harmful microorganisms are trapped, attacked, and destroyed by white blood cells. This is one of the body's primary and most efficient lines of defense.

Antibodies are manufactured in the lymph system. Antibodies are protective substances that the body produces in response to invasion by a hostile organism or the presence of a foreign substance. Antibodies counteract some invading bacteria and viruses by inactivating them so that they are powerless. Antibodies that neutralize toxins (poisons) produced by bacteria are called antitoxins.

The body's production of white blood cells and antibodies in response to an invading disease organism is called the immune reaction. Immunity is the body's ability to resist an invasion of disease-causing bacteria and viruses. Once antibodies have been made to fight a certain type of microorganism, that type usually no longer poses a threat to the body. That is why one attack of a disease often prevents the recurrence of that disease. The first attack causes antibodies to be produced, and these antibodies protect the system against subsequent attacks.

## Immunization

Immunity can be provided artificially by vaccination and other forms of immunization. A vaccine is a preparation containing the offending organism—usually in a weakened form that will not cause the actual disease. When introduced into the body, the vaccine stimulates the body to produce antibodies against the disease. These antibodies remain in the system for a long time (often for life), and the body is thus prepared to resist the actual disease.

A number of viral diseases can be prevented by immunization. There are vaccines against polio, measles, rubella (German measles), mumps, and some strains of influenza. Researchers are working on a vaccine against chicken pox and shingles; however, this vaccine is not yet available to the public.

## Medications

Besides vaccination, there are other measures that can be used to help the body's natural defenses fight off infectious diseases. Bacterial infections can often be conquered by medications called antibiotics. These are substances derived from living microorganisms that kill other microorganisms. Penicillin, for example, comes from a living mold called *Penicillium*. Penicillin is one of the most commonly used antibiotics, along with streptomycin, tetracycline, and erythromycin. Each of these is effective against specific diseases. Antibiotics work either by destroying bacteria or by preventing their reproduction.

Sulfonamides, or sulfa drugs, are synthetic antibiotic drugs

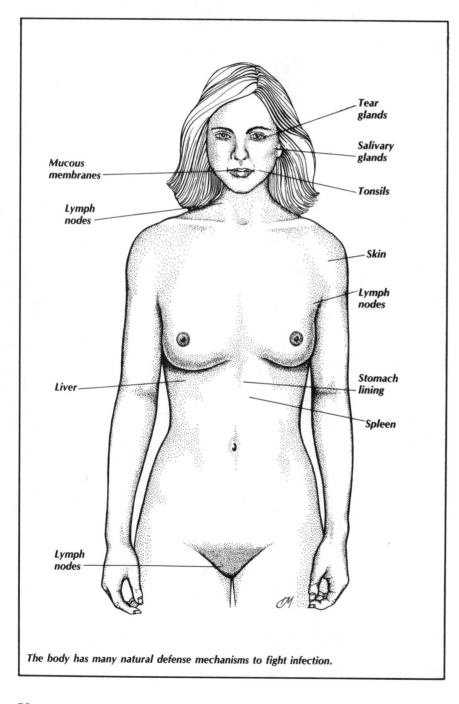

The body has many natural defense mechanisms to fight infection.

*Tear glands*

*Salivary glands*

*Mucous membranes*

*Tonsils*

*Lymph nodes*

*Skin*

*Lymph nodes*

*Liver*

*Stomach lining*

*Spleen*

*Lymph nodes*

that are also effective against infections. This type of drug is often prescribed for localized infections in the urinary tract.

Unfortunately, these medications do not attack viruses. Viruses, therefore, are responsible for many of the serious or fatal infectious illnesses today, since no generally effective cures have been developed.

Researchers are continually searching for new ways to help the body combat infectious diseases. Medical advances against these diseases have already been dramatic; not too many years ago, infectious diseases were uncontrollable and thus a constant danger. The control of infections has been one of medicine's greatest accomplishments.

The more common infectious diseases are discussed in greater detail in the following pages.

# Bacteria

Bacteria are one-celled microscopic organisms. Some kinds of bacteria cause disease in humans and animals, but many others are beneficial. Bacteria dispose of organic waste, enrich the soil, and are used to make wine, beer, vinegar, cheese, and yogurt. In human beings, certain beneficial bacteria live in the intestines, where they assist in digestion.

Bacteria are different from viruses in that they are able to multiply outside a living cell, whereas viruses can grow and multiply only in living cells. Bacteria are different from other causes of infection—protozoa (one-celled animals) and fungi (plantlike organisms)—in two ways: they have a primitive nucleus (center where genetic material is located), rather than a well-defined one with an enclos-

ing membrane and chromosomes; and they reproduce simply by splitting in two (binary fission), rather than by means of the more complex process, called mitosis, that is seen in higher organisms.

## Types

One way of classifying bacteria is by shape:

Rod-shaped bacteria are known as bacilli. They often have waving projections known as flagella, which they use to propel themselves. Some form thick-walled cells known as spores, which can survive for long periods even after the parent bacteria have been killed by freezing, disinfectants, or other harsh forces. When conditions are favorable, the spores are able to generate new bacteria. Typhoid fever is caused by bacilli.

Round or egg-shaped bacteria are known as cocci. They occur singly (micrococci), in chains (streptococci—the cause of strep sore throat), in pairs (diplococci), or in irregular bunches (staphylococci—the cause of many infections). Cocci do not form spores, nor do they usually move about.

Bacteria also exist as comma-shaped organisms called vibrios (the organisms responsible for cholera) and as spiral-shaped organisms, such as the spirochete that causes syphilis.

Another way to classify bacteria is by whether they can live in the presence of air. Those that can are called *aerobic;* those that cannot are called *anaerobic.* Some can live either with or without air and are called *facultative.* Tetanus (lockjaw) is an example of a disease caused by anaerobic bacteria that are commonly found in the soil. They

pose no danger to humans unless they enter the body through a wound, particularly a puncture wound (such as one made by a nail). The air then cannot get to the organisms to destroy them, and so they multiply within the body, unless the infected person has been vaccinated against tetanus.

## How bacteria are transmitted

Disease-causing bacteria enter the body in many different ways. Those that cause pneumonia and sore throat are carried in droplets that an infected person sneezes or coughs into the air; the bacteria are then inhaled and deposited on the mucous membranes of the throat or lungs of a healthy person, where they multiply and eventually cause disease, unless checked by the body's immune system. The bacteria that cause intestinal diseases like cholera and typhoid can be transmitted in foods that have been handled by an infected person or in water tainted by body wastes from an infected individual. Another important route for infection is any break in the skin, which is why it is important to clean any cut in the skin as soon as possible.

## Bacteria and the body's defenses

Once inside the body, bacteria do their damage in two main ways: by direct destruction of tissue and by producing toxins (poisons). Certain white blood cells, known as lymphocytes, produce substances called antitoxins, which neutralize the toxins of the bacteria, and antibodies, which destroy the invading bacteria themselves. Once created, the antibodies against a specific disease can persist in the body or be reproduced when needed, providing continuous immunity—sometimes for life. Still other white blood cells, known as phagocytes, entrap and destroy bacteria.

# Bubonic plague

Known as the "Black Death" in the Middle Ages, bubonic plague is said to have killed three-fourths of the population of Europe and Asia in 20 years during the fourteenth century. In recent times, only limited numbers of people have been infected, mostly in Southeast Asia. Cases are occasionally reported in the western and southwestern United States.

## Causes

The disease is caused by a bacterium, *Yersinia pestis,* which is carried by wild rodents, including rats, mice, prairie dogs, and squirrels. Infected fleas transmit the disease from animals to humans by their bite. Infected humans with plague sores in their lungs can pass the bacteria to other people when they cough. The result of direct infection of the lungs is known as primary pneumonic plague.

## Symptoms

In bubonic plague transmitted by flea bite, chills and high fever occur after an incubation period (the time between exposure to the disease and development of symptoms) that is usually two to five days (although it can vary from a few hours to 12 days). The chief symptom is the development of enlarged, painful lymph nodes (called buboes)

that fill with pus and may rupture. The patient is often restless, delirious, and uncoordinated. The plague bacteria rapidly spread to affect all organs of the body. Without treatment, 60 percent to 90 percent of victims die, usually within three to five days.

Primary pneumonic plague kills even more quickly. Two or three days after being infected, the victim experiences high fever, chills, rapid heartbeat, and headache. A cough develops, with blood specks in the mucous discharge, which eventually turns red and foamy. Breathing becomes rapid and irregular as pneumonia develops. Untreated persons usually die within 48 hours.

## Treatment

Immediate treatment as soon as plague is suspected can reduce the death rate to below 5 percent. An antibiotic, such as streptomycin or tetracycline, is given every six hours around the clock for seven to ten days. Patients with primary pneumonic plague must be isolated and watched closely. Anyone who is in contact with a plague victim should also be closely watched for the development of fever, cough, and painful lymph nodes. Preventive antibiotics, to prevent the onset of the infection, should generally be given to those exposed to plague victims.

## Prevention

Insect repellents help prevent bites from infected fleas, and avoidance of contact with wild rodents is always advisable. Rodent control measures can re-

duce the source of infection. Travelers to the parts of Southeast Asia and India where bubonic plague is present should be immunized with inactivated plague vaccine.

# *Candida albicans*

*Candida albicans* is a fungus that is normally present on the skin and on membranes of the mouth, throat, intestines, and vagina. It becomes an infecting agent only when there is some change in the body environment that allows it to grow out of control.

## Causes

The most common cause of infection may be the use of antibiotics that destroy beneficial as well as harmful microorganisms in the body and permit *Candida* to multiply in their place. The resulting condition is known as candidiasis, candidosis, or moniliasis. In the mouth, it becomes thrush; on the skin, an inflamed rash such as diaper rash; in the vagina, vaginitis, moniliasis, or yeast infection; and in or next to the nails, candidal onychomycosis or paronychia, respectively. Candidal infection can also affect the esophagus (food tube) and the digestive tract. In rare instances, when body resistance is low, *Candida albicans* enters the bloodstream and causes serious infection of the vital organs.

## Those at risk

Drug addicts, diabetics, and patients receiving chemotherapy are especially at risk. So are those whose natural defenses are weakened by drugs that suppress the immune system (such as those given to recipients of organ transplants). Pregnant women are often susceptible to moniliasis, and thrush may develop in babies who passed through an infected birth canal.

### Symptoms and treatment

The symptoms and treatment for the various forms of *Candida* infection are as follows:

- Vaginitis is characterized by a white or yellow discharge, with inflammation of the walls of the vagina and of the vulva (external genital area). A white, curdlike substance may cling to the walls of the vagina. Treatment is with an antifungal drug, such as nystatin, which is inserted deep in the vagina and, if necessary, applied to the entire region around the entrance to the vagina. The infection is often passed to the woman's sexual partner, causing irritation, redness, and soreness of the head of the penis and sometimes a slight discharge. Both partners should use the medication when one has a recurring infection. Otherwise, the disease may pass back and forth between them.
- Thrush appears as creamy-white or bluish-white patches on the tongue, which is also inflamed and sometimes beefy red; on the lining of the mouth; or in the throat. Treatment is usually with nystatin oral solution or drops five times a day until all patches have disappeared and then for a few days afterward.
- Diaper rash caused by *Candida* can be treated by keeping the baby as dry as possible with frequent diaper changes. In se-

vere cases, an antifungal ointment may be prescribed.
- Infections of the fingernails and toenails appear as red, painful swelling around the nail; later, pus develops. After the area has been treated with hot compresses and drainage, if necessary, and the nail has been cut back, an antifungal lotion is applied. The nail itself may be involved (appearing hard, yellow, and dull), making treatment more difficult and perhaps necessitating long-term use of oral drugs. Newer oral drugs, such as ketoconazole, are reserved for more severe or resistant infections.
- Systemic infection (when infection enters the bloodstream and affects the kidneys, heart, lungs, eyes, or other organs) can result in high fever, chills, anemia, and sometimes a rash or shock. Disease in the lungs can cause bloody sputum (mucous discharge); in the kidneys, blood in the urine; in the brain, seizures; in the heart, murmurs and valve damage; in the eye, pain and blurred vision. An antifungal medicine is usually given intravenously.

In all cases, the underlying condition that caused the outbreak of *Candida* must be removed, if possible. This may mean stopping the use of antibiotics or controlling diabetes. The same approach is used to prevent future infections.

# Chicken pox

Chicken pox is an extremely contagious disease that is characterized by a blistery rash. It occurs most frequently in children between the ages of five and eight; less than 20 percent of the cases in the United States affect people over 15 years old. Chick-

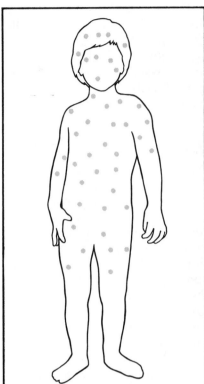

*The first symptom of chicken pox is usually an itchy rash that begins as small red spots on the trunk. Within hours, the spots become larger, fluid-filled blisters and begin spreading out from the trunk to the face, scalp, arms, and legs.*

en pox is transmitted so easily that almost everyone gets the disease at some time.

### Causes

Chicken pox is caused by infection with the varicella zoster virus.

Chicken pox is contracted by touching an infected person's blisters or anything that has been contaminated by contact with them. The virus is also thought by some researchers to be airborne, since it may be caught from an infected person before the rash develops. Another way to get chicken pox is by exposure to shingles, which is a nerve disorder caused by the same virus.

The incubation period (the time between exposure to the illness and the appearance of symptoms) of chicken pox is 10 to 21 days. Chicken pox is contagious for about six to eight days after the rash appears.

## Symptoms

The first symptom of chicken pox is usually a rash, which can be very itchy. It begins as small, red spots on the trunk. Within hours, the spots become larger, fluid-filled blisters and begin spreading out from the trunk to the face, scalp, arms, and legs. Over the next few days, the blisters continue to fill with pus, burst, and then form a scab or crust. New spots appear periodically during a two- to six-day period. They may spread to the soles and palms. The rash may even affect the eyes, mouth, throat, vagina, and rectum.

Another main symptom is a mild fever (101°F to 103°F) that rises and disappears as the rash comes and goes. Some children have a slight fever and feel sluggish a few days before the rash begins; however, this warning is more common in adults.

Adults usually have higher fevers, a more severe rash, headaches, and muscle aches, and they take longer to recuperate than children. Recovery from all symptoms takes ten days to two weeks.

## Complications

Complications of chicken pox seldom develop in otherwise healthy people. The most common complication is bacterial infection of the blisters, which may occur if the blister is scratched and the skin is broken. In some instances, the rash spreads to the eyes and causes pain and possible damage. Generally, the chicken pox rash heals without leaving scars, unless the blisters have been scratched and become infected. A doctor should be consulted if breathing problems, high fever, extreme drowsiness, severe headache, vomiting, or unsteadiness occurs within the course of the disease or within several weeks of recovery. These symptoms may indicate further complications.

## Treatment

Since there is no known cure for chicken pox, treatment consists in reducing the effects of the symptoms. A soothing lotion, such as calamine lotion, lessens itchiness. Baths in warm (not hot) water keep the skin clean and reduce the risk of infection in the rash. If itching is severe, the fingernails should be trimmed and gloves should be worn at night to minimize unconscious scratching. Children may need to wear mittens and socks all day for the duration of the rash.

An association has been established between aspirin use during a viral infection and Reye's syndrome (brain inflammation accompanied by deterioration of the liver) in children. It is recommended that aspirin not be given to a child with chicken pox. A doctor can suggest an aspirin substitute if needed for discomfort or fever.

## Prevention

Although almost everyone contracts chicken pox once, most people do not get it again because the body manufactures antibodies to combat the virus. Nevertheless, the same virus may cause shingles later in life. Researchers are working on a vaccine against chicken pox and shingles; however, this vaccine is not yet available to the public.

# Diphtheria

Diphtheria is a sudden, severe, and highly contagious disease that primarily affects the tonsils, upper airways, and larynx (voice box). Diphtheria bacteria destroy the outer layer of the mucous membrane of the throat or larynx; the slush of dead cells, bacteria, and white blood cells that remains forms the grayish membrane covering the tonsils and throat that is the chief sign of the disease. Complications may include inflammation of the heart muscle (myocarditis), which sometimes results in heart failure, and temporary neuritis (nerve inflammation). Diphtheria bacteria also infect skin wounds, but cannot invade intact skin.

## Cause

Diphtheria is caused by the bacterium known as *Corynebacterium diphtheriae*, which is transmitted via droplets of moisture from the throat and nose of an infected person. It is most common during the colder months, when schools are in session and people are in closer contact. Frequently, the bacteria are transmitted by carriers—people who have no symptoms and do not even know that they harbor the disease. The incubation period (the time between exposure to the infection and appearance of the first symptom) is one to seven days.

## Symptoms

Early symptoms include a mild sore throat, hoarseness, a rasping cough, pain on swallowing, and a mild fever. Children may be nauseated, vomit, and have chills and headache as well as fever and other symptoms. The membrane that forms is typically tough, adheres tightly, and causes bleeding if removed. It appears in patches and can vary from yellowish to grayish green or dirty gray (the most common color). Some people have little or no characteristic membrane. If the membrane extends from the throat to the trachea (windpipe), larynx, or bronchi (air tubes in the lungs), it can become detached and obstruct the passage partially or completely, choking off the air supply. Signs of this life-threatening emergency are rapid breathing, high-pitched breathing sounds, and blue lips and fingertips. Narrowing of the air passage may also be caused by edema (swelling of fluid-filled tissue) of the lining of the larynx and throat.

## Treatment

Treatment is with diphtheria antitoxin (a solution of refined and concentrated protective antibodies obtained from the blood of horses that have been immunized against the poisons created by the diphtheria bacteria). This should be done at once, after a skin test to determine that the patient is not allergic to horse serum (blood fluid). (A patient who is found to be allergic is desensitized with a series of diluted doses of antitoxin.) After the antitoxin has been administered, antibiotics, such as penicillin and erythromycin, are given for at least a week to eliminate the diphtheria organisms. The patient is isolated until two cultures obtained 24 hours apart indicate that the infection is gone.

Because of the possible severe or even fatal complications of diphtheria, patients with symptoms need to be placed in a hospital intensive care unit for complete rest and careful observation. If signs of airway obstruction occur, a tracheotomy (surgical creation of a hole in the neck) will be performed immediately so that a tube can be passed into the lungs to supply oxygen. Frequent checking of the heart and nervous system is needed to identify complications. In severe cases, these can include heart irregularities, cardiac arrest (heart stoppage), and nervous system disorders, such as swallowing difficulty caused by paralysis of swallowing muscles due to inflammation of their nerves.

Those who have been close contacts of the patient and who have not been immunized should receive throat cultures and be immunized with vaccine. These people should be watched carefully for the development of symptoms and be given antitoxin should symptoms occur. Another approach is to give antitoxin immediately (after allergy has been ruled out). In people who have been immunized, a booster of vaccine will be sufficient. Cultures of the nose, throat, and any open wounds should be obtained from all contacts of patients with diphtheria. Carriers of diphtheria should be given seven to ten days of treatment with an appropriate antibiotic (usually erythromycin). If the organism is still present, another course of drug therapy should be given. If this fails, a tonsillectomy may be needed.

## Prevention

Fortunately, widespread immunization has made diphtheria a rare disease. To maintain this status, children should be immunized, beginning in infancy. The diphtheria vaccine is usually given in combination with the vaccines against tetanus and pertussis (whooping cough)—the DTP immunization.

# Enteroviral infections

The enteroviruses are a group of viruses that cause a wide variety of usually brief, but occasionally serious, illnesses that are particularly common in children. Included in the group are the coxsackieviruses, the echoviruses, and the polioviruses.

Enteroviral infections occur most often in the summer and fall and can be spread by contact with infected human feces or respiratory secretions. Although they produce a great deal of temporary discomfort, most of the enteroviral infections generally do not cause lasting illness. Often, the only treatment possible is to make the patient comfortable, with plenty of liquids, bed rest, lukewarm sponge baths, and nonaspirin pain-relievers, such as acetaminophen, to control fever until the illness has passed. Careful hand washing and proper disposal of human wastes can help prevent the spread of infection.

The following diseases are caused by enteroviruses:

### Aseptic meningitis

This inflammation of the membrane covering the brain causes

headache, pain and stiffness in the neck and back, fever, nausea, vomiting, drowsiness, and a general sick feeling. Most patients recover in a week or so, but the disease may be fatal for newborns.

## Hand, foot, and mouth disease

In this disease, which is common in young children, little blisters erupt all over the mucous membranes in the mouth, on the hands and feet, and sometimes in the diaper area.

## Herpangina

An epidemic disease in infants and young children, herpangina is marked by sudden high fever, headache, sore throat, vomiting, and the appearance of grayish spots on the soft palate (rear roof of the mouth), tonsils, or throat. The spots become shallow ulcers and heal in three to six days.

## Myocarditis and pericarditis

Possibly fatal heart failure in newborns may result from myocarditis (inflammation of the heart muscle) caused by coxsackieviruses or echoviruses transmitted to the baby by the mother. Myocarditis and pericarditis (inflammation of the sac around the heart) in older children and in adults may also be caused by a coxsackievirus; patients usually make a complete recovery, although congestive heart failure can occur.

## Paralytic disease

Various echoviruses, coxsackieviruses, and polioviruses pro-

duce muscle weakness or paralysis that is similar to the paralysis of poliomyelitis and is treated in the same manner.

## Pleurodynia (Bornholm disease)

Sudden, recurrent pains in the lower chest or abdomen signal the onset of this illness, which is often accompanied by fever, headache, nausea, abdominal tenderness, and sore throat. The disease may spread to cause pleuritis (inflammation of the membrane sac surrounding the lungs and the lining of the chest cavity), pericarditis, or aseptic meningitis.

## Poliomyelitis

Poliomyelitis (also known as polio and infantile paralysis), caused by the three types of polioviruses, is a serious infection of the spinal cord, which can result in paralysis of all the muscles. The symptoms include muscle soreness and stiffness of the neck and spine. With the development of the polio vaccine, polio has been virtually eradicated in the United States, but the threat of polio epidemics remains if children are not routinely immunized.

## Respiratory disease

The enteroviruses cause respiratory illnesses accompanied by head cold, fever, sore throat, and sometimes vomiting and diarrhea.

## Rubellalike rash

A mild rash like that of rubella (German measles), but lasting

longer, this usually occurs in epidemic form and only on the face, neck, and chest. Fever is common, and meningitis can develop, but usually this is a mild disease.

# Histoplasmosis

Histoplasmosis is an infection that follows the inhalation of spores from the fungus *Histoplasma capsulatum*. The parts of the body principally affected are the lungs, the liver, and the spleen.

## Cause

The *Histoplasma capsulatum* spore is found in soil and in the air. There is no practical defense against breathing the spores. Development of symptoms seems to be a matter of individual immune system response.

## Symptoms

In most instances, histoplasmosis does not reach the point at which symptoms appear. People may have the disease but, because of the action of their immune system, never have enough damage to make the symptoms noticeable, much less to create an acute condition. However, if symptoms do appear, they can be serious, especially when left untreated. The most common symptoms are as follows:
• Acute pneumonia (inflammation of the lungs)
• Influenzalike illnesses, with lethargy, cough, fever, and lung involvement
• Enlargement of the liver and the spleen, with accompanying interruption of normal function

- The development of fibrous scar tissue in affected organs, particularly the lungs

Histoplasmosis can become inactive and then be reactivated at a later date. In cases of reactivated histoplasmosis, the lungs, meninges (coverings of the brain and spinal cord), heart, peritoneum (lining of the abdominal cavity), and adrenal glands can be involved.

Most affected people probably have histoplasmosis in a dormant form (present within their bodies, but not at the stage at which symptoms are evident). Fatalities occur only in cases of massive infection (which also implies massive breakdown or malfunctioning of the body's immune system).

### Diagnosis

Treatment for histoplasmosis begins with diagnosis. The best procedure is to cultivate growths of *Histoplasma capsulatum* organisms from tissue or fluid samples. Another method is to note the rise in the body's production of antibodies (the protective substances produced by the body).

### Treatment

An antifungal medication, such as ketoconazole or amphotericin B, is usually used to treat chronic cases. These drugs help control the disease but appear to have little effect on the fibrous scarring that often occurs in advanced cases.

# Influenza

Influenza, more commonly called the flu, is a contagious disease that is accompanied by

*Using a vaporizer to add moisture to the air in the patient's room will help to relieve nasal congestion.*

respiratory problems and fever. A bout of influenza is unpleasant, but it is usually not dangerous to otherwise healthy people.

### Causes

Two types of viruses cause influenza: influenza A virus and influenza B virus. Each type encompasses several different strains, which are named for the place where they were first identified, for example, Hong Kong flu virus and Russian flu virus.

The unusual characteristic of the flu viruses is that once a strain has spread throughout a population, it changes in structure, becoming capable of causing a new form of influenza. The antibodies produced by the body

to combat the virus are no longer effective because the virus has taken on different qualities. Scientists are generally able to predict what type of altered virus to expect each year, but about every ten years an entirely new strain appears.

Because influenza is thought to be transmitted by airborne particles from an infected person's respiratory tract, large numbers of people in a community or even in a country can easily contract the disease in a relatively short period of time. Overcrowded living conditions promote the transmission of the virus. Since flu spreads most easily when temperatures and humidity are low, most cases of influenza occur in the fall and winter months.

## Symptoms

Flu symptoms usually develop one to three days after exposure to the virus. Some people experience symptoms in as short a time as 18 hours. Fever, chills, headache, muscle aches, and total exhaustion can occur suddenly. Fevers generally do not exceed 104°F, but they may rise to 106°F.

Frequently, people experience a dry cough and a runny or congested nose as their initial symptoms begin to subside. These respiratory symptoms worsen and remain for three to four days. The cough and fatigue may persist for two weeks or more after the other symptoms have disappeared.

## Complications

The most common complications are those that involve parts of the respiratory system—for example, pneumonia (infection of the lungs), which affects both adults and children, and croup (infection of the larynx), which affects young children. If the patient has extreme difficulty in breathing, blood in the coughed-up mucus, bluish skin, or a barklike cough, a physician should be consulted immediately.

One life-threatening complication of influenza that affects children and adolescents between the ages of 2 and 16 years is Reye's syndrome. It is a type of encephalitis (inflammation of the brain) that is accompanied by deterioration of the liver.

## Treatment

In most cases, influenza cannot be cured and is treated only by relieving symptoms. The antiviral drug amantadine can be used to prevent and treat some forms of influenza A infection. This drug can produce unpleasant side effects, however, so physicians usually prescribe it only when a patient is susceptible to additional complications.

Treatment for flu is generally the same as treatment for a bad cold or fever. Physicians recommend bed rest, extra fluids, and an aspirin substitute to reduce fever and muscle aches. Because an association has been established between aspirin use during a viral infection and Reye's syndrome in children, it is recommended that aspirin not be given to a child with influenza. Acetaminophen, however, has not been linked to Reye's syndrome and can be used. Nasal sprays or drops, when used sparingly so that nasal tissues are not damaged, and cough medicines help relieve coldlike symptoms. Using a vaporizer in the patient's room to add moisture to the air relieves congestion.

## Prevention

Each year, researchers prepare an influenza vaccine in an attempt to prevent spread of the virus. The vaccine is composed of inactivated organisms from several virus strains and provides protection against influenza caused by these strains. Unfortunately, protection is not necessarily afforded against new or different strains. Vaccines are typically between 67 percent and 92 percent effective.

Some people have reactions to the vaccine that range from inflammation at the injection site to mild flu symptoms. On rare occasions, nervous system disorders result. Vaccination is not usually recommended for children unless they are in a high-risk group, such as those with heart or lung conditions.

# Measles

Measles (also called rubeola) is a contagious disease that mainly affects the respiratory system, skin, and eyes. It was once considered one of the more dangerous childhood diseases because the threat of serious complications was so great. Fortunately, development of a vaccine to prevent measles has drastically reduced its occurrence.

## Causes

Measles is caused by a virus. The virus is transmitted via droplets of moisture from the respiratory tract of an infected person that travel through the air. Some researchers contend that the virus enters the body through the eyes.

The incubation period (the time between being exposed to the infectious organism and actually showing symptoms) for measles is 8 to 12 days. An infected person is contagious for up to four days before symptoms appear and for up to six days after the rash develops.

## Symptoms

Measles usually begins much like a cold, with a runny nose, nasal congestion, sneezing, a dry cough, and a fever of 102°F to 104°F. After three or four days, the eyes may become sensitive to bright light as they grow red and swollen. Then the fever drops, and red spots with tiny white centers (called Koplik's spots after the physician who first identified them) appear in the mouth.

By the fourth or fifth day, the fever increases again, and a rash appears. The rash usually starts on the face and neck and behind the ears, and then spreads to the rest of the body. As the spots multiply, they grow larger, become raised, and sometimes blend together. They turn dark red and then brown before the skin begins to fall off in small flakes. This process takes about one week after the rash first emerges, although skin discoloration can last as long as two weeks. Other symptoms usually disappear within seven to ten days after the appearance of the first symptoms.

## Complications

Breathing problems, increased coughing, earache, or extreme drowsiness may indicate complications that warrant consulting a doctor immediately. The more serious complications are pneumonia (inflammation of the lungs) and encephalitis (inflammation of the brain). Subacute sclerosing panencephalitis, a rare but often fatal disease of the brain, has also been linked to measles. Severe ear infections can occur, particularly in young children. In addition, bronchitis, laryngitis, and swelling of the lymph nodes in the neck can prolong the course of the illness or make it appear to return.

## Diagnosis

Generally, physicians diagnose measles by the initial symptoms. To confirm diagnosis, nasal discharge, blood, or urine can be tested for the virus.

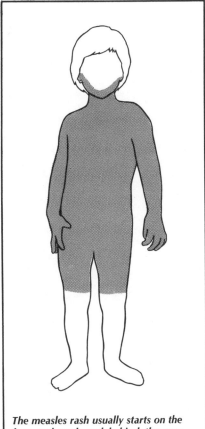

*The measles rash usually starts on the face and neck and behind the ears and then spreads to the rest of the body.*

## Treatment

Since measles is caused by a virus, it does not respond to antibiotics, and treatment must focus on relieving the patient's discomfort. A vaporizer in the patient's room will ease coldlike symptoms by adding moisture to the air. If the eyes are irritated, warm compresses may relieve the inflammation. Also, dim lights are easier on the eyes. Soaps that may irritate the skin should not be used. The doctor may suggest adding baking soda to bath water or applying a soothing lotion, such as calamine lotion, to the rash to relieve itching.

An association has been established between aspirin use during or immediately after a viral infection and Reye's syndrome (inflammation of the brain accompanied by deterioration of the liver) in children. It is recommended that aspirin not be given to a child with measles. A doctor can suggest an aspirin substitute, such as acetaminophen, if needed for relief of discomfort or fever.

## Prevention

Today, measles has been almost eliminated because of a vaccine given to children as an injection when they are about 15 months of age. The vaccine, which is prepared from measles virus, stimulates production of antibodies (protective substances) in the body. Because the vaccine effectiveness rate is very low in young infants, babies are not vaccinated before 15 months of age. The infants of women who are immune to measles (either because they have had measles or have been immunized against it) acquire temporary natural immunity that lasts for about the first six months of life. If a baby is exposed to measles, however, a doctor should be consulted. Measles is dangerous for anyone under three years of age and for anyone with a chronic (longterm) illness.

# Mononucleosis

Infectious mononucleosis, or "mono," is a contagious viral disease that initially attacks the lymph nodes in the neck and the throat. When these tissues become less effective in fighting infection, sore throat, swelling of the lymph nodes, and fever result.

## Cause

Mono is caused by the Epstein-Barr virus, which is named after the scientists who first identified it in the mid-1960s. The virus enters the lymph nodes and attacks the lymphocytes (the white blood cells manufactured there). As the white blood cells come into contact with the virus, they change shape and multiply. At first there are no symptoms, because it takes several weeks before enough of the altered cells can accumulate to generate a reaction. Gradually, however, symptoms appear. First, there is a mild sore throat, sluggishness, and fever. The symptoms worsen as the body tries to fight the infection by creating more white blood cells. The symptoms usually diminish and disappear about six to eight weeks later.

Mono spreads by contact with moisture from the mouth and throat of an infected person. Kissing, sharing drinking glasses and toothbrushes, or touching anything that has been near the mouth of an infected person may result in transmission of the disease.

## Those at risk

Teenagers and young adults seem most susceptible to mono. Sometimes, children become infected, but the disease is much less common in persons over the age of 35.

## Symptoms

In all cases, the infection develops so slowly with such mild symptoms that it may be initially indistinguishable from a cold or the flu. However, a sore throat that lasts two weeks or more; swollen lymph nodes in the neck, throat, armpits, and groin; a persistent fever (usually about 102°F); and tiredness may indicate mono. Mono symptoms can be mild or so severe that throat pain impedes swallowing and fever reaches 105°F. Some people also experience a rash, eye pain, and photophobia (discomfort in bright light).

## Complications

Most cases of mono run an uncomplicated course. Occasionally, however, the infection spreads to other parts of the body besides the throat and lymph nodes. For example,

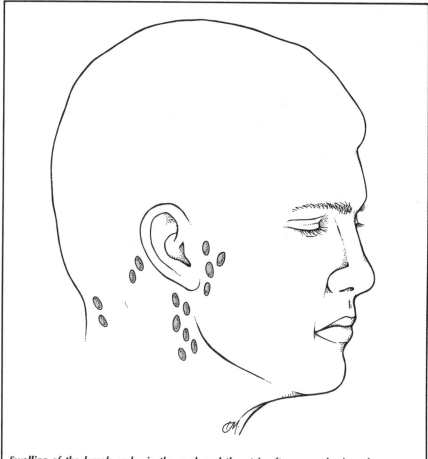

*Swelling of the lymph nodes in the neck and throat is often an early sign of mononucleosis.*

mono may lead to hepatitis (inflammation of the liver). Jaundice, a symptom of this complication, appears as a yellow discoloration of the skin and whites of the eyes. Another sign that the infection has traveled is pain or tenderness in the abdomen. This discomfort may mean a swollen spleen (an organ in the lymph system), which could burst. Any of these symptoms should be reported to a physician for immediate attention.

## Diagnosis

To diagnose infectious mononucleosis, blood samples are analyzed to detect the presence of antibodies to the Epstein-Barr virus and to determine overall blood cell count. Inflammation of the liver can also be detected and followed up with blood tests.

## Treatment

As long as there are no complications, the best treatment is to rest, drink plenty of liquids until the temperature returns to normal, and then gradually resume normal activities as strength returns. If the patient feels well enough, complete bed rest is probably not necessary or beneficial.

Antibiotics are ineffective against mono, since it is a viral infection and viruses do not respond to antibiotics. However, mono is often accompanied by a streptococcal infection of the throat, in which case an antibiotic will be prescribed to treat that condition. In severe cases, corticosteroid drugs that reduce swelling are prescribed. If the spleen is swollen, the doctor may recommend avoiding strenuous activities, such as lifting and pushing, which may cause sudden rupture of the spleen. Hospitalization is necessary if there is a serious complication, such as rupture of the spleen.

Most people recover in six to eight weeks, but some cases take as long as six months for complete recovery. A tired feeling, which may include depression, is the last symptom to disappear. Mono may return in a milder form within a few months. Fortunately, mono almost never reappears in its full-blown form after a year. However, in a related condition, chronic Epstein-Barr virus infection, symptoms of mono recur periodically over a period of years.

# Mumps

Mumps is a contagious viral disease that is usually contracted during childhood. More than 85 percent of the cases occur before the age of 15, especially between the ages of six and ten years.

## Cause

Mumps is caused by a virus that attacks cells of the parotid salivary glands. This invasion results in painful swelling of the face beneath the ear along the jawline. Mumps virus spreads by contact with airborne moisture from an infected person's nose or throat. Sometimes, the infection comes from someone who has the disease without symptoms or who is not yet aware of the symptoms. The disease occurs most often during the spring months, although it can happen at any time of the year.

## Symptoms

Symptoms can be so mild that they are almost nonexistent, or they can be very severe. Fever (101°F to 103°F), headache, and loss of appetite usually develop first, followed by earache; then the characteristic swelling of the salivary glands appears. Swelling may start on one side of the face and then appear on the other side within a few days. Sometimes, however, only one side swells. The inflammation may cause soreness and difficulty in eating or swallowing.

The sex glands may become swollen as well. Orchitis (inflammation of one or both testes) can cause considerable pain. Affected testes may shrink somewhat, but contrary to popular belief, it is not common for mumps to lead to sterility in males. Girls may have swelling in the ovaries, but there is seldom any severe discomfort. In addition, swelling may occur in

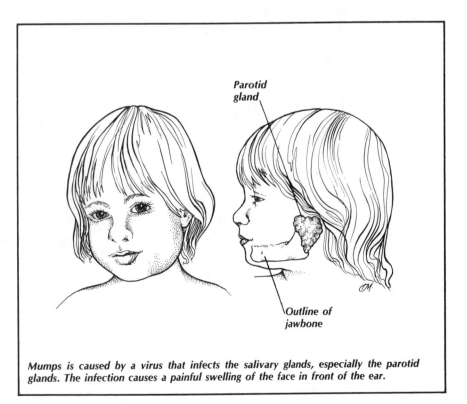

*Parotid gland*

*Outline of jawbone*

*Mumps is caused by a virus that infects the salivary glands, especially the parotid glands. The infection causes a painful swelling of the face in front of the ear.*

other glands and organs, including the breasts, other salivary glands, the liver, and the brain.

## Complications

Although mumps can be unpleasant, it rarely has long-term complications. Encephalitis (inflammation of the brain) is the most dangerous complication of mumps because it carries the risk of death. Another possible consequence of mumps encephalitis is hearing loss or even deafness. Hearing may return to normal after several months, however. A milder complication is meningoencephalitis (inflammation of the brain and its covering, the meninges). This disease causes a stiff neck, headache, high fever, drowsiness, sensitivity to bright light, and sometimes delirium; these symptoms usually disappear without damage to the brain.

Pancreatitis (inflammation of the pancreas) can also result from mumps. Symptoms of pancreatitis include stomach pain, vomiting, chills, fever, and extreme weakness. Although these signs usually vanish and leave no damage, diabetes can result in rare cases. Other complications of mumps include nerve inflammation, heart problems, and nervous system disorders—all usually temporary. Symptoms of any of these conditions should be brought to the attention of a doctor.

## Diagnosis

A doctor diagnoses mumps on the basis of the characteristic form and texture of the swollen parotid glands. Boys may have swelling and tenderness in the testes. Exposure to the disease is also a clue. The incubation time (the time between exposure to the virus and the appearance of signs and symptoms) is 14 to 21 days. If mumps is suspected, secretions from the salivary glands can be tested for mumps virus.

## Treatment

Treatment for mumps involves relieving the discomfort of the symptoms, since there is no cure for the disease. Bed rest is usually not necessary. Soft foods and liquids may be easier to swallow. However, fruit juices with a high acid content, like orange and grapefruit juice, may sting the mouth.

If the glands are severely swollen, a physician may prescribe painkilling drugs. Steroid drugs may be recommended for men or boys with extremely swollen testes, but these drugs may prove ineffective. Warm or cold compresses or an ice pack may relieve some pain. Most mumps symptoms disappear within about ten days.

## Prevention

There is a vaccine that is 95 percent effective in preventing mumps. The vaccine stimulates the production of antibodies to resist the disease. Mumps vaccine is usually combined with measles and rubella (German measles) vaccines and given to children by injection when they are 15 months of age.

# Reiter's syndrome

Reiter's syndrome is characterized by the occurrence of urethritis (inflammation of the urethra, which is the tube from the bladder to the outside of the body), conjunctivitis (inflammation of the membrane that covers the front of the eyeball and the insides of the eyelids), and arthritis (joint inflammation). It affects males more often than females.

## Cause

It is thought that Reiter's syndrome is caused by a bacterial infection that is often sexually transmitted.

## Symptoms

Reiter's syndrome exhibits multiple symptoms, any one of which might be mistaken for a sign of another disease. The conjunctivas become inflamed, with corresponding discomfort around the eyes. Urethritis causes discomfort during urination. Arthritic symptoms appear, with joint swelling and pain. Furthermore, many victims have a fever; diarrhea; sores on the palms of the hands, the soles of the feet, the trunk, the mouth, and the penis; and inflammation of the iris (the part of the eye that gives it color).

## Treatment

Treatment for Reiter's syndrome is similar to that for rheumatoid arthritis: aspirin or, if aspirin is ineffective, another nonsteroidal anti-inflammatory drug, such as ibuprofen, indomethacin, or naproxen. The antibiotic tetracycline may help control the urethritis. Conjunctivitis can be treated with eye drops.

# Rubella

Rubella, or German measles, is a relatively mild viral infection with coldlike symptoms and a short-lived rash. The disease is contagious; however, rubella outbreaks have become infrequent since the development of a vaccine to prevent the illness. It is usually not dangerous, unless it occurs during pregnancy, when it can cause serious birth defects.

## Cause

Rubella is caused by a virus. The virus spreads from one person to another via airborne droplets from an infected person's respiratory system. The incubation period (the time between exposure to the infection and appearance of symptoms) is usually 14 to 21 days. An infected person can spread the virus as early as one week before the rash appears and as late as five days after the rash has faded. A child with congenital (present at birth) rubella syndrome can transmit the virus until he is about 12 to 18 months old. Second infections have been reported, but they are rare.

## Complications

Although rubella is generally a mild infection, some complications can arise. Encephalitis (inflammation of the brain) occurs in one in 5,000 cases. Thrombocytopenic purpura, a blood disease characterized by a lowered platelet count, can prove fatal when it accompanies rubella. High or prolonged fever and extreme fatigue should be reported to a physician to prevent further complications.

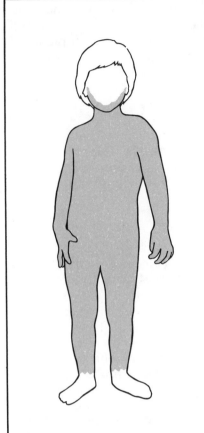

The rubella rash usually first appears on the face and neck and then gradually spreads over most of the body.

Congenital rubella syndrome occurs when the disease is transmitted to the fetus during pregnancy. Rubella virus may cause one or more serious organic and growth disorders in the fetus, particularly if contracted during the first three months of pregnancy. The most common problems include congenital heart defects, hearing and vision problems, blood disorders, and mental retardation and other brain disorders.

## Symptoms

The first symptoms of rubella are a runny nose, swollen lymph nodes in the neck, and a low-grade fever (up to 101°F). About two days later, a rash of very small red or pink spots appears on the face and neck. The spots are flat initially. They then become slightly raised and fade within a day or two. As the first spots fade, more spots develop until the rash has spread over most of the body. The rash lasts only two to three days, but swelling of the lymph nodes may persist for as long as a week. All other symptoms have usually disappeared by then. When there is joint pain, as is common with older women, discomfort may last another week.

## Diagnosis

Under normal circumstances, rubella is difficult to diagnose because the symptoms are so mild and variable. Sometimes there is no rash, and the disease resembles a cold. Other cases may be so severe that the infection may be confused with measles. A doctor can identify the virus by testing a blood sample. Tracing a history of exposure to the disease also helps to establish the diagnosis.

## Treatment

Most patients require little or no treatment for rubella because the symptoms are so mild. An aspirin substitute may afford relief from joint pain. Otherwise, drugs are not needed. Some patients may want bed rest, but most people feel well enough to be somewhat active.

## Prevention

Rubella rarely occurs now because children routinely receive rubella vaccine at about 15 months of age. The vaccine is usually combined with measles and mumps vaccines in one injection. The rubella vaccine works in the body to stimulate the production of antibodies (protective substances) that fight the disease.

Women who want to become pregnant should have a blood test to determine whether they are already immune to rubella; if not, they can be vaccinated. Vaccination is not recommended during pregnancy because of the risk of infection to the fetus. Doctors also caution women to wait at least three months after rubella vaccination before trying to become pregnant.

# Scarlet fever

Scarlet fever (also known as scarlatina) is a highly contagious disease caused by *Streptococcus* bacteria.

## Symptoms

The symptoms of scarlet fever include fever; sore throat; widespread scarlet rash beginning in the armpits and groin and spreading to the neck, chest, back, extremities, and even the tongue; and peeling and scaling of the skin, even on the palms of the hands and the soles of the feet. The incubation period (the time between exposure to the disease and the appearance of symptoms) is two to four days.

## Treatment

In the past, scarlet fever was often fatal, but today it is easily treated with penicillin, and complications are rare. Bed rest and a nourishing diet with plenty of fluids help speed recuperation.

# Septicemia

Septicemia, often called blood poisoning, is a form of bacteremia (invasion of the blood circulation by bacteria).

## Causes

The cause of septicemia is sometimes traceable to a surgical procedure, to the use of intravenous devices or catheters, or to childbirth injury complicated by infection. Septicemia is also a common effect of intravenous drug injections, particularly in drug abusers. Other diseases and disorders associated with septicemia include endocarditis (inflammation of the lining of the heart), genitourinary tract infections, and diseases of the skin, bones, and joints.

## Symptoms

Because few symptoms are unique to septicemia, it is often confused with other illnesses. Fever is generally present, although it may be variable and intermittent. Chills may occur at the onset of the disease. Skin eruptions are common and may be petechial (small red dots or splotches) or purpuric (purple and bruiselike) or may take any of several other forms. Septicemia often begins abruptly with chills, fever, nausea, vomiting, and diarrhea, leading to collapse.

Complications may include secondary infections of the organs and bones.

## Diagnosis

The diagnosis of septicemia is established by testing cultures of blood and other tissues for various kinds of bacteria. Normally, there should be no bacteria in the blood. A single negative culture does not exclude septicemia, particularly in some patients who have had antibiotic therapy.

## Treatment

Septicemia is treated by intravenous administration of antibiotics. Therapy should continue until the patient has been free of symptoms for at least one week.

# Shingles

Shingles, or herpes zoster, is a painful viral infection of one or more nerves. The infection produces a blistery, itchy skin rash on the area of skin supplied by the affected nerve. Shingles rash looks identical to the rash of chicken pox, which should not be surprising because shingles and chicken pox are both caused by the varicella zoster virus.

## Causes

Shingles usually occurs only in persons who have already had chicken pox. Some scientists believe that after a case of chicken pox has run its course, the varicella zoster virus lies dormant in the body, but can be reactivated by injury to the affected area or emotional or physical upset. Others believe that the number and strength of antibodies produced by the body to fight the varicella zoster virus diminish with time, making the person

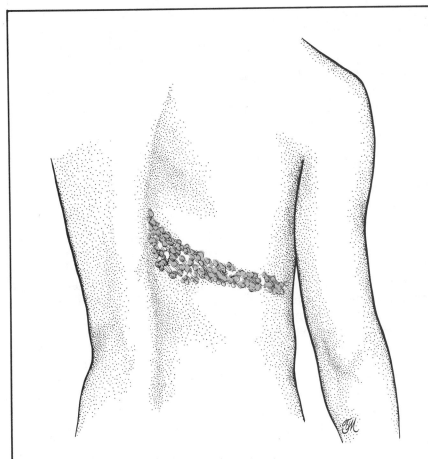

*Shingles is an infection of a nerve characterized by a blistering skin rash following the path of the affected underlying nerve. The rash itself is identical to that of chicken pox, since both diseases are caused by the same virus.*

back, neck, arms, and legs; however, facial nerves are frequently involved. The rash appears in a band or strip following the distribution of the nerve, usually on one side of the body. The rash persists for two to three weeks before clearing; the pain continues for about three or four weeks. In persons over age 60, pain may persist for months to years after the rash has disappeared; this condition is called postherpetic neuralgia.

### Complications

Occasionally, the shingles rash spreads over the entire body. This develops most often in people who have some underlying disease, such as Hodgkin's disease (cancer of the lymph system) or leukemia (cancer of the blood). When these serious disorders already exist, shingles can cause death, but this is rare. A signal that such extreme illness may be present is recurrence of shingles, since the condition seldom occurs more than once.

The most common complication of shingles is bacterial infection of the rash. This can prolong the rash and cause scarring of the skin.

Less common complications follow a shingles attack on facial nerves. Eye disorders and Bell's palsy (a disorder that temporarily paralyzes one side of the face) can result. Shingles in other parts of the body can cause similar temporary paralysis of the area over the affected nerve.

### Treatment

Since there is no known cure for shingles, treatment focuses on reducing pain. An analgesic (painkilling drug) may relieve the

susceptible to another attack of the virus; because some antibodies endure, the person gets shingles rather than chicken pox. If an adult who has not had chicken pox is exposed to the virus, he will get chicken pox, not shingles.

The incidence of shingles increases with age. It rarely occurs in people under the age of 15. More than 50 percent of those who get shingles are over 45 years of age.

### Symptoms

Shingles begins with prickling or tenderness in the skin over the affected nerve. Burning or shooting pain in the same area is also an early symptom. Within two to four days, a rash of small, red spots appears over the affected part of the body. As the spots enlarge, they blister and sometimes blend together. Eventually they fill with pus, burst, and crust over, much the same as with chicken pox rash. With shingles, however, the process takes longer and is confined to the skin area above the affected nerve.

The shingles rash is very itchy. Pain increases as the area beneath the rash becomes redder and more swollen. Shingles most often attacks nerves of the chest, burning sensation. Some physicians prescribe steroid drugs to reduce nerve inflammation in older patients. In order to be effective, steroids must be taken soon after shingles begins. Steroid treatment is usually not recommended for persons with underlying disease because steroids can interfere with resistance to infection. Acyclovir, an antiviral drug given in ointment, oral, and intravenous forms, has been shown to shorten the course and decrease the severity of the illness in many cases.

Preventing infection is also important. Baths in warm (not hot) water soothe and clean the skin. If itching is severe, patients should cut their fingernails and wear gloves when asleep to control unconscious scratching.

# Tetanus

Tetanus is an infectious disease, commonly associated with improperly cleaned deep wounds, that causes severe muscle contractions.

## Cause

Tetanus is caused by toxins (poisonous substances) that are produced by *Clostridium tetani* bacteria. These bacteria may be present on the skin at the time of the injury or may enter the body through a wound caused by an object that has been in contact with material, such as soil, in which bacterial spores are present. Puncture wounds and animal bites, because of their depth, are especially vulnerable to tetanus infection since they are difficult to clean and medicate.

## Symptoms

Tetanus symptoms are varied, depending on the extent of the infection and the body part that is affected. A common symptom is lockjaw, in which the muscles of the jaw go into severe, continuous contraction, thus rendering the jaw immobile. Other symptoms include bowing or arching of the body (a rare occurrence) because of contraction of lower back muscles, back muscle spasms, and throat spasms, which can cause blockage of the airway. The affected body parts become immobile because of the simultaneous and continuous contraction of opposing muscles.

In severe cases, the contractions involve most of the fibers in an affected muscle, similar to what would be required to lift a heavy weight or to marshal all the potential force of a muscle against a great resistance. Such violent and prolonged muscle contractions can be very painful.

## Treatment

Treatment includes muscle relaxant drugs, such as diazepam, to ease the contractions. Antimicrobial drugs, such as penicillin, are used to fight the infection. Tetanus antitoxin is injected intramuscularly (into a muscle) in the hope of lessening the severity of the disease. However, the antitoxin does not counteract the toxin already in the nervous system, nor does it act to relieve symptoms already present.

## Prevention

Immunization with the tetanus vaccine is the best preventive against the disease. Also, wounds should be attended to immediately, especially puncture wounds and animal bites. Tetanus booster shots should be administered periodically, especially if small skin wounds are a common occurrence in the course of the workday.

# ALLERGIES AND THE IMMUNE SYSTEM

Immunity is the body's ability to defend itself against harmful organisms and substances. Essentially, it is a resistance to infection that may be inherited or acquired naturally or artificially.

Immunity develops when foreign organisms or substances called antigens enter the body, causing particular specialized cells to react either by attacking the antigen directly or by producing proteins (specialized molecules essential to living cells) that neutralize the foreign agents. The most common types of antigens are forms of bacteria (microscopic organisms that have the potential to attack body tissues or secrete poisonous substances called toxins) and viruses (the smallest infective agents, responsible for a variety of diseases).

## Lymph system

The lymph system is the body's drainage system. It is composed of a network of vessels and small structures called lymph nodes. The lymph vessels convey excess fluid collected from all over the body back into the blood circulation. Along the way, however, these fluids are forced to percolate through the lymph nodes so that they can be filtered. Harmful organisms are trapped and destroyed by the specialized white blood cells called lymphocytes that are present in these nodes. Lymphocytes are also added to the lymph that flows out of nodes and back to the bloodstream.

## Antibodies

Antibodies are manufactured by the lymph system. Antibodies are specialized proteins that the body produces in response to invasion by a foreign substance. The process of antibody formation begins when an antigen stimulates specialized lymphocytes, called B cells, into action. Antibodies then counteract invading antigens by combining with the antigen to ultimately render it harmless to the body. Some antibodies coat the harmful organisms so that the body's scavenger cells can destroy them more easily. The antibody molecule combines with the antigen molecule by matching combining sites; they fit together like the pieces of a jigsaw puzzle. Other antibodies that neutralize toxins produced by bacteria are called antitoxins.

During periods of active antibody production, lymph nodes often enlarge and become tender to the touch. For example, a vaccination (injection of a natural or artificial antigen to stimulate the body to produce protective antibodies) in the arm can cause swelling of the nodes in the armpit, while mononucleosis causes enlargement of nodes that can be felt under the skin of the armpits, groin, and neck. The spleen (an organ located in the upper left part of the abdomen) is also important in the production of antibodies.

## Immune response

Production of white blood cells and antibodies in reaction to an invading disease organism is called an immune response. This response is one of the body's primary and most efficient lines of defense. Once antibodies have been produced to fight a certain organism, it no longer poses a great threat to the body. That is why one attack of a disease often prevents that same disease from infecting the body again—the first attack causes production of antibodies that protect the body against subsequent attacks. With measles, for example, the antibodies produced as a result of having the disease or of being immunized with the measles vaccine resist a second attack of the disease, providing protection against recurrence.

Antibodies are not always beneficial. For example, when tissue from another body, such as a transplanted heart, is introduced, antibodies are produced to destroy the "invader." Transplants usually are made possible only by means of drugs that act against the body's natural immune response, which would attempt to destroy the transplanted organ. Also, when blood is transfused from one person to another, it must be of a matching type; otherwise, the recipient's immune system will manufacture antibodies to destroy the transfused blood.

Sometimes, the immune system causes reactions that make the body unusually sensitive to foreign material. When the immune response is disruptive to the body in this way, it is called an allergic reaction.

## Allergic reaction

An allergy is a state of special sensitivity to a particular environmental substance, or allergen. An allergic reaction is the body's response, directed by the immune system, to exposure to an allergen.

Although an allergy can be present almost immediately after exposure to an allergen, it usually develops over time, as the immune system forms antibodies against the foreign substance.

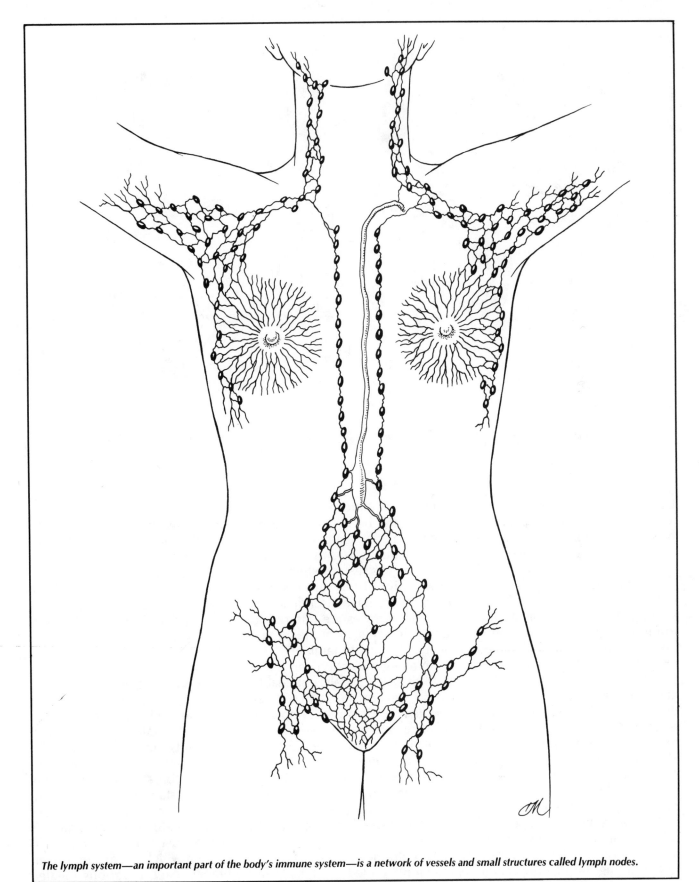

*The lymph system—an important part of the body's immune system—is a network of vessels and small structures called lymph nodes.*

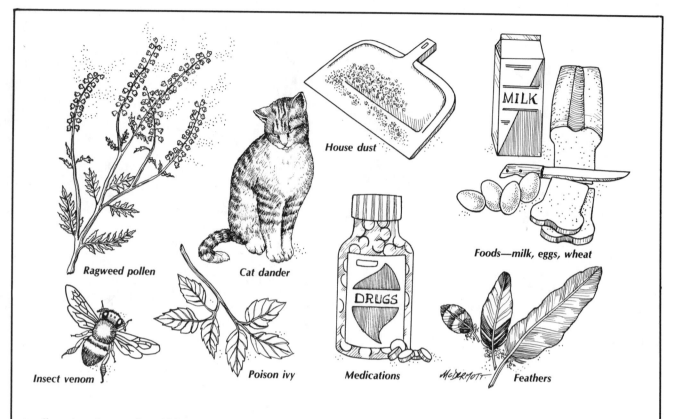

*Ragweed pollen*

*Cat dander*

*House dust*

*Foods—milk, eggs, wheat*

*Insect venom*

*Poison ivy*

*Medications*

*Feathers*

*An allergy is an increased sensitivity to an environmental substance. Some of the more common offending substances, or allergens, are shown here.*

Under normal conditions, such antibodies work to protect the body from further attack. In the case of an allergy, however, the antibodies and other specialized cells involved in this protective function trigger an unusual sensitivity, or overreaction, to the foreign substance. The antibodies stimulate specialized cells to produce histamine, a powerful chemical. Histamine causes the small blood vessels to enlarge and the smooth muscles (such as those in the airways and the digestive tract) to constrict. Histamine release can also cause other reactions, such as hives.

No one knows why allergies develop, but it is known that an allergy can appear, disappear, or reappear at any time and at any age. Allergic reactions rarely occur during the first encounter

with the troublesome allergen because the body needs time to accumulate the antibodies. Also, an individual's sensitivity to certain allergens seems to be related to a family history of allergies. People who have a tendency to develop allergies are referred to as atopic. This atopic tendency frequently runs in families.

An allergic reaction can be so mild that it is barely noticeable or so severe that it is life-threatening. Common symptoms of allergy are watery eyes, runny nose, itching or inflamed skin, and a swollen mouth or throat. Some allergic reactions may be accompanied by headaches, sinus stuffiness, a reduced sense of taste or smell, or difficulty in breathing.

An extremely severe allergic reaction, called anaphylactic

shock, is characterized by breathing difficulties (caused by swelling of the throat and larynx and narrowing of the bronchial tubes), itching skin, hives, and collapse of the blood vessels, as well as by vomiting, diarrhea, and cramps. This condition can be fatal if not properly treated.

**Types of allergens**

There are four categories of allergens: inhalants, contactants, ingestants, and injectants.

Inhalant allergens are those that are breathed in, including such substances as dust, pollen, feathers, and animal dander (small scales from an animal's skin). Hay fever is an inhalant allergy in which the mucous membranes react to various inhaled substances, usually the pollens associated with the changing seasons. Year-round "hay fever" may actually be a reaction to pet dander, feathers, mold, or dust. Hay fever symptoms include sneezing, headache, watery eyes, and itching of the nose, eyes, and roof of the mouth.

Contactant allergens are those that are touched, including such substances as poison ivy, poison oak, cosmetics, detergents, fabrics, and dyes. Contact dermatitis is an example of an allergic reaction to a contactant allergen. The skin may itch, burn, or become inflamed where it has come in contact with certain soaps, detergents, household cleaners, dyes, medications, or chemicals found in food or cosmetics.

Ingestant allergens are those that are swallowed. A variety of foods and medications can act as ingestant allergens. Food allergies occur more frequently in children than in adults. Some common ingestant allergens are milk, eggs, shellfish, fish, peanuts, chocolate, strawberries, tomatoes, and citrus fruits. Symptoms of food allergies include abdominal cramps, nausea, vomiting, and diarrhea. Hives, rash, headache, nasal congestion, and even anaphylactic shock can also be responses that indicate a food allergy.

Injectant allergens are substances that penetrate the skin, such as insect venom and drugs that are injected. For example, people who have severe allergic reactions to insect bites or stings are suffering from a reaction to an injectant allergen. Shortness of breath, coughing, wheezing, light-headedness, and strong, rapid heartbeat are common symptoms. The bite area swells and becomes tender or numb; in extreme cases, anaphylactic shock may occur.

## Diagnosis

Identifying an offending allergen may be uncomfortable, time-consuming, and expensive, but it is necessary to avoid future allergic reactions. A medical history, a record of any recent changes in daily habits, skin-scratch tests (in which small amounts of suspected allergens are applied to tiny scratches in the skin), and intracutaneous skin tests (in which allergens are injected under the skin) are used to help identify the troublesome foreign substance. A special study called radioallergosorbent testing (RAST) is sometimes performed to detect and measure antibodies in the blood that have been manufactured in response to invading substances.

## Treatment

Once the allergen has been identified, half the battle is won. Avoiding the troublesome substance is the first step toward relieving an allergy. If the allergen cannot be avoided or removed, medication or immunotherapy may be recommended. Three types of medications are commonly prescribed: antihistamine drugs, which combat the effect of the histamines in the body; corticosteroids, which reduce inflammation and swelling; and bronchodilators, which ease breathing by opening bronchial tubes.

Allergy immunotherapy, or "desensitization," consists of injections of an allergen in gradually increasing quantities. This allows the body to build up a tolerance to the offending substance. Immunotherapy works best in controlling allergies to pollen, insect venom, and house dust.

A little common sense goes a long way toward controlling allergies. Obviously, the offending allergen needs to be avoided. Natural fibers in the home can be replaced with synthetics. Air conditioners or air filters can be installed for hay fever sufferers. Those susceptible to insect bites can wear protective clothes and avoid wearing bright clothing and perfumes, both of which attract insects. Babies born into allergy-prone families should be breast-fed as long as possible to delay exposure to cow's milk, eggs, and citrus fruits.

## Prevention

In most cases, allergies cannot be prevented, but much can be done to help to control or diminish their effects on overly sensitive individuals.

# AIDS

Acquired immune deficiency syndrome (AIDS) is a condition in which the body's natural defense system is disabled, allowing organisms that are normally fought off to become deadly.

## Causes

This disease, discovered in 1979, is caused by a microorganism called the human immunodeficiency virus. This virus is carried and transmitted in bodily fluids. Sexual intercourse (heterosexual or homosexual), use of nonsterile hypodermic needles (a common practice among drug addicts), and infected blood transfusions have all been implicated as means of transmission of the AIDS virus. Transmission from a pregnant woman to her infant may also occur.

In Western countries, male homosexuals, drug addicts who inject drugs, and hemophiliacs who receive blood transfusions for their disorder are all at high risk of contracting AIDS. In Africa (where the disease seems to have originated), heterosexual transmission is apparently the most common route.

A widespread misconception has been that AIDS can be contracted by *giving* blood—this notion has been disproved. Since the introduction of a blood screening test for use in blood banks and hospital laboratories, acquisition of the AIDS virus by *receiving* blood products is now extremely unlikely.

### Symptoms

Initial symptoms include low-grade fever, swollen lymph nodes, weight loss, fatigue, night sweats, and long-standing diarrhea. Because of impairment of the immune system, AIDS patients easily fall prey to many diseases, including various types of cancer, skin infections, fungal infections, and tuberculosis. About one third of the victims develop a previously rare cancer known as Kaposi's sarcoma, which often appears as purplish bumps on the skin. Many suffer *Pneumocystis carinii* pneumonia (a serious lung infection).

### Diagnosis

The blood of AIDS patients contains an abnormally small number of specialized white blood cells called lymphocytes. Lymphocytes play an important role in combating infectious diseases and may also be instrumental in destroying malignant growths in their early stages. There are two types of lymphocytes actively engaged in coping with infection: T cells, which directly kill invaders, and B cells, which are involved in the production of infection-fighting antibodies. The finding that AIDS patients have decreased numbers of T cells, particularly a subtype called "helper" T cells, has proved useful in diagnosis.

A person may be a carrier of the disease without being aware of the fact and without having any of the symptoms. Blood tests for the detection of antibodies to the AIDS virus have recently been developed. The implications of a positive blood test are controversial, however. Although a positive blood test definitely indicates exposure to the disease, it is not known whether all individuals with positive test results will subsequently contract AIDS.

### Treatment

No cure for AIDS has been found yet. The recently released drug zidovudine (formerly called azidothymidine or AZT) acts by preventing replication of the AIDS virus in human cells. Although this drug has been shown to prolong survival and improve the quality of life for AIDS patients, it cannot be considered a cure.

Until a cure for AIDS is found, treatment is limited to countering the effects of the disease (for example, surgery to remove skin cancer, chemotherapy, and use of drugs to raise the body's resistance to diseases).

### Prevention

Since there is no cure for AIDS, prevention is critical. Limiting the number of one's sexual partners and using condoms decrease the risk of exposure to the AIDS virus. Avoiding contact with potentially contaminated hypodermic needles and with blood and blood products is also important. The evidence to date indicates that casual contacts, such as would occur in school and the workplace, are not responsible for transmission of the virus.

If a person has tested positive for the presence of the AIDS antibody, there are a number of precautions that should be taken to promote the effectiveness of his immune system and to prevent the possible spread of infection. Substances that will burden the immune system should be avoided. These include live-virus vaccines, such as those against measles, mumps, rubella, and polio; alcohol, tobacco products, and illicit drugs, such as marijuana and heroin; and possible sources of salmonella and other food-borne infections, such as unpasteurized milk and inadequately cooked meats. A physician may also recommend that immunosuppressive drugs, such as corticosteroids, some antibiotics, and certain anticancer drugs, be avoided, as well as aspirin and other painkillers, which may be immunosuppressive.

Among the activities that may place a strain on the immune system are changing cat litter (cats transmit toxoplasmosis), cleaning bird cages (birds transmit histoplasmosis and psittacosis), sharing razor blades and toothbrushes, and engaging in sexual activity without a condom or with a partner who might transmit cytomegalovirus, Epstein-Barr virus, syphilis, or AIDS virus. Pregnancy is also somewhat immunosuppressive. It is important that the immune system be bolstered by maintaining general health—the person should choose a balanced diet, get regular exercise and adequate rest, and avoid stress as much as possible.

Needless to say, the person should inform all sex partners and medical and dental personnel with whom he comes into contact of his immune status and should not donate blood, sperm, organs, or any other body tissues.

## Anaphylaxis

Anaphylaxis is said to be present if a person is extremely sensitive to a substance on first exposure. If the person is exposed to the substance again, the result may be anaphylactic shock, an explosive overreaction of the body's immune system. Anaphylactic shock is a violent allergic reaction characterized by itching skin, hives, breathing trouble, collapse of the circulatory system, and sometimes vomiting, diarrhea, and cramps in the abdomen.

### Causes

Anaphylaxis may be triggered by an insect sting, such as that of a bee or wasp; by animal serum used in a vaccine; by desensitizing injections; or by one of various drugs. The allergen (the substance that sets off the reaction) is usually a protein, called an antigen. When it first enters the body, certain body cells treat it like an invading microorganism and create antibodies, which are protective substances that fight infection. On subsequent exposures to the same antigen, the antibodies are ready for the "invader" and stimulate the release of certain chemicals. One of these chemicals, histamine, causes contraction of the muscle in the digestive and respiratory tracts, resulting in abdominal cramps and wheezing. Histamine also causes the small blood vessels to enlarge and lose plasma (blood fluid) to surrounding tissues. The decrease in the volume of blood in the vessels results in a drop in blood pressure, which may lead to shock (collapse of the circulatory system).

### Symptoms

Symptoms of anaphylactic shock develop rapidly. Within 15 minutes, the victim becomes uneasy, upset, and red in the face. Rapid heartbeat, prickling and itching sensations in the skin, throbbing in the ears, sneezing, coughing, and breathing difficulty are also likely. Vomiting, incontinence (involuntary release of urine and bowel contents), and even convulsions may occur. In another one or two minutes, shock may result, in which blood vessels collapse, the pulse becomes weak and rapid, and the person becomes cold, clammy, and faint. Without immediate medical aid, death may result.

### Treatment

In cases of anaphylactic shock, medical aid should be obtained as quickly as possible—call an emergency squad. Keep the patient's airway open. Have the patient lie down, with his legs elevated. Immediate treatment with the drug epinephrine is critical. It counteracts the action of the histamine released in the blood, which is causing the symptoms of anaphylactic shock. If a drug injection has caused the reaction, a tourniquet is applied above the site of the injection, and epinephrine is often injected into the site. Antihistamine drugs are also given. In extreme cases, especially when shock has occurred or there is great breathing difficulty, intravenous solutions are given to restore blood volume and raise blood pressure. Anyone with a severe reaction is usually hospitalized for at least 24 hours to guard against a recurrence of the condition.

### Prevention

A preventive measure against anaphylactic shock is routine allergy skin testing before the use of substances that may cause sensitivity or that have been known to cause anaphylaxis, such as animal serums in vaccines. In addition, anyone who has had an anaphylactic reaction to an insect sting should carry a kit containing a syringe of epinephrine and an epinephrine-filled nasal sprayer for prompt self-treatment if stung again. Desensitizing injections of the insect venom should also be considered to allow the body to build up a resistance to the venom, if the doctor feels that such injections will not trigger an anaphylactic reaction.

### Anaphylactoid reactions

Similar to anaphylaxis in effect (but not in cause) are anaphylactoid reactions, which can occur on the first injection of certain drugs, such as morphine, and of contrast media (special solutions used when performing certain x-ray studies). These are not allergic reactions in the pure sense, but they may be just as serious nevertheless.

# Autoimmune diseases

Autoimmune diseases are disorders in which the body's immune system reacts against some of its own tissue and produces antibodies to destroy it.

## Examples

Ailments believed to be autoimmune diseases include Hashimoto's thyroiditis and Graves' disease, which are disorders of the thyroid gland; systemic lupus erythematosus, which attacks multiple organ systems; myasthenia gravis, a neuromuscular disease; and autoimmune hemolytic anemia, in which red blood cells are destroyed before the end of their normal 120-day life span.

Diseases that probably are autoimmune disorders include rheumatoid arthritis, a connective tissue disease; pernicious anemia, a serious blood disorder; glomerulonephritis, a disorder that affects the kidneys; and Addison's disease, which attacks the adrenal glands.

Diseases that may be autoimmune disorders are chronic active hepatitis (a liver disorder), some forms of vasculitis (inflammation of blood vessel walls), and many other diseases that produce inflammation, degeneration, or wasting away of body tissues.

## Causes

An autoimmune disease can begin in several ways:
- Some body substance that ordinarily never enters the bloodstream may do so because of injury. For example, a disease known as sympathetic ophthalmia occurs when tissue from the inside of an injured eye is released into the bloodstream. The tissue is recognized as "out of place" or "foreign" by the body's immune system, and antibodies attack it, causing irritation in both the injured eye and in the noninjured eye. The reaction may be severe enough to cause blindness.
- A body substance may be altered by chemicals, sunlight, or a virus so that it seems foreign to the body's immune system. The substance is then attacked by antibodies. An example of this process occurs when the metal in a bracelet causes chemical changes in the skin on one's wrist. The body reacts against the "different" skin and attacks it, causing the rash of contact dermatitis.
- Infection may cause an immune response so strong that the body reacts against some of its own normal tissues.

Genetic factors may play a role. Women are affected more often than men.

## Treatment

Treatment is dependent on the particular autoimmune disease present. Many treatments involve decreasing the patient's immune response. Other cases require more aggressive therapy to allow repair of damage caused by the body's attack on itself.

# Contact dermatitis

Contact dermatitis is a type of allergy in which the skin becomes inflamed in the area where it has come in contact with an irritating substance.

## Causes

Contact dermatitis can be caused by a virtually limitless array of substances, among them soaps, detergents, metals, shaving materials, shampoos, hair colorings or sprays, solvents in household cleaners, chemicals in foods and cosmetics, dyes in household products, and certain plants, such as poison ivy and poison oak. Photodermatitis (a skin inflammation caused by light) is a type of dermatitis that develops when certain ingested drugs, such as some antibiotics, sensitize the skin so that a rash develops on skin that is exposed to the sun.

## Symptoms

The major symptoms of contact dermatitis are burning, swelling, severe itching, and stinging sensations on the area of the skin that has been exposed to the allergen. Blisters that ooze a clear fluid may form (a cloudy or yellow, foul-smelling fluid indicates that a bacterial infection, rather than contact dermatitis, is present).

## Diagnosis

Contact dermatitis is diagnosed by first identifying the allergen causing the trouble. The location of the rash often gives an important clue to the identity of the allergen. For instance, if the inflammation is on the scalp, the disorder may be assumed to be triggered by a shampoo, hair spray, or hair coloring. More specific identification of the allergen may be obtained with one of several available tests, including scratch tests, in which a small amount of the suspected allergen is applied to a scratch on the skin; intracutaneous tests, in which a small amount of the allergen is injected into or under the skin; and radioallergosorbent testing, a blood test in which antibodies produced in response to the allergen are measured.

### Treatment

Once the allergen has been identified, the best treatment for contact dermatitis is for the patient to avoid the allergen or to remove it from his environment. It is often possible to do this by switching brands of soaps or shampoos, wearing rubber gloves when using harsh detergents, and using unscented or hypoallergenic cosmetics. If the use of a drug cannot be discontinued despite a case of photodermatitis, sunscreens should be used and adequate clothing should be worn to shield the skin when outdoors.

Oral steroid drugs (such as cortisone) help to relieve the itching of contact dermatitis; however, these are reserved only for the most serious cases. Topical (applied directly to the skin) steroids and antihistamines are more commonly used.

### Prevention

There is no preventive treatment for contact dermatitis, but those susceptible to one or more contactant allergens can usually prevent outbreaks by avoiding exposure as much as possible.

# Food allergy

A food allergy is an unusual sensitivity to a specific food. A food allergy is not a food intolerance, which exists when the body lacks the enzymes that are needed to digest a certain food. A food allergy exists when the body's immune system manufactures antibodies as a reaction to the food. This food then becomes an ingestant allergen (an allergy-causing substance that is swallowed or eaten). Any food can become an allergen, but the foods most commonly found to cause allergic reactions are milk, eggs, shellfish, fish, peanuts, chocolate, tomatoes, strawberries, and citrus fruits.

### Symptoms

The symptoms of a food allergy most commonly arise in the digestive tract—cramps, nausea, vomiting, and diarrhea. Other signs that may also be present include hives, rash, headache, nasal congestion, and anaphylactic shock (a very serious reaction that can be fatal, characterized by breathing problems due to swelling of the larynx and collapse of blood vessels). Food allergies occur more often in children than in adults.

### Diagnosis

Food allergy is diagnosed by having the patient maintain a detailed record of all foods eaten, as well as of the times when symptoms appear. Elimination trials may also help identify the allergen; the patient eliminates one food at a time from the diet to see if the symptoms disappear. In addition, several tests are used to detect various types of allergens: scratch tests, in which a small amount of the suspected allergen is applied to a scratch on the skin; intracutaneous tests, in which a small amount of the allergen is injected in or under the skin; and radioallergosorbent testing, in which antibodies developed in response to specific allergens are measured in a blood sample.

### Treatment

There is no way to treat a food allergy other than to avoid eating the food and to treat the symptoms of a reaction should one develop. Fortunately, children usually outgrow these allergies.

Some doctors feel that infants who are breast-fed for up to a year are less likely to develop food allergies than babies who are formula-fed or who are breast-fed for only a couple of months. This continues to be a controversial issue.

# Gamma globulin

Gamma globulin preparations are derived from the blood of a person or animal and contain antibodies made by that person or animal in response to invasion by harmful agents, such as bacteria and viruses. These preparations are widely used for the prevention, modification, treatment, and diagnosis of many kinds of infectious diseases.

Gamma globulin is usually injected. Since it contains almost all the antibodies circulating in the blood, it can provide passive (borrowed) immunity that lasts for about six weeks.

Gamma globulin injections may be useful in preventing infectious hepatitis when given within about two weeks of exposure to intimate contacts of someone with hepatitis. Many physicians recommend that persons traveling to underdeveloped countries, particularly rural areas, should receive doses of gamma globulin before departure and during an extended stay.

Measles can often be prevented by the administration of gamma globulin injections within five days of exposure. The injections are especially important for children under three years of age, for pregnant women, for tuberculosis patients, and for those with impaired immune mechanisms. Even if measles is not prevented, a less serious case may result; however, gamma globulin is of no use once the symptoms have appeared.

Gamma globulin can also be used as a diagnostic tool. For example, one symptom of multiple sclerosis is an elevated level of gamma globulin in the cerebrospinal fluid.

# Hay fever

Hay fever is the name for acute (short-lived), seasonal attacks that are allergic reactions to pollen. Most often, spring attacks are reactions to tree pollen; summer attacks are reactions to grass pollen; and autumn attacks are reactions to weed pollen.

## Symptoms

The symptoms of hay fever are usually the same, regardless of

the allergen (irritating substance). Common symptoms include itching of the nose and roof of the mouth; a thin, watery discharge constantly draining from the nose; itchy, watery eyes; sneezing; headache; irritability; a feeling of exhaustion; insomnia; loss of appetite; and, in advanced cases, coughing and wheezing.

## Diagnosis

Hay fever, as with other allergies, is diagnosed by identifying the allergen. This is done by taking a medical history and reviewing the patient's environment, daily habits, and recent changes in lifestyle. Skin tests and blood tests may also be performed. These include scratch tests, in which a small amount of the suspected allergen is applied to a scratch on the skin; intracutaneous tests, in which a small amount of the allergen is injected in or under the skin; and occasionally radioallergosorbent testing, in which antibodies developed in response to specific allergens are measured in a blood sample.

## Treatment

A severe case of hay fever may be best treated by changing the environment, that is, by removing the allergen causing the trouble or reducing the patient's exposure to it. Those who react to weed pollen may need to move to a more urban location with a lower concentration of pollen in the air. Many hay fever sufferers will benefit from using an air conditioner, which filters the air and thus keeps pollen levels in the home to a minimum.

Several medications are available for the hay fever sufferer: oral antihistamines, which counteract the histamine that is released by the body in reaction to the allergen; corticosteroids, which reduce inflammation; eye drops, which relieve itching and redness; and desensitization shots, which cause the body to develop tolerance to the allergen.

## Prevention

There is no way to prevent hay fever, but avoiding the allergen as much as possible may at least help to relieve some of the discomfort.

# Hives

Hives (also called urticaria) is a reaction of the skin marked by intense itching and, most noticeably, by the rapid development of raised, smooth patches, or welts (also called wheals). Hives is most often a sign of an allergic reaction.

## Causes

Hives is often caused by an allergy to certain foods, particularly shellfish, tomatoes, strawberries, eggs, milk, and chocolate. It can also be a reaction to drugs, food dyes, molds, bacteria, and animal skin or hair. In a susceptible person, cold, the rays of the sun, and vigorous exercise have also been known to cause hives.

## Symptoms

Hives is characterized by an outbreak of red and white welts that vary in size and appear suddenly either in small areas or all over the body. They often appear and disappear, lasting anywhere from a few minutes to a day or two, but the outbreak can last for weeks. Accompanying symptoms may include intense itching, fatigue, fever, nausea, and difficulty in breathing if the allergic reaction has led to swelling of the mucous membrane lining the respiratory tract.

### Diagnosis

Diagnosing the allergy and pinpointing the allergen that is causing the trouble can require extensive testing, especially when a food may be involved. Eliminating many suspected foods and then reintroducing them one at a time sometimes helps to diagnose the cause of hives. This must be done under professional supervision and with caution.

### Treatment

Hives can be treated immediately by taking antihistamines. When taken several times a day at a prescribed dosage, the correct type of antihistamine will help control swelling by preventing the released histamine from triggering the hives. Drowsiness is a common side effect of antihistamines, so the type and dosage may need to be adjusted periodically. Other drugs (such as corticosteroids, which reduce inflammation) may be used to treat serious hives.

### Prevention

Hives can be prevented by avoiding contact with the allergen or stimulus once it has been identified.

# Immunization

Immunization is the means of producing immunity (resistance by the body) to a specific disease. There are two types of immunization, active and passive.

### Active immunization

Active immunization is accomplished by injecting weakened or killed viruses or bacteria into the body. This stimulates the body's natural defense system. Certain specialized white blood cells produce substances known as antibodies, which are carried in the bloodstream and are tailor-made to fight invading organisms. These antibodies remain in the body for years—sometimes a lifetime—to protect it against that particular disease.

### Passive immunization

Passive immunization involves injecting ready-made antibodies into the body. These antibodies are usually extracted from the blood of humans who are immune to a certain disease or of animals that have been immunized solely for the purpose of producing antibodies to be used in passive immunization. Passive immunization is borrowed immunity and is only temporary, but it serves to protect a person who may already be infected until the body has time to create sufficient quantities of its own antibodies.

Immunization can protect against diphtheria, measles, mumps, pertussis (whooping cough), polio, rubella (German measles), and tetanus.

### Children's immunizations

Every child should receive injections of the combined diphtheria-tetanus-pertussis (DTP) vaccine at 2, 4, 6, and 18 months of age. The child should also receive a dose of the oral polio vaccine (OPV) at 2, 4, and 18 months of age. At 15 months, a child should receive the combined measles, mumps, and rubella (MMR) vaccine and a test for tuberculosis (TB). Some doctors are also recommending that a relatively new vaccine against *Hemophilus influenzae* type B (HiB) infection be given to children at about two years of age, especially if they are in day care, where they may have a greater risk of exposure to infection. Booster shots of DTP vaccine and OPV should be given around the time of school entry (when the child is four to six years old). A diphtheria-tetanus toxoids (DT) booster shot should be given between 14 and 16 years of age.

### Immunization and testing schedule

| | |
|---|---|
| 2 months | DTP and OPV |
| 4 months | DTP and OPV |
| 6 months | DTP |
| 15 months | MMR and TB test |
| 18 months | DTP and OPV |
| 2 years | HiB |
| 4–6 years | DTP and OPV |
| 14–16 years | DT booster |

If the family does not have a physician, immunizations can usually be obtained through the local public health department.

## Adult immunizations

Adults need a tetanus shot once every ten years. Otherwise, there are no routine immunizations necessary for adults in the United States, with the possible exception of influenza shots given annually (usually in the fall) to the aged and to patients with heart, lung, or other chronic diseases. A vaccine that would protect against 80 percent of serious cases of pneumonia is available. Immunization against rabies is possible both before and after exposure.

There are precautions to consider. Immunizations should not be given routinely to pregnant women, nor in general to anyone whose immune system has been weakened by leukemia, cancer, fever, or prolonged x-ray or corticosteroid treatment.

## Vaccinations for foreign travel

Most persons traveling abroad in developed countries need no additional vaccinations. In general, in the United States, Canada, Australia, New Zealand, Japan, and Europe, the traveler is safe without vaccinations. Travel in Mexico and the less-developed countries of Africa, Asia, South America, Central America, the South Pacific, the Middle East, and the Far East may hold more risks, particularly in small villages and rural areas not usually visited by tourists.

In recent years, no vaccination has been necessary for direct travel from the United States to most countries or for return to the United States. However, some countries require proof of vaccination from travelers who have passed through infected areas, and it is best to get the shots before leaving home.

Any physician can give immunizations except for yellow-fever vaccinations, which must be given at an official "Yellow Fever Vaccination Center." Weeks before you plan to leave on your trip, call your local health department for the latest information about vaccination requirements and recommendations for all of the countries you plan to visit. The vaccinating physician must fill out and sign an "International Certificate of Vaccination," which must be validated by a health department or by an authorized physician.

Vaccinations against cholera, which is transmitted in contaminated food and water, and against yellow fever, which is transmitted by certain mosquitoes, are the shots most often required for foreign travel. Because no cholera vaccine is very effective and because the risk of acquiring cholera is small, the U.S. Public Health Service does not recommend vaccination against cholera unless the country to be visited requires it. However, yellow-fever vaccinations are strongly recommended, even if not required by law, for travel to infected areas (usually parts of Africa and South America) and for travel in countries in "yellow fever endemic zones" (areas in which the possibility of contracting the disease is always present).

In no case should anyone be immunized against smallpox. The World Health Organization has declared that smallpox has been eliminated from the world, and the vaccination itself is not without risk. Therefore, if you are traveling to a country that still requires proof of vaccination against smallpox, the U.S. Public Health Service suggests that you obtain a written statement from your physician recom-

mending against smallpox vaccination for health reasons.

Anyone not already immune to measles and mumps should receive vaccinations before traveling abroad, as should children not immune to rubella. Travelers to developing countries need diphtheria, polio, and typhoid immunizations, unless they are already immune, and a tetanus booster shot if they have not had one in the previous ten years.

Immunization cannot protect against malaria, a health threat in many developing countries. Travelers to infected areas should take along protective medications, sleep in well-screened areas, wear protective clothing, and use chemical repellents to ward off the long-legged *Anopheles* mosquito, which transmits the disease.

# Insect bites and stings

Insect bites and stings are minor inconveniences to most people, but to those who have an allergy to insect venom, the consequences can be serious.

## Symptoms

Reactions to insect venom show themselves in various symptoms—shortness of breath, rapid heartbeat, coughing, wheezing, and light-headedness. The affected area swells and becomes tender or numb. In extreme cases, anaphylactic shock (a severe, potentially fatal reaction characterized by breathing problems, hives, collapse of blood vessels, and sometimes vomiting, diarrhea, and cramps) can occur.

## Treatment

Serious reactions to bites and stings are treated by slowing the spread of the venom throughout the body and getting emergency medical treatment as soon as possible. The progress of the venom can be slowed somewhat by applying an ice pack or a tourniquet (but not so tightly as to stop the blood flow) to the affected area. Emergency medical treatment will usually consist of an epinephrine injection, an injection of antihistamine, and in some cases a corticosteroid. These serve to lessen existing symptoms and to halt progression of the reaction.

## Prevention

Prevention of recurrent allergic reactions to insect venom is accomplished with a course of desensitization shots; starting with an initially weak solution of insect extract, doses are gradually increased with each shot. This allows the body to build up tolerance to the effects of the insect venom.

Persons with known sensitivity to insect bites should carry kits with injectable epinephrine, which are available by prescription.

# THE BRAIN AND NERVOUS SYSTEM

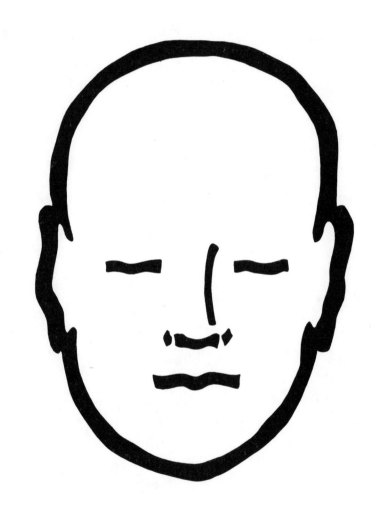

The nervous system is a complex network of specialized tissues that regulates thoughts, emotions, actions, sensations, and basic body functions.

## Nerve cells

The basic element of the nervous system is the nerve cell, or neuron. In combination, neurons form nerves, which transmit impulses throughout the body. A protective covering of myelin, a fatty substance, insulates parts of those fibers.

The action of nerve cells is both electrical and chemical. At the ends of each nerve cell there are specialized regions called synaptic terminals, which contain large numbers of tiny membranous sacs that hold neurotransmitter chemicals. These chemicals transmit nerve impulses from one nerve cell to another. After an electrical nerve impulse has traveled along a neuron, it reaches the terminal and stimulates the release of neurotransmitters from their sacs. The neurotransmitters travel across the synapse (the junction between neighboring neurons) and stimulate the production of an electrical charge, which carries the nerve impulse forward. This process is repeated over and over again until a muscle is moved or relaxed or a sensory impression is noted by the brain. These electrochemical events can be considered the "language" of the nervous system, by which information is transmitted from one part of the body to another.

## Nervous system

There are two major divisions of the nervous system: the central nervous system and the peripheral nervous system. The *central ner-*

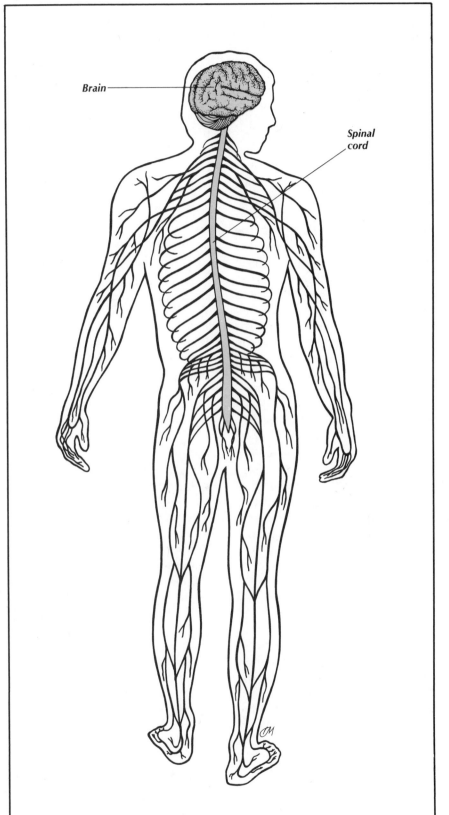

*The nervous system has two major divisions: the central nervous system (brain and spinal cord) and the peripheral nervous system (nerves that branch out from the brain and spinal cord).*

*vous system* consists of the brain and the spinal cord. The brain lies within the skull (the bony framework of the head). It governs body functions by sending and receiving messages through the spinal cord. Protecting the brain and spinal cord are bones, layers of tissue, and cerebrospinal fluid.

Once messages leave the central nervous system, they are carried by the *peripheral nervous system*. The peripheral system includes the cranial nerves (nerves branching from the brain) and the spinal nerves (nerves branching from the spinal cord). These nerves convey sensory messages from receptor cells in the body to the central nervous system. They also transport motor impulses from the central system out to the body, where muscles and glands can respond to the impulses.

The *autonomic nervous system,* which is part of the peripheral nervous system, regulates all activity that is involuntary but necessary for life, including activity of the internal organs and glands.

Working together, these divisions coordinate adjustment and reaction of the body to internal and external environmental conditions.

## Brain

The brain is the control center for the entire body. The brain sends messages to and receives stimulation from all parts of the body. More than ten billion interlinked brain cells regulate the functioning of the body during sleep and wakefulness.

Different areas of the brain control different body functions. At the back of the skull is the cerebellum, which controls coordination of movements, balance, and posture. Deep inside the brain is the thalamus, which

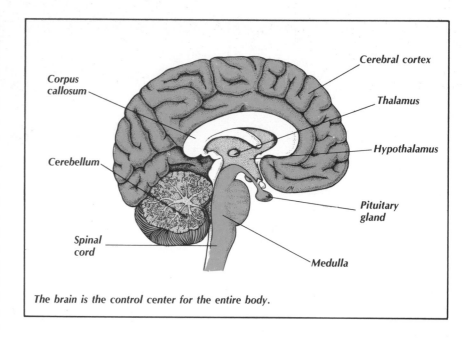

The brain is the control center for the entire body.

is the relay station for incoming impulses from the rest of the body, conveying sensations of pain, touch, and temperature to other parts of the brain. Around the thalamus is the hypothalamus, which governs involuntary (automatic) body operations, such as heartbeat and blood circulation. The pituitary gland is attached to the hypothalamus by a thin stalk. Because the pituitary gland controls most of the hormones in the body, the hypothalamus is considered a major influence on primary drives governed by hormones, such as sexual desire, hunger, and thirst.

Covering the inner parts of the brain is the cerebral cortex, which consists of two cerebral hemispheres. In these hemispheres are the nerve centers that regulate thought and voluntary action. Connecting the left and right cerebral hemispheres is a broad band of fibers called the corpus callosum. Because nerve fibers from the two cerebral hemispheres cross one another in a structure called the medulla at the base of the brain before progressing down the spinal

cord, each hemisphere generally controls functions in the opposite side of the body. For example, a region in the left hemisphere governs movement of the right arm.

The brain is the most complex organ in the body. Although research has identified many of its capabilities in memory, reasoning, and creative thought processes, many functions of the brain remain a mystery.

## Cerebrospinal fluid

Cerebrospinal fluid (CSF) is a clear, colorless fluid that surrounds the brain and spinal cord, cushioning them against injury.

The CSF is made of water containing small amounts of minerals and organic substances (especially protein). It is continuously being produced by a specialized network of capillaries (tiny blood vessels) known as the choroid plexus, which is located in the ventricles (chambers) of the brain. About one pint is produced every 24 hours, and approximately five ounces is circulating at any one time. From the two lateral (side) ventricles, the CSF flows into the third and fourth ventricles of the brain. It then passes into the space between the innermost and second layers of the tissue covering the brain, bathing the entire outer surface of the brain in fluid before passing downward around the spinal cord. Eventually the fluid returns upward, is absorbed into special tissue between the linings of the brain, and passes into the blood vessels.

Samples of CSF (drawn from around the spinal cord with a needle inserted in the lower back—a procedure known as a lumbar puncture) can be valuable in diagnosing disorders of the brain and spinal cord. The samples may indicate a hemorrhage or blood clot in the brain, various types of meningitis, a brain abscess, or a tumor of the brain or spinal cord.

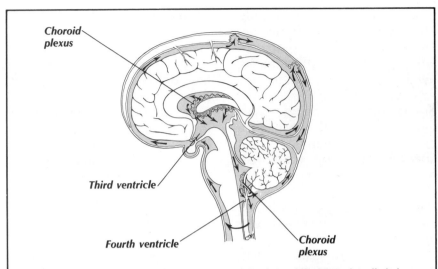

The cerebrospinal fluid is produced by a network of tiny blood vessels called the choroid plexus, located in the ventricles of the brain. From the two side ventricles, the fluid flows into the third and fourth ventricles and then passes into the space between the innermost and second layers of tissue covering the brain. The fluid bathes the outer surface of the brain and the spinal cord.

# Alzheimer's disease

Alzheimer's disease is a disorder in which there is a steady deterioration of brain function resulting in progressive loss of memory, of recognition of friends and family, of personality, and of mental powers. Although Alzheimer's disease may begin as early as age 40, it is most prevalent in the aged. It accounts for about half of all serious mental impairment in persons over age 65.

### Changes in the brain

In Alzheimer's disease, as in any senile (characteristic of old age) mental disorder, there is atrophy (shrinkage or wasting) of the cerebral cortex (the outer layer of the brain, which is mostly concerned with intellectual and social functioning). There are also more specific abnormalities, such as the presence of tangles of fibers within the nerve cells and of senile plaques, which are probably deposits of amyloid (a semisolid protein complex seen in many degenerative diseases). These abnormal changes are scattered throughout the cortex of an Alzheimer's victim and serve to distinguish the disease from other forms of senility. Because brain biopsy specimens (tissue samples taken from the brain for laboratory examination) are not obtained without very specific reasons and without intention of specific treatment, these changes are usually seen only after death.

### Causes

Theories abound as to the possible causes of Alzheimer's disease. So-called slow viruses (viruses acquired early in life that take many years to do their damage) have been considered, as have environmental factors and damage from previous diseases. Recently, a diminished amount of the enzyme choline acetyltransferase (which is necessary to manufacture the neurotransmitter acetylcholine) has been found in some patients, and theories about replacement of the enzyme or neurotransmitter are being formulated. Heredity seems to play some part, since a family member of an Alzheimer's victim is more likely than others to develop the condition. It is generally agreed that hardening of the arteries is not a cause. The disease does not appear to be contagious, nor is it caused by emotional upsets and stress.

### Symptoms

Symptoms vary considerably from one person to another and

may occur days or months apart. They begin with small memory lapses, almost always first involving loss of recall for recent events. Such lapses can happen to anyone, but in Alzheimer's disease they grow more serious with time. A person may forget a close relative's name, get lost coming home from the office, forget to turn off the oven, misplace articles, recheck to see if a task was done, or repeatedly ask questions that have already been answered.

Eventually, the gaps in memory and the failure to recognize friends and family members interfere with normal work and social life. The individual starts having trouble with figures when working on bills, with understanding what is being read, and with organizing the day's work.

As the disease progresses, the victim of Alzheimer's disease becomes confused, frustrated, and irritable. Although at first the person seems physically unaffected by the disease, as the condition advances the patient becomes restless, always moving about, and must be watched so that he or she does not wander away or into danger. Endless repetition of unnecessary actions, such as the opening and closing of drawers, is another characteristic of the disease. Some victims of Alzheimer's disease may become extremely agitated with little or no provocation.

The course of the disease, which eventually can result in damage to the rest of the nervous system and to other parts of the body and in loss of control over bladder and bowels, may range from 1 to 20 years. It may cut life expectancy by contributing to death from another cause, such as pneumonia or heart or kidney failure.

### Diagnosis

Other conditions can cause many of the symptoms of Alzheimer's disease, and many of these conditions are treatable. Therefore, it is very important for the patient to undergo a thorough medical evaluation, which may include extensive neurological and psychological examinations and other diagnostic studies, such as computed tomography (a special x-ray technique for obtaining cross-sectional images), electroencephalography (a study of brain waves), blood tests, and sampling of cerebrospinal fluid. These procedures can rule out or identify possible causes of nervous system malfunctioning, such as a series of "little strokes," brain tumors or infections, pernicious anemia (curable with vitamin $B_{12}$), overmedication with barbiturates or bromides, alcoholism, drug side effects, abnormal thyroid function, or hydrocephalus (blockage of cerebrospinal fluid in the head). Psychological depression is also an important—and treatable—cause of senile symptoms, such as apathy, slowness of thought, inattention, and poor concentration. Death of a spouse or a shock, such as moving to a nursing home, could cause such symptoms temporarily.

### Treatment

Medical science does not yet know how to prevent or treat Alzheimer's disease. However, it is important to find a physician who is able to help the patient and his family handle the many problems that are bound to arise. At times, tranquilizers can lessen agitation and anxiety and reduce the incidence of undesirable behavior.

Medication may also help to improve sleeping patterns and treat depression caused by the disease.

It is important that the patient continue the daily routine, exercise as usual, and keep in touch with friends. Memory aids, such as lists of daily chores, reminders about safety, and a large calendar, can help in day-to-day living. As care of the patient becomes more difficult, it may be best (for the patient and family alike) to move the patient to a health facility where a professional staff can provide around-the-clock care.

# Amnesia

Amnesia is the loss of memory and the inability to form new memories. It can be either temporary or permanent. The causes may range from brain damage to a psychological reason.

### Retrograde amnesia

This type of amnesia usually follows any severe head injury that produces unconsciousness. The patient is not able to recall what happened immediately before the accident that caused the injury, the accident itself, or some of the events of the recovery period. In most cases, this type of amnesia is not significant because no other memory is affected, and no treatment is needed.

### Korsakoff's syndrome

An inability to record new memory along with a defect in recent memory, usually accompanied by confabulation (storytelling of fabricated events), is known as Korsakoff's syndrome. It may be caused by head injury, stroke, encephalitis (inflammation of the lining of the brain), deficiency of vitamin $B_{12}$, cancer of the brain, or poor blood supply to memory tissue or pathways in the brain. However, heavy drinking of alcohol, with resultant brain damage, is commonly the cause.

Although there may be little or no loss of memory or skills that were acquired before the disease began, the person with Korsakoff's syndrome cannot effectively learn new skills or remember recent events. To hide this loss, from himself as well as others, the patient may describe imaginary or confused experiences to take the place of the missing experiences. Sometimes the stories are so convincing that the patient appears normal.

Treatment of Korsakoff's syndrome is limited to treating the condition that caused it. Permanent brain damage may make it incurable. Frequently, however, the condition will disappear with time, especially if it was caused by a concussion (a swelling in the head that puts pressure on the brain).

### Psychological amnesia

Amnesia of psychological origin is less common but more dramatic and newsworthy than other forms of amnesia. A person disappears from home, job, and family; he travels to a new place and assumes a new identity—all without being aware that anything has changed. After days or weeks, the person "awakens," becomes his old self, and wonders what happened. There is no memory of the period of amnesia.

Anxiety is the cause of this type of amnesia. The person is faced with an intolerable situation of high emotional stress or pain. To protect itself, the mind forgets the anxieties and everything related, including the person's identity.

Treatment may not be necessary, since most affected persons recover without help. However, if the problem that caused the amnesia still remains, it must be faced and solved. Family therapy and change of work or activities may help. Hypnosis may be used to bring back the memory of the "lost days" and unlock the ideas and feelings that caused the original flight from home and self.

# Ataxia

Ataxia is a condition characterized by muscular incoordination, producing irregular and inaccurate movements of the body. The result may be a clumsy manner of walking, with feet wide apart; a lack of balance; tremor (shakiness) of the arms; and slurring of speech.

### Causes

Ataxia may be caused by anything that affects the motor control centers of the brain or the nerve pathways leading from them. Drunkenness can produce a temporary staggering ataxia. Permanent ataxia is caused by damage to the brain, spinal cord, or spinal nerves.

Locomotor ataxia may be a late result of untreated syphilis. Its symptoms include sharp, stabbing pains, usually in the legs; an unsteady walk; and a feeling of walking on foam rubber. There may be an increased sensitivity of the skin, sometimes with burning, prickling, creeping, or crawling sensations.

Ataxia occurs in one case in ten of cerebral palsy, which is a movement disorder caused by damage to the brain or nerve pathways before or around the time of birth. Weakness, unsteadiness, clumsy walking, and difficulty with fine or rapid movements are typical. Physical and occupational therapy help patients handle daily life despite their condition.

Ataxia may also be caused by any one of a group of hereditary diseases that attack the central nervous system. They cause degeneration of the spinal cord and cerebellum (the portion of the brain responsible for fine control of muscle movements) and also frequently damage the brain stem (the portion of the brain that controls the most basic body functions, such as breathing and circulation) and various nerves. Inherited disorders of body chemistry and body chemicals are believed to be involved, but little is known about them. Only one of these disorders—Refsum's syndrome—can be treated, by reducing the excessive level of a body chemical known as phytanic acid.

### Symptoms

Symptoms of the hereditary ataxias include unsteadiness in walking, tremor of the arms, muscle weakness, and wasting away of muscles. Various other abnormalities may be present, depending on the disease. For example, Friedreich's ataxia, the most common form, causes scoliosis (curvature of the spine) and damages heart tissue.

### Treatment

All of these diseases continue throughout life. With the exception of Refsum's syndrome, none can be treated effectively.

# Bell's palsy

Bell's palsy is total or partial paralysis (loss of function or movement) of one side of the face. It is believed to be due to inflammation of the nerve that controls the facial muscles. The inflammation, often of unknown cause but suspected to be the result of viral infection, causes the nerve to swell and to be compressed inside its bony passage in the skull. This compression reduces the blood supply to the nerve and thus its ability to function.

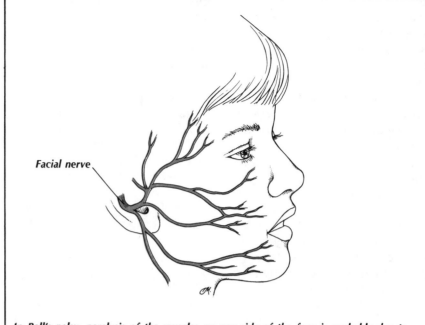

*In Bell's palsy, paralysis of the muscles on one side of the face is probably due to inflammation of the facial nerve and its branches.*

### Symptoms

This disorder can occur in someone of any age, but is most common from ages 20 to 50. The first sign may be an aching pain behind or below the ear. Paralysis may develop in a few hours or more slowly, causing the entire side of the face to be flat and without expression (this is different from the facial paralysis caused by stroke or brain tumor, in which the weakness is mostly below the forehead). The mouth droops on the weak side, with saliva drooling from the corner. The sense of taste may be impaired. The eyebrow cannot be raised. In most cases, the eye cannot be shut. When the patient tries to close the affected eye, it can be seen to roll upward (which also happens in a healthy person, but is not seen because the eyelid normally closes). Unprovoked tears may come from the affected eye.

### Diagnosis

In making a diagnosis, the doctor must determine if the paralysis might be caused by other disorders affecting the facial nerve, including ear infections, cancer, or a skull fracture. In such disorders, there is usually involvement of other nerves as well, and distinctive signs and symptoms are frequently present. X-ray studies of the head may be performed.

### Treatment

Primary treatment is aimed at reducing the inflammation of the nerve before any permanent damage is done to it. An oral corticosteroid drug, such as prednisone, may be given for this purpose. However, in many (if not most) uncomplicated cases, treatment with medication is unnecessary. After two weeks, if there has been no improvement in the ability of the muscles to move, the muscles of the weak side of the face may be stimulated electrically to maintain muscle tone.

The affected eye should be covered with an eye patch, especially when the patient is outdoors, and protected from dirt and wind. Application of moist, moderate heat on the affected side of the face can reduce pain. Brief periods of upward facial massage help maintain muscle tone, as do specific facial exercises.

Fortunately, most Bell's palsy patients recover in one to eight weeks. Elderly patients may take much longer—up to two years. Complete recovery usually follows within several months if the paralysis is partial.

# Carpal tunnel syndrome

Carpal tunnel syndrome is characterized by weakness, pain, tingling, numbness, or burning in the palm, the thumb, the index finger, the middle finger, and the ring finger, caused by entrapment of the median nerve in the wrist. (This condition, like any syndrome, is not a disease in itself but rather a collection of symptoms.) The condition most often affects women in their 30s, 40s, and 50s. It may develop or become worse because of work, such as scrubbing, that requires repeated grasping, twisting, or turning of the hand and wrist.

The carpal tunnel is formed by the bones of the wrist (*carpal* means wrist) and the tough band of connective tissue known as the transverse carpal ligament. Among the structures inside the tunnel are the median nerve and the tendons that flex the fingers and thumb. Any swelling or thickening of tissue within the tunnel can cause the median nerve to be compressed between the transverse carpal ligament and the tendons and other contents of the tunnel. The squeezed nerve, which controls the thumb, index finger, and third finger, cannot work as it should, and the symptoms of carpal tunnel syndrome result.

## Causes

Pregnancy and other conditions that produce generalized swelling of body tissues may be a cause of carpal tunnel syndrome, as can localized swelling caused by a dislocation, sprain, or fracture of the wrist. Rheumatoid arthritis can cause inflammation of the sheaths (coverings) of the tendons, causing compression. Other possible causes include an inflamed wrist joint, a benign (noncancerous) tumor, myxedema (tissue swelling due to lack of thyroid hormone), tuberculosis, amyloidosis (a disease characterized by abnormal deposits of the protein amyloid), acromegaly (overgrowth of connective tissue), and diabetes mellitus.

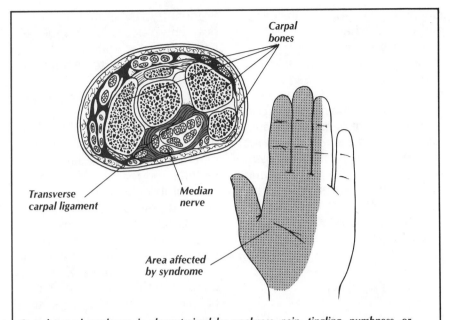

Carpal
bones

Transverse
carpal ligament

Median
nerve

Area affected
by syndrome

*Carpal tunnel syndrome is characterized by weakness, pain, tingling, numbness, or burning in the palm, the thumb, the index finger, the middle finger, and the ring finger. These symptoms are caused by entrapment of the median nerve within the carpal tunnel of the wrist. The carpal tunnel is formed by the carpal bones of the wrist and the tough band of connective tissue called the transverse carpal ligament.*

## Symptoms

Aching pain may travel up the forearm and even into the shoulder joint, neck, and chest. (This type of pain can usually be relieved by shaking the hand vigorously or dangling the arm loosely from its socket; occasionally, however, such pains are caused by compression of the median nerve in the forearm or upper arm.) Other signs include an inability to make a fist, deterioration of the nails, and dryness and shininess of the skin over the involved surfaces. The pains may occur in both hands at the same time. They may be constant or may come and go, and are increased by manual work or movement that flexes the wrist or palm. Weakness of the fingers occurs later than other symptoms and accompanies atrophy (wasting away) of the muscles. Symptoms are usually worse at night and in the morning.

## Diagnosis

Preliminary diagnostic tests include tapping the wrist, which causes tingling in the area of pain if carpal tunnel syndrome is present, and forced flexion of the wrist, which may also reproduce the pain. An x-ray examination may reveal abnormalities of the wrist bones. Testing of the conduction of nerve impulses is the most specific means of diagnosis.

## Treatment

Treatment is aimed first at relieving pressure on the median nerve. If soft-tissue swelling is a cause, elevating the hand may eliminate the symptoms. It may help to place the forearm in a splint at night, which keeps the hand turned upward, extending the wrist. If an inflammation inside the wrist is at fault, cortisone may be injected into the carpal tunnel. Other causes of the disorder are treated appropriately.

If conservative forms of treatment prove ineffective, surgery to release the transverse carpal ligament may be necessary to relieve the pressure on the nerve and prevent permanent damage. Usually, muscle strength gradually returns after such surgery, but if surgery has been delayed too long and muscles have severely deteriorated, full strength does not return. Symptoms usually disappear shortly after the operation.

# Concussion

Concussion is an injury to the brain, caused by a violent jar or shock, such as a blow to the head. The force of the shock causes the brain to strike against the inside of the skull, producing temporary brain swelling and malfunctioning and often loss of consciousness. The shock may even be strong enough to cause cerebral contusion (bruising of brain tissue), cerebral hemorrhage (bleeding between the covering of the brain and the skull or inside the brain covering), or formation of a hematoma (collection of clotted blood).

### Symptoms

Unconsciousness is a common symptom of concussion. Unconsciousness may last only a few minutes or as long as a few hours, but rarely more than 24 hours (a longer period of unconsciousness or a deep coma indicates more serious brain damage). The patient may then feel nauseated, irritable, "dragged out," or dizzy, or may have a severe headache; these symptoms may continue for days or weeks (or longer) after the accident.

Frequently, the individual cannot remember what happened just before the injury and later may not be able to recall anything that happened in the first few hours or on the day following the concussion.

A person who suffers an accident serious enough to cause a cerebral contusion; laceration (cutting and tearing) of nerve tissue, blood vessels, and brain covering; or edema (fluid build-up) within or around the brain often shows symptoms other than those accompanying a simple concussion. Signs of serious damage to the brain include partial paralysis of the body, posture with the arms and legs extended and with the jaws clenched, and unequal or pinpoint pupils of the eyes.

### Diagnosis

A simple concussion usually requires no special care. The purpose of the doctor's examination is to determine if any more serious injury may have occurred. The patient is observed for level of consciousness, mental sharpness (if awake), and proper nerve and muscle functions and reflexes. An x-ray study of the head may be performed to rule out a skull fracture (although most simple undepressed skull fractures are allowed to heal without treatment). If the patient acts strange or out of character or does not respond correctly to the tests, hospitalization and evaluation by a neurologist or neurosurgeon may be necessary.

### Treatment

Once a doctor has determined that a patient has had only a simple concussion, the patient may be allowed to return home without hospitalization. For the next 24 hours, the person is advised to relax and to take no medication stronger than an aspirin substitute (acetaminophen). It is best not to eat solid foods following any vomiting (which is common after concussion). A parent, roommate, or spouse is usually asked to wake the patient every two hours during

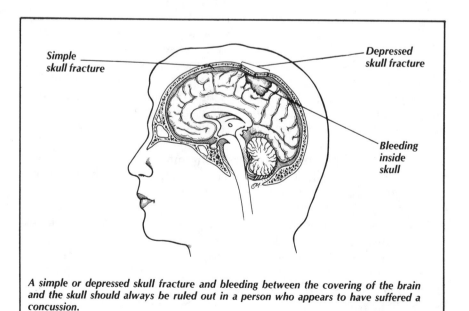

*A simple or depressed skull fracture and bleeding between the covering of the brain and the skull should always be ruled out in a person who appears to have suffered a concussion.*

the night and ask three questions: What is your name? Where are you? What is my name? If the patient cannot answer these questions, will not awaken, or has convulsions, he should be rushed to the hospital. The patient should return to the hospital immediately if any of the following danger signals is noted: a continuing or worsening headache, blurring of vision, extreme or constant vomiting, unusual eye movements, twitching, a staggering way of walking, or any change in personality. If none of these symptoms develops, the patient can resume his normal activities after a day or so of rest.

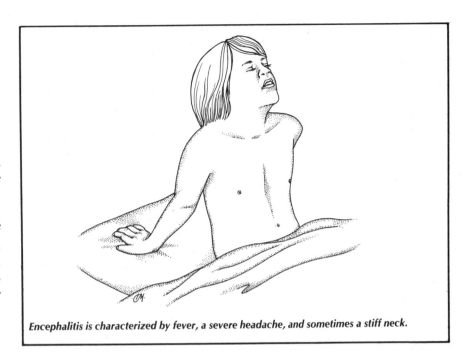

*Encephalitis is characterized by fever, a severe headache, and sometimes a stiff neck.*

# Encephalitis

Encephalitis is an inflammation of the brain. The term is usually used to describe an infectious process caused by bacteria, parasites, vaccines, and, most often, viruses. Noninfectious agents such as poisons, metabolic abnormalities due to liver or kidney failure, and tumors can cause conditions that closely resemble encephalitis.

### Causes

Viruses may cause encephalitis either as a primary disease or as a complication of an infection. Some of these viruses are mosquito-borne and afflict humans only in warm weather, when mosquitoes are in season. Many cases of encephalitis occur as complications of viral infections, such as measles, mumps, chicken pox, and rubella (German measles). These cases usually develop five to ten days after the onset of the original illness, but can develop as long as six weeks afterward.

### Symptoms

Encephalitis may be associated with meningitis (infection of the layers of tissue that cover the brain and spinal cord). There may be evidence of brain disturbances, such as alterations in mental state, personality changes, seizures, and paralysis. Edema (fluid buildup) in the brain is present, and there may be petechial hemorrhages (small, red spots that indicate bleeding) scattered throughout parts of the brain and spinal cord. As with meningitis, fever, headache, vomiting, a general feeling of illness, and a stiff neck may be the first symptoms to appear.

### Diagnosis

Prompt diagnosis and supportive treatment are essential in any case of encephalitis or suspected encephalitis. Even patients who have been seriously or critically ill with encephalitis often recover. One diagnostic problem is differentiating encephalitis from bacterial meningitis and other similar ailments. Even with ideal circumstances for diagnosis, the encephalitis virus is often not identified. Viruses can sometimes be isolated directly from cerebrospinal fluid or from the tissues. Since many forms of encephalitis, such as the mosquito-borne forms, have important public health implications, blood is often drawn whenever encephalitis is suspected; the sample is sent to the local department of health, which can provide a more precise diagnosis.

### Treatment

With a form of encephalitis called herpes simplex encephalitis, early recognition and treatment with a medication that inhibits the reproduction of viruses reduce the chances of death and neurologic impairment significantly. However, for maximal effectiveness, the drug should be given before coma or paralysis occurs. Supportive therapy involves bed rest and maintaining fluid balance to avoid dehydration (loss of body fluids).

# Epilepsy

Epilepsy is a disorder characterized by sudden surges of disorganized electrical impulses in the brain, which lead to seizures (attacks).

There are several categories of seizures; they can be so mild as to go almost unnoticed or so severe that, if untreated, they can cause serious harm.

### Causes

Epilepsy is usually divided into two categories: idiopathic (of unknown cause) and acquired (caused by some known factor, such as a brain tumor or an injury). Until the age of 25, idiopathic epilepsy is a very common cause of seizures. Seizures beginning after the age of 25 are more often a sign of acquired epilepsy due to injury, tumors, or other brain disorders (such as cerebral palsy, infection, and malformations of blood vessels).

Idiopathic epilepsy, although by definition of unknown cause, has several consistent attributes. It occurs with highest frequency between the ages of two and five years and again at puberty and tends to run in families.

### Symptoms

The symptoms of epilepsy vary according to the type of seizure experienced. Not all seizures are convulsions. A convulsion involves the nerves that control movement and is characterized by jerking, spastic muscle move-

ments. It is also marked by alterations in sensation and consciousness; loss of consciousness is common.

Seizures are classified according to the symptoms present. In the past, classifications were grand mal (French for "big sickness"), petit mal (French for "little sickness"), psychomotor, and focal. The current classification separates seizures into partial and generalized types, depending on the extent of brain involvement.

The four currently used categories (and their symptoms) are as follows:
- Simple partial seizures, confined to small areas of the brain, may be accompanied by feeling a tingling sensation in the arm, finger, or foot; perceiving a bad odor; seeing flashing lights; or speaking unintelligibly. The patient remains conscious.
- Complex partial seizures include episodes of "automatic behavior," in which the patient remains conscious but sits motionless or moves or behaves in a strange, repetitive, or somehow inappropriate way.
- Generalized convulsive seizures have a number of symptoms: the patient may cry out, stiffen and fall to the ground unconscious, lose urinary and bowel control, and have muscle spasms or thrashing movements that cause the limbs to jerk. Spasm of the jaw muscles can cause the victim to bite his tongue. After the convulsion, the patient falls into a deep sleep and then awakens dazed, often with a headache and no recollection of the seizure. A warning sensation, called an aura, may precede the seizure; this may be a headache, sleepiness, yawning, or tingling in the arms or legs.

- Generalized nonconvulsive, or absence, seizures are characterized by periods of staring into space, rhythmic blinking, and what appears to be daydreaming. The patient remains conscious but is totally unaware of the seizure. This type of seizure, which is most common in children, may be mistaken for a short attention span or a learning disability.

### Diagnosis

Epilepsy is diagnosed by observing the symptoms and by obtaining an electroencephalogram (EEG), which is a visual record of the electrical activity of the brain. Abnormal electrical discharges can be detected if they are present in the brain. However, an abnormal EEG in the absence of symptoms is by no means proof of epilepsy, nor does a normal EEG rule it out.

### Treatment

Nonmedical treatment of an epileptic seizure should be limited to preventing injury and keeping the patient comfortable by loosening clothing or placing a pillow under the head. The patient should not be left in any position in which vomit can be swallowed or inhaled or in any position in which he might suffocate. *Never* should an attempt be made to pry open the mouth or insert any object into the mouth of a person who is having a convulsion.

Epilepsy cannot be cured, but it can usually be controlled with a program of anticonvulsant drug therapy. Patients who tend to have seizures following emotional or physical stress may also benefit from tranquilizers. After two to five years of drug control of idiopathic epilepsy, the dosage is sometimes decreased and, occasionally, when enough time has elapsed during which no seizures have occurred, medication can be discontinued.

Epilepsy cannot be prevented, but once the seizures have been controlled by medication, epileptic persons can lead normal lives.

# Headache

A headache is a symptom, not a disease. A headache is rarely the symptom of a serious illness, but severe or frequent headaches can be exhausting and can affect daily life.

There are three basic types of headaches. The *vascular headache* occurs when blood vessels in the head enlarge and press on nerves, causing pain. The most common vascular headache is the migraine. The second type of headache is the *muscle contraction headache,* which results when the muscles of the face, neck, or scalp contract and tighten. A tension headache is an example of a muscle contraction headache. The third kind of headache is the *inflammatory headache.* Such a headache is the result of pressure within the head. The causes range from relatively minor conditions, such as sinusitis, to more serious problems, such as a brain tumor.

A more detailed description of each type of headache follows.

## MIGRAINE HEADACHE

One theory about migraine headaches is that they occur when the blood vessels in the head expand and press on the nerves, causing pain. However, another theory is that they result when the blood vessels first overreact to outside stimuli by constricting and thus blocking blood flow to parts of the brain; this may cause the visual impairment and numbness that often accompany or precede a migraine headache. The blood vessels then become full of blood and press on surrounding nerves, causing pain.

Women are more prone to migraines than are men, and a certain personality type—compulsive, perfectionist, excessively neat, and very success-oriented—seems to be more susceptible to this kind of headache.

## Causes

A number of physical and emotional factors may contribute to migraine headaches. Migraines may be triggered by a sharp reduction in caffeine intake or by allergies to certain foods or food additives (among them chocolate, coffee, fatty foods, alcohol, citrus fruits, monosodium glutamate, and nitrates). Emotional stress can also cause migraine headaches, as can drinking, smoking, or an interruption in routine eating and sleeping habits (all of which may be responsible for "weekend" headaches suffered by some patients). Cyclical, seasonal, or emotional factors, such as men-

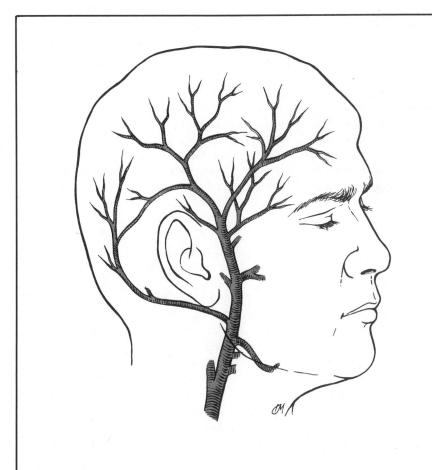

*A migraine headache occurs when the blood vessels in the head expand and press on nerves, causing pain.*

struation, for instance, may be associated with migraine. A tendency toward having this type of headache may also be inherited.

## Symptoms

The predominant symptom of a migraine headache is a sharp, pulsating, incapacitating pain on one or both sides of the head. Paleness, sweating, nausea, and sensitivity to light may accompany the pain.

A warning sensation (called an aura) may indicate an approaching migraine headache. Before the pain begins, some individuals may see flashing lights or "shooting stars," hear noises, smell fragrances or odors, or feel a tingling sensation in the arms or legs.

Cluster headaches, a form of migraine most commonly experienced by men, occur in groups of up to six a day, lasting for weeks or months. Their chief symptom is intense pain on one side of the head, accompanied by tearing of the eye and a runny nose on the same side. Drinking and smoking may aggravate these headaches.

## Diagnosis

Vascular headaches are diagnosed by a careful review of the circumstances surrounding the headaches as well as by a physical examination to rule out any other disorder that might be causing them. Elimination tests may be done to identify the exact cause of migraines suffered by people who seem to react to certain foods or changes in eating and sleeping habits. In an elimination test, all the substances that are suspected of causing the trouble are eliminated and then reintroduced one at a time to identify the cause of the headaches.

## Treatment

Treatment of a migraine already in progress usually consists of a drug therapy program chosen from a variety of painkillers, sedatives, and special drugs to combat migraine. For the occasional migraine sufferer, tranquilizers and sedatives may relieve some of the symptoms experienced during an attack.

## Prevention

Prevention of migraines is possible with several types of medication. One commonly prescribed is ergotamine, which constricts the blood vessels and thus prevents the swelling that causes pressure on the surrounding nerves. This drug is usually taken to stop an approaching migraine; it may have no effect on the aura symptoms some patients experience. Antidepressant drugs, taken in small doses, may prevent migraines in a patient who experiences them regularly.

A recent development in migraine treatment is the use of the drug propranolol, a beta-blocking drug. This drug works in the body to block what are called the beta effects, one of which is dilation (enlargement) of the blood vessels. Because propranolol blocks the dilation of blood vessels, it has been used to prevent, but not treat, acute attacks of migraine headaches. New drugs known as calcium-channel blockers, such as verapamil, nifedipine, and diltiazem, are also effective in prevention of migraine. They probably act by preventing the initial constriction of blood vessels.

## MUSCLE CONTRACTION HEADACHE

A muscle contraction headache occurs when muscles of the face, neck, or scalp remain contracted (tightened) for long periods. These muscles are then said to be in spasm.

## Causes

A muscle contraction headache usually occurs following a specific event that has caused the muscles to tense. The tension is then translated into physical discomfort in the form of a clenched jaw, aching neck, and tightened muscles of the face and head.

Muscle contraction headaches can also be brought about by abnormalities in the eyes, neck, teeth, or jaws or by poor posture—especially by holding the head at an awkward angle while reading, driving, or watching television, for example.

## Symptoms

The major symptom of these headaches is a tight, squeezing pain in the forehead or jaws or around the back of the head or neck. This constant, dull pain usually occurs on both sides of the head.

## Diagnosis

Diagnostic evaluation involves a review of the events that usually precede the headaches, as well as a physical examination to rule out any other disorder that might be causing them. A psychological examination may also be conducted to detect any emotional problems that may be contributing to the headaches.

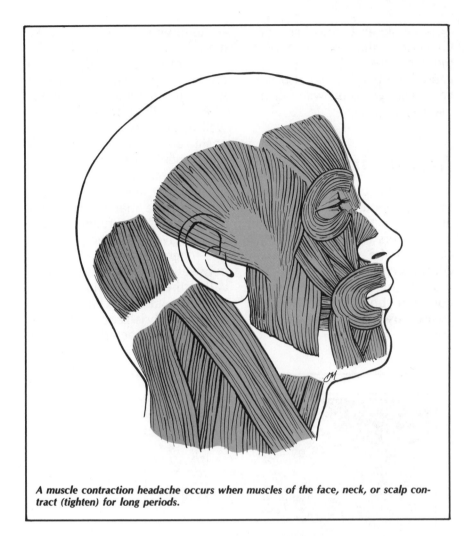

*A muscle contraction headache occurs when muscles of the face, neck, or scalp contract (tighten) for long periods.*

(a bulge in a blood vessel) in the head and a brain tumor. Aneurysms may not cause pain until they rupture or enlarge rapidly. Brain tumors are usually associated with swelling in the surrounding tissues, which causes increased pressure within the skull and, as a result, a dull, constant headache and sensation of pressing.

High blood pressure, which causes blood to rush through the vessels with too great a force; infections, which inflame sensitive tissue; and fever, which may enlarge the blood vessels, can also cause headache due to excess pressure within the skull.

### Symptoms

The symptoms of an inflammatory headache are a dull, aching pain, often occurring early in the day, accompanied by a feeling of pressure in the head. The pain is heightened by sneezing, coughing, bending over, or doing anything that increases the amount of blood in the head.

### Treatment

Eliminating the tension or correcting the physical problem that is causing the headaches is a good start in treating them. Painkillers, muscle relaxants, and tranquilizers may be used occasionally (although not on an everyday basis) to treat muscle contraction headaches. Also, antidepressant drugs may be effective in preventing these headaches in persons who suffer from them regularly.

### INFLAMMATORY HEADACHE

An inflammatory, or traction, headache is caused by pressure within the head, due to any of a variety of disorders.

### Causes

Clogged sinuses and sinus infections are probably the chief cause of this type of headache. The sinuses are the cavities, lined with mucous membranes, within the facial bones. When mucus, which normally flows freely through the sinuses and drains down the nasopharynx or out the nose, cannot drain properly, it collects in the sinuses and causes excess pressure on the surrounding tissues, leading to headache.

Other causes of inflammatory headaches include an aneurysm

### Diagnosis

This type of headache is diagnosed by determining first whether sinus problems are causing it. If not, the doctor may order an electroencephalogram (EEG), which is a visual record of electrical activity in the brain; x-ray studies; a computed tomographic (CT) scan, which provides a cross-sectional picture of the brain; or a magnetic resonance imaging (MRI) study, which yields images comparable with those obtained with CT but without the use of x-rays. These tests may detect the presence of a tumor, an aneurysm, or other abnormality in the brain.

## Treatment

Inflammatory headaches are treated according to their cause. Those triggered by a sinus infection can be treated with pain-killers; antibiotics, which fight the infection; or antihistamines and decongestants, which dry out and help drain the sinuses. Headaches resulting from more serious disorders, such as a brain tumor, brain abnormality, or aneurysm, will almost certainly require surgery.

## Prevention

Prevention of these headaches is sometimes possible if the cause is as simple as a sinus infection. Of course, the correction of a more serious disorder that has caused the pain should also prevent future problems with inflammatory headaches.

# Meningitis

Meningitis occurs when bacteria or viruses enter the spinal fluid and infect the meninges, the three layers of membranes that surround the brain and spinal cord. Meningitis can be fatal, although this is becoming less common because of the increased use of effective medications.

Meningitis seems to strike males more often than females and is most commonly seen in children up to the age of four years and in adults over the age of 60. Swelling of the brain, as well as epilepsy, blindness, amnesia, and deafness, can result when meningitis is not properly and promptly treated.

The three layers of meninges are the dura mater (the outermost layer), the arachnoid (the middle layer), and the pia mater (the innermost layer). The space between the inner two layers, called the subarachnoid space, is filled with clear cerebrospinal fluid, which is produced in the brain. When bacteria or viruses

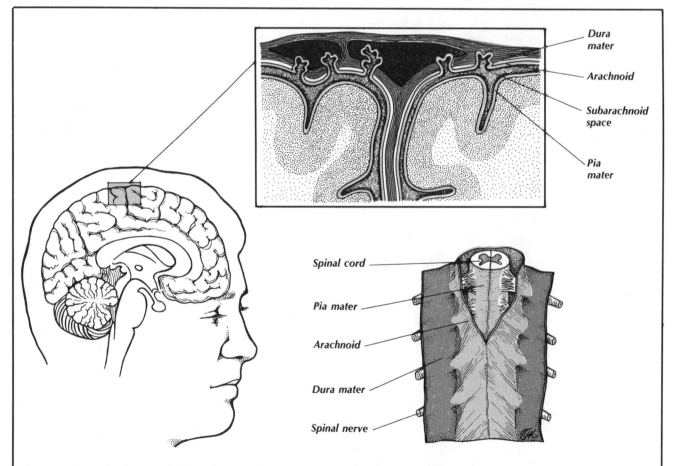

*The meninges are the three membranes that cover the brain and spinal cord: the dura mater (outer layer), the arachnoid (middle layer), and the pia mater (inner layer). Between the pia mater and the arachnoid is the subarachnoid space, which is filled with cerebrospinal fluid. Meningitis results when infection is spread from the cerebrospinal fluid to the meninges.*

invade this fluid and form pus, the surrounding membranes soon become infected, resulting in meningitis.

## Causes

Meningitis is caused by an infection that enters the system through a serious head wound or through the bloodstream from a source of infection in another part of the body. The bacteria may also reach the meninges from an abscess (localized infection) of the brain itself, but this is quite rare.

A deficiency in the immune system, which can be either inherited or acquired over time, may lead to a greater chance of contracting this disease. Also, newborns may be at a greater risk if the mother had a genital infection, such as herpes, during the last week of pregnancy, if the membranes of the uterus ruptured prematurely, or if labor was prolonged.

## Symptoms

The symptoms of meningitis are a "bursting" headache, high fever, rising pulse rate, irregular breathing, vomiting, and sensitivity to light. Pain extends down the neck and into the back and lower limbs; the neck may be stiff, and it will be difficult for the patient to bend forward. As the disease progresses, convulsions or coma may occur.

## Diagnosis

Unless increased pressure in the brain is suspected, meningitis is diagnosed with a test called a lumbar puncture, or spinal tap, in which a sample of the cerebrospinal fluid is withdrawn and examined to see if it is clear (normal) or cloudy (pus-filled) and to identify the bacteria causing the infection. A physical examination, blood cultures, and cultures from the secretions of the respiratory tract may also be useful in determining the type of bacteria present. A viral infection is much harder to diagnose; it may not show up on any tests.

## Treatment

Because immediate treatment is so important, medication may be prescribed before the specific infecting agent has been identified. Once the cause has been determined, a more appropriate medication, most often an antibiotic, can then be administered. The patient will be admitted to the hospital, where measures can be taken to reduce fever and control brain swelling.

Viral infections are much more difficult to treat. Fortunately, most cases run their course without causing serious consequences. Treatment is generally limited to hospitalization, so that supportive therapy can be administered.

## Prevention

Prevention of meningitis caused by certain strains of bacteria may be possible with some vaccines that are now available. Research continues on vaccines against other bacterial strains.

# Multiple sclerosis

Multiple sclerosis is a chronic disease of the central nervous system (the brain and spinal cord) in which the protective myelin sheath (the insulating covering) of the nerve fibers degenerates. When this protection disappears, body functions may become impaired. In some cases, the patient ultimately becomes wheelchair-bound or even dies. In other cases, the disease may flare up only once in a lifetime and leave the individual with no or only minimal disabilities.

## Causes

Researchers have not yet determined the exact cause of multiple sclerosis. Some studies indicate that the disease follows exposure to a virus that may lie dormant (inactive) until some factor, such as stress or a second exposure to the virus, triggers the disease.

Another theory suggests that multiple sclerosis affects people who have some defect in their immune system (the body system responsible for protection from foreign substances or infective agents). It is thought that following viral exposure, the immune system mistakenly identifies the myelin covering of the nerves as foreign tissue and tries to destroy it. The symptoms of multiple sclerosis may be the consequence of this destructive process.

## Symptoms

Initial attacks of multiple sclerosis are most common in people in their late 20s and early 30s. The disease begins with tingling and numbness in the arms and legs, muscle spasms, partial loss of vision, difficulty in walking, and impaired bladder

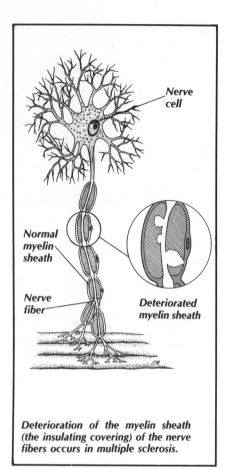

Nerve cell

Normal myelin sheath

Nerve fiber

Deteriorated myelin sheath

*Deterioration of the myelin sheath (the insulating covering) of the nerve fibers occurs in multiple sclerosis.*

control. After the first attack, there is usually a period of remission (a time without symptoms) for as long as two to three years.

Subsequent attacks occur at irregular intervals and cause gradually increasing disability. Frequent episodes cause weakness, general incoordination, impaired speech, and burning sensations. Sexual function deteriorates, and mood swings are common.

More extensive nerve damage may result in loss of muscle control and necessitate the use of a wheelchair. Usually, the earlier the onset of disease, the more slowly it progresses. Ten years after onset, fewer than half of patients with multiple sclerosis can continue regular daily activity. After 20 years, fewer than one fourth are able to function normally.

### Diagnosis

Physicians diagnose multiple sclerosis through physical examination and observation of symptoms. Often, diagnosis remains unconfirmed until a second attack occurs.

### Treatment

Since there is no cure for multiple sclerosis, treatment concentrates on relieving the symptoms. Muscle relaxants may ease muscle spasms, and corticosteroid drugs may shorten attacks by reducing nerve tissue inflammation. Many patients are more comfortable if they are well rested; afternoon naps and adequate sleep at night are advised. Cold temperatures sometimes relieve symptoms, whereas heat makes them worse.

# Myasthenia gravis

Myasthenia gravis is an uncommon disease of the nerves and muscles, characterized by great fatigue and weakness in the muscular system, most notably in the face and throat. Although the muscles do not atrophy (wither or waste away), there is slow and progressive paralysis. The disease is most likely to strike adults, especially women between the ages of 18 and 25 and men older than 40, but it can affect persons of any age.

### Causes

Myasthenia gravis is sometimes associated with thyroid disease, excessive growth of the thymus (a gland in the chest that is an essential part of the immune system), or tumors in the thymus.

The condition is a neuromuscular disorder; the muscles fail to receive messages from the nerves because of a lack of the important neurotransmitting chemical acetylcholine. Experts believe that the disorder originates in the immune system and causes the body to destroy or block the sites responsible for receiving acetylcholine.

### Symptoms

The muscular weakness first shows up in the face: the eyelids droop, often causing squinting and double vision; there is an inability to move the mouth and lips, with subsequent difficulty in talking, chewing, and swallowing; and the cheeks generally droop or sag. Sometimes the arms and legs are afflicted, affecting basic motor movements, like walking and standing, and the performance of simple tasks, like lifting a cup. The progressive muscular weakness can also impair breathing. The degree of paralysis or weakness varies from hour to hour and day to day, although it tends to be least severe in the morning and worst at night. Blood tests and chest x-rays aid in the diagnosis.

### Treatment

Myasthenia gravis is usually not curable, but drugs are available that restore nerve transmission to the muscles. The drugs neostigmine and pyridostigmine help to reestablish muscle strength and enable the patient with myasthenia gravis to live a more normal life. If a disorder of the thymus gland is found to be the underlying problem, the gland can be surgically removed. Corticosteroids are used to help regulate the immune system.

# Narcolepsy

Narcolepsy is a disorder in which a person is recurrently subject to an irresistible, uncontrollable desire to sleep.

## Causes

Narcolepsy is not necessarily related to any other abnormal condition, although it may be the result of an abnormality in the hypothalamus that causes a disorder in the endocrine system.

## Symptoms

The most obvious symptom is the pattern of uncontrollable lapses into deep sleep during waking hours, often at inopportune times. These episodes of sleep last only a few minutes; the person wakes up feeling refreshed but is likely to fall asleep again a few hours later. The condition may be associated with cataplexy, a disorder in which stress or an unexpected emotional reaction causes collapse due to a sudden attack of muscle weakness.

## Diagnosis

The diagnosis is confirmed by observation in a sleep laboratory or by special electroencephalographic (EEG) studies.

## Treatment

Central nervous system stimulants are often prescribed.

# Neuralgia

Neuralgia is pain that runs along the course of a damaged nerve. The condition ranges from mild and temporary to severe and chronic. The pain itself is sharp and extreme, lasting only a few seconds but tending to recur. There are various types of neuralgia.

### Carpal tunnel syndrome

Carpal tunnel syndrome is caused by compression of the large nerve that passes through the tunnel created by the bones and ligaments of the thumb side of the wrist. It is fairly common, especially in pregnant women. Numbness, tingling, and a burning pain in the hand at first awaken the patient at night and then begin to occur during the day. (For additional information on carpal tunnel syndrome, see pages 92–94.)

### Peripheral neuropathy

In peripheral neuropathy, impairment of the peripheral nerves (those outside the brain and spinal cord) occurs as a complication of another disorder, such as diabetes mellitus, alcoholism, certain vitamin deficiencies, anemia, or a tumor, or as a result of overexposure to particular chemicals or drugs (the typical cause for farm and industrial workers). The first symptom is frequently a tingling sensation in the hands and feet, which slowly spreads up the limbs to the trunk; numbness follows in the same pattern, the skin becomes sensitive, and neuralgic pain ensues. Numbness in the hands leads to a loss of dexterity and susceptibility to

accidents. A special risk is that a numbed part of the body can sustain an injury without the patient's awareness until it becomes infected or ulcerated. The muscles gradually atrophy (wither away), and paralysis may set in.

### Sciatica

Sciatica is caused by pressure on the sciatic nerve (the body's largest nerve, which runs from the spinal cord through the lower body and legs). The pressure is usually caused by a slipped disk between two vertebrae (bones of the spine). The pain is frequently described as a burning sensation through the buttocks and along the backs of the thighs. (For additional information on sciatica, see page 107.)

### Shingles

Shingles, or herpes zoster, is a viral infection characterized by intense pain and skin rash along the course of a nerve. Red blisters appear in a band, usually along one side of the chest, trunk, or abdomen. Shingles occurs almost exclusively in persons who have already had chicken pox (which is caused by the same virus) and appears during times of stress or after a subsequent exposure to the chicken pox virus. Shingles can often be diagnosed by sight. (For additional information on shingles, see pages 70–72.)

### Trigeminal neuralgia

Trigeminal neuralgia, or tic douloureux, primarily affects elderly persons (most commonly,

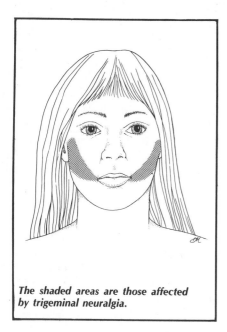

*The shaded areas are those affected by trigeminal neuralgia.*

those over age 70), although it may also occur in younger persons with multiple sclerosis. The pain arises from the trigeminal nerve, which controls sensation in the face, teeth, mouth, and nasal cavity and movement of the jaw. The pain, usually excruciating, covers one side of the face and can be set off by eating, by washing, or even by being exposed to a gust of air. With time, the stabbing pains occur more and more frequently, until they become constant. The cause is unknown. Although the condition is not life-threatening, it can become very disabling.

### Treatment

Treatment for the various types of neuralgia depends on the location of the damaged nerves, the severity of the pain, and the reason behind the impairment. Therapy may vary from cold or hot packs and aspirin to stronger prescription painkillers. For shingles, ointments may soothe and dry up blisters, and the antiviral drug acyclovir may shorten the

course of the illness. A physician may refer a patient with neuralgia to a neurologist (a specialist in problems of the nervous system). In rare instances, neurosurgery to sever a damaged nerve is necessary to eliminate the pain.

### Prevention

There is virtually no way to prevent neuralgia, except to treat underlying diseases that may precipitate nerve damage and to avoid overexposure to chemicals and drugs.

# Paralysis

Paralysis is the loss of the ability to move a part of the body, usually brought on by damage to either the muscles or to the nervous system. The condition can vary in severity and degree from paralysis of one small muscle to paralysis of almost the entire body. Irreversible and permanent paralysis results when a nerve is completely severed and destroyed, whereas paralysis caused by some diseases that cause inflammation without actual destruction of nerve tissue may diminish as the condition is treated and the body recuperates.

### Causes

There are numerous causes of paralysis. Brain damage resulting from disease or a stroke can lead to partial or total paralysis of various parts of the body. Such damage interferes with the transmission of nerve impulses from the brain to the muscles. Certain other diseases (for example, poliomyelitis, a viral infection of the central nervous system, and myasthenia gravis, a severe mus-

cular disorder of the neurochemical transmission system) and poisons (such as nerve gas and the toxin that causes botulism) also prevent nerve impulses from making contact with muscles, but do not necessarily cause complete loss of movement.

Damage to the spinal cord at the level of the middle or lower back can cause paralysis of the legs and the structures in the lower part of the body, including the bladder and rectum; this condition is called paraplegia. Injury to the spinal cord at the level of the neck affects both arms and both legs; this is known as quadriplegia.

Diabetes, cancer, alcoholism, vitamin deficiency, and drug reactions, among other conditions, can injure peripheral nerves (those outside the brain and spinal cord), occasionally weakening or totally immobilizing the muscles they control, as well as causing loss of sensation in the areas they serve.

### Treatment

Well-being and survival depend on the cause and extent of the paralysis. Obviously, paralysis that affects the muscles involved in breathing is life-threatening, and the job of breathing must be taken over by machines (called ventilators or respirators) until the paralysis improves or disappears.

Patients whose paralysis does not require artificial measures for survival may benefit from physical or occupational therapy. These patients can learn to reuse a muscle or to develop other muscles to compensate for a disabled muscle. All patients with disabled muscles require special attention to prevent muscle atrophy (withering away) and ulcers (pressure sores or bed sores).

# Parkinson's disease

Parkinson's disease is a progressive disorder characterized primarily by uncontrollable tremors in the limbs, a shuffling gait, and generalized muscular rigidity. It most often strikes people over the age of 60.

Parkinson's disease is usually not fatal, but it leads to changes in the entire body, making the patient more susceptible to other diseases. It can be present in a mild form for 20 or 30 years, but a severe form can lead to serious disability within five to ten years.

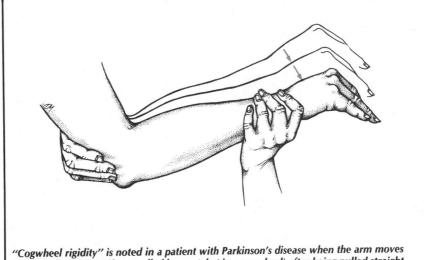

*"Cogwheel rigidity" is noted in a patient with Parkinson's disease when the arm moves in a jerky fashion (as if controlled by a ratchet in a cogwheel) after being pulled straight from a flexed position.*

### Cause

The cause of Parkinson's disease is unknown. No inherited, physiologic, or environmental factors have been identified as causes of the disease. It is known, however, that Parkinson's disease is a reflection of a chemical imbalance in the brain. Those with the disease have been shown to have low levels of a neurotransmitter called dopamine. (Neurotransmitters are chemicals in the brain that transmit impulses across junctions between neurons; the delicate balance of neurotransmitters in the brain is responsible for brain function and muscular control.) To date, no cause for this chemical deficiency has been found.

### Symptoms

The symptoms of Parkinson's disease are uncontrollable shaking of the limbs, stiff muscles, drooling, reduced blinking, an expressionless face, stooping posture, and a shuffling walk. Tremors may worsen during rest periods and times of increased anxiety. Interestingly, the tremors may decrease when the patient makes a conscious effort to perform some action.

As the disease progresses, speech slurs and sentences trail off into unintelligible muttering. Small muscle movements become increasingly difficult—reducing the ability to write, eat, chew, and swallow—and all movements seem overly stiff and slow. The term "cogwheel rigidity" is often used to describe the typical arm motion these patients display; when the arm is pulled straight from a flexed position, it seems to jerk up and down as if controlled by a ratchet in a cogwheel.

Excitement and tension can cause these symptoms to worsen, as can depression. Depression is common among Parkinson's disease victims, who are understandably upset by their loss of muscle control.

### Diagnosis

Diagnostic evaluation involves a history, physical examination, and observation of the symptoms. If tremors are the only symptom displayed, tests may be done to rule out the possibility that other disorders are causing the tremors, such as liver disease, multiple sclerosis (a debilitating nervous disorder), chronic alcoholism, or overactivity of the thyroid gland.

### Treatment

Treatment of Parkinson's disease consists of correcting the dopamine deficiency. Dopamine itself cannot be absorbed directly into the brain from the bloodstream, so a substance called levodopa is prescribed to help the brain manufacture more of its own dopamine.

Levodopa has several undesirable side effects, among them nausea (which is decreased if the drug is taken with meals), an uneven "on-off" effect (causing symptoms to disappear and then reappear), and a loss of effectiveness over time. Levodopa preparations are often given in combination with anticholinergic drugs, which decrease nerve-to-muscle transmission, thereby reducing tremor and rigidity, and also decrease drooling. Levodopa is most often prescribed in combination with carbidopa, a substance that prevents destruction of levodopa in the body before it reaches the brain, thus allowing the use of smaller amounts of levodopa.

Bromocriptine, a drug that enhances the effects of dopamine, has also been successful, as have other drugs.

Physical therapy and exercise are also important in a treatment program for patients with Parkinson's disease. In addition, emotional support and understanding are critical.

# Rabies

Rabies (formerly known as hydrophobia) is an acute infectious viral disease of mammals, especially carnivores (meat eaters), which is characterized by central nervous system irritation followed by paralysis and, in some cases, death. Human infection usually follows the bite of a rabid animal (dogs, skunks, cats, bats, foxes, and coyotes are among those that may be affected). In the later stages of the disease, it is marked by paralysis of the swallowing muscles and by throat spasms, which are set off by drinking or even the sight of liquids (hence the name hydrophobia, meaning fear of water). Convulsions, tetanus (a condition characterized by severe muscular contractions), and paralysis of the respiratory (breathing) muscles are other symptoms of the last stages. Fortunately, because of animal immunization programs, only a handful of cases of rabies are reported in the United States each year.

## Cause

Rabies is caused by a virus that is present in the saliva and respiratory secretions of rabid animals. Rabid animals transmit the infection by biting other animals or human beings. Rabies can also be acquired by exposure of a mucous membrane or an open skin wound to infected animal saliva or by inhalation of the virus.

The rabies virus travels from the site of entry to the spinal cord and brain, where it multiplies. It then spreads to the salivary glands and into the saliva itself. In human beings, the incubation period (the time between exposure to the virus and development of symptoms) may extend from ten days to one year, but the average incubation period is 30 to 50 days. The incubation period is shortest in persons who have been bitten on the head or trunk and in those who have multiple bites.

## Symptoms

The first symptom is a short period of mental depression, restlessness, and fever. In the next stage of the disease, the restlessness increases to uncontrollable excitement and hyperactivity. There is excessive salivation ("foaming at the mouth") and painful spasms of the throat muscles. The spasms can be easily initiated—by a breath of air, a slight breeze, an attempt to drink water. Generally, the patient experiences overwhelming thirst but cannot drink. In untreated cases, death occurs within three to ten days. However, patients often survive the disease if diagnosis and treatment are prompt.

## Diagnosis

In human patients, rabies is usually suspected if there has been a report of an animal bite or exposure to the saliva of a rabid animal. The diagnosis is confirmed by testing for the virus once the symptoms appear. A domestic animal with no symptoms that suddenly bites a human should be confined and observed by a veterinarian for ten days. If the animal still shows no symptoms, it was most likely not infectious at the time of the bite and is usually released. However, if the animal is apparently rabid or is a wild animal, it should be captured. The police or local health department should be notified so that they can capture and examine the animal. Only an experienced professional should attempt to capture an animal suspected of being rabid.

## Treatment

As soon as possible after the bite or exposure of an open wound to animal saliva occurs, the contaminated area should be cleansed thoroughly with soap and water or an antiseptic solution.

The next step is administration of antirabies serum or human rabies immune globulin for passive immunization. This is followed immediately by vaccine for active immunization. A new active immunization, called HDCV, is said to have only mild side effects for most people. Subsequent HDCV injections are given on days 3, 7, 14, and 28 after exposure. The World Health Organization recommends that a sixth injection be given routinely 90 days after the first injection.

### Prevention

The best preventive measure for rabies is to minimize contact with animals that may be rabid. In many cases, persons with a high occupational risk of animal bites receive preexposure injections. This is especially helpful for zoo personnel and persons whose work or hobbies take them into areas where they might encounter rabid animals.

As for domestic animals, restraining dogs and cats from contact with wild animals and impounding stray animals are important preventive measures. Immunizing 70 percent or more of the dog population of major cities has helped to restrict transmission of rabies, even in areas where wild animals have the disease.

Controlling rabies in wildlife areas is more difficult, although rabies as a disease is self-limiting, because it tends to kill off susceptible hosts in an area. Expensive control efforts are generally limited to areas where humans are apt to be exposed to wildlife—in campgrounds, parks, wildlife preserves, and so on.

# Sciatica

Sciatica is a condition characterized by pain that extends along the entire length of the sciatic nerve (which runs down the lower back and outer side of the thigh, leg, and foot), radiating across the back of the pelvis through the buttocks and into the thigh and leg.

### Cause

Sciatica is commonly associated with injury to or rupture of a lumbar disk, one of the cartilaginous disks located between the lumbar (lower back) vertebrae. When the injured disk exerts pressure against the sciatic nerve, pain radiates down the nerve.

*Sciatica occurs when pressure on the sciatic nerve in the area of the lumbar vertebrae causes pain to radiate along the path of the sciatic nerve.*

**Area of lumbar vertebrae**

**Path of sciatic nerve**

### Symptoms

The symptoms of sciatica vary in intensity, depending on the extent to which the injured disk presses on the sciatic nerve and according to the individual's susceptibility to pain. In mild cases, the pain may be a slight discomfort in the lower back and along the leg. In severe cases, the pain is excruciating and often completely immobilizes the victim. Since the cause is frequently a ruptured ("slipped") disk, it is difficult to know when an attack will begin. A sudden cough may cause the disk to move and press on the sciatic nerve, resulting in the pain that such pressure causes. It is commonplace for sciatica patients to be free from pain one moment and in agony the next.

Repeated problems with a ruptured lumbar disk can cause general inflammation of the sciatic nerve. In these cases, it is not a matter of pain that comes and goes. Instead, it is a matter of having somewhat less pain at one time than at another.

### Treatment

The primary treatment of sciatica is rest, to allow the inflammation of the nerve to subside. In an effort to alleviate the pain, various medications, such as analgesics and muscle relaxants, may be prescribed, or anesthetic agents may be injected into the spinal cord. In extreme cases, surgery may be necessary.

Physical therapy (under a doctor's supervision or according to a doctor's prescription) is often used to relieve the pain of sciatica. This treatment includes hydrotherapy, in which a stream of water is directed at the affected area. Many therapists advise their patients to overcome the effects of a ruptured disk by developing the core muscles (the four muscle groups that form the waist) in order to provide a supportive column of muscle that will help keep the disk in place.

# THE SKIN

The skin is the largest organ of the body, covering 18 square feet in area and weighing about seven pounds in an average adult. This waterproof barrier affords protection from invasion by dirt, bacteria, and other harmful substances and helps to regulate body temperature.

The skin is composed of three layers—the epidermis, the dermis, and the subcutaneous layer.

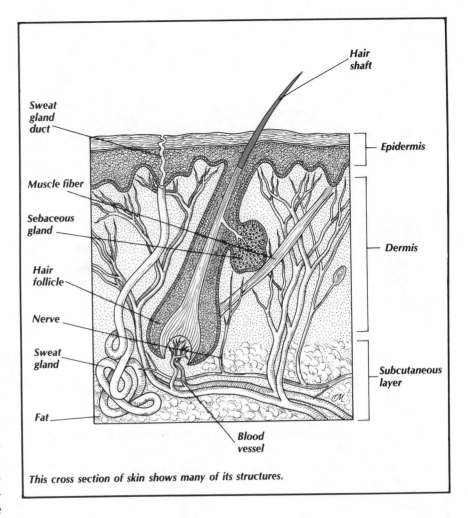

This cross section of skin shows many of its structures.

### Epidermis

The outermost layer of skin is the epidermis. The epidermis contains pigment cells that determine skin color and shield the skin against damaging sun rays. Specialized cells within this layer manufacture keratin, a tough substance also found in hair and nails.

Epidermal cells are continuously being worn away and replaced. This reconstruction process is usually invisible, except when skin becomes irritated, as in psoriasis, a disease that appears as scaly red patches. Since the outer skin layer repairs itself quickly, any injury to the epidermis rarely causes injury to the body as a whole.

### Dermis

The dermis contains blood vessels, nerve endings, hair follicles, sweat glands, and sebaceous (oil) glands. Damage at this level can send infection into the bloodstream and throughout the body.

Within the dermis, blood vessels and sweat glands help the body regulate heat. If the temperature of the blood rises, the brain stimulates secretion by the sweat glands. Sweat then flows to the surface of the skin through ducts and cools the skin by evaporating. The sebaceous glands prevent excessive evaporation by coating the surface of the skin with an oily substance called sebum.

### Subcutaneous layer

Beneath the dermis is the subcutaneous layer, in which the sweat glands originate and fat is stored. This layer also supports the blood vessels and nerves that supply the outer layers of the skin.

Because the dermis and the subcutaneous layer are rich with nerve endings, the skin is also a sensory organ. Nerves throughout these layers transmit tactile perceptions to the brain.

## Acne

Acne is a condition of the skin that ranges in appearance from small raised bumps to pustules (large cysts and pimples). Acne is so common that more than 80 percent of the population will have some form of it at some time in their lives.

### Causes

Although there are several theories about what causes acne, authorities generally believe that acne is a by-product of

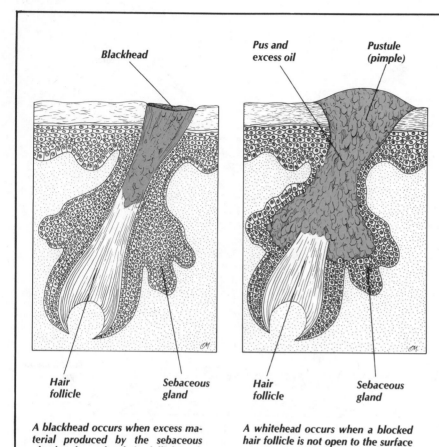

**Blackhead**

**Hair follicle**

**Sebaceous gland**

*A blackhead occurs when excess material produced by the sebaceous glands clogs the hair follicle. Although the follicle is still open to the skin surface, the normal release of material from the sebaceous gland is blocked.*

**Pus and excess oil**

**Pustule (pimple)**

**Hair follicle**

**Sebaceous gland**

*A whitehead occurs when a blocked hair follicle is not open to the surface of the skin. The follicle may rupture internally, discharging its contents into surrounding tissues and causing an inflammatory response.*

hormonal changes in the body during puberty—that period of life when a child develops the secondary sex characteristics (such as facial and body hair, deepened voice, and increased muscle mass in boys and breast development and menstruation in girls). At this time, production of hormones (particularly the male hormone testosterone) increases and stimulates the sebaceous glands to produce more sebum (an oily secretion). Most excess oil produced by these glands leaves the skin through the hair follicles (the tubelike structures from which hairs develop). Sometimes, oil clogs these tubes and creates

comedones (blocked hair follicles). Comedones are what form the initial lumps in acne.

If comedones are open to the surface of the skin, they are called blackheads. They contain sebum from the sebaceous glands, bacteria, and any skin tissue that accumulates near the surface. Comedones that are closed at the surface are called whiteheads. Plugged follicles can rupture internally, resulting in a discharge of their contents into the surrounding tissues. This process begins an inflammatory response that sets the stage for the development of acne.

The role of bacteria in acne is unclear. Bacteria may act by

causing chemical reactions in the sebaceous fluid, leading to the release of very irritating compounds called fatty acids. These in turn may cause inflammation that increases susceptibility to infection.

Authorities disagree about the role of diet as a cause of acne. Diet alone does not cure acne, nor does acne stem from an allergic reaction to a specific food. However, some cases of acne appear to improve after eliminating certain foods, particularly chocolates and fats. In addition, emotional stress seems to increase the severity of acne in certain cases.

## Symptoms

Acne causes raised swellings, most frequently on the face, neck, back, chest, and shoulders. In severe cases, there may be pus-filled sacs that break open and discharge fluid. Soreness, pain, and itching may accompany the bumps. These symptoms could be acne, or they could indicate other skin reactions to such substances as cosmetics, medications, and grooming or cleaning products.

Since puberty plays a role in the onset of acne, the condition usually appears during the teenage years. However, it can extend to age 25 and over, particularly in women. Although acne is not life-threatening, it can be problematic. If untreated, comedones can leave permanent scars, which can cause embarrassment and emotional stress.

## Treatment

Acne has no prevention or cure, but there are several treatments. The simplest home remedy is to wash the affected areas thoroughly at least twice a day with warm water and mild soap. Washing gently will not dry or irritate sensitive skin. Regular shampooing also helps, especially if the hair is oily. Use of makeup should be limited. In addition, skin may heal with exposure to the sun. However, sunlamps and ultraviolet lamps should be used very cautiously, and only under a doctor's supervision.

One form of treatment not recommended is picking or squeezing pimples, since more inflammation and scarring may result. Also, the risk of infection is increased.

Some over-the-counter acne medications, particularly lotions or creams containing benzoyl peroxide, can help troubled skin. However, most of these preparations tend to dry the skin if the manufacturer's directions are not followed carefully.

For persistent acne, a doctor may prescribe an antibiotic preparation that can be applied to the surface of the skin or an oral antibiotic, such as tetracycline or erythromycin. These antibiotics act to suppress bacterial growth, which may be a factor in worsening acne.

Another drug, tretinoin (vitamin A acid), has reduced acne in more than 50 percent of the persons who have tried it. This drug can be taken independently or in combination with an antibiotic, and must be used under a doctor's supervision. A newer drug, isotretinoin, is related to tretinoin and is used to treat severe cystic acne. It is usually not prescribed, however, unless all other acne treatments have failed. These drugs work by temporarily suppressing the production of secretions by the sebaceous glands.

# Athlete's foot

Athlete's foot (known medically as *tinea pedis*) is a fungal infection of the foot. It is also known as ringworm of the foot, although it is not caused by a worm.

## Symptoms

Athlete's foot causes itching, burning, and stinging sensations. The skin between the toes reddens, cracks open, and crumbles. In extremely long-lasting cases, the toenails may become infected, discolored, and overgrown. The fungus may spread to the underside of the foot, beneath the arch, producing groups of itching blisters and peeling of the skin.

## Diagnosis

It is important to rule out other causes of similar symptoms. For example, hot, tight shoes may make the feet sweaty in warm weather; the moisture and friction may cause softening and peeling of the skin on the soles. Dyes, adhesive cements, and other substances inside the shoes may cause irritation, as may powders and nail polishes. Eczema, psoriasis, and scabies are other possible causes of similar symptoms.

## Treatment

Most people can treat athlete's foot at home using one of several good salves, powders, or liquids obtainable without a prescription from the drugstore. These include undecylenic acid ointment, tolnaftate, and miconazole. Clotrimazole is another

effective medication, but it must be prescribed by a physician. Directions usually call for application morning and night, to continue until one week after all symptoms have vanished. As long as loose skin remains, the feet should be soaked before the ointment is applied, and the loose skin removed carefully.

If sweaty feet are the cause, athlete's foot ointments should not be used. Instead, you should ask your doctor for suggestions about controlling the excessive sweating; there are ointments and solutions that can help. Changing shoes may eliminate the problem if the feet are sensitive to chemicals inside the shoes.

Severe cases of athlete's foot call for treatment by a physician. To relieve symptoms, the doctor may prescribe soaking the feet three times a day in a solution of aluminum sulfate and calcium acetate (often called Burow's solution), with an antiseptic solution added if a secondary infection is present.

## Prevention

Athlete's foot can recur despite any treatment, especially during the hot summer months. The organisms that cause athlete's foot thrive in a hot, moist setting. However, there are several things you can do to help prevent the disease. You can keep your feet clean, dry between your toes after bathing, and change socks frequently. Use dusting and drying powders to keep the feet dry. Separate your toes with small wads of cotton when you are sleeping. Wear wooden or rubber clogs in motel and community showers and sandals, open-toed shoes, or no shoes at all during hot weather.

# Baldness

Baldness (or alopecia, as it is known medically) is partial or complete loss of hair on the head. This may be caused by an inherited tendency or by aging, fever, drugs, radiation, or disease.

## Male-pattern baldness

Male-pattern baldness is the most common form. There seems to be an inherited tendency toward it, and androgen (a male hormone) contributes to it. However, the exact mechanism by which it occurs is not known. Hair loss is gradual, occurring at the forehead, on either side of the front (sometimes leaving a center tuft known as a "widow's peak"), and on top of the head. It can begin as early as age 15 or 16, in which case it may indicate that considerable baldness is likely later (however, male-pattern baldness does not usually advance at a steady or predictable rate).

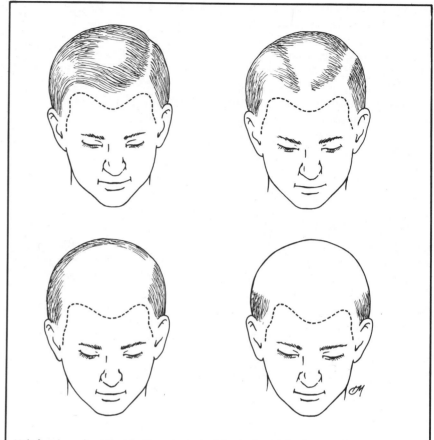

*Hair loss in male-pattern baldness is gradual, beginning at the forehead on either side of the front and continuing to the top of the head.*

## Female-pattern baldness

Female-pattern baldness is fairly common in menopausal women and usually involves only the area around the crown of the head. Like male-pattern baldness, it is believed to be due to hormonal causes.

## Temporary baldness

Temporary baldness sometimes occurs up to three or four months following a severe illness, especially one with fever, such as scarlet fever. It can result from decreased activity of the pituitary or thyroid gland, early stages of syphilis, pregnancy, use of birth control pills and certain other medications, "crash" dieting or malnutrition, or a diet containing too much vitamin A. When the cause is removed, the missing hair usually returns.

## Spotty baldness

Spotty baldness, or alopecia areata, may affect areas of the head and beard. The cause is unknown. It often clears up after a few months if there are just a few spots and if it first occurs in adulthood; it may recur, however. The outlook is less favorable if it begins in childhood or if hair loss is widespread. Occasionally, all body hair is lost. If there is no apparent cause, such as fever or severe illness, the hair is not likely to return.

## Permanent baldness

Permanent baldness occurs when the scalp is scarred as a result of burns, other injury, or disease. Conditions that can cause scarring baldness include severe bacterial and fungal infections, tuberculosis, ulcers, lupus erythematosus, and certain slow-growing tumors.

## Treatment

There is no totally satisfactory medical treatment at this time to cure or prevent baldness. However, hair transplants can be effective. Scalp plugs containing active hair follicles are taken from the back of the head, which is not affected by male-pattern baldness. The transplanted follicles continue to produce hair just as before, despite the new location.

A topical form of the antihypertensive drug minoxidil has recently been released for use in treating baldness. This preparation has been shown to stimulate hair growth; however, it must be applied on a continuous basis.

# Boils

A boil, or furuncle, is caused by a bacterial infection and irritation of the skin and its underlying structures. It is a painful swelling in the skin that is easily detected by touch. When a group of boils interconnects below the surface of the skin, a carbuncle forms.

## Causes

Boils develop when *Staphylococcus* bacteria enter the skin through a hair follicle and multiply in its warm, moist environment. Bacteria continue to grow while producing substances that invade surrounding cells. White blood cells (which attack and kill invading organisms) travel to the infected hair follicle and enclose bacteria. As more white blood cells gather, they eventually consume the bacteria and eliminate the infection. This counterattack by the white blood cells is what produces the pustule in the center of the boil, because of the buildup of white blood cells. When the pustule ruptures, pus and dead skin cells killed by the bacteria drain out, and the boil heals.

*Staphylococcus* bacteria are often found in the nose and throat, where washing cannot reach them. They can spread to a hair follicle from there or from another site on the body. They can also be transmitted by contact with an infected person or by contact with an infected article, such as a washcloth or towel. In most cases, however, other persons who come in contact with bacteria do not get boils.

## Those at risk

Persons who are run-down or who suffer diseases such as anemia (deficiency of red blood cells), diabetes, or infections that weaken their natural defenses against bacteria seem more susceptible to boils. Those who work with greasy or oily substances are more likely to develop boils because these materials trap bacteria against the skin. Poor bathing habits, especially in the summer months, when sweaty skin provides the moist climate conducive to bacterial growth, also invite infection.

## Symptoms

Boils can develop anywhere on the skin. They appear most frequently on the neck, face, and back, and they can erupt in several places at once. Although boils vary in size, they characteristically form white or yellow pustules. As the infection progresses, the pustule becomes red

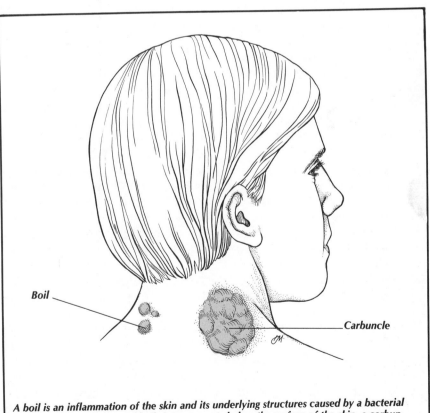

*A boil is an inflammation of the skin and its underlying structures caused by a bacterial infection. When a group of boils interconnects below the surface of the skin, a carbuncle forms.*

and hot. Excess fluid in the boil produces pressure on the nerves underneath, which can result in considerable pain. When boils contain little pus, they are called blind boils; the inflammation recedes slowly without rupturing, but sometimes it leaves a scar.

If boils are large or extensive, the person may also experience fever and a general feeling of weakness. Sometimes, the infection gets into the bloodstream and spreads throughout the body. The same bacteria that cause the boil may also produce a toxin (poison) that causes blood clots, usually in the blood vessels around the boil.

## Treatment

Any treatment plan for boils and carbuncles emphasizes that they should *never* be squeezed, particularly if they are on the face. Squeezing may force the infection deeper into the skin and possibly into the bloodstream. Only a physician should lance a boil to encourage drainage. Afterward, the doctor may prescribe an oral antibiotic, such as penicillin or erythromycin, to fight further infection.

Many boils will rupture and heal on their own. However, holding a soft cloth soaked with warm water against the boil for 15 to 20 minutes at least four times a day will speed the process. These warm compresses increase blood flow to the area and encourage pustule formation. Since bacteria from the boil are contagious, the cloth should be disinfected in boiling water or in the hot cycle of a washing machine.

When a boil bursts, the infected area should be washed thoroughly and covered with an antibiotic cream and sterile gauze. If the boil does not heal within a few days, or if the boil is located on or near the face, a physician should be consulted.

## Prevention

To prevent new eruptions, the skin needs to be kept cool and dry. Sometimes, physicians advise washing the entire body with an antiseptic (germ-fighting) soap twice a day. If boils frequently recur, underclothing and bed linen should be changed every day.

# Calluses

Calluses are thickened areas of the skin. They develop most often on the balls and heels of the feet and on the hands.

## Causes

Skin buildup is the result of excessive friction or pressure against the surface of the skin. As pressure mounts, dead skin cells accumulate, and the skin thickens. Wearing shoes that fit improperly or holding pencils too tightly can create the problem. Since calluses often follow blisters on the same site, they are considered to be the body's way of shielding the area against further injury.

Flat-footed persons have a greater incidence of calluses. Because of the abnormal shape of the foot, the small bones in the front portion of the foot are forced downward against the skin of the sole with great pressure during walking, creating pressure points. Those who wear high heels promote growth of calluses by increasing pressure on the balls of their feet.

## Symptoms

Calluses vary in size and shape depending on where they grow and how much skin is affected. Sometimes, calluses grow so thick and irregular in shape that the skin becomes inflexible and cracks.

When pressure is relieved, calluses usually produce no pain. However, continued irritation, especially involving areas where the skin is split, can cause enough discomfort to interfere with physical activities.

## Treatment

Immediate treatment involves removal of the pressure that caused the callus in the first place. Extremely persistent or painful calluses should be examined by a doctor. In rare instances, surgery may be necessary to alleviate intense pressure. In milder cases, calluses can often be eased by padding the exposed area to reduce further friction.

There are over-the-counter remedies that soften the callused tissue, making it easier to remove. Salicylic acid plasters, which are sold in medicated sheets, can be placed over the callus after bathing and secured with tape. The pad should be removed just before the next bath so that the softened skin can be gently removed with a pumice stone or a special implement with a rough surface designed for that purpose.

Home remedies should not be used by persons who have diabetes, atherosclerosis, or other circulatory disorders because their risk of infection is greater. They should consult their doctor before attempting any form of treatment.

# Canker sores

Canker sores (medically known as aphthous ulcers) are inflamed tissue cavities, usually found in the mouth. They can be quite painful, often inhibiting eating ability. Even though up to one out of every four persons develops canker sores, they are not contagious.

## Causes

Researchers differ about the cause of canker sores. One unconfirmed theory suggests that the sores are the result of an autoimmune response, whereby the body develops antibodies to its own tissue. Other factors that have been said to trigger canker sores include fever, menstruation, fatigue, tension, and allergies. Some people get canker sores after eating certain foods. Poor dental hygiene, ill-fitting dentures, and injuries from stiff toothbrushes may also lead to the condition. All of the above may be contributing factors; however, the true cause of canker sores is unknown.

## Symptoms

Canker sores may occur singly or in groups. They can be found almost anywhere in the mouth—inside the cheek and on the tongue, lips, or gums.

A canker sore begins as a small blister. After the blister breaks, a small ulcer develops and enlarges until there is a bright red sore surrounding a whitish-yellow cavity. This sore can last about 10 to 14 days before healing. Canker sores leave no scars. However, they often recur, sometimes every few weeks or months.

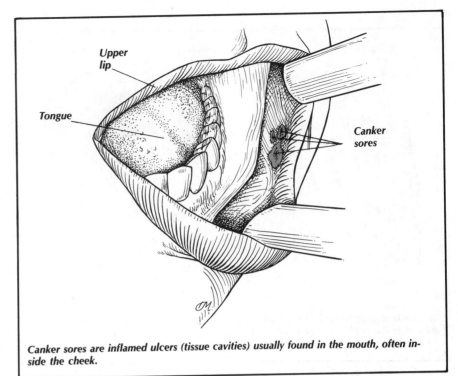

*Canker sores are inflamed ulcers (tissue cavities) usually found in the mouth, often inside the cheek.*

## Treatment

Canker sores have no cure, but there are several treatments that may relieve pain. Some physicians prescribe the antibiotic tetracycline for canker sores. Treatment involves dissolving the capsule in an ounce of warm water and swishing the mixture in the mouth for five to ten minutes, three or four times a day for five to seven days. Sometimes, therapy includes soaking a cotton wad in the solution and applying it directly to the sores.

There are also various over-the-counter preparations designed to reduce discomfort. However, they are of uncertain value, and you should always check with your doctor before using them.

## Prevention

Persons who have repeated attacks of canker sores should see a physician or dentist. Recurrence may be lessened by improving oral hygiene or by avoiding certain foods or other substances.

# Corns

Corns are small, round mounds of firm, dead skin that form on or between the toes. Their hard, waxy cores, which bore down into the skin and press on the underlying tissue and nerves, can cause extreme pain. Corns sometimes are associated with bursae (fluid-filled sacs), which can become irritated, resulting in bursitis.

## Causes

Corns are caused by a great deal of pressure or friction on the toes (as are calluses, their basis), usually from ill-fitting shoes or high heels. Since the skin acts as

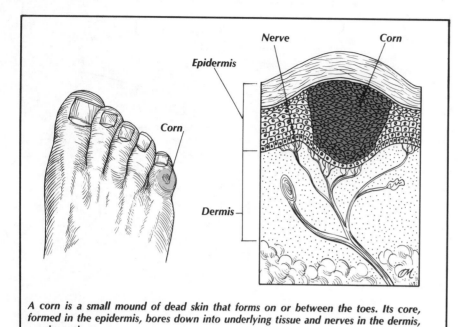

A corn is a small mound of dead skin that forms on or between the toes. Its core, formed in the epidermis, bores down into underlying tissue and nerves in the dermis, causing pain.

the body's protector from the outside environment, corns form when the body attempts to protect the troubled area from more pressure by building up a mass of dead skin cells and secreting a hard substance called keratin. Persons who have abnormal bone structure in their feet or certain types of arthritis tend to develop corns. Generally, however, those who avoid wearing high-heeled or tight-fitting shoes should be able to avoid the development of corns.

## Symptoms

Corns are usually regular in shape, and can be white, gray, or yellow. They most often form on the outside of the first or fifth toes, since that is where pressure most often occurs. Corns that form between the toes are called soft corns; they are not as firm as other corns because of the moistness of the environment between the toes.

## Treatment

Corns are best treated by first eliminating the cause of the pressure. Over-the-counter preparations are available. These include padding to reduce the friction on the area, ointments, and medicated pads, which will soften and blister the skin layers, making them easier to remove and reducing the pain. Severe or persistent corns must be treated by a doctor, but only rarely do they necessitate surgery. Persons with diabetes, atherosclerosis, or other circulatory diseases should *never* treat a corn themselves, as the risk of infection is much greater for them.

# Cyst

A cyst is an abnormal sac or membrane containing a fluid or semisolid material.

Cysts may develop virtually anywhere in the body. They may form around a foreign body, such as a particle in the lung or beneath the skin, or around a parasite. They may entrap an escaping body liquid, such as blood hemorrhaging into tissue or fluid leaking from a bursa (a sac containing lubricant for a joint).

### Types and treatment

Perhaps the most common cysts are those of the skin and mucous membranes.

A *sebaceous cyst* occurs when a sebaceous gland (the tiny oil gland at the base of each hair root) becomes plugged. Ordinarily, this plugging results in a blackhead or, if the blackhead becomes infected, a pus-filled pimple. Occasionally, however, the pimple does not break, and the swelling becomes entrapped beneath the surface of the skin. Sebum (oil from the sebaceous gland) continues to flow into the sac that forms in the cavity, and the cyst grows to the size of a marble or larger. Sebaceous cysts—which can occur in any part of the body where there is hair, including the neck, scalp, and back—can easily be removed surgically if bothersome; if they become infected, they must be drained and removed. A type of tiny cyst known as *milium,* which usually occurs on the face and scrotum, can simply be opened and drained. Larger cysts must be removed completely, or they will recur.

*Mucous cysts* that occur in the mouth, on the tongue, or on the lower lip are caused by plugged mucous glands and may grow to the size of a pea or larger. They may be removed in the same manner as sebaceous cysts.

*Traumatic epithelial cysts* usually result from the trapping of a piece of skin, a blood clot, or foreign material beneath the skin because of some injury. In some cases, they may not need to be removed.

# Dermatitis

Dermatitis is an inflammation of the skin. There are many different kinds of dermatitis and a great variety of causes.

## Chronic dermatitis

This often occurs on the hands or feet, and may simply be the result of continued irritation, especially by contact dermatitis. It is marked by thickened skin, inflammation, and scaling. It is sometimes caused by excessive hand washing or by accumulation of soaps or detergents under rings. Occasionally, a fungal infection is the cause.

## Contact dermatitis

This is a skin inflammation caused by a substance that has touched the skin. This may be a harsh chemical or a detergent or soap that irritates directly, or it may be a substance that produces an allergic reaction that does not appear until five or six days after the contact. Less commonly, the reaction appears only after years of repeated use. Common causes of allergic contact dermatitis are poison ivy, chemicals in shoes and clothing, metal watchbands and rings, antibiotic salves, and cosmetics. There are also cases in which a substance, such as a shaving lotion or cosmetic, produces a "photoallergic" reaction— that is, a rash develops when the skin under the substance is exposed to sunlight.

## Eczema

This inflammation of the skin is marked by small blisters (when severe), redness, fluid in the tissue, oozing, scales, crusts or scabs, burning or itching, and sometimes dryness. The skin of flexor surfaces (those subject to bending movements, such as the back of the knee and the top of the elbow) is most commonly affected. There are several different forms of eczema. One of the more common types is atopic dermatitis, which is an itching skin inflammation due to an allergy. Susceptible persons often have a family history of allergic diseases, such as asthma or hay fever. Typically, it begins in infancy, subsides by age 3, and may reappear by age 10 or 12. Certain foods (such as wheat, milk, and eggs) and other substances (such as pollen and fur) often bring on symptoms; if so, they must be avoided.

## Exfoliative dermatitis

This condition produces shedding of skin all over the body, together with hair loss. The entire skin surface is red, scaly, and thickened. The cause is unknown in most cases, but it sometimes occurs following a less severe case of dermatitis or as a side effect of a drug. Hospitalization is frequently necessary because the condition can be life-threatening. A first step is to consult a doctor about any medications and to ask about stopping or changing them.

## Localized neurodermatitis

This condition is characterized by thick, sharp-bordered, scaly breaks in the skin, occasionally

with little blisters. This condition is caused by habitual scratching of an insect bite or other real or imagined irritation of the skin and is corrected by covering the area and stopping the scratching. In the case of an itch in the area around the openings of the vagina and colon, however, warts, pinworms, hemorrhoids, infections, or certain diseases may be the cause.

## Nummular dermatitis

Coin-shaped patches of blisters that later ooze and crust over mark this condition, which usually is accompanied by dry skin and itching. Most often, it appears on the legs and sometimes the buttocks and trunk of middle-aged persons.

## Seborrheic dermatitis

This is a scaling and inflammation of the scalp and sometimes the face and other parts of the body. This is the cause of dandruff in adults and cradle cap in infants.

## Stasis dermatitis

This stubborn skin inflammation of the lower legs is usually the result of poor blood return from the area. There is redness, mild scaling, and brown discoloration of the skin. If the condition is neglected, the skin swells and may become infected, or ulcers (eroded skin sores) may develop.

## Treatment

Because there is such a bewildering variety of skin diseases and because some can be dangerous if neglected, it is important to seek medical care for any dermatitis. In general, this care usually begins with very simple measures. Dry skin needs lubricating agents, while moist or oily skin may require powders or other drying substances. Inflamed skin is commonly treated with cortisone-type creams; cool, wet dressings; or baths.

Hardened, dried skin may be peeled off with strong substances available only by prescription. If possible, the cause of the dermatitis is sought with the patient's help and eliminated. Cortisone creams are often used to make the patient more comfortable by reducing inflammation, although continuous use is not usually recommended. Antibiotics are employed promptly to eliminate any infections before they can spread to other parts of the body. Patients must resist the constant temptation to scratch itchy areas or remove scabs, because that will simply prolong and even worsen the problem. In addition, while cleanliness is desirable, some patients need to be told to reduce hand washing and the number of baths they take, because they may be washing away natural oils that protect the skin. Along the same lines, patients should not use any medication that has not been recommended by a doctor or use it more frequently than directed. Overmedication of skin diseases may be worse than undermedication in some cases.

# Fever blisters

Fever blisters, also called cold sores, are fluid-filled blisters that appear on the border of the lips and on or around the nose. They are the result of a very conta-

gious virus that affects most of the population at one time or another.

## Cause

Fever blisters are caused by a type of herpes simplex virus. It enters the body most often through the mouth or nose areas, where the skin is easier to penetrate.

At first, characteristic blisters may not result. Antibodies (protective substances) in the body defend against the invading virus. The inactivated virus withdraws to a nearby nerve, where it remains until stress to the body or a diminished capacity to fight off infection triggers a recurrence. When the virus is reactivated, it overruns the body's protective system and progresses back along the nerve to the general area of original infection. Factors that seem to favor the appearance of blisters include fever, colds, menstruation, skin injury from dental work, excessive sun and wind exposure, and emotional stress. Cold sores can return every few weeks for several weeks or not at all.

## Symptoms

Initially, the virus may present no symptoms, so some people are unaware of infection. For others, the infection begins with numbness or tenderness in the affected area. Then small, fluid-filled blisters appear. These blisters break, encrust, and heal within one to two weeks.

## Complications

Occasionally, excessive pain or swelling of lymph nodes

develops. These symptoms may indicate a secondary bacterial infection that needs a doctor's attention.

Other complications can be more serious. Herpes simplex keratitis is a painful viral infection of the cornea (transparent covering) of the eye that can result in blindness if not treated. When inflammation of the eyes accompanies fever blisters, a physician should be consulted immediately. Steroid (cortisone-type) medications should not be used near the eyes during a herpes attack without consulting a doctor, since these preparations can encourage spread of the virus to the eye.

Other serious complications can occur in infants and extremely ill patients who contract herpes virus if the infection travels to the lungs, brain, or other internal organs.

## Treatment

Treatment involves relieving symptoms, since there is no known cure for fever blisters. Some over-the-counter remedies may relieve pain and help dry blisters. Topical corticosteroid creams, however, should not be applied unless prescribed by a physician; the possibility of spreading infection increases because the corticosteroid can depress the immune response.

Healing time may be shortened by certain newer prescription drugs, such as acyclovir, but these drugs should not be used for routine fever blisters.

# Frostbite

Frostbite is damage to skin tissue resulting from exposure to low temperatures. The condition can affect any part of the body, but most often involved areas (such as the face, hands, and feet) have the poorest blood circulation and the greatest exposure to cold.

## Causes

When exposed to cold, the body naturally tries to protect vital organs. Blood vessels near the surface of the skin constrict to preserve internal body heat. This tightening causes blood to be diverted from the outside of the body, thereby reducing the supply of blood to skin tissues. As a result, skin tissue freezes from the lack of a warm blood supply and dies. Frequently, frostbite develops after prolonged exposure to cold. Extremely low temperatures or forceful winds can also cause the condition. Wearing insufficient or improper clothing increases susceptibility to frostbite. Skin can freeze to the surface of a metal object and block circulation to the area. In addition, any health problem that weakens the body or reduces circulation increases the likelihood of frostbite.

## Stages of frostbite

Frostbite develops in three stages, and each stage can produce varying degrees of pain. First-degree frostbite appears as whiteness or slight yellowness of the skin accompanied by burning or itching sensations. In this stage, symptoms can be reversed if the affected area is gradually rewarmed.

Should exposure to cold continue, sensation in the affected area ceases. Disappearance of pain and reddening and swelling

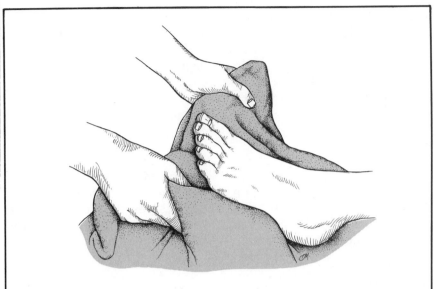

*If the person must remain outdoors for a time, the frostbitten area should be wrapped in a warm, dry blanket.*

of the tissue signal second-degree frostbite. At this stage, warming the area may produce blisters and skin peeling. The blisters may persist for weeks, and the tenderness may linger for months.

Skin with third-degree frostbite becomes waxy and hard. At this stage, skin tissue dies and edema (collection of fluid within the tissues) may occur. Severe frostbite can damage muscles, tendons, and nerves. Blood clots may form in small blood vessels and inhibit or block circulation, which can lead to gangrene.

## Treatment

Initial treatment focuses on what *not* to do, since there are many misconceptions about the proper course of action. Frostbitten tissue should not be rubbed with snow. In fact, the affected part should not be rubbed at all, because further damage to tissue can result. Exercising the frostbitten area will aggravate the condition.

To reduce tissue loss and avoid complications, frostbitten tissue should be immersed in lukewarm water rather than exposed to the extreme heat of a radiator, stove, or fire. Ideally, water temperature should be between 100°F and 110°F. Any temperature above 110°F can burn skin that lacks sensation, and thawing that is too rapid may produce pain, redness, and blisters. Gently patting (but not rubbing) the skin dry helps prevent additional injury.

If the patient remains outdoors, affected areas can be warmed by placing them in contact with warm portions of the body, such as under the armpits or between the thighs. The area can also be wrapped in a warm, dry blanket. Frozen areas should be kept clean to prevent infection. Warm, nonalcoholic drinks aid circulation. Smoking should be avoided because it causes constriction of blood vessels.

Once frozen tissue has been rewarmed, the affected area should be elevated to promote increased blood circulation and maintain the skin at room temperature. All cases of frostbite should be examined by a physician, who may prescribe medication to prevent infection or formation of clots in blood vessels.

### Prevention

The best prevention of frostbite is to wear adequate clothing to protect the skin. Feet, hands, and parts of the face need covering since these areas are likely to have the poorest blood circulation and are the most exposed. When weather is unusually cold or windy, remaining indoors or keeping outside trips short to limit exposure is recommended.

# Head lice

Infestation with head lice (or pediculosis capitis, as it is known medically) has become a relatively common occurrence among school-age children; however, persons in all age groups are susceptible. Sometimes erroneously thought to be an indication of an unsanitary lifestyle, lice infestation can actually afflict anyone, without regard for distinctions of social status or personal hygiene.

### Cause

Head lice are tiny parasites, less than one-eighth inch long. They are grayish-white, almost transparent, six-legged creatures that live exclusively on humans. Lice can be passed easily from one person to another (for example, by using the comb or wearing the hat of an infested person). Head lice live on or close to the scalp, where they bite and

suck blood. Their eggs, which are called nits, are milk-white and about the size of a flake of dandruff.

### Symptoms

Head lice cause itching of the scalp and sometimes a red, scaly rash on the back of the neck at the hairline. Scratching may cause sores on the scalp. The lymph nodes at the base of the skull may be enlarged.

### Diagnosis

Unless hundreds are present, it is difficult to see lice in the hair. However, the nits attached to the shafts of the hairs are usually clearly visible. Although nits are about the same color and size as flakes of dandruff, they can be easily distinguished from dandruff: flakes of dandruff can be blown or brushed away; nits can be removed with the fingernails only with difficulty.

### Treatment

Both prescription and non-prescription medicated shampoos (called pediculicides) are used to combat lice infestations. It is important to remember that these substances can be poisonous if swallowed or absorbed through the skin or if they come in contact with the eyes. Care must be taken to use them exactly as directed and neither more nor less often than recommended. Sometimes a vinegar rinse is recommended to loosen the nits after using the special shampoo. The nits can then be removed with a fine-tooth comb.

If infected sores on the scalp or enlarged lymph nodes at the

base of the skull accompany a lice infestation, this must be called to the attention of a physician.

### Prevention

The best preventive measure is to avoid sharing combs, brushes, towels, and hats with others.

If one member of the family has head lice, it is usually necessary to treat the rest of the family as well (a physician may have special recommendations for infants and pregnant women). Lice cannot be transmitted by pets, however. All combs and hairbrushes should be discarded or thoroughly cleaned in boiling water. Bed linen, hats, and clothing that may have been in contact with an infested person should be cleaned by washing in very hot water.

# Heat rash

Heat rash, or prickly heat, is a mild skin condition that produces an itchy, burning sensation. It is found most often in infants and in overweight persons who have overlapping folds of fat.

### Causes

The sweat glands in the skin normally work along with the blood vessels to regulate the body's heat. When the blood temperature rises, the brain triggers a reflex in the sweat glands to encourage secretion of sweat. Sweating reduces body temperature by releasing sweat to the surface of the skin, where it evaporates and cools the skin. However, when skin surfaces press together, the sweat ducts,

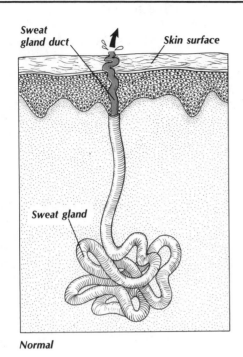

Sweat gland duct

Skin surface

Sweat gland

Normal

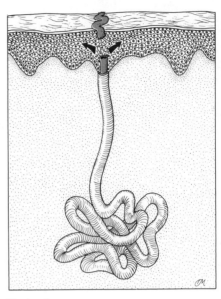

Heat rash

*A sweat gland normally releases sweat through its duct onto the skin surface. When perspiration cannot reach the surface, the sweat may break through the duct wall and become trapped beneath the skin, causing inflammation and a rash.*

which carry secretions from the sweat glands to the skin's surface, become temporarily blocked. If sweat cannot reach the skin's surface, it may break through the duct wall and remain trapped in an inner layer of the skin, where it can cause inflammation and a rash.

Heat rash can result any time the body is unable to perspire adequately. Most often, hot weather or exertion triggers the reaction. Wearing tight clothing or overdressing, even in cold weather, may compound the problem.

Heat rash in infants occurs primarily because their sweat glands are immature and cannot transport large amounts of perspiration to the surface of the skin. The sweat remains trapped within the skin, which causes the characteristic inflammation and irritation.

## Symptoms

Usually, heat rash (known medically as miliaria) appears on moist parts of the body where skin surfaces can touch, such as on the neck, under the arms, and between the legs. An infant can have the rash under a tight-fitting diaper. The rash looks like tiny, pinhead-sized red pimples, and it can cause itching and a prickling or burning sensation.

Heat rash is sometimes confused with a condition called chafing because the symptoms are similar. However, chafing is caused by friction between two skin surfaces rubbing together and not by obstructed sweat ducts. Under extreme conditions, the warm, moist areas where heat rash develops can become breeding grounds for microorganisms that cause secondary infection.

## Treatment and prevention

Treatment and prevention of heat rash involve reducing or eliminating the stimulus for sweating. The affected person needs to stay in a cool environment and refrain from exertion. Cool showers followed by thorough drying can also help, as can wearing light, loose-fitting clothes. Once sweating stops, the rash may disappear in a few hours.

Babies who suffer from heat rash should be bathed in clear water and dried thoroughly. Cloth diapers are more likely to allow the natural evaporation process to occur than are disposable diapers. If discomfort becomes prolonged or extreme, a doctor should be consulted in order to rule out the possibility that some other disorder is causing the symptoms.

# Leukoplakia

Leukoplakia is a tough, fibrous lesion that occurs on a mucous membrane. When it occurs in the mouth, it is often referred to as a smoker's patch or smoker's tongue. Although these oral lesions are generally not painful, they may cause difficulty and discomfort when the person talks or swallows.

### Causes

The oral condition may be caused by badly fitted dentures, excessive smoking, overconsumption of alcohol, or a diet of highly spiced foods. Leukoplakia may also be a symptom of syphilis and may develop into a cancerous growth.

### Symptoms

Leukoplakia most often appears in the form of a white patch on the lips, tongue, or gums or in other areas that are lined by mucous membranes, such as the female genital organs.

### Diagnosis

If a person notices these persistent white patches, a physician should be seen immediately. A biopsy specimen is often obtained because the presence of cancer cannot be determined by merely looking at the lesion.

### Treatment

One should never attempt to self-treat leukoplakia. After a physician has examined the lesion, he may advise having dentures refitted or cutting down on smoking and the consumption of alcohol and excessive amounts of spicy foods. These patches should be examined by a physician frequently, since cancer may develop in the future. In most cases, however, the physician will probably advise that the lesion be entirely removed surgically.

# Mole

A mole is a cluster of cells, usually pigmented (colored), that appears on the skin. Moles are sometimes present at birth, but more often they appear during childhood, adolescence, or pregnancy. Although moles, which are commonplace, can become cancerous, they seldom do.

### Symptoms

Moles vary in size, shape, and color. They may be large or small, flat or raised, smooth or warty. They may be the same color as the skin, or their color may vary from yellow-brown to black. Some moles have one or more hairs in them.

The most common type of mole is the intradermal nevus, which forms in the lower layer of skin. It is a raised cluster of cells that ranges in color from skin-tone to black. Other types of moles include the lentigo nevus (a flat, uniformly pigmented brown or black spot), the junctional nevus (a flat or slightly raised blemish that ranges in color from light brown to nearly black), the compound nevus (a raised mole that is usually dark in color), and the halo nevus (a pigmented mole in the middle of a ring of skin from which the pigment has been lost).

### Treatment

Moles are often removed for cosmetic reasons. However, any mole that enlarges suddenly, becomes darker, begins to bleed, or changes in any other unexplained way should be removed by a physician and examined microscopically.

# Onychogryphosis

Onychogryphosis (or onychogryposis) is unusual growth of the fingernails or toenails, to the extent that they begin to resemble claws or horns.

### Causes

Injuries due to going barefoot or wearing tight shoes are the usual cause of onychogryphosis, but the condition can be hereditary. It may also be related to congestive heart failure, in which there may be a shortage of blood circulation to the feet; peripheral neuritis, which affects nerves in the legs, causing decreased sensation in the feet and thereby increasing the chance that the foot will be injured; dry, scaly skin; hormonal disorders; syphilis; and stroke.

### Symptoms

The nail becomes thick, long, horny or raised, and green or black in color with an opaque surface. This condition occurs most often in toenails, especially on the big toes.

### Treatment

Properly fitting shoes, hot baths, massage with warm oil or

hydrogen peroxide, or treatment of the underlying disease may clear up the condition. Trimming or removal of an abnormal nail should be done only by a physician or podiatrist; serious complications can arise if this is done improperly.

# Onychomycosis

The most common of inflammatory nail disorders, onychomycosis is a fungal infection of the nails that is prevalent among persons with a low resistance to infection (diabetics and patients taking corticosteroid or other hormonal drugs), those who work with their hands in water and are prone to paronychia (inflammation of the skin around the nail), and those with ingrown toenails. Onychomycosis is caused by a number of fungi and is often associated with paronychia.

### Symptoms

The condition is chronic but painless. The affected nails look dull, opaque, and brittle; are marked with grooves or ridges; and appear flaky. The surrounding cuticle may become red, tender, and swollen, and may ooze pus if a bacterial infection accompanies the disorder. The fungi can be identified by examining nail scrapings in the laboratory.

### Treatment

The condition is sometimes treated with griseofulvin, an antifungal drug that can be taken orally or applied topically. However, it may take months to cure. Furthermore, the condition may

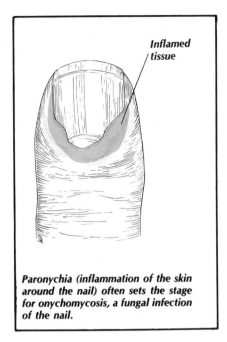

*Paronychia (inflammation of the skin around the nail) often sets the stage for onychomycosis, a fungal infection of the nail.*

never clear up at all, especially if the toenails are affected. Cutting the nails short or having the entire nail removed by a physician can help the healing process.

### Prevention

To prevent onychomycosis, fingernails and toenails should be dried thoroughly after bathing, because fungi thrive in a moist environment. Footwear should be changed often if the feet tend to perspire.

# Photosensitivity

Photosensitivity is an abnormally increased sensitivity of the skin to the rays of the sun.

### Causes

The causes of this condition are not fully understood, although it is known that certain substances, when combined with ultraviolet light, produce

the reaction. Among those substances are contraceptive pills, hexachlorophene (a skin antiseptic), sandalwood oil, coal tar, certain perfumes and soaps, sunscreening agents, and a variety of orally administered drugs, including chlorothiazides, phenothiazines, sulfonamides, and tetracyclines.

### Symptoms

The symptoms of photosensitivity include burning reactions similar to those ordinarily suffered after prolonged exposure to the sun, rashes, scaling, welts (raised areas) on the skin, dizziness, nausea, and vomiting. The most common symptom is a rash.

### Treatment

The most effective treatment is to discover the basic cause of the heightened sensitivity and to eliminate it. If, for example, photosensitivity is a reaction to a contraceptive pill, a different kind of pill or form of contraception could be prescribed. Treatment of photosensitivity symptoms is similar to that used for sunburn: ointments, topical anesthetics, and creams. It should be remembered that these treatments are standard topical therapy for the skin but do not eliminate the underlying causes of photosensitivity.

If it is impossible to isolate the cause of photosensitivity, the next best step is to avoid exposure to sunlight by wearing light-colored clothing, white gloves, and broad-brimmed hats. Commercial sunscreen products are also helpful. Obviously, contact with the substances already listed should be avoided.

# Psoriasis

Psoriasis is a persistent skin disease characterized by thick, red eruptions, often covered by silvery scales, either in small patches or over large areas of the body. Psoriasis is fairly common, affecting 1 percent to 2 percent of the population. The condition often first appears between the ages of 15 and 30 years and usually requires life-long treatment.

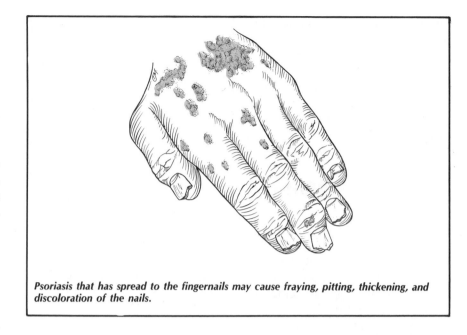

*Psoriasis that has spread to the fingernails may cause fraying, pitting, thickening, and discoloration of the nails.*

## Cause

Psoriasis is not contagious. The cause of psoriasis is unknown, but researchers believe that the condition is related to a malfunction in the process of skin growth and regeneration (cell replacement). With normal skin, old cells are continuously being shed from the epidermis and replaced by new cells formed in the deeper layers. Cells live for about one month before they die and flake off. With psoriasis, the rate of cell growth accelerates. Skin cells may move to the surface and die in as short a time as four or five days. Increased cell growth causes buildup that can be extremely dry and irritating. The normal shedding process is usually unnoticeable, but psoriasis can produce very obvious blemishes.

Psoriasis seems to involve a strong hereditary factor although only one-third of its victims can recall having a relative with the disease. There seems to be some relationship between the condition and a certain type of arthritis as well.

Once psoriasis develops, outbreaks of the disorder can be triggered in several ways. Injury to the skin, such as a cut or burn, may provoke a flare-up, usually 8 to 18 days after the trauma. Seasonal changes may also affect psoriasis, with the disease worsening during winter months. Many patients have greater problems during periods of physical and emotional stress. Infections, particularly upper respiratory tract infections, may aggravate psoriasis.

## Symptoms

Psoriasis is characterized by reddened, raised patches of skin with silvery scales called plaques. These clearly defined plaques appear most commonly on the elbows, knees, trunk, and scalp, although the underarm and genital areas may also be involved. Patches on the scalp shed large, silver-white scales at the hairline that resemble severe dandruff. Those patches found in moist areas, such as the underarms, are usually less scaly and less red. All patches may itch. If fingernails are involved, they may be pitted, frayed, thickened, or discolored; in more advanced cases, the nails may be separated from the nail beds.

Usually, psoriasis produces no general health problems. Sometimes, however, the disease becomes so severe that chills, painful reddening of the skin, cracking of the skin around the joints, and shedding of large areas of scaled skin result. This condition, called exfoliative psoriasis, may necessitate hospitalization for intensive therapy.

## Treatment

As yet, there is no known cure for psoriasis, and treatment offers only temporary relief from symptoms. Normal cleaning of the skin around the affected areas is important to prevent infection. Over-the-counter lotions and creams can cleanse irritated skin and reduce itching as well. These preparations often contain small amounts of coal tar and other ingredients designed to remove scales. If the skin becomes sensitive after application, use of these preparations should be discontinued. Many patients find regular and controlled exposure to sunlight helpful. Where sunlight is scarce, a special sunlamp may be used, but only under a doctor's supervision.

Various drugs have recently been shown to be effective in relieving the symptoms of psoriasis. Cortisone and newer steroids (hormonally based medications) can clear plaques in about 50 percent of the cases when applied directly to the affected skin. Many physicians recommend covering the treated areas with a thin plastic wrapping in addition to the cream. This is called occlusive therapy.

Some drugs slow the growth rate of cells. The most commonly used of these drugs, methotrexate, reduces symptoms in severe cases. Because its side effects may be severe, however, the drug is prescribed for use only under the close supervision of a physician.

Another form of treatment is called PUVA therapy, which combines medication and ultraviolet light treatments. The benefits of this form of therapy should be carefully weighed against the premature skin aging and skin cancer that it may cause.

# Purpura

The term purpura refers to a group of bleeding disorders that are all characterized by purplish or brownish-red discolorations, easily visible through the skin's outer layer, that are caused by hemorrhaging (internal bleeding) into the tissues.

## Common purpura

Common purpura (also called simple purpura or senile pur-

pura) is the most widespread of such disorders and is marked by easy bruising and increased blood vessel fragility. It is an inherited condition that occurs mostly in women, particularly following menopause. The condition often affects thigh tissue and produces large bruises rather than hemorrhages. The bleeding is usually under the skin and may be intensified by surgery or injury.

## Henoch-Schönlein purpura

Henoch-Schönlein purpura (also known as allergic purpura and anaphylactoid purpura) most often affects children. The condition may be associated with arthritis, gastrointestinal disorders, kidney failure, and erythema (redness of the skin).

## Purpura fulminans

Purpura fulminans is most often seen in children, mainly after an infectious disease. It is

marked by fever, shock (dangerous, sudden lowering of blood pressure), anemia, and rapidly spreading symmetrical skin hemorrhages in the lower limbs, as well as by intravascular thrombosis (blockage of a blood vessel by a solid mass) and gangrene.

## Thrombocytopenic purpura

Thrombocytopenic purpura is a disorder in which the number of platelets (the tiny elements in the blood that are vital to clotting) is decreased, whether because of a primary disease or as a consequence of another blood disorder. This form of purpura is characterized by anemia, side effects in the nervous system, and blood clots in tiny blood vessels.

## Causes

Causes vary with the type of purpura. Common purpura in postmenopausal women appears

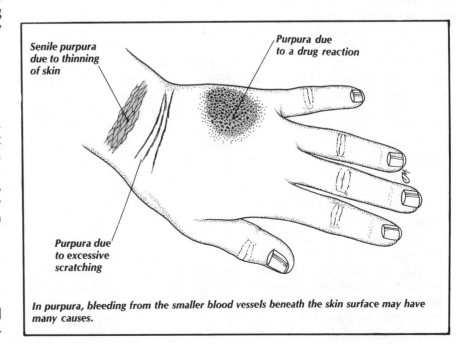

*Senile purpura due to thinning of skin*

*Purpura due to a drug reaction*

*Purpura due to excessive scratching*

*In purpura, bleeding from the smaller blood vessels beneath the skin surface may have many causes.*

to result from decreased estrogen (female hormone) levels and thinning of the deep layers of the skin. Henoch-Schönlein purpura may result from the development of sensitivities following an infection or allergic reaction. Purpura in the elderly is often due to the fragility of their skin. There are also temporary forms of purpura in which vascular bleeding occurs as a result of fever, hypothyroidism (a condition characterized by low output of thyroid hormone), generalized illness, defects in the small blood vessels, or a drug reaction to certain medications, such as aspirin. Purpura can sometimes stem from wearing overly tight clothing or from sustaining an injury, such as a black eye.

### Diagnosis

Laboratory testing is essential in all cases of possible purpura in order to exclude other causes. Perhaps the most difficult of the forms of purpura to diagnose is Henoch-Schönlein purpura. Joint pain and bouts of abdominal pain in this disorder may mimic acute abdominal conditions or forms of arthritis. Later, kidney involvement during the course of this form of purpura may cause a misdiagnosis of kidney disease.

### Treatment

In the case of allergic purpura, it is advisable to eliminate the possible allergic cause. Corticosteroid medications (artificial hormones) are often prescribed, but may produce disappointing results. Immunosuppressive therapy (suppression of the immune system by means of drugs) is sometimes useful. If the purpura is thrombocytopenic, the spleen (an abdominal organ that is a component of the circulatory system) may be removed if it is hoarding too many platelets. Milder cases of purpura often improve spontaneously.

### Prevention

Estrogen therapy has proved helpful in preventing or relieving common purpura in postmenopausal women. Other than preventive measures to avoid infections or allergic reactions, there is little that can be done to prevent purpura.

# Ringworm

Ringworm is a skin infection caused by a fungus, not a worm. The name originated because the infection is often characterized by round patches that enlarge as healing proceeds from the center, leaving red rings that persist on the skin for a few months.

### Types

There are several different types of ringworm, each caused by a different type of fungus. Ringworm of the scalp, or *tinea capitis,* appears as scaly patches with stubs of broken-off hairs or as bald areas. Ringworm of the body, or *tinea corporis,* appears as round or oval, scaly, red patches on the torso. Ringworm of the groin, or *tinea cruris* (popularly referred to as "jock itch"), is characterized by a scaly, red or brown rash on the crotch and the genital area. Ringworm of the feet, or *tinea pedis,* is more commonly called athlete's foot (for more information on athlete's foot, see page 111).

### Cause

Ringworm spreads by direct contact with an infected person or pet or by contact with contaminated objects, such as combs, pillows, towels, and clothing. Tight-fitting clothing, obesity, and heavy perspiration may be contributing factors in the development of ringworm of the body and the groin.

### Diagnosis

Ringworm infections are generally unsightly rather than threatening to general health. However, several other skin infections resemble ringworm, so it is important that a physician make the diagnosis. The doctor may want to examine the rash under ultraviolet light and obtain a skin scraping to be examined microscopically.

### Treatment

An antifungal ointment to be applied to the skin may be prescribed for ringworm of the body or the groin. Special medicated shampoos are available to treat ringworm of the scalp. In some especially resistant cases, an oral medication called griseofulvin may be necessary as well.

### Prevention

To prevent spread of the infection, personal articles that have been in contact with infected areas, such as hats, combs, and bed linen, should be discarded or laundered in very hot water.

# Sunburn

Sunburn is an inflammation of the cells of the skin caused by overexposure to the ultraviolet radiation of the sun or a sunlamp. Damage to the skin can be either insignificant or serious, depending on the intensity of the light source, the length of exposure, and the sensitivity of the individual to ultraviolet radiation.

### Causes

Sunburn is caused by overexposure to ultraviolet radiation. Certain substances (such as deodorants, soaps, perfumes, cosmetics, and certain medications) may produce heightened sensitivity to ultraviolet radiation, with a corresponding increase in the severity of the burn. While light-skinned people usually burn more easily than swarthy or dark-skinned people, skin color is not always a dependable guide to individual susceptibility.

### Symptoms

Irritation of the skin and a prickling sensation mark the onset of sunburn; the skin also feels hot to the touch. Capillaries (tiny blood vessels) in the skin become congested because of the release of certain inflammatory agents, thus producing the characteristic redness. Oral contraceptive users may develop irregularly shaped dark splotches, and some sensitive individuals may have allergic reactions in the form of rashes or welts.

As the burn progresses in severity, the skin will feel tight, swollen, and dry or brittle, and may become hypersensitive to touch. Overheating and loss of fluids through the damaged skin may also produce dizziness, nausea, vomiting, hyperventilation (rapid breathing, which causes excessive loss of carbon dioxide from the blood), impaired vision and hearing, irregular heartbeat, and loss of consciousness.

The aftermath of severe sunburn often includes blistering and peeling, as well as permanent freckling, splotching, or scarring of the skin. Long-term effects may include premature skin aging, marked by chronic dryness, wrinkling, leathery texture, and loss of elasticity. In some cases, melanoma (a form of skin cancer) may be induced by chronic overexposure to sunlight.

### Treatment

Minor sunburn can be effectively treated by a wide variety of nonprescription ointments, oils, powders, creams, and sprays that restore fluids and prevent further drying, relieve discomfort, and promote healing. Many over-the-counter medications contain mild anesthetics to relieve stinging and suppress the desire to scratch itching areas. One of the most common complications is the infection of blistered and peeling areas of the skin. This condition should be treated by a physician.

In the case of severe sunburn, overheating and dehydration (loss of too much fluid) must be avoided. The victim should be taken out of the sun immediately and placed in a cool, shaded area until medical attention can be obtained. Cool (but not cold), wet cloths can be applied to the arms, the head, and the legs. Chills should be avoided. Ice water and other cold drinks may trigger unwanted responses. If the victim is perspiring profusely, a fan may help evaporate the water on the skin's surface, thus aiding a natural cooling process.

### Prevention

The best prevention of sunburn is simply to avoid prolonged exposure to the direct rays of the sun or a sunlamp. When this is not possible, the first line of defense is to cover the skin completely, preferably with loose-fitting, light-colored clothes made of loose-weave fabrics. Wearing a wide-brimmed hat will also help.

The second line of defense is a sunscreen, available as an oil, cream, paste, or liquid. Most sunscreens are intended to block ultraviolet rays. Many contain para-aminobenzoic acid. This compound may affect some individuals adversely, particularly those with photosensitivity (abnormal sensitivity of the skin to light) who are taking certain drugs. For these people, opaque (light-blocking) creams, pastes, and lotions are available, as well as other chemical sunscreens known as benzophenones. Anyone who is uncertain about a possible interaction between sunlight and a medication that has been prescribed should contact his doctor before exposure to sunlight.

# Warts

Warts are infectious growths in the outer layers of the skin. Because they are contagious, they can spread from person to person or from one site to another on the same person. Most frequently, warts appear on the hands and fingers and on the soles of the feet. However, they can emerge anywhere on the skin, including the genital and anal areas.

### Causes

Common warts are caused by exposure to a virus called the human papilloma virus. The virus can remain inactive for up to six months after contact before causing the eruption of abnormal skin masses.

The virus is transmitted to another person or another site on the body by direct contact. For example, brushing or combing the hair can spread the virus from a wart on the scalp. Shaving or scratching a given area on the body and then touching another area will also transmit the virus. In addition, moist parts of the body, such as the soles of the feet, provide a breeding ground for growth of the virus.

As people become older, they seem to develop an immunity or resistance to the wart virus. For this reason, children tend to acquire warts more frequently than adults. Nevertheless, warts can occur at any age.

### Symptoms

Usually, warts appear as firm gray masses that feel tender or itchy. Their size and shape vary depending on the location and severity of the viral infection. Children are most likely to have flat warts, particularly on the face. This variety looks smooth, flat, and yellowish brown.

Plantar warts grow on the soles of the feet, where they can become as large as two inches in diameter. These warts cause considerable pain because the

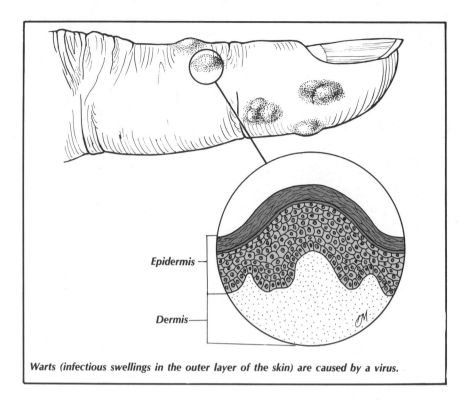

*Epidermis*

*Dermis*

*Warts (infectious swellings in the outer layer of the skin) are caused by a virus.*

tissue swelling pushes inward with the pressure of each step; the discomfort from plantar warts feels like walking with a pebble in your shoe.

Most warts are not health-threatening. However, they can be so extensive in number as to cause extreme sensitivity or pain.

### Treatment

Studies have shown that two out of every three warts disappear on their own within two years. Consequently, physicians usually recommend leaving warts alone unless they cause discomfort or obstruction.

Doctors sometimes treat one or two warts and find that other warts on the same person also clear up. A possible explanation is that the original treatment stimulates manufacture of antibodies (protective substances) that fight the virus in other warts.

There are over-the-counter preparations to aid removal of warts. Most of these remedies contain a form of acid, which is dangerous if not used according to directions. Although some of these drugs are effective, only a doctor should remove a wart.

Physicians may try a variety of topical preparations to loosen the warts. A solution containing cantharidin, a substance that causes blistering, may be applied directly to the wart. About one week after application, the doctor should be able to remove the wart with a surgical knife or scissors. Corn plasters containing salicylic acid soften the wart so that it can be scraped away.

When a wart persists, physicians may advise surgery to remove affected tissue. Electrosurgery dissolves wart tissue with electric current. Cryotherapy freezes the area with dry ice or liquid nitrogen; freezing allows the wart to be lifted off easily.

# BONES AND MUSCLES

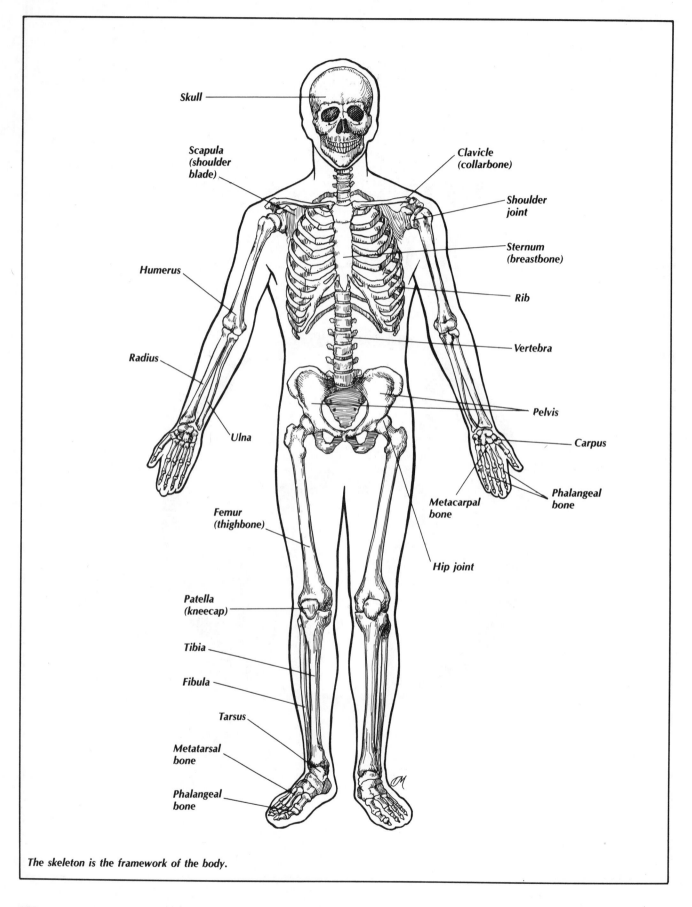

Skull

Scapula
(shoulder
blade)

Clavicle
(collarbone)

Shoulder
joint

Sternum
(breastbone)

Humerus

Rib

Radius

Vertebra

Ulna

Pelvis

Carpus

Metacarpal
bone

Phalangeal
bone

Femur
(thighbone)

Hip joint

Patella
(kneecap)

Tibia

Fibula

Tarsus

Metatarsal
bone

Phalangeal
bone

*The skeleton is the framework of the body.*

The musculoskeletal system is an intricate structure of interconnecting parts. Every movement of the body is the result of the coordination of the bones and muscles, as well as the tendons and ligaments.

## Bones

Bones are hardened masses of living tissue that have several functions. They collect calcium for the entire body, storing 99 percent of this mineral, which is required to keep all bones firm and strong. Within some bones is a substance called marrow, which produces red and white blood cells and platelets.

There are 206 bones in the skeleton, or framework, of the body. The skeleton maintains the body's shape and protects internal organs from injury. For example, the bones in the skull shield the brain, and the bones in the rib cage encircle the lungs and heart.

The place where two or more bones meet is called a joint. This juncture usually allows movement of the bones that are involved. However, movement is governed by ligaments (bands of fibrous tissue) attached to the bones and cartilage (elastic tissue) covering the ends of the bones. Ligaments connect one bone with another. Cartilage cushions and protects bones with the aid of various joint fluids and bursae (small sacs containing lubricating fluid that encompass the joints). Other bands of connective tissue called tendons attach bones to muscles. Muscles are specific kinds of tissues that have the ability to contract. It is this contraction that pulls on the tendons and makes movement possible. In order to move any part of the skeleton, coordination of ligaments, tendons, and muscles is necessary.

## Muscles

There are three types of muscles: striated, smooth, and cardiac. Striated, or striped, muscle consists of layers of tissue divided into bundles of interwoven fibers that run parallel to one another. These layers are attached to the skeleton, and they aid the body in voluntary movement.

Smooth, or organic, muscle is present in several of the internal organs, including the intestines and the bladder, and in the larger blood vessels. This type of muscle functions under involuntary control by the autonomic nervous system. Among its various functions, smooth muscle helps circulate blood and glandular secretions throughout the body, move material through the digestive tract, and regulate breathing. Smooth muscle contains elongated, spindly cells arranged parallel to one another, and grouped into bundles.

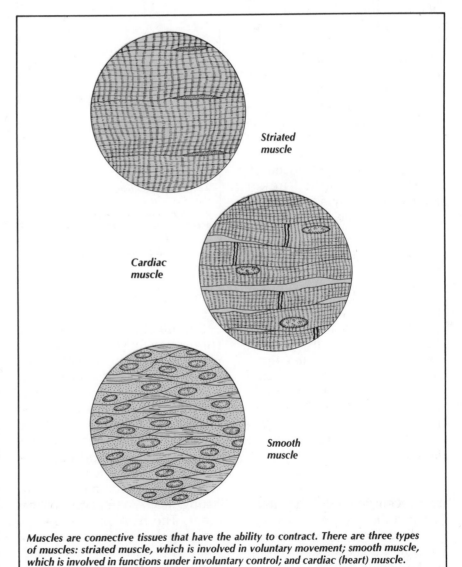

*Muscles are connective tissues that have the ability to contract. There are three types of muscles: striated muscle, which is involved in voluntary movement; smooth muscle, which is involved in functions under involuntary control; and cardiac (heart) muscle.*

Cardiac muscle is the muscle of the heart, and its job is to pump blood within and from the heart. The unique characteristic of this muscle is that although it is striated (like the muscles of the skeleton), it is controlled by the autonomic nervous system (like the muscles of the internal organs).

# Ankylosing spondylitis

Ankylosing spondylitis is a form of arthritis, mainly affecting the sacroiliac joints, the spine, and nearby structures. Joints become inflamed and eventually stiff and immovable. The elastic cartilage disks between the vertebrae (bones of the spine) become dense, as does adjacent connective tissue, and bony connections between the vertebrae are formed. The lower vertebrae may become fused together, creating a straight "poker spine," frequently accompanied by a curve in the upper spine.

### Cause

The cause of ankylosing spondylitis is unknown, but there appears to be an inherited tendency toward the disease. The disease affects men ten times more often than women, and many are born with a certain trait, called HLA-B27, in their blood. Persons carrying this trait are more likely to suffer the disease.

Ankylosing spondylitis is predominantly a disease of young men, occurring most commonly between the ages of 15 and 40. The disease may progress slowly for 10 to 20 years and then stop or slow down.

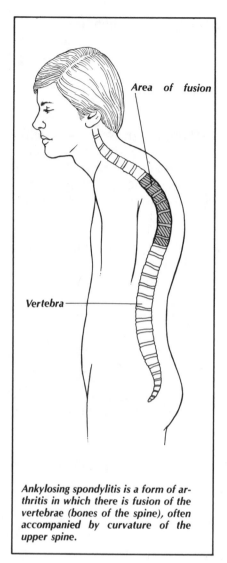

*Ankylosing spondylitis is a form of arthritis in which there is fusion of the vertebrae (bones of the spine), often accompanied by curvature of the upper spine.*

### Symptoms

Chronic low back pain and stiffness in a young man is a chief sign of the disease; hip pain is also quite common, as is an inflammation of the eye known as anterior uveitis. Symptoms begin gradually, usually as low backaches. There may be morning stiffness and pain extending down the leg along the sciatic nerve, commonly alternating from one side to the other. The back pain and stiffness eventually affect the upper spine and sometimes the neck. In up to a third of the cases,

large joints (such as those of the hips and shoulders) are affected. Knees and other smaller joints are affected less often, with symptoms matching those of rheumatoid arthritis. The heart is affected in up to 3 percent of cases (after many years of disease), and inflammation of the lining of the eye occurs in about 25 percent of the cases. As the disease progresses, it is more difficult for the patient to flex the back and expand the chest, and neck movements may be limited. X-rays of the back-related joints—especially those between the upper portion of the hip bone and the sacrum (the bony structure at the base of the spine)—reveal changes typical of ankylosing spondylitis. A sign of advanced disease is "bamboo spine," in which bony bands around the disks cement the vertebrae together.

### Treatment

Although there is no cure for ankylosing spondylitis, certain measures can lessen the effects of the disease. These include rest, breathing exercises, and exercises to maintain posture, to help with curvature of the upper spine, and to keep the back as flexible as possible. To prevent curvature of the upper spine, sleeping on the back on a firm mattress with a small pillow or with no pillow is advised. Locking the fingers behind the head and pushing the elbows back as far as possible is a good way to straighten the upper back and stretch the chest muscles. Painkillers and anti-inflammatory drugs may be given. Corticosteroid drugs are generally not prescribed because of their many side effects. Surgery is rarely needed.

# Arthritis

Arthritis is an inflammation of the joints (the junctures where the ends of two or more bones meet).

## Types

Inflammation develops in one of two ways. With *osteoarthritis,* there is gradual wearing away of cartilage in the joints. Healthy cartilage is the elastic tissue that lines and cushions the joints and allows bones to move smoothly against one another. When this cartilage deteriorates, the bones rub together, causing pain and swelling. Permanent damage and stiffness of the joints are possible. Although osteoarthritis can result from direct injury to the joint, it commonly occurs in adults over the age of 55, because of long-term wear and tear on the joints.

*Rheumatoid arthritis* can attack at any age. This form of arthritis affects all the connective tissues in the body. The precise cause of rheumatoid arthritis is unknown. Some researchers believe that a virus triggers the disease, causing an autoimmune response whereby the body develops an allergy to its own tissues. However, evidence for this theory is inconclusive as yet. What is confirmed is the progression of the condition. First, the synovium (the thin membrane lining and lubricating the joint) becomes inflamed. The inflammation eventually destroys the cartilage. As scar tissue gradually replaces the damaged cartilage, the joint becomes misshapen and rigid.

If left untreated, rheumatoid arthritis may damage the heart, lungs, nerves, and eyes. Osteoarthritis can cause permanent

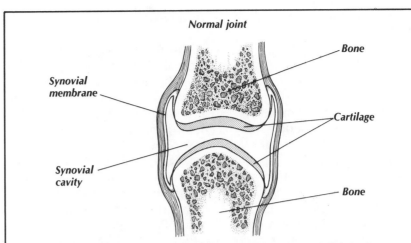

*Normal joint*

The normal joint is lined by a synovial membrane, which produces the lubricating synovial fluid that fills the synovial cavity. The bone ends are covered by cartilage.

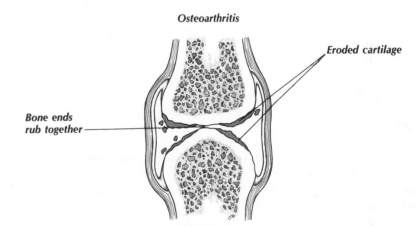

*Osteoarthritis*

In osteoarthritis, the cushioning cartilage at the bone ends is eroded (worn away), allowing the bone ends to rub together, which causes swelling and pain.

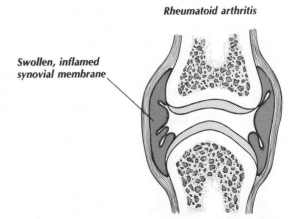

*Rheumatoid arthritis*

Rheumatoid arthritis is characterized by swelling and inflammation of the synovial membrane.

damage and stiffness of the joints.

### Those at risk

Arthritis is not an inherited disease. Nonetheless, people who have a family history of arthritis are more likely to develop the disease. Women are at greater risk than men, although the reason for this is unclear. Excess body weight may promote osteoarthritis because of increased load on the joints. Constant sports- or job-related joint abuse may encourage arthritis, but inactivity can also cause the problem.

### Symptoms

Symptoms of arthritis include swelling, tenderness, pain, stiffness, and redness in one or more joints. For many patients, pain is greatest in the morning and subsides as the day progresses. Damp weather and emotional stress do not cause arthritis, but they can make symptoms worse.

With rheumatoid arthritis, these symptoms may be accompanied by more generalized feelings of fatigue and fever. This form of arthritis may go into periods of remission, when symptoms disappear. When symptoms return, however, they are often more severe.

### Diagnosis

To diagnose arthritis, a physician observes the symptoms and administers a standard physical examination. X-ray studies and laboratory tests may be recommended for confirmation of joint swelling and determination of the extent of damage.

### Treatment

The most effective treatment program for arthritis consists of drug therapy, exercise, and rest. Treatment should begin early after diagnosis to prevent permanent damage.

Aspirin is the drug most commonly administered for arthritis. Taking two or three tablets several times a day is often recommended to reduce inflammation and relieve pain. If stomach irritation is a problem, aspirin may be taken after meals or in a coated-tablet form. Nonaspirin pain-relievers and nonsteroidal anti-inflammatory drugs (such as ibuprofen, naproxen, tolmetin, and sulindac) may also be prescribed. Corticosteroids relieve inflammation, but they can cause adverse side effects. Sometimes, a doctor needs to try several different drugs before finding an effective one that produces few side effects.

Moderate daily exercise, such as swimming, walking, or physical therapy, is critical to maintaining mobility in arthritic joints. A supervised exercise program interspersed with rest periods helps to reduce joint inflammation. To lessen pain while increasing movement, moist heat often helps. In addition, maintaining correct posture and body weight reduces the burden on sore joints.

Some severe cases of rheumatoid arthritis may require surgery to remove inflamed synovial tissue. With either form of arthritis, artificial joints may be implanted to replace those damaged beyond repair.

# Backache

A backache is generally a gripping pain near the inward curve

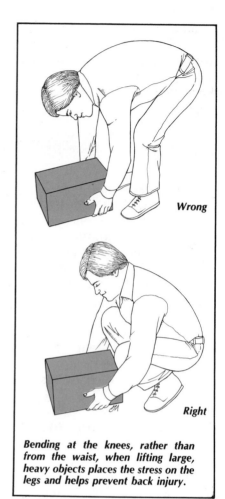

*Wrong*

*Right*

*Bending at the knees, rather than from the waist, when lifting large, heavy objects places the stress on the legs and helps prevent back injury.*

of the back above the base of the spine. It is one of the most common physical ailments, affecting about 80 percent of the population at some time in their lives.

### Causes

Pain results from a variety of causes. Strains are especially common when overworked or underexercised back muscles perform beyond their normal capacity. The muscles will then contract or go into spasm and become a tight mass of tissue. Meanwhile, the body transmits a sharp pain signal as nearby muscles tighten in an effort to protect strained muscles and prevent further damage. Strain of back muscles can be due to participation in a sport, a sudden jerking motion (such as a car braking), or reflex actions like sneezing.

Overweight is a leading factor in backache because it increases the stress on back muscles. Similarly, pregnancy can produce back pain because of the weight or position of the fetus. For some women, menstruation is also associated with back discomfort.

Many people experience back pain as they age and their joint tissues deteriorate or shift. Psychological tension, stress, or anxiety about everyday problems can also lead to backache. In addition, back pain can result from diseases of the kidneys, heart, lungs, intestinal tract, or reproductive organs.

Backache occasionally stems from a congenital (present from birth) malformation. In such cases, pain generally results from the unusual stresses that the deformity imposes on surrounding muscular structures rather than from the abnormality itself. For example, if one leg is shorter than the other, the muscles in the lower part of the body are forced out of alignment, causing back pain.

### Symptoms

Backaches can appear abruptly after physical activity or may develop slowly. The pain may feel like a sharp jab or a dull ache. The pain sometimes becomes so piercing that a person who is bending over may not be able to straighten up. Severe back pain may also be accompanied by pain or numbness radiating down one or both legs. Most muscular back pains disappear within a week or two of their onset, while some will last one to two months. Pain may recur unless preventive measures are taken.

### Diagnosis

Prolonged back pain (lasting for more than one or two weeks) should be brought to the attention of a physician, who will check for underlying disorders, such as kidney or lung problems, that may be causing the backache. Once other medical causes have been ruled out, an orthopedic surgeon (a physician who specializes in bone and muscle conditions) may be able to determine the cause of the discomfort.

During the examination, the physician asks questions about the type of pain and its location, general health, previous illnesses, and physical activity routines. The patient walks, sits, stands, and performs exercises while being observed. An x-ray study may reveal adverse changes in the spine.

### Treatment

If there are no apparent physical causes for the backache, physicians usually recommend an exercise program to strengthen weak muscles. Losing weight can also relieve the pressure on the back.

For immediate treatment of symptoms, using a heating pad at the site of the pain will usually reduce soreness. Nonprescription analgesic creams containing methyl salicylate (oil of wintergreen) or a similar ingredient may produce a soothing warm sensation when applied to the pain site. Muscle-relaxant drugs may also be prescribed.

When backache is the result of some deformity, surgery may be necessary to correct the problem. Braces, corsets, or shoe lifts sometimes improve the condition. Exercises to strengthen affected muscles and counter stress may be prescribed.

Almost all types of musculoskeletal backaches respond well to complete bed rest, which allows muscles to relax and inflammation to subside. Time is often the best healer.

### Prevention

To prevent back pain, stress to the spine should be avoided. Good posture, when awake and asleep, relieves tension on the spinal column. Wearing properly fitted shoes encourages good posture, as does sleeping on a semifirm bed. Contrary to popular belief, a hard mattress distorts the alignment of the spine and causes back problems as much as a soft mattress does. A semifirm mattress is recommended because it conforms to the arch of the back and maintains spinal alignment.

Good posture is also important when performing daily activities. Bending at the knees, rather than from the waist, when lifting large, heavy objects places the stress on the legs and helps prevent back injury. One should avoid looking down for long periods of time while seated at a desk, as well as watching television with the chin on the chest.

# Bunion

A bunion is a swelling on the foot, usually at the joint of the big toe. Often, a bony protuberance is present at the joint of the big toe, which gives the bunion its bulging appearance.

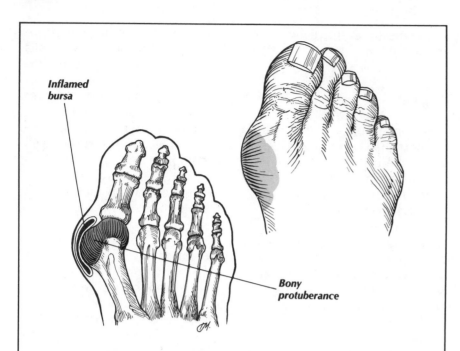

**Inflamed bursa**

**Bony protuberance**

*A bunion is a swelling on the foot, usually at the joint of the big toe. Often, a bony protuberance is present at the joint of the big toe, and there is inflammation of the bursa (the fluid-filled sac that acts as a cushion for the joint). A bunion is most often caused by friction or pressure on the joint.*

### Causes

Bunions are most often caused by wearing poorly fitting footwear, but they can also be the result of inherited deformities in bone structure. In a normal foot, the two main bones of the big toe must align to fit together. However, some people have loose joints in the foot that allow their big toes to point toward the other foot. This inherited condition causes problems when footwear encloses the foot. The shoe forces the big toe inward and the big-toe joint outward so that the joint rubs against the inner surface of the shoe. Friction from such rubbing produces a bunion. The same action results when a pointed-toe or tight shoe puts pressure on the joint—regardless of whether the person has the predisposing inherited tendency to have large joints in the foot.

### Symptoms

A bunion is characterized by swelling at the big-toe joint, which may be accompanied by pain and tenderness. Bunion formations can be acute or chronic. Acute bunions are a type of bursitis, which is an inflammation of a bursa (a fluid-filled sac that cushions the juncture where two or more bones meet). With an acute bunion, the bursa covering the big-toe joint becomes inflamed from friction at the joint, often producing considerable pain. Chronic (long-term) bunions develop into inflexible bony protrusions.

### Complications

Complications can occur if the bunion grows and increases pressure on the big toe. This pressure may force the other toes

to overlap, encouraging the development of corns (mounds of dead skin found on toes) or other problems that could result from friction on the skin of the distorted toes.

### Diagnosis

A physician diagnoses a bunion by general physical examination. To identify bone problems, an x-ray examination may be necessary.

### Treatment

Surgery is the only permanent cure for bunions. It can entail simple removal of the excess bone or more complex realignment of the affected bones, muscles, and tendons. A doctor can sometimes remove a bony protrusion in the office. Local anesthetic can be used, the incision is often only about an inch long, and pain is minimal. With this treatment, the patient has full use of the foot in about six weeks.

For more extensive surgery, the patient is admitted to the hospital, and recuperation time is longer. Usually, an orthopedic surgeon performs this type of surgery.

Nonsurgical devices can often relieve the pain and discomfort of bunions. Padding can be used to shift the weight of the foot in the shoe, lessening friction. Protective shields can also prevent contact between the bunion and the inside of the shoe.

### Prevention

Wearing properly fitting footwear is the best preventive measure. Even a child's first shoes should have a sturdy sole and be wide enough to accommodate all the toes without cramping, since early childhood is when most foot problems begin.

When buying shoes, the width and length of each foot need to be measured separately. If one foot is larger than the other, the shoe size should correspond to the size of the larger foot. A one-inch gap between the big toe and the tip of the shoe allows enough space for movement. Even more room is needed with pointed-toe shoes. Shoes should be comfortable from the first wearing—no breaking-in period should be necessary. Women who wear stylish high-heel or pointed-toe shoes may be damaging their feet. Heels about one inch in height are actually best for feet. However, if higher heels are chosen, open-toe styles cause fewer problems.

# Bursitis

Bursitis is an inflammation of a bursa (a fluid-filled sac that cush-ions the juncture of two or more bones). Bursae (the plural of bursa) contain lubricating fluid that normally eliminates friction in the area and maintains smooth muscle movement over the bones.

Bursitis seems to be more common in men than in women, possibly because of greater phys-ical activity. Continual stress on a particular joint increases the probability of injury and inflam-mation. In advanced cases, swelling and calcium deposits within a joint may render it im-mobile.

## Causes

The inflammation can result from either sudden extreme pres-sure or from continual strain. Some occupations and sports that require constant use of cer-tain joints contribute to acute or chronic bursitis. For example, "typist's shoulder" and "base-ball pitcher's elbow" are forms of chronic bursitis. Acute bursitis can develop suddenly and may be triggered by physical stress or injury.

## Symptoms

Inflamed bursae produce ten-derness and swelling near the af-fected joint. Pain from bursitis can be so severe that movement becomes impossible. Any joint in the body can be the site of bursitis, but shoulders, knees, and elbows are most commonly affected.

## Diagnosis

To diagnose bursitis, an x-ray examination may be ordered to determine whether there are cal-cium deposits in the bursa. In the case of stress-related bursitis, however, such a study will show only swelling of the bursa.

## Treatment

Acute bursitis may heal with time if the joint is immobilized.

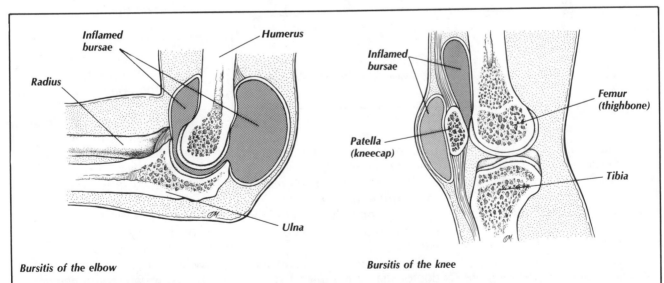

Bursitis of the elbow

Bursitis of the knee

*Bursitis is an inflammation of a bursa (a fluid-filled sac that cushions the juncture of two or more bones). Bursae (the plural of bursa) contain lubricating fluid that normally eliminates friction and maintains smooth muscle movement over the bones. The elbow and the knee are common sites of bursitis.*

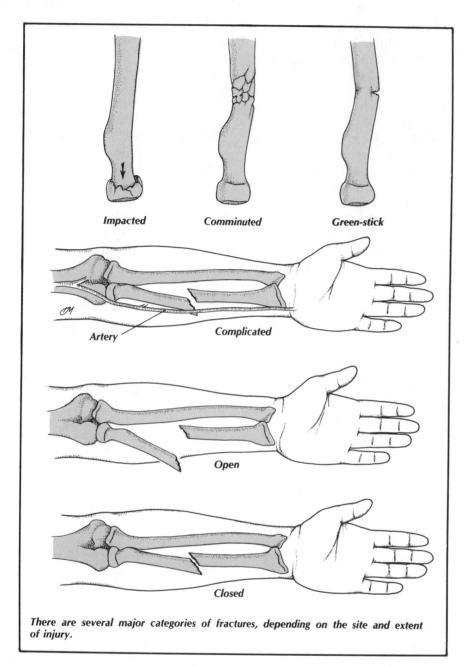

Impacted    Comminuted    Green-stick

Artery    Complicated

Open

Closed

*There are several major categories of fractures, depending on the site and extent of injury.*

tion by removing all or part of the bursa.

# Fracture

A fracture is a break in a bone or a cartilage. Among the possible consequences of a fracture are infection and damage to nearby nerves, blood vessels, and internal organs.

### Causes

Most often, fractures are caused by direct stress, such as a blow from a heavy object, or a severe strain, such as a violent twist. They can, however, be the result of an indirect cause. A fall on a hand, for example, may result in a fracture of the collarbone. There are also pathological fractures, in which disease softens the bone, making it vulnerable to a break.

### Types

There are many different types of fractures, among them the following:
- Closed fracture—one in which the skin is not broken
- Comminuted fracture—one in which the bone is broken into several pieces
- Complicated fracture—one in which significant injury has been done to internal organs, blood vessels, or nerves
- Green-stick fracture—one in which only one side of the bone is broken and the bone is not severed
- Impacted fracture—one in which the ends or fragments of bone are jammed together
- Open fracture—one in which one or more of the broken ends of the bone pierce the skin

Complete bed rest or use of a sling or crutches may be recommended to relieve pressure on the affected area.

Applying moist heat to the area of the inflamed joint frequently reduces the discomfort of bursitis, although some patients find cold compresses more effective. Aspirin and other over-the-counter pain relievers may also help. In some cases, anti-inflammatory corticosteroid medications may be injected directly into the inflamed area, but these drugs must be used judiciously since they have been known to cause adverse side effects.

For severe cases of bursitis, a doctor may recommend surgery by an orthopedic surgeon to remove calcium deposits or free the area from chronic inflamma-

## Those at risk

Fractures are common among children and the elderly. Children have relatively soft, elastic bones; breaks in their bones are often incomplete, that is, they may be on only one side of the bone. Elderly persons have brittle bones that tend to break easily; hip fractures are particularly common.

## Symptoms

Among the symptoms of a fracture are pain, swelling, loss of strength, abnormal movement, and a grating sound when the broken pieces of bone rub together. Shock may occur with a severe fracture if large amounts of blood have been lost.

## Treatment

Bone fractures are treated by closed (nonsurgical) or open (surgical) reduction. Reduction is a procedure in which the broken bone is manipulated (for example, by pulling or bending) so that its ends will be in the best position for healing. Most fractures are treated through closed reduction. However, open reduction may be necessary when damage to bones, joints, ligaments, tendons, or other internal parts is severe or extensive. In open reduction, the pieces of bone are often held together by pins, metal plates, or rods; some are left in the body, and others are removed after healing has taken place.

# Gout

Gout is a form of recurrent acute arthritis. Most gout victims are

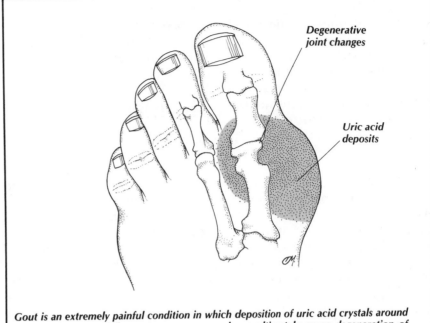

*Gout is an extremely painful condition in which deposition of uric acid crystals around a joint triggers an inflammatory response and can ultimately cause degeneration of the bone.*

middle-aged men. It usually appears in women only after menopause.

## Cause

The underlying cause of gout is a defect in the body's processing of uric acid, a chemical normally found in the blood and urine. If the body does not properly process uric acid, the level of uric acid in the blood becomes elevated. The excess uric acid may crystallize and become deposited in and around the joints and their tendons. An acute attack of gout is caused by the body's inflammatory response to the deposits of uric acid crystals.

The high levels of uric acid can also lead to deposition of crystals in areas of the body other than the joints, most notably the skin and the kidneys. Uric acid deposits in the kidneys may form kidney stones. About 20 percent of patients with chronic gout also have kidney stones. If the kidneys become blocked by stones, kidney failure may result.

## Symptoms

Gout usually first appears as a sudden and extremely painful attack in a single joint, usually the big toe. Later attacks can involve several joints, such as the ankle, knee, wrist, and elbow. The pain, which commonly begins at night during sleep, may occur without warning or may be preceded by excessive alcohol consumption or unusual exercise earlier in the day. The pain grows in intensity and is often described as throbbing or crushing. Inflammation follows, with swelling, warmth, redness, and tenderness over the affected joint. The pain is sometimes so severe that the individual cannot tolerate the weight of a bed sheet over the joint. Other symptoms that may accompany the joint pain and swelling include fever, rapid heartbeat, chills, and an overall feeling of being unwell. Uric acid deposits in the skin may be noted as white lumps under the skin, most often appearing in the hands, the feet, the elbows, and the rims of the outer ears.

The first attacks usually last only a few days, but if the disorder goes untreated, later attacks may last for weeks. Symptoms eventually disappear, and joint function returns to normal between attacks. As the disease progresses, the periods of remission become shorter and shorter as more and more attacks occur each year.

### Treatment

The treatment of gout is twofold—to relieve the symptoms of an acute attack and to prevent recurrences. The drug colchicine has traditionally been used to relieve a gout attack, but nonsteroidal anti-inflammatory drugs are now more often prescribed to relieve the inflammation and pain. These drugs are quite effective. However, they do have side effects, so they should be used only under close and continuous medical supervision.

Once the acute attack is under control, prevention of future attacks is the main goal. This can be done with the drug allopurinol, which interferes with the production of uric acid and thus prevents the deposition of uric acid crystals in the body. Allopurinol usually has to be taken for long periods of time to maintain normal blood levels of uric acid. There are also other drugs, called uricosurics, that speed up the excretion of uric acid by the kidneys. These drugs, however, cannot be used if there is known kidney damage.

# Hernia

A hernia is an abnormal protrusion of part of an organ through the tissues that normally contain it. In this condition, a weak spot or opening in a body wall, often due to laxity of the muscles, allows part of the organ to protrude. A hernia may develop in almost any part of the body; however, the muscles of the abdominal wall are most commonly affected.

### Types of hernias

A hernia can be congenital (present at birth) or acquired (often the result of some stress or strain on the body wall involved). Although there are a wide variety of types of hernias, the following are some of the most common:
- Umbilical hernia—protrusion of part of the intestine at the umbilicus (navel). This type is seen mostly in infants.
- Inguinal hernia—protrusion of a loop of intestine into the groin (where the folds of abdominal flesh meet the thighs). This type of hernia, which accounts for about 75 percent of all abdominal hernias, is often the result of increased pressure in the abdomen because of lifting, coughing, or straining.
- Scrotal hernia—an inguinal hernia that has passed into the scrotum (the sac containing the testes).
- Femoral hernia—protrusion of a loop of intestine into the femoral canal, which carries nerves and blood vessels from the abdomen into the thigh. This type of hernia is more common in women than in men.
- Incisional hernia—a hernia that occurs at the site of a surgical incision. This type of hernia is often due to strain on healing tissues due to excessive muscular effort, lifting, coughing, or extreme pressure.
- Hiatal hernia—protrusion of part of the stomach through the diaphragm and into the chest (for more information, see pages 243–245).

### Symptoms

The symptoms will vary slightly, depending on the cause and the structures involved. However, most hernias begin as small breakthroughs that are hardly noticeable. At first, they may be soft lumps under the skin, a little larger than a marble; there is usually no pain. As time goes by, the pressure of the internal contents against the weak containing wall increases, and the size of the lump increases.

In the early stages, the hernia may be reducible, that is, the protruding structures can be pushed gently back into their normal places. If those structures cannot be returned to their normal locations by manipulation, the hernia is said to be irreducible, or incarcerated.

If an incarcerated hernia progresses, bulging out farther through the weakest points in its containing wall, the opening in the wall will close behind it, forming a narrow neck. If the neck is pinched enough to cut off the blood supply to the protruding tissue, the hernia will swell quickly and become strangulated—that is, the blood supply will be totally cut off. Unless treated, a strangulated hernia can cause tissue death. Fortunately, the symptoms of strangulation of a hernia are usually detectable. When a hernia suddenly grows larger, becomes tense, will not go back into place, and is accompanied by pain and nausea, the hernia is most likely strangulated. Sometimes, however, there is no pain or tenderness when this happens, especially in elderly patients.

### Diagnosis

Diagnosis of a hernia can usually be made by thorough examination and by studying the patient's medical history and symptoms.

### Treatment

For small nonstrangulated and nonincarcerated hernias, various supports and trusses may offer temporary, symptomatic relief. However, the best treatment is herniorrhaphy (surgical closure or repair of the muscle wall through which the hernia protrudes). When the weakened area is very large, some strong synthetic material may be sewn over the defect to reinforce the weak area. Postoperative care involves protecting the patient from respiratory infections that might cause coughing or sneezing, which would strain the suture line. Recovery is usually quick and complete.

### Prevention

Avoiding strain or pressure on any body wall, especially the abdominal wall in men, is the only real preventive measure against hernias.

# Lupus erythematosus

Lupus erythematosus is a disorder that frequently affects the skin and the connective tissues (particularly the joints and muscles) but that can affect every tissue and organ in the body. The disorder occurs in two different forms—discoid lupus erythematosus and systemic lupus erythematosus.

### Discoid lupus erythematosus

Discoid lupus erythematosus is a chronic disease of the skin that is characterized by a red rash that appears on the cheeks and nose, as well as on other parts of the body. It often appears for the first time after the skin has been exposed to sunlight. Discoid lupus erythematosus is usually treated with drugs commonly used in the treatment of malaria (even though the two conditions are not at all related).

### Systemic lupus erythematosus

Systemic lupus erythematosus is a widespread inflammatory disease of the blood vessels and connective tissues. The condition affects the joints, skin, and numerous other organs in the body, including the heart, lungs, liver, intestines, and kidneys. Red patches that resemble an open-winged butterfly appear on the cheeks and nose. Symptoms may also include severe pain in the joints, intermittent fever, and unusual fatigue. The inflammation may cause severe and irreversible damage to the blood vessels and to the kidneys.

Cortisone and other steroids are used to control the inflammation in the joints and in other parts of the body; aspirin and other analgesics are used to control the pain. As with discoid lupus erythematosus, antimalarial drugs are used in the treatment of the rash.

This disease may be mild, or it may progress rapidly to seriously affect many organs. Death may result in severe cases.

# Osteoporosis

Osteoporosis is a relatively common disorder characterized by a decrease in the calcium content of the bones, which leaves them thin and susceptible to fracture.

### Causes

The causes of osteoporosis are largely unknown. However, chances of acquiring the disease seem to increase dramatically with age, especially for women. One prevailing theory maintains that osteoporosis results from a loss of the female hormone estrogen, which affects the calcium content of the bones. Menopause (cessation of menstruation) may lead to osteoporosis because the body's production of estrogen is reduced at that time. Almost one-third of all women over 60 years of age have the disease to some extent.

For reasons not entirely known, osteoporosis is more likely to affect white and Oriental women than black women. In addition, slender women, especially those with fair skin, run a higher risk than stouter, darker-skinned women.

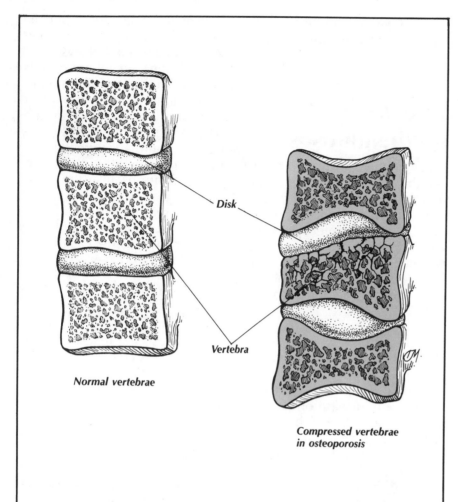

*Normal vertebrae*

*Disk*

*Vertebra*

*Compressed vertebrae
in osteoporosis*

*Osteoporosis, a condition in which the bones weaken and break easily, may lead to
compression of the vertebrae (bones of the spine).*

Osteoporosis can also occur as a result of other conditions. Surgical removal of both ovaries (the female sex glands, which produce estrogen), chronic arthritis (inflammation of the joints), and Paget's disease (a disorder of unknown origin that results in bone destruction) may lead to osteoporosis. People who are inactive, either by choice or due to confinement because of illness, seem more susceptible to the disorder. A diet deficient in nutrients, especially calcium (which promotes bone development), may also contribute to osteoporosis.

## Symptoms

Depending on the strength of the bones, osteoporosis may initially cause either no symptoms or extreme pain. If there is pain, it is most commonly in the lower back. The disease is not life-threatening, but it may lead to fractures, which, for the elderly, can result in serious complications. Initially, sudden back pain may follow fracture of the vertebrae (the bones of the spine). Pain from the fracture itself may subside but discomfort from osteoporosis may continue. This pain may lead to further inactiv-

ity, which may weaken additional vertebrae. Hence, a vicious cycle develops whereby pain leading to inactivity encourages osteoporosis, which in turn increases bone fragility.

As the disease progresses, the spinal column may decrease in length, causing a height loss of as much as several inches, or may become curved, producing the characteristic "dowager's hump." These changes are the result of successive fractures due to the pressure of body weight on the deteriorating vertebrae.

## Diagnosis

Often, osteoporosis progresses undetected until a bone is fractured and an x-ray is taken. At that time, a physician may notice that bone thinning has become a generalized condition throughout the body.

## Treatment

Physicians urge patients with osteoporosis to follow an exercise program that will strengthen the muscles supporting weakened bones. To protect bones in the spinal column, however, lifting heavy objects should be avoided. For advanced cases, a back brace may be necessary to help support body weight while sitting or standing. Crutches, walkers, or a cane may assist walking.

Physicians sometimes prescribe estrogen to women to decrease bone loss. Women taking this medication need careful supervision because the hormone may cause adverse side effects. Anyone receiving estrogen therapy should have a physical examination and a Pap test (examination of cells scraped from the vagina and cervix to detect cancer) every six months because of a suspected link between estrogen supplements and uterine and breast cancer. Men may be given the male hormone testosterone, which stimulates growth of body tissues, to treat osteoporosis.

For people prone to injury from osteoporosis, a balanced diet is an important factor in preventing or controlling the disease. Foods rich in vitamins and minerals, particularly calcium and vitamin D, encourage bone formation. When the diet is deficient in these nutrients, vitamin and mineral supplements may be prescribed by a doctor.

# Paget's disease

Paget's disease (known medically as osteitis deformans) is a disorder in which the normal process of breakdown and replacement of bone tissue is greatly accelerated. The disease develops in three stages. In the first, or destructive, stage, bone tissue breaks down and is replaced with blood vessels and dense fibrous tissue, making the bones very vascular (having a greater than normal number of blood vessels). During the second, or mixed, stage, new bone formation takes place at a rate geared to the breakdown process. In the third, or sclerotic, stage, the breakdown process slows, allowing the hardening of new bone, which becomes quite dense.

Although any bone can be affected, Paget's disease most commonly invades the pelvis, skull, thighbones, shinbones, vertebrae (the bones of the spine), collarbones, and ribs.

The condition affects about 1 percent to 3 percent of the adult population. Men are more commonly afflicted than women. The incidence of the condition is higher in some European countries than in others; it is rare in Asia, Africa, and South America. The cause is unknown.

## Symptoms and complications

Bone pain is one of the most prevalent symptoms. Complications sometimes develop. The thickened, enlarged bones are susceptible to fracture, particularly during the destructive phase of the disease. When the disease attacks the skull bones, the auditory nerve, which relays signals from the ear to the brain, is often compressed, causing deafness. Heart failure can result from the stress of the increased blood flow through the bones. Malignant bone tumors are another complication, but fortunately they are uncommon. The disease can affect appearance if it enlarges the head, bends the back, or bows the legs. In some severe cases, particularly if the person is immobile, calcium levels in the blood and urine increase and may lead to formation of kidney stones.

## Diagnosis

A history and physical examination, blood tests, and particularly x-ray studies are used to confirm the diagnosis of Paget's disease.

## Treatment

Although there is no cure, analgesics (painkillers) like aspirin offer some relief. Severe pain and other complications are sometimes managed with drug therapy. Injections of calcitonin (a hormone normally produced in the thyroid gland, which promotes calcification of bone) may help to block excessive breakdown of bone.

# Slipped disk

A slipped disk is a back problem involving the disks of elastic tissue located between the vertebrae (the bones of the spine). The vertebrae are loosely strung together by bands of connective tissue called ligaments, which allow body movement and flexibility. The function of each disk is to prevent friction between adjacent vertebrae as the body moves.

When this intricate spinal structure experiences strain and overexertion, the rim of a disk may weaken and tear, causing part of the gelatinous center of the disk to be forced out of position (or "slip"). In its new location, the protruding material often presses against an adjacent spinal nerve, which causes pain along the path of the affected nerve.

## Causes

Often, a slipped disk occurs when bending and straightening the back to lift heavy objects results in strain or injury. Damage to the disk may not be realized for many months, however. People with the problem frequently have a history of damage to the same area.

Disks also seem to disintegrate with age. They lose some of their fluidity and become more compressed. This form of degeneration usually results in only mild pain and intermittent backache and stiffness.

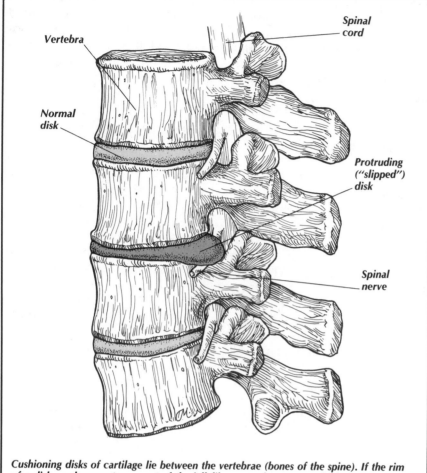

*Vertebra*

*Normal disk*

*Spinal cord*

*Protruding ("slipped") disk*

*Spinal nerve*

*Cushioning disks of cartilage lie between the vertebrae (bones of the spine). If the rim of a disk weakens or tears, part of the jellylike center becomes pushed out. This protruding "slipped" disk presses on a nearby spinal nerve, causing pain along the path of the nerve.*

an x-ray study obtained after the injection of dye into the space surrounding the spinal cord and nerve roots. Discography gives much the same information as myelography; before this x-ray study, dye is injected directly into the disks.

### Treatment

The first course of treatment for a slipped disk involves complete bed rest on a firm mattress. Rest relieves pressure exerted by the disk on the nerve and may shrink the protruding material. Some form of back support may improve comfort when moving about. Under no circumstances should a patient lift heavy objects.

For severe pain, a physician may prescribe a pain-reliever. As pain subsides, an exercise program may be recommended to gradually strengthen muscles in the region.

Partial or complete relief from the pain of a slipped disk can usually be obtained without surgery. However, in some cases, surgical removal of the disk provides the only remedy.

# Tendinitis

Tendinitis is an inflammation of a tendon (a band of fibrous tissue connecting muscle to bone). The condition appears most often as a result of physical activity. It also can be a symptom of a more generalized inflammatory disease, such as rheumatoid arthritis.

### Causes

Improper activity, lack of conditioning, and poor athletic

### Symptoms

Symptoms of slipped disk may vary with the location of the disk. The most common site for a slipped disk is the lowest movable disk in the small of the back. Injury to this disk causes pain along the sciatic nerve, a condition called sciatica. Mild or disabling pain and tenderness may result. Any straining, such as coughing or moving, can aggravate the discomfort. Weakness, tingling, or numbness in parts of the arms, legs, or feet may also result from damage to a particular disk in the neck or back.

### Diagnosis

To determine the source of back pain, a physician obtains a medical history; observes the patient sitting, walking, and bending; and explores for sensitive areas by maneuvering the patient's legs in different positions, checking ankle and knee reflexes, and testing muscle strength. Structural changes in bones, joints, or disks (but not the disks themselves) can be seen on an ordinary x-ray study.

To locate a particularly problematic disk or to prepare for a surgical procedure, special tests are necessary. A myelogram is equipment encourage the development of tendinitis. Non-athletes who suddenly begin long-distance jogging or another athletic activity and athletes who resume strenuous sports after a period of inactivity are especially susceptible. In addition, people who wear shoes with run-down heels put needless tension on the Achilles tendon, which joins the two major muscles on the back of the leg to the back of the heel bone. Similarly, women who wear high-heel shoes may have problems with inflamed Achilles tendons because the angle created by the shoes considerably shortens the tendons.

### Symptoms

A tendinitis attack causes pain in the affected tendon, which is worsened by activity. The tendon may grow thicker than normal and be tender to the touch or very painful. When minor injuries are continually placed under stress, an already inflamed tendon can rupture and become a greater problem.

### Diagnosis

Physicians diagnose tendinitis problems by first acquiring an exercise history to determine the patient's normal activity and to identify any changes in routine. Muscle lengths in the area of inflammation are also evaluated because unusually short or inflexible muscles are often the cause of tendinitis.

### Treatment

Treatment for tendinitis begins with resting the affected area.

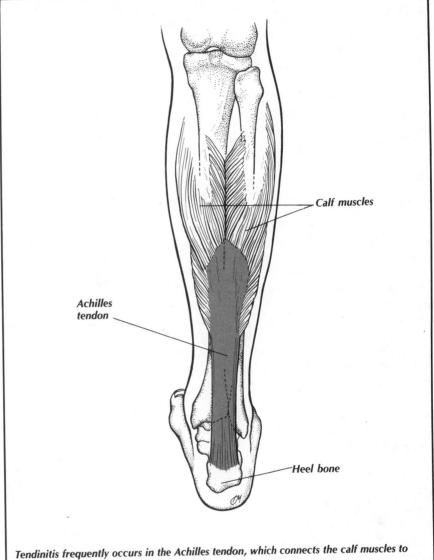

*Tendinitis frequently occurs in the Achilles tendon, which connects the calf muscles to the heel bone.*

Pain-relievers and anti-inflammatory drugs are used to ease immediate symptoms, but these preparations will not by themselves cure the condition or keep it from recurring.

In rare cases, surgery is necessary to remove damaged tendons. In the past, tendons were replaced with artificial tissues that never achieved the strength and flexibility of natural tissues. More effective techniques and materials have since been developed.

### Prevention

People participating in sports can prevent tendinitis by taking time for warm-up prior to exercise. For example, stretching the leg and calf muscles before and after running may help prevent inflammation of the Achilles tendon.

Wearing supports in shoes during physical activity can correct instability of the foot and lessen pain when tendinitis does occur.

# Tic

A tic is a spasmodic movement or twitching that is generally a brief, repetitive, purposeless, semivoluntary or involuntary muscle contraction, most commonly seen in the face, shoulders, or arms.

## Causes

Tics are caused by involuntary muscle contractions, but, with the exception of the tics that develop as a result of nerve or brain damage and other specific conditions, the physiological basis of most tics is largely unknown. They often accompany emotional upset or some hidden psychological problem. Tics in children may be a sign of Gilles de la Tourette's syndrome, a disorder marked by multiple tics and compulsive use of profane language (for more information, see pages 349–350).

## Symptoms

A typical "nervous tic" is a twitching of the corner of the eye or the mouth, grimacing, blinking, or making repetitive motions with the arms or shoulders. Tics in children often occur between the ages of five and ten years and may gradually disappear as the child grows older; however, they can persist into adulthood. When nervous tics first arise, they can usually be voluntarily controlled, but persistent tics often become automatic after a period of time.

## Diagnosis

Many tics are, at the beginning, hard to distinguish from many neurologically based illnesses.

## Treatment

For mild childhood or adult tics, tranquilizers or muscle relaxants may be prescribed. Gilles de la Tourette's syndrome sometimes responds to medication. Psychotherapy may help to relieve the emotional stress that precipitates attacks or intensifies the symptoms of some tics.

# Trichinosis

Trichinosis is a condition caused by the infestation of the body by *Trichinella spiralis,* a parasitic worm sometimes found in pork.

## Cause

Trichinosis is most commonly caused by eating pork that has not been cooked for a sufficient length of time or at a sufficiently high temperature to kill the *Trichinella spiralis* worms. The worms are encapsulated in the meat itself. When the meat is eaten, the worms emerge from it and begin their life cycle in the human host. This begins in the small intestine, where the larvae (an immature form of the worms) mature within two days after they emerge from the meat. The adults breed, the males die, and the females produce more larvae, which invade the tissues of the bowel and are then dispersed to muscles throughout the body, where they lodge. The muscles around the eyes, the tongue, and the diaphragm (the muscle separating the chest cavity from the abdomen) and the muscles between the ribs are the most commonly affected.

## Symptoms

Quite often, the patient is entirely unaware of the presence of trichinosis. When large infestations do occur, however, they are accompanied by symptoms. One to two days after consumption of the contaminated meat, a severe flulike illness consisting of fever, nausea, vomiting, diarrhea, and abdominal pain occurs. Tenderness and swelling around the infested muscles are common. After about a week, rash, swelling of the eyelids, and neurologic disorders may develop. Myocarditis (inflammation of the heart muscle) can also occur at this stage. Eventually the larvae in the muscles die and become calcified. Symptoms gradually disappear within a few months.

## Treatment

Since there is no way to get the larvae out of the muscles, treatment is aimed at relief of discomfort. Analgesics, such as aspirin, are administered for pain, and anti-inflammatory steroids (cortisonelike drugs, such as prednisone) are administered for allergic symptoms, myocarditis, and central nervous system involvement. Thiabendazole (which tends to kill worms such as the *Trichinella*) is often given with good results. A close watch is kept for fever, abdominal pain, vomiting, and dermatitis (skin inflammation).

## Prevention

The only preventive is to make sure that pork is sufficiently cooked (to an internal temperature of at least 170°F) to kill the larvae.

# THE EYES AND VISION

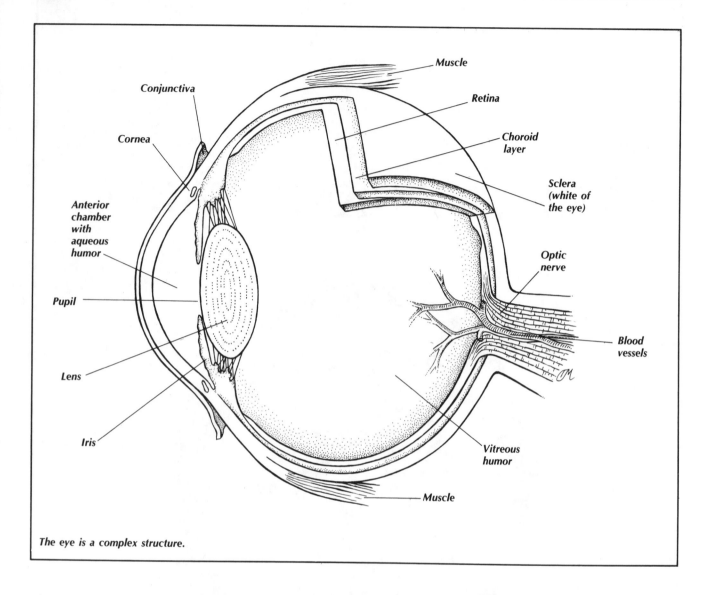

*The eye is a complex structure.*

The eye is the organ of sight. This complex structure works by capturing light and transforming it into impulses that the brain can interpret as images providing information about the environment.

In order to understand visual perception, it is important to know the functions of the various parts of the eye. The eye includes the eyeball and all the structures within and surrounding its almost spherical mass. This delicate organ is nestled within the bony socket of the skull. A layer of fat cushions the socket, and the eyebrow, eye-lashes, and eyelid provide a barrier against incoming irritants. Lining the inside of the eyelid and continuing over the exposed surface of the eyeball is the conjunctiva, a thin protective membrane. Tears released from the lacrimal glands moisten the conjunctiva and keep the eyeball clean. The cornea is a transparent covering over the area that admits the light. The sclera is the tough outer covering of the eyeball. The choroid layer contains blood vessels that nourish the eye.

Light enters the eye through the cornea. Behind the cornea is a pigmented (colored) structure called the iris. The iris surrounds an opening known as the pupil. The iris changes the size of the pupil, depending on the amount of light present in the environment: if the surroundings are relatively dark, the pupil is enlarged to admit more light; if the environment is bright, the pupil is made smaller. Behind the iris is the lens, a transparent structure held in place by elastic, muscular-type tissue. That tissue can change the shape of the lens to accommodate the available light and to focus on objects at varying distances.

Between the cornea and the lens is a space, the anterior chamber, which is filled with a fluid called aqueous humor. Aqueous humor contains nutrients that nourish the cornea and the lens. The fluid also allows light rays to pass through the area easily.

The chamber of the eyeball behind the lens holds a clear jelly called vitreous humor. In the retina (the innermost layer of the eyeball) are the specialized cells, called rods and cones, that convert light focused from the lens into electrical impulses. Sensitive nerve endings then transmit these impulses to the brain via the optic nerve, which extends from the rear of the eyeball to the brain.

*Lazy-eye amblyopia may be corrected by using a patch to hinder the vision in the good eye, thus forcing the lazy eye to work.*

# Amblyopia

Amblyopia is the name for diminished vision in one or both eyes, usually without any obvious defect. (Amblyopia is not the same as nearsightedness, farsightedness, or astigmatism, which can be corrected with eyeglasses or contact lenses.)

There are two main types of amblyopia: "lazy-eye" amblyopia and toxic amblyopia.

### LAZY-EYE AMBLYOPIA

Lazy-eye amblyopia occurs frequently in young children whose eyes do not line up correctly (a condition known as strabismus). In order to prevent double vision (in which the patient sees two images of everything instead of one), the brain suppresses the sight of one eye; the other eye does all the work. The brain structures dependent on the eye that is not working may atrophy (waste away) or fail to develop.

### Symptoms

Unfortunately, there are usually no obvious symptoms of this form of amblyopia. By the time the condition is recognized, the eye may be permanently damaged. Usually, the child appears to see as well as the next boy or girl. Sometimes, however, the condition that causes the amblyopia is very noticeable: the eyes may turn either inward or outward, or one eye may be looking up while the other is looking down.

### Treatment

To fully restore sight in the lazy eye, treatment must begin before the child is four to six years of age. If the eyes are out of focus because some of the muscles of the eye are weaker than others, the condition may be corrected by wearing special glasses or contact lenses, by doing eye exercises, by using eye drops or a patch to diminish the ability of the normal eye to focus (and thereby force the lazy eye to work), or by surgery. Periodic reexaminations are needed until the child is at least ten years of age.

### Prevention

Prevention of lazy-eye amblyopia can begin soon after birth. If the eyes of a baby are continually out of alignment in the first weeks of life or are still out of alignment from time to time at six months of age, the condition should be investigated. A simple eye test given in the doctor's office should show whether one eye is not working properly. Evaluation should not be delayed. The child will not "grow out" of either strabismus or amblyopia.

### TOXIC AMBLYOPIA

Toxic amblyopia, which usually occurs in both eyes, can result from excessive drinking of alcoholic beverages over a long period of time (and may be due mainly to the poor nutrition of heavy drinkers, who get most of their calories from alcohol and so do not eat enough nourishing food). It may also be found in heavy cigarette smokers and in people exposed to various chemicals and drugs, including lead, methanol (wood alcohol), digitalis, chloramphenicol, and arsenic. The toxic substance causes swelling and irritation of the optic nerve around the site where it leaves the eyeball. If the irritation continues, it can cause lasting damage to the nerve and even total blindness.

## Symptoms

Symptoms include pain on moving the eyeball and an increasing area of poor eyesight in or near the center of the field of vision.

## Treatment

Treatment is to stop exposure to the poison, if it can be discovered. In the case of lead poisoning, the patient is given medicine that combines with the lead and draws it out of the body tissues (this treatment is known as chelation therapy). If the cause is removed at once, vision may improve—unless there has been permanent damage to the optic nerve.

# Astigmatism

Astigmatism is a type of distorted vision caused by a defect in the curvature of the cornea or lens of the eye. This prevents the rays of light entering the eye from being

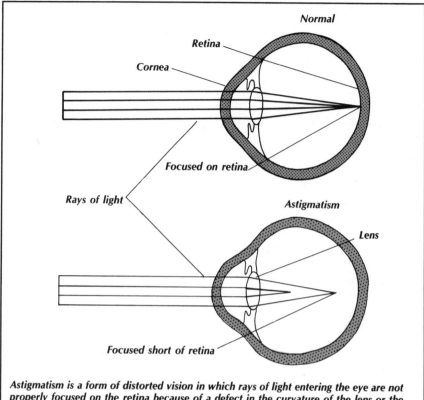

*Astigmatism is a form of distorted vision in which rays of light entering the eye are not properly focused on the retina because of a defect in the curvature of the lens or the cornea. This defect can be corrected by wearing eyeglasses or contact lenses.*

properly focused onto the retina at the back of the eyeball. Some rays are misplaced, causing the image to be partially out of focus.

## Types

Most people with astigmatism can see clearly those objects directly in front of them, but their peripheral vision is defective. They may have vertical astigmatism, in which the areas above and below their direct gaze are imperfectly visualized. They may have horizontal astigmatism, in which the right and left sides of their field of vision are warped (for example, a straight horizontal line may appear curved to the right and to the left). The astigmatism may also be diagonal.

## Treatment

Fortunately, a defect in the curvature of the cornea or lens is usually uniform and can be easily corrected by eyeglasses or contact lenses. The fault is usually in the shape of the cornea (the clear "window" in front of the iris and pupil), which may be slightly flattened vertically or horizontally. The eyeglass lenses or contact lenses worn by a person with astigmatism are made so that they do not bend the rays entering the areas of clear vision, but are curved to adjust the angle of rays entering regions of the eye that are defective.

Although most people with astigmatism were born with a tendency toward the condition, a few cases are caused by eye disease or injury. These may be more difficult to correct. Regardless of the cause, astigmatism—as with any vision problem—should be corrected as early as possible. Children, in particular, are at risk for development of permanently defective vision if astigmatism goes uncorrected.

# Blepharitis

Blepharitis is an inflammation of the edges of the eyelids, with redness and thickening. Scales and crusts or shallow ulcers (eroded areas) may also appear. The disease is common, especially in children, and often affects the upper and lower eyelids of both eyes.

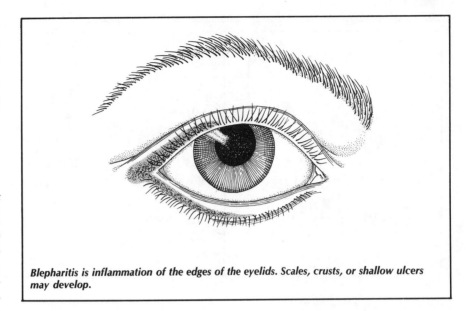

*Blepharitis is inflammation of the edges of the eyelids. Scales, crusts, or shallow ulcers may develop.*

### Causes

Infection of eyelash follicles and oil glands by *Staphylococcus* bacteria causes blepharitis with ulcers. The nonulcerous variety may be due to an allergic reaction, or it may be linked to seborrheic dermatitis, an inflammatory scaling of the scalp, eyebrows, and sometimes ears. The nonulcerous form is occasionally caused by lice, which irritate lid margins.

### Symptoms

Symptoms of blepharitis include itching, burning, "red-rimmed" eyes; swelling of the lids; loss of eyelashes; and irritation of the underside of the lid, as if dirt or sand were underneath. The eyes may tear and be sensitive to light. In ulcerous blepharitis, the tough, dry crusts that form leave a bleeding surface when removed. In nonulcerous blepharitis, greasy, easily removed scales appear on the edges of the lids.

### Treatment

Blepharitis caused by a bacterial infection can be treated with an antibiotic ointment, such as erythromycin or bacitracin, that is specially formulated for use around the eyes. The medication is usually applied three times a day to the eyelash margins with a cotton-tipped swab, after the margins have been softened with warm compresses for ten minutes and the crusts have been removed. Medicated eye drops may also be used to combat irritation or other types of infection.

If an allergy to a cosmetic is the cause, its use should be discontinued. If there is scaling on the eyebrows and scalp due to seborrheic dermatitis, the doctor is likely to recommend a special shampoo, such as a sulfur or tar shampoo, for control of dandruff and to prescribe a cortisone lotion or cream to be rubbed into hairy areas. Absolute cleanliness of hair, scalp, eyebrows, and eyelid margins is necessary during treatment.

If the blepharitis is caused by lice, the nits (louse eggs) should be carefully removed with tweezers, and steps should be taken to keep the patient free of lice.

Both of the principal varieties are difficult to cure and often recur. Nonulcerous blepharitis causes no permanent damage. However, ulcerous blepharitis, if it recurs often enough, can cause scarring of the eyelids, loss of the eyelashes, and even ulcers of the cornea.

### Prevention

Meticulous cleanliness may help prevent the disease. If it is treated promptly when it occurs, permanent damage can probably be prevented.

# Cataract

A cataract is a clouding of the lens of the eye that results in obscured vision. Because people with this defect see their environment as if they were looking through a waterfall, the condition was named *cataract* from the Greek word for waterfall.

Normally, the lens is clear. Its function is to direct light into the

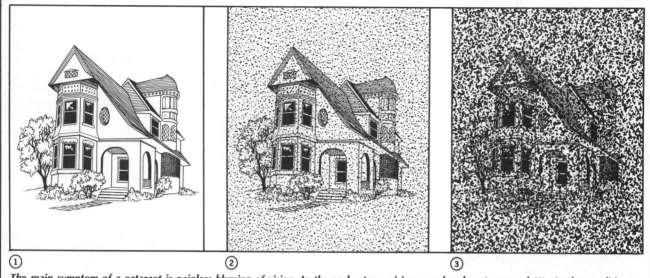

*The main symptom of a cataract is painless blurring of vision. In the early stage, vision may be close to normal (1). As the condition progresses, vision gradually worsens (2) and eventually becomes extremely blurred (3).*

eye so that objects at various distances can be seen clearly. If the lens becomes hazy, however, incoming light is scattered and vision blurs.

## Causes

The exact cause of cataracts is unknown. Aging may play a role in development of cataracts, but the condition also occurs in newborns whose mothers contracted German measles during pregnancy and in other young persons.

Diabetes (a disorder characterized by inability to use carbohydrates), glaucoma (a condition in which there is increased pressure within the eyeball), and detachment of the retina (the innermost layer of the eye) may lead to cataracts. Injury to the lens, prolonged use of certain drugs, and high doses of radiation (for example, from prolonged exposure to x-rays) may also trigger the condition.

Although the condition is usually curable, cataracts can cause

blindness. In addition, the shadowy lens prohibits a clear view of the interior of the eye. Because of this obstruction, a physician may not be able to detect other potentially serious eye disorders, such as changes in the retina and damage to the optic nerve (which transmits information from the eye to the brain).

## Symptoms

The main symptom of cataracts is painless blurring of vision, occurring most often in only one eye. During the initial stages of development, cataracts can cause the person to experience glare in bright light, since the clouded lens scatters, rather than focuses, incoming light. As the condition progresses, the lens becomes milky white, and vision worsens.

## Treatment

Successful treatment begins with surgical removal of the af-

fected lens. With the aid of a microscope, the surgeon opens an area in the front of the eye and removes the lens. The use of local anesthetic eye drops makes the procedure relatively painless. After the patient has recuperated for a few weeks, special cataract eyeglasses or a contact lens are prescribed to help correct the vision. These aids are by no means perfect and require an adjustment period.

Many doctors now recommend the implantation of an intraocular lens in the eye after cataract removal. The lightweight plastic lens is relatively free of distortion and affords vision that is closer to normal than eyeglasses or contact lenses can provide because it occupies the exact position of the natural lens. Nevertheless, not everyone can benefit from an intraocular lens. Doctors advise patients with glaucoma, detached retina, or eye disorders caused by diabetes to wear eyeglasses or contacts to restore vision.

In 95 percent of cases, surgery for cataracts is without complications. Restoration or substantial improvement of vision results after surgery in the majority of cases. If vision remains unimproved, a disorder that was not detected due to the presence of the cataract may be the cause. Generally, however, cataracts can be removed successfully, and the patient can resume a normal life.

# Color blindness

Color blindness is an inability to distinguish certain colors. By far the most common type is inherited red-green color blindness, which affects 8 percent of men and boys but only 0.5 percent of women and girls. Total color blindness, which is very rare, and pastel-shade blindness are believed to be inherited. Other types, including blue-yellow blindness and red-green blindness, can be either inherited or acquired. Disease or injury affecting the retina sometimes causes color blindness.

## Description

Color blindness results from a defect in the cone-shaped light-sensitive cells of the fovea (the tiny, yellowish pit at the rear of the eye, which is the center for perceiving color). The 7 million cone cells differ from the 130 million rod-shaped cells in the rest of the retina in that, while the rod cells register only black and white, the cone cells contain pigments for red, green, and blue—the colors that can combine to produce all the colors of the spectrum. The pigments become more vivid or fade in response to colors that the eye sees. The changes in pigmentation produce tiny flashes of elec-

tricity, which are carried by means of the optic nerve to the visual center of the brain. There, the electrical signals are combined into a full-color picture. In the color-blind person, for unknown reasons, the cones are effective in some ways, but the process for one or more color pigments simply does not work correctly. No cure is known.

### Inheriting red-green color blindness

Why is red-green color blindness inherited by boys more often than by girls? The reason is that the defective gene, which directs production of the defective pigment, is carried on the same pair of chromosomes that determines the sex of the child. In a female child (who has two X sex chromosomes), a defective gene on one X chromosome is

almost always counteracted by a normal gene on the other X chromosome; as a result, the girl is born with normal color vision. In a male child (who has an X and a Y sex chromosome), there is no matching normal gene to block the defect on the only X chromosome the boy has; the boy is, therefore, born color-blind.

Red-green color blindness cannot be passed from a father to his sons, nor will his daughters be color-blind, unless the mother carries the defective gene. However, his daughters will all be carriers of the defective gene, and the daughters' sons will have a 50 percent chance of being color-blind.

# Conjunctivitis

Conjunctivitis, or pinkeye, is an inflammation of the conjunctiva.

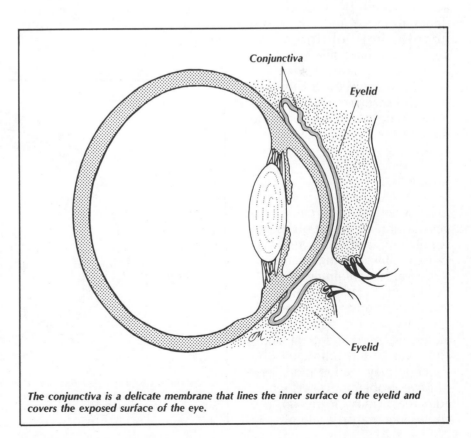

*The conjunctiva is a delicate membrane that lines the inner surface of the eyelid and covers the exposed surface of the eye.*

The conjunctiva is a delicate membrane that lines the inner surface of the eyelid and covers the exposed surface of the eye.

## Causes

Most cases of conjunctivitis result from disease-causing microorganisms such as bacteria, fungi, and viruses. Allergies, chemicals, dust, smoke, and foreign objects that irritate the conjunctiva may also lead to conjunctivitis. Swimming may also be associated with conjunctivitis, due to exposure to chlorine in a pool or to contaminated water. Occasionally, a sexually transmitted disease can cause pinkeye if the eyes are rubbed after the hands have touched infected genital organs.

Children are most often affected by conjunctivitis. Measles, a viral disease, may be accompanied by this eye inflammation. In addition, those people, both children and adults, who have allergies, such as hay fever, or who work and live in areas where they are exposed to chemicals or other irritants are more susceptible to noninfectious conjunctivitis.

## Symptoms

Conjunctivitis may cause redness, a grating sensation, burning, itching, and light sensitivity. Occasionally, tearing occurs, or a discharge containing pus will be present. Symptoms can last a few days or up to two weeks.

Conjunctivitis usually produces no permanent damage. However, if left untreated, the infection may lead to more serious eye problems. Ulcers (eroded areas) may form on the cornea (the transparent covering across the front of the eye). If these ulcers persist, they can scar the eye and interfere with vision.

## Treatment

Treatment depends on the cause and resulting symptoms of the conjunctivitis. If the inflammation is environmentally caused, simply removing the irritant may be sufficient to eliminate the condition. For more difficult cases, a physician may prescribe antibiotic, steroid, or combination eye drops to be used several times a day as directed. Frequent use is necessary because the drops tend to be washed away by the natural cleansing action of the tears.

Sensitive eyes should be rested and shielded from bright lights. When the discharge glues the eyelids closed, bathing them with warm water and wiping with a clean cloth will loosen them.

A most important fact about conjunctivitis is that its infectious form is highly contagious. Individuals with infectious conjunctivitis should not share handkerchiefs, towels, or washcloths and should be careful to avoid touching the unaffected eye after contact with the infected eye.

# Detached retina

Normally, the retina is firmly attached to the choroid, an underlying layer of tissue that is rich in blood vessels. If blood or other fluid collects between the retina and the choroid, the retina may become partially or totally detached. Fluid from the vitreous cavity (the fluid-filled space within the eye) may penetrate beneath the retina because of a small hole in the retina. Fluid leaking out of certain blood vessels in the eye may also penetrate beneath the retina to cause detachment.

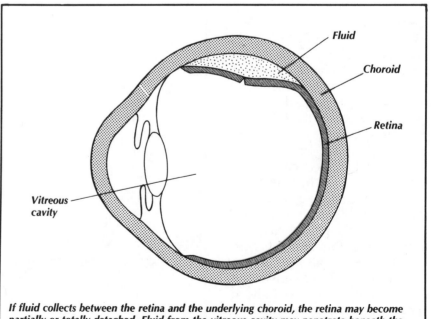

Fluid

Choroid

Retina

Vitreous cavity

*If fluid collects between the retina and the underlying choroid, the retina may become partially or totally detached. Fluid from the vitreous cavity may penetrate beneath the retina through a small hole in the retina.*

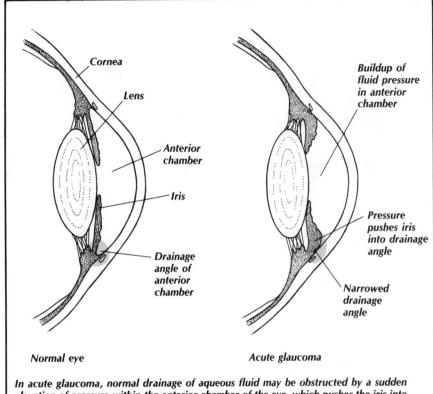

## Causes

Cataract surgery, severe myopia (nearsightedness), and injury can cause retinal detachment. Although injury can be the primary cause of this condition, it is more likely to accelerate a detachment that has already begun. Conditions that increase susceptibility to retinal detachment are inflammation or tumors of the eye, high blood pressure, and vitreous hemorrhaging.

## Symptoms

Initial symptoms include seeing floating dark spots or flashes or streaks of light and experiencing blurring of vision. As the condition progresses, a curtain or veil seems to fall over part or all of the field of vision.

## Treatment

A detached retina can be treated by using a laser to fuse the retina to the choroid. It can also be treated by diathermy (repair using heat), cryotherapy (repair using extreme cold), or microsurgery (surgery using a microscope). Left untreated, the detachment may increase and lead to loss of sight.

# Glaucoma

Glaucoma is an eye disorder caused by increased pressure within the eyeball, which builds up because fluids are unable to drain normally.

## Cause

Although glaucoma is understood to be a problem with the fluid-regulating mechanism of the eye, its precise cause is unknown. In the healthy eye, aqueous fluid in the anterior chamber of the eyeball (between the lens and the cornea) is under a slight degree of pressure. If the delicate fluid balance changes, internal pressure rises in the eye. This buildup produces damage to the sensitive structures and nerve endings within the eye.

## Forms of glaucoma

Depending on the type of defect in the fluid-regulating system, one of two primary forms of glaucoma results. *Chronic,* or *open-angle, glaucoma* develops when pressure is elevated gradually, and normal fluid drainage slows but is not obstructed at the drainage angle (the network of tissue between the iris and the cornea, through which fluid can normally pass). *Acute,* or *closed-angle, glaucoma* occurs when pressure mounts suddenly and forces the iris into contact with the cornea, thereby blocking fluid drainage from the anterior chamber of the eye.

## Those at risk

Both forms of glaucoma are more common in adults over 40 years of age. Statistics indicate that people with a family history of glaucoma have a greater risk of acquiring the condition, but inheritance has not been proved. Some evidence suggests that glaucoma may be linked to long-term use of certain drugs, especially steroids, which can alter body fluid levels. Glaucoma can

The figure shows labels: Cornea, Lens, Anterior chamber, Iris, Drainage angle of anterior chamber (Normal eye); and Buildup of fluid pressure in anterior chamber, Pressure pushes iris into drainage angle, Narrowed drainage angle (Acute glaucoma).

*In acute glaucoma, normal drainage of aqueous fluid may be obstructed by a sudden elevation of pressure within the anterior chamber of the eye, which pushes the iris into the angle where the iris meets the cornea.*

① ② ③

*Normal vision (1) will deteriorate gradually if glaucoma is not treated. Loss of peripheral vision may slowly progress as central vision remains normal (2). Untreated glaucoma can lead to partial or complete vision loss (3).*

also follow other eye disorders, such as infections and cataracts.

### Symptoms

Chronic glaucoma begins with no noticeable symptoms. Vision deterioration is so gradual and painless that this form of glaucoma has been termed the "sneak thief of sight." Sometimes, loss of peripheral vision slowly progresses as central vision remains normal. As the disorder advances, other symptoms (which may be intermittent or constant) include foggy or blurred vision, difficulty in adjusting to brightness and darkness, and slight pain in or around the eye, usually on one side. The one symptom indicative of chronic glaucoma is the perception of a faint white circle or halo surrounding a light, which is most easily visible when looking at a distant light while in the dark.

Acute glaucoma brings sudden and severe symptoms of extreme eye pain and abrupt vision

blurring. Frequently, the pain can be so intense that it causes nausea and vomiting. Fortunately, acute glaucoma is rare, but when it does occur, medical attention is needed immediately to prevent permanent blindness. Usually, however, the symptoms are so severe that medical help is promptly sought.

### Diagnosis

If left untreated, glaucoma can lead to partial or complete vision loss. However, if diagnosed early, treatment can usually halt the process. Because chronic glaucoma has no warning signs, it is particularly important that persons over the age of 40 be tested for glaucoma every two or three years. In addition, physicians recommend that persons with a family history of the disease be screened every year beginning even before the age of 40.

Glaucoma testing is a relatively simple office procedure. The doctor uses a special device

called a tonometer to measure the amount of pressure within the eyeball. The doctor also inspects the interior of the eye through an instrument that allows a view of the angle where the iris and the cornea meet. This part of the examination shows whether there is blockage in the drainage system or damage to the optic nerve. Peripheral vision is tested by measuring the point at which objects enter the field of vision.

### Treatment

Glaucoma treatment is usually effective if started early in the course of the disease. Oral drugs work by decreasing production of eye fluid, while daily applications of eye drops promote fluid drainage. Because some medications cause constriction of the pupils of the eyes, which can be misconstrued as a symptom of drug overdose, many glaucoma patients carry an identification card that describes their medical history in case of emergency.

Beta-blocker eye drops reduce production of eye fluid without altering the size of the pupil. However, beta-blockers can affect the heart rate and cause narrowing of the breathing passages, which makes these drugs unsuitable for patients with heart or respiratory disease.

Although chronic glaucoma responds to medication, some patients (fewer than 5 percent) require surgery to open new pathways for fluid drainage. Laser therapy is a relatively new surgical technique under investigation. The laser uses an intense light beam to slightly modify tissues in the region in order to allow better fluid drainage.

### Prevention

The best way to prevent serious complications of glaucoma is to undergo periodic screening for early diagnosis.

# Keratitis

Keratitis is an inflammation of the cornea (the transparent covering over the iris and pupil of the eye), which commonly produces redness, tearing, tenderness, sensitivity to light, and blurred vision.

### Interstitial keratitis

Interstitial keratitis is often caused by congenital (present at birth) syphilis in children or by tuberculosis. This type of keratitis produces deep deposits of scar tissue, which cause the cornea to become hazy and give it a ground-glass appearance. There is little that can be done for this condition, although the inflammation and redness usu-

ally diminish after a month or two. Vision may or may not be impaired thereafter.

### Herpes simplex keratitis

A common type of keratitis is caused by the herpes simplex virus, the same virus that produces cold sores. Herpes simplex keratitis is usually not painful, although at first there is a sensation that foreign matter may be present. If the infection is left untreated, all feeling in the cornea will eventually be lost. Like a cold sore, the infection tends to come and go, but it should be taken care of when the first sign—a whitish lesion on the cornea—appears. Treatment usually consists of applying eye drops or ointment, but some specialists prefer to scrape the cornea, after which they cover the affected eye temporarily.

### Traumatic keratitis

Traumatic keratitis occurs when scar tissue remains after a corneal injury has healed. If a

considerable amount of scar tissue covers the pupil, blindness may result. This condition can generally be cured by corrective surgery or corneal transplantation.

# Macular degeneration

Macular degeneration is the deterioration of the macula (the yellowish depression in the back of the retina of the eye). The macula is the part of the eye with the greatest density of visual receptor cells. As light enters the eye, the image that is focused on the macula is the one that is most accurately perceived in the brain. The function of the macula is to distinguish fine detail in the central visual field. Consequently, degeneration of the macula leads to blurring of central vision.

### Causes

Macular degeneration is often a result of another eye disorder.

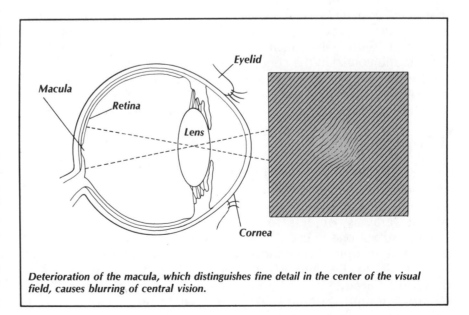

*Deterioration of the macula, which distinguishes fine detail in the center of the visual field, causes blurring of central vision.*

The condition is usually hereditary; however, one form is not hereditary and occurs primarily in persons more than 60 years of age. In many of these cases, the blood vessels of the eye narrow, possibly as a result of atherosclerosis, and the blood supply to the macula is diminished. Because the cells of the macula require a plentiful blood supply, any deficiency of blood causes deterioration of the region.

### Symptoms

Macular degeneration develops slowly and painlessly. Therefore, the blurring of central vision is gradual. If both eyes are affected—as is almost always the case—activities requiring sharp vision, such as reading and driving, usually have to be curtailed. Eventually, all central vision disappears, although peripheral vision is unaffected.

### Treatment

There was no treatment for macular degeneration until recently. It has now been found that about 5 percent of affected individuals may be helped by treatment with laser beams. Early in the course of the condition, vision may be improved by special powerful eyeglasses.

# Myopia

Myopia, or nearsightedness, is a common optical defect in which close objects can be seen clearly but faraway objects look blurred. About one in every five persons is myopic. The condition tends to be hereditary, developing around age 12 and progressing until about age 20.

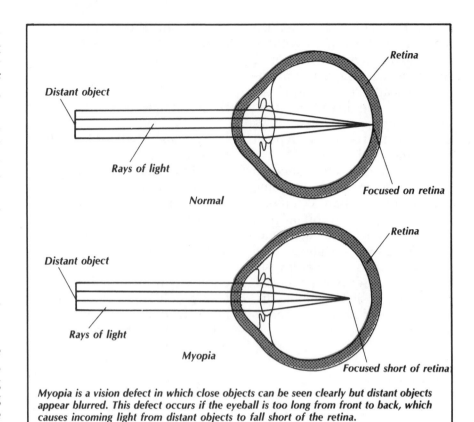

*Myopia is a vision defect in which close objects can be seen clearly but distant objects appear blurred. This defect occurs if the eyeball is too long from front to back, which causes incoming light from distant objects to fall short of the retina.*

### Cause

The defect occurs if the eyeball is too long from front to back. Normally, the cornea and the lens (the disk-shaped structure just behind the front of the eye) refract (bend) light coming from a viewed distant object so that the image is focused on the retina (the layer of specialized, light-sensitive cells that line the back of the eyeball). In myopia, the focused image falls short of the retina because of the greater length of the eyeball, resulting in a fuzzy image.

### Types

There are several kinds of myopia. *Curvature myopia* occurs when there is an excessive curve of the refractive (light-bending) surfaces of the eye,

which causes light to enter the eye in an abnormal path. The curvature is in the front surface of either the cornea or the lens. In *index myopia,* there is an increase in the light-refracting properties of the lens. It is sometimes associated with future development of cataracts or iritis (inflammation of the iris). *Progressive myopia* is an uncommon form in which the eyeball continues to elongate throughout a person's life, eventually leading to degeneration or detachment of the retina.

### Diagnosis

Blurred or fuzzy vision should be evaluated by an ophthalmologist (a physician who specializes in eye disorders), who will look inside the eyes with a special instrument called an ophthalmoscope, diagnose any disorders, and test the acuity (sharpness) of vision.

## Treatment

Nearsightedness is easily corrected with a concave (inwardly curved) lens that pushes the images back toward the retina and focuses them clearly.

A surgical procedure known as radial keratotomy corrects myopia. It involves cutting numerous ''spokes'' into the corneal surface, coming out from the center; the cornea flattens as it heals, which counteracts the problem. This procedure is still considered controversial.

Myopia rarely progresses after age 30. In fact, the onset of middle age sometimes lessens the severity of the condition.

# Night blindness

Night blindness, or nyctalopia, is a condition in which a person can see well in good light but not in dim or fading light.

The retina contains a layer of photoreceptors (specialized, light-sensitive cells) that lines the interior of the eyeball. These photoreceptors make the adjustments that are responsible for adaptation to varying degrees of light. There are two types of photoreceptors—cones and rods. Cones, concentrated in the center of the retina (the region called the macula), distinguish fine detail and color, while rods, which predominate around the edges of the retina, are sensitive to the intensity of light and do most of the work of seeing in dim light. Rods contain the pigment rhodopsin, or visual purple, which becomes temporarily bleached by bright light. The

speed at which rhodopsin adjusts to darkness depends on a sufficient supply of vitamin A in the body.

## Causes

Night blindness is caused either by a severe deficiency of vitamin A or by retinitis pigmentosa, an inherited degenerative disorder of the retina. In cases of extreme vitamin A shortage, the cornea may soften or start to dissolve (a condition called keratomalacia), or the eyes may become excessively dry (a condition called xerophthalmia).

## Treatment

A vitamin A deficiency can be treated with doses of the vitamin. However, consuming large doses of vitamin A without a doctor's recommendation and without documentation of a deficiency can be extremely dangerous.

## Prevention

The only preventive measure is to obtain enough dietary vitamin A (for example, from liver, egg yolks, yellow and darkgreen vegetables, butter, and cream).

# Nystagmus

Nystagmus is the involuntary, rhythmic, and rapid movement of the eyeballs in a horizontal, vertical, or rotary direction. The eye movements of a person who sits in a moving vehicle and watches the scenery flashing by are an example of normal nystagmus.

### Abnormal nystagmus

Abnormal nystagmus is brought on by one of three problems: defective vision, such that the eye does not receive enough stimulation to concentrate on one object; disturbances in the elaborate mechanisms in the inner ear responsible for balance; and diseases of the nervous system, especially those affecting the parts of the brain responsible for eye movement and coordination. Generally, the only symptoms of abnormal nystagmus are double vision, vertigo, and dizziness. Treatment depends on the underlying cause.

# Retinitis

Retinitis is an inflammation of the retina, the light-sensitive innermost lining of the eye.

## Types and causes

There are several types of retinitis. *Toxoplasmic retinitis,* which may be either acquired or congenital (present at birth), is caused by a microorganism. If the condition is congenital, the microorganism was passed to the fetus through the placenta (the temporary organ in the uterus that nourishes the fetus during development). A similar type of retinitis is caused by a blood-borne infection that settles in the eye. *Exudative retinitis* stems from unknown causes, but may result in detachment of the retina from the internal surface of the eyeball. *Retinitis pigmentosa* is an inherited disorder in which excessive amounts of a substance called phytanic acid accumulate and cause extensive damage to the retina. This form of retinitis also usually accompanies the rare inherited disorder of fat metabolism called Refsum's syndrome.

## Symptoms

The symptoms of retinitis pigmentosa are night blindness, inflammation of the retina, marked limitation of the field of vision (tunnel vision), loss of kinesthetic sense (sense of body movement), shrinkage of the retina, clumping of retinal pigment, and dislodging of the blood vessels of the retina. Many of the same symptoms are found in the other forms of retinitis. They are sometimes accompanied by cloudiness of the vitreous humor (liquid filling the eyeball). This can be detected by a physician examining the interior of the eye with a special lighted instrument called an ophthalmoscope.

## Treatment

In the case of retinitis pigmentosa, there is little that can be done. If the retina is detached (a condition often caused when a hole in the retina allows fluid to seep into the eye and create a pocket), surgery is usually the treatment. The pocket is eliminated either by freezing or by heat, sometimes with a laser. If retinitis is the result of blood-borne infection, that condition must be treated first.

## Prevention

Other than genetic counseling for persons with a family history of retinitis pigmentosa, there are no clear-cut preventive measures that can be taken against retinitis.

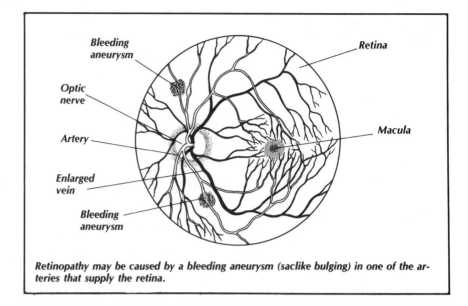

*Retinopathy may be caused by a bleeding aneurysm (saclike bulging) in one of the arteries that supply the retina.*

# Retinopathy

Retinopathy is a condition in which deterioration of the retina is caused by damage to or overproduction of the blood vessels in that structure.

## Causes

The vast majority of cases of retinopathy are due to diabetes. Although fewer than 5 percent of all diabetic patients completely lose their sight because of retinopathy, diabetes is one of the leading causes of irreversible blindness today. Other conditions that increase susceptibility to retinopathy include high blood pressure (because retinal arteries and veins may be either constricted or entirely blocked); hemorrhaging due to sudden vessel blockage by a blood clot, fat globule, or cholesterol plaque; and chronic kidney failure.

If a sudden hemorrhage is triggered, total blindness in the eye can strike swiftly; immediate medical attention is necessary. In cases of retinopathy due to hypertension (high blood pressure) or diabetes, vision usually worsens over time.

## Treatment

Hypertensive retinopathy is primarily treated by strict control of the blood pressure through diet and, in many cases, medication (depending on the severity of the condition). Diabetic retinopathy is also treated through diet and medication; if diabetic patients continually allow their glucose levels to exceed normal bounds, retinal damage can be extensive and may require laser treatments to seal off leaking blood vessels.

# Sty

A sty is an inflamed or infected swelling of the sebaceous (oil-producing) glands in the eyelid.

## Cause

The infection is commonly caused by *Staphylococcus* bacteria. An external sty appears on the surface of the skin at the edge of the eyelid. An internal sty is due to inflammation, infection, or obstruction of a sebaceous gland on the inner surface of the eyelid. This type of sty is often seen as a protrusion or lump on the eyelid without visible pus or redness.

### Symptoms

Initially, a sty feels like a foreign object in the eye. Tearing, redness, swelling, and tenderness in or around a particular area of the eye soon follow. The eye may be sensitive to light and touch. In addition, pustules (small, yellow bumps filled with pus) may develop. These pustules often burst, release the pus, and begin to heal. Once the pressure has been released, the pain usually subsides.

### Treatment

Treatment for a sty often involves antibiotic eye drops

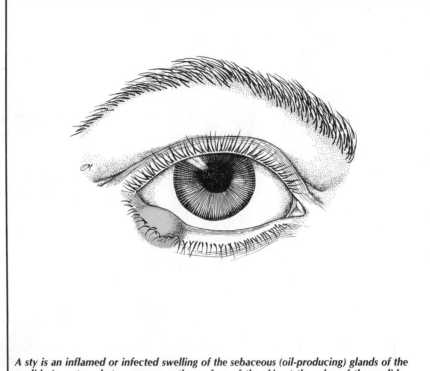

*A sty is an inflamed or infected swelling of the sebaceous (oil-producing) glands of the eyelid. An external sty appears on the surface of the skin at the edge of the eyelid.*

or ointments. Applying warm, moist compresses to the eye for about ten minutes three or four times a day may encourage the sty to burst. In some cases, particularly if there is an internal sty, surgical opening may be needed to cure the condition. One should never attempt to open a sty on his own, as the risks of spreading and worsening the infection are quite high.

# EARS, NOSE, AND THROAT

The ears, nose, and throat are interconnected, and for this reason they are usually grouped together in the field of medicine. Because they are joined, infection in one structure often spreads into one of the others.

## Ears

The ear consists of three parts: the outer ear, the middle ear, and the inner ear. The outer ear consists of the pinna, or external ear, which captures sound waves and directs them inward, and the ear canal, which leads to the eardrum. In the middle ear, sound waves vibrate through three tiny bones commonly called the hammer, the anvil, and the stirrup. The vibrations continue into the inner ear, where a structure called the cochlea transforms them into nerve impulses. These impulses are conveyed to the brain via the auditory nerve.

The eustachian tube in the middle ear connects the ear with the nasopharynx (the upper part of the throat). This tube allows the air pressure in the middle ear to equalize with the pressure outside the body, thus helping to prevent rupture of the eardrum. However, the eustachian tube also provides a passageway for infecting microorganisms to enter the middle ear from the nose or throat.

The semicircular canals (also called the labyrinth) within the inner ear serve as the organs of balance by detecting motion of the head and conveying this information to the brain.

## Nose

The nose is a specialized structure that serves dual func-

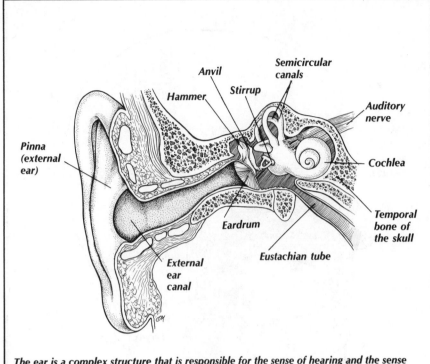

The ear is a complex structure that is responsible for the sense of hearing and the sense of balance.

tions as the organ for the sense of smell and as an entry to the respiratory tract.

Nerve receptor cells within the nose detect odors that enter via the nostrils and transmit signals to the brain through the olfactory nerve. The sense of smell also enhances the sense of taste. The ability to smell is more refined than the ability to taste; therefore, when a cold blocks nasal passages, food may seem bland and tasteless.

As part of the respiratory tract, the nose moisturizes and warms incoming air and filters out foreign materials. Small glands within the lining of the nose secrete mucus, a sticky substance that lubricates the walls of the nose and throat. Mucus humidifies the incoming air and traps bacteria, dust, and other particles entering the nose. Many bacteria are either dissolved by chemical elements in the mucus

or transported to the entrance of the throat by tiny, hairlike structures called cilia. The bacteria are then swallowed and killed by acids and other chemicals produced in the stomach. This efficient line of defense protects the body against the billions of bacteria that continually enter the nose.

Connected to the nose are the sinuses—air-filled cavities lined with mucus-secreting glands that are located within certain facial bones. There are four groups of sinuses—frontal, sphenoidal, ethmoidal, and maxillary.

## Throat

The throat, or pharynx, is a passageway connecting the back of the mouth and the nose to the esophagus (the tube between the mouth and the stomach) and to the trachea, or windpipe (the

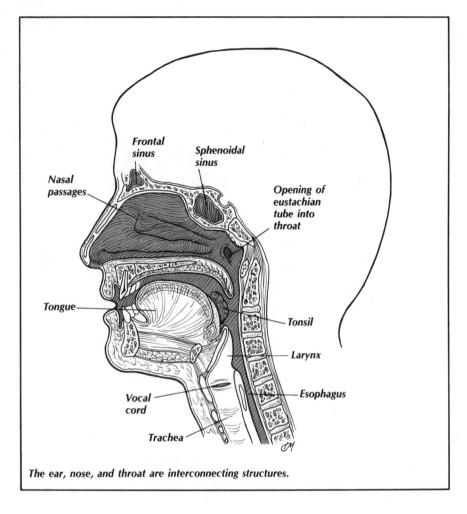

*The ear, nose, and throat are interconnecting structures.*

tube between the mouth and the lungs). Because air and food pass through the throat, the throat is considered to be a part of both the respiratory and the digestive systems.

Three sections make up the throat. The nasopharynx is the upper part of the throat, which opens into the nose. The oropharynx is the middle portion, which opens into the mouth. The lower section of the throat, or laryngopharynx, connects the other sections with the larynx, or voice box.

Within the throat are two small, almond-shaped masses of lymphoid tissue called tonsils. The tonsils help fight disease by destroying bacteria that enter the throat.

# Adenoids

Adenoids are masses of protective lymphoid tissue located in the lining of the nasopharynx. Like the tonsils located below them, the adenoids (technically known as the nasopharyngeal tonsils) are lymph nodes containing the specialized white blood cells that help localize and destroy harmful bacteria and viruses. They thus provide an important defense against diseases of the respiratory system.

## Enlarged adenoids

It is normal for adenoids to become enlarged during throat infections, just as the tonsils do,

and then to diminish in size after the infection has passed. Sometimes, however, as a result of continuing infection or allergies, the adenoids remain enlarged. The resulting obstruction of the nasal passage may cause mouth breathing, the characteristic "nasal" voice, and continuing drainage of pus-filled mucus down the throat. It may also cause a blockage of the eustachian tubes, which connect the throat to the ears, resulting in retention of fluid in the middle ear, impaired hearing, earache, and recurring ear infections.

## Treatment

Treatment of infection of the adenoids is with antibiotics, taken by mouth. Surgery may be recommended when the infected or enlarged adenoids themselves are the source of the disease (usually the tonsils beneath are infected as well and are removed in the same operation). This would be the case if recurrent or continuing infection of the adenoids could not be eliminated with antibiotics, if the adenoids caused repeated ear infections, or if cancer or an abscess (a mass of pus in a cavity) was present. If chronically infected adenoids increase susceptibility to a serious condition, such as rheumatic fever or nephritis (a kidney disease), surgical removal of the adenoids may be recommended. However, surgery is generally not performed during an acute attack of tonsillitis, because it may worsen the infection.

Surgery may not be the answer to prevent snoring, mouth breathing, or the nasal voice caused by enlarged adenoids, since the enlargement usually diminishes after childhood.

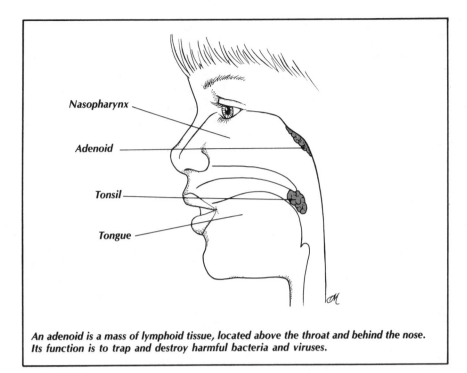

*An adenoid is a mass of lymphoid tissue, located above the throat and behind the nose. Its function is to trap and destroy harmful bacteria and viruses.*

## Prevention

Adenoid infection and enlargement cannot always be prevented. In fact, enlarging in order to trap and fight infectious organisms is a normal function of the adenoids. Good general health measures can help, however, as can the use of antibiotics prescribed by a physician when the adenoids become infected and enlarged.

# Common cold

A simple common cold is a collection of familiar symptoms signaling an infection of the upper respiratory tract, which includes the nose, throat, and sinuses.

Colds are self-limiting diseases, meaning that their symptoms last a certain length of time (or "run their course," as is often remarked) and then disappear without leaving lasting ill effects. A cold is a mild but commonplace disease, contracted by adults about two to four times a year and by children about six to eight times a year. Adults with children at home are more likely to catch colds than are those who do not have children. Children are especially susceptible to colds because they have not yet developed immunity or resistance to the many viruses that can cause colds. Small children gradually build up immunity to the viruses in their homes; when they go to school and have close contact with many other children, they are exposed to new viruses. Similarly, adults who travel frequently or have a high number of close contacts outside their community are more likely to contract colds or encounter new cold viruses to which they are not immune than are those who lead more isolated lives.

## Complications

A cold can be a minor irritation, but it can increase suscep-tibility to more serious conditions, especially in the very young, the very old, and the very weak. Pneumonia, an infection of the lungs, is probably the most serious. Ear infections, sinus infections, and bronchitis are other possible complications. A few days after a cold, children sometimes develop croup, recognized by a harsh, barking cough that signals swelling of the airways to the lungs.

## Causes

At least five major categories of viruses cause colds. One of these groups, the rhinoviruses, includes a minimum of 100 different types of viruses. Various combinations of symptoms and possible complications can develop from each of these viruses. It is not known exactly how viruses spread, but it seems to be a combination of physical contact and the presence of both virus particles and moisture in the air. A virus can be spread by hand-to-hand contact, for example, or by the passage of droplets from an infected person's nasal passages and throat into the air. Colds have an incubation period of 48 to 72 hours, meaning that it takes that long after the virus enters the body for early symptoms to appear.

## Symptoms

Early symptoms of the common cold include a stuffy or runny nose, sneezing, a sore or scratchy throat, a cough, and occasionally a mild fever. Usually, as the cold progresses, other symptoms—burning or watery eyes, loss of the senses of taste and smell, pressure in the ears or

# EARS, NOSE, AND THROAT

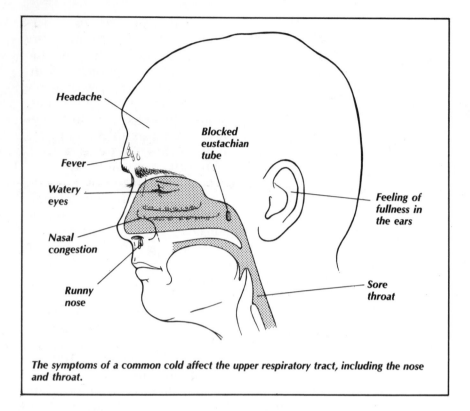

The symptoms of a common cold affect the upper respiratory tract, including the nose and throat.

for the symptoms actually present and to carefully follow directions on the medication package. Overuse of an otherwise effective remedy can backfire and actually make the symptoms worse, and treating symptoms that are not there can complicate matters. For example, the overuse of an antihistamine or other drying agent for nasal congestion can make a cough more uncomfortable, and the use of a nasal decongestant for more than three days can actually increase congestion when the blood vessels can no longer remain constricted and relax in a rebound fashion. Anyone who is pregnant or has a chronic disease should check with a doctor before using cold preparations, even seemingly harmless over-the-counter drugs.

sinuses, nasal voice, and tenderness around the nose—may appear.

Symptoms vary in type and severity from one viral infection to another, so a cold can begin with any symptom or combination of symptoms. Most colds last about a week, but about 25 percent of all colds last two weeks. Smokers and those with chronic respiratory diseases tend to have more severe symptoms and longer-lasting colds and to experience complications more readily than do those who do not fall into these categories.

## Diagnosis

Since common colds are mild diseases, the physician, in diagnosing a cold, will actually be looking for symptoms indicating a condition more serious than a common cold. Material from the patient's throat or nasal passages

may be tested for bacterial infections. A blood test may be recommended to check for mononucleosis, a disease characterized by a long-lasting sore throat and swollen lymph nodes. An x-ray examination of the sinuses may be necessary if sinusitis (an infection of the sinuses) is suspected.

## Treatment

Getting plenty of rest, drinking lots of fluids to prevent dehydration, and using a humidifier or vaporizer can help relieve the irritating symptoms of a cold. Nevertheless, the common cold cannot be cured, and no known treatment will actually hasten recovery. Many over-the-counter (nonprescription) medicines and preparations are available that will at least ease the discomfort of a cold. However, it is best to take specific medications only

## Prevention

There is no known preventive for the common cold. Vitamin C has been said to help prevent colds, but many studies have shown that it has no measurable effect in this regard. Avoiding exposure to viruses, when possible, may be the only means of avoiding the common cold.

# Deafness

Deafness is a term used to describe complete or partial loss or absence of the ability to hear.

## Types

There are three major types of deafness:

*Conductive deafness* is caused by a defect in the outer or middle ear, which prevents normal transmission of sound. It may be present at birth as the result of an

# Headache
Fever
Watery eyes
Nasal congestion
Runny nose
Blocked eustachian tube
Feeling of fullness in the ears
Sore throat

166

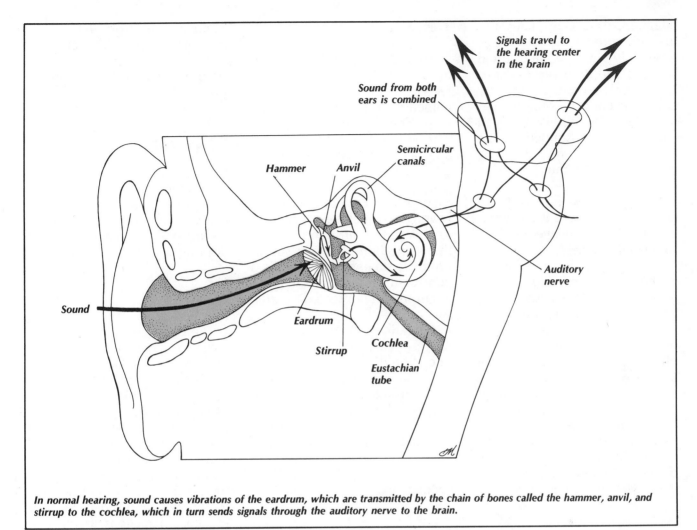

*In normal hearing, sound causes vibrations of the eardrum, which are transmitted by the chain of bones called the hammer, anvil, and stirrup to the cochlea, which in turn sends signals through the auditory nerve to the brain.*

inherited defect, an abnormality in development, or an infection of the fetus in the womb. It may be produced by an injury that perforates the eardrum or that breaks up the linkage of the three tiny bones—hammer, anvil, and stirrup—that normally transmit sound from the eardrum through the middle ear to the inner ear. Inflammation of the middle ear, a condition known as otitis media, is another important cause of conductive deafness. Infection from an upper respiratory tract ailment, such as strep throat or the flu, can produce a buildup of pus in the middle ear so great that it ruptures the eardrum. Also, a plugged eustachian tube (the tube leading from the back of the throat to the ear) may trap fluid in the middle ear, creating temporary deafness. Conductive deafness in the middle and later years is most often caused by otosclerosis. In this inherited condition, new spongy bone grows over the stirrup bone, preventing it from vibrating when sound travels to it through the hammer and anvil bones.

*Sensorineural deafness* is a type of hearing loss that occurs because of damage to the structures of the inner ear, to the auditory nerve carrying sound messages to the brain, or to the hearing center of the brain itself, which is located in the temporal lobe. It may be due to a head injury during birth, the effects of a woman's rubella infection on her unborn baby, a skull fracture affecting the inner ear or the auditory nerve, fever, bacterial or viral infections (such as mumps and meningitis), tertiary (final-stage) syphilis, Meniere's disease, tumors, multiple sclerosis, a hemorrhage or blood clot in the inner ear, drug side effects, normal aging, prolonged or repeated exposure to intense noise, or edema (fluid buildup) caused by a thyroid deficiency. Most sensorineural deafness is not nerve deafness, the popular term for it. It is usually sensory deafness, caused by defects in the structure of the inner ear, especially in the fluid-filled cochlea and its organ of Corti. The cochlea contains sensory cells that convert sound waves into electrical impulses, which can then be transmitted via the auditory nerve to the brain, where they are interpreted as sounds.

*Mixed deafness* is a relatively common condition. It is a combination of conductive and sensorineural deafness.

People with pure conductive deafness simply need louder volume to hear all sounds. Those with defects in the inner ear usually can hear low-pitched sounds more easily than high-pitched sounds, and some sounds may be distorted. When there is damage to the hearing center in the brain, the person may be able to hear sounds, but has trouble recognizing them and understanding words (this problem can also occur with the other types of deafness).

### Diagnosis

When hearing loss is suspected, a complete examination of the ears, nose, and throat is necessary to identify infections or abnormalities that may be present. Infections of the adenoids or tonsils, as well as sinus or nasal infections, may be linked to ear infections.

Testing of hearing is important for all ages, but especially for infants. Many times, partial deafness in a baby is not discovered until the child fails to learn to talk, a direct result of the hearing loss. Babies who were born prematurely or ill or whose mothers had certain viral infections, such as rubella, during pregnancy are in special need of testing.

### Treatment

Although inborn hearing defects usually cannot be corrected, deaf children can be helped to deal with their handicap. Starting very early, they can be fitted with hearing aids and can be instructed in lipreading, speaking, and sign language.

Surgery to correct conductive hearing loss includes operations to replace the stirrup bone or all three tiny bones with tissue or synthetic material, to repair a punctured eardrum, and to clean a chronically infected middle ear.

A hearing aid can often help to restore hearing. However, one should be purchased only after thorough testing by a specialist in audiometry, who can suggest the most appropriate type. Classes in lipreading and listening can also be helpful.

### Prevention

It is far easier to prevent deafness than to cure it. Antibiotics have made it possible to eradicate most of the middle ear infections that have been the major source of conductive hearing loss in children. Middle ear problems are sometimes eliminated by treating allergies that cause the eustachian tubes to close up or by removing infected adenoids. Nerve deafness caused by continued exposure to intense industrial noise, gunshots, rock music, or aircraft engines may be avoided by wearing earplugs or other ear protectors. Some lost hearing may return after several months of relief from intense sound. Drugs that can cause hearing loss, including some antibiotics and certain diuretics (drugs that

remove water from the blood), need to be used with care, and signs of hearing loss should be brought to a doctor's attention.

# Glossitis

Glossitis is an acute (short-term) or chronic (long-term) inflammation of the tongue. It may exist either as a primary disease or as a symptom of another disease or disorder.

### Causes

The causes of glossitis can be either local or systemic (affecting the entire body). Local causes include immediate irritants, such as jagged or broken teeth, badly fitting dentures, poor oral hygiene habits, biting of the tongue (such as during convulsions), and external irritants, such as alcohol, tobacco, hot or spicy foods, and even mouthwashes, toothpastes, and breath fresheners. Local infections, burns, and injuries may also produce symptoms of glossitis. Systemic causes may include certain vitamin deficiencies (especially vitamin B deficiencies, such as pellagra), anemia, syphilis, and generalized skin diseases.

### Symptoms

Symptoms vary widely, ranging from simple redness of the tip and edges of the tongue (if the cause is pellagra, anemia, or irritation from smoking or a tooth with a rough surface) to painful ulcers and whitish patches. In the later stages of pellagra, the entire tongue may be fiery red, swollen, and ulcerated. In iron deficiency and pernicious anemia, the tongue is pale and smooth. Painful ulcers on the tongue may indicate a number of diseases, including herpes, tuberculosis, and streptococcal infection. White patches suggest candidiasis (a type of yeast infection), syphilis, or simple mouth breathing (which dries out the mucous membrane of the tongue). Very smooth and painless areas may be what is called geographic tongue, or benign (harmless) glossitis. So-called hairy tongue often follows antibiotic therapy, a high fever, excessive use of certain mouthwashes, or a simple reduction in saliva secretion.

Severe acute glossitis, which can result from local infection, burns, and injury, can cause tenderness, pain, and swelling sufficient to make the tongue protrude from the mouth into the back of the throat—creating the danger of airway obstruction and even suffocation. In severe cases, the patient may not be able to chew, swallow, or speak. Steroid drug treatment usually reduces the swelling and helps relieve symptoms.

Patients may also complain of a painful burning tongue without other symptoms of inflammation. This is a common complaint among postmenopausal women. Diabetes, anemia, nutritional deficiencies, and malignant conditions should all be considered as possible primary causes.

**Treatment**

The patient should be reassured that redness and most lesions of the tongue are usually harmless and respond well to treatment. Such complaints as ulcers and hairy tongue often recur periodically, however; if

an ulcer does not respond to treatment after several weeks, a biopsy (removal of a tissue sample for examination under a microscope) may be performed.

In treating glossitis, specific causes, such as jagged teeth and ill-fitting dentures, should be corrected. Irritants, including hot or spicy foods, tobacco, alcohol, mouthwashes, and toothpastes, should be avoided once they have been identified as the source of the trouble. A bland or liquid diet, preferably cool or cold, will often have a soothing effect. Good oral hygiene is necessary in all cases.

Tiny brown growths on the tongue are usually caused by contact with tobacco or certain bacteria; the treatment is to stop smoking or otherwise correct the underlying cause and also to brush the tongue with a toothbrush.

Symptomatic relief for large lesions includes rinsing the mouth with a medicated mouthwash before meals. Application of topical anesthetics, such as lidocaine and benzocaine, can also bring relief. Patients with

complaints of painful burning should be tested to rule out vitamin $B_{12}$ deficiency, diabetes, and some types of anemia.

**Prevention**

Prevention of glossitis involves avoiding irritants, correcting nutritional and vitamin deficiencies, and treating primary infections that produce glossitis as a secondary symptom.

# Laryngitis

Laryngitis is an inflammation of the mucous membrane lining the larynx (voice box), which is located in the upper part of the respiratory tract. It causes hoarseness and possibly a temporary loss of speech.

**Causes**

Laryngitis may result from a bacterial or viral infection, such as a cold or the flu; from an irritation of the mucous membrane

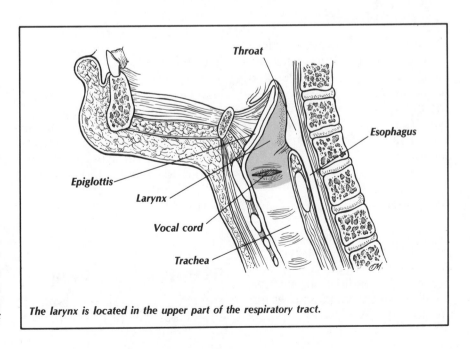

*The larynx is located in the upper part of the respiratory tract.*

of the larynx, such as that caused by smoking; or from overuse of the voice.

Chronic or persistent laryngitis is most often caused by smoking, air pollution, dust, or smoke. It may also stem from tonsillitis, tuberculosis, the early stages of some forms of cancer, or paralysis of the vocal cords. Because laryngitis may be a symptom of a more serious condition, persons who consistently suffer from it should consult a physician.

### Symptoms

Hoarseness, loss of the voice, dryness and scratchiness of the throat, coughing, and pain on speaking are common symptoms.

### Treatment

Laryngitis is best treated by totally resting the vocal cords. Pain may be eased with throat sprays, steam inhalations, and mild pain-relievers, such as aspirin and acetaminophen.

# Mastoiditis

Mastoiditis is a bacterial infection of the mastoid air cells (small, air-filled cavities located in the mastoid process, which is the bulge in the skull behind the ear). Mastoiditis is most often a complication of a middle ear infection.

### Symptoms

Mastoiditis is characterized by ringing in the ear, a discharge of pus from the ear canal, and fever. Other indications include swelling and tenderness over the mastoid process.

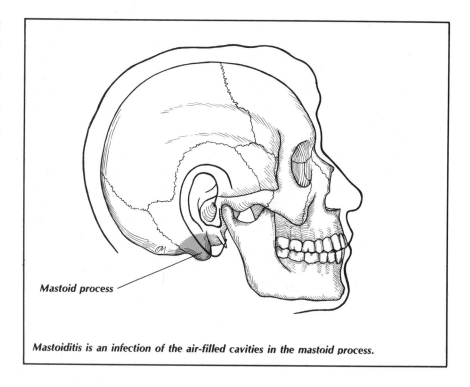

*Mastoid process*

*Mastoiditis is an infection of the air-filled cavities in the mastoid process.*

### Complications

In severe cases, an abscess may develop in the mastoid process. This is a serious complication because it carries the risk that infection will spread to the interior of the skull and cause meningitis (inflammation of the membranes that cover the brain).

### Treatment

Because antibiotics are so effective against ear infections and mastoid infections, mastoiditis is fortunately now rare. Sometimes, however, surgery is required to remove the infected cells if antibiotic treatment is started too late or is not effective.

# Meniere's disease

Meniere's disease is the result of an increase in pressure in the inner ear because of a buildup of fluid in the labyrinth (the semicircular canals of the inner ear, which control balance and equilibrium). This buildup of pressure distorts and sometimes ruptures the lining of the labyrinth wall.

### Causes

The cause of Meniere's disease is unknown, although it is thought that the pressure changes may be brought on by an infection, a small hemorrhage in the ear, or an allergic response. It occurs most commonly in men aged 40 to 60.

### Symptoms

The symptoms of Meniere's disease include recurring and violent attacks of vertigo or dizziness, ringing in the ears, muffling or distortion of noises, and nausea that is sometimes accompanied by vomiting. Deafness in one or both ears may eventually develop.

Mild attacks of Meniere's disease may last from a half hour to several days before fading away naturally. They may recur regularly at intervals of weeks, months, or years. Severe attacks may last for several weeks, requiring the person to be confined to bed. In such cases, almost any movement of the head will result in bizarre and disturbing sensations that the floor and the furniture in the room are spinning around. Severe cases may also be accompanied by anxiety attacks and migraine headaches.

### Treatment

The use of certain drugs, such as diuretics and antihistamines, may help to relieve severe and recurrent attacks. In severe cases, surgery may be necessary.

# Middle ear infections

The ear can become infected in any one of its three parts—the inner ear, the middle ear, or the outer ear. However, ear infections most commonly settle in the middle ear. The medical term for middle ear infection is otitis media.

Ear infections are much more likely to affect children than adults; children are most susceptible between the ages of six months and six years. Children who contract ear infections in their first year are more likely to have chronic (long-term) ear infections later in life. By the age of eight, almost every child has had at least one ear infection.

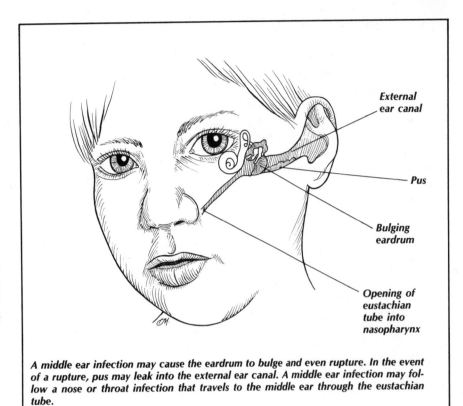

External ear canal

Pus

Bulging eardrum

Opening of eustachian tube into nasopharynx

*A middle ear infection may cause the eardrum to bulge and even rupture. In the event of a rupture, pus may leak into the external ear canal. A middle ear infection may follow a nose or throat infection that travels to the middle ear through the eustachian tube.*

### Causes

Middle ear infections develop when viruses or bacteria in the nose or throat travel to the ear through the eustachian tube, which connects the middle ear to the nose and throat. The middle ear also can become infected when infection spreads from a severe outer ear infection or injury.

### Symptoms

Middle ear infections can be recognized by severe throbbing pain in the ear, fever as high as 105°F (102°F in adults), hearing loss, and possibly dizziness, nausea, vomiting, or sore throat. The eardrums may bulge out or may even burst, oozing blood and pus into the outer ear and relieving the pain. Symptoms may worsen over a period of

hours or days. A child too young to talk may seem ill or feverish or may pull on an ear.

### Diagnosis

Ear infections are diagnosed by an inspection of the eardrum. If it is red and swollen or bulging, middle ear infection can usually be confirmed.

### Treatment

Middle ear infections are usually quickly eliminated by treatment with an antibiotic, often a form of penicillin. Decongestants may also be used. If a viral infection is present, however, antibiotics are not used, since viruses do not respond to antibiotics. If the eardrum is bulging and the pain is severe, the doctor may make a small cut in the eardrum (called a myringotomy) to relieve the pressure. If the eardrum bursts, the outer ear must be kept clean to prevent infection from spreading.

The development of more effective antibiotics has lessened the need for surgery. In rare cases, however, the infected tissue may have to be surgically removed.

Middle ear infections usually clear up quickly, but the more severe or persistent infections can lead to a variety of serious complications, including temporary or permanent hearing loss, infection of the semicircular canals in the inner ear, facial paralysis, brain abscess, meningitis (infection of the covering of the brain), and infection of the mastoid process (the bulge in the skull behind the ear).

# Nosebleeds

A nosebleed occurs when there is a break in the blood vessels in the inner lining of the nose, causing bleeding from the nose. Nosebleeds seldom require medical attention, but it is possible, although relatively rare, for nosebleeds to be symptoms of serious illnesses.

### Causes

Nosebleeds can be caused by an injury to the nose, breathing dry air for prolonged periods, repeated blowing or picking of the nose, tumors in the nose, high blood pressure, and certain blood diseases.

### Treatment

Very persistent or frequently recurring nosebleeds will require

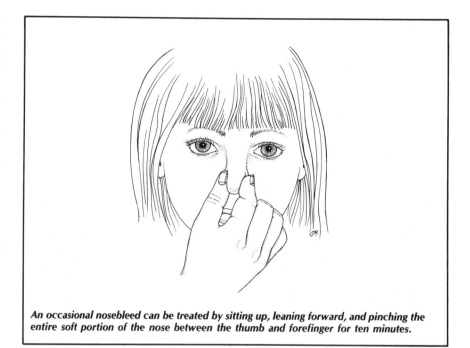

*An occasional nosebleed can be treated by sitting up, leaning forward, and pinching the entire soft portion of the nose between the thumb and forefinger for ten minutes.*

the attention of a doctor, who may cauterize (use heat or the chemical silver nitrate to seal off) the blood vessels in the back of the nose.

However, occasional nosebleeds can be treated simply by sitting up and leaning forward, so as not to swallow the blood, and pinching the entire soft portion of the nose between the thumb and forefinger for ten minutes. If the bleeding does not stop, cold packs can be applied to the bridge of the nose for 15 to 20 minutes. If bleeding still persists, a doctor should be notified.

Frequent nosebleeds from breathing dry air may be relieved by the use of a humidifier. Also, those who have frequent nosebleeds should not blow the nose too harshly or blow through one nostril.

When nosebleeds occur along with colds or other respiratory infections, a nasal decongestant may help to temporarily shrink the blood vessels in the nose. However, these decongestants should not be used by anyone with high blood pressure, heart disease, diabetes, or thyroid disorders, because decongestants also shrink blood vessels in parts of the body other than the nose, which can lead to complications for these patients.

# Otosclerosis

Otosclerosis is a condition in which an abnormal spongy overgrowth of bone in the middle ear leads to totally or partially muffled hearing or deafness. The excess bone grows at the entrance to the middle ear, where it immobilizes the base of the stapes (a tiny, stirrup-shaped bone, which is one of three interconnected bones that transmit sound waves to the inner ear). As a result, sound-conducting vibrations are diminished and impaired hearing results. In most cases, both ears are eventually affected. The cause of otosclerosis is unknown, but the condition tends to be hereditary.

## Symptoms

Hearing loss generally begins in the late teens or early 20s; the rate of deafness may accelerate and stabilize several times, but ordinarily the loss is complete within 10 to 15 years—sooner if the disease began in childhood. In some cases, the hearing loss stops just short of deafness and the affected person can still hear loud sounds. Otosclerosis usually affects one ear before the other and is preceded by tinnitus (ringing in the ear). Special hearing tests aid in diagnosis.

## Treatment

The only way to halt or reverse otosclerosis is surgery, which is successful about 70 percent of the time. Although a hearing aid can help, most doctors prefer to operate. In a procedure called a stapedectomy, a surgeon folds back the eardrum, removes the affected stapes and replaces it with a synthetic or wire substitute that restores the conductive vibrations of the middle ear. Because the bones involved are the tiniest in the body, the surgery is very delicate and entails a risk of failure. In most cases, the operation is done on only one ear at a time, thereby reducing the risk.

After surgery, the hearing of most patients is greatly improved within two to three weeks. In some cases, a residual blood clot at the site of the surgery temporarily blocks hearing until it dissolves. Patients with advanced otosclerosis in both ears are usually advised to undergo stapedectomy as soon as possible.

# Sinusitis

Sinusitis is an infection (usually bacterial) of one or more of the sinuses. It occurs more commonly in adults than in children.

The sinuses are air-filled cavities located within the facial bone structure and connected to the nose. There are four major groups of sinuses: frontal, ethmoidal, sphenoidal, and maxillary.

The sinuses are lined with mucous membrane and are normally kept clear when mucus

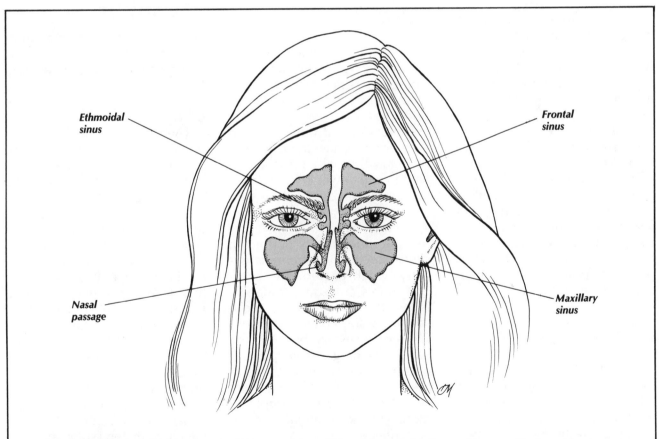

*The sinuses are air-filled cavities within the facial bone structure, which are connected to the nasal passages. The four major groups are the frontal, ethmoidal, sphenoidal, and maxillary. The sphenoidal sinuses (not shown here) are located behind the ethmoidal sinuses.*

drains through them into the nasal passages. If they are obstructed for any reason, such as from the congestion present during a cold, normal drainage cannot occur, and infection of the sinuses can result.

## Complications

It is rare but possible for long-lasting sinusitis to lead to more serious disorders. A persistent infection may travel to the brain, causing meningitis (inflammation of the membranes surrounding the brain), or to the bone, resulting in osteomyelitis (inflammation of a bone and its marrow).

## Causes

A sinus infection may be triggered by anything that prevents the mucus in the sinuses from draining properly into the nasal passages. Possible causes include swimming and diving, injuries, abnormal structure of the facial bones, congestion from the flu or a cold, allergies, or an abscess (inflamed pocket of pus) in a tooth, which may penetrate the sinuses and allow bacteria to enter them. Many different types of bacteria can cause sinusitis, including some of the same strains that lead to pneumonia, laryngitis, and middle ear infections.

## Symptoms

Sinusitis is characterized by pain and tenderness above the infected sinus, which is felt in the face and forehead, behind the eyes, in the eyes, near the upper part of the nose, and even in the upper teeth (but not in a single tooth). This facial pain may be accompanied by headache, slight fever, chills, sore throat, nasal obstruction, and a discharge of pus from the nose.

Sinusitis usually lasts about two weeks, with the pain often subsiding in the morning and worsening as the day goes on, or fluctuating as the patient moves about and changes positions.

## Diagnosis

The sinuses cannot be seen directly by a doctor, so diagnostic evaluation may include an x-ray examination to check for the presence of fluid or abnormalities in the sinuses and to determine which sinuses are infected.

## Treatment

Sinusitis is treated by encouraging drainage of the sinuses so as to remove the bacteria that are causing the infection. Nasal decongestants, hot compresses, and moist heat all work to aid sinus drainage. The doctor will usually prescribe an antibiotic that will kill the bacteria that most commonly trigger sinusitis.

If these treatments bring no relief, the doctor may perform a sinus puncture to determine exactly which bacteria are present. In this procedure, a needle is inserted into the sinus, and a sample of the fluid is removed. (This is necessary because the nasal discharge may contain bacteria different from those in the sinuses.) On the basis of analysis of the fluid sample, a more specific antibiotic may be prescribed.

In severe cases, codeine may be prescribed to dull the pain,

and the doctor may clear the sinuses by injecting a solution through the nose to flush out the bacteria.

In some cases, surgery may be necessary to remove a nasal polyp (a mass of swollen tissue), repair abnormal bone structures, or remove infected sinus tissue.

## Prevention

There is some evidence that smokers are more likely to suffer from sinusitis than are nonsmokers. Those who frequently have colds are also more susceptible to sinusitis. Avoiding smoking and exposure to persons with colds may help to prevent sinusitis.

# Tonsillitis

Tonsillitis is an inflammation or infection of the tonsils. It occurs most commonly in children from 5 to 15 years old, and only rarely in those under the age of two.

The tonsils are two small, almond-shaped lumps of specialized lymph node tissue located in the throat at the back of the mouth. They are barely visible in infants, increase in size during the preschool and early school years, and shrink by adulthood.

The function of the tonsils has not been pinpointed, but scientists believe that they perform at least two vital jobs: they release antibodies (protective agents) into the throat to prevent infection from spreading into the lungs (a useful service to children, who are highly susceptible to ear, nose, and throat infections); and they attract bacterial infection, thereby stimulating the production of antibodies, which accumulate in the body and are

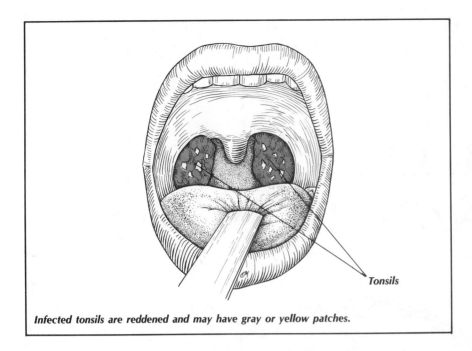

*Infected tonsils are reddened and may have gray or yellow patches.*

**Tonsils**

then available to prevent future, and potentially much more serious, infections. (Antibodies normally do not develop unless infection is present.) If the tonsils do indeed perform these two functions, then each attack of tonsillitis may help immunize a child against disease; once resistance has been developed, the function of the tonsils is complete.

There are two types of tonsillitis: acute tonsillitis, in which the infection flares up and then disappears in a short time; and chronic tonsillitis, in which the tonsils seem to be permanently inflamed and have abscesses (pus-filled cavities) on them.

## Causes

Tonsillitis is caused by many different infectious agents, both viral and bacterial. The *Streptococcus* bacterium is the most common bacterial cause; acute tonsillitis is usually a ''strep'' infection. Chronic tonsillitis, however, is more of a mystery; it

is not known why chronic tonsillitis occurs in certain people or what causes it.

## Symptoms

The symptoms of acute tonsillitis are a sore throat, fever (up to about 101°F), chills, headache, and muscle aches. These symptoms worsen for one to three days and then subside. Nausea, vomiting, stomachache, and swelling of lymph nodes in the neck may also occur and may last for about a week.

The symptoms of chronic tonsillitis include a persistent or recurrent sore throat, difficulty in swallowing or breathing, and foul breath.

## Diagnosis

Tonsillitis is diagnosed by examination of the tonsils for redness, swelling, and the presence of gray or yellow infectious material. The doctor will take a sample of this material with a

cotton swab in order to identify the organism causing the infection.

## Treatment

Bed rest or reduced activity and the use of antibiotics, often penicillin, are recommended to treat tonsillitis if the inflammation is due to bacteria. Gargling with warm salt water can help relieve sore throat.

Surgical removal of the tonsils (called a tonsillectomy) is performed only if the tonsils are abscessed (filled with pus) or so enlarged that they are blocking the air passages. Tonsillectomies are seldom performed today, because research has found that even when tonsils are enlarged, they almost always shrink over time. Furthermore, removing the tonsils does not necessarily prevent recurrent sore throats and colds, as was once believed.

## Complications

Complications resulting from tonsillitis seldom occur today because of effective, fast-acting antibiotics, but rheumatic fever and infections of the sinuses, ears, and kidneys are rare but possible complications.

## Prevention

Since it is not yet known why some people suffer from chronic tonsillitis, preventive measures have not been established. Because episodes of acute tonsillitis may be useful in the development of immunities in the body, prevention of such episodes may not be appropriate. More research is needed in this area.

# THE LUNGS AND
# RESPIRATORY SYSTEM

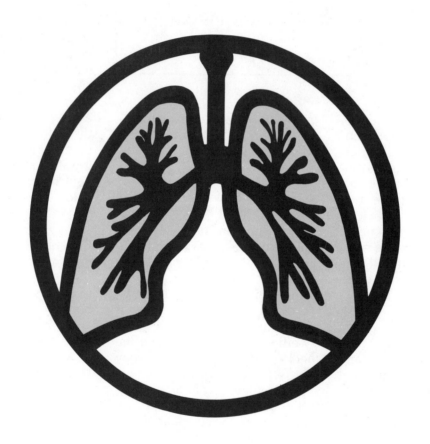

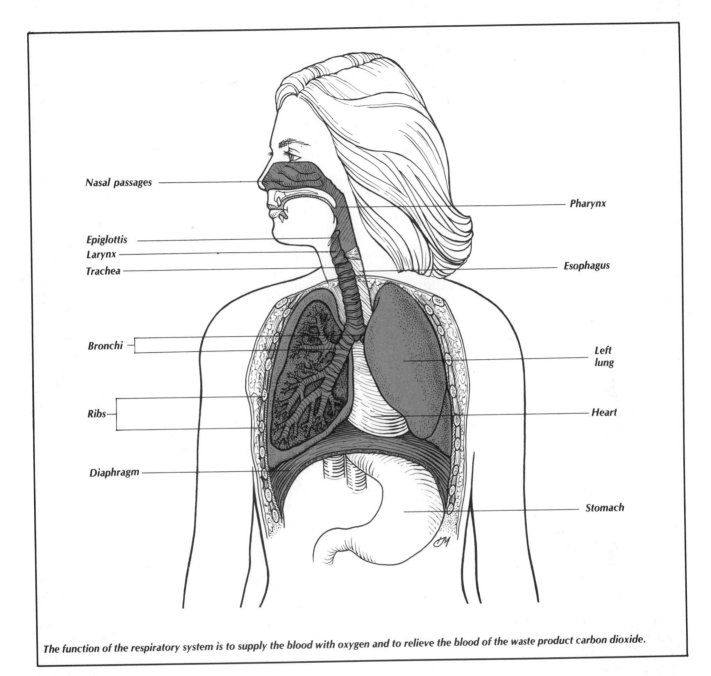

Nasal passages

Pharynx

Epiglottis
Larynx
Trachea

Esophagus

Bronchi

Left lung

Ribs

Heart

Diaphragm

Stomach

*The function of the respiratory system is to supply the blood with oxygen and to relieve the blood of the waste product carbon dioxide.*

The respiratory system includes the nose, the throat, the larynx, the trachea, the bronchi, and the lungs. The function of the respiratory system is to supply the blood with necessary oxygen and to relieve the blood of the waste product carbon dioxide. This exchange of oxygen and carbon dioxide occurs in the lungs. Air from the outside enters through the nose, where it is warmed, moistened, and filtered before it passes through the throat and past the larynx (voice box) into the trachea (windpipe). The trachea divides into two main bronchi (passageways leading into each lung). Within each lung, the bronchi divide and subdivide, forming progressively smaller passageways called bronchioles. The smallest bronchioles end in small, cup-shaped sacs called alveoli. It is in the alveoli that the exchange of oxygen and carbon dioxide takes place. Each alveolus is served by numerous tiny blood vessels called capillaries. Oxygen in the alveolus crosses the thin alveolar and capillary walls to enter the blood, while carbon dioxide passes from the blood through the capillary walls into the alveolus. The oxygen is then

177

carried by the blood to cells throughout the body, and the carbon dioxide is exhaled.

During inhalation and exhalation, the lungs are expanded and contracted by movements of the rib cage and the diaphragm (the large muscle separating the chest and abdominal cavities). During inhalation, the diaphragm contracts, which causes it to descend and the chest cavity to expand. At this point, the air pressure inside the chest cavity is less than that of the air outside the body; consequently, air from the outside rushes into the lungs. During exhalation, the diaphragm relaxes and moves upward, reducing the chest capacity and pushing air out of the lungs. The friction caused by expansion and contraction of the lungs is eased by the pleurae (thin, moist membranes that cover the lungs and line the chest cavity), so that the surfaces of the lungs and chest cavity can move past each other smoothly.

# Apnea

Apnea is strictly defined as the absence of breathing. The term is also used to refer to an interruption in breathing that occurs in some premature babies and also during the sleep of some children and adults. The usual cause in infants is immaturity of the brain centers that regulate breathing. In children and adults, most often the cause is obstruction of the upper airway; the second most common cause is malfunction of the breathing control centers in the brain.

## Apnea in infants

Apnea in a tiny baby is frightening. From time to time, the infant suddenly stops breathing completely and turns blue. If the baby is stimulated in some way (for example, by a flick of the finger on the bottom of the foot), he will usually start breathing normally at once. Seldom is it necessary to use first-aid measures or a mechanical respirator to restart breathing. However, because a history of apnea is one of the factors that may be associated with sudden infant death syndrome (SIDS), physicians sometimes recommend monitoring of high-risk infants with special equipment that sounds an alarm if any stoppage of breathing is detected (for more information on SIDS, see page 361). In some cases, the tendency toward apnea disappears a few weeks after birth, when the breathing control centers have matured. In other cases, especially if there have been a number of episodes of apnea, home monitoring may continue for months.

## Apnea in children and adults

Apnea in children and adults is generally less immediately life-threatening than apnea in infants, but it can be physically exhausting and in a severe form it can cause cardiovascular and respiratory problems. In some patients, episodes of sleep apnea can cause the concentration of carbon dioxide in the blood to build up to a dangerously high level.

Recognition of the problem generally cannot be made by the patient himself. A spouse or parent may be the first to notice an abnormal sleep pattern—for example, loud snoring, followed by silence (when the breathing stops), and then a loud choke or gasp as the sleeper partially awakens, clears the air passage, and resumes breathing. Such a pattern may be repeated many times during the night. As a result, persons with sleep apnea are likely to be drowsy during the day and irritable due to lack of sleep, with decreased memory and attention span. A definitive diagnosis can be made after observation in a hospital sleep laboratory.

The problem may occur because of a disorder in the breathing control centers in the brain, or it may be a result of physical abnormalities of the chest, neck, and back due to obesity, the presence of a disease process, or an inborn structural defect. If apnea is due to an abnormality of the breathing control centers, drugs may be prescribed, or stimulation of the diaphragm (the muscle separating the chest and abdomen, which is instrumental in breathing) with an electronic pacemaker may be tried. Obesity is a common cause of sleep apnea in adults because the presence of excess tissue may block the airway in certain sleeping positions; the disorder may disappear after weight loss. If a physical abnormality due to disease or a structural defect is the cause, surgical treatment may be necessary; for example, enlarged tonsils and adenoids that are partially obstructing the upper airway may be removed. In extreme cases of airway obstruction, the only solution may be tracheostomy (surgical creation of a hole in the trachea and neck, through which the patient can breathe).

# Asthma

Asthma is a respiratory disorder characterized by unpredictable periods of acute breathlessness and wheezing. Asthma attacks can last from less than an hour to a week or more and can strike frequently or only every few years. Attacks may be mild or severe and can occur at any time, even during sleep.

The difficult breathing occurs when the small respiratory tubes called bronchioles constrict or become clogged with mucus or when the membranes lining the bronchioles become swollen. When this happens, stale air cannot be fully exhaled but stays trapped in the lungs, so that less fresh air can be inhaled.

## Causes

Asthma attacks can result from oversensitivity of the bronchial system to a variety of outside substances or environmental conditions. Approximately half of all attacks are triggered by allergies to such substances as dust, smoke, pollen, feathers, pet hair, insects, mold spores, and a variety of foods and medications. Attacks not related to allergies can be set off by strenuous exercise, breathing cold air, emotional stress, and infections, particularly those of the respiratory tract. Heredity may play a part in the tendency to develop asthma; if one or both of a child's parents are asthmatic, he has up to a 50 percent chance of developing the condition.

Asthma is rarely fatal, but it can be a very serious condition, especially in young children. Attacks often become less frequent and less severe as a child grows.

## Symptoms

Common symptoms of an asthma attack include tightness

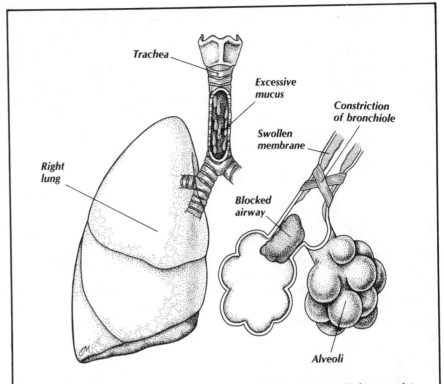

*The difficult breathing characteristic of asthma occurs when the bronchioles constrict or become clogged with mucus or when the membranes lining the bronchioles become swollen. Stale air is trapped in the alveoli, and less fresh air can be inhaled.*

in the chest, difficulty in breathing, coughing, and the characteristic wheezing, which is caused by the effort to push the flow of air through the narrowed bronchioles. As the attack progresses, muscles surrounding the bronchioles constrict further, breathing becomes even more difficult, and mucus collects in the airways.

## Diagnosis

Diagnostic procedures may include a complete physical examination and medical history, chest x-ray, and allergy testing.

## Treatment

Asthma cannot be cured, but it can be controlled with a vari-

ety of drugs. Epinephrine or isoproterenol may be administered by injection or as an aerosol during an acute attack in order to enlarge the bronchioles; however, these drugs may overstimulate the heart and so cannot be used for long periods of time. Similar drugs, such as metaproterenol and terbutaline, can be taken orally. They exert much less of a stimulating effect on the heart than epinephrine and isoproterenol do and can, therefore, be administered for longer periods of time. However, it is usually recommended that these drugs be taken for only a few days after an attack, because constant use may result in the development of drug tolerance, thus making the next attack more difficult to treat.

For long-term therapy, the drug theophylline can be used to

help keep the bronchioles open. Its dosage, however, must be closely supervised because its rate of absorption into the body varies widely among patients: some persons eliminate the drug so quickly that it is almost ineffective; in others, the drug accumulates in the body, at times to toxic levels. Nausea, vomiting, and agitation are common side effects.

Corticosteroids can control asthma, but patients may become dependent on them and may experience such undesirable side effects as weight gain, ulcers, and high blood pressure. Stunting of growth and development has been reported in children.

Cromolyn, a drug that actually prevents attacks, acts to inhibit the release of histamines (the substances produced by the body during an allergic reaction). Cromolyn, however, cannot relieve an attack already in progress and is usually used only for mild cases.

Regardless of which drug is prescribed, all asthmatic patients should drink plenty of water to replace fluids that may be depleted by the use of drugs.

If an allergy is causing the attacks, the troublesome foreign substance (called an allergen) must be removed from the patient's environment. If this cannot be accomplished, allergy shots to reduce the patient's sensitivity to the allergen may be beneficial. The use of antihistamines may also bring some relief.

### Prevention

Several precautions can be taken to reduce the possibility that asthma will develop. Since the tendency to develop asthma is inherited, babies of asthmatic parents should be fed breast milk or soy protein formula, since these are less likely than cow's milk to cause allergic reactions. Smoke and pet hair, as well as rugs, drapes, and overstuffed furniture, which tend to attract dust, can be removed from the home. Moderate exercise is a good preventive method, although strenuous exercise may cause an attack.

# Bronchiectasis

Bronchiectasis is a lung condition in which some of the bronchi and bronchioles have lost their elasticity and have expanded and filled with fluid.

### Causes

Most often, bronchiectasis follows pneumonia, whooping cough, tuberculosis, or another lung disease. (Fortunately, the use of antibiotics has reduced the number of cases due to lung infection.) Other causes include obstruction; clogging of the airways by the thick, mucous secretions of cystic fibrosis; and Kartagener syndrome, which is a condition in which the cilia do not work properly (the cilia are hairlike projections that line the bronchial walls and wave mucus, pus, and dirt upward).

### Symptoms

Bronchiectasis is a chronic condition that persists for life. The individual almost always has some symptoms, which will worsen if an acute infection occurs. The most typical symptom is a chronic cough that produces thick, white or green sputum (discharge). The sputum may be foul-smelling and abundant and may also contain blood. The individual generally coughs up large amounts of sputum after changing position (for example, after rising from bed).

### Diagnosis

The doctor, listening to the chest with a stethoscope, can hear abnormal sounds inside the lungs as the patient breathes. An x-ray obtained after the injection of dye into the bloodstream or directly into the bronchi will show the characteristic appearance of the disease. Chronic bronchitis (continued inflammation of the mucous membranes in the bronchi) must be ruled out as a cause, along with tuberculosis, certain fungal infections, a tumor, and the presence of an inhaled object that is lodged in one of the bronchi.

### Treatment

Treatment of an active case of bronchiectasis includes fighting the infection with an antibiotic, such as penicillin or tetracycline, and eliminating the fluid with postural drainage. In the latter procedure, the patient lies face down in bed, with pillows elevating the hips, and a therapist strikes the back over the lungs with cupped hands to loosen mucus. The treatment, which can be taught to a family member, requires two to four ten-minute sessions a day. Inhaling warm mists may also help to moisten the thick mucous secretions that are clogging the airways, so that the secretions can be more easily expelled. The patient should avoid anything that can irritate the lungs, such as

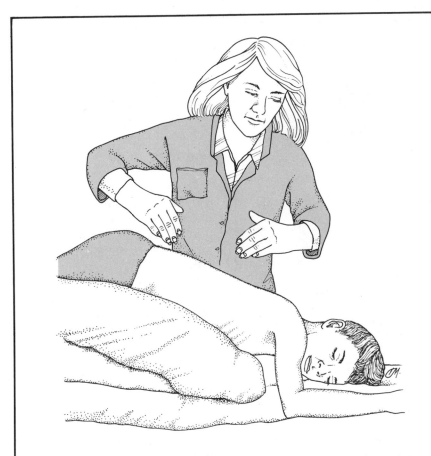

*To perform postural drainage, the therapist positions the patient head down with pillows elevating the hips and then strikes the patient's back over the lungs with cupped hands.*

smoke (especially cigarette smoke), fumes, and dust.

In the relatively few cases in which the infection is confined to a small part of the lung and is progressing despite antibiotics and other forms of therapy, it may be best to surgically remove the affected portion of the lung.

### Prevention

You can prevent progression of the disease by being immunized against flu and pneumonia, avoiding anyone with a cold or cough, and stopping smoking. Prompt treatment with antibiotics can help to control new infections.

# Bronchitis

Bronchitis is a respiratory disease characterized by inflammation and swelling of the bronchi (the main airways connecting the windpipe and the lungs). When the mucous membranes lining these tubes become inflamed, the mucous glands in the membranes expand and release more mucus. The bronchi, already narrowed by the swelling, become further clogged by the excess mucus. This mucus must then be coughed up in order to keep the breathing tubes free for normal airflow into the lungs.

When the condition is of short duration, it is called acute bron-

chitis; when the coughing lingers, it is called chronic bronchitis. In either case, the coughing stops only when the source of inflammation has been removed or overcome and the inner linings of the bronchi have returned to normal.

### Complications

Bronchitis alone is rarely fatal, but it may lead to another condition that proves fatal. For example, the functioning of lungs that have been severely damaged by bronchitis over a long period of time is so limited that the heart is deprived of adequate oxygen, ultimately resulting in death from heart failure. Also, bronchitis can be very serious when combined with other respiratory diseases. Such is the case for people who suffer from a category of respiratory conditions called chronic obstructive pulmonary disease (COPD). Bronchitis, emphysema, and several other diseases are included in this category. Patients may suffer from two or three of the COPD conditions, or one may lead to another.

### Causes

Bronchitis occurs when the bronchial tubes are infected or irritated. A cold, the flu, or strep throat may lead to acute or chronic bronchitis if these infections occur often enough. However, chronic bronchitis is more commonly triggered by the constant irritation of environmental substances such as cigarette smoke, air pollutants, and occupational dusts.

Cigarette smoking is the predominant cause of chronic bronchitis. Seventy-five percent of all

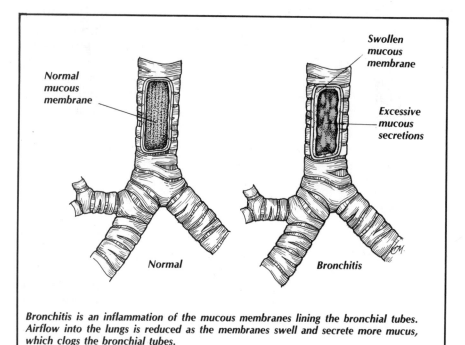

Normal mucous membrane

Normal

Swollen mucous membrane

Excessive mucous secretions

Bronchitis

*Bronchitis is an inflammation of the mucous membranes lining the bronchial tubes. Airflow into the lungs is reduced as the membranes swell and secrete more mucus, which clogs the bronchial tubes.*

those who suffer from bronchitis are cigarette smokers. When tobacco smoke reaches the bronchial linings, it stops the action of the cilia (the hairlike projections that sweep mucus out of the lungs, carrying with it dust and bacteria). When the cilia are stilled by smoke, particles remain trapped in the stagnant mucus, irritating the delicate bronchial tubes and eventually creating a breeding ground for infection.

Some degree of bronchitis occurs in about 90 percent of all smokers who live in polluted environments or who are exposed to occupational dusts. Babies and young children with chronic bronchitis usually overcome the condition, but they are more likely to contract it again later in life. People who are undernourished, inadequately housed, or often fatigued are more likely to contract bronchitis. This disorder tends to occur within certain families, but the reason is not yet known.

## Symptoms

Bronchitis can be recognized by its major symptom, the persistent cough in an effort to bring up the excess mucus. Acute bronchitis may be accompanied by hoarseness, chest discomfort, slight fever, wheezing, and shortness of breath. In children, chronic bronchitis may establish itself after several short-term infections. In adults, the beginning of chronic bronchitis is signaled by regular coughing and clearing of the throat the first thing each morning; the coughing will become more persistent and the mucus more plentiful as the disease progresses, and these symptoms may be accompanied by wheezing, shortness of breath, chest infections, and heavy panting after exercise.

As the years pass, chronic bronchitis may cause the bronchial tubes to become severely obstructed and the breathing to be irreversibly impaired. The heart sometimes becomes en-

larged because it must pump harder than normal to deliver needed oxygen to the rest of the body. The nails, lips, and skin may develop a blue tinge due to lack of oxygen.

## Diagnosis

To diagnose bronchitis, the doctor will obtain the medical history, do a physical examination of the chest with a stethoscope, and perhaps order a chest x-ray. Special machines can measure the amount of air flowing in and out of the lungs, and others can measure how well oxygen is being transported from the lungs to the bloodstream.

## Treatment

Bronchitis is treated by removing the irritants from the patient's surroundings, clearing the lungs of mucus, and trying to prevent infections. A patient with chronic bronchitis will need to quit smoking and to avoid constant exposure to pollutants or hazardous dusts. Humidity plays a large part in treating bronchitis; patients should drink plenty of water and other liquids, and breathe warmed, humidified air from a vaporizer or humidifier. Humidity acts to moisten mucus trapped in the airways, allowing it to be brought up from the lungs and thereby promoting what is known as a productive cough. A bronchodilator drug, which relaxes the walls of the air passages, may be prescribed.

## Prevention

Bronchitis can best be prevented by avoiding the irritants that cause it, namely cigarette smoke, air pollutants, and dusts. Patients with chronic bronchitis can prevent further irritation by maintaining good health and eating habits to avoid infections. Other lung disorders may precipitate the condition; antibiotics may be prescribed to treat bacterial infections, and vaccinations against influenza and pneumonia may be recommended.

# Dyspnea

Dyspnea is a sensation of "air hunger." It is usually accompanied by difficult, labored breathing and discomfort. Dyspnea is a symptom that may occur in a variety of diseases and conditions, ranging from congestive heart failure to emotional upset.

## Causes

Dyspnea may be caused by inadequate delivery of oxygen to the tissues, as in severe anemia; by failure of the heart to keep up with the needs of the body, as in congestive heart failure; by overexertion; by obstruction of the airways (for example, by an inhaled foreign object); by narrowing of air passages, such as occurs in asthma; or by restriction of lung capacity, which may be caused by a chest deformity. Emphysema (in which many of the small air sacs of the lungs have been weakened or destroyed) is commonly associated with dyspnea. It can also occur if there is fluid in the lungs, as in pneumonia or congestive heart failure, because the entry of oxygen into the alveoli (the tiny air sacs in the lungs, where gas exchange takes place) is blocked by the fluid, thereby preventing oxygenation of the blood.

A nighttime form of dyspnea is called paroxysmal nocturnal dyspnea, in which the patient awakens gasping for breath and can breathe only by sitting up or standing. Usually this is caused by congestive heart failure.

Another type of dyspnea, called psychogenic or hysterical hyperventilation, is a physical response to stress, anxiety, or emotional upset. In this condition, excessive breathing results in exhalation of too much carbon dioxide, which causes lightheadedness, numbness and tingling of the hands and toes, and fainting. (For more information on hyperventilation, see page 369.)

## Symptoms

Signs of dyspnea include noisy breathing; an anxious, distressed expression; dilated nostrils; gasping; a protruding abdomen; an expanded chest; and blue lips and fingertips.

## Treatment

Treatment involves controlling whatever condition is causing the dyspnea, including the anxiety responsible for psychogenic hyperventilation.

# Emphysema

Emphysema is a chronic, progressive lung disease. Emphysema develops when the small air passages leading to the alveoli (the tiny air sacs in the lungs, where gas exchange takes place) become distended and the walls dividing the alveoli are injured or destroyed. Spaces form where alveoli had been, and lung tissue becomes nonfunctional. Emphy-

sema is commonly associated with chronic bronchitis, in which the airways become inflamed, causing specialized cells within them to secrete abnormally large amounts of mucus. The inflammation, swelling, and excessive mucus production result in obstruction to airflow and entrapment of air within the lungs.

## Effect on the body

As the disease progresses, many complex changes take place, ultimately leading to diminishment of the amount of oxygen in the blood, frequently associated with an increased amount of carbon dioxide. As the lung tissue deteriorates and loses its elasticity, changes also occur in the blood vessels carrying deoxygenated blood to the lungs for a fresh supply of oxygen. The net effect is that the right side of the heart, which is responsible for collecting deoxygenated blood from the veins of the body and pumping it through the lungs, must work much harder. As the process continues, the muscle of the right side of the heart is weakened by this extra work and becomes less able to pump blood into the lungs. The blood "backs up," causing increased pressure in the veins. This, in turn, causes fluid to recede into the tissues, resulting in severe swelling of the feet, ankles, and legs. If this rightsided heart failure (also known as cor pulmonale) is very severe, the abdomen will become distended with fluid.

## Causes

External factors that irritate the lungs, such as tobacco smoke

183

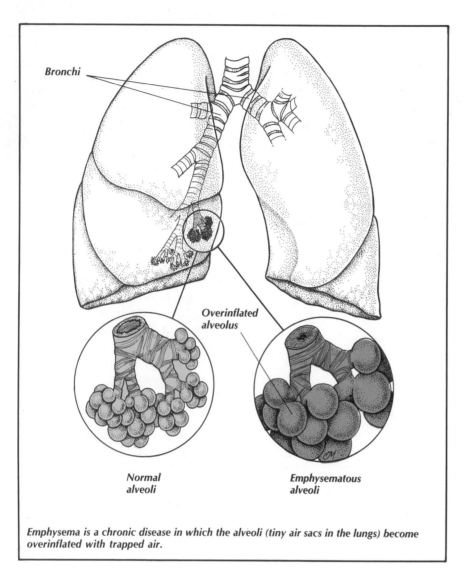

Bronchi

Overinflated alveolus

Normal alveoli

Emphysematous alveoli

*Emphysema is a chronic disease in which the alveoli (tiny air sacs in the lungs) become overinflated with trapped air.*

and air pollutants, are commonly linked to emphysema, but no single cause has been determined. Unlike many respiratory diseases, emphysema is not caused by a viral or bacterial infection. However, it is often aggravated by a case of bronchitis or another lung infection.

In a minority of cases, emphysema is a result of a genetic deficiency or an inherited lack of a specific blood protein, which leads to loss of elasticity in the alveoli.

Those afflicted with emphysema are most likely to be white men over the age of 50, al-though women are becoming equally susceptible because of an increase in smoking among women during recent years.

## Symptoms

Emphysema is characterized by one major symptom—shortness of breath. Patients may also have a persistent, racking cough, which either brings up mucus or is overly dry. Patients experience difficulty in breathing, often taking twice as many breaths as others to get enough oxygen. It has been found that advanced emphysema sufferers exert tremendous amounts of energy just to breathe. They also tire quite easily and require more calories to maintain their weight than healthy individuals do. An enlarged, rounded "barrel" chest often develops due to overinflation of the lungs and excessive growth of the chest muscles used in breathing. Lips, ear lobes, skin, and fingernails may be tinged blue from lack of oxygen in the blood.

## Diagnosis

There is no single test that can pinpoint the condition. Breathing tests to measure the amount of air being inhaled and exhaled will not reveal the disease in its early stages. A blood test may be performed to determine the red blood cell count (when emphysema causes diminished oxygenation of the blood, more red blood cells are produced in an effort to increase oxygen transport; because of this compensation, the red blood cell count is elevated). A chest x-ray may be taken to search for specific changes in the lungs that may point to advanced stages of the disease; however, a chest x-ray is not diagnostic of early emphysema. Thus, emphysema is diagnosed by putting together a collection of findings.

## Treatment

There is no known cure for emphysema, nor is it reversible. However, the progress of the disease can be checked by removing irritants, particularly cigarette smoke, from the patient's environment. Patients are encouraged to drink large amounts of fluids to help thin out the mucus that may block the airways. Adequate rest, a balanced diet, and moderate regular exercise are recommended. Vaporizers, humidifiers, and air conditioners help to moisturize and filter the air. A physical therapist can teach an emphysema patient how to use his chest and abdominal muscles to breathe more efficiently.

Several drugs may aid the emphysema patient. They act to loosen mucous secretions or to relax and expand the air passages. Antibiotics are sometimes prescribed if infection exists. In advanced cases, oxygen may have to be administered continuously. However, an emphysema patient must be particularly careful to use only the amount of oxygen prescribed. Too much oxygen can suppress the drive to breathe, thereby causing respiratory failure and possibly death. In addition, sedatives and sleeping medications should be avoided by patients with severe emphysema, as these can also lead to a dangerous slowing of breathing.

Emphysema is a very serious condition. However, with the help of modern treatments, breathing aids, and medications, patients can lead a reasonably comfortable life. It is, however, necessary for these individuals to stop smoking and avoid air pollutants as much as possible.

# Legionnaires' disease

Legionnaires' disease is a severe bacterial infection of the respiratory tract. The first identifiable outbreak of Legionnaires' disease occurred in 1976 in Philadelphia. More than 180 people attending or visiting the state convention of the American Legion became afflicted with the disease, and 29 of them died. Other outbreaks have since occurred in the United States and Europe. Studies have also shown that outbreaks of respiratory diseases later identified as Legionnaires' disease, occurred as early as 1947.

## Cause

Legionnaires' disease is caused by the *Legionella pneumophila* bacterium, which was not identified by scientists until the 1976 outbreak of the disease. The major environmental source of the infection is water from reservoirs and cooling units of air-conditioning systems. Lakes, creeks, and areas of excavation also may harbor the bacteria. Transmission is by breathing in droplets of contaminated water. Person-to-person transmission has not been documented.

## Those at risk

Cigarette smokers, the elderly, and persons receiving drugs that diminish the power of the immune system are more likely to contract Legionnaires' disease than are other people. Persons who have some other medical problem—heart trouble, cancer, respiratory illness, or kidney disease—are also believed to be particularly susceptible.

## Symptoms

Legionnaires' disease has symptoms similar to those of many other respiratory diseases, making it difficult to differentiate and diagnose. Symptoms include dry coughing, high fever, chills, diarrhea, shortness of breath, chest pains, headaches, excessive sweating, nausea, vomiting, and abdominal pain. Occasionally, bloody sputum is produced. Lethargy and confusion may occur in progressive, serious cases.

Although Legionnaires' disease is uncommon, it should be considered in the case of anyone (particularly an elderly or chronically ill person) who has a respiratory tract infection that worsens over a period of about four days. The disease can initially be mild and appear to be an episode of the flu. The diagnosis is made from the history and physical examination, chest x-rays, and special tests of the blood and sputum that determine the presence and changing numbers of antibodies (protective substances that fight off infection).

## Treatment

If an antibiotic (usually erythromycin) is given early in the course of the illness, the outlook for recovery is good.

## Prevention

There is as yet no preventive vaccine against Legionnaires' disease. If an outbreak is suspected, public health officials may search for and attempt to eliminate the source of infection.

# Pleurisy

Pleurisy, or pleuritis, is an inflammation of the pleurae (the membranes that cover the outside of the lungs and line the chest cavity). The pleurae normally reduce the friction between the chest structures as the lungs expand and contract. Inflammation of the pleurae causes breathing to become painful and less effective.

### Types and causes

There are two types of pleurisy: dry pleurisy and wet pleurisy. In dry pleurisy, the more common condition, the inflamed pleurae rub directly against each other. In wet pleurisy, fluid oozes from the inflamed tissue into the space between the lungs and the chest wall. This fluid may compress the lungs, making breathing difficult.

Both types of pleurisy often occur as complications of respiratory tract infections, such as pneumonia and tuberculosis, and are more likely to develop in persons who are highly susceptible to such infections. They can also be caused by tuberculosis, a tumor, or an injury. Some cases are due to certain liver diseases, which can inflame the diaphragm (the muscle separating the organs of the chest region from those of the abdomen) and the portions of the pleurae that cover the diaphragm.

### Symptoms

The major symptom of dry pleurisy is a sharp, stabbing pain toward the side and lower part of the chest. The pain may also be felt along the shoulders, neck, and abdomen. Any movement involving the chest, such as breathing or coughing, will aggravate the pain, which may be accompanied by shortness of breath, a dry cough, and fever. Wet pleurisy is characterized by similar symptoms, but there may also be difficulty in breathing.

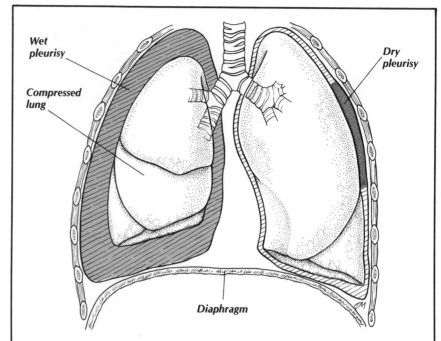

*Pleurisy is an inflammation of the pleurae (the membranes that cover the lungs and line the chest cavity). In dry pleurisy, the inflamed pleurae rub directly against each other, causing painful breathing. In wet pleurisy, fluid oozes from the inflamed tissue into the space between the lungs and the chest wall, compressing the lung.*

### Diagnosis

A diagnosis of pleurisy usually begins with a physical examination, during which the doctor listens to the chest with a stethoscope for the low-pitched, grating sound that occurs with each breath in a case of dry pleurisy. The skin near the affected area is often found to be tender. If wet pleurisy is suspected, a sample of the fluid oozing from the pleurae will be analyzed. A tuberculin skin test may be done to learn whether tuberculosis is a factor. An x-ray study may be useful in detecting the presence of pleural effusion.

### Treatment

To treat pleurisy, the doctor will first need to treat the underlying infection or disease, often with antibiotics. The symptoms

of pleurisy can be relieved somewhat by bed rest and by use of a humidifier or vaporizer to add moisture to the air. Strapping the chest firmly with nonadhesive elastic bandages is sometimes recommended; however, it may prevent deep breathing and coughing up of mucus, both of which are necessary to clear the respiratory tract. Painkillers may help to relieve chest discomfort at least enough so that the patient will not need to stifle the painful coughing that is necessary to loosen the mucus.

# Pneumonia

Pneumonia is an infection of the lungs in which the alveoli in one or more sections of the lungs become inflamed and filled with fluid and white blood cells, which try to fight off the infection. Pneumonia can be fatal, especially in the very young and the very old.

## Types

There are several types of pneumonia, distinguished by the location and extent of infection. Lobar pneumonia is an infection in only one lobe (section) of the lungs. Double pneumonia is an infection of both lungs. Bronchial pneumonia is an infection in the areas of the lungs near the bronchi (the airways connecting the windpipe and the lungs). Walking pneumonia is a general term often used to describe a relatively mild form of pneumonia that is not at first recognized as a lung infection.

Pneumonia most often strikes the person whose resistance is lowered, frequently by an upper respiratory tract infection or a systemic (affecting the body generally) disease. It is commonly a secondary disease stemming from inadequate defense mechanisms, from a cold or the flu, or from long-term diseases, such as chronic bronchitis, emphysema, asthma, diabetes, cancer, or sickle cell anemia. In the elderly, pneumonia is a much-feared consequence of being bedridden for long periods of time, especially following injuries due to falls (such as broken bones).

## Causes

Viruses, bacteria, fungi, and other microorganisms may cause pneumonia. It may also develop if a person inhales certain chemicals or if food, vomit, or a foreign object passes through the trachea (the windpipe) instead of the esophagus (the passageway from the mouth to the stomach)

and settles in a lung. Smoking, excessive drinking, a prolonged period of being bedridden, anesthesia, and use of sedatives and drugs that suppress the immune system may make an individual more susceptible to pneumonia if he is exposed to an infectious organism. Pneumonia is most common during flu and cold epidemics and during the winter months, when people are more likely to be indoors, where bacteria and viruses are easily spread.

## Symptoms

Pneumonia is generally characterized by four major symptoms: chest pain, a sudden rise in temperature, coughing, and

difficulty in breathing. Viral pneumonia is signaled by coughing and other cold symptoms, as well as by general fatigue. Bacterial pneumonia generally comes on suddenly with shaking chills; a rapid, steep rise in temperature; shallow breathing; and a cough that brings up bloody, dark yellow, or rust-colored sputum. An oxygen shortage, which is sometimes a result of bacterial pneumonia, will be indicated by other symptoms, such as headache, nausea, vomiting, and cyanosis (bluish discoloration of the lips and fingertips).

## Diagnosis

Pneumonia is diagnosed by listening to the chest with a

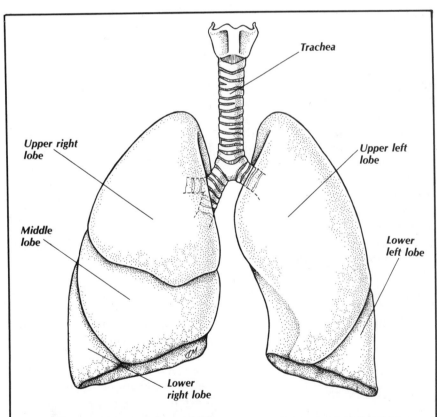

The lungs consist of five sections, called lobes. If there is an infection in only one lobe, the condition is called lobar pneumonia; if at least one lobe in each lung is affected, it is called double pneumonia.

stethoscope in order to detect the presence of fluid in the lungs. An analysis of the sputum and an x-ray examination may also help to identify the type and location of the infection.

## Treatment

Viral pneumonia is generally treated by staying in bed, drinking lots of fluids, maintaining a light diet, and using painkillers to combat discomfort. Hospitalization is not usually necessary.

Bacterial pneumonia is treated with antibiotics, such as penicillin. Patients also need to stay in bed or, if the case is serious enough, enter the hospital for care and supervision. If breathing difficulty worsens, oxygen may be administered.

## Prevention

There are vaccines that may help in preventing some types of pneumonia. Pneumonia caused by certain bacteria may be prevented with a vaccine, which is especially recommended for the elderly or for those with chronic diseases that may weaken the respiratory system. Pneumonia caused by one type of influenza virus may also be prevented with a vaccination.

The very young, the very old, and the chronically ill are the most likely to contract pneumonia, so care must be taken to protect them from respiratory infections.

## Psittacosis

Psittacosis is a rare form of pneumonia caused by a microorganism called *Chlamydia psittaci,* which may be transmitted to humans by certain birds. The disease is often called parrot fever because it was first found to be transmitted by members of the parrot family, including parakeets and lovebirds. It may also be transmitted by other birds, such as seagulls, pigeons, canaries, and poultry, in which case it is more correctly called ornithosis.

## Causes

Infection usually takes place when a person inhales dust from the feathers or droppings of infected birds. It can also be transmitted directly to a person by a bite from an infected bird. Person-to-person transmission is rare. Eating poultry has not been reported as a source of infection.

## Symptoms

The incubation period (the time between exposure to the illness and the appearance of symptoms) is one to two weeks. The disease usually begins with fever, chills, headache, muscle aches, and loss of appetite. Nausea, vomiting, and enlargement of the spleen may also be present. The patient's temperature continues to rise, and a dry cough develops. Coughing brings up mucus and pus in the later stages. Chest x-rays made during the first week of noticeable symptoms often show inflammation of the lungs. During the second week, the typical symptoms of pneumonia develop. The patient's temperature will remain above normal for at least two weeks and then will begin to fall slowly. A steady increase in the pulse and breathing rate may be serious. About 30 percent of untreated cases end in death. Recovery of those people who receive treatment may be gradual.

## Treatment

The drug most commonly used to treat psittacosis is oral tetracycline, an antibiotic. Complete bed rest is necessary in most cases. Cough preparations with codeine are also advised. In severe cases, tetracycline may be given intravenously.

## Prevention

Flocks of infected pigeons or other birds, dust from feathers, bird-cage contents, and sick domestic birds or fowl should be avoided. Specially treated feed is often used to prevent the spread of infection among imported parrots, parakeets, and lovebirds, as well as among turkeys raised for market.

# Pulmonary embolism

Pulmonary embolism occurs when an embolus (a bubble or clump of matter) blocks a blood vessel in the lungs.

## Causes

Emboli (the plural of *embolus*) may be solid (detached blood clots, clumps of tumor cells, or bits of foreign objects); liquid (globules of fat); or gaseous (air). Pulmonary emboli most often are venous thrombi (blood clots that form in the veins) that have originated in the lower extremities and pelvis, usually as the result of injury, surgery, and blood vessel diseases. Such thrombi are common in persons on prolonged bed rest, particularly after surgery, due to the lack of movement of blood in the legs.

## Symptoms

The presence of a pulmonary embolus may be indicated by the sudden development of wheezing, dyspnea (labored or difficult breathing), chest pains, and hemoptysis (spitting up of blood).

## Diagnosis

Diagnostic procedures for detection of pulmonary embolism may include an electrocardiogram and analysis of arterial blood obtained from the wrist, arm, or groin. The definitive diagnostic procedure is pulmonary angiography, which is an x-ray scan of the lungs after the introduction of a special dye into the bloodstream.

## Treatment

Initial treatment may include administration of oxygen, pain-relievers, and medication to maintain cardiovascular functions. Anticoagulant medication (usually intravenous heparin or oral warfarin) is given to prevent the development of additional emboli.

If it is determined that the embolism was caused by a venous thrombus and there is some reason why anticoagulants should not be used, the inferior vena cava (the main vein for the lower limbs and the pelvis) may be deliberately blocked with an "umbrella filter" or a clip to

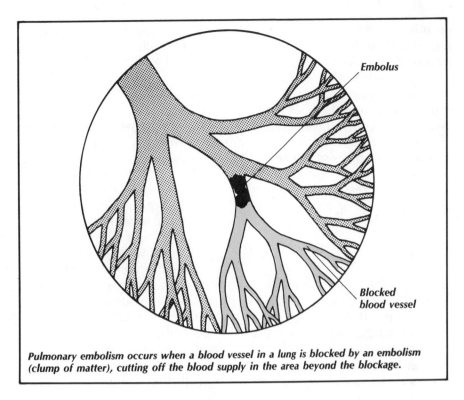

*Pulmonary embolism occurs when a blood vessel in a lung is blocked by an embolism (clump of matter), cutting off the blood supply in the area beyond the blockage.*

keep other venous thrombi from traveling to the lungs. Surgical removal of the embolus is done only when the patient has low blood pressure as a side effect of the embolism and when surgery can be performed soon after occurrence of the blockage.

As serious as pulmonary emboli can be, only a small number are lethal.

## Prevention

The best prevention of pulmonary embolism is early detection and treatment of venous thrombosis. Persons predisposed to embolism may be given injections of heparin or low doses of oral warfarin to prevent the formation of thrombi.

# Tuberculosis

Tuberculosis is a bacterial infection caused by *Mycobacterium tuberculosis* organisms. Because the body's defense system has difficulty fighting this type of bacterium, it attempts to wall off invading organisms within small nodules, called granulomas or tubercles, which contain both the infecting bacteria and the tissue produced by the body in reaction to them.

Of all persons who are infected by tuberculosis bacteria, 80 percent will never experience the symptoms of the disease. Usually, the body is able to surround the offending bacteria with granulomas; the tuberculosis bacteria then lie dormant in the body, and active disease does not develop. However, because the body cannot kill the bacteria—only contain them within granulomas—the infection can become active at a later time, often when some other disease has weakened the body's defenses.

Of the 20 percent of infected persons in whom an active case of tuberculosis does develop, only half will become sick within three months of contracting the infection; the other half will suffer from the disease at some time in their lives, perhaps years later. Tuberculosis usually affects the lungs, but it can also involve other parts of the body, such as the spine, the kidneys, the digestive tract, and the lining of the heart.

## Causes

Tuberculosis is contracted when a person breathes in droplets containing *Mycobacterium tuberculosis* organisms that have been coughed or sneezed into the air by an infected person. Tuberculosis is contagious, especially for persons living in crowded conditions. Also highly susceptible to this disease are those who are undernourished, in poor health, or living in poor urban areas, as well as the very young, the very old, and those in the medical professions. Anyone who has been in close contact with a tuberculosis patient should be tested for the disease.

## Symptoms

Early signs include fever, fatigue, loss of appetite, and weight loss. Later signs include coughing up of blood-tinged sputum, chest pain, and shortness of breath.

## Diagnosis

The symptoms of tuberculosis are similar to those of many other diseases, and its characteristic symptoms do not appear until the disease is in its advanced stages. For these reasons, coupled with the fact that the incidence of tuberculosis has been declining in recent years in the United States, this disorder often remains untreated or misdiagnosed for some time before the patient is finally tested for it. Tuberculosis may be accompanied by an infection due to *Streptococcus* bacteria, which often further complicates diagnosis.

Patients can be tested for tuberculosis with a tuberculin skin test. If the bacteria are present, whether active or inactive, the patch of skin that has been treated with dead tuberculosis bacteria will swell. Chest x-rays or sputum analysis may also help to identify the site of active or inactive infection.

## Treatment

Tuberculosis is treated with a variety of antibacterial drugs simultaneously. Each medication acts on a different portion of the tuberculosis bacterium; only in combination do these drugs have the greatest probability of eliminating the infection. The drugs are usually prescribed for a long period of time, perhaps 9 to 18 months, but usually after two weeks the patient is no longer contagious and can resume normal activities. With this type of treatment, the disease is rarely fatal. Severe side effects, such as liver or hearing damage, can result from certain antituberculosis drugs.

## Prevention

An active case of tuberculosis can be prevented in some high-risk persons by the administration of certain antituberculosis drugs, but these drugs are likely to have undesirable side effects. (High-risk persons include those under the age of 35, especially children, who have been exposed to the disease, as well as those with chronic diseases that have weakened their respiratory systems.) Liver damage from these drugs is more likely to occur in those over the age of 35, so people in this age group seldom receive these drugs.

Regardless of age or physical condition, anyone who has been in close contact with a person who has an active case of tuberculosis should be tested for the disease.

# THE HEART AND CIRCULATORY SYSTEM

The circulatory system, which includes the heart, the blood vessels, and the blood, brings nutrients and oxygen to every part of the body and carries away wastes.

## Heart

The heart is a hollow, muscular organ that maintains blood circulation throughout the body. It lies behind the sternum (breastbone), between the lungs. Its size in most adults approximates that of the clenched fist. A heartbeat is a rhythmic contraction of the heart muscle as it pumps blood. A normal heart usually beats 60 to 90 times per minute when the person is at rest.

The heart has four chambers, through which the blood passes. Valves control the movement of blood within these compartments. The blood flows from two large veins (the superior vena cava and the inferior vena cava) into the right atrium (upper chamber). The blood continues down to the right ventricle (lower chamber). From this chamber, the blood is pumped to the lungs, where carbon dioxide (a waste product from the cells) is exchanged for oxygen (an element necessary for cell life). The rejuvenated blood then returns to the left atrium. From there, the blood passes to the left ventricle, which forces the blood away from the heart through the aorta (the main artery, which extends through the chest and abdomen) to the other arteries, which carry the blood to all the tissues of the body.

## Blood vessels

Blood vessels form the network of passageways that trans-

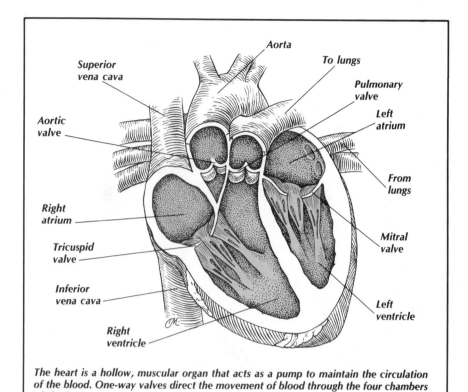

The heart is a hollow, muscular organ that acts as a pump to maintain the circulation of the blood. One-way valves direct the movement of blood through the four chambers of the heart.

port blood throughout the body. The blood leaves the heart and passes through arteries of progressively smaller diameter. When the blood reaches the smallest blood vessels, called capillaries, oxygen and nutrients are exchanged for carbon dioxide and other waste products. The "used" blood then continues on its journey back toward the heart through veins of progressively greater diameter.

## Blood

Blood is the fluid that courses through the blood vessels of the body. It consists of plasma (a yellowish liquid composed of proteins and water) and three formed elements—red blood cells, white blood cells, and platelets—that are visible only under a microscope. These elements are manufactured by the

bone marrow (the soft tissue in the center of some bones).

Red blood cells carry oxygen from the lungs to the various body tissues. Oxygen travels attached to hemoglobin, a pigmented substance in red blood cells that contains iron. When the amount of hemoglobin in each red blood cell or the total number of red blood cells falls below a certain level, anemia is said to be present. Normally, there are about 25 billion red blood cells in one teaspoon of blood.

The job of the white blood cells is to protect the body from invading organisms. Whenever the body becomes wounded or infected, white blood cells attack and kill disease-causing agents in the affected area. In addition, certain white blood cells produce antibodies. These substances counteract harmful agents by destroying or inactivat-

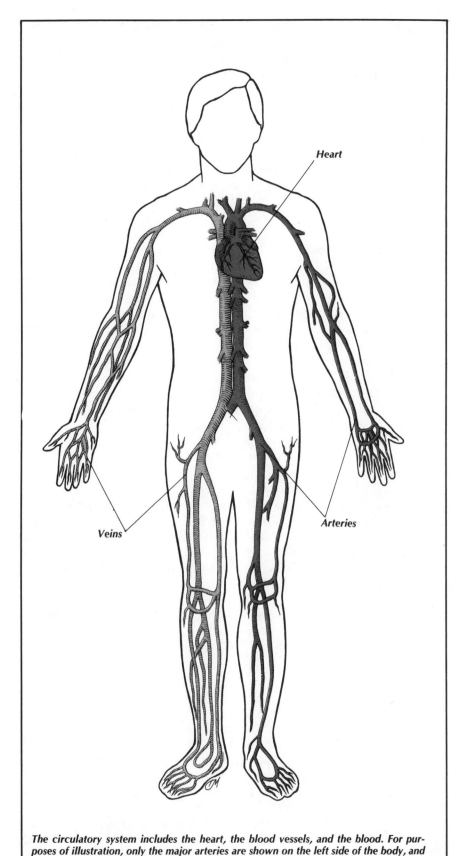

*The circulatory system includes the heart, the blood vessels, and the blood. For purposes of illustration, only the major arteries are shown on the left side of the body, and only the major veins are shown on the right side.*

ing them. Because the body produces more white blood cells than usual in response to infection, an increase in their number signals disease. From 25 million to 45 million white blood cells are normally present in one teaspoon of blood.

Platelets are small, colorless disks numbering approximately one and a half billion in a single teaspoon of blood. They work to help the blood clot.

### Antigens and blood types

An antigen is a substance that can provoke an immune (protective) response by the body. An antigen promotes the manufacture of antibodies that will interact only with that antigen. On the surfaces of all cells are numerous antigens, which cause production of different antibodies. The major blood groups (types A, B, AB, and O) are differentiated on the basis of the presence on the red blood cells of two of those surface antigens: type A blood has antigen A, type B has antigen B, type AB has both antigen A and antigen B, and type O has neither antigen A nor antigen B. A person's blood type must be identified before a blood transfusion can be given because his blood may reject transfused blood of the wrong type. Type A blood plasma, for example, does not contain any anti-A antibodies. It does, however, contain anti-B antibodies. If type B blood is transfused, the anti-B antibodies in the plasma will destroy the type B red cells, which have type B antigens.

# Anemia

Anemia is a general term referring to a shortage of red blood cells or a reduction in their hemoglobin content. (Hemoglobin is the pigment in the blood that carries oxygen in the red blood cells.) A shortage of red blood cells or hemoglobin means that the blood is unable to carry adequate amounts of oxygen to all parts of the body.

### Causes

Anemia can be caused by vitamin deficiencies or inability to absorb certain vitamins, the destruction of red blood cells, inherited abnormalities in the blood, or the failure of the bone marrow to manufacture enough red blood cells. Such diverse conditions as bleeding ulcers, drug allergies, cancer, and exposure to radioactivity can also lead to anemia. People with poor diets or histories of alcoholism are likely to suffer from one of the types of anemia caused by vitamin and mineral deficiencies. A tendency toward certain types of anemia (for example, sickle cell anemia) can also be inherited.

### Symptoms

Among the many symptoms of anemia are fatigue, shortness of breath, pounding heartbeat, rapid heart rate, headaches, loss of appetite, dizziness, ringing in the ears, weakness, and faintness. Burning of the tongue or a change in its appearance may also be a clue. Another sign of anemia may be paleness in the creases of the palms, under the fingernails, and in the lining of the eye. Very severe cases may be signaled by swollen ankles; rapid, weak pulse; pale, clammy skin; and a feeling of fullness in the neck or abdomen.

### Diagnosis

Diagnosis is based on the findings from a physical examination and tests of the blood (and sometimes the bone marrow) to detect shortages of red blood cells or hemoglobin. A specific diagnosis is necessary because each type of anemia has a different cause and, therefore, a different treatment.

### Iron deficiency anemia

Iron deficiency anemia is caused by a shortage of the mineral iron, which is necessary to produce hemoglobin. This shortage can be caused by a variety of conditions, among them a drastic blood loss, such as from an accident; a chronic blood loss, such as from a bleeding ulcer; hookworm infestation; and choosing a diet lacking in good sources of iron, such as dark-green vegetables, egg yolks, meats (especially liver), fish, seafood, and dried peas and beans. Women are particularly susceptible to iron deficiency anemia because of regular loss of blood during menstruation as well as depletion of iron by the fetus during pregnancy. This type of anemia can be treated with iron supplements (ferrous sulfate or ferrous gluconate tablets).

### Folic acid deficiency anemia

Folic acid deficiency is caused by insufficient dietary folic acid, which is necessary for hemoglobin production. This deficiency may be caused or aggravated by malnourishment or alcoholism. Some disorders of the small intestine, such as inflammatory bowel disease, may also cause

it. It is treated with folic acid and sometimes additional supplements.

### Pernicious anemia

Pernicious anemia arises if the body is unable to absorb vitamin $B_{12}$, which is necessary for the production of red blood cells in the bone marrow. A substance called intrinsic factor, which helps to absorb vitamin $B_{12}$, is lacking in the stomach of persons suffering from this condition. Inability to absorb vitamin $B_{12}$ can also be caused by some parasites, inflammatory bowel disease, and diseases of the small intestine. Pernicious anemia is treated with vitamin $B_{12}$ injections directly into the bloodstream, bypassing the stomach completely.

### Aplastic anemia

Aplastic anemia is a serious condition caused by the inability of the bone marrow to produce white and red blood cells and platelets. Bone marrow function can be inhibited by cancer or exposure to radioactivity, hazardous chemicals, or some drugs. This variety of anemia is treated with blood transfusions and bone marrow transplants.

### Hemolytic anemias

Hemolytic anemias are caused by the destruction of red blood cells. These anemias can be either acquired (developed over time) or congenital (present at birth).

Acquired hemolytic anemias can be caused by mismatched blood transfusions, a drug allergy, cancer, or a serious infection. Treatment of the primary condition is necessary to treat the resulting anemia. Blood transfusions can treat the condition temporarily.

Congenital hemolytic anemias are caused by an inherited abnormality in the red blood cells. The most common type is sickle cell anemia, a disorder that predominantly affects black persons. In this form of anemia, the red blood cells, which are sickle-shaped instead of disklike, cannot carry enough oxygen throughout the body. These cells are also very fragile and hemolyze (break down) easily. This disease is characterized by crisis periods of severe joint or abdominal pain and can lead to complications, such as kidney disease, gallstones, and heart failure. Sickle cell anemia is treated with painkillers, oxygen, and transfusions. Avoiding situations in which oxygen may be scarce, such as high altitudes, is advisable. (For more information on sickle cell anemia, see pages 384–385.)

## Prevention

There are no specific methods to prevent anemias other than selecting a balanced diet to prevent anemia caused by vitamin and mineral deficiencies and obtaining genetic counseling if a hereditary condition is a possibility.

# Aneurysm

An aneurysm is a bulge in a blood vessel, usually an artery, due to a weakness in the vessel wall, particularly in the elastic, muscular middle layer of the artery wall. An artery has three layers: the intima, which is the

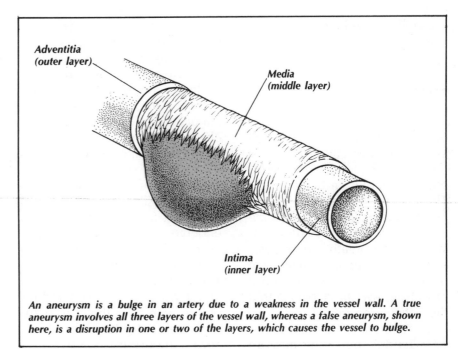

*An aneurysm is a bulge in an artery due to a weakness in the vessel wall. A true aneurysm involves all three layers of the vessel wall, whereas a false aneurysm, shown here, is a disruption in one or two of the layers, which causes the vessel to bulge.*

smooth inner layer; the media, or middle layer; and the adventitia, which is the tough outer layer. A true aneurysm involves all three layers, whereas a false aneurysm is a disruption or clot in one or two of the layers, causing a bulge in the vessel. A dissecting aneurysm occurs when blood separates the layers, thereby creating an extra channel, sometimes extending the full length of the artery, through which blood flow is diverted from the organs or tissues served by that vessel. This dangerous condition can develop in a matter of hours or days.

The main danger of most untreated aneurysms is rupture, causing death due to loss of blood. Even if death does not occur, blood loss may so decrease blood flow to the heart that it cannot work properly.

## Causes

There are various causes of aneurysms. Those occurring in

the arteries of the brain are often due to an inherited defect—a weakness or lack of elastic tissue in the media. If an aneurysm in the brain ruptures, a stroke can result. Aneurysms in the small arteries may be caused by blood vessel infections that weaken the vessel wall. Penetrating wounds occasionally can cause aneurysms.

The sexually transmitted disease syphilis may also be a cause of aneurysms. Syphilis can cause vasculitis (inflammation of the smaller arteries that feed a large one). When this occurs, these small arteries are lost, thereby denying nourishment to parts of the large arterial wall and causing scarring and death of tissue. This process leads to weakness of the wall and consequent formation of an aneurysm.

Dissecting aneurysms usually occur in the aorta. Atherosclerosis (hardening of the arteries) is the most common cause, especially in the elderly. If a young person is affected, the condition is usually caused by an inherited defect.

### Symptoms

Symptoms of dissecting aneurysms of the aorta, if in the chest, include sudden, severe pain in the area of the aneurysm, often resembling a heart attack. There may be pain under the breastbone or in the back of the neck, difficulty in swallowing, shortness of breath, hoarseness, or a heavy cough. An aneurysm in a neck artery may create a pulsating, swishing sound that the patient can detect.

Evidence of an aneurysm can be a tender, pulsating mass in the abdomen or a painful, tender mass at the back of the knee (the latter can lead to blood clots that can travel downward and may result in death of tissue in the toes). Symptoms of a dissecting aneurysm in the abdomen can include sudden, severe central or low abdominal pain radiating to the back; a loss of blood flow to the legs; and shock (collapse of circulation, signaled by fainting, pale and clammy skin, and rapid, weak pulse). Death can result quickly.

### Diagnosis

X-ray and ultrasound studies of affected areas are used to locate aneurysms and determine their extent. The most reliable test is an arteriogram (also called an angiogram), which is an x-ray study after the injection of a special dye.

### Treatment

Treatment of most aneurysms, especially dissecting aneurysms, should begin as soon as possible. Patients with dissecting aneurysms belong in an intensive care unit. Drugs are given to lower high blood pressure (which worsens a dissecting aneurysm) and thus reduce the chances of rupture. Occasionally, a dissecting aneurysm heals itself if pressure is lessened. Long-term medication that keeps blood pressure low is standard treatment for those who cannot undergo surgery. Surgery, however, is by far the most satisfactory solution when it is possible. The damaged portion of the blood vessel is removed and replaced with a synthetic or natural vessel. Patients with ruptured aortic aneurysms need emergency surgery, as do most patients with dissecting aneurysms. Rapid replacement of blood is necessary, as is intensive monitoring. Surgery for aneurysm repair is usually long and difficult. However, with newer methods of diagnosis, many more people are being spared the risks of surgery by correction of the aneurysm before it becomes a life-threatening problem.

# Angina pectoris

Angina pectoris, usually referred to simply as angina, is a dull, suffocating pain in the center of the chest that indicates that the heart muscle is not getting enough blood and, as a result, is not getting sufficient oxygen. When, during a period of stress or exertion, the oxygen needs of the heart muscle are greater than its blood supply from the coronary arteries can meet, angina is a mechanism for slowing down the body.

An angina attack is not a heart attack. Its pain is usually not as severe or as long-lasting as that experienced during a heart attack, and it does not destroy the heart muscle, as does a heart attack. However, those who suffer from this condition are probably more prone to heart attack than are those who do not.

### Causes

Angina can be caused by any number of factors that prevent the heart muscle from getting enough blood. By far the most common cause of angina is coronary artery narrowing due to atherosclerosis. The coronary arteries supply the heart muscle itself with blood. When an increased demand is placed on the heart by the body, for instance, by exercise, the heart must work harder to supply blood (and thereby oxygen) to keep the muscles and organs nourished. This increased work effort causes the heart muscle itself to require more blood. When narrowing of a coronary artery is present, the areas of heart muscle supplied by that artery cannot get enough blood to keep up with the demand. When this occurs, the muscle reacts by causing the pain of angina. Exercise, stress, and even cold weather can trigger an attack.

This pain usually occurs during or after physical exertion or emotional stress, lasts only three to five minutes, and is relieved by resting or relaxing. If the pain does not go away within five minutes or if the pain increases, the condition causing it may not be angina. It may be another disorder unrelated to the heart, or it may be a heart attack.

Overeating and smoking can also trigger and aggravate an-

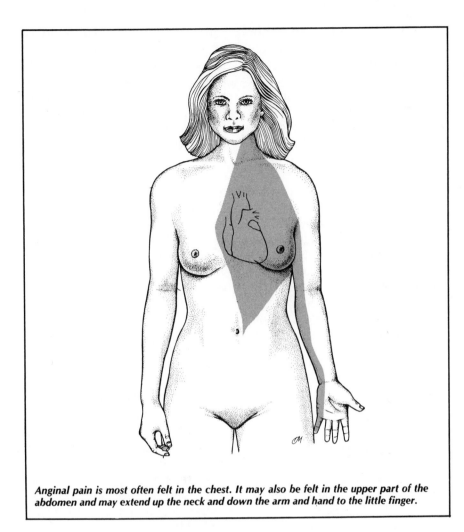

*Anginal pain is most often felt in the chest. It may also be felt in the upper part of the abdomen and may extend up the neck and down the arm and hand to the little finger.*

along the neck, in the upper part of the abdomen, and extending down the arm and hand to the little finger. The location and severity of the pain vary among angina sufferers, but in a given patient the same symptoms usually recur with each episode.

## Diagnosis

Angina is diagnosed by first eliminating the possibility that the pain is originating from some other disorder, such as gallbladder disease, rib injury, muscle spasm, or pleurisy (an inflammation of the membrane that covers the lungs). The doctor will take a complete medical history and perform a physical exam and probably a stress test, in which an electrocardiograph (an instrument that records the electrical impulses generated in the heart) is used to evaluate heart function during exercise. This test can indicate abnormalities in the blood supply to the heart.

The most definitive test for the diagnosis of coronary artery disease is cardiac arteriography (also called cardiac angiography). In this test, a radiopaque (able to be seen on x-rays) dye is injected through a catheter (tube) placed into the heart through an artery in the leg or arm. Once the dye has been injected, x-ray films are taken, and areas of obstruction to the dye within the coronary arteries can be clearly seen. During this procedure, other important information, such as the overall condition of the heart muscle, can also be obtained.

## Treatment

Angina is often treated by recommending changes in the pa-

gina—overeating, by drawing much-needed blood to the full stomach to aid in digestion; smoking, by causing the coronary arteries to constrict, thus reducing their capacity for carrying blood.

## Risk factors

Several risk factors are associated with the development of coronary artery disease and angina. A family history of heart attack, smoking, high cholesterol levels, and high blood pressure are among the best known. There is much controversy in medicine regarding the degree of impact these factors have. It has

not yet been clearly established whether alteration of the last three factors will definitely prevent or delay the onset of heart disease. However, there is much evidence favoring their reduction. Furthermore, common sense would dictate that one attempt to do so.

## Symptoms

The major symptom of angina is the sensation of pressure, squeezing, or burning in the center of the chest behind the breastbone. This discomfort in the chest is often compared to that accompanying indigestion. Angina pain may also be felt tient's lifestyle to reduce the strain on the heart and by administering medication to modify the relationship of the heart muscle and its blood supply.

A change in lifestyle will be necessary for patients who smoke, overeat, or overexert themselves. Certain types of exercise may be too stressful, but regular exercise is necessary to improve collateral circulation (the natural development of a system of small blood vessels that detour obstructions in the arteries and supply blood directly to the heart).

The medication most often used to treat angina attacks is nitroglycerin, which may act by expanding blood vessels to increase blood flow or by altering the volume of blood in the heart. Nitroglycerin is taken in the form of a tablet that dissolves under the tongue. Pain should stop within three or four minutes; if it does not, the pain may not be due to simple angina. Nitroglycerin can also be prescribed as an ointment or patch. These are used for the prevention of attacks, not for the treatment of an acute episode.

Surgery to bypass the obstructions in the coronary arteries is performed only when angina cannot be controlled with medication or when its pain is becoming increasingly severe. (For information on coronary bypass surgery, see pages 201–202.)

In recent years, the technique of angioplasty has become widely used to treat obstructions that are causing angina pectoris. This procedure consists of inserting a balloon-tipped catheter into an artery and inflating the balloon at the site of narrowing, thereby decreasing the obstruction. The advantage of this technique is that it saves the patient from having to undergo an oper-

ation. Unfortunately, it is not useful in all types of coronary artery disease and can be associated with complications that necessitate emergency surgery. Also, the artery frequently becomes obstructed again.

### Prevention

Incidents of angina can be prevented with several drugs: nitrates (such as nitroglycerin); calcium antagonists (such as diltiazem, nifedipine, and verapamil), which act by blocking the constricting action of calcium on arterial muscle); and beta-blockers (such as nadolol and propranolol), which decrease the work of the heart, thereby lessening its oxygen needs.

# Atherosclerosis

Atherosclerosis is a slow, progressive disease of the arteries in which fatty deposits partially clog or totally block blood flow. Atherosclerosis is the most common form of arteriosclerosis (hardening of the arteries) and a major cause of coronary artery disease.

Atherosclerosis occurs when the normally smooth, firm linings of the arteries become roughened, thickened, and clogged by deposits of fat, fibrin (a protein involved in blood clotting), calcium, and cellular debris. The condition develops gradually. Lipids (fats), necessary for the production of certain hormones and tissues and as an energy reserve, are constantly present in the bloodstream. When the lipid concentration is greatly increased, however, fatty streaks form along the artery walls. These streaks, harmless in them-

selves, can cause small nodules of fatty deposits of cholesterol to jut out from the normally smooth linings of the artery walls. Fibrous scar tissue grows under these nodules and attracts calcium deposits. Accumulated calcium develops into a hard, chalky film (called plaque) that cannot be removed. This permanent lining inside the arteries hampers their ability to expand and contract properly and slows the blood flow through the narrowed channels. Clots may then form easily, hindering or preventing the blood from traveling through the artery.

### Causes

The exact cause of this process has not been pinpointed, but three major risk factors have been identified: hyperlipidemia (abnormally elevated concentrations of lipids in the blood), hypertension (high blood pressure), and a history of smoking. Hyperlipidemia seems to result from choosing a diet high in saturated fats (fats that are usually solid at room temperature, including all animal fats, such as those found in butter and meats). Hypertension increases the risk of atherosclerosis because it puts constant strain on the arteries, which speeds up the clogging and hardening process. Smoking narrows the arteries, thus restricting blood flow and setting the stage for atherosclerosis.

### Symptoms and complications

Atherosclerosis alone has no visible symptoms. The disease often remains undetected until the arteries leading to a vital organ are blocked. The symptoms that then become apparent

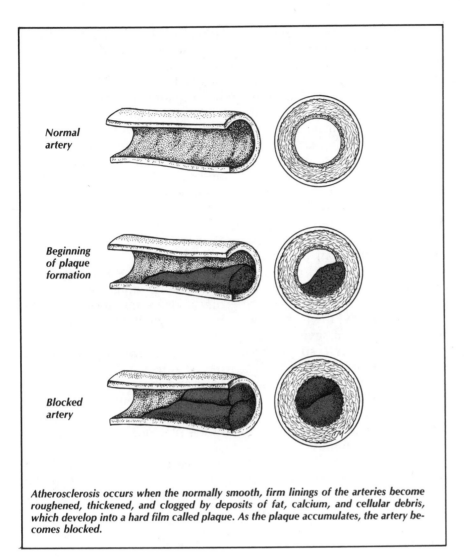

Normal
artery

Beginning
of plaque
formation

Blocked
artery

*Atherosclerosis occurs when the normally smooth, firm linings of the arteries become roughened, thickened, and clogged by deposits of fat, calcium, and cellular debris, which develop into a hard film called plaque. As the plaque accumulates, the artery becomes blocked.*

are those of the specific condition caused by arterial blockage in that organ. For example, if an artery supplying the heart is partially blocked, angina (chest pain) may be felt; if the artery is totally blocked, heart attack can result. If atherosclerosis affects an artery in the head, the person may experience dizziness, blurred vision, and faintness or may suffer a stroke. Kidney disease can develop from obstruction in the arteries leading to the kidneys. Blindness can result from obstruction of vessels leading to the eyes. Diseases of the extremities can result from blockage of their arteries.

## Diagnosis

Diagnostic evaluation begins with a medical history, physical examination, and analysis of the blood, particularly the cholesterol level. An exercise tolerance test, or stress test, using an electrocardiograph (an instrument that measures the electrical impulses generated by the heart) may indicate whether areas of the heart muscle are damaged or have inadequate blood supply. Nuclear medicine studies after the injection of radioactive isotopes into the bloodstream and arteriography (an x-ray study after the injection of a special

dye) may pinpoint obstructions in blood vessels or areas of the body that are insufficiently supplied with blood.

## Treatment

Treatment of this disorder is aimed at reducing the strain on the heart and increasing blood flow to affected organs. Medications, changes in lifestyle and eating habits, and surgery may each be helpful.

Anticoagulants may be prescribed to prevent clotting of the blood. If atherosclerosis has led to angina, nitrates (such as nitroglycerin) and calcium-channel blockers (such as diltiazem, nifedipine, and verapamil) may provide relief by expanding the arteries and increasing blood flow. If high blood pressure contributes to the problem, antihypertensive medication is prescribed. There are not yet any medications that will actually dissolve deposits that are clogging arteries.

Lifestyle changes include quitting smoking, reducing cholesterol intake, losing weight (obesity puts a strain on the heart), and maintaining a moderate (but not strenuous) exercise program (exercise helps develop the collateral circulation, a system of small blood vessels that can bypass the partially blocked arteries and directly supply organs with blood).

Delicate surgical procedures, called endarterectomies, may be performed to remove deposits that are blocking arteries to vital organs. These procedures can be performed on relatively large vessels entering the brain, heart, kidneys, and legs, but cannot remove deposits in small blood vessels of these structures. If the patient suffers from severe and recurrent chest pain that is not relieved by medication, surgery may be performed to bypass major obstructions in arteries.

# Congestive heart failure

Congestive heart failure (also called left ventricular failure or simply heart failure) is a condition in which the heart weakens and fails to keep the blood moving adequately. As a result, the supply of blood to the body's tissues decreases, lowering efficiency and endurance. With poor circulation, the kidneys fail to remove enough water, salt, and wastes from the blood. In addition, the kidneys, because of the decreased blood flow presented to them, retain even more salt and water in an effort to increase blood volume. The increased blood volume makes more work for the already overworked heart, which may enlarge and beat faster in an attempt to satisfy the body's hunger for oxygen-rich blood. The veins distend with fluid, and the balance of pressures between fluids inside and outside the veins shifts, which causes fluid that normally stays in the bloodstream to leak into surrounding tissue. This fluid leakage, the reduction of forward blood flow, and the backflow of blood are primary factors responsible for pulmonary edema (accumulation of fluid in the lungs), as well as the swelling of the abdomen and legs that often accompanies this condition.

## Causes

The usual cause of congestive heart failure is a diseased heart that just cannot pump enough blood. The most common reason is severe coronary artery disease, which decreases flow of blood to the heart muscle. If the person has suffered a heart attack, the resultant nonworking scar tissue further reduces the efficiency of the heart as a pump. Leaky or narrowed heart valves, due to a birth defect or rheumatic fever, are another cause of heart failure. A large cardiac aneurysm (a bulge caused by thinning of the wall of the left ventricle of the heart) may also decrease the pumping ability of the heart.

Less frequently, the root of the problem is one of several heart muscle diseases; some are caused by poisons like excessive alcohol, some by a viral infection, and others by the deposition in the heart tissue of iron or a fibrous protein called amyloid. Cardiac arrhythmias (disturbances of the normal rhythm of the heart) can also lead to heart failure.

## Symptoms

Early signs of congestive heart failure include unexplained rapid heartbeat, unusual fatigue during exertion, shortness of breath during stair climbing or other mild exercise, and inability to withstand cold. Attacks of shortness of breath and coughing when lying in bed that are relieved by sleeping with pillows under the back to tilt the chest are also early symptoms. Sometimes, a person is actually awakened by a sensation of "air hunger" and must sit or stand to breathe more easily. These symptoms are caused by increased fluid pressure in the lung circulation. The relief obtained by assuming a more erect position is due to a shift of blood volume to the lower half of the body, easing the burden of the heart. In advanced congestive heart failure, shortness of breath and a severe cough with reddish-brown or brownish sputum are common. There may also be swelling of the legs and ankles and a feeling of fullness in the neck or abdomen.

## Diagnosis

Usually, congestive heart failure can be diagnosed after a physical examination, on the basis of symptoms. However, a chest x-ray is commonly taken to determine how much the heart has become enlarged by its overload and to see if fluid has accumulated within the lungs. An electrocardiogram (a recording of the electrical impulses generated in the heart) may reveal damage due to a previous heart attack and irregularities in the heart rhythm.

## Treatment

Treatment for congestive heart failure includes rest, oxygen, medication (such as digitalis) to strengthen the pumping ability of the heart, and medication to prevent irregular heart rhythms. Diuretic medications are given to help the kidneys remove more salt and water from the blood and thus decrease the volume of blood the heart must pump, and a low-salt diet is prescribed to prevent water buildup in the blood and tissues (salt tends to cause fluid to accumulate in the body). In more severe or chronic cases, a drug may be given to expand the blood vessels and thus make it easier for the heart to pump blood through them.

In some cases, the original cause of the congestive heart failure can be corrected. For example, bypass surgery may be performed on the coronary arteries to improve blood supply to the heart muscle. Surgery may also be done to replace or correct a faulty heart valve or to repair an aneurysm. Contributing factors to be controlled or eliminated include high blood pressure, anemia, excess salt or alcohol intake, fever, an overactive thyroid gland, and stress due to overexertion.

## Prevention

The prevention of congestive heart failure rests on those good health habits that help prevent heart disease in general: choosing a well-balanced diet with moderate or low intake of fats; maintaining appropriate body weight; getting plenty of exercise, rest, and sleep; avoiding tobacco and excess alcohol intake; and having periodic medical checkups to detect conditions, such as high blood pressure, that might eventually overload or injure the heart and thus lead to congestive heart failure.

# Coronary bypass surgery

Coronary bypass surgery is performed on one or more of the coronary arteries, which lie on the outer surface of the heart and supply the heart muscle with the oxygen and nutrients it needs. In coronary artery disease, a section or sections of the arteries gradually become obstructed by a buildup of cholesterol, calcium, and scar tissue. The pur-

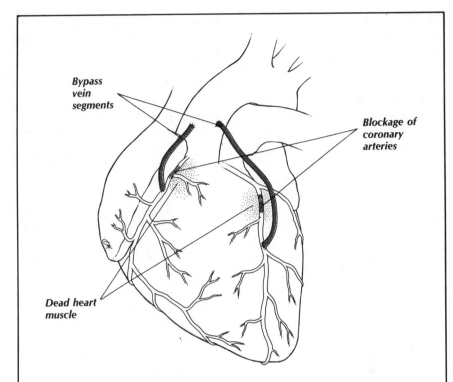

*Coronary bypass surgery is performed if a section of one of the coronary arteries has become obstructed by a buildup of cholesterol, calcium, and scar tissue. A section of a blood vessel (usually a vein taken from the leg) is sewn into a small hole in the aorta and then attached to the affected vessel. This operation permits the return of free blood flow.*

pose of the operation is to bypass the obstructed area to permit free blood flow. Without the procedure, heart muscle beyond the obstruction is starved for blood and oxygen, especially during exercise. This condition causes the chest pains known as angina. If one or more of the coronary arteries become completely obstructed, the result may be a heart attack, in which a portion of heart muscle becomes so starved for blood that it dies.

## Indications and alternatives

Bypass surgery is usually considered when a person suffers frequent, severe chest pains from angina. However, not all persons with angina need bypass surgery. Advances are being made in using medication to control angina. Furthermore, some angina is caused by spasms (sudden, violent contractions) of the coronary arteries, which bypass surgery may not prevent or ease.

Obstructions in the coronary arteries can now sometimes be eliminated by methods that do not require cutting open the chest, such as percutaneous transluminal coronary angioplasty, in which a long tube with a balloon tip is threaded through the arteries to the site of the obstruction and the balloon is inflated to open a clogged vessel. Even without outside help, and given enough time, the heart may create its own partial bypass via collateral circulation (a system of blood vessels that detour the blood around the obstruction).

If a patient often has severe chest pains that cannot be controlled by medication, the doctor may decide to order x-ray motion pictures of the heart. Through a thin, woven plastic catheter (tube) inserted into an artery in the arm or leg and passed through large blood vessels to the heart, x-ray contrast medium is injected so that it flows into the coronary arteries, outlining them on an x-ray screen. The pictures show exactly where and to what extent the blood vessels are narrowed or blocked. Thus, the doctor can determine whether bypasses are needed and, if so, where. The most urgent reason to operate is the obstruction of 50 percent or more of the left main coronary artery, which supplies two-thirds of the blood to the heart muscle.

### Procedure

First, the surgeon makes several incisions in one leg to obtain a long section of a large vein for use as bypass tubing. Next, the surgeon makes an incision down the middle of the chest, divides the breastbone with an electric saw, and separates the two sides of the rib cage enough to expose the beating heart. The heartbeat is then stopped using electric shock, ice water, or certain drugs. A heart-lung machine is connected to the large vessels that carry blood to and from the heart, and takes over the job of adding oxygen, removing carbon dioxide, and pumping the blood through the body.

The surgeon then cuts through the pericardial sac (a thin bag of tissue that surrounds the heart) to expose the coronary arteries, which lie on the surface of the

heart. A small hole is made in the aorta, and one end of the vein segment to be used as bypass tubing is sewn to it. The other end is attached to the affected vessel beyond the obstruction. Thereafter, blood will flow freely around the obstructed portion of the artery to nourish the heart muscle, which should decrease the patient's risk of chest pains and heart attacks.

The bypass surgery operation takes about four or five hours, depending on the number of bypasses. A double bypass operation is one in which portions of two vessels are bypassed, a triple bypass means that portions of three vessels are bypassed, and so forth. Usually the patient can walk about three or four days following the operation and return home in little more than a week.

### Results

Considering that the procedure is such a major operation, the death rate is very low— less than 1 percent in some hospitals. In 80 percent of cases, angina pains are eliminated, and the patient can return to a normal life. Life expectancy may improve, but it cannot be guaranteed in all cases. There has been much controversy surrounding coronary bypass surgery, mainly centering on the question of whether this procedure can increase life expectancy for those with coronary artery disease and angina. At present, there is no question that the surgery relieves pain and allows for greater exercise tolerance in the majority of patients who undergo it for severe angina. In certain patterns of disease, such as obstruction of the left main coronary artery, the op-

eration definitely prolongs life expectancy. In other patterns, such as triple vessel disease, in which branches of the coronary arteries (except for the left main coronary artery) are involved, the procedure most likely allows a longer life. In still other patterns, the question remains unsettled. Whether the surgery will prevent a heart attack has also not been determined.

# Cor pulmonale

Cor pulmonale, or right heart failure, is the enlargement and failure of the right ventricle of the heart, due to poor functioning of the lungs. The right ventricle is affected because its main job is to pump blood returning from the veins of the body into the lungs, through the pulmonary artery. When the lungs are not working properly—for example, when many of the capillaries (tiny blood vessels) in the lungs have been destroyed or constricted by disease—not enough blood can get through the lungs. The blood backs up, and the pressure rises in both the pulmonary artery and the right ventricle, which become enlarged. Blood pressure also rises in the veins leading to the heart.

In addition, because not enough blood is getting to the lungs and because of disease or destruction of the alveoli (the oxygenating units of the lungs), the oxygen content of the blood decreases. This causes the bone marrow to produce more red blood cells, which in most circumstances would allow the blood to carry more oxygen. However, in this case it only makes matters worse. The excessive numbers of red blood cells thicken the blood, making it harder to pump. The result of this entire process is failure of the right ventricle to perform effectively.

## Causes

In nearly six cases out of seven, the lung condition that has led to cor pulmonale is chronic obstructive pulmonary disease (COPD), which is a breakdown in lung function resulting from emphysema, chronic bronchitis, asthma, or a combination of these diseases. Some of the other causes are cystic fibrosis, recurrent blood clots in the blood vessels of the lungs, loss of lung tissue because of surgery or injury, extreme obesity that prevents normal breathing, diseases of the nerves controlling the breathing muscles, and insufficiency of oxygen from living at high altitudes (chronic mountain sickness). Almost always, the cause of cor pulmonale is a chronic, lifelong condition. One exception is acute (sudden and severe) cor pulmonale resulting from a massive blood clot in the lungs; the clot can sometimes be removed by surgery. Another, more common exception is acute worsening cor pulmonale resulting from a severe infection of the respiratory tract in someone with a chronic lung condition; appropriate treatment of the infection usually can bring this type of cor pulmonale under control.

## Symptoms

Symptoms of cor pulmonale include increasing fatigue, drowsiness, fainting on exertion, ankle swelling, a feeling of fullness in the neck and abdomen, enlarged neck veins, and an enlarged and tender liver. As in the more common congestive heart failure, the patient may wheeze, cough, and find breathing difficult and painful. At times, the lips, nails, fingertips, and face may appear bluish due to lack of oxygen.

## Diagnosis

X-ray or ultrasound images will reveal the enlargement of the right ventricle and pulmonary artery. A markedly increased number of red blood cells, exceeding 50 percent of the blood volume, is a telltale clue. Heartbeat patterns indicating right ventricular failure can be seen on the electrocardiogram (a visual record of the electrical impulses generated in the heart).

## Treatment

Medical management of cor pulmonale is twofold, treating the heart failure and treating the lung condition at the same time. Heart failure therapy includes administration of oxygen to make the patient more comfortable, to reduce the elevated blood pressure in the pulmonary artery, and to prevent elevation of the red blood cell count. Salt and water restriction and diuretics can reduce excess fluid in the tissues. Bed rest reduces the load on the heart.

In general, treatment of the underlying lung condition is much the same as it was (or should have been) before cor pulmonale occurred. The patient should not smoke; in most cases, smoking helped to cause the original condition, and smoking worsens the present condition. Once home from the hospital, the individual should regularly practice breathing exercises and may need oxygen and suction treatments to relieve symptoms. The patient should rest frequently, watch for ankle swelling and other signs of fluid build-up, avoid people with colds, and report early signs of infection.

## Prevention

You can help to prevent the lung condition leading to cor pulmonale by not smoking; by having periodic physical examinations, including lung function testing; and by seeking prompt medical treatment by a physician for any chronic cough or recurring respiratory infection. It is especially important to observe these precautions if you come from a family that has an inherited tendency to suffer from certain chronic respiratory diseases.

# Cyanosis

Cyanosis is a bluish discoloration of the skin and mucous membranes due to inadequate oxygenation of the blood. The abnormal coloration is easily seen in these areas because of both their rich blood supply and their relative transparency.

Blood rich in oxygen from the lungs is bright red. This is because of the red, iron-containing pigment known as hemoglobin, which is found in the erythrocytes (the disk-shaped red blood cells). When blood passes through the blood vessels of the lungs, oxygen from the air in the lungs combines with the hemoglobin, which causes it (and consequently the blood) to turn a very bright red. After the blood releases its oxygen to the cells of the body and picks up carbon dioxide and other waste products, the hemoglobin fades and the blood turns dark. However, if the lungs are not working well or if for some other reason the red blood cells are not being oxygenated, the blood appears bluish.

Cyanosis can be due to asthma, choking, pneumonia, and lung collapse. It can also be a sign of certain inborn heart defects, of severe cor pulmonale, or of abnormally excessive production of red blood cells. It is seen most frequently in cold weather when lips, toes, and fingers turn blue from extreme cold, the result of sluggish surface circulation of the blood (in this case, it may be a normal phenomenon and does not necessarily indicate disease).

# Defibrillation

Defibrillation is a technique to correct fibrillation of the heart, an abnormal condition marked by very rapid, disorganized twitching or trembling of the heart muscle in place of the normal rhythmic beat. Ventricular fibrillation produces a condition called cardiac arrest, in which no heartbeat, pulse, or blood pressure can be detected. Death or permanent brain damage follows within a few minutes unless this condition is corrected or unless first-aid measures maintain blood circulation and breathing until help can arrive.

### Causes of fibrillation

The most common cause of fibrillation is a heart attack. When this happens, certain parts of the heart will start contracting independently of the normal heartbeat. Other causes of fibrillation are severe electrical shock

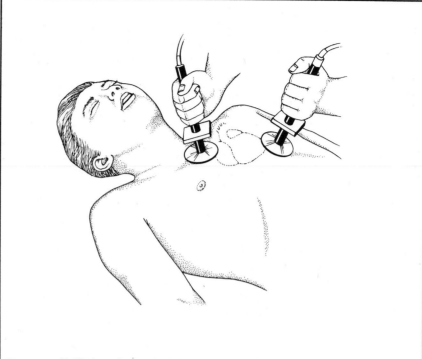

*To correct fibrillation (disorganized twitching or trembling of the heart muscle), the metal paddles of the defibrillator are placed on the chest, and a jolt of electricity is directed through them into the heart to shock it back into its normal rhythm.*

and prolonged exposure to cold temperatures.

### Defibrillation treatment

An electrical device called a defibrillator is used to correct fibrillation. A pair of metal paddles are placed on the patient's chest, and a jolt of direct-current electricity from the defibrillator is directed through them into the heart to shock it back into its regular rhythm. The shock stops the independent action of individual muscle fibers and allows the natural pacemaker of the heart to take over again.

Once the normal heartbeat has been restored, other measures are taken. A drug such as lidocaine is injected to prevent further fibrillation. An intravenous tube is inserted to administer sodium bicarbonate (to neu-

tralize acids in the blood) and defibrillating medication. A breathing tube is passed into the lungs; it is attached to a mechanical pump that forces air in and out of the lungs. Then the patient is taken to a hospital cardiac intensive care unit, where monitoring devices constantly keep track of the patient's condition and sound an alarm if danger threatens. An electrical defibrillator is close at hand if needed in an emergency.

Electrical defibrillation is also used to restart a heart that has been stopped for purposes of heart surgery.

# Embolism

An embolism occurs when some part of the circulatory system is either partially or completely blocked by some obstructing

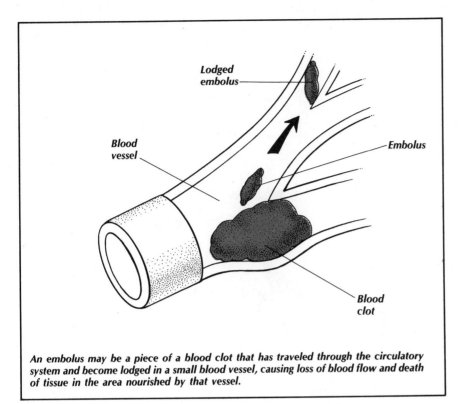

An embolus may be a piece of a blood clot that has traveled through the circulatory system and become lodged in a small blood vessel, causing loss of blood flow and death of tissue in the area nourished by that vessel.

mass that has traveled through the system. The occurrence of such an obstruction is called an embolism, while the mass causing the embolism is called an embolus.

## Types

Emboli (the plural of *embolus*) are classified into three major groups:
- Solid emboli, which are made up of a variety of substances, such as clumps of tissue, tumor cells, or pieces of blood clots
- Liquid emboli, which are made up of globules of fat or amniotic fluid (fluid that surrounds the fetus in the uterus)
- Gaseous emboli, which are made up of the various constituents of air

Emboli may be further categorized according to their origin and the location of the blockage that they cause:

- Arterial emboli, which originate either from the heart or the artery itself, travel downstream, and become lodged in a smaller blood vessel, preventing the flow of fresh blood to whatever area or organ is normally supplied
- Paradoxical emboli, which originate in the venous system, pass into the arterial system (usually through a defect in the walls separating the chambers of the heart), and block an artery anywhere in the body
- Pulmonary emboli, which block vessels in the lungs (for further information on pulmonary embolism, see pages 188– 189)
- Coronary artery emboli, which block the coronary arteries of the heart
- Cerebral emboli, which block vessels in the brain but usually originate in the heart or the carotid arteries in the neck, which lead to the brain

## Causes

The most common cause of emboli is blood clots from within the heart or blood vessels. Arterial emboli also commonly originate from plaques or other accumulations on the valves of the heart, from aneurysms, and from plaques or clots within arteries. Fat emboli can result from injury to the bones (particularly the long bones of the legs) or from damage to cells in fat tissue. Air emboli can develop if a very large amount of air is admitted during an intravenous infusion or during surgery, especially in operations on the neck or the chest (in the latter cases, air enters vessels that are open because of the surgery). However, the oxygen in air is not the only gas involved in gaseous emboli. When divers ascend from high-pressure levels in deep water to normal-pressure levels too quickly, or when pilots in planes without cabin pressurization climb from normal-pressure levels to low-pressure levels, there is always the possibility that nitrogen bubbles will arise in the bloodstream because of too rapid decompression. If any of these gaseous emboli find their way into the central nervous system, the results can be catastrophic.

## Symptoms

The symptoms produced by an embolism vary according to the site at which the embolism occurs. An embolism deprives the affected area of its blood supply, which can cause damage or death of tissue in the area. An embolism in a brain artery may produce the symptoms of a stroke, such as unsteadiness, slurring of speech, and numbness or weakness in the face, arm, or leg on one side. If an embolism occurs in the leg, the area beyond the blockage may become white and painful. Pain may be the first symptom of embolism in other areas.

### Treatment

Emboli resulting from blood clots are often treated with a variety of anticoagulants (agents that inhibit normal clotting mechanisms in the blood). Common anticoagulants, such as heparin and warfarin, do not dissolve clots, but instead prevent additional clots from forming and embolizing. There are newer drugs that do dissolve clots, but their use is restricted to special situations. If an embolism is in an accessible location, such as an artery in a limb, and tissue is threatened, surgery to remove the clot is the preferred method of treatment to save the limb. In cases of massive embolism in the lung in which life is threatened, surgery can also be attempted. If an individual has clots in the deep venous system of the lower half of the body and for some reason anticoagulants cannot be prescribed (for example, because of a recent hemorrhage in the brain or other vital organ), blocking devices, such as clips, can be placed on or in the inferior vena cava (the main vein receiving blood from the lower part of the body) to prevent emboli from reaching the lungs.

# Endocarditis

The heart is made up of three cellular layers: the epicardium (outermost layer), the myocardium (middle, muscular layer), and the endocardium (innermost

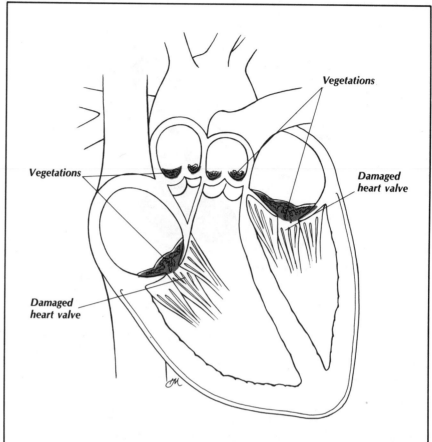

*Abnormal areas in the heart, such as valves that have been damaged by rheumatic fever or calcium deposition, are common sites for the development of vegetations (collections of platelets, fibrin, and other debris of the circulatory system).*

layer). The endocardium lines all of the chambers and valves of the heart, and its cells are continuous with those of blood vessels leaving the heart. Endocarditis is an inflammation of the endocardial layer of the heart.

### Causes

The most common form of endocarditis, infectious endocarditis, is caused by microorganisms. *Staphylococcus* and *Streptococcus* bacteria are most often the infectious agents, but viruses, fungi, and other bacteria may also be responsible.

Infective endocarditis usually occurs in persons with congeni-

tal (inborn) or acquired defects in the walls or on the valves of the heart. An example of a congenital defect would be a hole in the wall between two chambers of the heart. An example of an acquired defect would be damage to the heart valves caused by rheumatic fever or calcium deposition. Such abnormalities make the heart more susceptible to infection.

Bacteria probably circulate through the bloodstream of all people at some time or another. However, certain procedures, such as dental work and surgery, may lead to serious bacteremia (the presence of large numbers of bacteria in the bloodstream). The bacteria accumulate on these abnormal areas in the heart and cause inflammation or infection that serves as a foundation for the collection of platelets, strands of fibrin (clotting material), and other debris of the circulatory system. The clump of material that forms is referred to as a vegetation.

## Symptoms

Infective endocarditis is a serious systemic disease with a wide spectrum of symptoms and signs. Patients may complain of fevers, weakness, and weight loss. Anemia (deficiency of red blood cells) may also be present. Pieces of vegetations may break off and travel through the bloodstream to other areas of the body, causing symptoms of obstruction (for example, a stroke if the brain is affected, or microscopic blood in the urine if a kidney is affected).

## Diagnosis

The diagnosis is made on the basis of the history, the physical examination, and the results of laboratory studies, such as blood cultures, to identify the microorganisms present.

## Treatment

Once the infectious agent has been isolated, appropriate antibiotics can be administered. Antibiotic administration is by the intravenous route, at least at first, and usually continues for long periods (up to eight weeks).

If infection of a heart valve is particularly severe or if a prosthetic (artificial) valve is involved, the valve may have to be replaced.

## Prevention

Persons with abnormal heart valves, prosthetic valves, and other structural abnormalities must be given antibiotics before and after any procedure likely to disperse bacteria throughout the body (for example, dental work, surgery of the urogenital tract or large intestine, or opening of an abscess). The antibiotics serve either to prevent the passage of microorganisms through the bloodstream or to lessen their number, thereby decreasing the chance that endocarditis will develop.

# Extrasystole

An extrasystole is a contraction of the heart caused by a stimulus or impulse somewhere in the heart other than in the sinoatrial node, the natural pacemaker of the heart. In some ways, the condition is like static in an electrical circuit.

While physicians have for years debated the importance of extrasystoles, recent thought on the subject has led to a reassessment of the seriousness of the phenomenon. In many cases of sudden death attributed to severe cardiac arrhythmia (abnormal rhythm and rate of the heartbeat) in patients with severe underlying heart disease, the arrhythmia may have actually been triggered by ventricular extrasystoles.

## Causes

While the immediate cause of an extrasystole is an accidental signal telling the heart muscle to contract, the real causes lie elsewhere. For example, strenuous activity, especially if there are existing heart problems, can trigger extrasystoles, which, in turn, may trigger an episode of heart arrhythmia that leads to more serious complications. Coffee, nicotine, and certain drugs, as well as anxiety and sudden shocks or frights, are thought to play a role in causing extrasystoles. It is important to note, however, that extrasystoles also occur in normal hearts and, in these cases, are quite harmless and do not necessarily indicate underlying heart disease.

## Symptoms

The symptoms of extrasystoles are familiar to anyone who has ever been startled and felt that his heart had "skipped a beat." The extrasystole sometimes presents itself as one or two extra heartbeats. On other occasions, there will be a beat followed by a long silence, then a couple of quick beats. Some people experience a feeling of giddiness, shortness of breath, and weakness, with momentary feelings of blacking out. These symptoms, if prolonged (particularly if associated with loss of consciousness) usually indicate that a sustained arrhythmia is occurring, which should be reported to a doctor.

## Diagnosis

The primary diagnostic tool is the electrocardiograph (an instrument that records the electrical impulses generated in the heart). One method of documenting the occurrence and nature of extrasystoles is continuous ambulatory electrocardiographic monitoring with a device called a Holter monitor. The monitor, which is like a combination tape recorder-electrocardiograph, is worn by the patient for as long as 24 hours. A diary is furnished so that the patient can record his activities and symptoms. The patient goes about his usual routine during the test. After the specified time period, the tape is translated into a continuous electrocardiographic record. Comparison of this record with the diary allows a diagnosis to be made as to the presence and type of arrhythmia.

## Treatment

Any treatment program must be based on the underlying cause of the extrasystoles, as revealed by electrocardiographic studies. Treatment may involve medications to regulate the heartbeat, lifestyle changes (such as restriction of tobacco use and caffeine intake), or implantation of an artificial cardiac pacemaker. If the electrocardiographic studies indicate that the extrasystoles do not reflect any disease process, no treatment is necessary.

# Gangrene

Gangrene is a term that refers to the death of body tissue due to diminishment or loss of blood supply, leading to nutrient and oxygen deprivation.

There are three major types of gangrene: moist, dry, and gas gangrene. Although gangrene usually affects the extremities of the body, it can sometimes affect the internal organs.

## Causes

Moist gangrene is generally caused by a sudden stoppage of

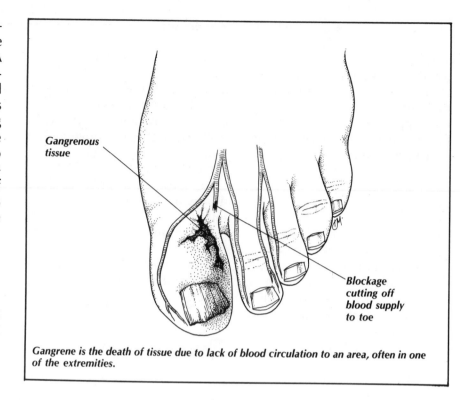

Gangrenous tissue

Blockage cutting off blood supply to toe

*Gangrene is the death of tissue due to lack of blood circulation to an area, often in one of the extremities.*

blood flow to a body site, usually resulting from burning by heat or by acid, from severe freezing, from a physical accident that destroys the tissues, from keeping a tourniquet in place too long, or from a blood clot or other blockage. The tissue death that results from loss of blood supply is accompanied by decomposition due to bacterial action. The gangrenous infection is likely to spread rapidly as toxins (poisons) are formed in the affected tissues and absorbed.

Dry gangrene usually occurs gradually and results from a slow, progressive reduction of blood flow in the arteries. There is generally no bacterial decomposition; the tissues simply become dry and shriveled. This type of gangrene occurs only in the extremities. It may occur as a secondary effect of arteriosclerosis in the elderly, of advanced stages of diabetes, or of Buerger's disease (an inflammatory condition that affects the blood

vessels of the limbs, primarily the legs).

Gas gangrene is often caused by infection of a wound by anaerobic (able to live without air) bacteria, which are commonly found in soil. It can follow rapidly after contamination of deep wounds. The bacteria break down tissues, giving off gas and toxic by-products.

Gangrene in an internal organ can be caused by any condition that cuts off blood supply to an area. For example, if a loop of intestine is caught in an opening in the abdominal wall, the blood supply to that part of the intestine may be cut off (causing what is called a strangulated hernia), and gangrene may then occur in that section of the tissue. In acute appendicitis, areas of gangrene may occur in the walls of the appendix, with rupture of the appendix through the gangrenous area. In severe cholecystitis (inflammation of the gallbladder, usually associated with gallstones), gangrene can develop in areas where the stones compress the mucous membrane, cutting off the blood supply.

## Symptoms

Moist gangrene is characterized by a purplish-red, bruised appearance; by swelling; and, often, by blisters.

Dry gangrene is marked by gradual shrinking of the tissues, which first grow cold and lack a pulse, then turn brown, then black. Usually there is a sharp line of demarcation where the gangrene stops because the unaffected tissue nearby is continuing to receive blood. This type of gangrene is sometimes called mummification of tissue because of the dry, shriveled, and dark appearance.

The initial symptoms of gas gangrene are swelling, paleness of skin, and a thin, bloody (but not foul) discharge. The characteristic foul smell comes later in the progression of this form of the disorder. It is an acute, painful condition in which the muscles and tissues under the skin become filled with gas and a thin, brownish-black fluid.

Symptoms of gangrene in an internal organ may include pain, tenderness over the organ, and fever.

## Diagnosis

The appearance of the affected area usually suggests the diagnosis to the physician. Laboratory analysis of a tissue specimen will allow the identification of the infective microorganisms, which is necessary for selection of an appropriate antibiotic. Areas of gas gangrene may be seen on x-ray studies.

## Treatment

Treatment of gangrene generally involves cleaning of the area and administration of antibiotics. The effectiveness of antibiotic therapy seems to depend on the time elapsed between injury or infection and the beginning of treatment.

In the case of gangrene caused by deterioration in the blood supply of the elderly or gangrene associated with appendicitis, hernia, diabetes, or Buerger's disease, the treatment begins with the diagnosis and treatment of the underlying condition.

## Prevention

Preventing gangrene in an open wound begins with cleanliness. All dirt and particles in an open wound should be removed as soon as possible, and the wound should be cleansed with a soap solution and water. Burned skin requires careful, antiseptic handling to avoid infection. Frostbite also is dangerous because freezing impairs the circulation of the skin, making it tender and easily damaged. Frostbitten skin, especially on the fingers, toes, and earlobes, must be handled with great care to avoid gangrenous infections.

# Heart attack

A heart attack, or myocardial infarction, occurs when an area of the heart muscle is damaged or dies because a coronary artery (an artery that delivers blood to the heart muscle itself) has been blocked and the oxygen-rich blood supply to that area of the heart has been drastically reduced. The damaged muscle tissue of the heart is replaced with scar tissue, which does not function as muscle, but rather as a kind of patch. If the area of damage is large enough, the ability of the heart to pump blood is seriously diminished.

Although the chances of surviving a heart attack are now better than ever and complete recovery is common, heart attack is still the number one cause of death in the United States. Heart attacks that do not result in death may lead to serious complications, including shock, cardiac arrhythmia (irregularity of the heartbeat), and congestive heart failure, in which the heart cannot pump enough blood to meet the body's needs.

## Causes

Heart attack is caused by the blockage of a coronary artery by a thrombus (blood clot) or by atherosclerosis, a disease in which the arteries become clogged by fatty deposits. Damage to the heart muscle occurs when the narrowed coronary arteries are unable to deliver the extra oxygenated blood needed by the heart during emotional stress or physical exertion.

## Risk factors

A number of factors have been associated with an increased risk of heart attack. Hypertension (high blood pressure) increases the resistance in the blood vessels, forcing the heart to pump harder to push blood through the body. Smoking acts to constrict and damage the arteries and reduce blood flow to the heart muscle. Use of birth control pills, especially by women over the age of 35 and by women who smoke, has been linked to an increased incidence of heart attack. Stress increases the oxygen requirement of the heart muscle. A diet high in saturated fats (fats that are usually solid at room temperature, including those animal fats found in butter and meats) has been found to increase the serum cholesterol level in the blood and thus the chances of developing atherosclerosis. The lack of moderate, regular exercise results in poor tone of the heart muscle and may also prevent the development of collateral circulation (the system of smaller blood vessels that bypass a blocked artery and increase the blood supply to the area served by that artery).

## Symptoms

The major symptom of a heart attack is a crushing pain in the middle of the chest, behind the breastbone; the pain can also extend down one or both arms and into the neck, back, teeth, or jaws. Fatigue, heavy perspiration, dizziness, difficulty in breathing, and fever may accompany this pain. The pain may be somewhat similar to that due to angina pectoris, but the pain of a heart attack is more intense, will not be relieved by nitroglycerin, and will not go away within a few minutes, as angina pain will. Also, a heart attack may take place during sleep, which is uncommon for angina pain.

Heart attacks may be very mild, signaled only by slight discomfort, faintness, and nausea. In very serious cases, a heart attack may be accompanied by cardiac arrest (cessation of the heartbeat) or ventricular fibrillation (degeneration of the normal, steady heartbeat to a useless

Right coronary artery

Left coronary artery

Clot in artery

Damaged area

*A heart attack occurs when an area of the heart muscle is damaged or dies because the coronary artery supplying the area has been blocked by a blood clot or advanced atherosclerosis.*

quivering that prevents blood from being pumped through the body).

## Diagnosis

Heart attack is diagnosed on the basis of the medical history, the physical examination, and test results. The electrocardiograph (an instrument that records the electrical impulses generated in the heart) will show disturbed patterns of heart activity because the impulses must travel around the damaged area. The white blood cell count may also be elevated because the body's immune system increases the number of white blood cells in

order to remove damaged tissue from the heart. Measurements of certain enzymes (special proteins) in the blood may signal that heart muscle has been damaged, although these tests may not confirm that a heart attack has taken place until 24 to 72 hours after the event.

## Treatment

There is no home treatment for a heart attack—other than emergency first-aid resuscitative measures—cardiopulmonary resuscitation (CPR)—if the patient loses consciousness. The only recommended plan of action is to summon emergency medical assistance as soon as a heart attack is suspected. Until help arrives, keep the patient warm and comfortable (generally sitting up rather than lying down).

Many deaths could be prevented if heart attack victims or their families, acting on their behalf, did not delay seeking medical attention. Studies have shown that, on the average, heart attack victims wait three hours before seeing a doctor.

In almost every case, hospitalization will be necessary following a heart attack. Treatment in the hospital will probably begin in the cardiac care unit, with limited physical activity at first and a gradual return to normal activities.

A variety of medications are used to treat heart attack patients: antiarrhythmics, which inhibit irregularities in the heartbeat; diuretics, which reduce strain on the heart by removing excess water from the blood; antianginals, which diminish chest pain; sedatives, which relax the body; and beta-blockers, which ease the strain on the heart by decreasing its work. Another category of drugs, calcium-channel blockers, also appear to be effective in reducing injury to the heart muscle and risk of death due to a heart attack.

Interventional therapy during the first few hours after a heart attack has become common. Usually, an angiogram is performed first: through an artery in the groin or arm, a special dye is injected directly into the heart and coronary arteries, and x-rays are taken to delineate the area of obstruction. Once the area has been localized, it may be possible to inject drugs to dissolve an obstruction. In other cases, percutaneous transluminal coronary angioplasty may be performed:

in this procedure, a long tube with a balloon tip is threaded through the arteries to the site of the obstruction, and the balloon is inflated to open a clogged vessel.

Lifestyle changes will also help heart attack victims. Patients may be advised to stop smoking, lose weight, and partake in regular, moderate exercise.

### Prevention

Prevention of heart attack begins with sensible health and dietary habits. Those who do not smoke and do not overeat or overindulge in saturated fats, but who do exercise regularly and eliminate as much stress as possible from their lives, are much

less likely to become heart attack victims. Those who have already suffered one or more heart attacks may be able to prevent further attacks by changes in their living habits along these lines.

# Heartbeat irregularities

Heartbeat irregularities (also called cardiac arrhythmias) are deviations from the normal, steady beating of the heart.

Minor irregularities in the heartbeat are common, but more serious arrhythmias can lead to fainting, angina pectoris, or heart attack. The most devastating heartbeat irregularity is called ventricular fibrillation,

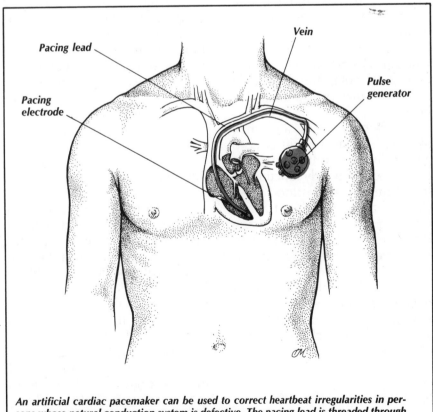

*An artificial cardiac pacemaker can be used to correct heartbeat irregularities in persons whose natural conduction system is defective. The pacing lead is threaded through a vein until the pacing electrode at the tip of the lead rests within the heart. The electrical pulse generator is then sewn in place under the skin.*

which occurs when the normally steady pumping action of the heart is reduced to a useless quivering.

## Causes

Arrhythmias are usually caused by damage to the heart muscle or to specialized heart tissue called the conduction system. The first part of the conduction system, called the sinus node, serves as the natural pacemaker of the heart; it is responsible for establishing and maintaining a healthy, steady heartbeat.

Heartbeat irregularities can also be caused by improper use of certain drugs (among them drugs prescribed for arrhythmia, which can actually cause arrhythmia if the dosage is too high), excessive smoking (the nicotine in cigarettes alters the heartbeat), or consumption of large quantities of caffeine (the amounts found in coffee, tea, chocolate, cola, and some cold medicines may overstimulate the heart).

Heartbeat irregularities may also develop as a result of congenital (present at birth) damage to the heart, a poorly functioning left ventricle, high blood pressure, or a previous heart attack (because the resulting scar tissue interferes with transmission of the nerve impulses governing the heartbeat).

Ventricular fibrillation often occurs after a myocardial infarction (heart attack) or some other serious injury, such as a severe electrical shock.

## Symptoms

Some heartbeat irregularities have no noticeable symptoms. Others will be signaled by lightheadedness, fainting, pounding of the heart, dizziness, and chest pain.

## Diagnosis

Arrhythmias are diagnosed primarily with the electrocardiograph (an instrument that records the electrical impulses generated in the heart). A normal heart will produce a record of regular peaks and valleys; an arrhythmic heart will show an uneven pattern. Continuous recording of the heartbeat can be done on an outpatient basis with a Holter monitor, which is like a combination tape recorder-electrocardiograph. This small device can be worn by the patient for as long as 24 hours. Electrocardiographic wires are taped to the patient's chest, and recordings of the heartbeat are made on magnetic tape. The patient makes a note of his activities and of any symptoms he experiences during the testing period, and these reports are later correlated with the recorded heartbeat rhythm.

## Treatment

Occasionally, cardiac arrhythmias are so mild that no particular treatment is required. However, most irregularities are treated with medication, defibrillation, or implantation of an artificial pacemaker. All of these methods act to steady the heart rhythm and to maintain a healthy, steady heartbeat.

Medications commonly used include digitalis, which slows the heartbeat; beta-blockers, which correct extra beats originating in the lower chambers of the heart; and antiarrhythmics, which act on specific problems of the heartbeat.

A defibrillator is a device applied to the chest that electrically jolts a quivering heart in a state of ventricular fibrillation back into a normal pattern of beating.

For those whose arrhythmia is caused by a faulty conduction system, an artificial cardiac pacemaker may be implanted in the chest. The pacemaker incorporates a small electrical generator, which causes the heart to beat when its own conduction system fails and steadies an abnormal heartbeat by sending out electrical impulses similar to those emitted by the heart.

Lifestyle changes will probably be recommended to patients suffering from heartbeat irregularities; they may need to quit smoking, lose weight, exercise more regularly, and reduce their caffeine intake. These precautions may also be taken in an effort to prevent arrhythmias.

# Heart murmurs

Heart murmurs are extra whishing sounds—in addition to the regular "lub-dub" sounds of the heartbeat—that are made as blood flows through the chambers and valves of the heart. In most cases, heart murmurs are quite harmless and represent no cause for concern. In other cases, however, heart murmurs can be a symptom that first alerts a doctor to the presence of heart disease or a structural abnormality in the heart.

## Causes

Heart murmurs can be heard in many healthy persons, especially children, teenagers, and pregnant women. These murmurs are normal sounds caused by the blood rushing through the heart and do not indicate a heart condition. They are called innocent, functional, or insignificant heart murmurs.

In contrast, organic, or structural, heart murmurs are caused by narrowing or obstruction of the heart valves or by incomplete closure of the valves, which allows blood to seep back into the upper or lower heart chambers. Such heart murmurs can be congenital (existing at birth) or acquired, due to damage to the heart valves caused by rheumatic fever, atherosclerosis, syphilis, or other ailments. Heart murmurs also occur when there are holes in the walls separating the chambers of the heart.

### Symptoms

Heart murmurs can be detected only by physical examination. By listening to the heart through a stethoscope, a doctor can usually distinguish any extra sounds and judge (by their quality, intensity, location, and timing) whether they signify a serious problem.

### Diagnosis

If the heart murmur is considered to be organic, the doctor will order special studies (for example, chest x-ray, electrocardiography, cardiac catheterization, and echocardiography) to evaluate the cause and extent of the condition.

### Treatment

An innocent heart murmur does not require any medical treatment or special care, and a person with such a murmur can live a completely normal life. In fact, it is very important that a child with an innocent murmur be treated as the normal, healthy child that he is. Parents are sometimes frightened by the idea of a heart murmur and overprotect a child unnecessarily, which is not good for the child's emotional well-being. Most innocent murmurs detected in children disappear or become undetectable by adolescence; only 15 percent to 20 percent of such murmurs continue into adulthood.

If a murmur is organic, the underlying condition can usually be corrected surgically.

## Hemoglobin

The role of the red blood cells is to carry oxygen throughout the body. The red blood cells are enabled to perform this task by the presence of hemoglobin, the pigment (coloring agent) that is formed when the red blood cells develop in the bone marrow.

Each hemoglobin molecule is made up of a protein molecule called globin and four pigmented molecules of a compound called heme. Each heme molecule has one atom of iron, and there are four heme molecules in a single molecule of hemoglobin; hence, a single molecule of hemoglobin has four atoms of iron. This structure makes it possible for one hemoglobin molecule to join with four oxygen molecules to form a substance called oxyhemoglobin. This reaction is reversible, enabling hemoglobin to pick up oxygen when the blood is in the lungs and to release oxygen in the cells when the blood is pumped to the tissues.

In general, the blood of men usually has a greater concentration of hemoglobin than that of women. Men have about 14 to 16 grams of hemoglobin per 100 milliliters of blood, whereas women have only about 12 to 14 grams per 100 milliliters of blood. (One hundred milliliters is approximately equal to three and one-half ounces.)

A number of blood disorders have to do with hemoglobin abnormalities. In many forms of anemia, there is not enough hemoglobin in the red blood cells (for more information, see pages 193–195). In polycythemia, there is too much hemoglobin in the blood (for more information, see pages 218–219). In other conditions, such as thalassemia, the abnormal chemical composition or production of hemoglobin molecules reduces the oxygen-carrying or oxygen-releasing capability of the red blood cells.

## Hemorrhage

Hemorrhage is the technical term for bleeding, often referring to substantial blood loss or uncontrollable bleeding, either externally or internally. The effects of hemorrhage depend on the part of the body that is bleeding and the total amount of blood that is lost. Hemorrhage can be a symptom of a number of serious, sometimes fatal, disorders.

### Causes

Hemorrhage occurs when blood vessels are torn or broken. Normally, blood will clot within seconds or minutes, stopping the blood flow. However, when serious injuries or other disorders (such as hemophilia, peptic ulcer, and cancer) are involved, the body's normal blood-clotting mechanism may be inadequate or may malfunction. If blood loss is not quickly stopped, death may result.

### Symptoms

Severe external hemorrhage is associated with the following symptoms: rapid pulse, dizziness or faintness, collapse, a drop in blood pressure, a rise in pulse rate, and pale, cold, clammy, or sweaty skin.

Internal hemorrhage may also show symptoms, even if the bleeding is slight. Black, tarry stools may signal bleeding in the intestinal tract from a peptic ulcer; blood in the vomitus indicates bleeding in the stomach; and blood in the urine means that bleeding is occurring in the kidneys or urinary tract.

Blood in the stool, urine, or vomitus should always be reported to a doctor at once, as should external bleeding that occurs frequently or that cannot be stopped within minutes.

### Treatment

Treatment for internal hemorrhage involves correcting the cause of the bleeding, possibly with surgery. External hemorrhage is treated by applying pressure to the wound with a sterile bandage (or, in an emergency, just pressing it with the fingers) until the bleeding stops. If bleeding cannot be stopped, the patient will almost certainly have to be hospitalized, so that lost blood can be replaced with transfusions of blood products and, in some cases, so that damaged blood vessels can be surgically tied off and sealed.

# Hypertension

Hypertension, or high blood pressure, refers to persistently elevated pressure of blood within the arteries, which carry blood from the heart through the body. The exertion of excessive force on the artery walls may cause damage to the arteries themselves and thereby to the heart, kidneys, and brain, leading to heart attack, kidney failure, and stroke.

### Causes

Although many people believe that hypertension is caused by extreme activity or tension, this theory has not been proved. When no underlying cause is discovered, the disease is called primary, or essential, hypertension. If another disease, such as kidney or heart disease, causes the elevated blood pressure, the condition is labeled secondary hypertension.

### Risk factors

Contrary to popular belief, there is no typical hypertensive person. However, some people are more susceptible to developing high blood pressure than others. Heredity appears to play a role; persons whose parents are hypertensive are at greater risk of becoming hypertensive themselves. In the past, hypertension was attributed to aging, but current evidence indicates that age is not a primary factor. The incidence of hypertension in black persons, both children and adults, is about twice that in white persons.

Overweight, prolonged stress, smoking, drinking, and excessive sodium in the diet (which

causes fluid retention) may increase blood pressure, especially in persons prone to hypertension. There are also indications that use of oral contraceptives may contribute to increased blood pressure; however, this is more likely to occur in women who are overweight, whose parents are hypertensive, or who have other hypertensive risk factors.

### Symptoms

Hypertension has been called the "silent disease" because it often has no obvious symptoms. A person may have high blood pressure for years without noticing any symptoms. Symptoms may include headache, fatigue, dizziness, flushing of the face, ringing in the ears, thumping in the chest, and frequent nosebleeds. However, these symptoms may result from other conditions.

### Diagnosis

To diagnose hypertension, a simple, risk-free, painless test using a stethoscope and a sphygmomanometer (a device for measuring the blood pressure) is used. Blood pressure is measured in a main artery of the arm by first shutting off and then releasing the flow of blood in the artery with the inflatable cuff of the sphygmomanometer while listening to the arterial pulse with the stethoscope.

The blood pressure measurements are given as the systolic pressure (the pressure at which the first beat of the pulse can be heard as gradual deflation of the cuff begins) over the diastolic pressure (the pressure at which steady flow through the artery

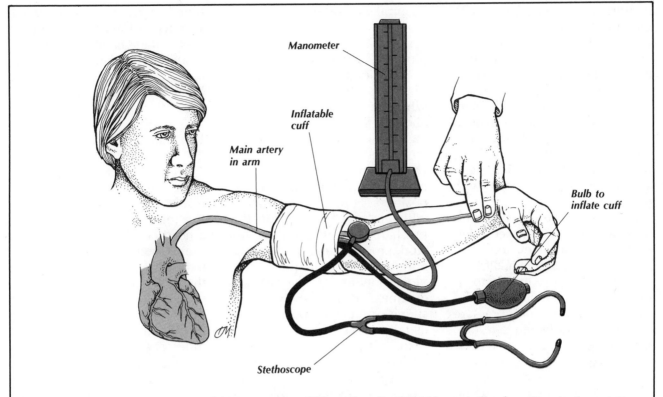

*Blood pressure is measured by using a sphygmomanometer, which consists of an inflatable arm cuff and a manometer (a pressure-measuring instrument). The pulse is listened to with a stethoscope while the blood flow in a main artery of the arm is shut off by inflating the cuff and then released by deflating the cuff.*

can be heard as the cuff is deflated)—for example, 150/95. The systolic pressure essentially measures the pressure of the heart during a contraction. The diastolic pressure is that which exists when the heart is filling between beats. Although diastolic pressure is considerably lower than systolic, there is still pressure in the body when the heart is filling. Both values have diagnostic importance. An unusually high systolic pressure may mean that the heart is pumping too hard or the arteries are stiff; a high diastolic pressure means that the arteries have abnormally high muscular tone or resistance.

Normal blood pressure is about 80/46 at birth and climbs as age increases. The normal adult pressure is around 120/80.

## Treatment

Fortunately, hypertension responds well to treatment, although female hypertensive patients seem to do better than male patients. When the condition is mild (a blood pressure of about 140/90) and there is no indication of other disease, a doctor may suggest lifestyle changes before prescribing medication. These changes may include weight loss, a regular exercise program, and strict limitation of sodium intake, which affects fluid balance and volume and therefore blood pressure. Controlling sodium in the diet requires restriction of table salt as well as careful scrutiny of all food and drug labels.

If medication is indicated, a physician may prescribe several drugs in a "stepped care" program. Step one generally begins with a diuretic (a drug that promotes elimination of water). Step two is the addition of a beta-blocker (a medicine that reduces the work of the heart) or a "centrally acting" drug that lowers blood pressure by affecting the blood pressure center in the brain. Step three is the addition of a vasodilator (a drug that widens narrowed blood vessels) to decrease resistance to blood flow. If the first three steps prove ineffective, a more potent drug may be used.

Recently, there has been some controversy over the necessity of stepped care. With new drugs, only one medication may be necessary, which decreases the risk of side effects from multiple medications and increases the likelihood of compliance with prescribed treatment.

While tension and stress do not directly cause hypertension, these factors do affect the condition. Persons with hypertension are urged to avoid high-pressure situations and to learn to deal with stress. Biofeedback, self-hypnosis, and meditation have proved useful for reducing stress, and may help someone with hypertension.

Blood pressure can be monitored at home with a special kit. If three separate elevated readings (above 140/90 in adults) are obtained, a trip to the doctor is in order. Furthermore, everyone should have his blood pressure measured by a health-care professional at least once a year. Persons with a history of hypertension or with any of the risk factors for hypertension should carefully follow their physician's recommendations for periodic blood pressure checks. It is also recommended that children of hypertensive parents begin to receive regular blood pressure measurement early in life.

# Hypotension

Hypotension is low blood pressure. Unlike chronic high blood pressure, which can be a serious health problem, low blood pressure usually need not be a cause for concern or even treatment.

Blood pressures vary, depending on such factors as age, race, sex, and environment. On rare occasions, individuals may have medical problems that cause low blood pressure. Among such conditions are some types of heart disease, hormonal deficiencies, and malnutrition. In these cases, the hypotension will be corrected by the treatment of the medical problem.

## Postural hypotension

Postural hypotension, or orthostatic hypotension, is a form of low blood pressure in which dizziness or faintness occurs when a person stands up abruptly from a sitting or reclining position. Normally, when an individual stands up, the blood vessels contract to maintain normal blood pressure in the new position. However, in persons with postural hypotension this mechanism probably does not work properly, and on standing, a temporary reduction in the blood flow to the brain leads to dizziness. Rising slowly from a sitting or reclining position will usually prevent the symptoms. Also, if a person stands in one position too long, blood pools in the leg veins, decreasing the amount of blood available to be pumped to the brain.

Sometimes postural hypotension results from taking a medication for high blood pressure; in these cases, the physician may reduce the dosage or change the medication.

# Ischemia

Ischemia is a deficiency of blood in a specific part of the body, caused by an obstruction of the blood vessels supplying that area. The obstruction may be due to narrowing, compression, or destruction of arteries caused by such conditions as blood clots and atherosclerosis (clogging of the arteries). The resultant oxygen deprivation leads to tissue death in the affected area.

## Ischemia in the brain

An ischemic attack in the brain occurs when the supply of blood to the brain is reduced. This type of attack resembles a stroke. If the brain is deprived of blood for more than several minutes, the result is irreversible brain damage and often death.

## Ischemia in the heart

When the blood supply to the heart is reduced, angina pectoris results. When the blood supply to a region of the heart is cut off, a heart attack occurs. The lower the blood supply that gets through to the heart, the greater the severity of the attack. If a weakened heart is unable to pump an adequate supply of blood to the rest of the body, the other organs will also work at less than capacity.

## Treatment

Ischemic attacks can be controlled by vasodilator medications, which widen blood vessels. Angina pectoris is often managed in this way. In many cases, surgery to remove or to bypass the obstruction is recommended.

# Lymphocytes

Lymphocytes are a type of white blood cell. They are produced in the bone marrow and lymph nodes and stored in the thymus gland, spleen, and lymph nodes.

Lymphocytes play an important role in the body's immune system. Lymphocytes make their way through the lymph channels into the bloodstream, where they identify and "memorize" the characteristics of foreign elements called antigens. There are two types of lymphocytes—B cells and T cells. B cells manufacture antibodies (highly specialized proteins that destroy the antigens by combining with them). T cells, which make up 70 percent of the lymphocyte total, regulate antibody production and oversee immune responses.

Lymphocytes are the second most numerous type of white blood cell, normally constituting between 22 percent and 28 percent of the white blood cells in an adult's circulation. In cases of infection, especially those caused by viruses, the percentage of lymphocytes in the blood may increase to above 50 percent.

# Necrosis

Necrosis is the death of individual cells, groups of cells, or areas of tissue. The tissue dies because it has not survived the ravages of an infection or because it has been cut off from its blood supply by any one of several diseases or conditions. Necrosis can occur in tumors that outgrow their blood supply; in any area of the body where the nurturing blood vessels have been blocked by fatty deposits (atherosclerosis), clots, or emboli; in small areas of the heart following a heart attack; or in bones in which osteomyelitis (inflammation of the bone due to infection) has choked off the arteries supplying the bone.

The symptoms and management of necrosis vary widely, depending on the underlying infection or blockage.

# Pericarditis

Pericarditis is an inflammation of the pericardium (the membranous bag surrounding the heart).

The inflammation is often accompanied by development of an effusion (a collection of fluid) between the membrane and the heart, which may lead to complications.

## Causes

The inflammation commonly stems from an infection, such as bacterial pneumonia, tuberculosis, or a viral infection. Pericarditis can also occur in noninfectious diseases, such as connective tissue disorders and chronic kidney failure. Pericarditis sometimes follows a heart attack or chest injury.

Occasionally, long-term pericarditis arises from a chronic condition, most notably tuberculosis. The chronic inflammation causes thickening and contraction of the pericardium to the point that it restricts the heartbeat. Called constrictive pericarditis, this condition is no longer common because of the decrease in the incidence of tuberculosis, but it is a severe condition calling for immediate attention.

## Symptoms

Pain in the center of the chest (and possibly the shoulders, neck, and upper arms) that worsens with coughing, lying flat, or breathing and is relieved by leaning forward may signify pericarditis. Since this type of pain is a symptom of a number of serious illnesses, a doctor should be consulted about any severe chest pain.

Constrictive pericarditis is signaled by difficulty in breathing, swelling of the veins in the neck, and edema (fluid accumulation) in the legs and abdomen.

## Diagnosis

A chest x-ray, electrocardiogram, and blood tests, along with the medical history and physical examination findings, are used to diagnose pericarditis. If an effusion is present, a sample of the fluid may be obtained to identify the infectious agent, if any.

## Treatment

When a large effusion exists, the motion of the heart may be restricted, thereby preventing it from filling and pumping effectively. This life-threatening condition must be corrected as soon as possible. The fluid may be drained by inserting a needle through the chest wall into the pericardial sac.

Once the underlying cause of pericarditis has been identified, the doctor can treat it (for example, by using dialysis in kidney failure or antibiotics for bacterial infection).

Constrictive pericarditis cannot be corrected without a surgical procedure, called pericardiectomy, to remove scarred tissue.

# Platelets

Platelets (also called thrombocytes) are tiny, disk-shaped, cell-like structures that play a critical role in the process of blood coagulation (clotting). They are manufactured in the bone marrow and usually survive for about ten days.

## Role in coagulation

Blood coagulation is a complex process requiring the pres-

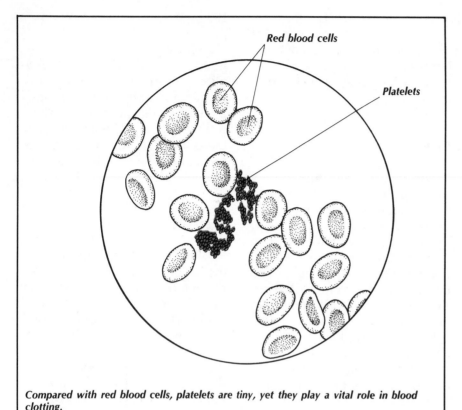

*Compared with red blood cells, platelets are tiny, yet they play a vital role in blood clotting.*

ence of many substances in the blood besides platelets. However, without platelets, coagulation would be impossible. Platelets initiate the coagulation process by aggregating (clumping together). The usual amount of time for adequate coagulation is five minutes or less.

The number of platelets per unit volume of blood plays an important role in proper platelet function. The normal number ranges between 200,000 and 500,000 platelets per cubic millimeter of blood.

### Low platelet count

A low platelet count may be seen with many different diseases, including certain liver diseases, uncommon forms of anemia caused by vitamin deficiencies, and certain cancers (such as leukemia) of the blood-forming organs. Use of certain drugs also may cause a low platelet count.

The most common cause of a low platelet count is destruction of platelets by the body's immune system. For some unknown reason, the immune system mistakenly identifies the platelets as foreign and forms antibodies to destroy them.

When a lack of platelets prolongs bleeding time, several types of treatment may be attempted, depending on the cause of the low platelet count. The usual method of immediately increasing the number of platelets in the blood is by transfusion (this procedure is generally reserved for patients with severe platelet deficiencies). Care must be taken to avoid increasing the platelet count too much, however, because emboli (clots that obstruct blood vessels) may develop.

Care should be taken by any patient whose platelet count is low, since bleeding will be prolonged and coagulation will not occur within normal time limits. For this reason many physicians recommend that until normal platelet counts are attained, patients should not take aspirin and should avoid doing anything that may cause bleeding, such as vigorous toothbrushing, eating abrasive foods, and having enemas. They should also avoid contact sports and exercise caution regarding personal injury.

## Polycythemia vera

Polycythemia vera is a relatively rare chronic disorder characterized by an increase in red blood cell mass and in the concentration of hemoglobin (the substance in red blood cells that carries oxygen). Polycythemia literally means "many blood cells."

### Cause

The immediate cause of polycythemia is excessive production of red blood cells by the bone marrow, but the underlying cause remains unknown. The condition is most often seen in the elderly and in persons of Jewish descent.

### Symptoms

The initial symptoms include fatigue, difficulty in concentration, headache, drowsiness, forgetfulness, and dizziness. About half of the patients with polycythemia vera complain of itching, especially after a hot bath. Reddish skin color, or flushing, may be observed; however, patients may have completely normal skin color, with redness only of the mucous membranes, especially the inner lids of the eyes. Patients may complain of blurred vision, ringing in the ears, and circulatory disturbances.

### Diagnosis

Diagnosis can usually be made on the basis of a physical examination and medical history and analysis of the blood.

### Treatment

Phlebotomy (withdrawal of blood from a vein) to counterbalance the overproduction of red blood cells is probably the safest treatment since it does not interfere with the functioning of the bone marrow. Radiation therapy to suppress bone marrow activity may also be useful.

# Raynaud's disease

Raynaud's disease involves spasm of the arterioles (small artery branches), especially in the fingers and hands and occasionally in other parts of the body, such as the nose and tongue. It is often accompanied by intermittent paleness or cyanosis (bluish discoloration) of the skin.

### Causes

Attacks of Raynaud's disease are most often precipitated by exposure to cold temperatures or by emotional stress. When the symptoms are caused by another condition, such as scleroderma (a connective tissue disorder), a nerve disorder, a drug reaction, or pulmonary hypertension, the condition is called Raynaud's phenomenon. Raynaud's disease is most common in young women.

### Symptoms

The color changes in the skin in the classic form of the disease come in three stages—pallor (extreme paleness), cyanosis, and then extreme redness, called reactive hyperemia. Sometimes the color changes may go through only two stages, cyanosis and then redness. Normal color and sensation are restored when the hands are warmed. Color changes in the hands do not affect the joints and seldom affect the thumb. Pain is usually not present, but numbness, tingling, and burning are common complaints. Ulcers (open sores) may appear on the tips of the fingers. Raynaud's disease differs from Raynaud's phenomenon in that both sides of the body are involved.

A wide range of other symptoms may be associated with Raynaud's phenomenon, depending on the underlying disease process.

### Treatment

Therapy for Raynaud's phenomenon depends chiefly on correctly diagnosing and then treating the underlying disorder.

Mild cases of Raynaud's disease can be relieved substantially by protecting the body and extremities from exposure to cold. This is extremely important because prolonged spasm of the small arteries leads to severe tissue injury. Mild sedatives, taken orally, can sometimes be of help. The patient is always advised to stop smoking, since nicotine acts as a constrictor of blood vessels. Drugs known as calcium-channel blockers, such as nifedipine, verapamil, and diltiazem, are of great benefit in relieving symptoms but do not cure the condition.

A more extreme measure, which is not often used, is regional sympathectomy (an interruption of certain portions of the nerve pathways). This operation is reserved for patients with progressive disability; while it abolishes the symptoms, the relief may last only for a year or two. Results of the surgical procedure are usually better in patients with Raynaud's disease than in those with Raynaud's phenomenon.

# Restless legs syndrome

Restless legs syndrome (also called Ekbom syndrome, "jimmy legs," and "jitter legs") is a feeling of uneasiness, shakiness, twitching, and restlessness that affects the legs after a patient has gone to bed for the night. Insomnia is almost always a result of the syndrome.

### Causes

The precise cause of the syndrome is not known, although some authorities consider it to be brought about, or intensified, by poor blood circulation. Some physicians believe that it is more common in hyperactive patients;

others say that it can be brought about by intense activity, especially physical activity, just before bedtime.

## Symptoms

The patient often has difficulty falling asleep in the evening because of an uncomfortable feeling or a jerking sensation within the legs, usually in the thighs and calves. The discomfort is often relieved by moving about, but as a result normal sleep is largely prevented. Consequently, the person may be excessively tired the next day. The condition most commonly affects middle-aged women.

## Diagnosis

The diagnosis can generally be made on the basis of the patient's medical history and report of symptoms. The physician will perform a physical examination to rule out more serious disorders.

## Treatment

Since the syndrome has been connected with circulatory disorders, drugs that increase the circulation to the lower extremities may prove helpful. A mild sedative at bedtime may also be useful.

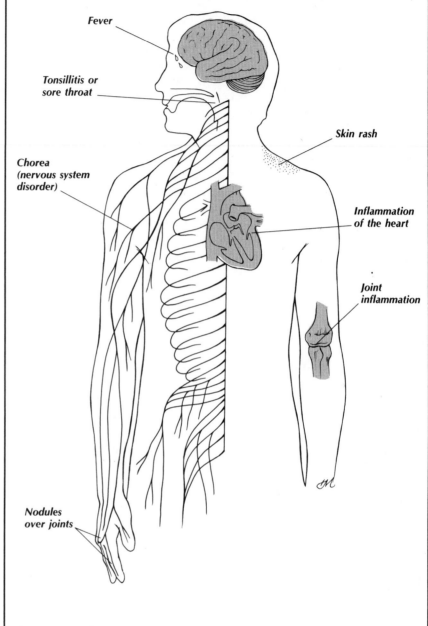

Fever

Tonsillitis or sore throat

Skin rash

Chorea (nervous system disorder)

Inflammation of the heart

Joint inflammation

Nodules over joints

*Rheumatic fever begins with a sore throat or tonsillitis and can have effects throughout the body.*

# Rheumatic fever

Rheumatic fever is the result of a bacterial disease characterized by inflammation, swelling, and soreness of the joints—especially the ankles, knees, and wrists—and inflammation of the heart. Occurring most commonly in children and adolescents, it is a serious illness that can result in permanent damage to the heart. The attacks of fever may recur over a period of years and last from a few weeks to several months.

## Cause

The disease is considered to be a late stage of a streptococcal infection, such as strep throat; however, not all species of *Streptococcus* bacteria cause rheumatic fever. In some cases, the earlier infection may have been so minor that it cannot be recalled. Some researchers believe that rheumatic fever is an autoimmune disorder, in which the immune system forms antibodies to attack the body's own healthy tissues, such as those of the joints and the heart. The disease is more prevalent in some families than in others, but whether this indicates a hereditary factor or is due simply to sharing the same environment and living habits is not clear. Because only 1 percent of all cases of streptococcal infection in children and adolescents are followed by rheumatic fever, it is believed that a special susceptibility may be involved.

### Symptoms

Rheumatic fever should be immediately suspected when a child or teenager develops an unexplained fever with joint inflammation a few weeks after a throat infection or tonsillitis, even if that preceding condition was very mild. The joints become inflamed one after another. A peculiar skin rash of large, reddened, nonitchy areas with irregular borders develops, lasting a day or two. Nodules may emerge over the elbows, kneecaps, and other bony prominences; they may also form within the heart. Chorea (involuntary movements of the limbs and facial features) may occur if the infection spreads to involve the brain. Chorea leaves no lasting brain damage and passes after some time, even without treatment.

### Effects on the heart

The acute stage of joint involvement leaves no permanent deformity or crippling, but damage to the heart is permanent when it involves destruction of heart valve tissue. Scar tissue is then eventually formed on the valves, so that they cannot open and close properly. The heart, unable to efficiently carry out its function of pumping blood through the circulatory system, must work harder and becomes enlarged. Blood clots may form on its inner lining and may be carried in the blood throughout the body, often lodging in a blood vessel and blocking it.

### Diagnosis

Joint inflammation, heart abnormalities, chorea, and the appearance of the rash and the nodules are the most common manifestations of rheumatic fever, but these signs may appear alone or in a number of different combinations. Because no single laboratory finding or symptom is common to all cases of rheumatic fever, the diagnosis is made presumptively on the basis of the total clinical picture.

### Treatment

The chief treatment for rheumatic fever is the use of antibiotics for an extended period of time to eliminate any remaining *Streptococcus* bacteria. Aspirin is commonly used to bring down fever and relieve inflammation and pain. Corticosteroid drugs are sometimes given if there are signs of heart involvement, and sedatives may be prescribed if chorea becomes severe. The long periods of immobilization in bed once recommended are now believed to be unnecessary, although bed rest during acute attacks may be prescribed. Seri-

ously damaged heart valves can often be repaired surgically or replaced by prosthetic (artificial) valves.

### Prevention

The only preventive measure is prompt diagnosis and adequate treatment of all streptococcal infections, especially those involving the throat and ears. Since dental procedures can sometimes be a source of bacterial infection, special precautions (such as the administration of antibiotics) may be recommended for persons whose heart valves have been injured.

# Rheumatic heart disease

Rheumatic heart disease consists of a variety of abnormal cardiac conditions, including heart valve scarring and endocarditis (inflammation of the lining of the heart).

### Cause

This disease is a potential aftermath of rheumatic fever, once one of the prime killers of children. Rheumatic fever may cause inflammation of the heart valves and scarring of the valve leaflets. This scarring can result in valve leakage, allowing blood to flow backward, or severe narrowing of the valve, restricting blood flow out of the heart.

### Symptoms

The most common symptom is a heart murmur, caused by abnormal blood flow across a scarred valve. There may be hemorrhaging (excessive bleeding) and impairment of vision if microscopic blood clots that have formed in the heart block tiny blood vessels in the eye. Kidney function may deteriorate in middle or later life. Muscle shrinkage due to inactivity may be accompanied by lack of muscular and cardiovascular endurance. Irregular pulse, shortness of breath, and fainting spells are also common.

### Treatment

Many persons who have suffered rheumatic heart disease have gone on to live long and extremely active lives, despite heart murmurs, heart enlargement, and damaged valves. Although rheumatic heart disease is a serious matter, regular exercise, a sensible diet, and determination can mean the difference between a sedentary and an active life.

Supervision by a physician is a necessity for anyone who suffers from rheumatic heart disease and wants to embark on a regular exercise program. In some cases, however, it may be impossible for a patient to participate in vigorous physical activity, especially if the heart damage is advanced or severe. For some of these individuals, surgery to implant an artificial valve can offer relief.

Persons with rheumatic heart disease must consult their physicians about antibiotic treatment before undergoing any dental or surgical procedures.

# Rh factor

Rh factor refers to a specific antigen present in the blood. ("Rh"

is derived from the name of the rhesus monkey, in which the factor was discovered.) An antigen is a substance that can induce the production of antibodies, which are crucial to the functioning of the body's immune system. Rh-positive blood has the antigen on its red cells; Rh-negative blood does not. An estimated 85 percent of the population has Rh-positive blood, that is to say, they possess Rh antigens.

### Dangers of anti-Rh antibodies

Blood normally has no anti-Rh antibodies. Anti-Rh antibodies can develop in Rh-negative blood, however, if Rh-positive blood is introduced into the bloodstream. This can come about in two ways: if a person with Rh-negative blood receives a transfusion of Rh-positive blood, or if a woman with Rh-negative blood conceives a child with Rh-positive blood (inherited from the father) and some of the Rh-positive cells from the fetus find their way into the bloodstream of the mother. In either case, the Rh-positive red blood cells will stimulate the person's body to form anti-Rh antibodies. If this happens, the blood will form clumps and a potentially lethal situation will develop: the clumps may block the blood vessels, leading to death.

If difficulties do not appear with the formation of these antibodies during the first transfusion or the first pregnancy, they will surely appear if Rh-positive blood is ever again introduced into the person's bloodstream. The antibodies are already present, and the introduction of additional Rh-positive blood will result in a mobilization of existing antibodies and the produc-

tion of even more. In addition to clumping of blood, other problems will arise. For example, hemolysis (the breakdown of red blood cells and release of their hemoglobin) will make it impossible for those cells to carry oxygen, resulting in anemia.

There are potential dangers to the fetus if the mother's blood contains anti-Rh antibodies. If the fetus has Rh-positive cells, anti-Rh antibodies may pass through the placenta from the mother's bloodstream to cause hemolysis of the child's blood cells. Once born, the baby may need to have massive, possibly even total, transfusions of Rh-negative blood to prevent clumping of the red blood cells and hemolytic anemia. This situation is now relatively rare because injections containing anti-Rh antibodies are routinely given to an Rh-negative mother after the birth of her first Rh-positive baby. These injections inhibit the formation of the potentially dangerous antibodies.

# Stroke

Stroke is a nervous system disorder of abrupt onset caused by interruption of the blood supply to an area of the brain, resulting in malfunction or loss of function in those parts of the body that the damaged area controls. Generally speaking, each side of the brain controls the motor and sensory functions of the opposite side of the body (for example, damage to cells on the left side of the brain will impair function on the right side of the body). Stroke can have a wide range of consequences, among them temporary or permanent loss of memory and difficulty in speaking, walking, and controlling emotions.

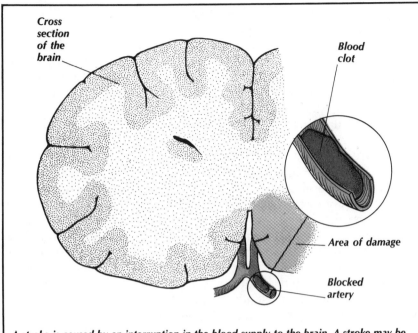

Cross section of the brain

Blood clot

Area of damage

Blocked artery

*A stroke is caused by an interruption in the blood supply to the brain. A stroke may be caused by a blood clot blocking an artery leading to the brain.*

## Causes

Stroke can be caused by several conditions. One is called cerebrovascular embolism, which occurs when a blood clot formed elsewhere in the body (usually in the heart or in one of the carotid arteries in the neck) lodges itself in an artery in the brain or leading to the brain. Interruption of blood flow also occurs when a clot is formed in the arteries that supply blood to the brain, usually due to atherosclerosis (clogging of the arteries by various deposits).

Stroke can also be caused by cerebral hemorrhage, in which a diseased artery in the brain bursts, depriving the cells that are normally nourished by that artery, as well as flooding the surrounding tissue with blood. This accumulation of blood forms a clot, which displaces and compresses brain tissue and thus interferes with brain function. This type of stroke often afflicts people who have both hypertension (high blood pressure) and atherosclerosis.

A third condition that can lead to stroke is rupture of an aneurysm (a bulge in an artery because of a defect in its wall), which interrupts blood flow to an area of the brain and floods the area with blood. The formation of aneurysms is sometimes associated with hypertension. Congenital (present at birth) aneurysms are often the cause of cerebral hemorrhage in young people.

## Those at risk

People who have both hypertension and atherosclerosis are the most likely to suffer a stroke, since both diseases weaken and damage the arteries. Hypertension probably also encourages hemorrhage. Heredity may play a role in stroke, since the tendencies to develop both hyper-tension and atherosclerosis appear to be inherited. Black persons are more susceptible to stroke because high blood pressure is about twice as common in the black population as in the white population.

Smoking, diabetes, and high blood cholesterol levels may also contribute to stroke. Stroke is more likely to occur if there is a history of mild strokelike episodes called transient ischemic attacks (TIAs), which are like mild strokes that clear up within 24 hours leaving no residual effects.

## Symptoms

A stroke can present itself in many ways, but some of the more common symptoms are sudden weakness or numbness in the face, arm, and leg on one side of the body; loss or slurring of speech or difficulty in understanding others; unexplained unsteadiness; and persistent falling to one side. It is possible to suffer a mild stroke and experience minor degrees of these symptoms.

## Diagnosis

Stroke is diagnosed mostly from the history and physical examination. Sophisticated x-ray techniques are also employed. For example, arteriography (an x-ray study after the injection of a special dye into a main artery) will show damage or clots in the arteries in the brain or leading to the brain, and computed tomography provides cross-sectional images that may indicate whether the stroke was caused by a hemorrhage or by blockage of blood flow. Tumors, which can cause symptoms identical to those of stroke, are also frequently diagnosed by these means.

## Treatment

Treatment of stroke begins with immediate hospitalization. Blood pressure is normalized, and drug therapy to prevent further damage, as well as to reduce swelling of the brain tissue, is often begun. Anticoagulants (drugs that inhibit the normal clotting of blood) are sometimes administered in the hope of limiting the progress of the stroke or preventing additional strokes. After the acute period, rehabilitation is begun by speech, physical, and occupational therapists.

## Prevention

For those who have experienced TIAs or other warning signs of stroke, precautions can be taken to prevent an actual stroke. After a TIA, some form of arteriography is usually performed to locate obstructions or ulcerated areas of the carotid arteries. Depending on the results of the arteriogram, the general condition of the patient, and many other factors, surgery to "clean out" the arteries or treatment with anticoagulants or other medications may be elected.

Prevention of stroke mainly involves control of high blood pressure and other risk factors, such as smoking and high cholesterol intake.

# Thrombocytopenia

Thrombocytopenia is a disorder characterized by a decrease in the number of platelets in the blood. Platelets are tiny components of the blood that act to promote clotting when there is an injury or another problem that requires bleeding to be stopped. Normally, about five to ten times the number of platelets needed for clotting circulate in the bloodstream; this amounts to about 200,000 to 500,000 per milliliter. In general, thrombocytopenia is considered to be present when the platelet count is less than 100,000. Abnormal bleeding commonly does not occur, however, until the count is less than 50,000, and serious or unprovoked bleeding usually does not occur with counts above 20,000.

## Causes

There are basically two mechanisms whereby thrombocytopenia occurs: decreased production of platelets and increased destruction of platelets. In the former, the elements in the bone marrow responsible for the production of platelets may malfunction or be severely diminished. Increased destruction of platelets occurs in essential, or idiopathic (of unknown cause), thrombocytopenia. In this disorder, which is most common in children, antibodies are made against the person's own platelets, thereby causing their destruction. Thrombocytopenia can also be due to the use of some medications. Severe, overwhelming infection can cause increased destruction of platelets. In pregnancy, platelets from the fetus can sometimes enter the circulation of the mother, causing antibody formation and the consequent destruction of fetal platelets, with abnormal bleeding at birth.

## Symptoms

An obvious sign of thrombocytopenia is a rash of reddish to reddish-purple spots. These are due to bleeding within and underneath the skin. Abnormal or easily provoked bleeding is the most dangerous symptom of thrombocytopenia. This bleeding may be minor, such as oozing from the gums while brushing the teeth or bruising caused by merely leaning on or brushing up against something. The bleeding can be much more serious, however, as in spontaneous internal bleeding, which may go unrecognized until the person goes into shock.

## Diagnosis

Laboratory evaluation of the blood is the basis of a diagnosis of thrombocytopenia. Examination of a sample of bone marrow may also be performed.

## Treatment

Treatment depends on the cause. If infection is present, this must be remedied; usually, the platelet count will then return to normal on its own. In essential thrombocytopenia, corticosteroids (cortisone or prednisone) are the initial treatment. In drug-induced thrombocytopenia, the first step is generally to discontinue the drug. This will usually result in improvement; if not, corticosteroids may be helpful. In severe immune thrombocytopenia of the newborn, exchange transfusion (whereby all or most of the blood is exchanged with transfused blood) may be necessary. If the platelet count in any of these conditions is dangerously low (around 20,000 per milliliter), transfusion of platelets may be indicated until the disease process has been controlled.

## Prevention

Thrombocytopenia may not be preventable in most cases, but early recognition of symptoms, such as rash and easy bleeding, may lead to prevention of serious complications.

# Thrombophlebitis

Thrombophlebitis is a condition in which both inflammation and blood clots exist in a vein. This can be caused by a number of factors. Commonly, when a person is immobilized, blood stagnates in the veins of the legs; this induces clotting, which in turn prevents blood from returning to the heart. The blood below the clot remains there, causing a buildup of pressure that forces fluid into the tissues, resulting in swelling. Simultaneously, the veins and surrounding area may become quite inflamed and tender. This condition is most often found in the deep veins of the legs, but it can also occur in veins of the pelvis and arms.

Thrombophlebitis itself may not be too serious, but it can lead to a life-threatening condition called pulmonary embolism if a blood clot formed in a deep leg vein breaks loose, travels through the bloodstream, and becomes lodged in a blood vessel in the lung. Pulmonary embolism can lead to chest pain, shortness of breath, coughing up of blood, and even death.

## Causes

The development of thrombophlebitis is favored by any condition that inhibits the free flow of blood through the veins, such as prolonged bed rest or inactivity, perhaps following illness or surgery; congestive heart failure, which affects the ability of the heart to pump blood throughout the body; and injury or infection that damages a vein. Other factors that may lead to an increased tendency toward thrombophlebitis are pregnancy, the use of birth control pills by susceptible individuals, occupations that require long periods of standing or sitting, obesity, old age, and chronic infections. In some cases, thrombophlebitis may indicate the presence of a blood disorder or a tumor in the pancreas or lung.

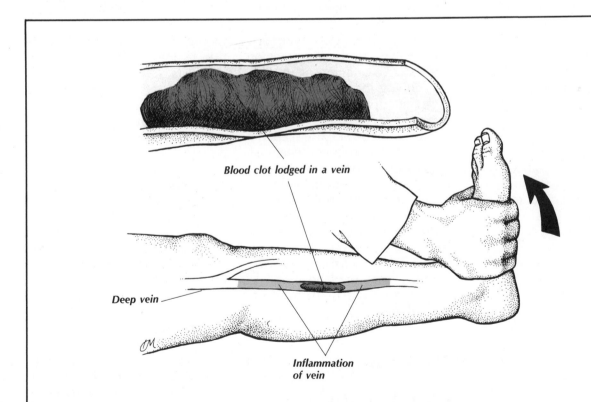

*Blood clot lodged in a vein*

*Deep vein*

*Inflammation of vein*

*Thrombophlebitis (inflammation of a vein accompanied by the formation of a blood clot) often occurs in the deep veins of the legs. The condition is suspected if moving the foot forward or backward causes pain.*

### Symptoms

Symptoms of deep-vein thrombophlebitis (which often appear only in advanced cases) are swelling, aching, and a feeling of heaviness in the leg or affected area. The skin may appear white and will be painful to the touch. If the veins of the leg are affected, the condition is characterized by increased pain when walking or when the foot is flexed backward or forward.

### Diagnosis

Thrombophlebitis of a surface vein (known as superficial thrombophlebitis) can be diagnosed by a simple physical examination, which usually reveals a red, warm, tender cordlike vein.

Diagnostic tests for thrombophlebitis include Doppler imaging (a technique used to detect obstructions by changes in the sounds made by flowing blood), nuclear medicine scans, plethysmography (a test to measure the resistance to flow in the veins), and venography. Venography involves the injection of a special dye into the veins so that a clot will be visualized on an x-ray if one is present. This is the most sensitive and specific test for thrombophlebitis.

### Treatment

Treatment of the superficial form of thrombophlebitis begins with bed rest with elevation of the leg. Warm compresses are also helpful, as are anti-inflammatory drugs. Superficial thrombophlebitis rarely, if ever, leads to pulmonary embolism.

Deep-vein thrombophlebitis, because of the potential for pulmonary embolism, is treated much more aggressively. The patient is usually hospitalized and put on bed rest with the leg elevated. Heparin (an anticoagulant, which inhibits the normal clotting mechanism of the blood) is given intravenously, usually for about seven days (up to ten days if pulmonary embolism has occurred). The patient is also usually given the oral anticoagulant warfarin for about six weeks (three to six months if pulmonary embolism has occurred). These drugs do not dissolve an existing clot, but serve to prevent new clots from forming while the old ones are resolving. Newer drugs do dissolve clots, but are still used only in special situations.

### Prevention

Prevention of thrombophlebitis is a controversial subject. In hospitalized patients who are immobilized for long periods or are about to undergo major surgery, doing leg exercises, wearing long support stockings, and increasing activity as soon as feasible may be helpful. Heparin therapy has also been beneficial in preventing deep-vein thrombophlebitis in certain patients. For nonhospitalized patients who are susceptible to this condition, regularly exercising the legs, elevating the legs when lying down, and wearing support hose may be helpful. Heparin or warfarin may be prescribed.

# Transient ischemic attacks

Transient ischemic attacks (TIAs) are neurologic deficits (such as loss of vision in one eye, inability to speak, paralysis, or weakness of one side of the body) of sudden onset that last for less than 24 hours. Although they are symptomatically similar to minor strokes, they do no discernible lasting damage to brain function.

The major importance of TIAs is their role as a predictor of stroke. When a person describes a "light stroke," it is often a TIA that is meant. If left untreated, TIAs can indeed lead to major strokes, with permanent damage to all parts affected, as well as to the possibility of sudden death.

### Causes

TIAs are probably due to a temporary interruption in blood flow to an area of the brain. They can be caused by a narrowing in the carotid arteries (the arteries in the neck that supply the brain with oxygenated blood). This narrowing is usually due to the presence of atherosclerosis (clogging of the arteries). Blood vessel spasms and showers of tiny emboli (clots that travel through the bloodstream) are also possible causes.

### Symptoms

The symptoms of TIAs are both varied and frightening to the victim. They can include weakness on one side of the face, numbness in various parts of the body, blindness in one eye, weakness in the arms or legs on one side, difficulty in speaking and understanding speech, and a prickling ("pins and needles") sensation in parts of the body. Vertigo (a sensation of spinning) combined with any of these or other symptoms can also be due to TIAs. Fainting

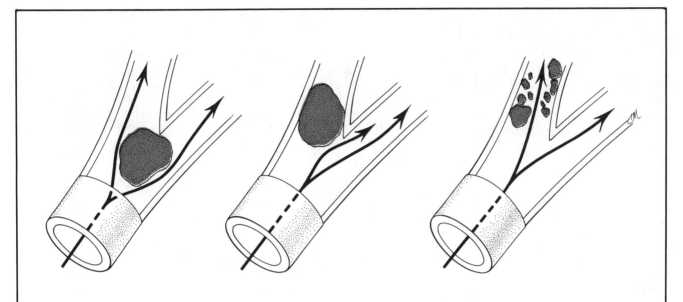

*A transient ischemic attack is caused by an interruption in blood flow to an area of the brain. This could be the result of a blood clot that temporarily blocks an artery into the brain before breaking up and restoring blood flow.*

spells alone and light-headedness are usually not due to TIAs.

### Diagnosis

The first step in diagnosis is a complete examination, including a history and physical, neurologic, and eye examinations. Bruits (noises caused by narrowing in an artery) may be heard in a carotid artery. Detailed testing, commonly with arteriography (an x-ray study after injection of a special dye into an artery) is performed to pinpoint the problem.

### Treatment

Treatment of TIAs is aimed at preventing stroke. There are two basic methods of treatment: medical, with anticoagulant drugs; and surgical, with the opening and "cleaning out" of the obstructed arteries. Which of these methods is more effective in preventing further TIAs or a

stroke is dependent on many factors and is a subject of considerable controversy. TIAs can be an indication of serious problems and must be brought to the attention of a physician immediately.

# Varicose veins

Varicose veins are swollen, stretched veins in the legs, close to the surface of the skin, caused by pooling of blood. Varicose veins alone are not too serious, but they may lead to a more serious condition, such as a skin ulcer, phlebitis (inflammation of a vein), or thrombosis (blood clot formation).

### Causes

Blood from the legs must return to the heart uphill, against the force of gravity, so the veins in the legs have one-way valves to prevent blood from flowing back down toward the feet.

When pressure on the veins stretches them, the valves cannot close properly, and some blood travels back down. This blood accumulates in pools, which stretch the veins even more.

Varicose veins are caused by a number of factors that put excess pressure on the veins in the legs: prolonged standing; prolonged sitting, especially with the legs crossed; lack of exercise; confining clothes; a diet low in fiber (the pressure needed to excrete hard stools puts extra stress on the veins); obesity (which puts excess pressure on the legs and contributes to the inability of the muscles to push blood upward); heredity (a tendency toward weak vein walls and valves seems to be inherited); and even height (tall people may be more susceptible because their blood needs to travel farther in its return trip to the heart).

Women are more susceptible to varicose veins than men, largely due to hormonal factors. Pregnancy accentuates this difference because special hormones released at this time tend to relax the walls of the veins. Also, varicose veins often appear during the last few months of pregnancy due to the increased strain from the weight of the growing uterus. These veins may recede, however, after the birth of the baby.

## Symptoms

Varicose veins are very noticeable since they form close to the skin. They appear as bulging, bluish, cordlike lines running down the legs. Symptoms that accompany varicose veins are feelings of achiness, heaviness, and fatigue in the legs, especially at the end of the day; itchy, scaly skin covering the affected areas; and, in advanced cases, swollen ankles, pain shooting down the leg, and leg cramps at night.

## Diagnosis

Diagnosis can most often be made on the basis of physical examination because the affected superficial veins can be readily seen and palpated. If involvement of deeper veins is suspected, Doppler imaging (a technique used to detect obstructions by changes in the sounds made by flowing blood) may be performed.

## Treatment

Varicose veins are usually treated by wearing elastic stockings, which act like muscles to

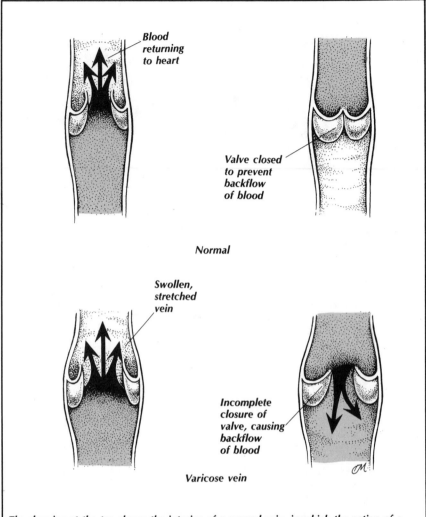

*The drawing at the top shows the interior of a normal vein, in which the action of a valve prevents blood returning to the heart from flowing backward. In the drawing of a varicose vein, the valve has been weakened and cannot completely close, causing the blood to accumulate.*

help push the blood upward. Severe cases may require a surgical procedure called vein stripping, in which the afflicted veins are tied off and removed; other healthy veins in the area will take over the job of pushing blood toward the heart. A chemical can also be injected into the veins, closing them off and forcing the blood to find other channels to the heart.

Those with varicose veins may need to lose weight, increase the fiber in their diets, exercise regularly, and stretch their legs or put their feet up whenever possible. Exercises to improve circulation in the legs may help relieve pressure.

Varicose veins tend to recur, particularly if adequate preventive measures are not undertaken.

# THE DIGESTIVE SYSTEM

Digestion is the process by which the body converts food into basic substances that can be either absorbed in the bloodstream as nutrients or passed out of the body as waste. This process of breakdown and assimilation occurs within the digestive tract, a convoluted tube more than 30 feet long that is lined by a mucous membrane. The tract includes several hollow organs—the mouth, esophagus, stomach, small intestine, and large intestine (colon)—each of which has a specific function in digestion. The muscles of these organs move the food through the system, while mucus lubricates the tract and prevents irritation. Other organs—the liver, gallbladder, and pancreas—are also critical in digestion.

Food first enters the digestive tract through the mouth. Movement of the jaws allows the teeth to cut and grind the food into smaller pieces, which are mixed with saliva (a secretion of the glands in the mouth). Saliva moistens food for easier swallowing and contains an enzyme (a special type of protein) that begins the chemical breakdown of starches.

From the mouth, food passes down the throat and into the esophagus, the muscular tube through which the food is conducted to the stomach. The stomach is a large pouch in the abdominal cavity, where food is combined with acid- and enzyme-containing digestive juices secreted by glands within the stomach walls. The food becomes semifluid, which allows it to pass easily into the small intestine.

In the first ten inches of the small intestine (called the duodenum), digestive juices from the liver and pancreas continue the process of breaking down the

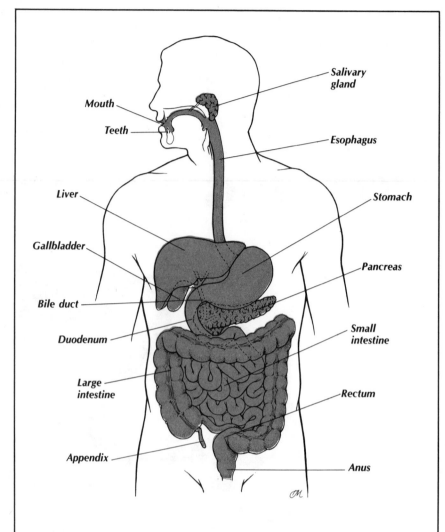

The digestive system includes the mouth, esophagus, stomach, small intestine, large intestine, liver, gallbladder, and pancreas—each of which plays a specific role in digestion.

food into its constituent nutrients, which can then be absorbed into the bloodstream in the remainder of the small intestine.

Aiding digestion is the liver, an accessory organ of digestion. The liver produces bile, which is necessary for absorption of fat in the small intestine. The liver also removes some wastes from the blood, produces and stores glucose (a form of sugar), and processes many drugs.

The gallbladder, located on the underside of the liver, is

another organ that performs an indirect digestive function. The gallbladder stores the bile manufactured by the liver. As bile is needed, the gallbladder contracts and releases the fluid into the duodenum.

Other digestive juices required by the small intestine to digest and absorb food, particularly fats and starches, come from the pancreas, an organ located just under the stomach. The pancreas also secretes insulin and other hormones into the blood. Insulin is the hormone responsible for aiding absorption and use of glucose.

Whatever substances are not assimilated into the bloodstream through the small intestine move into the large intestine. Within the large intestine, waste material is processed into stool (feces), and water and certain chemicals are absorbed into the bloodstream to preserve the body's fluid balance.

The fecal matter continues to move through the colon to the rectum (the lower part of the large intestine). Once in the rectum, waste is ready to be passed out of the body through the anus (the opening at the end of the digestive tract), thus completing the process of digestion.

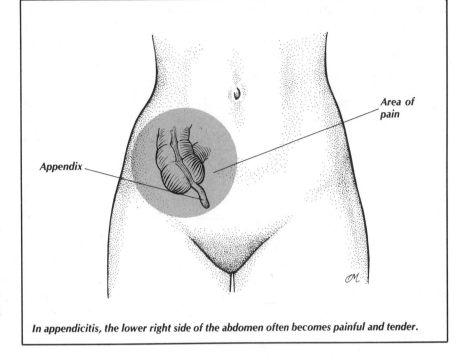

*In appendicitis, the lower right side of the abdomen often becomes painful and tender.*

# Appendicitis

Appendicitis is an inflammation of the appendix, which is usually a consequence of a bacterial infection.

The appendix is a small, wormlike pouch located at the juncture of the small and large intestines. Although it may have had a function at some point in evolutionary development, the appendix serves no purpose now.

## Causes

Despite its uselessness, the appendix can cause problems when it becomes inflamed. Inflammation occurs when the hollow, tubular structure becomes clogged with masses of waste matter, intestinal worms, or other material that can prevent normal drainage. The blockage provides a fertile environment for bacteria to grow and multiply, thereby causing infection and inflammation.

## Symptoms

In the beginning, appendicitis may produce a dull or sharp pain in the navel area of the abdomen. Any movement, coughing, or sneezing can intensify the pain. In the early stages, patients may also feel nauseated and be unable to eat. Constipation usually accompanies appendicitis; however, about 10 percent of patients have diarrhea instead. Adults may run a mild fever (up to 102°F), but children generally experience higher fevers. Occasionally, the pulse rate accelerates to about 100 beats per minute.

Within hours, the pain becomes continuous and moves to the lower right side of the abdomen over the appendix. Because the location of the appendix may vary from one individual to another, pain may emanate from the back, side, or pelvis—or even from the opposite side of the abdomen. The entire area around the appendix becomes extremely tender as abdominal muscles tighten.

As the fever rises and the pain grows more intense, chances of rupture also become greater. Rupture results when the appendix becomes so swollen and filled with pus that it bursts, spreading infection to surrounding organs. One serious complication of rupture is peritonitis (inflammation of the lining of the abdominal cavity).

Any fever with nausea and abdominal pain should be reported to a physician. More severe pain is an immediate medical emergency that must be evaluated and treated to prevent potentially fatal complications. Appendicitis can affect anyone, but the disease is more prevalent among persons between 10 and 30 years of age.

## Diagnosis

When confirming appendicitis, the doctor checks for tenderness over the appendix. A blood test determines whether there is an elevated white blood cell count (in response to infection, the body produces extra white blood cells to help fight the disease). The doctor may perform additional tests to rule out disorders sometimes mistaken for appendicitis, such as inflammation of the gallbladder, kidney stones, or a kidney infection. In women, a twisted ovarian cyst (the formation on an ovary of a sac filled with fluid or semisolid material) or a ruptured ectopic pregnancy (a pregnancy that develops outside the uterus) may produce symptoms similar to those of appendicitis.

### Treatment

Although appendicitis cannot be prevented, prompt diagnosis can lead to effective treatment. Patients who suspect appendicitis should not eat, drink, or take drugs to relieve pain until a doctor has been consulted. Eating or drinking any substance, especially taking a laxative, will stimulate activity by the intestine, which may cause the appendix to rupture.

The most common treatment for acute appendicitis is surgery to remove the inflamed organ. To ensure against further infection, antibiotics will also be prescribed.

# Bile

Bile is a fluid produced by the liver and discharged into the small intestine, where it helps in the digestion of food, particularly fats. Bile is made up of water, salts, bile acids, cholesterol (a fatlike substance), and lecithin (a fatty acid).

### Functions

Bile acts like a detergent to break down fat in the intestine into tiny globules that can be dissolved and suspended in water so that they can pass through the walls of the small intestine into the bloodstream (to provide fuel for the body). The bile salts are also absorbed through the walls of the intestine but are returned to the liver to form new bile. The yellow-green or golden color of bile is due to the pigments bilirubin and biliverdin. Bilirubin is a yellow pigment derived from decomposed red blood cells. Biliverdin is a green pigment derived from conversion of bilirubin by a chemical reaction. These pigments are also responsible for some of the coloration of body wastes.

Bile is produced continuously in the liver and passes through ducts to be stored in the gallbladder until mealtime, when it is emptied into the duodenum. Digestive disturbances result if the flow of bile is stopped or reduced, either because of a liver disorder or because a duct has been blocked by inflammation or a gallstone (a solid mass of material—usually composed of calcium, cholesterol, bilirubin, or a combination thereof—formed in the gallbladder). Any of these conditions can also cause jaundice, in which the pigments bilirubin and biliverdin accumulate in the blood. Jaundice is a sign of trouble, not a disease in itself, and shows up as yellow staining of the skin, eyes, and body fluids.

# Cholecystitis

Cholecystitis is an inflammation of the gallbladder. The gallblad-der is a small, pear-shaped organ that stores the bile produced by the liver and releases it as needed to help digest foods—particularly fats—in the small intestine. Cholecystitis may be either acute (sudden and severe) or chronic (recurring but less severe).

### Acute cholecystitis

In about 90 percent of cases, acute cholecystitis results when the outlet of the gallbladder or the duct leading from it is plugged by a gallstone, which is formed in the gallbladder from cholesterol (a fatlike substance), calcium, bile pigments, or a combination of these substances. Unless the stone becomes dislodged, inflammation and pressure build up behind it. In severe cases, the swollen gallbladder may not receive enough blood, resulting in tissue death. The gallbladder may become perforated, causing bile to spill into the abdominal cavity. An abscess (a collection of pus within a cavity) usually forms, and bacteria may colonize the region. Occasionally, the resulting leakage of infected bile causes peritonitis (a generalized infection of the entire area around the abdominal organs). However, not all gallbladder attacks progress to this extreme; they may subside only to be repeated another time. Cholecystitis may also result from a blockage caused by enlargement of the veins in the common bile duct, which the gallbladder shares with the liver. Only rarely does infection spread to the gallbladder from the nearby pancreas.

Acute cholecystitis often begins following a meal rich in fats, such as one containing fried foods, chocolate, or cream. The individual may awaken in the middle of the night with indigestion, gas, and a sharp pain in the upper right quarter of the abdomen, which is often hard and tender to the touch. Pain may also be felt in the middle of the abdomen and may spread to the tip of the right shoulder blade. The pain is steady and severe, gradually decreasing and finally disappearing in 12 to 18 hours unless there are complications. Vomiting is likely and provides some relief. If fever is present, infection of the gallbladder or bile duct is likely. If jaundice (yellowing of the skin, caused by bile pigment in the blood) is present, the symptoms are probably due to blockage of the common bile duct by a gallstone.

Radionuclide scanning confirms the diagnosis of cholecystitis. (In this procedure, a radioactive material is administered, and its distribution in the affected area is recorded on x-ray film.) X-ray examination and ultrasonography (a technique that uses sound waves to create images of internal structures) may also be used to confirm the diagnosis and to locate gallstones.

Treatment of an acute attack may include rest, intravenous feeding, painkilling drugs, and antibiotics. Because attacks are likely to recur, however, the usual solution is surgical removal of the gallbladder. This is done immediately if complications develop. Preferably, however, it is performed a few days after the attack has subsided. If the patient has another illness, it should be brought under control before the operation is performed.

The mere presence of gallstones found incidentally during tests for other problems does not always mean that surgery is necessary, however. In many cases, gallstones can be present for life without ever causing acute cholecystitis.

## Chronic cholecystitis

Chronic cholecystitis is a continued inflammation of the gallbladder, with repeated attacks over time that are similar to, but milder than, those of acute cholecystitis. Gallstones are usually present; whether they develop before or after the emergence of the disease is unknown. The causes of chronic cholecystitis are not entirely understood, although occasionally bacterial infection is the reason. Diet, heredity, and hormones appear to be involved, and the disease is more likely to affect women than men.

The pains of chronic cholecystitis commonly appear over the pit of the stomach and in the upper right quarter of the abdomen. They may range in intensity from mild to unbearable. Pains usually come on suddenly and are steady, but may be separated by pain-free intervals of 15 minutes to an hour. The pains may disappear after 15 minutes or continue for several hours; the average attack lasts about an hour. Although the pains may appear together with nausea, gas, and belching, and may occur after eating fatty foods, these indications may not be directly related to the disease.

Diagnosis is based on the symptoms and sometimes can be confirmed with an x-ray study. The patient swallows a special chemical (designed to show up on an x-ray film) that is absorbed by a normal gallbladder but not by an inflamed one. If the gallbladder does not show up on the x-ray, the patient may have the disease. The other studies used for diagnosis of acute cholecystitis—radionuclide scanning and ultrasonography—may also be helpful. The doctor must make a careful investigation of other possible causes of the symptoms, including peptic ulcer (which occurs in the stomach or the beginning of the small intestine), inflammation of the pancreas, and bowel disease.

The ideal way to treat chronic cholecystitis is to remove the gallbladder, together with any gallstones in the duct leading from the liver to the duodenum (the first part of the small intestine). If it is not clear that the symptoms are caused by gallbladder inflammation, or if the patient cannot withstand an operation, other methods are used. These include a low-fat diet (which lowers the need for bile), weight reduction, and use of antacids and other medications.

# Cirrhosis

Cirrhosis is a disease in which cells throughout the liver are progressively destroyed. They are replaced by nodules (swellings) containing normal new cells but also by much connective tissue, which alters the structure of the organ. The flow of blood and lymph through the damaged liver is much less efficient, and eventually the liver fails.

## Causes

Cirrhosis represents an attempt by the liver to rebuild itself and continue despite injury. The injury may be a sudden and massive infection, as in acute hepatitis, or it may occur in a

233

less severe manner over a period of months or years, as in chronic active hepatitis or obstruction of the bile ducts within the liver. The process of obstruction starts with inflammation and progresses to scarring and then closure of the ducts. A similar condition is caused by obstruction of the external bile ducts by a stone, scar, inborn defect, or tumor. The damage may be done over an even longer time, slowly and steadily, by alcohol abuse, which is by far the most common cause of cirrhosis. Other causes include the following:

• Use of certain powerful medications, such as methotrexate, an anticancer drug; halothane, an anesthetic; and oxyphenisatin, a substance used in enemas
• Inborn errors in physical or chemical processes of the body
• Syphilis
• Passive liver congestion, caused by a clot blocking the hepatic vein (a large vein that carries blood from the liver to the heart) or by inability of the heart to accept a normal flow of blood from the liver

### Symptoms

Frequently, cirrhosis is not suspected until it is well advanced, because it imitates many other diseases. Symptoms include general weakness, a vague feeling of being unwell, loss of appetite, loss of weight, and a loss of interest in sex. There may be a dull abdominal ache, nausea, constipation, or diarrhea. In a malnourished patient, the tongue may be inflamed. Many symptoms are the result of high blood pressure in the portal vein, which brings blood from the intestinal area to the liver. In cirrhosis, the liver cannot handle a normal flow of blood, so the pressure in the portal vein rises. One result is that fluid from the blood is lost into the abdominal cavity. The fluid may accumulate and press against the diaphragm (the muscular wall separating the abdominal and chest cavities) and interfere with breathing. Collateral blood vessels form to carry away the excess blood into the general circulation. There may be bleeding in the esophagus or stomach when these smaller collateral vessels burst under pressure. The patient may vomit blood. Serious, life-threatening hemorrhage may occur.

The liver may be enlarged and firm or, in advanced cases, shrunken. Other symptoms include an enlarged spleen, mottled redness of the mound at the base of the thumb, "spider veins" on the skin of the upper body; loss of hair from the chest and the pubic area, diminished size of the testes, and tingling sensations in the skin of the hands and feet.

### Diagnosis

Proof of cirrhosis of the liver is furnished by liver biopsy. A hollow needle is inserted through the skin and into the liver itself to obtain a tissue sample for analysis. Examination of tissue from a diseased liver reveals destruction of cells and scarring. Other diagnostic procedures include radionuclide scanning, in which radioactive material is administered and its distribution to the liver is recorded on x-ray film. X-ray pictures are taken of the gallbladder and of bile ducts inside the liver and leading from it. Important clues that may be found on blood and urine tests include the presence of bile pigments in the blood, a low red blood cell count, vitamin and mineral deficiencies, and protein in the urine.

### Treatment

Treatment is aimed first at removing the cause of the original injury. For example, an alcoholic patient is told to stop drinking; is placed on a well-balanced, moderate- to high-protein diet; and is given larger than usual doses of vitamins, including A, B complex, D, and K (which cannot be stored in the diseased liver) and folic acid. If a stone is obstructing an external bile duct and thus causing liver damage, it can be removed. Fluids and salt are usually restricted, to prevent fluid buildup in the body.

Good care includes getting plenty of rest; having frequent small meals, rather than fewer large ones, to reduce the work load of the liver; and avoiding infection, which places stress on the liver.

### Prevention

Many of the various causes of cirrhosis of the liver cannot be predicted and guarded against, but the major one can be. Drinking moderately or not at all is the best way to reduce the risk of contracting this serious disease.

# Colostomy

Colostomy is the creation of a stoma (opening) in the wall of the abdomen to which an opening in the colon is attached. Thereafter, the contents of the colon are eliminated through the stoma instead of through the rec-

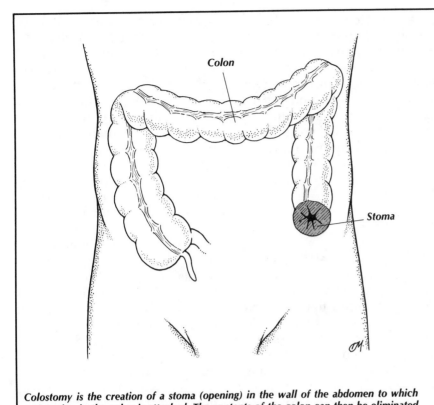

*Colon*

*Stoma*

*Colostomy is the creation of a stoma (opening) in the wall of the abdomen to which an opening in the colon is attached. The contents of the colon can then be eliminated through the stoma rather than through the rectum and anus.*

tum and anus (the normal opening to the outside of the body).

The opening may be permanent (as in some operations for cancer of the rectum, which eliminate the normal exit of the bowel), or it may be temporary (as in the surgical correction of Hirschsprung's disease).

### Correction of Hirschsprung's disease

In Hirschsprung's disease, an inherited disorder of newborns, the last portion of the bowel lacks specialized nerves and cannot function normally. The healthy portion of the bowel above this segment is connected to a stoma. Elimination takes place via this route for several months until the baby is strong enough for a second surgical procedure, in which the defective portion of the bowel is removed and the healthy portion is connected to the anus, permitting normal bowel movements.

### Permanent colostomy

Having a permanent colostomy does not prevent a person from leading a nearly normal life. The patient is taught how to empty the colon once a day by using irrigations (enemas) and a special collecting device. By manipulating the diet, it becomes possible to anticipate bowel movements. At first, patients wear a pouch over the stoma to collect any leakage from the colon. An adhesive is used to form a tight seal around the opening of the pouch and the stoma, and a deodorant in the pouch controls odor. After a while, many patients with so-called dry colostomies need only wear a stoma cap or a small gauze patch over the stoma to absorb mucous secretions. Physical activities can be resumed, with or without a pouch, including swimming, other noncontact sports, and sexual relations. The only exceptions are heavy lifting, which could cause a hernia through the weakened abdominal muscles, and any activity that could injure the stoma or abdomen.

To avoid infection of the stoma and irritation of the skin around it, the patient needs to wash the surrounding skin area with mild soap and water each day and then rinse and dry it. Special adhesive materials that protect and soothe the skin have become available. These are applied after cleaning the skin.

Support, encouragement, and practical advice from those who have undergone the operation are available through local chapters and the national headquarters of the United Ostomy Association.

## Crohn's disease

Crohn's disease (also known as regional enteritis and ileitis) is characterized by inflammation of a section or sections of any part of the digestive tract—most often, the ileum (the last third of the small intestine). The disease may begin as patches of tiny ulcers in the innermost lining of the intestine, with swelling of nearby tissues. The inflammation eventually extends through all layers of the intestine, which becomes thickened, hard, and brittle. Deepening ulcers, scarring, and swelling may obstruct the intestinal tract.

### Causes

The cause of Crohn's disease is unknown. However, research indicates that infection, immune disorders, or an inherited defect may play a part. There is some evidence of an increased incidence of Crohn's disease in Jews; black persons are least likely to have the disease. The disease usually begins between the ages of 15 and 35, but can occur at any age.

### Symptoms

Symptoms usually develop gradually, with spells of diarrhea (four to six stools a day, frequently bloody), low fever, weight loss, loss of appetite, general weakness, and steady or colicky pains in the abdomen, commonly on the right side. Milk, milk products, and coarse foods may make symptoms worse.

Occasionally an acute (sudden and severe) case resembles appendicitis, with sharp pain in the lower right portion of the abdomen, cramping, nausea, fever, and diarrhea. There may or may not be bloody stools. An acute case can resemble infectious diarrhea.

### Diagnosis

While probing the abdomen and pelvis, the doctor may detect a tender mass of thickened or matted loops of intestine. The chronic form of the disease can occasionally be mistaken for other problems, such as irritable bowel syndrome. However, an x-ray of the small intestine taken after administration of the contrast medium barium may reveal the characteristic pattern of narrowed portions of the bowel sharply differentiated from healthy portions. The doctor may use a sigmoidoscope (a lighted, hollow instrument inserted through the anus) to inspect the intestinal lining for patchy areas of inflammation or to perform a biopsy (obtain a sample of tissue from the lining for microscopic examination).

### Complications

Complications include abscesses (pus-filled cavities) and fistulas. Fistulas are abnormal connecting channels that originate from inflamed portions of the bowel and commonly extend into and around adjacent tissue. In the anorectal area, they may sometimes be seen as openings in the skin. They can also extend from one section of the bowel to another, from the bowel to the bladder or vagina, and from the bowel to the abdominal wall. Fistulas are often infected and discharge pus.

Perforation of the intestine can also occur, leading to peritonitis (inflammation of the lining of the abdominal cavity). This is marked by severe abdominal pain and rigidity of the abdomen, and is most often a surgical emergency. On occasion, a small perforation may become walled off, creating an abscess.

Malnutrition is a very common complication of Crohn's disease because areas of inflamed intestine cannot properly absorb nutrients. The risk of cancer of the colon and rectum is also increased.

### Treatment

At present, there is no cure for Crohn's disease. Surgery is sometimes necessary to remove an entire section of diseased bowel, drain an abscess, or eliminate a fistula. This relieves the condition for a time, but symptoms almost always recur, and another operation may be necessary. Treatment of the disease is directed at making the patient as comfortable and functional as possible by reducing the severity of his symptoms.

A diet rich in calories and vitamins with adequate protein is desirable, to compensate for the patient's poor absorption of nutrients from the intestines. Individuals with severely inflamed or obstructed bowels may be placed temporarily on intravenous feeding or a special no-residue diet. Patients with anemia may need supplements of vitamins and minerals (such as iron, folic acid, and vitamin $B_{12}$) and sometimes blood transfusions; those with severe diarrhea or dehydration (loss of body fluids) may need intravenous fluids.

Cramps and diarrhea are frequently controlled by various medications that relax the bowel wall, while preparations such as psyllium may help to firm stools.

Antibiotics are used on a short-term basis to treat abscesses and infected fistulas. Sulfasalicylate combination drugs may be used on a long-term basis to curb inflammation and prevent acute episodes, particularly in disease involving the large intestine. The steroid drug prednisone is a mainstay in treating flare-ups of symptoms.

# Diverticulosis and diverticulitis

Diverticulosis is the occurrence of diverticula (little pouches) that

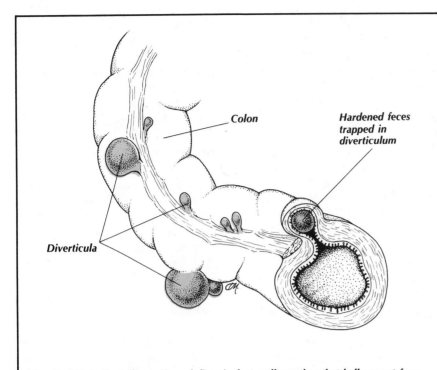

*Diverticulitis is the inflammation of diverticula (small pouches that balloon out from the colon wall when the inner lining is forced through weak spots in the muscular lining). Inflammation often develops when a mass of hardened feces becomes trapped in a diverticulum, reducing the blood supply to the pouch wall and making it more susceptible to infection by bacteria in the colon.*

form when the inner lining of the colon (large intestine) is forced, under pressure, through weak spots in the muscular outer layer of the colon. Diverticulosis may be present in about one-third of persons over 60 in the United States, and both its incidence and the frequency of complications increase with age. Diverticulitis is inflammation of the diverticula.

## Causes

One theory about the cause of diverticulosis is that abnormal movement of the colon (possibly because of too little bulk in the diet) produces intense pressure, which forces the intestinal lining through weak spots in the muscular layer. Most people with simple diverticulosis have no symptoms. Occasionally, however, a pouch next to a blood vessel may ulcerate, causing it to bleed. If the vessel is an artery, severe bleeding can result, seen as bleeding from the anus. Shock and even death may result if the condition is not treated.

It has been estimated that about one-fifth to one-fourth of the persons who have diverticulosis will suffer from diverticulitis. Diverticulitis develops when a mass of hardened waste matter (called a fecalith) forms in a pouch and reduces the blood supply to the thin walls of the pouch (by means of pressure against the wall), making them more susceptible to infection by the bacteria of the colon. The inflammation that follows can lead to perforation, formation of an abscess (an enclosed sac of pus around the perforation), or peri-

tonitis (infection of the lining of the abdominal cavity). Not infrequently, the inflamed section of bowel becomes attached to the urinary bladder or vagina, burrowing out from the colon to create a fistula (abnormal channel), which leaks infectious material into the other organ. Repeated inflammation can cause thickening of the wall of the colon, narrowing the colon and causing partial or sometimes total obstruction.

## Symptoms

Symptoms of diverticulitis include intermittent crampy abdominal pains and tenderness, usually on the lower left side, but sometimes in other areas of the lower abdomen, in which case the pains may resemble those of appendicitis. Pain that worsens during urination may indicate that the inflamed colon has become attached to the bladder. Stool (feces) or air in the urine may indicate a colon-to-bladder fistula. Constipation or constipation alternating with diarrhea is common. Fever is usually present with acute attacks.

## Diagnosis

The diagnosis of diverticulitis usually is made if there is a history of pain in the left lower section of the abdomen, accompanied by fever and a change in bowel habits. A physical examination may reveal a mass in that area, along with extreme tenderness. After the acute episode has subsided, the doctor may insert a proctoscope (a lighted, tubelike instrument) through the anus and into the colon to see if there is any evidence of cancer that might be causing the symptoms. X-ray studies are usually done to further rule out cancer of the colon and to locate diverticula, obstructions, and fistulas.

### Treatment

Treatment of severe diverticulitis begins with bed rest in a hospital and intravenous feeding; no food is given by mouth, to give the intestines a rest. Antibiotics are given if there is fever or other evidence of infection. If peritonitis develops, it may be necessary to operate. The inflamed section of the colon may simply be cut out, and the remaining sections joined. More often, a temporary colostomy (a surgically created opening in the abdominal wall, which allows the colon to empty to the outside of the body) is necessary. Later, after all inflammation and infection have subsided, the redirected portion of the colon is reconnected to the remaining portion of the colon or the rectum.

### Prevention

Choosing a diet with plenty of bulk appears to be a way to avoid diverticulosis. Persons who have diverticulosis should eat a relatively high-fiber diet. Supplements, such as psyllium, that increase bulk may be recommended to move the stool through the colon at a normal rate.

# Food poisoning

The term "food poisoning" generally refers to an illness caused by the ingestion (taking into the body) of food that is either poisonous itself (such as certain kinds of wild mushrooms) or that has been contaminated, usually by bacteria or their toxic (poisonous) by-products.

The symptoms commonly associated with food poisoning—nausea, vomiting, and diarrhea—are unpleasant but not generally life-threatening and usually subside within a relatively short period of time without treatment. However, for some groups—the very old, the very young, and the seriously ill—food poisoning can be extremely serious, and some forms, such as botulism and mushroom poisoning, are potentially fatal for anyone.

In general, bacterial food poisoning can be prevented by careful observance of proper procedures in food processing and preparation, especially hand washing by food handlers, prompt refrigeration of food, and cleanliness in food preparation areas.

### Botulism

The *Clostridium botulinum* bacterium produces a toxin which, when ingested, prevents the transmission of nerve impulses to muscle. Nausea, vomiting, and abdominal cramps are also common. The effects on the nervous system begin in the head, causing double or blurred vision and difficulty in swallowing, and then proceed downward as paralysis of the arms, the muscles that aid in breathing, and eventually the legs. These symptoms usually appear 4 to 36 hours after ingestion of the toxin, but can be delayed as long as eight days.

The foods most commonly implicated in botulism are home-canned preparations, and the best way to prevent botulism is to strictly follow established guidelines when home canning. Contaminated foods sometimes have a foul odor, but this warning is not always present. Also, honey should not be given to infants because it has been reported as a source of fatal botulism in that age group.

With the availability of botulism antitoxin, fewer than 10 percent of cases are now fatal. However, suspicion of botulism should still be considered a medical emergency.

### Salmonellosis

The term salmonellosis refers to a number of diseases caused by *Salmonella* bacteria. One of those diseases is typhoid fever, which fortunately is now uncommon in the United States. A very common form of salmonellosis is *Salmonella* gastroenteritis.

The foods that most commonly harbor *Salmonella* bacteria are meat, poultry, milk, and eggs. *Salmonella* bacteria are frequently transmitted by contact with human or animal fecal material or by eating food contaminated with such material. The symptoms of *Salmonella* gastroenteritis include nausea, abdominal cramps, and diarrhea. In severe cases, mucus and blood are present in the stools. The symptoms usually appear 12 to 24 hours after ingestion of contaminated food. Most cases occur in children during the summer and early fall. The illness is generally mild, usually lasting two to five days. However, salmonellosis can be fatal for very young infants, seriously ill patients, and the elderly.

Treatment of most *Salmonella* infections involves replacing the fluids lost because of diarrhea. If fluid loss is severe, hospitalization and intravenous fluid supplementation may be necessary. Use of antibiotics is reserved for patients with severe symptoms because, if used indiscriminately, such drugs can actually prolong the illness and create a state of unknowingly harboring the bacteria. Antidiarrheal medications can also prolong the illness and should be used only to control the most severe symptoms. Laboratory analysis of stool and blood samples may be necessary to establish the diagnosis and prescribe the appropriate treatment. Cultures of the stool should be performed after the illness has passed to confirm that the bacteria are not still being shed, creating the potential for spread of infection.

### Staphylococcal gastroenteritis

Gastroenteritis caused by the *Staphylococcus aureus* bacterium is a very common form of food poisoning. Foods cooked at low temperatures and then allowed to cool at room temperature for long periods of time are most often the source.

The symptoms—excessive salivation, nausea, diarrhea, abdominal cramps, and vomiting—usually occur within two to four hours after eating the contaminated food. The illness usually lasts less than 24 hours and requires no treatment in otherwise healthy individuals. Antibiotics and antidiarrheal medications can, in fact, prolong the illness. In elderly or ill persons, hospitalization and intravenous fluid replacement may be necessary. Symptoms of dehydration, such as dryness of the mouth and light-headedness, merit prompt medical attention.

### Other bacterial causes

*Clostridium perfringens* is a bacterium commonly found in raw meat and poultry. Its growth in foods is encouraged by slow cooking at low temperatures. Symptoms of infection—abdominal cramps, nausea, and diarrhea—usually appear about 8 to 12 hours after ingestion of contaminated food, but can be delayed as long as 24 hours. The illness generally lasts less than one day and requires no treatment other than getting plenty of fluids.

Infection with the *Vibrio parahemolyticus* bacterium is most often associated with ingestion of raw or improperly refrigerated seafood. This illness usually occurs during the warmer months and is most common in the coastal regions of the United States. The primary symptom—severe, watery, occasionally blood-tinged diarrhea—generally occurs 12 to 24 hours after eating the contaminated food. The illness rarely lasts more than two days. In severe cases, antibiotics may be necessary.

*Bacillus cereus* infection is commonly associated with rice products, particularly fried rice and unrefrigerated boiled rice. The primary symptoms—nausea and vomiting—are usually mild.

### Mushroom poisoning

It is all but impossible for anyone but the most highly trained expert to discriminate nontoxic mushrooms from the more than 50 species of toxic wild mushrooms. Therefore, all wild mushrooms should be avoided. The illness usually begins 6 to 24 hours after ingestion of the mushrooms. Starting with severe abdominal cramps, nausea,

vomiting, and diarrhea, the illness rapidly progresses to involve the liver, kidneys, and heart and can be fatal.

# Gallstones

Gallstones are hardened masses that consist mainly of cholesterol (a substance found predominantly in animal fats), blood, bile (fluid produced in the liver and stored in the gallbladder, which is required for fat absorption in the small intestine), and other substances. The stones form in the gallbladder or in the bile duct leading from the gallbladder into the small intestine, where food is digested and nutrients are absorbed into the bloodstream.

### Causes

When bile contains excessive amounts of cholesterol, the unnecessary cholesterol separates from the solution and forms stonelike masses. Unfortunately, since the body itself produces cholesterol, formation of these types of stones cannot be prevented merely by controlling cholesterol intake in the diet.

Pregnancy, obesity, diabetes, liver disease, and certain forms of anemia can increase the risk of gallstones. Overweight people who frequently lose and gain large amounts of weight seem more susceptible to gallstones, as do women who have had two or more children. Although the reasons are unclear, twice as many women as men over age 40 develop gallstones.

### Symptoms

By themselves, gallstones often produce no signs of disease.

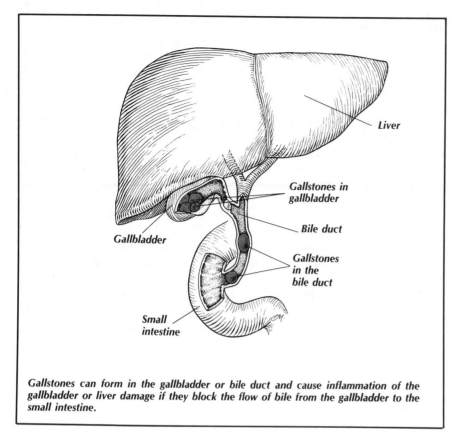

*Gallstones can form in the gallbladder or bile duct and cause inflammation of the gallbladder or liver damage if they block the flow of bile from the gallbladder to the small intestine.*

About half the people with gallstones have no symptoms. Symptoms that do appear are usually chronic (long-term) in nature, including discomfort and pain in the upper abdomen, indigestion, nausea, and intolerance of fatty foods. Sometimes stones pass through the bile duct into the intestines to be excreted naturally.

However, symptoms can occur if the stones lodge in the bile duct. In an acute gallbladder attack, a sharp pain (often on the right side of the upper abdomen) may travel to the back and under the right shoulder blade. Frequently, the pain develops suddenly after a meal and leads to fever, chills, vomiting, and possibly jaundice (yellowing of the skin and whites of the eyes caused by the presence of excess bile pigment in the bloodstream). These symptoms occur when a stone that had been floating in the gallbladder becomes trapped in the bile duct.

### Complications

Serious complications of liver damage or jaundice may develop if stones block the flow of bile. Pressure from the stones may also cause inflammation and damage to nearby organs.

When gallstones remain in the gallbladder, the organ may become inflamed. This condition, called chronic cholecystitis, may cause no symptoms. However, in most cases, repeated attacks of pain occur.

### Diagnosis

Gallstones that cause no symptoms may be detected on an x-ray study of the gallbladder, called a cholecystogram. A cholecystogram is performed after the patient has swallowed a tablet containing dye that outlines the gallbladder and any stones that may be present. Some physicians prefer to use ultrasound (a technique that uses sound waves to create images of internal structures). Some studies using radioactive isotopes can be used to differentiate between acute and chronic cholecystitis.

### Treatment

For acute attacks of gallstones with severe and prolonged symptoms, doctors generally recommend a cholecystectomy (surgical removal of the gallbladder). This treatment is one of the most common forms of abdominal surgery. Since the gallbladder is not necessary to maintain life, many doctors suggest removing a gallbladder containing stones that are not causing symptoms if there is a history of gallbladder disease.

Researchers are investigating a drug to dissolve cholesterol gallstones, which could be used as an alternative to surgery. Research is also being conducted to see if gallstones can be dissolved with localized forms of high-intensity radiation.

# Gastroenteritis

Gastroenteritis is an inflammation of the lining of the stomach and the intestines.

### Causes

Gastroenteritis can be caused by bacteria or viruses; by allergic reactions to certain foods or drinks; by infectious diseases, such as typhoid fever and influenza; by food poisoning; by overconsumption of alcohol; or by certain drugs.

## Symptoms

Symptoms include headache, nausea, vomiting, diarrhea, and gas pains in the stomach and the intestines. Often, the individual will feel that gas is "caught" in certain portions of the intestine. On occasion, cramps may produce severe pain.

## Diagnosis

The first task in treating gastroenteritis is to identify the cause or causes of the inflammation. Blood tests and cultures for viruses or bacteria may be done. If the problem is caused by an allergic reaction, the source of the reaction may be identified by allergy tests.

## Treatment

Antibiotics can be used to treat bacterial infections. A variety of medicines (many of them nonprescription) can ease the effects of stomach cramps and gas pains. Diarrhea may necessitate replacement of lost water. Elderly or extremely ill persons may have to be hospitalized for intravenous replacement of fluids.

## Prevention

Maintaining a clean kitchen, eating in restaurants where the kitchens are kept clean, washing fresh foods thoroughly, and cooking foods carefully are all safeguards against bacterial and viral infections. Identification of allergy-causing foods and moderation in alcohol consumption also help prevent gastroenteritis, if these are the causes of the problem.

# Hemorrhoids

Hemorrhoids (often called piles) are enlarged veins inside or just outside the anal canal, which is the opening at the end of the large intestine. As veins swell, they cause severe inflammation and discomfort.

## Causes

In some cases, hemorrhoids are the result of poor toilet habits. Habitual postponement of bowel movements can lead to loss of rectal function and undesirable straining during elimination. Straining irritates veins and slows the flow of blood, thereby contributing to swelling and inflammation of veins. If bowel movements are postponed, the stools retained in the bowels may lose moisture. When feces become dry and hard, the added strain of constipation stimulates the development of hemorrhoids.

Another source of hemorrhoid irritation comes from pressure on the veins due to diseases of the liver or heart or from a tumor. Pregnancy may also contribute to the development of hemorrhoids because the enlarged uterus increases pressure on the veins. Moreover, prolonged pressure from pushing during labor and delivery can inflame the anal area.

Diet plays a major role in the development of hemorrhoids. A diet containing a high proportion of refined foods, such as white flour and sugar, rather than foods with natural roughage, increases the likelihood of constipation and, therefore, the likelihood of hemorrhoids.

Hemorrhoids seem to be more prevalent in some families. However, this tendency has been attributed to similar dietary and personal habits.

## Symptoms

Hemorrhoids may take years to develop and almost always cause irritating symptoms. The first signs of hemorrhoids include itching and discomfort during and after bowel movements. Continued straining during elimination will eventually produce slight swelling of the lining of the anal canal. This swelling may not be noticed until hard stools scrape the anal lining and cause bleeding—an early clue that a hemorrhoid has developed.

With prolonged straining, a portion of the anal canal may jut out of the anus during a bowel movement. As long as the elastic connective tissue is still strong enough to pull the hemorrhoid back into the anal canal unassisted, the individual may not notice the growing problem. However, with persistent pressure, the protruding tissue may remain outside the anus after a bowel movement and need to be manually returned to the anal canal. Once outside the anal canal, the hemorrhoid creates a dull, aching sensation.

A more involved problem develops when the hemorrhoid is difficult or impossible to return within the anal canal, and permanent swelling at the anal opening interferes with elimination. The patient may then postpone bowel movements in an effort to avoid pain. Instead of helping, this intensifies the problem because it leads to constipation.

## Diagnosis

To diagnose a hemorrhoid, a physician inspects the anal canal, often with special instruments. An anoscope (a short, lighted, tubelike instrument) inserted into the anus can reveal the condition of the rectal lining. The sigmoidoscope, a longer instrument, provides a view of the lower portion of the colon.

## Treatment

Painful hemorrhoids can be treated at home by applying cold-water compresses directly to the anal area for five to ten minutes. Pain and swelling can be reduced by taking hot baths. Over-the-counter preparations cannot cure hemorrhoids, but they can relieve itching and swelling. Should symptoms worsen after application of any remedy, its use should be suspended and a doctor consulted. Chemicals in these preparations may produce an allergic reaction. Nonirritating laxatives may be useful in softening stools and easing bowel movements.

In the early stages of hemorrhoid development, adjustment of personal habits may prevent progression of the condition. A bowel movement should never be delayed once the urge is felt. During bowel movements, straining should be avoided. A diet including plenty of roughage—natural grains, fresh fruits, and vegetables—also softens stools.

For severe cases of hemorrhoids, a doctor may recom-

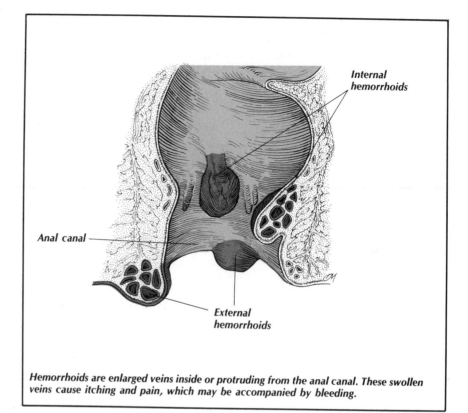

*Internal hemorrhoids*

*Anal canal*

*External hemorrhoids*

*Hemorrhoids are enlarged veins inside or protruding from the anal canal. These swollen veins cause itching and pain, which may be accompanied by bleeding.*

mend a surgical procedure called hemorrhoidectomy to remove dilated portions of the affected veins and to tie off the remaining parts of the vein. Newer procedures, such as cryosurgery and laser surgery, remove the hemorrhoid, but with less pain and fewer postoperative complications. Laser surgery uses an intensified beam of light to burn off the hemorrhoid. With cryosurgery, the hemorrhoid is frozen with an extremely cold probe. The frozen tissue dies, and the hemorrhoid falls off within several days. Physicians can perform cryosurgery in their offices in a matter of minutes. The only postoperative complaint is a slight watery discharge from the anal canal for a few days.

Another technique used to eliminate hemorrhoids is rubber-band ligation. With this procedure, which can be performed in the physician's office, the blood supply of the hemorrhoid is cut off by tying a rubber band around the swollen tissue. The hemorrhoid drops off within three to nine days. Unfortunately, this procedure is not suitable for all patients.

Recurrence of hemorrhoids after any type of treatment is not uncommon.

# Hepatitis

Hepatitis is an inflammation of the liver, usually caused by a viral infection, which is characterized by jaundice (yellowing of the skin and the whites of the eyes).

## Causes and types

The disease is caused by several viruses, but the most common are those that cause hepatitis A (infectious hepatitis) and hepatitis B (serum hepatitis). The hepatitis A virus and the hepatitis B virus both attack cells in the liver.

Hepatitis A is transmitted from person to person via contaminated food or water or contact with the stools of an infected person. This disease may occur in epidemics where sanitation is poor and the water supply is contaminated. The incubation period (the time between exposure to the disease and the appearance of symptoms) is between 14 and 40 days. Sometimes, hepatitis A is so mild that symptoms never appear, but the infected person can still be a carrier and transmit the disease to others.

In hepatitis B, the virus enters the bloodstream via contact with contaminated blood or other body fluids, such as semen, or use of contaminated hypodermic needles. Hepatitis B begins more gradually than does hepatitis A, so the disease may be present 40 to 180 days before the onset of symptoms. Because the virus can live in almost all body fluids, including saliva, semen, urine, and tears, hepatitis B can be transmitted by sexual contact or, more rarely, by casual contact.

Hepatitis may also result as a complication of the viral infection called infectious mononucleosis.

## Symptoms

Early signs of hepatitis include general fatigue, joint and muscle pain, and loss of appetite. Nausea, vomiting, and diarrhea or constipation may follow, with a low-grade fever of 101°F or less. As the disease develops, the liver enlarges and becomes tender. Chills, weight loss, and distaste for smoking appear along with the characteristic jaundice. Jaundice results from an accumulation of yellow bile pigment in the blood, which turns the skin and whites of the eyes yellow.

In hepatitis A, the disappearance of jaundice generally signals the beginning of recovery. However, in hepatitis B, the virus may persist for years or even a lifetime.

Any sudden rise in fever, extreme drowsiness, or severe prolonged pain requires immediate medical attention to avoid permanent liver damage. Chronic (long-term) hepatitis can lead to irreversible liver failure or cirrhosis (a condition in which normal cells of the liver are replaced by fibrous scar tissue that inhibits liver function).

## Diagnosis

To determine the extent and severity of hepatitis, a physician analyzes blood and urine specimens from the patient. If the disease has progressed, the patient may have yellow skin and soreness in the upper abdomen over the liver.

More severe chronic hepatitis may necessitate a liver biopsy—a diagnostic procedure in which a needle is inserted into the liver to obtain a sample of liver tissue. A local anesthetic is usually first injected into the upper abdomen to reduce discomfort from the procedure.

## Treatment

There is no cure for viral hepatitis. Even treatment is limited, especially for acute hepatitis. Once the virus attacks, recovery is usually up to the body's natural defense mechanisms.

To encourage the healing process, physicians advise patients to avoid strenuous activity. Bed rest is most important during the acute phase of hepatitis. More serious cases may require hospitalization to ensure adequate nutrition. All hepatitis patients must avoid alcoholic beverages, because processing alcohol puts a tremendous strain on the liver.

## Prevention

Persons exposed to hepatitis may prevent or minimize the severity of the disease by obtaining an injection of gamma globulin, a disease-fighting substance derived from blood. Gamma globulin usually defends against hepatitis A virus and may offer modest protection against hepatitis B virus. Antibody against hepatitis B is available and may be useful in preventing that disease if given at an appropriate time.

A hepatitis B vaccine is now available. (A vaccine is a preparation of a disease-causing agent that stimulates the body to produce antibodies to fight the disease.) Hepatitis B vaccine is recommended for persons who are in direct contact with hepatitis carriers, for health-care workers, and for persons in certain other high-risk groups (for example, travelers to regions where hepatitis is prevalent and hemophiliacs who receive pooled blood products).

# Hiatal hernia

A hernia is a protrusion of a body part through the structures that surround it. A hiatal hernia (also called a hiatus or diaphragmatic hernia) occurs when a portion of the stomach protrudes above the diaphragm (the muscular wall separating the chest and abdominal cavities) into the chest.

### Sliding hiatal hernia

Normally, the esophagus (the passageway from the throat to the stomach) passes through a tight muscular collar, called a hiatus, that prevents the stomach from squeezing up into the chest cavity. However, if the collar is too large or if it relaxes, a sliding hiatal hernia may occur. Pressure in the abdominal cavity (such as may be caused by obesity, pregnancy, tight clothing, bending or other changes in position, coughing, or straining) causes the top part of the stomach to herniate (slide through the opening) along with the gastroesophageal junction (the junction of the stomach and the esophagus). This condition is very common, especially in women and older persons. It is often without symptoms. Surgical treatment is recommended in only the most severe cases, and is aimed at restoring the functional ability of the lower esophageal sphincter (the muscular valve that keeps stomach contents from regurgitating upward).

Until recently it was believed that the mere presence of a sliding hiatal hernia causes regurgitation (backward flow) of food and harsh stomach acid into the esophagus, which produces the burning sensation of heartburn. Current thinking, however, is that regurgitation and heartburn are the result of loss of the functional ability of the esophageal sphincter.

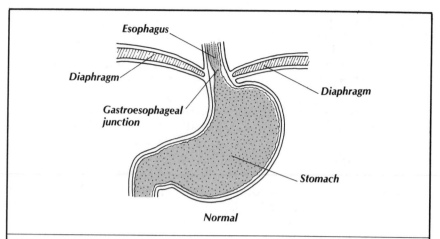

**Normal**

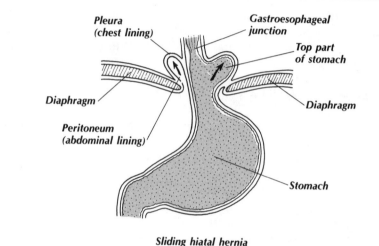

**Sliding hiatal hernia**

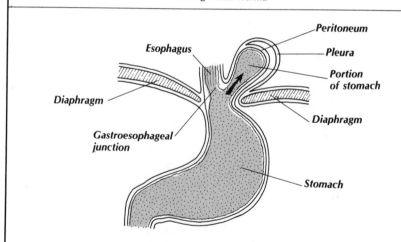

**Paraesophageal hiatal hernia**

*A hiatal hernia occurs when a portion of the stomach protrudes through the hiatus (the tight muscular collar that normally prevents the stomach from pushing through the diaphragm into the chest). In a sliding hiatal hernia, the top part of the stomach and the gastroesophageal junction (the junction of the stomach and the esophagus) move upward through the hiatus. In a paraesophageal hiatal hernia, the gastroesophageal junction retains its normal position while a portion of the stomach and its peritoneal covering roll up through the hiatus.*

### Paraesophageal hiatal hernia

A relatively uncommon but quite dangerous type of hiatal hernia is the paraesophageal, or rolling, hiatal hernia. In this type, the gastroesophageal junction retains its normal position while a portion of the stomach and part of its peritoneum (covering membrane) rolls up through the opening in the diaphragm, alongside the junction. The danger is that the herniated section may become trapped in the chest with its blood supply choked off, thereby causing death of stomach tissue. Bleeding is also a common complication. Although dangerous, this condition may have no symptoms and is usually found accidentally on an x-ray taken for another purpose. The only common symptom is a sense of fullness in the chest after eating.

Because of the potential complications of the paraesophageal hernia, many authorities recommend surgery, even in the absence of symptoms. Surgery for a paraesophageal hernia involves entering the abdomen and pushing the herniated portion of the stomach back into its proper position while removing the sac of peritoneum around it. After this, the muscular collar of the diaphragm is tightened by stitches.

# Ileostomy

An ileostomy is the surgical creation of an opening, or stoma, through the abdomen into the ileum (the lower part of the small intestine). An ileostomy is performed if the large intestine and rectum must be removed because of disease or abnormality. The opening into the small intestine then becomes an artificial anus through which waste material is expelled, since waste matter can no longer travel through the normal anus.

The waste matter that is discharged through the stoma is collected in a bag that the patient wears continuously. Because this waste matter does not pass through the large intestine, where water is absorbed from the waste matter, the material excreted through the stoma is watery.

Patients learn to care for their stomas in the hospital after the operation. Equipped with this knowledge, a patient can lead a nearly normal life after an ileostomy.

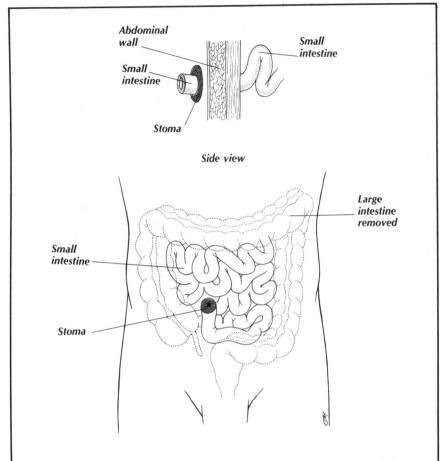

Abdominal wall

Small intestine

Small intestine

Stoma

Side view

Small intestine

Large intestine removed

Stoma

*An ileostomy is the surgical creation of an opening through the abdomen into the ileum (the lower part of the small intestine). Waste matter can then be expelled through that opening. An ileostomy is performed when the large intestine must be removed.*

# Intestinal and gastric bypass surgery

Intestinal bypass surgery and gastric bypass surgery are methods of treating massive obesity. Because of their potential dangers, such methods are usually limited to persons who are at least 100 pounds over their ideal weight and who have failed to lose weight by other means, such as diet and exercise. These persons are at serious risk for diabetes, high blood pressure, heart disease, arthritis, and other major disorders.

Various types of operations have been tried to detour digesting food around a long section of the small intestine, thus limiting the area of intestine that can absorb fats and carbohydrates from the food. The most recently devised operation is the jejunoileal bypass—named for the jejunum (the middle portion of the small intestine) and the ileum (the final portion of the small intestine). In this procedure, all but 18 inches of the 240 inches of the small intestine is bypassed (the unused portion remains in the body and drains into the colon). The method is very effective in reducing weight—from 80 to 150 pounds in most patients—but frequently produces persistent diarrhea, severe liver disease, imbalances in body salts, kidney stones, bladder stones, mental disturbances, and joint inflammations. Because the mortality rate associated with those complications may be as high as 5 percent, many physicians believe that the intestinal bypass method should no longer be used. This surgery is now seldom performed since there are safer treatment methods.

Replacements for the intestinal bypass procedure, which are reported to have far fewer complications, are gastric bypass and gastric stapling. Both are designed to reduce the capacity of the stomach so that only a small amount of food can be eaten at one time. In the gastric bypass operation, the lower part of the stomach is cut off, and the remaining top part is connected to the upper portion of the small intestine. In the gastric stapling operation, stomach capacity is reduced by stapling off most of the fundus (the uppermost portion of the stomach).

Recently, a nonsurgical technique for reducing stomach capacity has been developed. A specially designed balloon is placed in the stomach and then inflated. Since the balloon takes up a significant portion of the volume of the stomach, there is less room for food. The patient feels full after eating a relatively small quantity of food. This technique has the advantage that it is readily reversible: the balloon can be removed easily if problems arise or the patient reaches the desired weight.

The long-term results and side effects of gastric bypass, gastric stapling, and gastric balloon placement, when known, will determine whether these procedures are widely employed. Until then, it should be remembered that they all carry the risk of potentially serious complications.

# Irritable bowel syndrome

Irritable bowel syndrome, also called spastic colon and mucous colitis, is a collection of symptoms caused by irritability and irregularity in the movement of both small and large intestines. The syndrome is usually influenced by emotions. Feelings of nervousness, anxiety, guilt, depression, or anger may bring on or aggravate this very common disorder. Coffee, raw fruits and vegetables, hormones, drugs, and overuse of laxatives can promote it, as can an inability of the body to digest the natural sugar in milk.

## Symptoms

Irritable bowel syndrome is not a disease, but a collection of symptoms that includes both constipation and diarrhea, often alternating and sometimes accompanied by abdominal cramps and straining during elimination. Stools may be loose or compacted and may include mucus, which is produced by the bowel lining in greater than usual amounts as a response to irritation. Gas, bloating, nausea, headache, and fatigue may accompany the other symptoms.

There are two main types of irritable bowel syndrome. The first type, spastic colon, is marked by cramps or a dull, aching pain in the abdomen, usually the lower part. The discomfort often begins at mealtime and may disappear after a bowel movement. The second type of irritable bowel syndrome is characterized by painless diarrhea, especially an urgent need for a bowel movement on awakening or during or right after a meal. Fecal incontinence (loss of voluntary bowel control) can occur.

## Diagnosis

If a patient appears to have irritable bowel syndrome, the doctor will first want to rule out diseases with similar symptoms. The patient may be asked to bring in a stool specimen to be examined for traces of blood and microorganisms. The colon may be x-rayed following a barium enema. The doctor may examine the lower portion of the colon with a sigmoidoscope (a lighted, tubelike instrument, which is inserted through the anus) to check for serious disorders, such as ulcerative colitis.

## Treatment

If no organic disease is found, the doctor will reassure the patient and discuss ways in which the symptoms can be relieved. There may be methods by which the patient can reduce the anxiety or depression that may be causing the syndrome. The doctor may prescribe a tranquilizer, sedative, antidepressant, or antispasmodic medication—but only on a short-term basis, so that the individual does not become dependent on the drug. Long walks, bike rides, or other exercise may help to relax the person while promoting better bowel action.

If constipation is a problem, the doctor will advise the patient to add bulk, such as whole bran, to the diet; to stop depending on laxatives; and to take pills that absorb water, add bulk, and help to stabilize the large intestine. If diarrhea is present, avoiding laxative foods, such as prunes, may help. Patients bothered by gas will be warned against foods such as cabbage and beans. Milk may be barred from the diet. Most people, with the general exception of those of northwestern European origin, lose some or all of the ability to digest lactose, the natural sugar in milk, by the time they are 20 years old. A test for this is an oral dose of lactose. If it results in diarrhea and bloating, it is a tip-off that the symptoms could have been caused by drinking milk.

If irritable bowel syndrome continues despite treatment, it is important to remember that it is not dangerous. However, to be on the safe side, regular physical checkups should be scheduled with a doctor, especially after the age of 40.

# Jaundice

Jaundice is a yellowish discoloration of the skin, the whites of the eyes, the mucous membranes, and other tissues of the body, which is caused by the abnormal accumulation of the bile pigment bilirubin in the blood.

Bilirubin consists primarily of the hemoglobin of used red blood cells and is found in bile, a bitter, yellow-green fluid that aids in digestion by breaking down fat. Bile is secreted by the liver, stored in the gallbladder, and discharged into the small intestine when it is needed for digestion.

### Causes

In many cases, jaundice occurs when bile is prevented from being discharged into the small intestine by an obstruction. The obstruction may be caused by gallstones, tumors, or parasites in the bile ducts. Jaundice may also be a sign of hepatitis, in which the inflamed or damaged liver cannot process the bilirubin it receives. Occasionally, jaundice appears if red blood cells are destroyed too rapidly, sometimes as a result of anemia, and the liver cannot accommodate the excess. Jaundice is also associated with many other diseases in which the functioning of the liver is disrupted, including various forms of cancer and certain viral and parasitic infections. More than 50 percent of full-term newborn infants and 80 percent of premature newborn infants show signs of jaundice by the third day after birth. In most of these cases, the condition is nothing to worry about and disappears in a week or so.

### Symptoms

Usually when jaundice occurs, the liver has become enlarged and is functioning less than optimally. Bowel movements may be clay-colored, and urine can vary in hue from light yellow to brownish green. Jaundiced skin ranges in color from lemon yellow to olive green.

### Diagnosis

Routine blood testing will determine the origin of most cases of jaundice, but occasionally it is necessary to examine the bile ducts by means of an x-ray study. Certain dyes injected into the blood will collect in the liver and bile ducts so that an obstruction can be visualized on an x-ray film. Other alternatives include ultrasound, in which sound waves are used to create images of internal structures, and CT scanning, a special x-ray technique that provides cross-sectional pictures of an area.

### Treatment

Surgery may be necessary if an obstruction is present. Otherwise, treatment depends on the underlying condition.

# Occult blood

Occult blood is blood that is present in an amount so small that it is detectable only with a chemical test or microscopic examination. The term is generally used to refer to blood in the stools that indicates bleeding along the gastrointestinal tract.

### Symptoms

Often, the only symptom of occult bleeding is fatigue due to loss of oxygen-carrying red blood cells. A significant amount of blood can be passed in one stool with no visible indication that it is present.

## Diagnosis

Occult bleeding is not always constant, so tests are typically performed on stool samples obtained on three separate occasions if a problem is suspected. The patient must not eat red meat for three days before the samples are obtained because even cooked blood from meat that has been eaten can cause a positive test result. Aspirin can also cause minute amounts of blood to appear in the stools and should not be taken for at least several days before starting to test for occult blood in the stools.

# Pancreatitis

Pancreatitis is an inflammation of the pancreas.

The pancreas has many functions. The endocrine portion of the pancreas secretes hormones directly into the bloodstream, such as the hormones insulin and glucagon, which are critical to the processing of glucose (the form of sugar used by the body for energy). The exocrine portion of the pancreas secretes digestive enzymes (proteins that promote chemical reactions), such as amylase, which aids in the breakdown of starches, and lipase, which aids in the breakdown of fats.

## Causes

Pancreatitis commonly results from an obstruction of the pancreatic ducts, which convey enzymes to the small intestine.

Why these blockages occur is often hard to determine; however, most cases of pancreatitis are related to gallbladder disease or alcoholism. Acute attacks are frequently associated with gallstones or alcoholic binges. If hereditary factors are involved, the disease may begin in childhood, as early as eight or ten years of age. Direct blows to the abdomen or injury during an operation may also lead to pancreatitis, sometimes a year or more after the event. Mumps and other viral infections; use of certain drugs, including steroids, thiazide diuretics, and oral contraceptives; and tumors have all been associated with pancreatitis.

## Symptoms

The disease is characterized by the sudden onset of steady, severe, piercing, upper abdominal pain (frequently radiating to the middle portion of the back) accompanied by nausea and persistent vomiting. Eating—or even the sight of food—may bring on the pain or make it worse. Vomiting provides no relief, a feature that distinguishes pancreatitis from some stomach and intestinal disorders. Fever, shock (circulatory collapse), jaundice (yellowish discoloration of the skin and whites of the eyes), dehydration (excessive fluid loss), bleeding, and infection may occur in severe attacks.

## Diagnosis

The existence and degree of inflammation in the pancreas may be hard to determine, not only because of the hidden position and dual purpose of the gland, but also because the

symptoms are easily confused with those of other abdominal disorders. Blood and urine tests, as well as microscopic tissue examination, may be inconclusive, but can at least be helpful in excluding other abdominal disorders.

A special x-ray study, endoscopic retrograde cholangiopancreatography, may be used to inspect the pancreatic ducts. The technique is performed by inserting a gastroscope (a lighted, tubelike instrument) through the mouth and stomach into the duodenum. In the duodenum is the opening to the common bile and main pancreatic ducts. A special device is inserted through this opening, and x-ray contrast material is injected. Obstructions, tumors, and characteristic ductal patterns associated with chronic pancreatitis can be seen on the x-ray films obtained. This test is usually not performed within several weeks of an attack of pancreatitis.

## Treatment

The patient is usually hospitalized for 3 to 14 days for a mild to severe acute attack. Correction of an underlying problem (for example, removal of stones) improves the chances for complete recovery.

Initial treatment is aimed at relieving the pain and reducing stomach secretions, which can stimulate the pancreas. To allow the pancreas to rest, eating and drinking are replaced by intravenous feeding, and stomach acids are suctioned out through a tube inserted through the nose.

During convalescence, a lowfat, high-protein diet should be followed, and antacids may be prescribed. If the disease is chronic, it may be necessary to use pancreatic extracts to supplement the insufficient quantities of enzymes secreted by the diseased pancreas. This helps to normalize digestion and maintain adequate nutritional status.

After an acute episode of pancreatitis, tissue debris, blood, and pancreatic enzymes may form a pseudocyst (an internal space filled with a collection of material but not within a sac). Rupture or enlargement of a pseudocyst can be a very serious or even fatal event. If a pseudocyst does not clear up spontaneously, surgery is necessary to drain it.

Chronic pancreatitis is an indication of continued degenerative tissue damage, which may impair pancreatic function. In some cases of recurrence, surgical exploration might be considered to locate a previously unidentified blockage or to remove diseased tissue; however, surgery is unlikely to help the patient who continues to drink excessive amounts of alcohol. Recently, procedures to remove stones or otherwise relieve obstruction have been successfully performed through a gastroscope, eliminating the need for surgery.

# Periodontal disease

Periodontal disease (also known as periodontitis or, less accurately, as pyorrhea) is a progressive deterioration of the gums, bones, and other tissues around the teeth.

## Causes

One theory is that the condition begins with an accumula-

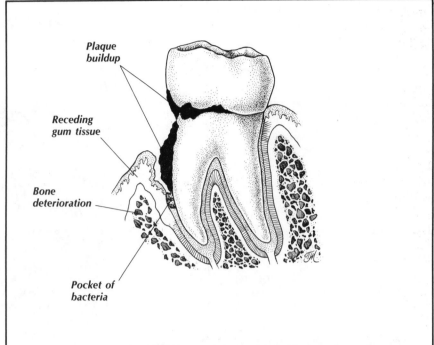

*The left side shows the plaque buildup and degeneration of bone and gum tissue associated with periodontal disease. The right side shows healthy tooth, bone, and gum tissue.*

tion of bacteria and food particles within tissues surrounding the teeth. These bacteria emit toxins (poisons) that cause gum tissues to swell, bleed, and deteriorate.

## Stages of periodontitis

Gingivitis (inflammation of the gums) is the first stage of periodontitis. The second stage results when the soft tissues become separated from the bone and teeth, leading to "pocket" formation. Pockets of bacteria and pus accumulate around the teeth, leading to weakening of the tissues holding the teeth in their sockets, as well as to destruction of the bone supporting the teeth. As the disease advances, teeth become loose and fall out. They may also move out of alignment with one another, causing problems with chewing.

## Symptoms

In the early stage of periodontal disease, gums become sore, red, and slightly swollen. They may be sensitive to the touch and may bleed when brushed or flossed. The presence of pus in the gums around the teeth signals the beginning of the second stage. If pus remains in the gum tissue without draining, extreme pain and swelling can result.

## Diagnosis

The diagnosis of periodontal disease is based on the presence of swollen gums and deposits of plaque around the teeth.

## Treatment and prevention

Once periodontal disease has been detected, continued care of the mouth at home can help prevent extension of disease and reduce gum problems.

Oral hygiene to prevent gum disease is the same as treatment to prevent tooth decay. Ideally, the mouth should be cleaned after every meal. At the least, a thorough cleansing at bedtime is necessary to reduce the risk of gum disease. Dentists suggest brushing with a soft-bristled toothbrush. Gentle movements within the crevices dislodge decay-causing material, and firm strokes over the teeth remove plaque.

Flossing is recommended to clear plaque from between teeth. After brushing and flossing, vigorously rinsing the mouth with mouthwash containing an antimicrobial agent (a substance that kills bacteria) can also help eliminate bacterial growth, but mouthwash alone cannot prevent plaque formation.

For self-checking, a dental mirror provides a view of the teeth and gums in the back of the mouth. Disclosing wafers, which discolor plaque when chewed, reveal any invisible film that needs to be removed.

In advanced cases, a dentist may scrape the affected tissue pockets and apply antiseptics (germ-killers) every few months in an effort to kill the bacteria. Should this procedure fail to check the spread of the disease, surgery by a periodontist (gum specialist) may be needed to remove deep pockets in the gums. Once the bacteria have been eliminated, good oral hygiene should control the disease.

# Peritonitis

Peritonitis is a term used to describe an inflammation of the peritoneum (the thin, double-

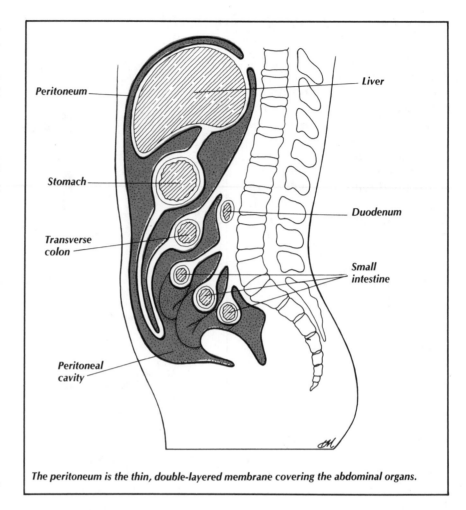

*The peritoneum is the thin, double-layered membrane covering the abdominal organs.*

layered membrane covering the abdominal organs).

## Causes

The condition occurs when the peritoneum is invaded by bacteria or irritated by toxins (poisons), bile (a substance produced by the liver and stored in the gallbladder), blood, or urine. Because the peritoneum is well sealed, it can be infiltrated only when one of the hollow organs of the abdomen ruptures; when a solid organ is somehow damaged, causing it to leak; or when there is a penetrating injury from the outside. For example, if the bladder is ruptured in an accident, urine is discharged into the peritoneal cavity. Although normally germ-free, the urine is quite irritating and causes chemical peritonitis. If the colon is perforated, feces, which contain bacteria and toxins, are discharged, causing bacterial peritonitis. Both of these conditions are extremely serious and must be treated immediately.

## Symptoms

A main symptom of peritonitis is severe pain that intensifies with any movement and often forces the person to lie very still with the legs drawn up. The abdominal area becomes very tender and rigid; commonly there is vomiting, fever, and dehydration (excessive loss of body fluids). When the peritoneum is inflamed, fluid begins to leak out of the blood vessels into the peritoneum. If this condition is not corrected, it may lead to shock (failure of the circulatory system because of loss of blood volume). Swelling of the abdomen is a danger sign that the intestines have become paralyzed and bloated with air.

## Treatment

The symptoms of peritonitis call for immediate medical care, including intravenous administration of antibiotics to fight infection. Intravenous fluids are also given to replace lost fluids. In addition, a tube is usually inserted through the nose and into the stomach to relieve bloating and remove pooled fluids. After the patient's condition has been stabilized, surgery is performed to remove or repair the cause of peritonitis. Chances for recovery are usually excellent.

# Pyloric stenosis

Pyloric stenosis is a constriction (narrowing) of the passage between the stomach and the small intestine. The stomach has two openings—one at the top, where it joins with the esophagus (the food passage between the mouth and the stomach), and one at the bottom, where it joins with the small intestine. The lower opening is called the pylorus.

## Causes

Pyloric stenosis can be caused by many conditions, including cancer, spasm, a nearby ulcer in the part of the intestine di-

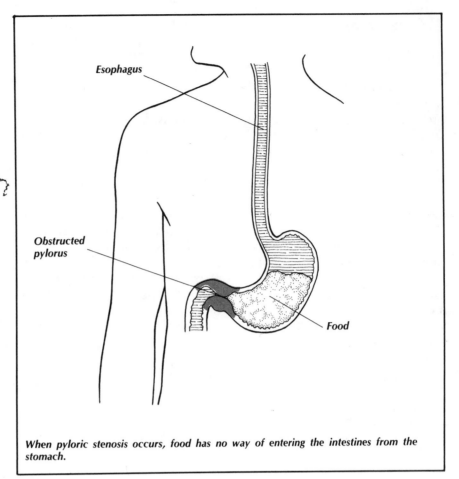

*When pyloric stenosis occurs, food has no way of entering the intestines from the stomach.*

rectly below the pyloric opening, gastritis (inflammation of the stomach), and enlargement of the pyloric sphincter (the muscle that rings the pyloric opening and controls its movement).

## Symptoms

In the case of congenital (present at birth) pyloric stenosis, ten days to three weeks after birth the infant will experience regurgitation ("spitting up" of part of the stomach's contents), projectile vomiting (vomiting with great force), weight loss, and dehydration (excessive loss of body fluids) without appetite loss. Adults with pyloric stenosis experience discomfort in the upper and middle portions of the abdo-

men, pain, bloating of the abdominal area, nausea, vomiting, and weight loss.

## Treatment

In mild cases of temporary pyloric stenosis, such as that due to an ulcer, the condition can be treated by offering only small meals, restoring normal fluid levels, and administering anticholinergic drugs (drugs that block the strength of the nerve impulses that are making the pyloric muscle contract).

In severe cases, a pyloromyotomy (a lengthwise incision into the pyloric muscle) may be indicated. A portion of the pyloric sphincter may also be removed.

# Tooth decay

Tooth decay (dental cavities, or caries) is the gradual process of destruction and mineral loss that affects the enamel (outer layer) and dentin (the bony second layer) of a portion of a tooth, causing it to become soft, discolored, and porous.

## Causes

A combination of factors causes tooth decay. A substance called plaque, made up of sugars, starches, bacteria, and proteins, builds up on dental surfaces, especially near the gums and in other hard-to-clean areas. The plaque prevents the saliva from performing its natural protective function. The bacteria in the plaque feed on the sugars and starches that cling to the teeth and produce acid as a by-product of their metabolism. That acid is probably the actual agent of destruction of dental tissue.

## Symptoms

When the cavity has progressed into the dentin or the surface of an exposed root, the tooth becomes sensitive to touch and rapid temperature changes. Sweet foods can cause pain as dissolved sugar enters the cavity. Bacteria may pass through tiny channels in the dentin and inflame the pulp, which contains blood vessels and nervous tissue, producing toothache.

## Diagnosis

The cavity reveals itself to the examining dentist as a darkened area or as an area of softness when probed with a sharp instrument. It is also apparent on an x-ray examination.

## Treatment

Cavities are treated by drilling out the decayed material and replacing it with a filling. In front teeth, where appearance is important, the filling may be of porcelain or a plastic resin (which is also used to fill pits and tiny cracks in the enamel). In other teeth, the filling is usually silver-colored or an alloy of gold, which is the most durable material. When a tooth is badly damaged, with involvement of the root, the dentist removes all decay, fills the cavity and root canal with dental cement, then grinds and tapers the outer surface and covers it with what is known as a gold crown. On teeth toward the front, the gold

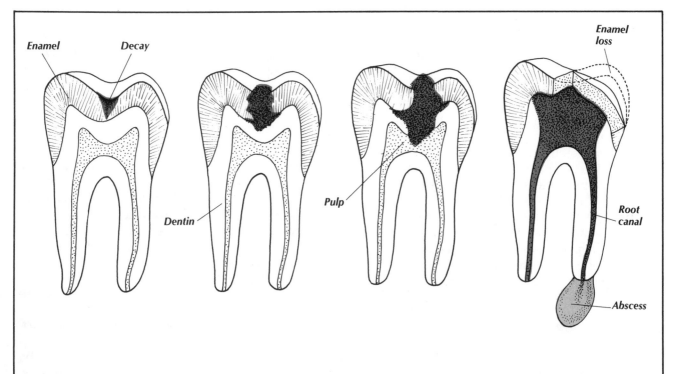

*Tooth decay, if untreated, can progress from the surface enamel to the dentin, then to the pulp, and finally through the root canal to form an abscess (pus-filled cavity).*

crown is overlaid with porcelain to provide a natural appearance.

## Prevention

To prevent decay, teeth should be cleaned daily with a soft-bristled brush, preferably after each meal, to remove food particles and plaque. Equally important is the use of dental floss to remove debris between the teeth. Avoiding sweet, sticky foods, or at least rinsing or brushing shortly after eating them, may also help prevent decay. A child's teeth will be more resistant to decay if the child drinks water containing the proper amount of fluoride in the first 12 years, while the teeth are developing. If the water supply is not fluoridated, a vitamin supplement containing fluoride can be taken daily. Adults and children alike can benefit by using a fluoride-containing toothpaste or mouthwash.

# Traveler's diarrhea

Of all the illnesses likely to afflict travelers to foreign countries, the most common is "traveler's diarrhea." This disorder, an intestinal infection caused by microorganisms to which the traveler is unaccustomed, is characterized by loose, watery stools (bowel movements), often accompanied by nausea and abdominal cramps.

## Causes

The organism most commonly responsible is probably the *Escherichia coli (E. coli)* bacterium. This bacterium is a normal inhabitant of the intestines, but in some areas of the world it has evolved into a strain called enterotoxigenic (poisonous to the intestines) *E. coli*, or ETEC, which can cause moderate to severe diarrhea. Other organisms that can cause traveler's diarrhea include *Campylobacter, Salmonella,* and *Shigella* bacteria; parasitic protozoa (one-celled organisms), such as *Entamoeba histolytica* (a cause of amoebic dysentery) and *Giardia lamblia;* and a number of viruses.

## Symptoms

The major symptom of the illness is, of course, diarrhea, which can range in intensity from mild (three to four loose, watery stools per day) to severe (10 to 20 bloody stools per day). The severity of traveler's diarrhea is largely dependent on the type of organism that is causing the infection and the health status of the individual. Traveler's diarrhea caused by bacteria usually begins a few days after the beginning of the trip and may last for several days to a few weeks if not properly treated. *Campylobacter* and *Shigella* infections commonly are marked by severe, bloody diarrhea. The diarrhea caused by *Giardia* organisms is usually characterized by abundant stools (rarely blood-tinged) and can be associated with other symptoms, such as fever, weight loss, and weakness. Traveler's diarrhea caused by protozoa can be mild or very severe, with involvement of other organs, such as the liver.

## Diagnosis

Knowledge of which foreign countries have been visited recently will help the doctor in making a preliminary diagnosis. Because it is very difficult to differentiate among the various infectious causes of diarrhea, laboratory studies, such as stool cultures and blood tests, are often needed. Parasitic diarrhea is especially difficult to diagnose; occasionally, multiple cultures are necessary, as well as proctoscopy (visual examination of the rectum with a special instrument).

## Treatment

Prescription antidiarrheal medications are often sought by individuals about to leave on a trip so that they can treat themselves if they suffer some form of traveler's diarrhea. Physicians are justifiably reluctant to prescribe these medications routinely because in many forms of diarrheal illness, such drugs can actually worsen the symptoms, cause complications, and prolong the course of the disease. These medications should never be taken except on the advice of a physician.

Mild cases of traveler's diarrhea usually clear up without treatment in a few days. Diarrhea that lasts for more than several days or that is associated with persistent fever or with the presence of blood, pus, or mucus in the stools calls for immediate medical attention.

## Prevention

Much has been written in recent years about prevention of traveler's diarrhea by taking medication before and during the trip. It must be remembered that all medications have potential side effects and that the indiscriminate use of antibiotics and antidiarrheal medications can be dangerous. Except in special circumstances (for example, a person with severe health problems, for whom an episode of severe diarrhea could be catastrophic), routine prophylaxis (preventive treatment) with antibiotics is not recommended.

Because there are no vaccines or universally effective prophylactic drugs to use against traveler's diarrhea, caution should be exercised when eating or drinking in many foreign countries. Avoid unboiled water (and ice made from unboiled water). Be careful of water that you use to brush your teeth, too. Do not assume that bottled water available locally is safe. Lettuce and other fresh vegetables are common culprits. Fruit with intact skin is usually safe if you peel it yourself before eating. Beer, wine, and carbonated beverages are usually safe, but it must be remembered that the addition of alcoholic beverages to water does not kill infectious organisms. Food obtained from local street vendors should be avoided.

# Ulcer

An ulcer is an erosion (open sore) on the surface of an organ or tissue. Ulcers most commonly erupt in the digestive tract, in which case they are known as peptic ulcers. Peptic ulcers may appear in the esophagus, the stomach, or the duodenum (the first segment of the small intestine).

### Causes

Although the cause of peptic ulcers has not been fully estab-

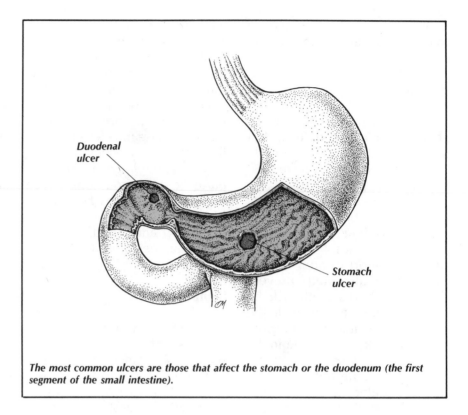

*The most common ulcers are those that affect the stomach or the duodenum (the first segment of the small intestine).*

lished, scientists believe that the more common duodenal ulcers may result from the presence of excessive amounts of digestive juices produced by the stomach. The stomach may increase acidic secretions after coffee, alcohol, aspirin, and certain medications are consumed or after cigarettes are smoked. Therefore, these substances are thought to contribute to ulcers.

The less common stomach ulcers may be due to an inherent weakness in the wall of the stomach. However, this weakness may result from the same environmental conditions that aggravate duodenal ulcers.

Emotional stress may play a role in ulcer development. However, physicians distinguish between stress as a factor by itself and certain ways of dealing with stress that may increase susceptibility to ulcers.

Heredity plays an important role in contributing to ulcers.

Persons who have a family history of ulcers seem to have a greater likelihood of acquiring the condition, as do persons with type O blood. In addition, liver disease, rheumatoid arthritis, and emphysema may increase vulnerability to ulcers.

### Symptoms

Ulcers can produce mild symptoms resembling heartburn or severe pain radiating throughout the upper portion of the body. The most common discomfort of ulcers is a burning sensation in the abdomen above the navel that may feel like hunger pangs. Pain comes about 30 to 120 minutes after eating or in the middle of the night when the stomach is empty. At this time, the acidic stomach juices are more apt to irritate the unprotected nerve endings in the exposed ulcer. Usually, pain subsides after eating or drinking something or taking an antacid to neutralize stomach acid.

Some people experience nausea, vomiting, and constipation. Blood in the feces (discoloring them black), blood in the vomit, extreme weakness, fainting, and excessive thirst are all signs of internal bleeding, and may appear in more advanced cases.

While ulcers are not usually life-threatening, they can cause serious damage if left untreated. Ulcers may corrode nearby blood vessels and cause internal seepage of blood or hemorrhage (massive internal bleeding). A perforated ulcer may penetrate an adjoining organ, causing infection. In addition, scar tissue growing around the ulcer may lead to an intestinal obstruction.

### Diagnosis

Physicians diagnose peptic ulcers primarily on the basis of an x-ray examination after the patient has swallowed a special chalky substance called barium. The barium makes the digestive tract visible on x-ray film, allowing the doctor a view of any abnormalities.

A second diagnostic technique is called gastroscopy. The doctor inserts a gastroscope (a long, flexible, lighted, tubelike instrument) through the mouth and down the esophagus to directly view the lining of the stomach. A gastroscopic examination and a biopsy (removal of a tissue sample for analysis) are necessary to confirm that an apparent ulcer is not actually a cancerous growth.

### Treatment

Treatment of ulcers involves relieving the irritation so that healing is able to progress naturally. Antacids counteract stomach acid and relieve symptoms, but they can cause complications. For example, sodium bicarbonate, a primary antacid ingredient, contains large amounts of sodium, which can aggravate kidney disease or high blood pressure.

For treatment of more problematic ulcers, a physician may prescribe other preparations to promote healing. Anticholinergic drugs delay emptying of the stomach and protect the lining against acidity. Antispasmodic drugs relax digestive tract muscles and relieve tension if stress is a contributing factor. Sucralfate lines the stomach, protecting it against gastric acid. Cimetidine and ranitidine inhibit gastric acid secretion.

Although recent studies have shown that a bland diet is not necessary for ulcer management, such a diet may be recommended until acute symptoms disappear. Thereafter, many doctors suggest avoiding only those foods known to cause stomach distress.

The effect of milk on ulcers is also questionable. Its neutralizing action on stomach acid is mild and temporary at best. Nevertheless, people who substitute milk for known irritants, such as alcohol and caffeine, are less likely to irritate their ulcers.

Most ulcers heal within two to six weeks after treatment begins. To prevent recurrence, patients should still refrain from use of cigarettes, caffeine, alcohol, and other substances that stimulate stomach acid production or irritate the digestive tract lining.

When drug therapy and diet cannot cure an ulcer, surgical repair may be necessary. Surgery is appropriate for ulcers that recur or are life-threatening, such as perforated ulcers. Sometimes, surgeons remove a portion of the stomach and parts of the vagus nerve (which controls digestive secretions) to reduce stomach acid production. Usually, ulcers do not reappear after surgery.

# Ulcerative colitis

Ulcerative colitis is a chronic inflammatory disease of the colon characterized by bloody diarrhea and the development of erosions (open sores) on the lining of the colon.

### Causes

Although there is a familial tendency to develop ulcerative colitis, the cause of the disorder is unknown. Any age group may be affected, but it tends to begin in persons between the ages of 15 and 40.

Among possible contributing factors are infection, immunologic derangement (a breakdown in the body's defense system), lack of protective elements in the bowel wall, nervous or psychological disturbances, and alterations in the connective tissue in the colon.

### Symptoms

The first sign of ulcerative colitis is usually a series of attacks of bloody diarrhea. The attacks can vary in intensity and duration and are usually interspersed with periods of normal bowel movements. The onset of the attacks may be severe, with sudden violent diarrhea, high fever, symptoms of abdominal inflammation, and bacterial invasions. Often, an attack will be preceded by mild lower abdominal cramps and the appearance of small amounts of blood or mucus in the feces.

If ulceration is confined to the rectum and the terminal portion of the colon, the bowel movements may be normal or very hard and dry, with discharges of mucus containing red and white blood cells between stools. If the disorder extends to other portions of the colon, however, stools become looser and more frequent (perhaps 10 to 20 per day), and the patient suffers severe cramps, watery stools, fever, anemia (due to blood loss), and loss of appetite.

### Complications

If the condition persists in a severe form, hemorrhage (internal bleeding) is the most common complication. In toxic colitis, a serious complication, the colon loses muscular tone and dilates almost completely, resulting in perforations of the organ. The risk of colon cancer and cancer of the bile ducts is also increased in patients with ulcerative colitis.

### Diagnosis

Ulcerative colitis is diagnosed with the use of a stool examination and sigmoidoscopy (in which a lighted, flexible, tube-like instrument is inserted into

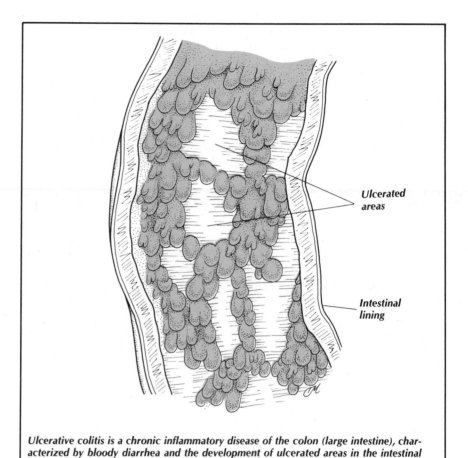

Ulcerated areas

Intestinal lining

*Ulcerative colitis is a chronic inflammatory disease of the colon (large intestine), characterized by bloody diarrhea and the development of ulcerated areas in the intestinal lining.*

the colon for a visual examination of the interior). X-ray studies after a barium enema are indicated, except in cases in which risk of perforation makes the barium enema procedure a potential danger for the patient.

### Treatment

Mild cases of ulcerative colitis may sometimes be treated with adequate physical and mental relaxation (since the disease appears to be stress-related in some patients); a diet low in milk, milk products, nuts, kernels, and seeds; and antidiarrheal medication. More severe cases may respond to the drug sulfasalazine. In cases that do not respond to sulfasalazine therapy, hydrocortisone (an artificial hormone) may be given by enema, along with oral cortisone.

# THE KIDNEYS AND URINARY SYSTEM

The urinary system includes those organs of the body that produce and eliminate urine (a combination of water and waste products that passes out of the body as fluid). By controlling urine flow, the system maintains proper water balance throughout the body. Individual parts of the urinary system monitor the concentration of salts and other necessary nutrients.

## Functions of urinary system organs

The organs most responsible for the control of the balance of chemicals and water in the blood are the two kidneys. The kidneys are bean-shaped structures located in the back of the abdomen. Their chief functions are to filter wastes from the blood and to ensure reabsorption of essential chemicals back into the bloodstream. In the kidneys, waste products combine with water and salts to form urine.

Urine passes from each kidney into the bladder through tubes called ureters. The bladder stores the urine prior to elimination from the body. A sphincter muscle around the exit from the bladder prevents urine from escaping. When the bladder is about half full, the body feels an urge to empty the organ. At this time, the muscle can be relaxed voluntarily to release the urine.

The urethra is a tube that conveys urine from the bladder to the exterior of the body. The female urethra is about an inch and a half long and is enclosed within the body. The male urethra passes through the penis and is approximately eight inches long. For the male, the urethra serves the dual function of transporting urine and semen

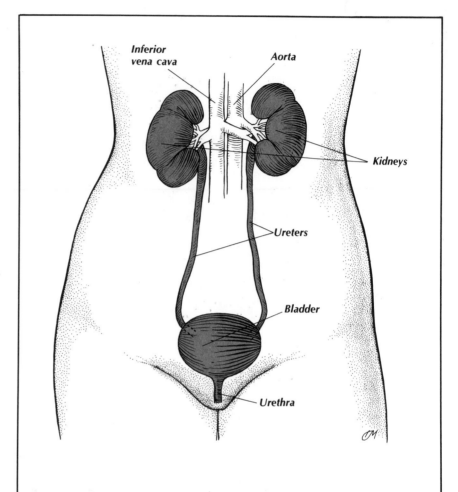

*The role of the urinary system (the female urinary tract is shown here) is to cleanse the blood. Arterial blood is filtered through the kidneys and returned to the circulation. Waste products, plus excess water, are sent through the ureters to the bladder, to be excreted as urine.*

(the fluid from the male reproductive organs). Semen is released during sexual intercourse, at which time urine is blocked from leaving the bladder.

## Disorders of the urinary system

Changes in urine and urinary habits that do not seem to have an obvious cause may be symptoms of disease. Some symptoms that require medical attention are changes in frequency, timing, and control of urination; changes in the quantity and color of urine; and the presence

of pain accompanying urination. A doctor should be contacted immediately if any of the following symptoms is noted: extreme pain while urinating, blood in the urine, a noticeable decrease in frequency of urination (a symptom of kidney failure), marked changes in the color of the urine, or cloudiness in the urine accompanied by pain or fever.

Changes in urine or urinary habits may be caused by a variety of disorders involving the kidneys, urinary tract, bladder, and prostate (a gland that surrounds the male urethra).

Increased frequency may be caused by inflammation of the kidneys, bladder, or urethra; diabetes (a disorder of carbohydrate utilization); or an enlarged prostate gland.

A change in timing of urination, usually in the form of very frequent nighttime awakenings accompanied by the urge to urinate (called nocturia), is often coupled with painful urination, a poor stream, or difficulty in starting urination. These may be symptoms of an enlarged prostate gland or an inflammatory or infectious disease within the urinary tract, as well as tumors or other disorders that result in increased pressure on the bladder.

Difficulty in controlling, starting, and maintaining the flow of urine may also be symptoms of an inflammation of the prostate gland. Inability to hold back urine is a common problem of elderly people, as their control of the sphincter muscle of the bladder weakens. Also affected by this problem are women in the late stage of pregnancy, when the enlarged uterus continuously presses on the bladder.

Changes in the quantity of urine normally produced can also signal disease. Producing an excessive amount of urine (called polyuria) may be a symptom of kidney disease, diabetes, or glandular disorders. Decreased production of urine may indicate the presence of dehydration, internal hemorrhaging, or acute renal failure.

Slight changes in the color and clarity of the urine from day to day are normal, but strikingly obvious color changes and extreme cloudiness may signal infection, tumors, kidney stones, prostate problems, or other abnormalities in the urinary tract.

Pain while urinating, most commonly in the form of a burning sensation felt along the urethra, may be a sign of a lower urinary tract infection. Excruciating pain across the abdomen or the back may signal the presence of kidney stones.

Treatment of urinary problems usually involves treating the underlying cause of the change, which can range from a mild infection to a very serious disease. An accurate diagnosis by a physician is the first step to proper treatment of these disorders.

# Cystitis

Cystitis is an inflammation of the urinary bladder; the term, however, is commonly used to mean bladder infection.

## Causes

Cystitis is usually caused by bacteria that have invaded the urethra and entered the urinary bladder. Women are more susceptible than men because their urethras are so short (approximately one and a half inches long, compared with about eight inches in men), thus presenting less distance for the bacteria to travel. Also, in women the anus and the external openings of the urethra and the vagina (birth canal) are so close together that bacteria can easily migrate from one to another. Almost always, the bacteria responsible are types that normally live harmlessly in the human intestine but that can cause infection if they invade the area around the opening of the urethra and enter the bladder.

Obstruction is also a common cause of urinary tract infection. When obstruction occurs, the bladder may not empty properly. The urine remaining in the bladder can then create a breeding ground for bacteria to multiply. Causes of obstruction include tumors, kidney stones, and an enlarged prostate gland.

The urethral lining may have a defect that allows bacteria to enter the urinary tract. For example, frequent intercourse may traumatize the urethra, disrupting its lining and making it more susceptible to infection.

Cystitis in men is uncommon. When it does occur, the usual cause is an infection that has spread from an inflamed prostate gland or that has developed in the bladder because of an enlarged prostate.

Urethritis, an infection or inflammation of the urethra, often sets the stage for the development of cystitis. Urethritis occurs in both men and women and is usually acquired through sexual intercourse with an infected individual. Gonorrheal and nongonococcal urethritis are the two most common types.

## Symptoms

The symptoms of cystitis include a painful sensation or burning on urination, a frequent and often urgent need to urinate (sometimes causing nighttime awakening), and, occasionally, low back pain. These symptoms, along with bloody urine, indicate hemorrhagic cystitis, which is relatively common in women. Although quite frightening, this is most often a minor, easily treatable condition. In men, however, bloody urine is not usually attributable to hemorrhagic cystitis and demands immediate investigation. With the exception of visibly bloody urine, all of the symptoms mentioned can be present in urethritis, which is also commonly ac-

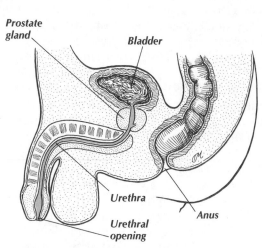

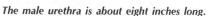

Prostate gland

Bladder

Urethra

Anus

Urethral opening

*The male urethra is about eight inches long.*

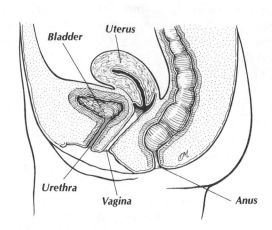

Bladder

Uterus

Urethra

Vagina

Anus

*The female urethra is about an inch and a half long.*

*Cystitis is nearly ten times more common in women than in men. Because the female urethra is much shorter than the male urethra, infecting bacteria have a shorter distance to travel in women.*

companied by a discharge. High fever, chills, and back pain (usually one-sided), with or without any other symptoms, usually indicate pyelonephritis (kidney infection), which demands the immediate attention of a doctor.

## Diagnosis

The diagnosis of urinary infection rests on the urinalysis and urine culture results. The presence of moderate to large numbers of white blood cells, along with at least 100,000 colonies of any one type of bacterium in a culture, provides conclusive evidence of infection.

Not infrequently, it is difficult to determine which part of the urinary tract is infected, or if there is infection at all. In women, some white blood cells and bacteria are usually present at the opening of the urethra. Therefore, in order to keep the urine specimen free of these contaminants, a midstream spec-

imen is usually requested. The first spurt of urine is thought to wash away the urethral contaminants, and the rest of the urine sample is then normally uncontaminated. For the vast majority of cases of simple cystitis, this procedure is adequate; however, if a question exists as to the validity of the specimen or if for some reason the specimen must be absolutely free of contaminants, a catheter (thin, flexible tube) may be inserted into the bladder through the urethra. In women, this is an easy procedure and eliminates vaginal and anal contaminants. If the catheterized specimen is free of pus and bacteria, the symptoms are the result of another condition—commonly vaginitis or urethritis. In a man, the procedure is somewhat more difficult and often not necessary. If prostatitis is the suspected cause of the infection, the physician can insert a gloved finger into the anus and feel the gland directly. A specimen of prostatic fluid is usually obtained

(by massaging the gland at the time of examination) through the urethra for culture.

Appropriate treatment is dependent on correct identification of the site of infection of the urinary tract. The experience of the physician, the patient's history of signs and symptoms (such as discharge, back pain, or fever), and the findings obtained with more sophisticated diagnostic techniques are all important in making the correct diagnosis.

In difficult chronic cases of cystitis in both men and women, in which the cause of recurring infection may be an obstruction or a drainage problem, special x-ray studies are necessary; contrast material is placed in the bladder by means of a catheter, and x-ray pictures are taken of the bladder and the urethra during urination. With such studies, narrowing of a portion of the urethra, the presence of kidney stones, and incomplete emptying of the bladder (which promotes cystitis) may be detected.

The bladder may also be examined by cystoscopy (an examination by means of a flexible, lighted, tubelike instrument called a cystoscope, which is inserted through the urethra). Most often these procedures are preceded by an intravenous pyelogram, in which contrast material injected through a vein is eliminated by the kidneys, providing an x-ray picture of the kidneys, ureters, and bladder.

### Treatment

Treatment of first-time cystitis is usually by means of antibiotics taken by mouth for seven to ten days. Occasionally, large single doses of drugs are used. Recurrences may be treated in the same way if they are due to a different organism. If the same organism is causing the trouble, the condition may require larger doses of medication or long-term treatment (for up to four to six weeks). If cystitis persists, daily doses of medications may be necessary for up to six months. It is important that dosage instructions be followed exactly, because a person is vulnerable to a new infection or reinfection if the entire course of recommended drug therapy is not completed.

Some individuals are prone to repeated episodes of cystitis or upper urinary tract infection. If there is an anatomic defect, such as a narrowed urethra, dilation (enlarging) may be needed. If stones are present, they may have to be removed. If an infected prostate is the source of infection, antibiotics are usually tried first; surgery is a last resort. If no obvious cause of recurrent cystitis is found, low doses of antibiotics may be prescribed for long periods of time (this is called prophylactic, or preventive, therapy).

### Prevention

Women may be able to guard against recurrent cystitis by front-to-back wiping with toilet tissue and cleansing with soap and water after each bowel movement. They should also try to urinate immediately after sexual intercourse to wash away infecting bacteria that might enter the urethra. Loose, absorbent underclothes allow evaporation and absorption of body fluids and thus help prevent infection. Both men and women should drink plenty of fluids and urinate frequently, completely emptying the bladder each time.

# Dialysis

Dialysis is the removal of wastes and other undesirable substances from the blood by means of a special membrane that is selective in what it allows to cross. In the healthy body, this task is performed by the kidneys.

### Hemodialysis

In a patient suffering from temporary or permanent kidney failure, cleansing of the blood can be done with an artificial kidney machine; this is known as hemodialysis. Two plastic tubes, one connected to an artery and one to a vein, are implanted in the patient's arm or leg. During dialysis, which can take three to five hours per treatment, blood from the artery tube enters the machine and comes into contact with a thin membrane. Wastes from the blood pass through the membrane into circulating fluid on the other side of the membrane. The blood cells themselves, along with other protein elements, cannot cross the membrane. The cleansed blood is then piped back into the patient through the vein tube.

### Peritoneal dialysis

In peritoneal dialysis, the patient's own peritoneum (lining of the abdominal cavity) is used as the dialysis membrane. A sterile plastic catheter (tube) is passed into the abdominal cavity, and a solution of glucose (a form of sugar) and mineral salts is periodically injected into and withdrawn from the cavity. The fluid comes into contact with delicate blood vessels in the peritoneum. Because of the difference in concentration of certain chemical elements in the blood and the dialysis solution, wastes from the blood are forced through the membrane of the peritoneal wall. The dialysis liquid is periodically withdrawn and replaced with fresh solution.

### Continuous ambulatory peritoneal dialysis

A new method called continuous ambulatory peritoneal dialysis has greatly lowered the cost of dialysis and made it more convenient. It can be done at home by the patient without the complex equipment and the skilled supervision that has made machine dialysis so expensive. A tube is surgically implanted in the patient, just below the navel. About every four to five hours and just before bedtime, the patient drains out the old fluid and empties a bag of fresh dialysis fluid into the abdominal cavity through a tube. The fluid remains in the cavity, soaking up wastes from the blood, while the patient sleeps or goes about his usual daily activities. The procedure takes only about 30 minutes each time, and enables the patient to be independent and mobile.

## Glomerulo-nephritis

Each kidney contains more than a million filtering units called nephrons, in which wastes are drawn from the blood to form urine. In each nephron is a network of capillaries (tiny blood vessels) called a glomerulus. Glomerulitis is an inflammation of the glomeruli (the plural of glomerulus), which interferes with the normal functioning of the kidney. First described in 1827 by the English physician Richard Bright, the condition used to be called Bright's disease, but doctors today are more likely to refer to it as glomerulonephritis (from *glomerulus; nephro,* referring to the kidney; and *itis,* meaning inflammation).

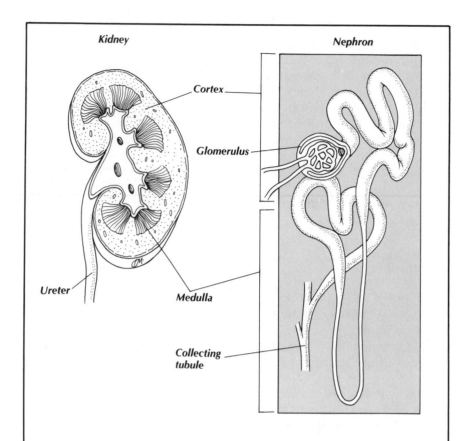

Each kidney contains more than a million filtering units called nephrons, in which wastes and excess water are drawn from the blood to form urine. In each nephron is a network of tiny blood vessels called a glomerulus. The glomeruli (plural of glomerulus) are located in the cortex (outer portion) of the kidney; their tubules lead into the medulla (central portion), from which the urine drains into the ureter.

### Causes

Glomerulonephritis can be caused by an infection in the kidneys, but most often it is due to an allergic or immune response to infections in other parts of the body. Although many different kinds of infections can lead to glomerulonephritis, including pneumonia, bacterial infection of the heart, syphilis, malaria, hepatitis, and measles, the most common cause is infection of the throat, tonsils, or skin by certain types of *Streptococcus* bacteria. The immune response to the infec-

tion occurs as an inflammation of the capillaries in the glomeruli. The capillaries become congested and surrounded by blood cells and pus. Fluid builds up in surrounding tissues, sometimes causing the kidneys to enlarge. Protein, which should remain in the blood, is discharged into the urine through the diseased glomeruli, and there is edema (fluid buildup) in body tissues. These two signs—edema and the presence of albumin (a type of protein) in the urine—are the chief indicators of the disease.

If the disease continues to progress, the tiny arteries in the kidneys become thickened and scarred so that some can no

longer carry blood. The parts of the kidneys that they serve shrink. The eventual result of this process over many years may be total kidney failure. The disease affects both kidneys.

### Symptoms

Symptoms of glomerulonephritis usually begin one to three weeks after an initial infection, such as strep throat. The patient has headaches, a mild fever, a puffy face, pain in the area between the ribs and the hips, and decreased urine output. The urine may be bloody, smoky, or coffee-colored. Shortness of breath may occur, together with increased heartbeat and a rise in blood pressure. Detection of protein and red blood cells in the urine confirms the diagnosis. In extreme cases, bloating due to accumulation of fluids can cause the symptoms of heart failure, including rapid heartbeat, heart enlargement, and congestion of the lungs.

### Treatment

Treatment consists of bed rest until one to two weeks after tests of blood, blood pressure, and the urine indicate that the kidneys are back to normal. Sodium and protein may be restricted or even forbidden for a time. Fluids are restricted until the output of urine returns to normal. Heart failure is treated with restriction of salt and water and with use of oxygen and the drug digitalis. Any infection is treated promptly with antibiotics. The overwhelming majority of patients with glomerulonephritis due to streptococcal infection recover fully.

Guarding against infection, injury, and fatigue can help prevent flare-ups of the disease. Intake of protein may have to be limited, depending on how well the kidneys are working. A return to normal activity is desirable, but strenuous exercise should be avoided, to prevent fatigue.

If the disease is still present after one to two years, it may be considered chronic. Fortunately, this occurs in only 5 percent to 20 percent of patients. Typically, the damage to the kidneys continues to progress, but so slowly that the patient is without symptoms; the only evidence may be the presence of protein and red and white blood cells in the urine. A normal life may be possible for 20 or 30 years, until the kidneys can no longer function. At that time, replacement with a kidney transplant or periodic cleansing of the blood with dialysis is necessary.

# Incontinence

Urinary incontinence is the loss of voluntary bladder control. It occurs frequently in children and in older persons.

### Causes

Most often, incontinence is caused by some underlying condition, such as obstruction, infection, or inflammation of any portion of the urinary tract. Successful treatment of the underlying cause clears up the problem of incontinence.

Stress incontinence is the leakage of urine on coughing, sneezing, straining, or laughing. This type of incontinence is common in women whose sphincter muscles have been weakened by childbirth.

### Treatment

Although the first step in treating incontinence is to detect and correct any underlying problem, it is important to remember that many children do not establish complete bladder control before they are four or five years old. Children of any age may have occasional accidents, especially if they are ill or exhausted.

Persons who have problems with incontinence can help themselves by going to the bathroom often and regularly, by arranging sleeping and living quarters near bathrooms, and by wearing clothes that can be removed quickly and easily. It may also help to keep a bedpan or urinal next to the bed and to drink only a small amount of water, if any, before going to bed.

Drugs are available to aid in controlling urination in certain conditions.

# Kidney failure

Kidney failure occurs when certain abnormalities within the kidneys prevent them from functioning normally, leading to chemical imbalances and the buildup of toxic (poisonous) substances and fluid within the body. This may eventually lead to organ damage and possibly death.

### Forms of kidney failure

There are two forms of kidney failure. In the acute form, there is a sudden malfunction of the kidneys, leading to a rapid buildup of toxins and fluid within the body, often within several hours. In the chronic form of kidney failure, there is a slow, progressive malfunction of the kidneys, leading to a buildup of toxins and fluid, often occurring over several months to years.

### Causes

Numerous conditions can cause kidney failure. High blood pressure, kidney stones or other urinary tract blockage, adverse reactions to chemicals or drugs, serious injury, infectious disease, shock following surgery, heart attack, blood transfusion with incompatible blood, severe dehydration (excessive loss of body fluid), complications during pregnancy, immunologic disease, and congenital (existing from birth) kidney defects may all lead to kidney failure.

## Symptoms

The most characteristic symptoms of kidney failure are a reduction in the volume of urine produced and edema (excessive accumulation of fluid in the tissues). As a result, the feet and hands and the area around the eyes may swell and become puffy. The urine may be bloody, wine-colored, or cloudy.

More generalized signs of kidney failure include drowsiness and fatigue, loss of appetite, diarrhea, nausea, dry skin, and difficulty in breathing. Delirium, coma, and death will eventually occur in untreated cases.

## Diagnosis

Analysis of blood and urine samples is used to diagnose kidney failure. Urine tests may show that white blood cells, sugars, or protein has slipped through the normally efficient filtering system of the kidneys. Similarly, when the kidneys are not filtering waste materials from the blood, blood analysis will detect waste products remaining in the blood. X-ray studies or ultrasound scans of the kidneys may identify structural abnormalities or blockage.

## Treatment

In the case of acute kidney failure, treatment begins with diagnosing and correcting the cause of the kidney damage and restoring normal kidney function as rapidly as possible. For example, shock may be treated with blood transfusions, and kidney stones may be removed.

Bed rest is essential as the kidneys recover. Limiting fluid intake, except in cases of unusual fluid loss from diarrhea or vomiting, relieves the strain on the sensitive kidneys. Physicians often recommend a low-protein diet to reduce the extra strain required to process the waste products of protein metabolism in the kidneys.

Should these measures prove ineffective, the patient may be helped by dialysis. Dialysis is a process that cleans and filters toxic substances from the blood with an artificial kidney machine. Most dialysis patients receive treatment by traveling to the hospital three times a week. However, newer portable techniques allow more freedom for dialysis patients.

In the case of chronic kidney failure, destruction of the kidney has progressed so much that treatment cannot bring kidney function back to normal. Treatment of these patients involves a diet low in salt and protein and dialysis at least three times a week. Dialysis will offer a chance to prolong life, but it is not a cure; only surgically replacing the damaged kidneys will cure the condition. In recent years, methods of matching kidney donors with recipients have improved, thereby limiting transplant rejection and serious complications. Today, kidney transplants are a highly successful treatment for chronic kidney failure.

# Kidney stones

Kidney stones are deposits of mineral or organic substances that form in the kidneys. When abnormally high levels of certain minerals, such as calcium, are in the urine, they may condense into hard masses, forming stones in the kidneys or urinary tract. The stones may be as small as a tiny pebble or as large as a walnut.

## Causes

Increased levels of calcium in urine may come from drinking large quantities of milk. Eating foods rich in vitamin D, which helps the body absorb calcium, can also contribute to an overaccumulation of calcium. In addition, fractured bones can release extra calcium, which may condense into stones in the kidneys.

Certain disorders encourage buildup of mineral deposits in the kidneys. Gout is a joint disease that results from high blood levels of uric acid (a waste product from the breakdown of protein), which may crystallize into stones in the urine. Urinary infections that impede bladder function can also cause retention of urine, which then harbors higher concentrations of elements that can solidify into stones. In addition, overactive parathyroid glands (endocrine glands that regulate calcium absorption) permit increased mineral absorption into the body.

Middle-aged men and persons with gout or chronic urinary tract infections are more susceptible to the development of kidney stones. However, in many cases, no one can pinpoint the cause of the kidney stones.

## Symptoms

Kidney stones may be present for years and never produce any symptoms. Problems arise when

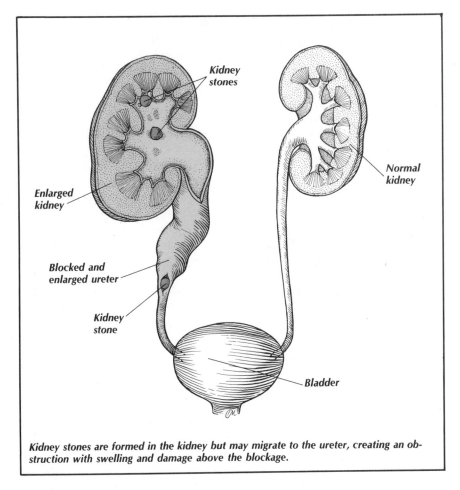

Kidney stones
Enlarged kidney
Blocked and enlarged ureter
Kidney stone
Normal kidney
Bladder

*Kidney stones are formed in the kidney but may migrate to the ureter, creating an obstruction with swelling and damage above the blockage.*

stones. Since calcium contributes to kidney stones in most cases, the diet should be low in milk products and foods containing vitamin D. Patients with gout should decrease their protein intake, since uric acid is a byproduct of protein digestion.

Medications may be taken to inhibit absorption of calcium from the blood, but there are no drugs that will dissolve kidney stones that have already formed. A painkiller may be prescribed if the pain from the movement of a stone is too great.

For kidney stones too large to pass, surgical removal may be necessary. A new, nonsurgical method of treating kidney stones called extracorporeal shockwave lithotripsy is becoming more widely available. With this technique, tiny shock waves are used to pulverize the stones so that they can pass out of the urinary tract relatively painlessly.

### Prevention

To prevent recurrence of kidney stones, patients need to drink about three or four quarts of water a day to dilute their urine. Drinking large amounts of fluids, sometimes throughout the night, reduces urine concentration so that stones cannot form. Surplus water can also flush the system of any small stones.

# Proteinuria

Proteinuria is a symptom of kidney problems marked by an excess of proteins in the urine.

### Causes

Proteinuria can be caused by, among other conditions, kidney

a stone becomes so large that it obstructs or irritates a part of the kidney or causes problems as it passes out of the kidney. Symptoms may include severe pain and tenderness over the affected kidney, frequent and painful urination, nausea, blood in the urine, fever, chills, and extreme exhaustion.

A more serious condition can develop if a stone becomes lodged in a ureter, producing excruciating pain across the back, abdomen, and reproductive organs. If blockage occurs in the urethra, urine output decreases. The trapped urine may back up, distending and injuring the urinary tract. This situation requires immediate medical treatment.

Kidney stones that are too small to be noticed may still cause damage to delicate tissues in the urinary tract.

### Diagnosis

To determine the type of kidney stone formation, a physician analyzes blood and urine samples. An ultrasound or x-ray study may reveal the location and nature of the stones.

### Treatment

The recurrence of kidney stones may often be controlled by diet. Reducing or eliminating intake of foods with high levels of stone-producing minerals can prevent worsening of the condition and the formation of new malfunction, heart disease, the consumption of certain foods, pregnancy, and overexertion from certain sports, such as jogging and marathon running.

## Symptoms

Most cases of proteinuria in adults are discovered unexpectedly in a routine physical examination. Usually, the person will have experienced no symptoms and will be essentially healthy, with no evidence of kidney disease.

## Treatment

Treatment of proteinuria depends on its cause and severity. In about half of the diagnosed cases, proteinuria ceases spontaneously within a year to several years. However, there are instances in which the patient continues to lose greater and greater amounts of protein in the urine. Eventually, high blood pressure and kidney failure may develop.

When proteinuria is constant, measurements of protein excretion should be made on a regular basis. Alteration in the protein level should be followed up with other appropriate testing of kidney function.

# Pyelonephritis

Pyelonephritis is an inflammation of both the kidney tissue and the renal pelvis (the funnel-shaped expansion of the upper end of the ureter where it joins the kidney).

There are two types of pyelonephritis, descending and ascending. In the descending type, the bacteria reach the kidney through the bloodstream, infecting first the kidney tissues themselves and then moving downward to infect the renal pelvis of the kidney. In the more common ascending type, the bladder is infected first, and the infection then spreads upward to the kidney.

## Causes

Most cases of pyelonephritis are caused by bacterial infection. Conditions that increase the likelihood of such an infection include scars from previous infections, urinary tract infections, abnormal growth of the prostate gland, kidney stones, tumors, stagnation of urine due to backflow from the bladder, diabetes mellitus (a condition characterized by the presence of excess sugar in the bloodstream), and pregnancy.

## Symptoms

Symptoms of acute pyelonephritis include fever, back pain, difficulty in urinating, a burning sensation on urination, mental confusion, nausea, vomiting, and, in extreme cases, loss of consciousness. Although some cases of chronic (recurring) pyelonephritis can be traced to an initial attack, many patients will have no evidence of past or current infections.

## Treatment

Acute pyelonephritis is treated with antibiotics given orally or intravenously. Recurrent episodes should be treated with an appropriate antibiotic. Chronic pyelonephritis requires careful management and frequent re-evaluation. Patients are generally treated with an antibiotic even during periods when they feel no symptoms and usually receive long-term therapy after that.

# THE ENDOCRINE SYSTEM

The endocrine system comprises a number of glands that produce hormones with a varied array of vital functions. Hormones are chemical substances that are secreted by organs or by cells of organs in one part of the body and are carried by the bloodstream to other organs or tissues, where they control or regulate the development or function of those structures.

Endocrine glands are also called ductless glands because they secrete hormones directly into the bloodstream. In contrast, exocrine glands release their secretions through ducts (for example, the sweat glands produce fluid that flows to the skin's surface through tiny tube-like sweat ducts).

Hormones can be considered chemical messengers. They are targeted at specific cells in the body, and their arrival in those cells causes specific activities to occur. One of the major tasks of hormones is to coordinate the activities of organ systems. For example, when a person has to run or do other physical exercise, the hormone epinephrine acts on the heart to increase its rate and force of contraction and on the blood vessels to increase blood flow to the muscles and decrease blood flow to the gastrointestinal tract (so that more blood will reach the muscles, where the need is temporarily greater). Hormones also help control the type and rate of body growth and metabolism, and they help the body maintain a consistent internal environment.

The endocrine system has a large influence on the way we feel and act. In turn, our energy and other needs in any given situation set the activity of the endocrine system. This feedback relationship is crucial in maintaining our general well-being.

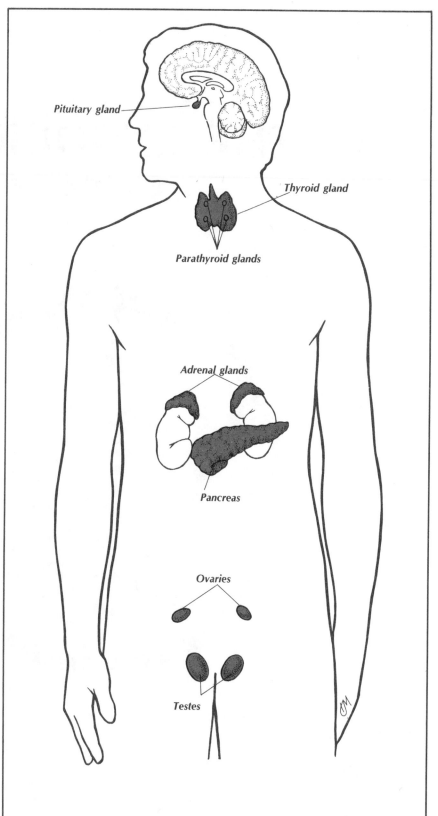

The endocrine system is composed of glands that release vital hormones into the blood. (On this illustration of the male endocrine system, the ovaries are shown only to indicate placement.)

## Adrenal glands

The adrenal glands are critical to normal body functions, such as maintenance of fluid balance, reaction to stress, and reproduction. There are two adrenal glands, each of which lies above a kidney. The adrenal glands have two distinct parts: the cortex (outer layer), which secretes steroid hormones, and the medulla (inner part), which secretes epinephrine and norepinephrine. The more than 30 steroid hormones regulate a wide array of processes throughout the body. Epinephrine and norepinephrine are responsible for the changes in heart rate, blood pressure, and level of usable glucose (a form of sugar) that are necessary to cope with stress.

## Pancreas

The pancreas is located within the abdominal cavity. Specialized cells in the pancreas produce two hormones, insulin and glucagon, needed to maintain stable blood sugar levels in the body. Insulin helps body cells utilize glucose for energy, thereby reducing the amount of sugar in the bloodstream. To balance this action, the hormone glucagon stimulates the liver to release its stored sugar into the blood, thereby raising the blood sugar levels.

The pancreas also functions in digestion. Nonendocrine cells in the pancreas produce special chemicals called enzymes, which are secreted directly into the small intestine through ducts. These enzymes help break down proteins, carbohydrates (sugars and starches), and fats in the small intestine.

This dual activity of the pancreas means that it functions as both an endocrine and an exocrine organ.

## Pituitary gland

The pituitary gland is a small organ located just beneath the base of the brain, between the two frontal lobes and directly above a cavity called the sphenoidal sinus. It is sometimes called the master gland because all other endocrine glands come under its control. Its job is to receive messages about the need for a particular hormone and to secrete either the hormone or substances that cause the manufacture and release of the hormone.

The anterior (front) lobe of the pituitary gland secretes somatotropin (also known as growth hormone), which affects the body's general growth; thyrotropic hormone (also known as thyroid-stimulating hormone), which acts on the thyroid gland to stimulate production of thyroid hormones; adrenocorticotropic hormone (ACTH), which stimulates the adrenal cortex; follicle-stimulating hormone and luteinizing hormone, which are necessary for maturation and release of egg and sperm cells; and prolactin, which acts on the mammary glands to promote the secretion of milk.

The posterior lobe of the pituitary gland secretes oxytocin, which stimulates smooth muscle tissue to contract and is of critical importance during childbirth, and vasopressin, which regulates kidney function with respect to water balance.

## Sex glands

The primary responsibility for hormone production for the reproductive system lies with the testes (male sex glands) and ovaries (female sex glands).

The testes are two oval organs in the scrotum (the pouch of skin behind the penis). They produce sperm and sex hormones that govern the male secondary sex characteristics, such as facial hair growth.

The two ovaries are located in the pelvis. They secrete the hormones estrogen and progesterone, which govern ovulation (monthly release of an egg from an ovary) and the female secondary sex characteristics, such as breast development.

## Thyroid and parathyroid glands

The thyroid gland is located in front of the throat above the top of the breastbone. It consists of two main lobes on either side of the trachea (windpipe), which are connected by a narrow band of tissue called the isthmus. The hormones secreted by the thyroid influence the rate of metabolism (the chemical processes in the body having to do with energy production).

The four parathyroid glands are located on the back and side of each lobe of the thyroid gland. Their secretion, parathyroid hormone, controls calcium levels in the blood.

# Addison's disease

Addison's disease is a condition that occurs when the adrenal cortex fails to produce enough of its hormones.

## Causes

Formerly, the cause of this disease in most cases was tuberculosis or a fungal infection. However, in recent years, the disease is more likely to be idiopathic (of unknown cause). One theory is that most cases are due to autoimmune destruction of the adrenal cortex (that is, the body produces antibodies against its own tissues). Other known causes include partial destruction of the adrenal cortex by cancer, surgery, degeneration of the tissue, or deposition of a substance called amyloid. A similar condition known as secondary adrenal insufficiency is caused by failure of the pituitary gland to produce enough adrenocorticotropic hormone (ACTH), which stimulates the adrenal cortex to produce its hormones.

### Symptoms

Early symptoms of Addison's disease are weakness, fatigue, and a tendency to become faint when rising suddenly from a bed or chair. Increased pigmentation of the skin, producing a "tan" all over the body, on exposed and unexposed areas alike, with even darker pigmentation on creases and bony pressure points, occurs in most cases. In certain places the tan may be broken by completely white patches, known as vitiligo. Black freckles appear on the forehead, face, shoulders, and neck. There may be discoloration around the nipples, and the mucous membranes of the mouth may have dark-blue patches.

Symptoms that may appear later include weight loss, dehydration (excessive loss of body fluids), low blood pressure, loss of appetite, nausea, vomiting, diarrhea, dizziness, and inability to keep warm.

The most alarming symptoms are those of a condition called adrenal crisis, which requires immediate attention and hospitalization. Signs of this are extreme weakness; severe pains in the lower back, abdomen, or legs; shock (collapse of the circulatory system); and renal shutdown (kidney failure). Such a crisis may be brought on by severe stress, such as may be caused by infection, injury, or surgery, or by a loss of salt through perspiration during hot weather.

### Diagnosis

One laboratory sign of Addison's disease is a high level of ACTH but a low level of cortisol (one of the adrenal gland hormones) in the blood. This indicates that the pituitary gland is working overtime, stimulating the adrenal cortex with ACTH to produce cortisol, but that the cortex is failing to produce it.

### Treatment

The basic treatment for Addison's disease is to provide steroid hormones, principally cortisone, to replace those not being produced by the adrenal cortex. An additional steroid drug may be prescribed to promote retention of salt, and thereby water, in tissues and blood, so that the low blood pressure of severe Addison's disease can be avoided.

The outlook for patients receiving hormone treatment is excellent. Continued medical supervision is necessary to prevent emergencies caused by a sudden withdrawal of treatment or by an increased need for hormones because of infection, injury, surgery, pregnancy, or other stress on the body. It is important to avoid infection and to treat infection that develops as soon as possible. At all times, patients should carry a card or wear a bracelet describing the condition and the need for cortisone. It is also critical to take the medication exactly as prescribed and to be monitored by a physician who can increase or decrease the dosage as the need arises. With proper care, a person with Addison's disease can lead a nearly normal life.

# Corticosteroids

Corticosteroids are hormones produced in the cortex of the adrenal glands in response to stimulation by adrenocorticotropic hormone (ACTH), which is secreted by the pituitary gland. There are more than 30 corticosteroids, which regulate essential processes throughout the body. They are divided into three groups: mineralocorticoids, glucocorticoids, and androgens (male sex hormones).

### Natural forms

Mineralocorticoids are involved in maintaining salt and water balance in the body. Without these hormones, the tissues and blood would become depleted of salt and water; the resultant decrease in blood volume would cause a drop in blood pressure that could lead to shock (collapse of the circulatory system).

Glucocorticoids help regulate the body's use and reserves of sugars and proteins, among other complex metabolic processes. They also participate in the inflammatory response and the body's reaction to stress. The most important of these hormones is cortisol, which plays a major role in protein breakdown and formation, blood sugar control, and reduction of inflammation, and is necessary to mount an effective response against severe stress due to disease or injury.

Androgens (which are also produced in the testes) stimulate the development of the male secondary sex characteristics, such as beard growth and increased muscle mass.

### Drug forms

Pharmacologic preparations of both ACTH and corticosteroids are used to treat disease in the same way that the natural hormones would or as substitute or supplemental hormones for patients who have lost the ability to manufacture their own. The primary difference is that ACTH acts less directly and more generally than corticosteroid drugs. ACTH stimulates the adrenal glands to enlarge and secrete more of all the steroids that they produce, rather than any one specific hormone. Corticosteroid drugs can be administered to the part of the body that needs them most. For example, a dab of hydrocortisone cream will eliminate a rash, and a hydrocortisone injection will diminish the swelling of a painful knee joint, generally with little effect on the rest of the body. Sometimes, however, corticosteroids are considered for generalized use throughout the body. Corticosteroids have an advantage over ACTH in that they can be taken by mouth and may be given in doses that far exceed what the adrenal glands can produce. ACTH must be injected because it would otherwise be destroyed by digestive enzymes, which do not affect the corticosteroids.

# Cushing's syndrome

Cushing's syndrome is a group of abnormalities resulting from an excess of the hormones produced by the adrenal cortex. The hormones produced in excess are chiefly cortisol, which has many complex functions; various hormones that regulate the body's use of sugars and proteins; male sex hormones; and a hormone that controls the distribution of fluids and salts in the body.

### Causes

In most cases, Cushing's syndrome is caused by excess production of adrenocorticotropic hormone (ACTH), which is normally manufactured by the pituitary gland to stimulate production of hormones by the adrenal glands. This excess of ACTH can be caused by an ACTH-producing tumor in another organ, such as the lung or pancreas; by overmedication with ACTH or corticosteroid drugs; by tiny, nonmalignant ACTH-producing tumors on the pituitary gland; or by a tumor (usually nonmalignant) on the adrenal gland. The effect of too much ACTH, for whatever reason, is overgrowth of tissue in the adrenal cortex, resulting in overproduction of all its hormones. Since these hormones regulate essential processes throughout the body, excess production causes widespread disorders.

### Symptoms

One of the most obvious signs of Cushing's syndrome is the

moon-shaped face, caused by excess fluid in the tissues. Because of deposition of excess fat, the trunk of the body is obese (although the arms and legs are thin), and there are fat pads over the shoulders and neck, producing a "buffalo hump." Purple "stretch marks" on the skin (usually of the abdomen), poor wound healing, easy bruising, muscle weakness, fractures in weakened bones, and emotional instability may also be part of the syndrome. Hairiness, acne, and decreased or absent menstruation may occur in women, due to the increase in male hormones. Diabetes and high blood pressure are also very common.

### Diagnosis

Diagnosis of Cushing's syndrome requires measurement of adrenal cortex hormones in the blood and urine. In normal persons, cortisol levels in the blood are high on awakening but decrease during the day; in the person with Cushing's syndrome, cortisol levels are high all the time. Various tests can determine whether the cause of the syndrome is a tumor of the pituitary gland (in which case the disorder is known as Cushing's disease) or is a tumor on the adrenal gland or elsewhere. Tumors on the adrenal glands may be identified by x-rays, ultrasound, and CT scanning (a special x-ray technique that provides three-dimensional images). CT scans and other special x-rays of the head can often locate tumors of the pituitary gland.

### Treatment

Cushing's syndrome is treated by restoring a normal balance of hormones. This may involve surgery, radiation treatments, or drugs. Tumors on the adrenal glands are removed by surgery. If there is a tumor on just one adrenal gland, the other gland usually shrinks and ceases normal productivity. Hormone supplements are usually given before surgery and must be taken for weeks or months after surgery until the second gland recovers normal function. In a rapidly worsening case of Cushing's syndrome in which the cortex is greatly enlarged on both sides, one treatment is to remove both adrenal glands. This is usually a last-resort measure, however; more commonly, another method, such as chemotherapy (drug treatments), radiation treatments of the pituitary gland (to weaken it and lower its output of ACTH), or removal of any adenomas (nonmalignant growths) on the pituitary gland, is tried first. If other measures fail, the adrenal glands are removed, and the patient must take daily supplements of adrenal cortex hormones for the rest of his life.

If Cushing's syndrome is being caused by production of ACTH by a tumor in a part of the body other than the adrenal glands, the cancer is removed, if possible. However, in many cases it is inoperable, in which case drugs to suppress production of the adrenal glands are given.

Cushing's syndrome is a very serious, possibly fatal, disease unless it is detected and treated early. The outlook is best for those whose condition is caused by noncancerous growths and who receive early treatment.

Those who must take replacement hormones after treatment should carry a medical identification card and immediately tell their doctor about any infections, injuries, or stressful situations that might require an increase in hormone dosage. They should also report signs of underdosage, such as weakness, dizziness, or fatigue, as well as signs of overdosage, such as swollen tissues and rapid weight gain. Anyone whose adrenal glands have been removed must always take replacement hormones; stopping these medications for any length of time is fatal.

# Diabetes mellitus

Diabetes mellitus, often called sugar diabetes, is a condition in which the body is unable to properly process carbohydrates (sugars and starches), which are the body's major source of energy.

## Cause

Normally, digestion causes carbohydrates to release a form of sugar called glucose into the blood. As the blood glucose level rises, the pancreas is stimulated to secrete the hormone insulin. Insulin acts to reduce the sugar content in the blood by transporting glucose from the blood to body cells, where it is used for fuel, or to the liver, where it is stored until needed for fuel.

When the pancreas produces insufficient insulin or the body

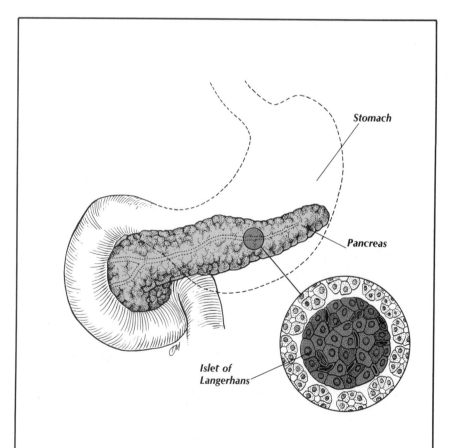

*The islets of Langerhans in the pancreas secrete insulin, the hormone that helps the cells utilize sugar as fuel. One type of diabetes results from a defect in the islets of Langerhans, which causes decreased production of insulin.*

cannot use the insulin it manufactures, diabetes results. The glucose concentration in the blood increases because glucose circulates throughout the body without being absorbed. Eventually, the kidneys filter glucose from the blood, and urine carries the excess sugar from the body.

## Types

There are two major forms of diabetes. Type I (or insulin-dependent) diabetes results from a defect of unknown origin in the islets of Langerhans (the areas in the pancreas where insulin is produced). This form of diabetes can develop in young children.

With Type II (or non-insulin-dependent) diabetes, either the pancreas functions inadequately or the body is unable to use insulin efficiently. Sometimes, a shortage of insulin-receptor cells (sites throughout the body where the interaction of glucose and insulin occurs) allows the insulin to be present in the bloodstream without working properly. Obesity often contributes to the problem because the presence of excess fat cells leads to increased resistance to insulin. Type II diabetes, which appears most often in adults over the age of 40, may evolve from a gradual slowing of insulin production within the pancreas. In addition, other disorders of the endocrine system may cause hormonal imbalances that disturb glucose regulation.

Research shows that people who have a family history of Type II diabetes may have a greater tendency to acquire the condition. Women are more likely to be affected, but for all adults, the risk of developing Type II diabetes doubles with every decade after the age of 40.

In some women, pregnancy triggers diabetes. The condition usually subsides after childbirth. However, women who show signs of diabetes during pregnancy and deliver babies weighing over ten pounds have a greater risk of diabetes later in life.

## Complications

Although patients with diabetes can usually control the condition, untreated diabetes can lead to serious complications. Extremely high blood sugar levels place great strain on other organs. Diabetes may accelerate atherosclerosis (clogging of the arteries). Insufficient blood supply contributes to heart attack, stroke, kidney disease, eye disorders, impotence, gangrene (death of tissue due to inadequate blood circulation), and even death.

## Symptoms

Symptoms of Type I diabetes are excessive thirst and urination, fatigue, altered vision, fainting, irritability, and slow healing of cuts and bruises. Weight loss may occur despite constant hunger and voracious eating.

The same symptoms may signal Type II diabetes, or no symptoms may appear at all. Physicians frequently detect this form when they perform routine examinations or tests for other problems.

## Diagnosis

Doctors can diagnose diabetes by analyzing blood samples for elevated sugar concentrations.

They may also test blood and urine for excess ketones (the chemical by-products of the breakdown of fat for energy). Since people with diabetes do not use glucose normally, their bodies burn fat for fuel, and as a result, ketones are eliminated in the urine.

## Treatment

Both forms of diabetes mellitus require a treatment plan that maintains normal, steady blood glucose levels. Once blood sugar levels have been brought under control with insulin injections, diet, or medication, a person with diabetes can usually lead a nearly normal life.

Type I diabetes requires injections of insulin to maintain blood sugar levels evenly all day. If the blood glucose concentration rises, imbalance may be signaled by weakness, fatigue, and thirst. These symptoms mean that more insulin is needed. However, if the blood glucose concentration falls too low, an insulin reaction sets in, causing dizziness, hunger, fatigue, headache, sweating, trembling, and (in severe cases) unconsciousness. A quick remedy for this problem is to give the person simple sugar, such as is found in orange juice and some kinds of candy. This should be done only if the person is conscious and alert, however; nothing should be given by mouth to an unconscious or semiconscious person, because of the risk of choking.

Ideally, a doctor can prevent these fluctuations of sugar levels by coordinating the type and timing of insulin injections with meal content and energy output. A special diet is important to balance daily insulin injections. Young children with diabetes, in particular, need sufficient calories to grow and develop normally. Insulin requirements for persons with Type I diabetes differ greatly. Some patients may maintain balanced blood sugar levels with one insulin injection taken before breakfast. Other patients may require several insulin injections per day. Insulin requirements may change as the patient grows older, undergoes surgery, becomes pregnant, or develops an unrelated illness.

Many people with Type II diabetes can regulate their condition with proper diet. Sometimes, oral antidiabetic drugs, which work by stimulating the pancreas to produce more insulin, may be prescribed.

Special attention to diet is critical for diabetes control. Overweight individuals need to lose weight. Thereafter, emphasis is on eating balanced meals that will sustain the recommended weight. Fats need to be limited to reduce susceptibility to atherosclerosis, and the diet should be low in simple sugars. The diet should include plenty of fibrous roughage, such as is contained in fruits, vegetables, and whole grains; fiber in the diet has been shown to reduce or slow sugar absorption in the digestive tract. A doctor can provide a medically approved diet plan, with enough flexibility to allow the diabetic patient to share in regular family meals while meeting his special dietary needs.

With either type of diabetes, follow-up is important to plan diet, determine changes in insulin dosage, and monitor blood sugar levels. Testing urine for sugar has been shown to be inaccurate, and the availability of home blood glucose monitoring has all but replaced urine sugar testing for most diabetic patients.

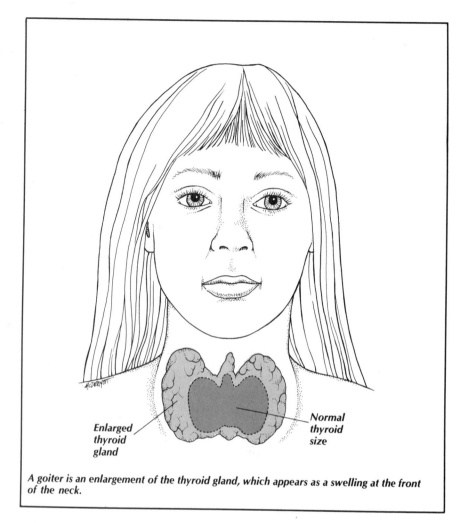

A goiter is an enlargement of the thyroid gland, which appears as a swelling at the front of the neck.

Enlarged thyroid gland

Normal thyroid size

Urine ketone testing, however, is still important.

# Goiter

A goiter is an enlargement of the thyroid gland, which appears as a swelling at the front of the neck.

### Causes

Goiter may be caused by a lack of dietary iodine, which is necessary for the production of thyroid hormone. In this case, the thyroid gland enlarges in an attempt to produce more hormone. When this happens, the cells in the gland enlarge, but do not increase in number.

Goiter was at one time common in areas where there is a lack of iodine in the soil and water. Since the ocean is the basic source of iodine, inland areas were the most deficient (in the United States, the Great Lakes region was such an area; in Europe, inhabitants of mountainous inland regions in the Alps often had an iodine deficiency). In recent times, however, the use of iodized table salt has solved this problem.

Some forms of goiter are associated with an overactive thyroid gland, that is, one that produces more hormone than the body needs.

## Symptoms

Often, the only symptom is the swelling in the neck. If the thyroid is overactive, nervousness, weight loss, bulging eyes, rapid heartbeat, and high blood pressure may be noted. If the thyroid is underactive, sluggishness, weight gain, dry skin and hair, and fatigue may be present.

## Diagnosis

The diagnosis is made primarily on the basis of the classic appearance and the dietary history of the patient. Blood tests to determine the concentration of thyroid hormones and a nuclear medicine study of the thyroid may be performed to rule out more serious thyroid disorders.

## Treatment

The chief objective of goiter treatment is reduction of the swelling. The first step is usually to suppress the overfunctioning of the thyroid gland. If the goiter is caused by simple iodine deficiency, small doses of iodine can be given. Sometimes, administering synthetic thyroid hormone, in an attempt to halt the increased efforts by the gland to produce the natural hormone, will reduce the enlargement. If treatment is started early enough, surgery to remove portions of the enlarged gland can be avoided. Surgery may be necessary if the size of the goiter interferes with normal breathing by pressing on the windpipe.

# Hirsutism

Hirsutism is excessive hair growth or hair growth in areas that are not usually hairy. In general, this condition is due to a hormonal imbalance.

## Causes

Some degree of hirsutism is present in about 30 percent of women, and it may be a symptom of some other disorder. Family and racial tendencies, however, account for a large percentage of cases of hirsutism in women. Many cases have no known cause. It is thought, though, that hirsute women may have hair follicles that are hypersensitive to normal female androgen levels. (Androgen is a male sex hormone, but it is normally present to a lesser extent in women as well.)

In some cases, hirsutism is only one sign of virilization (masculinization), which is characterized by acne, balding, and increased muscle mass, as well as by hirsutism. This condition may be due to overactive adrenal glands (which secrete some sex hormones), ovarian tumors, adrenal tumors, or use of steroid medications. However, the majority of hirsute women are not masculinized.

A common cause of hirsutism is polycystic ovaries; in this condition, the presence of numerous cysts on the ovaries leads to infrequent menstruation or absence of menstruation, absence of ovulation, obesity, and enlarged ovaries. Hirsutism is also seen in Cushing's syndrome, a condition that in women is characterized by excessive fat tissue in the face, neck, and trunk; absence of menstruation; convex (outward) curvature of the spine; high blood pressure; and muscular weakness. Mild hirsutism also appears in young girls with underactive thyroid glands. Ab-

sence of or damage to the pituitary gland, anorexia nervosa (an eating disorder characterized by self-inflicted starvation), and use of some drugs can also cause hirsutism.

## Symptoms

The only symptom of hirsutism is excessive growth of hair in men or women or growth of hair in normally hairless areas in women (for example, on the face, neck, breasts, chest, and abdomen). The hair may be soft and fine or coarse, depending on many factors.

## Diagnosis

Diagnosis is usually confirmed through visual examination and medical history.

## Treatment

The treatment of hirsutism is based on removing the cause. For example, adrenal hyperplasia (an abnormal increase in the number of cells in the adrenal gland) can be suppressed by corticosteroid drugs. Patients with polycystic ovaries can be treated with low-dose estrogen birth control pills or with other drugs.

Removing the cause does not always diminish the hair growth, however, and hair removal may be desired for cosmetic reasons. The only safe, permanent local treatment is electrolysis (destruction of individual hair follicles with an electric current). Other measures, such as plucking, shaving, waxing, or using a depilatory wax or chemical, will mask the problem only temporarily.

## Prevention

Other than prompt diagnosis and treatment of the primary cause or underlying disorder (provided there is one), there are no known preventive measures against hirsutism.

# Hyperthyroidism

Hyperthyroidism is a general term that encompasses several different disorders with the common feature of excessive production of thyroid hormone. The two most common forms of hyperthyroidism are Graves' disease and toxic multinodular goiter.

## Causes

The production of thyroid hormone is normally regulated by the pituitary gland, which secretes thyroid-stimulating hormone (TSH) when a need for thyroid hormone is present and ceases secretion of TSH when it senses an overabundance of the hormone. Generally speaking, some malfunction occurs in hyperthyroidism, and the thyroid is no longer sensitive to this regulatory mechanism. Graves' disease is probably due to the presence of an abnormal chemical stimulator of thyroid hormone production. In toxic multinodular goiter, nodules (lumplike clusters) of thyroid tissue form, for reasons that have yet to be determined, and secrete abnormally large amounts of thyroid hormone.

## Symptoms

Because thyroid hormone is involved in so many vital processes throughout the body, including maintenance of body tempera-ture, conversion of food to energy, and regulation of growth and fertility, the effects of an excess of that hormone are many and varied. The symptoms common to all forms of hyperthyroidism include rapid heartbeat, weight loss despite increased appetite and food intake, generalized hyperactivity, tremors (shakiness), increased sweating, severe nervousness and emotional instability, alterations of menstruation and fertility, and muscle weakness.

In addition to these symptoms, patients with Graves' disease often have bulging eyes. Their skin is characteristically warm, moist, and velvety, and there may be areas of raised, thickened, sometimes itchy skin with the texture of orange peel on the legs and feet. The thyroid gland is frequently enlarged, smooth, and soft. This disease occurs most often in those in their 30s and 40s. It is more common in women than in men.

In toxic multinodular goiter, the thyroid gland is lumpy but not uniformly enlarged. This condition occurs most often in the middle-aged and elderly.

## Diagnosis

The diagnosis of hyperthyroidism is made on the basis of the history and findings from a physical examination and various laboratory studies. Significant elevation of the level of thyroid hormone in the blood can be detected with special blood tests. The diagnosis can be further established through the use of nuclear medicine scans obtained after the injection of radioactive iodine, which becomes concentrated in the thyroid gland. The nuclear medicine study yields not only a picture of the gland, but also an estimate of the degree of hyperactivity.

## Treatment

Specific treatment of hyperthyroidism depends on which condition is present. However, treatment of the hyperthyroid state in general has several common elements. The drug propranolol, a beta-blocker, is commonly used to block the effects of the hormonal overstimulation that greatly contributes to the tremors, increased heart rate, and sweating. This drug, although it diminishes symptoms, does not get at the root problem of too much thyroid hormone. To decrease the amount of thyroid hormone being produced, an antithyroid drug, such as propyl-thiouracil, is used. Antithyroid drugs actually interfere with the production of thyroid hormone. However, this is only a temporary solution; when the drug is stopped, the excess production usually resumes. The definitive therapy for hyperthyroidism is the destruction or removal of most or all of the gland using radioactive iodine or surgery.

Graves' disease is usually first treated by blocking hormonal overstimulation with propranolol. Simultaneously, an antithyroid drug is started. Usually this drug is maintained for several years. If relapse occurs or if the level of thyroid hormone is not normalized, the question then is how to reduce the amount of thyroid tissue. Whether surgery or radioactive iodine is used depends on many complex factors. Both treatments frequently result in too little thyroid hormone in the blood, but this problem is easily remedied by supplementation with synthetic thyroid hormone.

The treatment of toxic multinodular goiter is less controversial. In addition to a beta-blocker and, frequently, an antithyroid drug, radioactive iodine is generally the therapy of choice.

# Hypoglycemia

Hypoglycemia is the state of having an abnormally low blood glucose level. (Glucose is a sugar released into the blood as a result of digestion of carbohydrates.)

The two main forms of this condition are reactive hypoglycemia and fasting hypoglycemia. To understand how both forms occur, it is helpful to understand how glucose utilization is normally regulated. During digestion, elevated blood glucose levels trigger the secretion of the hormone insulin from the pancreas. Insulin acts to reduce the sugar level in the blood by helping body cells absorb the glucose for fuel.

### Reactive hypoglycemia

Reactive hypoglycemia is caused by oversecretion of insulin and consequent rapid lowering of blood glucose levels in response to ingestion of glucose. Reactive hypoglycemia is also known as postprandial (after meals) hypoglycemia because it occurs only in response to ingestion of food.

The specific causes of reactive hypoglycemia are unknown in most cases. However, certain persons—for example, those in the early stage of adult-onset diabetes mellitus and patients who have had part or most of the stomach removed surgically—are particularly susceptible to reactive hypoglycemia.

### Fasting hypoglycemia

Fasting hypoglycemia is caused by insufficient production of glucose or overutilization of the glucose present in the blood. Often, these two factors combine to severely depress the blood glucose level. An insulin-producing tumor on the pancreas can also cause fasting hypoglycemia. Because alcohol disturbs the normal mechanisms of sugar storage and release within the liver, heavy drinkers are at greater risk of developing the disorder. Fasting hypoglycemia can also occur in anyone who has not eaten for an unusually long interval, but this is a temporary situation. Chronic (long-term) hypoglycemia is uncommon.

### Symptoms

The symptoms of both types of hypoglycemia include fatigue, nervousness, perspiration, dizziness, headache, hunger pangs, visual impairment, and accelerated heartbeat. The condition may also cause anxiety, difficulty in concentrating, confusion, and blackouts. If sugar deprivation continues unchecked, severe hypoglycemia may produce convulsions (short-term loss of consciousness, accompanied by jerking muscle movements) or deep coma (prolonged loss of consciousness).

True hypoglycemia is an uncommon condition. Since many of the symptoms of anxiety and hypoglycemia are alike, the two conditions are often confused.

### Diagnosis

To diagnose hypoglycemia, a doctor analyzes a blood sample to detect abnormally low sugar levels. Blood drawn during an attack of the condition allows the most accurate assessment, since symptoms can then be correlated with actual blood glucose levels.

### Treatment

Treatment for hypoglycemia is often aimed at the underlying cause of the disease. For example, surgical removal of a pancreatic tumor or adjustment of a diabetic patient's insulin dosage may be necessary. In most cases of reactive hypoglycemia, however, there is no known cure for the tendency of the pancreas to overproduce insulin when it is not needed. The most effective treatment is to avoid all foods that generate attacks.

A good diet for a patient who is susceptible to episodes of hypoglycemia is one that is low enough in sugar and starches to moderate the reaction of the pancreas to sugar intake and rich enough in protein to help maintain gradual elevations of blood sugar. Eating several smaller meals a day, rather than three large meals, may help to keep blood sugar levels stable.

# Hypothyroidism

Hypothyroidism is a disorder in which an underactive thyroid gland produces too little thyroid hormone.

### Causes

Hypothyroidism can result from chronic (long-term) thyroid inflammation or a deficiency of thyroid-stimulating hormone, which is secreted by the pituitary gland. Autoimmune disorders (in which the immune system destroys the body's own tissues) are also a common cause of hypothyroidism. In addition, heredity may play a role in the development of the condition. Women seem more prone to thyroid disorders, and in some women pregnancy triggers the hormonal imbalance. Hypothyroidism can also develop after suppression or partial removal of the thyroid gland as treatment for hyperthyroidism (a condition that results when an overactive thyroid gland produces too much thyroid hormone).

### Symptoms

Because thyroid hormone influences every tissue in the body (for example, by participating in maintenance of body temperature, conversion of food to energy, and regulation of growth and fertility), the effects of having too little of the hormone are many and varied. People with hypothyroidism may be overweight, easily exhausted, and subject to recurrent infection. They may also experience menstrual disorders, feel tingling in the hands and feet, be intolerant of cold, have dry skin and hair, exhibit puffiness of the hands and face, and suffer mental illness.

### Diagnosis

The diagnosis of hypothyroidism is based on laboratory tests of the blood. Determination of levels of thyroid and pituitary hormones is fundamental. Cardiac enzymes and cholesterol may also be measured. A special nuclear medicine study after the injection of radioactive iodine may be performed.

Chronic hypothyroidism may cause signs of reduced general body functioning. Anemia (deficiency of red blood cells) may result from diminished function of the bone marrow, where red blood cells are formed. Heart rate may decrease, and reflexes may become sluggish. An electroencephalogram may reveal irregular brain-wave patterns. Evaluation of growth patterns often provides the first clue to the diagnosis in children.

### Treatment

Since hypothyroidism develops from a shortage of thyroid hormone, the most effective treatment is generally thyroid hormone supplementation. Supplements are either natural hormones extracted from the thyroid glands of animals or synthetic hormones. Both types control the problem, but the newer, synthetic forms are much more efficient and their effects are more easily regulated. Although treatment provides the necessary hormone control, hypothyroidism often continues throughout life and the patient may require lifelong follow-up to monitor treatment.

Contrary to popular belief, the correction of hypothyroidism will not cause an obese person to lose a significant amount of weight.

# Ketosis

Ketosis is an abnormal condition that occurs when the body burns fat instead of glucose (the form of sugar that is the body's chief source of energy) and, as a result, produces more of the chemical substances called ketones than is normal.

### Causes

Ketones are the by-product of the chemical process that occurs in the cells when fat is broken down to produce energy. Under normal circumstances, ketones are in turn broken down into carbon dioxide and water by the liver and other organs. In ketosis, the body is producing more ketones than it can process. The buildup of ketones disrupts the chemical balance of the body; if left unchecked, this condition can prove fatal.

Ketosis occurs most often in persons with insulin-dependent diabetes mellitus, a disorder in which the pancreas produces little or no insulin (a hormone secreted into the bloodstream to regulate glucose levels). This deficiency prevents the body from absorbing enough glucose and forces it to obtain its energy by burning fat. If ketosis is allowed to progress in a diabetic patient, a condition called diabetic ketoacidosis may occur. This is a life-threatening disorder that involves severe dehydration (excessive loss of body fluids) and coma (prolonged loss of consciousness).

Ketosis is also a consequence of starvation (including the self-induced starvation of excessive dieting), in which the body must rely on stores of fat for energy.

### Symptoms

The most common symptoms are a slightly sweet breath odor (similar to the smell of acetone or nail-polish remover), extreme dryness of the mucous membranes, weight loss, increased thirst, urination, weakness, abdominal pains and generalized aches, nausea and vomiting, and breathlessness.

## Diagnosis

Ketosis is diagnosed by testing the glucose and ketone levels in blood or urine. The urine test is less accurate.

## Treatment

In insulin-dependent diabetics, administration of insulin corrects diabetic ketoacidosis. Diabetics are especially susceptible to ketosis before their condition is diagnosed, while they are fighting an infection, or when they neglect their diet or medication. Treatment of ketosis caused by starvation consists of feeding the patient substances that contain sugar or administering glucose solution intravenously.

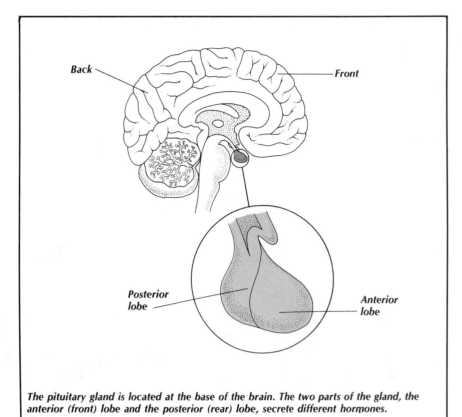

*The pituitary gland is located at the base of the brain. The two parts of the gland, the anterior (front) lobe and the posterior (rear) lobe, secrete different hormones.*

# Pituitary disorders

Because of the vital role of the pituitary gland in regulating many body functions, disorders of this gland (often due to tumors) can result in disastrous abnormalities in growth and body maintenance.

Persons who have excessive secretion of growth hormone by the anterior lobe during the years in which the skeleton is growing become giants; those who have deficient secretion at that time become dwarfs. If oversecretion occurs after a person has become an adult, a condition called acromegaly results, in which the victim's hands, feet, jaws, and facial bones grow disproportionately large.

A condition known as diabetes insipidus (which is related only symptomatically to the more common diabetes mellitus) is due to a malfunction of the posterior lobe. In this disorder, a deficiency of the pituitary hormone vasopressin results in abnormally high urinary output of water. Control can be regained with the use of synthetic vasopressin to inhibit excessive water release.

# THE MALE REPRODUCTIVE SYSTEM

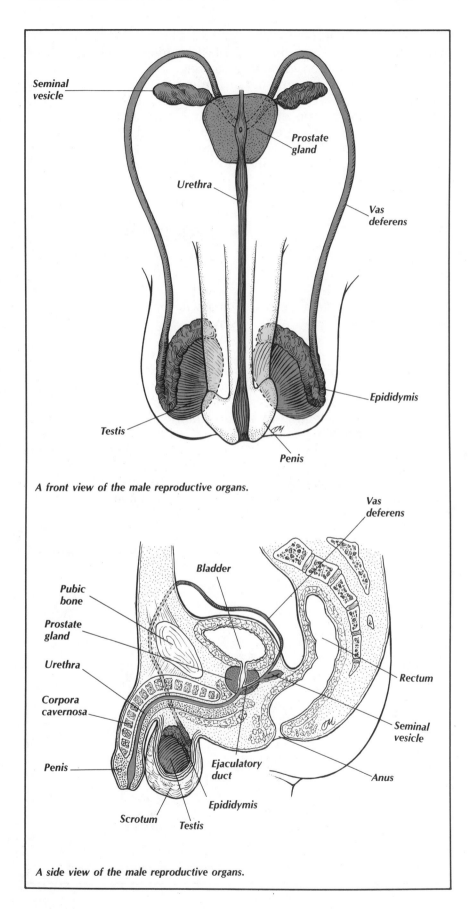

*A front view of the male reproductive organs.*

*A side view of the male reproductive organs.*

The male reproductive system consists of those structures in the male body designed to create life. The system includes the two testes, a network of ducts, the seminal vesicles, the prostate gland, and the penis.

The testes are two oval glands located in the scrotum (the pouch of skin that hangs behind the penis). They produce the male sex hormone testosterone and sperm (male reproductive cells). Sex hormones control the secondary male sex characteristics (such as growth of the penis and of body hair, voice change, and increased muscle mass), which begin to appear at puberty.

The testes discharge sperm into the epididymis, the first structure in the duct system. Other passageways include the two vasa deferentia (the plural of vas deferens), the ejaculatory duct, and the urethra (the tube that connects the bladder to the outside of the body).

The epididymis runs along the top and side of each testis. Inside the epididymis are several ducts that conduct sperm from the testis into the vas deferens. The vas deferens loops up into the body before descending into a duct in the seminal vesicle. This duct joins the ejaculatory duct, which extends through the prostate gland and enters the upper segment of the urethra. At different times, the urethra functions as a passageway for urine and for sperm.

As sperm travel through the duct system, they combine with fluids from the seminal vesicles, the prostate gland, and the urethra to form semen. The two seminal vesicles, which lie near the underside of the urinary bladder, discharge a thick, sticky fluid. The prostate gland is a small, doughnut-shaped organ that completely surrounds the urethra. The prostate gland secretes an alkaline substance that makes up the major portion of seminal fluid. The sperm are protected from acid (present both in the male urethra and in the vagina) by the alkalinity of the prostatic secretions. Sperm are also capable of the greatest mobility when in a slightly alkaline medium. Proper prostate secretion is thus essential to effective sperm action.

The penis is the external organ that propels sperm into the female during sexual intercourse. During sexual excitement, the corpora cavernosa (large internal spaces within the penis) become filled with blood, making the penis rigid enough to enter the vagina (the entryway to the female reproductive tract). The semen, which is formed in the urethra, then travels out of the penis during ejaculation (sudden discharge of fluid).

# Gynecomastia

Gynecomastia is excessive development of the breasts in a male. Breast enlargement is a normal, short-term occurrence in some newborn boys, whose breasts enlarge in response to female hormones they receive from their mother during pregnancy. The condition may also appear at puberty, when a boy's body is undergoing normal hormonal changes.

### Causes

In most cases, gynecomastia is the result of too much estrogen (a female sex hormone) in the male's body. Breast enlargement at birth and at puberty usually occurs because the estrogen

level has not yet adjusted to normal (both females and males normally have estrogen in their bodies). Abnormal gynecomastia occurs when some condition, such as a tumor of one of the testes or an estrogen-secreting tumor of one of the adrenal glands, results in abnormally high levels of estrogen.

### Symptoms

In addition to the obvious enlargement of the breasts, symptoms may include tenderness in the breast and, in extreme cases, secretion of milk.

### Treatment

Gynecomastia should always be brought to the attention of a doctor. It is especially important that tumors of the adrenal glands or testes be ruled out or treated. Such tumors are usually removed surgically. In severe or prolonged cases, the excess

breast tissue can be removed by plastic surgery, with no visible scarring.

In most cases, patients can be reassured that the condition is normal and temporary. Especially in need of such reassurance are teenage boys, who are often embarrassed and fearful that they are abnormal.

# Hydrocele

A hydrocele is an abnormal collection of fluid around a testis, which is noticeable as a soft mass in the scrotum. The term hydrocele literally means a sac of water.

There is normally a double-layered covering around each testis. Between these two layers there is usually just enough fluid for lubrication. Occasionally, however, the amount of fluid is increased, causing the swelling around the testis. As a rule, hydroceles are harmless. They are relatively common, especially in older men.

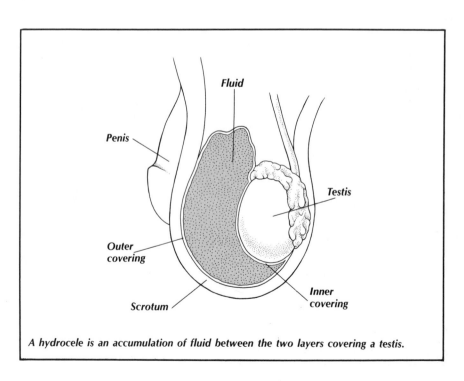

*A hydrocele is an accumulation of fluid between the two layers covering a testis.*

### Causes and types

If the hydrocele is caused by an injury or inflammation in the scrotum, it is called a secondary hydrocele. If there is no apparent cause, it is called a primary hydrocele.

### Symptoms

The most obvious symptom is the swelling. Although hydroceles are usually painless, pain may also be present.

### Treatment

A small, painless hydrocele often requires no treatment. However, care must be taken not to dismiss something more serious as a hydrocele. Only a physician can make the diagnosis. Therefore, any scrotal mass merits immediate medical attention. The treatment for hydrocele is surgical removal of the fluid. The condition can recur.

# Impotence

Impotence is the inability to achieve and maintain an erection of the penis, which is necessary to penetrate the vagina during sexual intercourse. The corpora cavernosa of the penis normally fill with blood during sexual excitement, which causes the penis to become rigid and erect. Impotence is a partial or total impairment of this function.

### Types

There are two types of impotence: primary impotence, in which a man is never able to have an erection adequate for sexual intercourse; and secondary impotence, in which a man quite often fails to complete intercourse to the satisfaction of both partners. Secondary impotence is the more common type.

Many men experience temporary impotence at some point in their lives, but chronic (recurring) impotence can lower a man's self-esteem and put a strain on his marriage or social relationships.

### Causes

Impotence can be caused by either physical or psychological problems. It may be brought on by job-related stress, fear of causing pregnancy, unresolved conflicts about sexuality, or fear of sex after a heart attack or major surgery. Drug and alcohol abuse are also among the leading causes of impotence.

Until recently, psychological problems were thought to be the only cause of impotence, but underlying physical factors are now also known to trigger the problem. These factors include the following: an imbalance in the hormonal system that causes a decrease in production of testosterone (the male hormone necessary for an erection); the use of certain drugs for the treatment of high blood pressure, particularly diuretics and beta-blockers; diseases of the nervous system, such as multiple sclerosis; structural abnormalities of the penis; injury to the penis; and malfunctioning of the circulatory system, which can interfere with the blood flow to the penis.

### Symptoms

The major symptom of impotence is inability to attain or maintain erection of the penis for sexual intercourse. This may be accompanied by a lack of interest in sex, but not necessarily infertility (the inability to father a child).

### Diagnosis

Several tests can help to diagnose the cause of impotence. A blood test will show whether adequate levels of testosterone are present. With a blood pressure cuff specially designed to wrap around the penis and ultrasound (a technique that uses sound waves to create images of internal structures), blood vessel problems in the penis can often be detected. Another test registers the size of erections that naturally occur during sleep; if erections do not occur during sleep, a physical, rather than an emotional, cause is likely.

### Treatment

If impotence has a physical basis, a number of treatments are available. Injections of testosterone and other hormones may relieve some problems. Surgery may be necessary to repair the arteries and veins that carry blood to and from the penis.

The use of penile implants is a successful new treatment for impotence, with several varieties now in use. One is a silicone rod that is implanted in the corpora cavernosa, resulting in a permanent partial erection. Another is a flexible silver wire surrounded by silicone, which allows manipulation of the penis to an erect position for intercourse. A third model consists of balloon-like cylinders implanted in the corpora cavernosa and connected to a container of fluid;

with the use of a hand pump, the cylinders may be filled with the fluid, in much the same way that blood normally fills the penis during an erection.

Counseling by psychologists or trained sex therapists may be recommended for men whose impotence seems to stem from emotional problems. Counseling may also help those with physical disorders in learning to deal with their impotence.

### Prevention

Avoiding the abuse of alcohol and drugs, as well as eliminating or coping with stress, should help to prevent at least some episodes of secondary impotence.

# Prostatitis

Prostatitis is an infection or inflammation of the male sex gland called the prostate. It predominantly affects older men, usually in the form of chronic (recurring) flare-ups. Though not a serious disorder, prostatitis can be irritating and uncomfortable because it disrupts normal urination; in advanced stages, it can cause bladder or kidney damage.

Located just below the bladder, the prostate is a small, doughnut-shaped gland that surrounds the neck of the bladder and the urethra. As men get older, the prostate often becomes enlarged, which may constrict the urethra. This will eventually develop into a condition called prostatism, which causes disruption of normal urination, marked by prolonged effort or repeated attempts to start the flow, decreased force, and dribbling toward the end of the flow. Some urine is almost al-

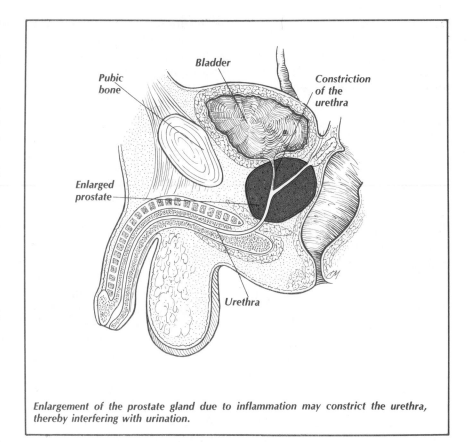

*Enlargement of the prostate gland due to inflammation may constrict the urethra, thereby interfering with urination.*

ways left in the bladder, providing a fertile breeding ground for bacteria. Bladder infection is a common consequence of prostatism, which may in turn cause prostatitis. Advanced cases of prostatitis may cause a sudden, total blockage of urine flow, requiring emergency treatment before the backup of urine can cause bladder and kidney damage.

### Causes

Sexually transmitted diseases and urinary tract infections are the most common underlying causes of prostatitis.

### Symptoms

The most common symptoms are trouble in starting the urine flow, reduced force in urination, dribbling at the end of urination, and increased frequency of urination. Prostatitis may be signaled by discomfort in the lower back and genital area, a burning sensation while urinating, fever, and chills.

### Diagnosis

Prostatitis is diagnosed by an examination of the prostate to check its size, shape, and firmness. An infected prostate will be tender to the touch; when it is massaged by the doctor, pus cells will be forced out and will then appear in the urine. A culture of the urine specimen will be examined for bacteria, although very often no bacteria are identified in a case of chronic prostatitis. However, a urinalysis may show some evidence of infection, and if a trace of blood is present, the urine may be additionally tested for the presence of malignant cells.

Enlargement of the prostate can be diagnosed by means of a procedure called an intravenous pyelogram (IVP), in which dye is injected into a vein in the arm and allowed to travel through the bloodstream to the kidneys and urinary bladder and out through the penis. The dye may show enlargement or obstruction in the ureters. The patient will then be asked to urinate; if the IVP shows a large quantity of urine left in the bladder, a partial obstruction caused by an en- larged prostate can generally be diagnosed.

### Treatment

Most prostate infections can be treated quite successfully with antibiotics. Chronic non- bacterial prostatitis, however, is not treated with antibiotics. In- stead, drinking large quantities of water and taking hot baths are often recommended.

Enlargement of the prostate gland that causes symptoms is normally treated by surgical re- moval of the excess tissue through one of two procedures: transurethral surgery, in which the center of the prostate gland is scraped out by an instrument that has been inserted into the penis; or prostatectomy, a more complicated procedure requiring an incision in the lower abdo- men or between the legs. There is little danger of impotence re- sulting from either of these surgi- cal procedures, but they may lead to retrograde ejaculation, a condition in which the semen is passed back into the bladder to be expelled with the urine, rather than being released during intercourse (although this condi- tion presents no health risk, it is a cause of infertility).

# THE FEMALE REPRODUCTIVE SYSTEM

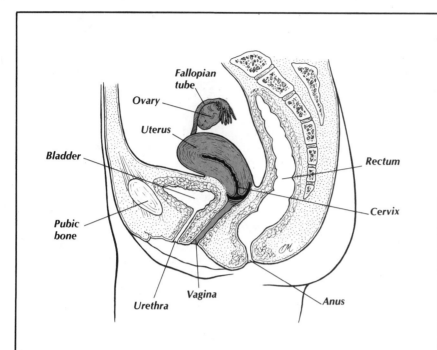

*Fallopian tube*

*Ovary*

*Uterus*

*Bladder*

*Pubic bone*

*Rectum*

*Cervix*

*Urethra*

*Vagina*

*Anus*

*A side view of the female reproductive organs.*

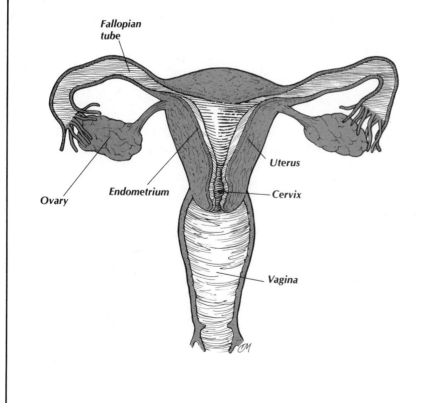

*Fallopian tube*

*Uterus*

*Cervix*

*Endometrium*

*Ovary*

*Vagina*

*A front view of the female reproductive organs.*

The female reproductive system consists of those structures within the female body that are designed to create and nourish new life. The system includes the ovaries, fallopian tubes, uterus, cervix, and vagina.

Although the breasts, or mammary glands, are actually a type of sweat gland, their function (supporting new life) is closely related to that of the reproductive system. For that reason, disorders affecting the breasts will also be considered in this chapter.

The reproductive process begins in the ovaries. The ovaries are small, egg-shaped glands located in the lower abdomen. These glands control the cyclic functions of the reproductive system—ovulation and menstruation. Ovulation is the monthly production and release of a mature egg (occasionally two or more eggs). This process and other reproductive functions are regulated by two hormones, estrogen and progesterone, which are secreted by the ovaries. Estrogen regulates the secondary sex traits of body hair growth, breast development, ovulation, and menstruation. Progesterone is responsible for preparing the uterus for pregnancy, as well as contributing to enlargement of the breasts during pregnancy and milk production after childbirth. The two hormones coordinate to control the menstrual cycle.

Once an egg has been released, it travels through the fallopian tubes, which extend from each ovary into the uterus. Their reproductive function is to contain the egg until fertilization (union of an egg and a sperm, or male sex cell) takes place and to provide a passageway leading the sperm to the egg and the fertilized egg to the uterus.

The uterus is a pear-shaped, hollow organ that is normally

287

about the size of a lemon. Its muscular walls are lined with rich, soft tissue called the endometrium. Each month the lining adds layers in anticipation of receiving a fertilized egg. Should fertilization occur, the lining nourishes the fertilized egg in the uterus until birth. However, if the egg remains unfertilized, the uterus sheds the endometrium and the egg, which leave the body as menstrual discharge.

The cervix is a narrow opening and inch-long canal connecting the lower end of the uterus to the upper portion of the vagina. This canal is the conduit for sperm on their way to fertilize an egg and for menstrual discharge and babies leaving the uterus.

The vagina, or birth canal, is a passageway leading from the uterus to the outside of the body. In the average adult woman, it measures four to five inches in length. Although the vaginal walls are normally close together, they separate to accommodate the infant during childbirth and the erect penis during sexual intercourse. The vagina continuously produces secretions that lubricate and cleanse it.

# Amenorrhea

Amenorrhea is the absence of menstruation. There are two categories of this disorder. Primary amenorrhea is the failure to begin menstruating by the age of 16. Secondary amenorrhea, the more common of the two conditions, is the absence of three or more periods in a row in a woman who has been menstruating for some time. Primary amenorrhea is specifically defined at the age of 16 and can go on indefinitely. Secondary amenorrhea is usually a temporary condition; the periods

generally resume when the underlying cause for the interruption has been corrected.

## Causes

Primary amenorrhea may be caused by an endocrine gland disorder (such as hyperthyroidism or hypothyroidism); genetic abnormalities; damaged or missing ovaries, uterus, or vagina; or an excessively thick hymen (the membrane that usually covers the vaginal opening in virgins), which blocks the outflow of the menstrual discharge.

Secondary amenorrhea is caused most commonly by pregnancy. It can also be triggered by strenuous sports training, poor nutrition, drastic weight gain, jet lag, certain medications (including corticosteroids, tranquilizers, and birth control pills), major surgery or serious disease, emotional shock, or the loss of a large percentage of body fat.

## Symptoms

Primary amenorrhea is commonly accompanied by abnormal or inhibited physical development; the young girl may fail to develop breasts or body hair, indicating that a genetic disorder may be preventing her from attaining sexual maturity. These girls are also usually short.

Secondary amenorrhea has no symptoms other than the absence of menstrual periods.

## Diagnosis

Diagnostic evaluation of both types of amenorrhea will probably include a test to rule out pregnancy, tests to detect genetic or hormonal disorders, and

x-rays to check the reproductive organs.

## Treatment

Primary amenorrhea may be treated with an extensive hormone therapy program to stimulate physical development. If the cause is a thick hymen, a minor surgical procedure may be performed to open the hymen. Some cases of primary amenorrhea, however, are untreatable (for example, those due to structural abnormalities of the reproductive organs).

Secondary amenorrhea may be treated with a hormone that will trigger ovulation and reestablish the menstrual cycle. However, quite often this condition will reverse itself without treatment, especially if the cause is merely an interruption in the patient's normal routine, an emotional upset, or pregnancy.

## Prevention

Maintaining good nutritional habits and a normal weight and avoiding overly strenuous sports can probably be beneficial in preventing secondary amenorrhea. No specific precautions can be taken, however, to prevent primary amenorrhea.

# Cystocele

A cystocele is a protrusion into the vagina of a portion of the urinary bladder.

## Cause

Cystocele is usually the result of damage to the wall of fibrous tissue that normally separates the

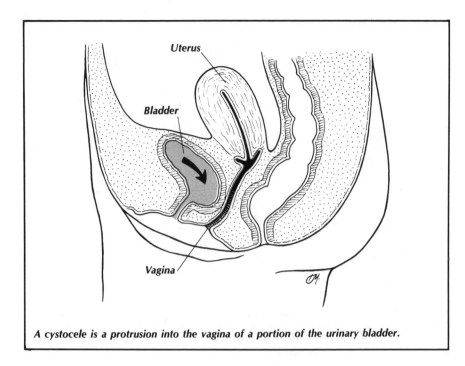

*A cystocele is a protrusion into the vagina of a portion of the urinary bladder.*

vagina and the bladder. Such an injury often occurs during childbirth and may happen with the birth of a baby of any size. However, women who have never given birth may also develop a cystocele. A cystocele may not appear until menopause, when the damaged area is weakened further, permitting the rear and base portions of the bladder to protrude into the vagina. A portion of the rectum (the final part of the large intestine), the small intestine, or the urethra (the tube through which urine leaves the body) may also bulge into the vagina, or prolapse of the uterus (in which the uterus drops through the vagina and in very severe cases protrudes through the vaginal opening) may occur.

The protrusion of the bladder into the vagina creates a pool of stale urine in the bladder, which cannot be easily emptied and as a result becomes a breeding ground for bacteria. Cystitis (inflammation of the bladder), signaled by painful and difficult urination, often results.

### Symptoms

A woman with a cystocele may feel a fullness in the vagina and may find it difficult to empty her bladder completely. However, many women with a cystocele have no symptoms at all.

### Diagnosis

Diagnosis is made by examining the inside of the vagina. If a bulge can be seen in front of the cervix, a cystocele is suspected. Also, if a catheter inserted into the bladder after urination can draw out more than two ounces of leftover urine, the diagnosis is even more likely. If a special x-ray study in which dye is injected into the bladder reveals a bulged-out section of the bladder, the diagnosis is confirmed.

### Treatment

The preferred treatment for cystocele is surgery to repair the damaged wall and put the protruding section of bladder back in its original place. A pessary (a device inserted into the vagina to support the vagina and reduce the cystocele) may be used in women who cannot or do not wish to undergo surgery. A cystocele does not always require treatment. However, if frequent bouts of cystitis occur, some form of treatment will be necessary.

# DES

Diethylstilbestrol (DES) is an artificial estrogen (female sex hormone) used to treat a variety of disorders. For nearly three decades, this drug was frequently prescribed to prevent miscarriage. In 1971, however, the Food and Drug Administration banned its use for this purpose because it had been found ineffective.

Use of DES has been linked to an increased incidence of adenocarcinoma (a rare cancer of the glandular cells of the reproductive organs) in the daughters of the several million women who took it to prevent miscarriage and other complications of pregnancy. Testicular cancer in male offspring has also been associated with maternal DES use. Persons exposed to DES before birth also have a higher than average incidence of benign (noncancerous) growths, structural changes involving the reproductive organs, and infertility problems. These abnormalities usually appear in the late teens to early 30s. Although the incidence of serious complications is small, physicians strongly advise that persons who were exposed to DES before birth should be routinely examined to detect any abnormalities.

Because of the potential problems, DES should not be taken by a woman who is pregnant or suspects that she is pregnant. DES may be used safely by non-pregnant women to treat a variety of disorders, including certain vaginal conditions and estrogen deficiency that may occur at menopause or after the surgical removal of the ovaries. Recently, DES has also been shown to be effective in some patients in reducing the growth of advanced prostate cancer. Since DES is a hormone that may produce a variety of effects in the body, its use must always be supervised by a physician.

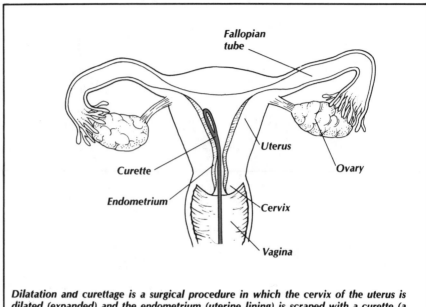

*Dilatation and curettage is a surgical procedure in which the cervix of the uterus is dilated (expanded) and the endometrium (uterine lining) is scraped with a curette (a loop-, ring-, or scoop-shaped instrument with a rodlike handle).*

# Dilatation and curettage

Dilatation and curettage, also called a D&C, is a surgical procedure in which the cervix of the uterus is dilated (expanded) and the endometrial lining of the uterus is scraped with a curette (a loop-, ring-, or scoop-shaped instrument with a long, rodlike handle).

### Purpose

This procedure is often used in the diagnosis of diseases of the uterus (such as cancer) and to halt excessive bleeding. It is also used to perform an abortion and may be employed after a miscarriage (involuntary expulsion of a fetus before it is able to live on its own) to remove any remaining tissue and thereby lower the risk of hemorrhage and infection.

Dilatation alone may be performed to enlarge the passageway out of the uterus. This might be done if a severely narrowed cervix is causing painful menstruation because of restricted flow of menstrual fluid. For treatment of this problem, multiple dilatations may be necessary since the cervix will often become narrow again after several months.

### The procedure

Although a D&C is a relatively minor procedure, hospital admission is sometimes recommended. Because the large intestine should be empty before the procedure, an enema is often given; the urinary bladder should also be emptied.

The procedure is performed in an operating room under sterile conditions. Anesthesia may be general (the patient is put to sleep) or local. The patient rests on her back with her feet in stirrups. The surgeon inserts metal dilators of progressively larger sizes into the cervix until it is open enough to permit the insertion of the surgical instruments.

(An alternative method of cervical dilatation employs a small tube of dried seaweed that is left in the cervical canal for 8 to 12 hours. As the seaweed absorbs moisture from the cervical canal, it expands and enlarges the canal.)

A curette is used to remove endometrial tissue. Special forceps may also be used to remove tissue. When the operation is finished, an absorbent pad is placed over the entrance to the vagina. The pad is checked every 15 minutes for two hours, and excessive bleeding is reported to the physician.

Mild painkillers should be enough to control discomfort from the operation. If there is pain in the abdomen that cannot be relieved in this way or that is continuous or sharp, it should be reported immediately. Some difficulty in urinating is to be expected immediately after the procedure.

In most cases, the patient stays in bed for one to two hours following surgery. Most women return home several hours after the operation or the next day. A return to many daily activities is possible immediately, and in a week all normal physical activities may be resumed. Sexual intercourse and use of tampons should not be attempted, however, until after the follow-up visit to the doctor (usually about two weeks after the procedure).

## Risks

The principal risks of a D&C are hemorrhage, infection, and perforation (puncture) of the uterus. The latter is more likely during pregnancy, when the uterine walls are especially soft and thin.

# Dysmenorrhea

Dysmenorrhea is the term for painful menstruation. It occurs most commonly in teenagers and in women who have never been pregnant.

There are two types of dysmenorrhea. Primary dysmenorrhea is a recurring condition, usually beginning shortly after the onset of menstruation in a young girl. Secondary dysmenorrhea develops later in life, after a woman has been menstruating for some time.

Dysmenorrhea is not a serious condition, but it can be annoying, uncomfortable, and even incapacitating. Since secondary dysmenorrhea usually indicates that another disorder is present, treatment should always be sought for this condition.

## Causes

The cause of primary dysmenorrhea is thought to be the release of prostaglandins from the lining of the uterus shortly before the beginning of a menstrual period. (Prostaglandins are substances that, among other functions, stimulate uterine contractions.) The resulting contractions constrict blood vessels in the uterus, causing pain in the same way that a decrease in blood supply to the heart causes chest pain. The reason for this excessive production of prostaglandins is not known. Dysmenorrhea is usually secondary to (a result of) another reproductive problem, such as fibroid tumors, a narrow cervix, or endometriosis (the displacement of tissue from the lining of the uterus to areas elsewhere in the body).

## Symptoms

The major symptoms of dysmenorrhea are cramps and pain in the lower abdomen, possibly extending around to the back. Nausea, vomiting, diarrhea, headache, fatigue, and nervousness are mainly associated with primary dysmenorrhea. These symptoms usually appear at the beginning of, or slightly before, the menstrual period, and may last several hours or several days.

## Diagnosis

Diagnostic evaluation will include a complete physical examination, as well as medical and menstrual histories. If the symptoms have been present from the onset of menstruation at puberty, primary dysmenorrhea is usually the diagnosis. If the symptoms appeared suddenly in a woman who has been menstruating for some years, secondary dysmenorrhea can be assumed. In that case, further diagnostic evaluation of the reproductive organs will then be necessary to identify the underlying disorder. Ultrasound examinations (in which the echoes of sound waves are used to create images of internal structures) or x-ray studies often prove useful.

## Treatment

Primary dysmenorrhea has been treated successfully with nonsteroidal anti-inflammatory drugs (such as ibuprofen, naproxen, meclofenamate, diflunisal, and mefenamic acid), which, when taken just before a period is to begin, act to suppress the release of prostaglandins and thereby reduce the intensity of the contractions that cause pain.

Secondary dysmenorrhea is treated by correcting the problem that is causing it. For instance, if endometriosis is the underlying problem, it may be treated with hormone therapy or surgery, thereby relieving the dysmenorrhea as well.

Home remedies often help to ease menstrual pain and relieve pressure. These include placing a hot-water bottle or heating pad on the abdomen, taking hot baths, and lying on the back with the knees bent. A woman who experienced dysmenorrhea before pregnancy may find that the problem is lessened after childbirth, possibly because of enlargement of the cervix or destruction of some nerve fibers in the uterus.

# Dyspareunia

Dyspareunia is difficulty or pain for a woman during sexual intercourse.

## Causes

Dyspareunia may be caused by a resistant hymen (the membrane that usually covers the opening to the vagina in virgins) or by inflammation of or injury to the vagina, the urethra (the tube that carries urine from the bladder to the outside), the vulva (the structures around the opening to the vagina), or the anus. It can be the result of formation of scar tissue around an episiotomy (a surgical cut to enlarge the opening of the vagina immediately before childbirth) or surgery to repair the vagina. Other organic causes include tight muscles in the area around the vagina, an "hourglass" contraction of the vagina, a divided vagina, inflammation of the cervix, prolapsed (fallen) uterus, infected fallopian tubes, and endometriosis.

Inadequate lubrication of the vagina is a common cause of dyspareunia. This deficiency may be due to inadequate arousal of the woman before insertion of the penis or to menopause, which is accompanied by a decrease in vaginal secretions and thinning of the vaginal lining. Unconscious tightening of the vaginal muscles, called vaginismus, is another possible cause—perhaps the result of fear, unreadiness or unwillingness to perform the sex act, or other psychological reasons. Improperly fitted or improperly lubricated birth control devices (condoms or diaphragms) and an allergy to contraceptive spermicides are other causes.

## Symptom

Pain during or following sexual intercourse is the primary symptom.

## Diagnosis

Diagnosis is made on the basis of both a physical and an emotional evaluation. In some cases, physical abnormalities can be detected during the physical examination. In other cases, careful inquiry into the patient's emotional state and sexual history may reveal factors that account for the discomfort.

## Treatment

Treatment for dyspareunia is correction of any underlying disease, injury, or structural defect, if such a problem exists. For some couples, counseling by a psychiatrist or sex therapist is helpful in removing psychological barriers to sexual closeness that may result in dyspareunia.

Water-soluble lubricating jelly (not petroleum jelly), obtainable in any drugstore, is a good vaginal lubricant. Estrogen creams can be used along with water-soluble jelly to restore lubrication to a dry vagina after menopause. Soothing creams and temporary avoidance of intercourse can relieve the soreness of dyspareunia.

# Endometriosis

Endometriosis is a condition in which tissue from the endometrial lining of the uterus becomes detached and grows in the abdominal cavity outside the uterus. It occurs only in women of childbearing age, especially in women between the ages of 30 and 40.

## Cause

During each menstrual cycle, the endometrium normally thickens and swells in preparation for

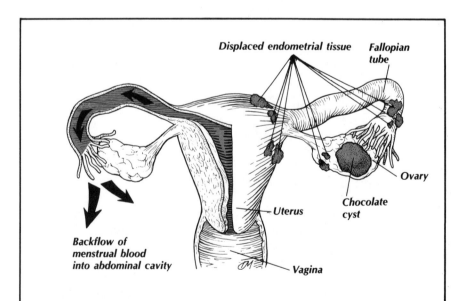

*Endometriosis is a condition in which tissue from the endometrium (uterine lining) becomes detached and grows outside the uterus, usually elsewhere in the abdominal cavity. One possible cause may be backflow of menstrual blood through one of the fallopian tubes into the abdominal cavity. Blood-filled pockets called "chocolate cysts" sometimes form when scar tissue surrounds accumulations of blood and displaced endometrial tissue.*

possible pregnancy. If no pregnancy occurs, portions of endometrial tissue break down and pass out of the uterus as part of the menstrual flow. When endometriosis develops, displaced endometrial tissue continues to swell and bleed each month in an abnormal location, but the blood has no outlet. The body responds to the presence of this accumulated blood by surrounding it with scar tissue, which builds up month after month, until blood-filled pockets, or cysts (often called "chocolate cysts"), are formed on the affected organs.

The exact cause of endometriosis is not known, but several conditions are thought to lead to its development: menstrual blood may flow backward through the fallopian tubes and into the abdominal cavity; the cervix or vagina may be blocked, so that the menstrual blood cannot flow out normally; or surgery or another condition may lead to the displacement of some tissue from the uterus.

### Symptoms

The symptoms of endometriosis are pain immediately before, during, or immediately after the menstrual period; pain during intercourse; discomfort in the lower urinary tract or intestine; irregular or excessively heavy menstrual flow; bleeding from the rectum; blood in the urine; and infertility. Some women may experience all of these symptoms, while others may experience only one or two.

### Diagnosis

Diagnostic evaluation begins with a complete medical and menstrual history. Pelvic examinations may be performed twice—once during menstruation and once between periods—to investigate the changes in the reproductive organs during the cycle. The doctor may also perform a laparoscopy, in which a small, lighted, tubelike instrument is inserted into the lower abdomen through a tiny incision, often allowing visualization of displaced tissues.

### Treatment

Treatment of this disorder consists of halting the condition, reducing the pain, and restoring normal menstruation and fertility. The best way to halt endometriosis is to modify the body's natural hormonal secretions with drugs in order to stop menstruation and ovulation for some time, thus allowing the endometrial tissue to shrink. Naturally, the patient will be unable to become pregnant during this type of drug therapy, but since endometriosis often causes infertility, many patients are already unable to conceive.

Two types of drugs are usually used in this treatment. Birth control pills, as well as several other medications that modify female hormonal secretions, are sometimes prescribed in doses high enough to stop menstruation and ovulation. However, an excessive dosage often brings with it undesirable side effects, such as nausea, fluid retention, and blood clotting. A synthetic hormone called danazol creates a condition similar to menopause, causing menstruation and ovulation to stop and the endometrial tissue to shrink almost immediately. Danazol does not have some of the side effects associated with other hormonal drugs. However, it is relatively expensive and is not effective in all cases.

If drug therapy is unsuccessful, surgery may be necessary, involving either the removal of scar tissue and endometrial tissue or, in advanced cases, the removal of the uterus and ovaries, rendering the patient sterile.

## Fibrocystic disease of the breast

Fibrocystic disease is a condition in which benign (noncancerous) lumps form in the breast, either temporarily or for the duration of the childbearing years.

This condition is not dangerous in itself, but it has been found that women with certain forms of fibrocystic disease may be two to four times more likely to develop breast cancer than other women are. To complicate matters, the presence of these benign lumps makes it difficult to detect any new, possibly dangerous growths.

### Cause

The exact cause of fibrocystic disease is not known. However, the tendency to develop it may be inherited. Also, it is seen more often in women who have never breast-fed a child; the reason for this is not known.

### Symptoms

The most noticeable symptom of this disorder is the presence of the lumps, which may take the form of either solid masses or fluid-filled sacs called cysts. Large cystic lumps near the surface can be moved about freely, unlike cancerous lumps, which are usually firmly attached to surrounding tissue. Changes in hormonal secretions during the menstrual period tend to slightly increase the size of the lumps, which causes additional pain, but the size of the cysts decreases following the period. Other symptoms may include a slight discharge from the nipple, as well as persistently heavy and tender breasts, not only before and during menstruation (as is commonly seen in healthy breasts) but all the time.

### Diagnosis

Diagnostic evaluation will begin with a physical examination. Mammography (a special x-ray study of the breasts) is often done to determine whether the lumps are fluid-filled cysts or solid masses. If they are found to be solid, a biopsy (the removal of a small piece of tissue for analysis) may be performed to detect the presence of cancerous cells.

The normal breast (seen on the left) contains some fibrous tissue, which supports the mammary (milk) glands. The fibrocystic breast (seen on the right) is characterized by the presence of extra fibrous tissue and solid masses or fluid-filled sacs (cysts).

### Treatment

Fibrocystic disease often requires no treatment. In some cases, the lumps may disappear in a few months. However, cysts that are unusually large or particularly bothersome may be drained of their fluid by the insertion of a hollow needle in a procedure called aspiration. If there are many small lumps or if there is continuous development of new ones, other forms of treatment may be necessary to prevent the formation of cysts. Birth control pills may be pre-

scribed, since they act to equalize the concentration of hormones in the body throughout the monthly cycle; however, birth control pills have also been found to cause cysts in some women. Large doses of vitamin E (taken under a doctor's supervision) have also been reportedly effective in treating this disorder.

### Prevention

Relieving or preventing fibrocystic disease may be promoted

by discontinuing or drastically limiting the intake of nicotine and a chemical called methylxanthine, found most commonly in coffee, tea, cola, chocolate, and some cold medications. It is thought that both nicotine and methylxanthine may promote the growth of fibrocystic tissue.

Because certain forms of this disorder carry a greater risk of breast cancer, women with fibrocystic disease should have a physical examination at least twice a year, report any new growths or enlargements of existing lumps, and perform self-examination of their breasts each month following the menstrual period.

# Fibroid tumors

Fibroid tumors are solid, noncancerous growths composed of smooth muscle fibers and connective tissue that grow in the walls of the uterus or out from the uterus. Only rarely do they appear on the cervix. Occasionally they fill the entire uterus, push through the cervix, and appear in the vagina. These tumors usually grow slowly and vary in size and shape.

Fibroid tumors are thought to be the most common type of abdominal tumor, found in about 25 percent of all women over the age of 30 (more frequently in black women). Cancer rarely develops in fibroid tumors; however, they do sometimes cause problems. For example, the tumors tend to enlarge during pregnancy, which can cause complications as the fetus grows.

### Cause

The cause of fibroid tumors is not known, but their growth seems to be related to the female hormone estrogen, since these tumors rarely appear before puberty and tend to recede by the menopause years. They most commonly appear in the middle to late reproductive years, when the estrogen level is at its peak.

Fibroid tumors may occur with other disorders, such as endometriosis (the displacement of tissue from the uterine lining to outside the uterus) or pelvic inflammatory disease (an infection of the fallopian tubes).

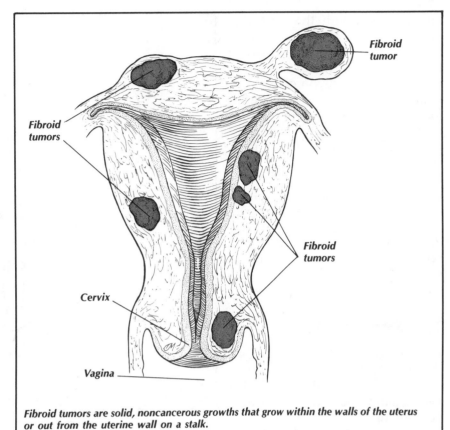

Fibroid tumors are solid, noncancerous growths that grow within the walls of the uterus or out from the uterine wall on a stalk.

### Symptoms

Common symptoms of fibroid tumors are dysmenorrhea (pain during menstruation) and gushing or flooding menstrual flow. Occasionally, there is abdominal pain; however, pain is not usually a symptom unless a complication develops (for example, if the tumor becomes twisted, cutting off its blood supply, there may be severe pain). If fibroid tumors become very large, they may press on surrounding organs, such as the intestines and bladder, which may result in constipation or frequent urination. If they extend into the uterus, heavy and prolonged menstrual periods may result. If the tumor is advanced, the abdomen may be noticeably enlarged. Sometimes, however, these tumors cause no symptoms at all and are simply discovered during a routine physical examination.

### Diagnosis

Diagnostic evaluation begins with a physical examination and may include curettage (scraping of the uterus walls) or endometrial biopsy (removal of some tissue from the lining of the uterus) to test for cancer. X-rays and ultrasound (a technique that uses sound waves to create an image of internal structures) may also be used to establish the location and nature of the tumor.

### Treatment

Fibroid tumors may require no treatment at all, other than regular checkups with the doctor. Those that are causing complications may require one of two types of surgery: removal of the tumor (called a myomectomy), which is usually recommended for women in their early reproductive years whose symptoms are somewhat mild and who desire a future pregnancy, or removal of the uterus (called a hysterectomy), which is usually recommended for older women and for those who do not want to become pregnant, since this operation makes pregnancy impossible.

# Hysterectomy

Hysterectomy is the surgical removal of the uterus, which causes the termination of menstruation and the ability to bear children.

A hysterectomy may be either total or partial. Total hysterectomy entails removal of the entire uterus, including the cervix. Partial hysterectomy, which is rarely done today, involves removal of only the body of the uterus but not the cervix. Oophorectomy (removal of one or both ovaries) and salpingectomy (removal of one or both fallopian tubes) may be performed at the same time as hysterectomy (for more information, see page 301).

Removal of the uterus may be done through an abdominal incision (cut) or through the vagina. In the latter procedure, the top of the vagina is stitched together after the uterus has been removed; this technique requires no external incision and, therefore, leaves no external scar.

Hysterectomies are most commonly performed when the uterus is diseased. Symptomatic fibroid tumors, uterine prolapse

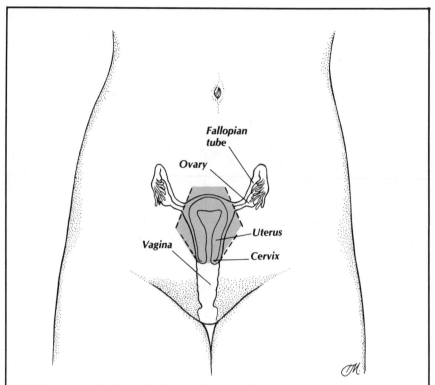

*Total hysterectomy is the surgical removal of the uterus and the cervix. Oophorectomy (removal of the ovaries) and salpingectomy (removal of one or both of the fallopian tubes) is sometimes performed at the same time.*

(falling of the uterus out of its normal position), and cancer of the uterus are common reasons for a hysterectomy.

Contrary to common belief, a hysterectomy, in and of itself, does not interfere with, or diminish the pleasure of, sexual intercourse, nor does it cause weight gain.

# Leukorrhea

Leukorrhea is an abnormal discharge from the vagina. All women have some normal discharge in the form of mucous secretions from the cervix and the vagina. This normal discharge helps to lubricate the vagina and, to some extent, prevent infection. This discharge is most noticeable at the time of ovulation (when an egg is released

from the ovary), but it is generally present during the entire menstrual cycle.

### Causes

Abnormal discharge is usually caused by an infection of the vagina by fungi, parasites, or bacteria. It may also be caused by an infection of the cervix, a tumor or other abnormal growth, the presence of foreign matter (such as a forgotten tampon) in the vagina, or an inflammation of the vagina caused by chemicals in douches or contraceptive creams or jellies.

### Symptoms

An abnormal vaginal discharge usually is heavy, is accompanied by itching of the genital organs and anal area, and has a disagreeable odor.

## Diagnosis

To diagnose the cause of the discharge, the doctor will perform a pelvic examination and will often take a sample of the discharge for microscopic examination. Sometimes a culture of the discharge may also be performed so that the organism causing the problem can be grown in the laboratory and identified.

## Treatment

Once the cause of the abnormal discharge has been identified, specific steps are taken to treat it. If the discharge is caused by a bacterial infection, oral antibiotics or antibiotic vaginal creams may be prescribed. Specific oral drugs or vaginal creams will be prescribed if the discharge is caused by a type of yeast or trichomonad (a single-celled parasite). In some cases, a biopsy of the cervix or vagina may be required if the doctor suspects that a tumor may be causing the discharge.

Douching with vinegar and water or other solutions available without a prescription generally will not cure the discharge, even though symptoms may improve for a few days. A woman with an abnormal vaginal discharge should consult her doctor rather than attempting to treat herself.

# Mastectomy

Mastectomy is the surgical removal of a breast or part of a

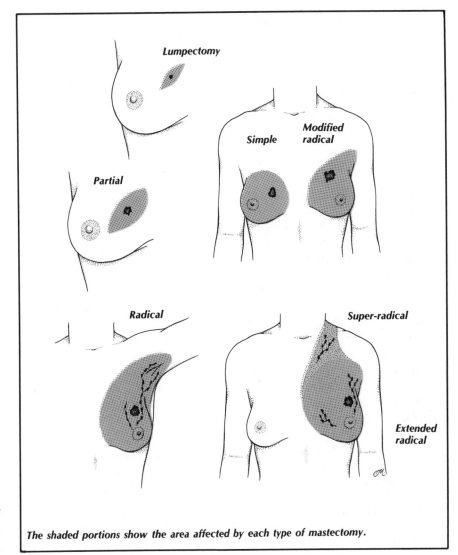

*The shaded portions show the area affected by each type of mastectomy.*

breast, usually as a treatment for cancer.

## Types

There are several types of mastectomy, each characterized by which muscles, glands, and other tissues are removed.

- Lumpectomy—removal of the tumor along with some of the surrounding breast tissue
- Partial mastectomy—removal of the tumor along with as much as one-half of the breast
- Simple mastectomy—removal of the entire breast

- Modified radical mastectomy—removal of the entire breast plus the armpit lymph nodes on the affected side
- Radical mastectomy—removal of the entire breast, the armpit lymph nodes, and the muscles below the breast
- Extended radical mastectomy—removal of the entire breast plus additional tissue in the chest, as well as the armpit lymph nodes and chest muscles
- Super-radical mastectomy—removal of the same tissues and muscles as in the extended radical mastectomy, as well as

some tissues and lymph nodes in the neck

### Choice of type

The type of mastectomy to be performed is determined by a multitude of factors, including the location, size, and type of tumor. The age and general health of the patient are also extremely important. A biopsy (removal of a small tissue sample for microscopic examination) will be performed prior to mastectomy. In addition, other tests may be done to determine if the cancer has spread to other areas of the body.

There is some question about how extensive the surgery should be. In recent years, the modified radical mastectomy has become the most frequently chosen procedure. However, there are differences of opinion in medical circles, and a woman facing a mastectomy should thoroughly discuss all of the procedures and available options with her doctor.

### Treatment

The operation is performed while the patient is under general anesthesia. Afterward the patient remains hospitalized for about a week and may begin physical therapy and radiation therapy or chemotherapy. Checkups every 6 to 12 months are recommended.

### Prevention of breast cancer

One of the best preventive measures a woman can take is establishing the habit of examining her breasts monthly. With this simple routine, a woman

can often detect a cancerous lump before cancer cells can spread beyond the breast. The effectiveness of breast self-examination is shown by the high percentage of breast tumors that are discovered by patients themselves during a monthly breast self-examination. (For instructions on breast self-examination, see page 393.)

Many experts recommend annual mammography (x-ray examination of the breasts) for women over the age of 50 and for women from 40 to 49 who are considered to be at high risk of developing breast cancer (those who have had breast cancer in the past or who have a mother or sister who has had the disease). A mammogram at the age of 35 is recommended for every woman to provide a baseline for later comparison.

# Menopause

Menopause is the normal, natural stage in a woman's life when her menstruation and ovulation cycles stop, ending her reproductive years. Also called the climacteric, or the change of life, it occurs around age 50 but can start anywhere between the ages of 40 and 60.

### Cause

Scientists do not fully understand what causes menopause, but they believe that it is triggered when the ovaries stop responding to the sex hormones that are secreted by the pituitary gland to control normal functioning of the ovaries. The subsequent decline in the production of the female hormone estrogen by the ovaries sets off the bodily changes.

### Symptoms

During the years immediately preceding the onset of menopause, menstrual periods may become irregular and menstrual flow scanty.

Other physical symptoms may include hot flashes (a warm and flushed feeling over the face, neck, and chest that lasts a few minutes and recurs throughout the day), excessive perspiration, dryness in the vagina (which can lead to painful or difficult sexual intercourse), pounding heartbeat, joint pains, headaches, itching skin, increased facial hair, and decreased armpit and pubic hair.

Nonphysical symptoms may include depression, anxiety, irritability, apprehension, decreased ability to concentrate, lack of confidence, and insomnia.

The duration of symptoms may range from a few weeks to more than five years. Not every woman experiences the same changes, other than an end to menstruation; about 25 percent notice no other changes, 50 percent discern some physical or psychological symptoms, and the other 25 percent are troubled by very uncomfortable or distressing symptoms.

### Diagnosis

It is important not to attribute all physical changes to menopause to the point of overlooking the symptoms of some disease. This is a good time to schedule an examination and discuss the bodily changes with a doctor. A woman should see a doctor immediately if she starts to bleed in between menstrual periods, bleeds excessively, or has another period six months or more after they had apparently stopped.

### Treatment

The primary treatment for the physical symptoms of menopause is replacement of the female sex hormones (commonly estrogen or a combination of estrogen and progesterone in the form of a tablet or vaginal cream). The lowest effective dose is administered (because of possible side effects) for the first few months and then tapered off (unless symptoms reappear) until the changes in the ovaries have been completed. Any treatment merely lessens the discomfort of menopause, however; it cannot stop or slow down the process.

Estrogen is not usually given to women with circulatory or liver disorders and is carefully controlled when prescribed to those with diabetes, epilepsy, or heart or kidney disease. Progesterone is not prescribed for women with liver disease and is carefully controlled in those with asthma, epilepsy, or heart or kidney disease. The benefits and hazards can be discussed with a doctor; other medication is available to treat certain menopausal symptoms in women who cannot take hormones.

Treatment for the psychological or emotional symptoms may include tranquilizers, antidepressants, sleeping pills, or psychotherapy. During this time, it may also be difficult for a woman to face the aging process and its physical ramifications—the end of the childbearing years and a sense of uselessness because of a possible decrease in family responsibilities. Some form of counseling may be helpful in such a situation.

Fertility and the need to practice birth control at this stage depend on a woman's age at the time of her last period. In general, a woman under the age of 50 may still be able to conceive for up to 24 months after the date of her last period; over 50, conception may be possible for up to one year.

After menopause, a woman is more liable to suffer osteoporosis (a disease that makes bones porous and brittle). This can often be prevented or controlled with estrogen therapy and calcium supplementation under medical supervision.

## Menorrhagia

Menorrhagia is a term referring to an abnormally long (more than seven days) or heavy menstrual flow, frequently accompanied by the passing of large blood clots.

The condition, which is especially common in women in their late 30s and 40s, seldom indicates the existence of a serious disorder. However, it may result in iron deficiency anemia because of excessive blood loss.

### Causes

Menorrhagia is a common problem, often caused by a disturbance in the hormones controlling the menstrual cycle. It can also be caused by fibroid tumors in the uterus, inflammation of the pelvic region, and hypothyroidism (underactivity of the thyroid gland).

### Diagnosis

If abnormal menstrual flow continues or recurs or if there is any chance of pregnancy, a physician should be consulted. The physician may perform a number of tests (including a Pap test) to determine whether there is a serious underlying cause. Biopsy (removal of a small tissue sample for laboratory examination) of the cervix or the uterine lining may be performed to check for cancer or other abnormalities. The physician may also do a blood test to check for iron deficiency anemia.

### Treatment

It is suggested that women who experience this disorder reduce the level of their activities during menstruation and be sure to get enough iron so that they will not become anemic.

## Menstruation

Menstruation is the monthly breakdown and discharge of portions of the endometrial tissue that lines the uterus.

### The normal process

Endometrial tissue thickens during each menstrual cycle to prepare the uterus for possible pregnancy. Approximately midway through the cycle, ovulation occurs. Ovulation is the process by which an ovary produces and releases an egg. The fingerlike projections at the end of the nearby fallopian tube sweep the egg into the tube, where it begins inching toward the uterus. If the egg is fertilized by a sperm, the fertilized egg moves to the uterus and becomes implanted in the rich uterine lining, where it grows for the next nine months. If the egg does not become fertilized, the thickened endometrial tissue breaks down and passes, along with the unfertilized egg, out of the cervix, through the vagina, and out of the body as the menstrual discharge. This monthly cycle is controlled by the female hormones estrogen and progesterone, which are secreted by the ovaries.

Young women start menstruating and ovulating at puberty, which usually occurs between the ages of 9 and 14. Thereafter, they normally menstruate and ovulate every month (except while pregnant) until they reach menopause.

### Menstrual disorders

Menstruation may be accompanied by complications of varying degrees of seriousness. Most women will experience at least one such problem at some point in their reproductive lives. The most common problems are dysmenorrhea (painful menstruation), amenorrhea (the absence of one or more menstrual periods), and premenstrual syndrome (a complex of physical and emotional symptoms that appear in the days before the period begins).

For many years the symptoms of these disorders have been attributed to emotional factors. Research has shown, however, that most are caused by very real physical changes, and many new methods of treatment have been developed.

Although the disorders themselves are generally not dangerous, they can be physically and emotionally incapacitating. Furthermore, they may be symptoms of disease in the reproductive organs. Therefore, to be on the safe side, medical treatment

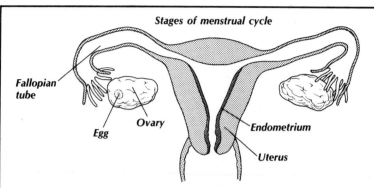

Stages of menstrual cycle

*While the egg (shown greatly enlarged, for purposes of illustration) is still inside the ovary, the endometrium (uterine lining) is fairly thin.*

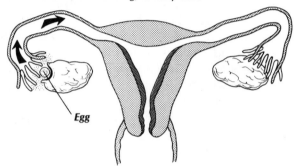

*When the egg is released and begins to move into the fallopian tube, the endometrium begins to thicken in preparation for a possible pregnancy.*

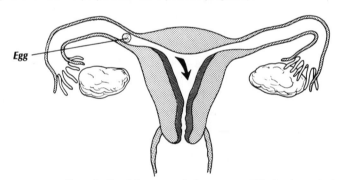

*The egg moves through the tube toward the uterus. This is the point at which conception may occur. The egg is met by the sperm cell in the fallopian tube, and the fertilized egg moves on to the uterus. During this time, the endometrium continues to grow.*

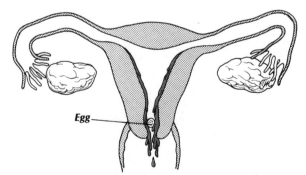

*If conception does not occur, the endometrium ceases to grow and thicken. At this stage, the endometrium breaks down and is discharged, along with the unfertilized egg, from the uterus as the menstrual discharge.*

for annoying symptoms accompanying menstruation should always be sought.

# Oophorectomy

Oophorectomy is the surgical removal of an ovary. An oophorectomy is a major operation, usually performed through either a vertical or a horizontal incision in the abdominal area, but occasionally performed through an incision in the vagina.

Removal of one ovary is called a unilateral oophorectomy. A salpingectomy (removal of all or part of the nearby fallopian tube) is usually performed at the same time. Removal of both ovaries is called a bilateral oophorectomy. A bilateral oophorectomy ends a woman's ability to conceive children and brings on menopause (if it has not already occurred). A hysterectomy (removal of the uterus) is generally performed in conjunction with a bilateral oophorectomy because the uterus has no purpose without both ovaries and, if left, can later harbor tumors.

### Purpose

Oophorectomy is used to correct a number of conditions in which the ovaries are the site of the trouble, including ovarian ectopic pregnancy (in which the embryo begins to develop in the ovary, rather than in the uterus) and benign (noncancerous) and malignant (cancerous) ovarian cysts and tumors. In women with recurrent cancer or endometriosis (a condition in which displaced parts of the uterine lining grow outside the uterus), oophorectomy is performed to stop the production of hormones, which tend to aggravate the problem.

Breast cancer, as well, may be dependent on hormones to grow; about one third of women with breast cancer show a decrease in breast cancer growth after removal of their ovaries.

### Pros and cons

Some physicians recommend a bilateral oophorectomy when a hysterectomy must be performed. There are pros and cons when it comes to removing healthy ovaries. Arguments for their removal are that it reduces the risk of ovarian cancer; that a small number of women will develop painful cystic ovaries, which would necessitate a second operation; and that for a woman in her 40s, the ovaries will naturally stop functioning within a few years anyway. Arguments against routine oophorectomy are that it causes the premature onset of menopause, which brings with it a greater risk of osteoporosis (loss of bone mass); that the abrupt end of hormone production is less natural than the gradual tapering off of natural menopause, provoking severe menopausal symptoms, such as hot flashes and vaginal shrinkage; and that estrogen, the hormone often prescribed after the procedure, may increase the risk of cancer of the reproductive system.

If a woman is in her childbearing years, her doctor will make every effort to save healthy ovarian tissue. Because the ovaries are fed by an excellent blood supply, they heal quickly and even a small bit of preserved ovarian tissue will function, secrete hormones, and release eggs. The woman remains fertile and avoids early menopause.

In women past menopause, for whom fertility is no longer an issue and in whom the ovaries are no longer producing estrogen anyway, both the ovaries and the uterus are commonly removed even if only one ovary is abnormal.

# Ovarian cysts

An ovarian cyst is an abnormal swelling or saclike growth on an ovary.

Ovarian cysts may be filled with liquid or may contain a semifluid substance. Most cysts are small, but they can vary in size from less than an inch in diameter to as large as 15 to 20 inches in diameter. Depending on their size, type, and location, they can cause severe pain and complications or no symptoms at all. They are common among women between the ages of 20 and 50. The cysts can grow alone or in groups and can form on one ovary or both. Approximately 85 percent are benign (noncancerous).

### Causes

The origin of most ovarian cysts is unknown. In some instances, they develop from an abnormal egg. Others originate as eggs in polycystic ovaries (ovaries in which the eggs are not released after they mature). Still others are related to abnormalities in the ovary. Women with endometriosis (a condition in which displaced uterine tissue grows outside the uterus) tend to develop growths on the ovaries. Dermoid cysts, which are most often found in women under the age of 30, arise from the ovarian cells that produce the eggs, and may contain fragments of hair, teeth, bone, and sweat and oil glands.

## Complications

Cysts can rupture during sexual intercourse, a fall, childbirth, or surgery, or for no apparent reason. The resulting effect depends on how irritating the cystic fluid is to the surrounding tissues. The situation can be dangerous if the fluid is infected, cancerous, or extremely irritating. Also, in response to the injury caused by cystic fluid, surrounding tissues may produce adhesions (fibrous, scarlike material), which can further complicate the situation.

## Symptoms

Symptoms of ovarian cysts vary with the type of growth. Some cause no symptoms at all and are discovered during a routine pelvic examination. Others cause firm, painless swelling in the lower abdomen; pain during sexual intercourse; frequent urination (if they press against the bladder); irregular vaginal bleeding; or pain, nausea, and fever (if the cysts rupture or grow on stalks that become twisted). Excessive and abnormal body hair growth and the development of acne may result from hormonal imbalances caused by polycystic ovaries.

## Diagnosis

Ovarian cysts are diagnosed by pelvic examination, ultrasound, or laparoscopy (a surgical procedure in which a tubelike instrument is inserted through the abdominal wall to view the pelvic organs). The condition may be difficult to diagnose accurately because the symptoms can resemble those of acute appendicitis or other abdominal problems. In addition, it can be hard to determine if a cyst is malignant and if it is actually on the ovary rather than some other pelvic organ. Ovarian cysts that develop during pregnancy are also difficult to diagnose.

## Treatment

Cysts that are small, are not creating any problems, or are likely to disappear on their own require no treatment. If treatment is necessary, cysts may be removed surgically. Removal involves either taking out the entire ovary (oophorectomy) or taking out only the cyst (cystectomy).

If the ovarian cyst is found to be cancerous, it is necessary to remove both ovaries, both fallopian tubes, and the uterus, since the cancer may have spread from the ovarian cyst to these other structures. This procedure is also performed if an ovarian cyst is found after menopause because these cysts are often cancerous.

# Ovulation

Ovulation is the process by which an ovary produces and releases an egg.

The egg develops within the ovary in a small, fluid-filled sac called a follicle. When the egg is mature, this sac ruptures, releasing the egg from the ovary. The fingerlike projections on the nearby fallopian tube sweep the egg into the tube, where it begins to inch toward the uterus. If the egg is fertilized by a sperm, the fertilized egg moves along the tube to the uterus and becomes implanted in the rich uterine lining, where it grows for

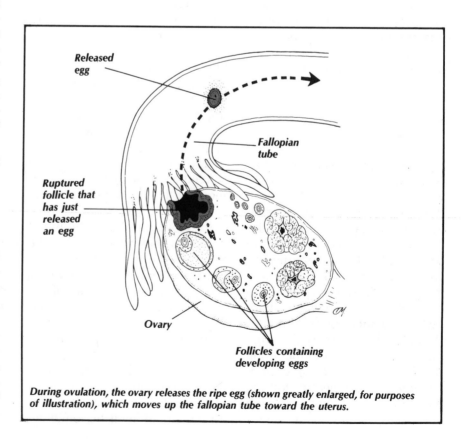

During ovulation, the ovary releases the ripe egg (shown greatly enlarged, for purposes of illustration), which moves up the fallopian tube toward the uterus.

the next nine months. If the egg does not become fertilized, the uterine lining breaks down and passes, along with the unfertilized egg, out of the cervix, through the vagina, and out of the body as the menstrual discharge.

Ovulation is regulated by a complex system of hormonal and chemical secretions from the ovaries, the hypothalamus (part of the brain), and the pituitary gland (the master gland, which controls most hormonal secretions). Ovulation and menstruation begin during puberty, which usually occurs between the ages of 9 and 14, and normally continue every month (except during pregnancy) until menopause occurs (around age 50).

One way to recognize when ovulation is happening is to take the body temperature with a basal thermometer (a special thermometer that will show even slight changes in body temperature) before rising in the morning. In most women, the body temperature rises slightly soon after ovulation occurs each month and does not return to normal until the menstrual flow begins. Another way is to count 14 days from the first day of the last menstrual period in an average 28-day cycle (count 15 days for a cycle that is normally 29 days long, 16 days for a cycle that is normally 30 days long, and so on). However, this method is less accurate than the thermometer method because the length of the menstrual cycle can vary from month to month. Some women feel cramps in the lower abdomen during ovulation.

A sperm that has been released into the vagina as long as two days before the release of a ripe egg can still fertilize it; and

an egg, once released, is capable of being fertilized for about two days. Because of this variability, there is a period of four to ten days in each menstrual cycle during which a woman can become pregnant. (For more information on the role of ovulation in family planning, see pages 313–314.)

# Pelvic inflammatory disease

Pelvic inflammatory disease (PID), or salpingitis, is an inflammation of one or both of the fallopian tubes. Although the term is widely used to refer to infections of other organs in the pelvic cavity, PID properly refers only to an inflammation of the fallopian tubes.

## Causes

Pelvic inflammatory disease is usually caused by certain bacteria transmitted during sexual intercourse, the presence of an intrauterine device (IUD) that has become a source of infection, or certain vaginal infections. One of the most common causes of PID is gonorrhea, a sexually transmitted disease.

Under normal circumstances, the cervix prevents bacteria in the vagina from entering the uterus. However, a woman becomes more vulnerable to PID if the opening of her cervix has been dilated (enlarged) by recent surgery, childbirth, or miscarriage.

## Symptoms

Symptoms include severe pain and tenderness in the lower ab-

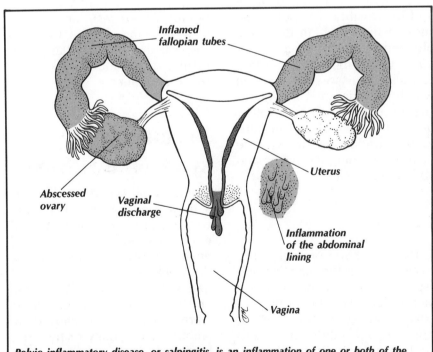

Pelvic inflammatory disease, or salpingitis, is an inflammation of one or both of the fallopian tubes, which can lead to an ovarian abscess, an inflammation of the abdominal lining, and blockage of the fallopian tubes. Vaginal discharge is a common sign of the condition.

domen, fever, a foul-smelling vaginal discharge, menstrual irregularities, pain during sexual intercourse, nausea, vomiting, fatigue, and pain during urination or defecation.

### Diagnosis

It is important to seek medical attention as soon as symptoms occur, so that the infection can be treated before it worsens and spreads. The physician will perform a physical examination and take a sample of fluid from the cervix to identify the infecting organism.

### Complications

If PID is not diagnosed and treated early, the infection can cause abscesses (pus-filled cavities) to form in the fallopian tubes or around the ovaries. The inflammation can also damage and irreversibly scar pelvic tissues. If the fallopian tubes are blocked, conception can become impossible. The infection can also result in septicemia (in which bacteria enter the bloodstream and are spread to other parts of the body) and in peritonitis (inflammation of the membrane lining the pelvic and abdominal cavities).

### Treatment

The doctor will prescribe antibiotics to fight the infection and aspirin or another painkiller for pain relief. The woman may be advised to rest in bed, abstain from sexual intercourse, and apply heat to the lower abdominal area. In some cases, the woman may have to enter the hospital to receive antibiotics in-

travenously. Laparoscopy (examination of the internal organs through a special tubelike instrument) or surgery to drain blocked tubes or abscessed tissue may be performed. Sometimes, the damage is too extensive, and the fallopian tubes, the uterus, and the ovaries have to be removed surgically.

### Prevention

When the cervix is dilated for any reason, a woman is more susceptible to PID for several weeks. Since the cervix is dilated in childbirth, abortion, miscarriage, and the surgical procedure called dilatation and curettage (D&C), a woman can minimize her chances of contracting PID by taking special precautions after any of those events. Such precautions include avoiding sexual intercourse, tub baths, and the use of douches and tampons. She should check with her doctor before resuming any of these activities. Also, if a woman suspects that she may have gonorrhea, she should seek treatment immediately.

# Premenstrual syndrome (PMS)

Premenstrual syndrome (PMS) is a term used to encompass the varying complex of physical and emotional symptoms experienced by some women during the week before their menstrual period begins. In the past, this and other menstrual problems were thought to be caused by emotional instability or hysteria, but current research, while not yet offering conclusive findings, indicates that there may be physical reasons for such disorders.

### Cause

Many researchers believe that PMS is caused by fluctuations in the production of female hormones during the course of the menstrual cycle. Hormonal changes influence the amounts of salt and fluid retained in the body, especially during the week before the period begins. Neither the exact cause for this fluid and salt retention nor the reason for its effect on certain women is fully understood.

### Symptoms

The symptoms of PMS appear during the week preceding menstruation and usually disappear as soon as the menstrual flow begins. In addition to nervousness and irritability, a bloated or puffy feeling that results from edema (fluid retention) often characterizes this disorder. Other possible symptoms include depression, headache, fatigue, tenderness in the breasts, and acne.

### Diagnosis

The diagnosis of premenstrual syndrome is based on a physical examination and the menstrual history. The occurrence of any of the symptoms with some regularity before each menstrual period and their disappearance soon after menstrual flow begins are the key diagnostic clues.

### Treatment

At present, there is no single or sure remedy for PMS. Depending on the symptoms present, various medications may be helpful. The edema is often treated by reducing salt intake or taking diuretics (medications that help to eliminate excess fluid from the tissues). Tranquilizers and psychological counseling may be recommended for patients in whom PMS causes emotional distress. A balanced diet, moderate exercise, and adequate rest may also be beneficial in treating the condition.

### Prevention

A reduction of salt intake may help to prevent the initial edema that often accompanies PMS. Self-treatment with diuretics without the advice of a physician is not recommended.

# Prolapse of the uterus

Prolapse refers to a collapse, descent, or other change in position of an organ in relation to surrounding structures. Prolapse of the uterus may be one of three types, depending on severity:
- First-degree prolapse, in which the uterus sags downward so that the cervix is flush with the entrance to the vagina
- Second-degree prolapse, in which the cervix is outside the vagina
- Third-degree prolapse, in which the entire uterus is outside the vagina

### Cause

Prolapse of the uterus occurs when the muscles and ligaments that normally hold the uterus in place become stretched or slack. This is most often due to a long or difficult childbirth or multiple childbirths.

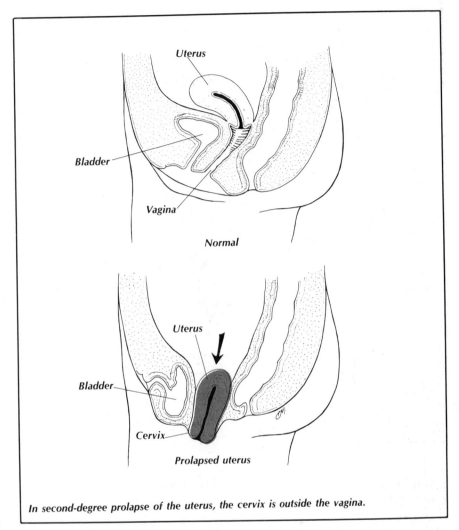

In second-degree prolapse of the uterus, the cervix is outside the vagina.

### Symptoms

There may be a feeling of heaviness in the vagina, backache, or inability to control urination.

### Diagnosis

Prolapse is apparent during a pelvic examination.

### Treatment

It is especially important to treat prolapse of the uterus because it can make childbirth difficult and may damage other organs. In mild cases, exercises for the muscles of the pelvic floor may be helpful. If the prolapse is the result of injury or stress, surgical repair may be indicated, in which the uterus is returned to its proper place and sewn or stapled into position. If the prolapse is due to disease or swelling, the underlying disorder must first be controlled or eliminated before the uterus can be returned to its original position and secured there.

# Rectocele

Rectocele is a condition in which a portion of the rectum

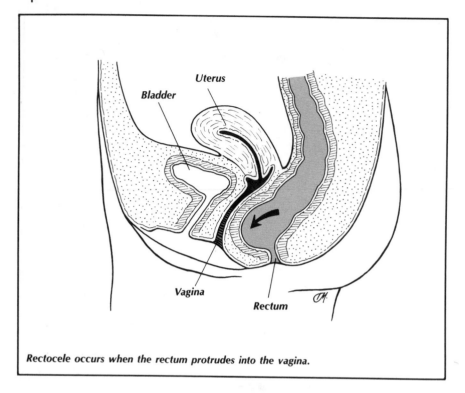

*Rectocele occurs when the rectum protrudes into the vagina.*

(the terminal portion of the large intestine) protrudes into the vagina.

## Cause

The usual cause of this condition is a weakening of the back wall of the vagina due to the stretching caused by childbirth.

## Symptoms

A minimal protrusion may produce no symptoms or only a mild pressure sensation during bowel movements. More severe protrusion of the rectum may lead to chronic constipation and painful bowel movements.

## Diagnosis

A rectocele is easily identified by the doctor during a pelvic examination. On straining or coughing, the rectum may be found to bulge into the vagina.

## Treatment

Rectocele is not a dangerous condition and generally requires no treatment. If severe constipation or painful bowel movements develop, surgical repair is often curative. Mild symptoms may be relieved by avoiding straining and heavy lifting and by ensuring soft bowel movements with use of drugs and careful selection of diet.

# Toxic shock syndrome

Toxic shock syndrome (TSS) is a rare, sometimes fatal disease that develops very suddenly and progresses rapidly when a bacterial infection spreads through the bloodstream. The disorder was first defined in 1978, when its link to the use of tampons was suspected. Most of the reported cases have occurred in menstruating women under the age of 30 who use tampons. A significant number of these cases have been fatal.

## Cause

Most researchers believe that TSS occurs when the *Staphylococcus aureus* bacterium enters the bloodstream and produces a toxin (poison) that causes leaks in blood vessel walls, allowing blood to seep into the tissues. This results in a sudden, very dangerous drop in blood pressure, shock, and sometimes death.

In serious cases, low blood pressure and weakening of the cell membranes can leave the victim susceptible to further complications, such as heart and liver damage. Often the body cannot produce enough antibodies (protective substances) to fight off the invasion of organisms through the weakened cell membranes, so TSS can easily recur.

Although the use of tampons is considered to be a definite risk factor, tampons do not actually cause the disease but rather promote the growth of bacteria that leads to the disorder. The tampons swell to fill the vagina and thereby inhibit the elimination of blood, creating a breeding ground for infection. Also, if tampons are left in the vagina for long periods of time, the chances for infection are increased. Tampon applicators, moreover, may scratch the walls of the vagina, allowing bacteria to enter.

Since about 25 percent of cases now occur in men and

nonmenstruating women, it is clear that the bacteria can enter the body in ways other than through the vagina. In these cases, TSS often occurs when the body has been weakened by major surgery, severe burns, or boils or abscesses. Also, women who have recently given birth are at a higher risk of contracting TSS because the vagina is more susceptible to the invasion of bacteria at this time.

## Symptoms

The symptoms of TSS are high fever, vomiting, diarrhea, a rash that looks like sunburn, peeling of skin on the soles of the feet and the palms of the hands, blurred vision, and disorientation.

## Diagnosis

The occurrence of the high fever, the characteristic rash, low blood pressure, and involvement of several organ systems strongly points to the diagnosis of TSS. Cultures of the blood and mucous membranes will be performed to search for evidence of infection by the *Staphylococcus aureus* bacterium.

## Treatment

Emergency medical treatment should be sought immediately. This will necessitate hospitalization, during which the patient will be given therapy similar to that administered to poisoning victims. Fluids or whole-blood transfusions are given to raise blood pressure, an ice blanket is used to reduce fever, and antibiotics are administered to fight the infection.

## Precautions

The best precaution is probably to discontinue or limit the use of tampons. Tampons can still be worn safely, but they should be changed every three to four hours and alternated with sanitary napkins as often as possible, especially before going to bed.

# Vaginitis

Vaginitis is an inflammation of the vagina, usually marked by burning and itching of the external genital organs.

## Causes

Vaginitis is most commonly caused by an imbalance of the microorganisms normally present in the vagina, resulting when some factor causes one of the strains to reproduce more quickly than the others. The microorganisms most often involved are the fungus *Candida albicans* (also called monilia), the bacterium *Hemophilus vaginalis,* and the protozoan (one-celled organism) *Trichomonas vaginalis.* Possible causes of overgrowth of microorganisms include the use of birth control pills, which produce changes in the vaginal lining; the use of certain antibiotics, which may kill some types of bacteria but allow others to flourish; and the presence of a warm, moist environment (such as may be created by wearing tight pants or pantyhose, nylon underwear, or a wet bathing suit), which acts as a breeding ground for infection. Vaginitis tends to occur more often in the summer, because excessive heat and moisture are known to promote the disease.

One variety of the disease, called noninfectious vaginitis, is not caused by overproduction of microorganisms, but rather by direct irritation of the vagina by some outside agent, such as the chemical irritation that arises from the excessive use of douches, feminine hygiene sprays, bubble baths, talcum powder, and scented or colored toilet paper.

Pregnant women and those who have diabetes or gonorrhea (a sexually transmitted disease) are at a higher risk of developing vaginitis than other women.

## Symptoms

Infection by *Candida albicans* causes severe itching of the external genital organs and pain during intercourse. Because of the thick, white vaginal discharge, which resembles cottage cheese in texture and has a "yeasty" odor, this condition is commonly known as a yeast infection. This is the type of vaginitis most frequently contracted by diabetic and pregnant women.

Infection by *Hemophilus vaginalis* causes a creamy white or grayish, foul-smelling discharge.

The presence of *Trichomonas vaginalis* is indicated by itching and burning, as well as by a greenish-white discharge and foul odor. These symptoms are likely to appear during or immediately following menstruation.

Noninfectious vaginitis is characterized only by irritation and dryness, usually with no discharge.

## Diagnosis

Vaginitis is diagnosed by determining which microorganism

is causing the infection. Microscopic examination of a sample, or "smear," of vaginal secretions is used to make the diagnosis.

### Treatment

Treatment will vary according to the type of causative microorganism. Fungal infections are generally treated with an antifungal cream, which is applied directly to the vagina or as a vaginal suppository.

Bacterial infections are treated with antibiotics, administered either orally or as vaginal suppositories. Because bacterial infections can be transferred between sexual partners, both are usually treated with oral antibiotics.

An oral antibiotic called metronidazole is given to women with protozoan infections and to their partners. Because some studies have linked this drug to cancer and genetic damage in laboratory animals, it should not be taken during the first half of pregnancy.

Noninfectious vaginitis is usually treated simply by avoiding the irritants that may cause it, such as perfumed soaps, chemical sprays, and scented tissues, and by not wearing tight-fitting clothing.

### Prevention

Some types of vaginitis can probably be prevented by using only nonscented, white toilet paper; wearing cotton underwear and loose-fitting pants; and avoiding the overuse of douches, feminine hygiene sprays, and scented toiletries.

# PROBLEMS OF COUPLES

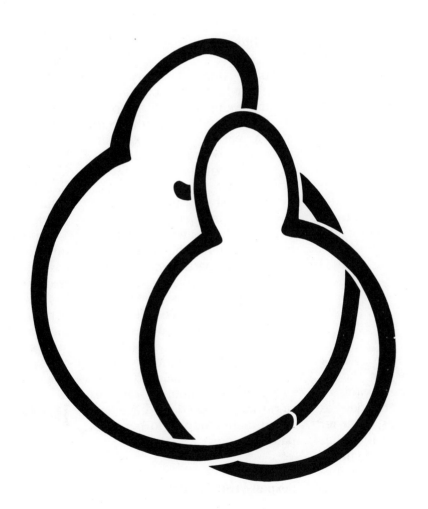

A couple can encounter health problems in three areas: contraception (birth control), infertility, and venereal (sexually transmitted) diseases. Decisions or problems in all three areas affect both partners.

Although sex is a topic that arouses considerable curiosity and interest, it unfortunately is also surrounded by many myths and misconceptions that can lead to needless anxiety. Fortunately, societal attitudes have been changing, and there is now more free and open discussion about subjects that used to be considered taboo.

The best approach to solving any problem includes two ingredients: an understanding by both persons involved in the relationship of how the male and female reproductive systems work and a willingness to communicate openly and honestly.

Responsibility for these areas of health should not be shouldered by either the man or the woman alone. Both partners need to work together to weigh consequences, consider alternatives, and provide mutual support.

### Birth control

Couples who want to delay or prevent pregnancy can choose from several different kinds of contraceptives: physical devices (intrauterine devices), barrier methods (condoms and diaphragms), chemical methods (spermicides and pills), a combination of physical and chemical methods (diaphragm with a spermicide), permanent birth control (vasectomy for men and blocking of fallopian tubes for women), and abstinence from intercourse during the woman's fertile period.

Some birth control methods require a doctor's prescription; others can be purchased over the counter. Methods vary in effectiveness, convenience, and safety. It's a good idea for a couple to discuss with a doctor the advantages and disadvantages of the various methods of birth control, especially the side effects, ease of use, and reliability. Choose the birth control method that best suits your needs as a couple; what works well for one couple may not appeal to another.

### Infertility

About one of every five couples who want to conceive a child are unsuccessful at doing so. If pregnancy does not occur after a year of regular sexual intercourse without contraceptives, the couple may want to consult with an obstetrician/gynecologist or a urologist who specializes in infertility.

During the last ten years or so, medical science has made tremendous inroads into diagnosing and treating causes of infertility and has thus given new hope to childless couples. Improved testing procedures, new drugs that stimulate ovulation, and surgical techniques that can correct female or male structural problems or sometimes reverse sterilization procedures have enabled many couples to become parents.

### Sexually transmitted diseases

One of the risks of intimate sexual contact, especially for men and women who have more than one partner, is infection with a sexually transmitted disease (STD), or venereal disease (VD). Despite improved diagnosis and treatment for these diseases, their incidence has increased, probably because of the sexual freedom of the last 20 years, which has resulted in large part from more reliable birth control.

Sexually transmitted diseases are caused by organisms that thrive in the warm, moist environment of the reproductive system and are transmitted by sexual contact. Gonorrhea is the most prevalent of the STDs, but herpes, syphilis, and nonspecific urethritis are common enough to be of concern to sexually active people. Although, with the exception of herpes, these diseases can be cured, the consequences of delaying treatment are too important to ignore. Permanent sterility can result.

STDs are particularly serious for pregnant women. The diseases can be transmitted to a baby passing through the birth canal and can critically affect the child.

A person who does become infected with any of these diseases must abstain from further sexual contact until the problem has been controlled. Any sexual partners need to be informed of the possibility of infection and must seek treatment, whether or not symptoms develop.

# Birth control

Birth control, also called contraception, is the voluntary prevention of pregnancy. A variety of methods are available for preventing pregnancy. Couples who use no contraceptive method have a 90 percent chance of achieving pregnancy over a 12-month period (provided that they have no underlying infertility problem).

## Condom

A condom is a thin rubber or synthetic sheath that the man fits over his erect penis just before sexual intercourse. A condom used alone is about 70 percent to 90 percent effective, depending on the care with which it is used. Several problems may occur with the use of the condom. For example, tiny holes or tears may develop in the sheath, causing leakage of sperm. Also, when the penis is withdrawn from the vagina as intercourse is completed, the condom sometimes breaks or partially unrolls inside the vagina, releasing its contents. However, a condom used regularly with a spermicide is approximately 95 percent effective in preventing pregnancy. Condoms have the great advantage of being readily available in any drugstore without a prescription. They also have the advantage of helping to prevent the spread of venereal disease and acquired immune deficiency syndrome (AIDS).

## Diaphragm

The diaphragm is a molded rubber cap that the woman places inside the vagina to cover the cervix. The cap blocks sperm from entering the uterus. It must be inserted for each act of intercourse and left in place for six hours afterward. Diaphragms come in different sizes and must be fitted by a physician. Used alone, diaphragms occasionally fail, either because they were not inserted correctly or because they shifted during sexual intercourse. Used with spermicides, however, diaphragms are quite effective, associated with only about a 3 percent chance of pregnancy.

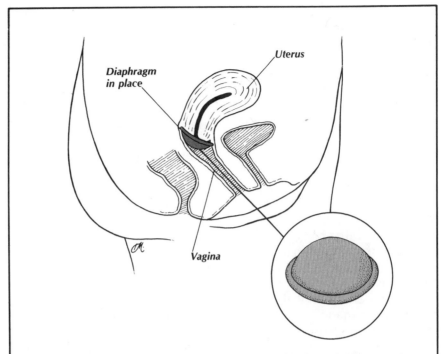

*The diaphragm is a molded rubber cap that is placed inside the vagina to cover the cervix (the opening at the lower end of the uterus) before sexual intercourse. Ideally, the diaphragm blocks sperm from entering the uterus, but it should not be relied on as the sole means of contraception.*

## Spermicide

Spermicide is a chemical foam, cream, suppository, or jelly applied to the woman's vagina to kill sperm. Used alone, a spermicide is about 75 percent to 85 percent effective. Some disadvantages of a spermicide are that it must be applied before each separate act of sexual intercourse, it has chemical odors, and it may irritate the vagina. A chief advantage is that spermicides are readily available at every drugstore without a prescription.

## Contraceptive sponge

The contraceptive sponge is a disposable, spongelike device saturated with spermicide. A woman inserts the sponge into the vagina up against the cervix, where the device works by continuously releasing spermicide for up to 24 hours. Additional applications of spermicide are not necessary, even for multiple acts of intercourse. There are other advantages as well: the sponge is available without a prescription; unlike a diaphragm, the sponge does not have to be fitted; and the sponge can be inserted ahead of time, which allows greater spontaneity in sex. The sponge has been found to be about 85 percent effective.

Because the contraceptive sponge is a relatively new product, some doctors think that more needs to be known about side effects. Cases of local irritation or allergic reaction have been reported; however, these have been mild and infrequent. There is also concern that the sponge could become a breeding ground for infection, especially if used improperly. You should consult your doctor about the contraceptive sponge and its proper use before trying this method of birth control.

### IUD

The intrauterine device (IUD) is a small plastic device inserted into the woman's uterus by a physician. The IUD has a string attached to it that hangs into the cervix, so that the woman or her partner can check to be sure that the IUD is still in place. Most researchers believe that the IUD prevents pregnancy by causing changes in the uterine lining that disrupt the normal environment of an egg. For the woman who can use an IUD, the advantages are great, because she does not have to worry about contraception each day. The effectiveness rate is high, with only about a 5 percent chance of pregnancy.

However, there are several disadvantages to use of an IUD. Severe menstrual cramps and increased menstrual bleeding may follow the insertion of an IUD. Sometimes these side effects lessen after a month or two. In other cases, severe cramps and prolonged bleeding continue, and the physician may advise removal of the IUD. The IUD is also thought to increase the probability of pelvic infections and ectopic (outside the uterus) pregnancies.

Due to severe problems caused by one brand of IUD, several types have been withdrawn from the market.

### Sterilization

A woman may be sterilized by an operation that blocks the fal-

lopian tubes (the structures through which eggs travel from the ovaries to the uterus). A man may be sterilized by a procedure called a vasectomy, in which each vas deferens (one of the two ducts through which the sperm travel from the testes to the urethra) is cut. These procedures may be reversed, but only by complicated surgery, which is not always successful. Therefore, physicians recommend sterilization only when a couple has decided, without reservation, that no further pregnancies are desired.

### Oral contraceptives

Oral contraceptives, or birth control pills, are the most effective reversible method of contraception. A woman taking the

pill has less than a 1 percent chance of getting pregnant.

The pill—which is available by prescription only—uses synthetic female hormones (estrogen and progestin) to override the natural hormonal regulation that results in the release of an egg. The pill signals the pituitary gland, which directs hormonal activity in the body, not to release the hormones that would normally stimulate the ovary to release an egg.

Each day you take one pill, at about the same time of day, removing it from a container that has the required number of pills for one cycle (usually 21). One to three days after you take the last pill for that cycle, your menstrual period begins. Menstrual periods may be lighter in flow, and cramps are reduced or absent.

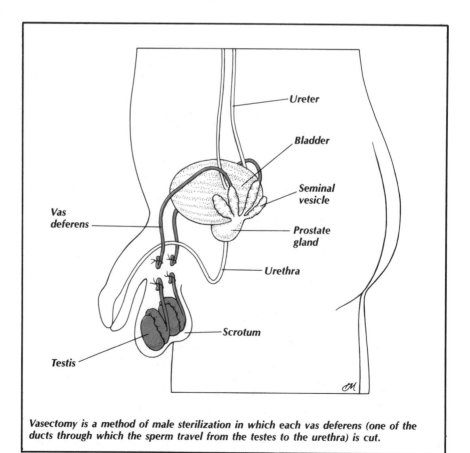

*Vasectomy is a method of male sterilization in which each vas deferens (one of the ducts through which the sperm travel from the testes to the urethra) is cut.*

If you forget to take one pill or more, menstrual bleeding may begin. In that case, you should continue taking the pills daily, but you should also use an additional contraceptive method, such as a condom, until after your next regular period.

Birth control pills are not recommended for women with a history of high blood pressure, blood-clotting problems, hepatitis, or cancer of the uterus or breast. A woman over age 35 who smokes heavily is advised to stop smoking if she wants to take the pill. Birth control pills should not be taken by a woman who suspects she may be pregnant. In addition, women with diabetes, epilepsy, heart disease, or thyroid disease may be advised not to take the birth control pill, depending on the nature and severity of the disease.

It is important for a woman taking birth control pills to report to her doctor if any of the following symptoms occurs: blurred vision; severe chest pain; sudden shortness of breath; abdominal pain; unusual bleeding or bruising; breakthrough vaginal bleeding (spotting); changes in menstrual flow; pain in the calves; depression; difficult or painful urination; enlarged or tender breasts; hearing changes; increase or decrease in hair growth; migraine headaches; numbness or tingling; rash; skin color changes; swelling of the feet, ankles, or lower legs; vaginal itching; weight changes; or yellowing of the eyes or skin.

### Natural family planning

Natural family planning is based on calculating when ovulation (release of an egg from one of the woman's ovaries each month) occurs. The couple then

*No mucus for several days after period*

*Thick, sticky mucus for several days before ovulation*

*Slippery, stringy mucus indicates that ovulation is occurring*

*Thick, sticky mucus or no mucus after ovulation*

*Mucus from the cervix (neck of the uterus) undergoes changes as hormone levels vary during the menstrual cycle. The mucus can be tested between the thumb and the forefinger to detect the changes shown here.*

abstains from intercourse during this fertile period.

A man's sperm can live in a woman's body for about two days. The egg can live for about 24 hours after ovulation. A few days are added to this fertile period for safety's sake because it is so difficult to determine just

when ovulation occurs. All told, a couple needs to abstain from intercourse seven to ten days a month in order to have the greatest chance of preventing pregnancy.

There are three methods a woman can use to determine when she ovulates. The temperature method is one of the most reliable. Each morning on awakening and before getting out of bed, she takes her temperature with a special basal temperature thermometer (which measures temperatures only between 96°F and 100°F) and records it on graph paper. Near the middle of the menstrual cycle, the temperature may drop slightly (indicating that ovulation is about to occur) and then rise rapidly and continue to climb for the next three days. The temperature will not return to preovulation levels until the beginning of the menstrual period. The "safe" days to have sexual intercourse are from four days after the sudden rise in temperature until three or four days after the end of the period. It is important to become familiar with the menstrual cycle by recording temperature levels for several months before relying on this method of birth control.

The mucus method may also help determine the time of ovulation. Each morning the mucus from the vagina and cervix is examined. Cervical mucus undergoes changes as hormone levels vary during the course of the cycle. To detect these changes, the vaginal area is blotted each morning with a facial tissue and then the mucus is tested between the thumb and forefinger. After the menstrual period there will be several days with no mucous discharge. This is followed by several days of a thick, sticky, yellow or white discharge. There will then be one or two days when the mucus becomes transparent and very slippery, with the consistency of raw egg whites. The mucus will form a string between the thumb and forefinger. This is when ovulation occurs. After ovulation, the mucus again becomes thick and sticky, or there may be no mucus at all. The fertile period begins with the thick, sticky, yellow or white discharge and continues until about three days after the phase when the mucus has the consistency of egg whites. Intercourse should be avoided during this time. In other words, the safe period is from three days after the slippery mucus stage to about three days after the end of the menstrual period. The use of certain medications (such as antihistamines), which alter mucus production throughout the body, will make determination of ovulation by the mucus method difficult.

The calendar method is also an option. A record of menstrual cycles is kept for one year or more. The doctor will then use the record to work out the probable day of ovulation, based on the fact that the average woman menstruates 14 days after she ovulates. However, any individual woman may vary from that average, so the calendar method is not precise.

Natural family planning does not require the use of mechanical aids or drugs. The effectiveness rate for this kind of birth control is up to about 80 percent, depending on the care with which the techniques are followed. However, even in women with regular cycles, such factors as illness, fatigue, stress, and use of certain drugs can delay ovulation or cause the techniques used to determine ovulation to become inaccurate,

thereby throwing off all careful calculations.

# Genital warts

Genital warts (known medically as condylomata acuminata) are viral growths that appear on the external genital organs. The condition is considered to be a sexually transmitted disease.

If left untreated, genital warts can grow quite large, causing discomfort during sexual intercourse, urination, and bowel movements. They are seen more frequently in uncircumcised men than in those who have been circumcised.

Pregnancy may make genital warts grow faster, but they usually shrink after the baby is born. They may even become large enough during pregnancy to block the birth canal, making a cesarean delivery necessary. The wart virus can be transmitted from a mother to her child during birth, but, unlike some other sexually transmitted diseases, there is no evidence that it causes any serious complications in infants.

## Cause

Genital warts are caused by direct sexual contact with an infected person. About 60 percent of all those exposed to genital warts will develop the condition. However, the warts will not appear until six weeks to eight months after the initial exposure.

## Symptom

The only symptom of genital warts is the warts themselves, which appear most frequently on the penis, vagina, and anus.

They may also be found in the mouth or on the cervix (neck of the uterus). They are soft, moist, and pink, occurring alone or in clusters; cluster formations tend to resemble cauliflower in their uneven, puffy appearance. They are seldom painful, but they can be irritated by sexual intercourse; in fact, they often grow on the parts of the sex organs that receive the most friction during sexual intercourse.

## Diagnosis

Genital warts can usually be diagnosed by a simple physical examination because their appearance is so distinctive. If there is any doubt, a sample of tissue from the wart can be tested to rule out other disorders, such as cancerous growths or the warts that often accompany syphilis (another sexually transmitted disease).

## Treatment

Genital warts are treated with a drug called podophyllin, which is applied directly to the warts and then washed off several hours later. More than one application may be necessary. Because podophyllin is toxic in large quantities, very large or troublesome warts are often removed by cryotherapy (a process in which liquid nitrogen is used to freeze the growths, which then fall off) or by heat treatments, which dry out and destroy the warts.

A person who has genital warts or any other sexually transmitted disease should abstain from sexual activity until all tests have indicated that the disease is no longer present. As is the case with all other sexually transmitted diseases, every sexual partner of the infected person needs to be examined and, if necessary, treated.

## Prevention

Genital warts can be prevented by avoiding sexual contact with someone who has the condition. Because the chances of contracting this and other venereal diseases increase with the number of sexual partners a person has, limiting the number of partners is the first step in prevention. Using condoms also helps to reduce the risk of contracting genital warts.

# Gonorrhea

Gonorrhea is one of the most frequently reported sexually transmitted diseases. It is a highly contagious bacterial infection, spread primarily through direct sexual contact.

Gonorrhea predominantly affects the penis in men, the vagina in women, and the throat and anus in both sexes. Left untreated, it can lead to a generalized blood infection, sterility (inability to conceive children), arthritis, and heart trouble. Additionally, in men it can spread throughout the prostate gland and the ducts of the reproductive system, causing painful inflammation.

Gonorrhea can also lead to eye infections if the genital secretions come in contact with the eyes—for instance, if a person rubs his eyes after handling infected genital organs. Because the infant passes through the potentially infected birth canal during the birth process, every state requires that a few drops of silver nitrate or penicillin be placed in

_In males, untreated gonorrhea may involve the prostate gland, the male duct system (including the epididymis, which connects each testis to its vas deferens, and the vas deferens, which conducts the sperm cells to the urethra), the bladder, and the uretha._

the eyes of all newborns to prevent infection and possible blindness.

## Symptoms

In females, this disease may exist entirely without symptoms, but in many cases it is marked by a discharge from the vagina and urethra; frequent, painful urination; cloudy urine; vomiting; and diarrhea. Gonorrhea often leads to pelvic inflammatory disease (PID), which results when the infection extends to the fallopian tubes; scar tissue that forms may block the tubes, preventing conception and often causing sterility. The symptoms of PID are lower abdominal pain, fever, chills, and vaginal discharge.

The primary symptom of gonorrhea in men is a yellowish discharge from the penis within two to ten days of exposure to the disease, accompanied by painful and burning urination.

Gonorrhea of the anus is marked by an often bloody or mucus-filled discharge from the anus and pain during bowel movements. Gonorrhea of the throat may have no noticeable symptoms or may reveal itself only as a scratchy, sore throat or a severe, flame-red sore throat.

## Diagnosis

Diagnosis is accomplished by taking a sample of the discharge, examining it under a microscope to identify the gonorrhea bacterium, and confirming the diagnosis by performing a culture (a technique in which a sample of the discharge is placed in a special substance that encourages the growth of bacteria).

## Treatment

Gonorrhea is usually treated with penicillin or tetracycline, either injected or taken orally.

Men being treated for gonorrhea should avoid alcoholic beverages because recent studies have shown that drinking may increase the chances of developing an inflammation of the urethra (the canal leading from the urinary bladder through the penis).

While under treatment, the patient should abstain from sexual activity until further tests have confirmed that gonorrhea is no longer present. This testing is usually done one week after the beginning of treatment and sometimes again two weeks later. If signs of the disease are still present, drug therapy can be reinstated at a higher dosage or perhaps with a different antibiotic.

Another sexually transmitted disease called nongonococcal urethritis (NGU) sometimes occurs simultaneously with gonorrhea, but NGU is not affected by penicillin. If symptoms persist after regular treatment for gonorrhea, it may be that the gonorrhea has cleared up, but NGU remains; in that case, NGU should be treated with another antibiotic, often tetracycline.

Every sexual partner of the infected person should be examined and, if necessary, treated.

### Prevention

Gonorrhea can be prevented by avoiding sexual contact with someone who has the disease. Because the chances of contracting this and other venereal diseases increase with the number of sexual partners a person has, limiting the number of partners is the first step in prevention. Using condoms helps to reduce the risk of contracting gonorrhea.

# Herpes

Herpes is a sexually transmitted disease—a highly contagious illness spread primarily through direct sexual contact.

Herpes infection can be treated but not cured. Its symptoms appear briefly and then disappear; the disease lies dormant in nerve cells, but it may be reactivated by stress or illness. It is contagious only during active periods, when blisters are present. Persons taking drugs that suppress the body's immune system (for instance, cancer or organ transplant patients) are at a higher risk of contracting herpes because their bodies are in a weakened state. There is also some evidence that links genital herpes with a higher rate of cancer of the cervix (the neck of the uterus) in women.

Herpes is spread primarily by direct sexual contact. It can also be transmitted to an infant during childbirth, causing brain damage or death. Therefore, if a woman shows signs of the active disease while in labor, the baby will be delivered by cesarean section (through an incision in the walls of the uterus and abdomen), rather than through the vagina, where the herpes blisters may be present.

### Cause

Herpes is caused by herpes simplex virus type 2, which is similar to the virus (herpes simplex virus type 1) that causes cold sores and fever blisters.

### Symptoms

The predominant symptom of herpes is the outbreak of painful, itching blisters filled with fluid

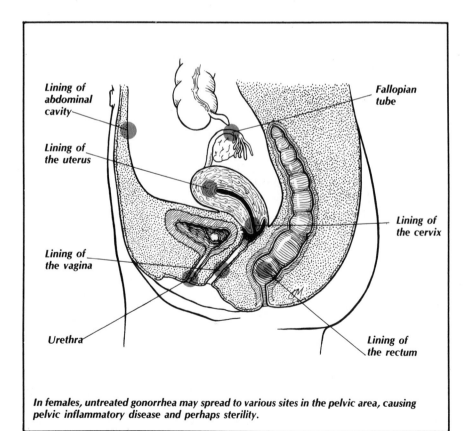

Lining of abdominal cavity

Lining of the uterus

Lining of the vagina

Urethra

Fallopian tube

Lining of the cervix

Lining of the rectum

*In females, untreated gonorrhea may spread to various sites in the pelvic area, causing pelvic inflammatory disease and perhaps sterility.*

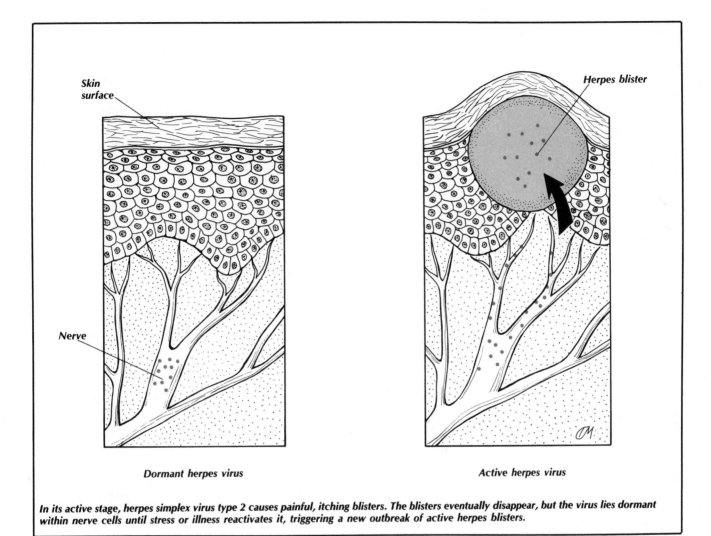

*Skin surface*

*Herpes blister*

*Nerve*

Dormant herpes virus

Active herpes virus

*In its active stage, herpes simplex virus type 2 causes painful, itching blisters. The blisters eventually disappear, but the virus lies dormant within nerve cells until stress or illness reactivates it, triggering a new outbreak of active herpes blisters.*

on and around the external sexual organs. Females may have a vaginal discharge. Symptoms vaguely similar to those of the flu may accompany these outbreaks, including fever and fatigue.

The blisters will disappear without treatment in about two to ten days, but the virus will remain, lying dormant among clusters of nerve cells until another outbreak is triggered by such factors as stress, a cold, fever, or menstruation. Many patients are able to anticipate an outbreak—they notice a warning sign, a tingling sensation called a prodrome, of the approaching illness. Herpes is contagious only during actual outbreaks, so sexual activity should be avoided while blisters or other symptoms are present.

### Diagnosis

Diagnosis of herpes is accomplished by microscopic examination and culture of the fluid contained in the blisters.

### Treatment

Unlike other sexually transmitted diseases, herpes cannot be cured, because any medication that will attack the virus while it lies dormant in the nerve cells will also damage the nerve cells. However, there is treatment for acute outbreaks now available that involves the use of either the antiviral drug acyclovir or laser therapy, both of which will heal blisters, reduce pain, and, most important, kill large numbers of the herpes virus organisms. Acyclovir has also been found to reduce the reproduction of the virus in initial outbreaks, thus possibly lessening the number of subsequent outbreaks. It should be noted, however, that to be effective, therapy must be started immediately after the first sores appear. Every sexual partner of the infected person needs to be examined and, if necessary, treated.

## Prevention

Herpes can be prevented by avoiding sexual contact with an infected person whose disease is in its active period. Because the chances of contracting this or any other sexually transmitted disease increase with the number of sexual partners a person has, limiting the number of partners is the first step toward prevention. Using condoms also helps to reduce the risk.

# Infertility

Infertility is defined as a couple's failure to conceive a child after one year of regular sexual intercourse without birth control. In about 40 percent of all cases of infertility, the problem lies with the man; in 60 percent it lies with the woman or with both partners.

Infertility is not sterility. The term infertility implies that the condition can be treated and reversed—that it may be a temporary problem. The term sterility is applied to a permanent, irreversible inability to have children.

Recent research has shown that a woman's fertility drops off significantly between the ages of 31 and 35 and continues to decline thereafter until menopause, when it ceases. A man's fertility also declines after the age of 40, although men can remain fertile until old age.

## Causes of male infertility

One of the major causes of male infertility is a low sperm count. It is measured by the number of active sperm present in a milliliter (there are approximately five milliliters in one teaspoon) of semen (the fluid ejected from the penis during intercourse). An average sperm count is 90 million sperm per milliliter. A count of 40 to 60 million is thought to be necessary for conception; when the count is less than 20 million, it is highly unlikely that the man can father a child (although, since only one sperm is needed to fertilize an egg, it is still possible).

A low sperm count can be caused by low levels of testosterone (the male sex hormone); by exposure to chemicals, pesticides, and radiation; by engaging in sexual intercourse too frequently, which depletes the sperm supply too quickly; and by heat (which slows sperm production) generated by wearing tight underwear or pants, sitting for long periods in hot cars or trucks, or working near ovens and kilns. Infertility can also result if sperm cannot propel themselves through the female reproductive tract to reach the egg, or if sperm are irregularly shaped (only sperm with oval-shaped heads can fertilize an egg).

In addition to problems with the sperm themselves, male infertility can be caused by any obstruction in the tubes that convey the sperm from the testes (the male sex organs where sperm are produced) to the penis. Infertility may also be caused by varicose veins in the scrotum (the pouch containing the testes), perhaps because the increased blood flow in these swollen veins brings extra heat to the area, or by a local infection or injury; the infertility problem will probably reverse itself when the condition is corrected. In addition, surgical removal of part of the prostate gland (one of the organs in which most of the fluid in semen is produced), as well as the use of certain drugs for high blood pressure, can lead to retrograde ejaculation (a disorder in which the semen is passed backward into the bladder, to exit with the urine, rather than out through the penis).

## Causes of female infertility

A woman may be infertile because of a variety of conditions. It may be that she is not ovulating (releasing an egg each month); this is true in about 25 percent of all cases of female infertility. The fallopian tubes (through which the eggs travel on their way from the ovaries to the uterus) may be obstructed, often as a result of pelvic inflammatory disease (PID), which irritates the tubes and causes scar tissue to form. PID can develop as a reaction to an IUD (intrauterine device used for birth control), a sexually transmitted disease, or an infection of the lower reproductive tract. Endometriosis (the displacement of tissue from the lining of the uterus to outside the uterus) may also cause the formation of scar tissue that blocks the fallopian tubes. An imbalance of the female hormones estrogen and progesterone or of other hormones secreted from the pituitary or thyroid glands can interfere with the reproductive cycle. A weakness in the cervix (the neck of the uterus), sometimes resulting from an abortion or surgery, may render it unfit to hold the weight of a pregnancy. A "hostile" cervix (one that creates an environment that in some way prevents sperm from surviving) may also be the cause of the infertility.

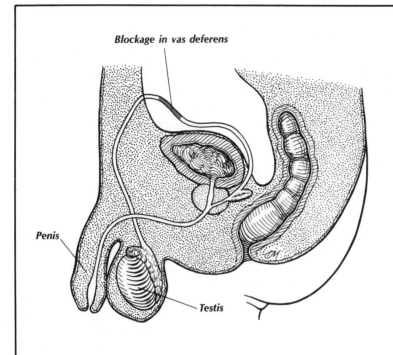

*Male infertility can be caused by a blockage anywhere in the tubes that convey sperm from the testes to the penis.*

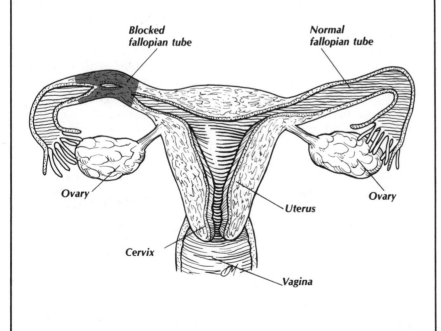

*Female infertility can be caused by an obstruction in a fallopian tube, through which the egg passes from the ovary to the uterus.*

## Diagnosis

Diagnosis of the reason for the infertility problem will usually begin with physical examinations and complete medical and sexual histories of both partners.

A fresh sample of the man's semen will be examined under a microscope to determine the quantity and quality of the sperm. This will provide a sperm count and will also indicate whether the sperm are adequately mobile and whether the heads of the sperm are oval, both of which characteristics are necessary for conception.

To determine whether ovulation is taking place in the female, the basal body temperature (the body temperature on awakening, before eating or drinking) will be taken every morning for several months. If the temperature rises by 0.6°F to 1.0°F for a few days in the middle of the menstrual cycle, ovulation is probably taking place. An endometrial biopsy, in which a sample of the lining of the uterus is obtained for examination, can also indicate whether ovulation is occurring and whether hormonal secretion is normal.

Obstruction of the fallopian tubes can be diagnosed by injecting a dye into the reproductive tract and then taking an x-ray. Another test consists of injecting carbon dioxide gas into the fallopian tubes and waiting for the patient to feel pain in the upper part of the body, indicating that the gas is passing through the fallopian tubes and that there are no obstructions.

A weakness in the cervix can be diagnosed through a physical examination and x-rays. A hostile cervix can be identified by a microscopic examination of the mucus in the cervix shortly after sexual intercourse to determine the rate of sperm survival. Endometriosis is diagnosed by inserting into the abdomen a laparoscope (a small, lighted instrument), through which the doctor can see the uterus, fallopian tubes, ovaries, and any displaced endometrial tissue that may be causing the infertility.

Hormonal imbalances in both men and women can be diagnosed with blood tests.

### Treatment

Treatment for a low sperm count caused by a testosterone deficiency is usually hormone therapy to increase testosterone levels. If the low sperm count is due to chemicals, radiation, or excess heat, exposure to these factors must be corrected or avoided. If the sperm count is low for some unknown reason, there is often little more that can be done.

If male infertility is caused by varicose veins, surgery may be necessary. If an obstruction exists somewhere in the tubes leading to and through the penis, microsurgery to open the blockage may correct the problem.

Failure to ovulate is often treated with a fertility drug called clomiphene, which stimulates production of the hormone that regulates ovulation. About 60 percent of the patients who receive clomiphene become pregnant, and the chances of multiple births are very low. A stronger drug, which is a combination of certain pituitary gland hormones, may also be prescribed, but it carries with it a greater risk of multiple births.

Obstructed fallopian tubes may require microsurgery to open the blockage, or a new procedure in which an egg is re-

moved and replaced beyond the point of the obstruction, where it may be fertilized normally. A hostile cervix can be treated with the female hormone estrogen, which stimulates the increased production of mucus, which is necessary to transport the sperm. Sometimes sperm can be placed directly into the uterus, bypassing the cervix completely. Endometriosis can be treated by the surgical removal of displaced tissue and the scar tissue that has formed around it. Hormonal imbalances can be corrected with hormone therapy.

Test-tube, or *in vitro,* fertilization is a relatively new technique in which an egg is removed from the woman's ovary and then placed in a test tube or special sterile dish containing the husband's sperm. Once the egg has been fertilized, it is placed into the woman's uterus, where it will continue to grow. This technique is used primarily in women whose blocked fallopian tubes cannot be opened by surgery.

Although recent advances in treating infertility have led to greater and greater success, about 15 percent of all female infertility problems and about 10 percent of all male problems remain undiagnosed and therefore untreatable.

### Artificial insemination

Artificial insemination is the introduction of semen (the fluid containing sperm) into a woman's vagina or uterus by means other than sexual intercourse (usually with a special syringe) at or before the time of ovulation in the hope of achieving fertilization. The semen may be from the woman's husband or from a donor.

Artificial insemination using semen from the husband is sometimes done when he has a low sperm count—that is, when there are not enough sperm per unit of fluid to be likely to fertilize an egg. To obtain enough sperm, several collections may be made over a period of days or weeks; the sperm obtained is frozen, pooled, and used in one insertion. Artificial insemination may also be used when one or the other partner cannot perform the sexual act in a normal manner, perhaps because of a physical condition or an emotional problem.

Artificial insemination using semen from a donor can be an alternative to adoption when the husband cannot father a child, whether because of low sperm count, absence of sperm, poor quality of sperm, or lack of motion by sperm or because of inability to perform sexual intercourse. It may also be considered when the husband carries an inborn defect that he does not want to transmit. The couple's physician arranges for the sperm to be obtained from a donor unknown to them. This procedure should never be done without the husband's permission; in fact, in most states it is illegal without the husband's written consent.

# Nongonococcal urethritis

Nongonococcal urethritis (NGU), also known as nonspecific urethritis, is a venereal (sexually transmitted) disease that causes inflammation of the urethra (the tube that carries urine from the bladder to the outside of the body). Like other venereal diseases, NGU is a highly contagious illness spread primarily through direct sexual contact.

## Complications

Left untreated, NGU can lead to prostatitis (inflammation of the prostate gland, where seminal fluid is produced) and epididymitis (inflammation of the ducts leading from the testes) in men and to pelvic inflammatory disease (an inflammation in the pelvic cavity affecting the fallopian tubes) in women. It can be transmitted from a mother to her baby during childbirth, resulting in ear infections and pneumonia; it has also been linked to an increased risk of stillbirths and sudden infant death syndrome (SIDS).

## Cause

NGU is transmitted by direct sexual contact with an infected person. It displays symptoms similar to those of gonorrhea, although it is not caused by the gonorrhea bacterium but by several others, including one called *Chlamydia*.

## Symptoms

Sometimes no symptoms are evident. In other cases, there is a discharge from the penis or vagina, painful and burning urination, and other symptoms similar to those of gonorrhea. In fact, NGU can occur with gonorrhea, so if symptoms persist after treatment for gonorrhea, they may be due to NGU.

## Diagnosis

Diagnosis of NGU is often difficult because there is no one simple test for it. A sample of secretions from the penis or vagina may be taken to determine if chlamydial infection is present, but many labs do not do this test and those that do may charge a very high fee. Therefore, NGU is often diagnosed by ruling out other disorders that may display similar symptoms, such as gonorrhea or cystitis (bladder infection). Noninfectious or postinfectious (occurring after an infection) inflammation of the urethra may also cause urethritis.

## Treatment

Penicillin has no effect on NGU, so this disease is treated with another antibiotic, such as tetracycline, erythromycin, or trimethoprim-sulfamethoxazole combination. This is why treatment of gonorrhea with penicillin will not affect a coexisting case of NGU.

A person who has NGU or any other sexually transmitted disease should abstain from sexual activity until all tests have indicated that the disease is no longer present. Every sexual partner of the infected person needs to be examined and, if necessary, treated.

## Prevention

NGU can be prevented by avoiding sexual contact with someone who has the disease. Because the chances of contracting NGU or any other sexually transmitted disease increase with the number of sexual partners a person has, limiting the number of partners is the first step toward prevention. Using condoms also helps to reduce the risk of contracting NGU.

# Syphilis

Syphilis is a serious, highly contagious disease spread primarily by direct sexual contact. Syphilis is caused by spiral-shaped bacteria called spirochetes.

Over time, syphilis can affect all parts of the body—the brain, bones, spinal cord, and heart, as well as the reproductive organs. If left untreated, blindness, brain damage, heart disease, and even death can result. Syphilis can also be passed from a mother to her unborn baby, causing congenital syphilis in the child, which may eventually result in blindness and deafness, among other serious consequences. Syphilis in a pregnant woman must be treated prior to the eighteenth week of the pregnancy in order to prevent passage of the disease to the fetus.

## Stages and symptoms

Syphilis is a progressive disorder that passes through three stages: primary, secondary, and tertiary.

Primary syphilis is characterized by the appearance of a painless, open sore (called a chancre) 10 to 90 days after exposure to the disease. As a rule, there is usually only one sore, appearing most commonly on the genital organs, but also at times on the rectum, cervix (the opening to the uterus), lips, tongue, fingers, or anywhere that direct contact was made. The chancre first appears as a red bump, sometimes surrounded by a red ring that oozes clear fluid; it soon turns into a painless ulcer and disappears within several weeks without treatment. Although the chancre is gone, the disease is still active in the body.

Secondary syphilis usually appears within six weeks to six months of initial contact. Symptoms resembling those of the flu (fever, sore throat, headache, fatigue, aching joints, and enlarged lymph nodes) are common. Secondary syphilis is also characterized by extremely contagious, red or reddish-brown erosions that can be seen on the lining of the mouth, the penis, the external female sex organs, the anus, and warm, moist areas, such as the underarms; by growths resembling warts in the genital area (not to be confused with the more common nonsyphilitic genital warts); and by a rash on the palms of the hands or the soles of the feet in the form of round, reddish spots that occur in patches and do not itch. These sores, growths, and rashes heal within three to six weeks without treatment, and the disease enters the third stage.

At the beginning of the third stage, all symptoms disappear and the disease becomes latent (present but not showing symptoms) for a time. The patient appears to be healthy, and the disease is probably no longer contagious (except in the case of pregnant women, who can still pass it on to their offspring). This latent stage can last indefinitely, but in about one third of patients the disease will most likely progress, and the entire body may come under siege. The brain, bones, spinal cord, and heart may be affected, resulting in blindness, brain damage, heart disease, or even death.

### Diagnosis

Syphilis is diagnosed on the basis of the patient's medical and sexual history and findings from the physical examination,

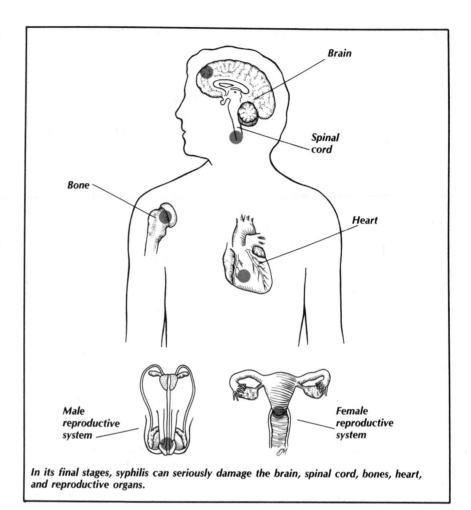

*In its final stages, syphilis can seriously damage the brain, spinal cord, bones, heart, and reproductive organs.*

blood tests, and microscopic examination of a sample taken from the sores or rash areas. Several blood tests may be necessary because the bacteria may not show up on blood tests during the first one to two weeks after exposure to the infection.

### Treatment

Treatment of syphilis is accomplished with the administration of penicillin (or another antibiotic, if a penicillin allergy exists). Some cases of late syphilis are so advanced, however, that they cannot be treated.

A person who has syphilis or any other sexually transmitted disease should abstain from sex-ual activity until all tests have confirmed that the disease is no longer contagious. Every sexual partner of the infected person needs to be tested and, if necessary, treated.

### Prevention

Syphilis can be prevented by avoiding sexual contact with someone who has the disease. Because the chances of contracting this or any other sexually transmitted disease increase with the number of sexual partners a person has, limiting the number of partners is the first step toward prevention. Using condoms also helps to reduce the risk of contracting syphilis.

# PREGNANCY AND CHILDBIRTH

## PREGNANCY AND CHILDBIRTH

This chapter considers the normal course of the childbearing process—from conception to childbirth—as well as common disorders that may arise during pregnancy.

### CONCEPTION

Conception is the union of a sperm cell from the father with an egg from the mother to begin a new life.

### Ovulation

During the course of her life, the average woman produces 350 to 400 eggs, or ova. The two organs in which the eggs are produced, known as ovaries, are located near the top and on either side of the uterus. Ducts known as fallopian tubes conduct the eggs toward the uterus. At the midpoint of the average 28-day menstrual cycle, an egg matures in one of the ovaries, is expelled from the ovary during the process called ovulation, and starts to travel through the nearby fallopian tube toward the uterus, propelled by the waving action of tiny hairlike structures, known as cilia, that line the tube. If the egg meets a sperm cell en route, conception may occur.

### Fertilization

Sperm cells—which look like tadpoles through a microscope—originate in the man's testes. At the climax of sexual intercourse, an average of 300 million to 500 million sperm cells, contained in a teaspoonful of thick white fluid, spurt from the tip of the man's penis deep into the woman's vagina. Imme-

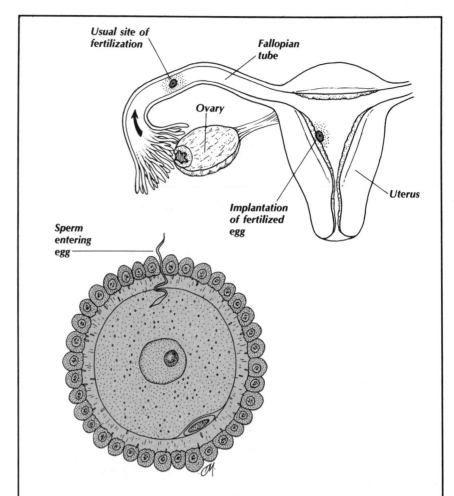

Once a month, one of a woman's ovaries releases an egg, which travels through the nearby fallopian tube toward the uterus. Conception occurs if a sperm unites with the egg. The fertilized egg then continues its progress toward the uterus, where it becomes implanted in the endometrial lining.

diately the sperm start swimming forward, propelled by their long, waving tails and aided by contractions of the muscles of the woman's vagina and uterus. The goal of the sperm is to swim through the cervix, into the uterus, and up one of the fallopian tubes to fertilize an egg.

Millions of sperm are killed by the acidic secretions of the vagina and the cervix or become trapped by mucus in the vagina. (During the middle of the woman's menstrual cycle, when the egg is moving along a fallopian tube, the secretions are thinner, less acid, and less of a

barrier; also, there are alkaline chemicals in the fluid accompanying the sperm, which act to neutralize the woman's acidic secretions.) The vast majority of sperm fail to pass through the uterus and up one of the fallopian tubes. During most of the woman's menstrual cycle, both tubes are empty and the sperm find nothing to fertilize. Only for a few days is an egg present in one of the tubes, and then it may be reached by only a few of the millions of sperm cells that began the journey. The sperm completely surround the egg, their tails waving furiously in an attempt to force their pointed heads into the female cell. Finally, one succeeds. The tail detaches, and the head moves toward the center of the egg. In seconds, a chemical change comes about in the egg that prevents the entry of any other sperm. Conception has occurred.

### The fertilized egg

Unlike all other cells in the body, the sperm and the egg each contain only 23 chromosomes (chromosomes are the chemical "blueprints" that together determine all of the inherited characteristics of an individual; all of the other cells contain twice that number). In the first 12 hours after conception, the 23 chromosomes from the mother and the 23 chromosomes from the father join to form a new nucleus of 46 chromosomes. This is the basic unit from which the new individual will develop.

During the next four or five days, as the fertilized egg, or zygote, drifts down the fallopian tube and into the uterus, the original cell divides and subdivides into anywhere from 16 to 48 cells. In another two or three days, the growing cluster of cells becomes implanted in the nourishing, blood-rich lining of the mother's uterus, which soon forms the beginning of a placenta around the baby-to-be, called an embryo at this stage. (The placenta is the structure through which oxygen and nutrients pass from the mother to the fetus and carbon dioxide and other waste products pass from the fetus to the mother.) Within about 17 days after conception, the placenta begins blood circulation to the embryo, in which var-

ious cells are specializing to form different parts of the baby's body. By the end of the seventh week of pregnancy, all of the basic structures of the body have been formed. The developing embryo now is called the fetus until birth.

## PREGNANCY

Pregnancy is the condition that exists in a woman between the time one of her eggs is fertilized by a sperm and the time her child is born.

### Physical changes

During normal pregnancy, many changes take place in a woman's body. The abdomen expands, and the breasts enlarge, grow sensitive, and prepare to produce milk for the baby. Blood volume increases by up to 30 percent. Breathing proceeds more from the chest and less from the abdomen. The bladder is pushed higher into the abdomen because of the increased abdominal space taken up by the growing fetus. The amount of blood flowing through the kidneys increases by 25 percent to 40 percent because wastes must be eliminated from both the mother and the fetus. There is a slight increase in the acidity of the saliva (this may be one of the causes of the nausea and vomiting that are so common). The nipples and external genitalia may darken, and brown spots or splotches may appear on the skin. A hormone called relaxin causes the ligaments (connective tissues that link bones together at joints) to begin to loosen during the tenth or twelfth week of pregnancy; this will be particularly impor-

tant in the pelvic area because it will allow greater flexibility at the time of delivery. Many of the glands increase in size.

### Symptoms

Usually the first symptom noticed by a pregnant woman is a missed menstrual period. Nausea and vomiting ("morning sickness") are also common symptoms of pregnancy.

The nine months of pregnancy are usually thought of medically as three three-month periods, or trimesters. During the first trimester, the woman may experience nausea and vomiting, her breasts and nipples will become enlarged, and her waistline may expand. In the second trimester, the uterus increases in volume, abdominal enlargement becomes more apparent, and the woman can feel the fetus move. Many women feel their best during this trimester. During the last three months, pregnancy tends to become a more cumbersome condition, and the woman may feel tired much of the time. The fetus often "drops" lower in the uterus in the last month.

### Prenatal care

Many women wait until they have missed a second period before consulting their doctor. Once the doctor has confirmed the pregnancy, a program of prenatal (before birth) care will be prescribed for the mother-to-be. Prenatal care consists chiefly of making sure that nothing goes wrong with this completely normal and natural process—in other words, that there are no complications.

Good nutrition is especially important during pregnancy. The

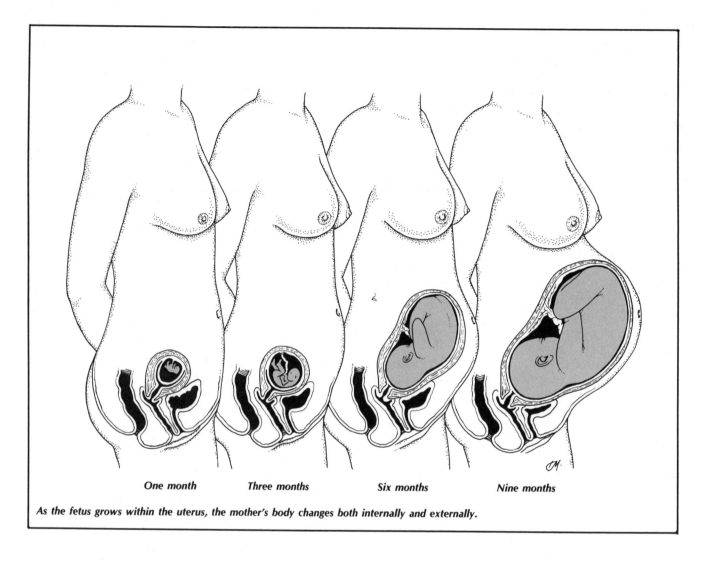

One month     Three months     Six months     Nine months

*As the fetus grows within the uterus, the mother's body changes both internally and externally.*

body's requirements for calcium and phosphorus, two essential minerals in food, almost double, and there is an increase in the demand for iron and many other elements. Gradual caloric increases are not only allowed but advisable, provided that the additional food does not consist of empty calories, such as excess starches and sugars. Fresh fruits and vegetables and appropriate amounts of high-protein, low-fat foods are good choices. Generally, if the woman was consuming 2,000 calories before pregnancy with no weight gain, she should raise her intake to 2,200 to 2,400 calories in early pregnancy; she may be advised to in-

crease that figure to 2,600 calories by the later stages.

If the baby's weight is included, most women should gain approximately 23 to 26 pounds by the ninth month. This additional weight puts more stress on the back and on the legs, sometimes resulting in such problems as swayback and varicose veins (swollen veins close to the skin surface) in the legs. These conditions can be eased by getting proper rest and exercise and by wearing special hosiery to alleviate or prevent varicose veins.

Once the initial period of nausea and vomiting is over (usually after two or three months), many

women increase their caloric intake too much, sometimes in a mistaken attempt to "make up for what the baby is taking." As a consequence, they experience a drastic gain in weight. At the other extreme are those mothers who cannot eat normally because nausea persists throughout pregnancy. In each of these cases, both the mother and the fetus may suffer. If any sudden weight gain or loss is experienced, the physician should be informed.

Due to either rapid weight gain or inadequate kidney function, some women experience significant swelling in the ankles and lower legs and, to a lesser extent, in the hands and fingers. Under no circumstances should nonprescription diuretics (drugs that increase urinary output) be taken for this condition. The doctor should be consulted.

Proper rest and exercise are important throughout pregnancy. In general, a woman can participate in most, if not all, of the activities and sports she was taking part in before her pregnancy. Her doctor can advise her about any limitations.

### Precautions

Many substances and organisms have been found to affect the development and survival of the fetus. It is estimated that 20 percent of all birth defects are directly related to environmental factors, such as drugs, viruses, and vitamin deficiencies. Another 60 percent are caused by the interaction of an environmental factor and an inherited predisposition. So it is important for every woman who is contemplating pregnancy or is already pregnant to beware of the possible hazards to which her baby may be vulnerable.

One of the most important aspects of prenatal care is safety in the use of medications and the ingestion of nonfood substances. A pregnant woman (or one who even suspects she is pregnant) should never take a medication without her doctor's recommendation or approval. This caution includes over-the-counter preparations—even aspirin—as well as prescription drugs. In addition, a woman should not smoke during pregnancy, and she should limit, if not eliminate, consumption of alcoholic beverages. Smoking has been linked to miscarriage (the expulsion of the fetus before it is capable of

surviving on its own), low birth weight, and prematurity. Alcohol, too, has been linked to miscarriage, and studies have shown that alcohol can affect the brain of the fetus. Products containing caffeine should probably also be limited. The best guideline to remember is that no drug or nonfood substance can be assumed to be harmless during pregnancy.

The fetus is also susceptible to infections that affect the mother-to-be, especially rubella (German measles) and certain sexually transmitted diseases, such as herpes. A pregnant woman should avoid immunizations with live viruses and postpone travel to foreign countries where infectious diseases are prevalent. Toxoplasmosis, an infection spread by eating or preparing uncooked meat or handling a cat's litter box, presents another risk. The parasite that causes toxoplasmosis is harbored in the bodies of some food animals (pigs, sheep, and cattle) and in the intestinal tracts of cats. A pregnant woman need not forgo meat or get rid of her cat. She should, however, be certain to cook meat thoroughly and to avoid emptying or cleaning the cat's litter box.

A woman's doctor may also advise against unnecessary x-rays during pregnancy.

As the medical profession has learned more about inherited diseases, it has been able to offer genetic counseling to couples concerned about the possibility of having a child with an inherited disease or abnormality. A genetic counselor or specialist in genetic disorders can estimate the likelihood that a couple's offspring will be afflicted by a problem due to an inherited trait or to the age of the parents. For some genetic disorders, tests can

determine whether one or both parents are carriers or can detect whether a defect is present in a fetus. However, genetic counseling cannot guarantee the health of a child; it can only be a source of advice.

### CHILDBIRTH

A normal pregnancy that has run its full course is called a "full-term pregnancy"—the baby is born after a full gestational (developmental) period of about 40 weeks. If the birth occurs earlier, it is considered premature.

There are three stages of normal labor and vaginal childbirth. During the first stage, contractions of the uterus open the cervix (the neck of the uterus). The plug of mucus that has been sealing off the uterus from the vagina for nine months is expelled. This is often followed by either a slow trickle or a sudden gush of amniotic fluid as the amniotic sac, in which the baby has been growing, breaks. At this point, the woman should notify her physician and go to the hospital.

The second stage begins when the cervix is completely dilated (opened). The contractions become much stronger, accompanied by an urge to bear down and push the baby along the birth canal. A doctor or midwife will instruct the woman to push down only during a contraction so that she conserves her energy and strength. After the baby has emerged, the umbilical cord, which connects the baby to the placenta, is tied and cut.

The baby, who usually gasps and cries on delivery, is immediately checked by the obstetrician or pediatrician. After being cleaned off, the baby may be given to the mother to hold.

Five or ten minutes later, the placenta, or afterbirth, is pushed out by more contractions of the uterus. After this third stage has been completed, the physician will stitch any tears or incisions that were made in the vagina and give the woman medication to stop excessive bleeding.

The entire birthing process can last anywhere from 5 to 24 hours; the average is about 12 hours. Childbirth usually takes longer if it is the woman's first delivery.

In about one of six pregnancies, vaginal delivery is not possible or desirable, and a cesarean section must be performed. The baby is delivered through an incision in the mother's abdominal wall. (For more information on cesarean delivery, see the following section.)

More and more expectant fathers are taking active roles in the birthing process by attending prenatal classes and participating in the delivery. Most hospitals now welcome fathers into the delivery room so that they can witness the miracle of childbirth and comfort and support the mother while she goes through labor.

### Anesthesia

Although once the norm, general anesthesia is now rarely used during vaginal childbirth because, among other reasons, it slows uterine contractions and causes sluggishness and the possibility of respiratory problems in the baby. Other forms of anesthesia that are used during childbirth include pudendal block, paracervical block, spinal, epidural, and caudal anesthesia.

In pudendal block, local anesthetic is injected through the wall of the vagina or through the skin of the buttock to reach the pudendal nerve. Blocking this nerve eliminates pain and feeling from the lower part of the vagina, the rear portion of the vulva (the external genitals), and the surrounding skin. It is often used when delivery is going well and the mother wants to push. Sometimes this type of anesthesia is used following a paracervical block, in which a local anesthetic is injected around the opening of the uterus.

Various types of spinal anesthesia are used in childbirth. In one method, a solution containing local anesthetic is injected between the fourth and fifth vertebrae of the lower back into the fluid-filled sac surrounding the spinal cord. The heavy solution mixes with the spinal fluid and settles downward, blocking off pain messages from below the waist for about an hour.

Epidural anesthesia has an effect similar to that of spinal anesthesia. The anesthetic is injected at the same place, but instead of being introduced into the spinal fluid in a single injection, it can be administered over a period of hours through a fine plastic tube with its tip resting against the tough dural membrane covering the spinal cord (the prefix *epi* means upon, hence the term epidural). The nerves are blocked where they enter the spinal cord to produce a numbing effect. Because the dural membrane is not punctured, the chance of complications, such as headache and infection, is reduced. Caudal anesthesia is the same as epidural except that the tube is introduced at the very tip of the spine (caudal comes from the Latin word meaning tail). Because both epidural and caudal anesthesia can slow labor if administered too soon, they are not given until the woman is in active labor.

# Cesarean section

Cesarean section is a way of delivering a baby by cutting through the external walls of the mother's abdomen and uterus and removing the baby through these incisions. Cesarean section is performed when a vaginal delivery would cause injury to either the mother or the baby.

In the United States today, about 10 percent to 20 percent of births are by cesarean section. While cesarean delivery is still considered major surgery, the availability of antibiotics, improved anesthetic techniques, and blood transfusions has made cesareans much safer than in the past. Nevertheless, the indications for performing a cesarean section and the disadvantages of the procedure should be weighed carefully by the woman and her physician.

### Types

There are two main types of cesarean section.

In the *classic cesarean,* an incision is made vertically on the skin of the abdomen, extending from the navel to the pubic bone. A vertical cut is also made directly down the center of the uterus in its thick upper section. This operation is generally used only if the baby is lying in an abnormal position or if the placenta is located in an abnormally low position in the cavity of the uterus.

The *lower-segment cesarean* is the more commonly performed procedure. The incision in the

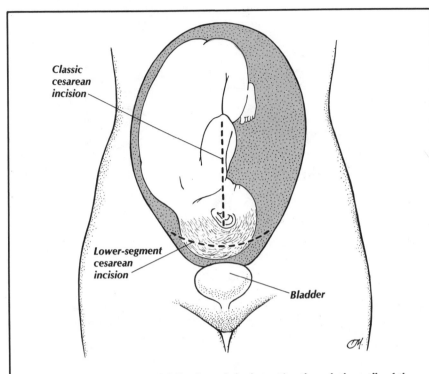

*A cesarean section is a way of delivering a baby by cutting through the walls of the mother's abdomen and uterus and removing the baby through these incisions. The incision for the classic cesarean is a vertical cut down the center of the abdomen and uterus. One type of incision for the lower-segment cesarean is a curved cut near the lower part of the abdomen.*

Classic cesarean incision

Lower-segment cesarean incision

Bladder

uterus is made in the lower, thinner section. This incision may be either a vertical cut down the middle or a curved, smile-shaped cut near the lower part of the abdomen.

The classic cesarean produces more bleeding than the lower-segment cesarean. Also, the incision is more difficult to repair, and the uterus is more likely to rupture during a future pregnancy. For these reasons, the classic cesarean is seldom used today unless there are specific reasons.

### Reasons

Some of the reasons for a cesarean section include the following:

- To save the baby's life when the umbilical cord (the fetus' sup-

ply line from the placenta) is being pinched off during the birth process, or any other time that the fetus is not getting enough blood and oxygen to survive. (These conditions may be indicated by abnormal heart rate patterns during fetal monitoring.)
- To prevent infection of the baby by a dangerous vaginal infection, such as herpes, gonorrhea, or syphilis.
- To prevent injury to the baby that may result from a breech birth, during which a baby emerges through the vagina buttocks or feet first rather than head first. (Many obstetricians believe that cesarean delivery is necessary for all breech births in first-time mothers and all premature breech births.)
- To ease the birth or prevent injury when the baby is too large

or the mother's pelvis is too small for a vaginal delivery.
- To deliver the baby if the mother fails to give birth after a long labor.
- To save the baby's life if problems with the placenta cause a decrease in the blood supply to the fetus.
- To facilitate delivery if immediate birth would allow more effective treatment of disease in the mother or the baby.
- To be safe if the mother has had a previous cesarean delivery. (The rule used to be that any woman who had one cesarean would have to have cesarean sections for all subsequent births; however, in recent years many vaginal deliveries have been performed successfully on women who had previous lower-segment cesarean sections.)

### Disadvantages

Risks of a cesarean section include possible infection, bleeding, and the formation of dangerous blood clots. There is a small chance that the uterus will rupture during a subsequent pregnancy, before or during birth. The cesarean may be inconvenient for the mother, requiring her to stay in the hospital for five to seven days instead of going home with her baby in three days or less. She may not be able to see the baby for a number of hours after delivery if she has undergone general anesthesia. Breast-feeding may be difficult if the mother is being given strong medications to relieve pain, which keep her asleep for long periods of time. There is pain from the abdominal incision, and the mother's activity is restricted once she arrives home. It takes up to six weeks for complete healing of the incision. The expense of the surgical procedure and the extra hospitalization is also a consideration. However, these disadvantages are relatively unimportant if they save the baby from permanent brain damage or save the life of the infant or the mother.

# Ectopic pregnancy

An ectopic pregnancy is one in which the fertilized egg develops outside the uterus. Usually it occurs in one of the two fallopian tubes, through which the egg travels from the ovary to the uterus. (In that case, it is also known as a tubal pregnancy.) However, on rare occasions the fertilized egg starts to develop in the ovary, on the cervix (neck of the uterus), or attached to the outside of a nearby organ in the abdominal cavity. (The ovary is not directly connected to the fallopian tube. There is a slight gap between them, which sometimes permits an egg to enter the abdominal cavity.)

### Causes

The usual cause of an ectopic pregnancy is an obstruction or narrowing of the fallopian tube that prevents the egg from passing through the tube to the uterus. The obstruction or narrowing is usually the result of inflammation or scarring from an infection, such as gonorrhea, but it may also develop after abdominal surgery or because of a growth, such as a pelvic tumor. Tubal infections can occur after miscarriage or childbirth or during the use of an intrauterine

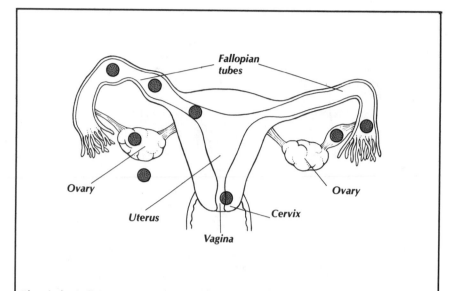

The circles indicate some of the possible sites of an ectopic pregnancy, in which a fertilized egg develops outside the uterus. The most common site is in one of the fallopian tubes, but development in an ovary, on the cervix, or attached to another organ in the abdominal cavity can also occur.

contraceptive device (IUD). If these infections are severe, blockage of the fallopian tube may result.

### Complications

An ectopic pregnancy may be fatal unless it is promptly treated. The danger of a tubal pregnancy is that it will not be detected until the tube enclosing the egg has ruptured (broken), causing massive bleeding. When a fertilized egg begins to develop in an area other than the uterus, such as the ovary or the cervix, nearby large blood vessels may be invaded, causing massive bleeding.

### Symptoms

Symptoms of ectopic pregnancy usually begin two to four weeks after a woman misses her menstrual period. She may be bothered by sharp, continuous pains on one side of her lower

abdomen and by slight bleeding from her vagina. When rapid bleeding occurs, which is usually not until after the sixth week of the pregnancy, she may experience sudden sharp pains in the lower abdomen, backache, low blood pressure, fainting, and even shock (collapse of the circulatory system).

### Diagnosis

The examining doctor may discover a tender swelling on one side of the pelvis. Movement of the uterus during a pelvic examination may cause pain. When ectopic pregnancy is suspected, the patient is hospitalized immediately. An ultrasound study may reveal the outline of the expanding mass. In most cases, there is slow bleeding from the end of the fallopian tube into the abdominal cavity, which may be detected by inserting a hollow needle through the wall of the vagina beneath the cervix. The diagnosis is confirmed by inserting a laparoscope (a lighted, tubelike instrument) through a small incision into the abdominal cavity to inspect the area directly.

**Treatment**

Treatment for ectopic pregnancy is surgical removal of the embryo and surrounding tissues. When the condition occurs in a fallopian tube, the entire tube and sometimes the ovary must be removed. It is sometimes possible to reconstruct the tube.

A woman who has had one ectopic pregnancy has about a 15 percent chance of having a second one. This does not mean that she should not try to become pregnant again; however, when she does try, she should be especially watchful for symptoms of ectopic pregnancy, and when she suspects that conception has occurred, she should see her physician immediately so that the location of the embryo can be determined.

# Episiotomy

An episiotomy is a surgical incision into the tissues surrounding the opening of the vagina during childbirth in order to make the delivery easier and to avoid extensive tearing of the tissues. The advantage of the procedure is that it substitutes a controlled surgical incision for excessive stretching and tearing of all the tissues. The incision itself is easier to repair later than a tear or break in the tissues would be.

Episiotomy is often performed in women who are having their first baby. With subsequent pregnancies, episiotomy may not be necessary, since the tissues surrounding the vagina

*An episiotomy is done to make childbirth easier and to avoid extensive tearing of tissues. The most common type of episiotomy is a midline incision from the midpoint of the vaginal opening directly downward toward the anus. Some doctors, however, prefer an incision at an angle, called a mediolateral episiotomy.*

have often been stretched sufficiently by the first delivery to allow an easy second delivery.

The most common type of episiotomy is an incision made with surgical scissors from the midpoint of the vaginal opening directly down toward the anus. An important risk with this type of incision is that during the birth, the opening might further extend into the anal sphincter (the ring of muscle surrounding the opening from the rectum) or the rectum itself; however, such a tear can be repaired relatively easily and will eventually heal itself. To avoid the risks of entering the rectum, some physicians prefer the mediolateral episiotomy, in which the incision is made at an angle, thus avoiding the rectum and anus.

# Hyperemesis gravidarum

Hyperemesis gravidarum is a term that refers to excessive

vomiting during pregnancy. This type of vomiting is more severe than that caused by ordinary morning sickness, which usually clears up on its own within a few months. In hyperemesis gravidarum, the vomiting leads to starvation, dehydration (excessive loss of water from the tissues), and a disruption of the chemical balance in the body.

Symptoms include loss of weight, dehydration, and jaundice (yellowing of the skin and the whites of the eyes). The condition is most often treated in the hospital through the use of anti-vomiting drugs and intravenous feeding to correct the possible malnutrition, dehydration, and chemical imbalance. A pregnant woman should not attempt to treat the vomiting with drugs without consulting her doctor.

# Mastitis

Mastitis is an inflammation of the breast, most often caused by bacterial invasion and infection.

331

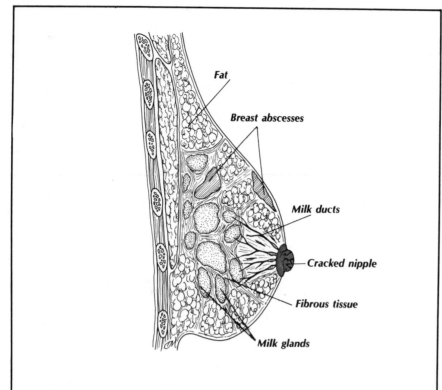

Mastitis is an inflammation of the milk glands and ducts, which occurs most frequently in breast-feeding mothers. The condition is caused by bacteria that enter the breast through cracked nipples.

## Causes

This condition occurs most frequently in nursing mothers and is caused by bacteria normally found on the skin and nipples. The bacteria enter the breast through the nipple and infect the milk glands and ducts. In many cases, the condition occurs on the third to fifth day after the birth of the baby because of the development of cracked nipples, through which the bacteria may enter the breast.

## Symptoms

Symptoms of mastitis include pain, swelling, redness, high fever, and a tender lump in the breast. Sometimes the lymph nodes in the armpit next to the affected breast may be tender and swollen. In cases of severe infection, there may be pus in the breast.

## Diagnosis

The diagnosis is generally made on the basis of the physical examination and the medical history. If there is a severe infection, signaled by the appearance of pus coming from the nipple, a specimen of the pus may be examined to identify the causative organism.

## Treatment

The treatment for mastitis is antibiotic medication to combat the infection. A breast-feeding mother can continue nursing from the unaffected breast, but her physician may recommend that she discontinue nursing from the infected breast and expel the milk by hand to prevent painful swelling of the breast. Even though most antibiotics will enter the breast milk in small quantities, this will not harm the baby. When the infection clears up, nursing from the previously infected breast can be resumed. If there is a great deal of pus, the pus may have to be drained.

## Prevention

A breast-feeding woman can reduce the risk of developing mastitis by keeping her nipples clean and dry between feedings and by wearing clothing that does not rub or irritate the nipples.

# Miscarriage

A miscarriage (in medical terms, a spontaneous abortion) is the ending of a pregnancy due to the premature delivery of the fetus before the beginning of the twentieth week of pregnancy. At that point, the fetus is not developed enough to survive outside the uterus on its own. (After the twentieth week of pregnancy, a spontaneous abortion is considered a premature delivery or, if the fetus is dead at delivery, a stillbirth. A pregnancy that is ended artificially is commonly known as an abortion, although the medical term is termination of pregnancy.) Most miscarriages occur within the first 14 weeks of pregnancy.

It is impossible to know the number of miscarriages that occur during the first month of pregnancy before a woman realizes that she is pregnant; the only indication is a slightly late menstrual period with a heavier than normal flow. However, about 12 percent of known pregnancies end in miscarriage.

## Types

There are several types of miscarriages. A *threatened miscarriage* is experienced by about one of every five pregnant women when vaginal bleeding occurs during the first three months. Although such bleeding may indicate a spontaneous abortion, it is rarely more than a threat, and the pregnancy will continue normally. An *inevitable miscarriage* refers to a situation in which bleeding occurs, the cervix begins to dilate (open), and the uterine contents are expelled. A *missed miscarriage* occurs when the fetus dies in the uterus but is not naturally expelled, and the woman has no bleeding or pain to signify that the pregnancy is not progressing; the physician usually diagnoses the condition when the uterus stops enlarging.

## Causes

The reason that a miscarriage occurs is not always understood, but it is believed that a fetus is usually aborted because it is not developing normally. Several factors can contribute to a miscarriage, including abnormalities in the father's sperm; disease in the mother (for example, an infection, a glandular disorder, high blood pressure, kidney or heart disease, or diabetes); uterine abnormalities; the mother's poor nutrition or use of cigarettes, alcohol, or drugs; and exposure to environmental pollutants. Because the fetus is so well protected within the uterus, a fall or other trauma suffered by the mother is rarely, if ever, the cause of miscarriage.

The expulsion of the fetus resulting from an abnormality is thought to be a chance event, not due to a problem or defect in either parent. Of women who miscarry once, most (about 80 percent) have a successful subsequent pregnancy.

## Symptoms

The symptoms of miscarriage are vaginal bleeding (from a few drops to a heavy flow) and cramps (either dull and constant or sharp and intermittent) in the lower abdomen or back. The bleeding can start suddenly or follow a brownish discharge. A solid clot of material or tissue may pass from the vagina. If possible, this should be saved for the doctor, who may be able to examine it and determine a reason for the expulsion. A miscarriage can be complete (the uterus expels all the tissue) or incomplete (tissue remains inside the uterus).

A pregnant woman who starts bleeding or experiences pain should contact her physician immediately.

## Diagnosis

Depending on the type of miscarriage, diagnosis may be made on the basis of the medical history, physical examination, analysis of any discharge, blood and urine tests (to detect the presence of infection or anemia caused by hemorrhage), or x-ray or ultrasound studies (to establish the absence of a fetus or the presence of an abnormal fetus or parts of a fetus).

## Treatment

There is no medical treatment to stop or avert an inevitable miscarriage. (The drug diethylstilbestrol, or DES, used to be prescribed to deter miscarriages until it was discovered that it had little effect and could cause fetal abnormalities.) The physician generally directs the woman with symptoms to rest in bed and abstain from sexual intercourse.

After an inevitable, incomplete, or missed miscarriage, any remaining fetal or placental tissue must be removed by a surgical procedure known as dilatation and curettage (D&C), in which the physician expands the cervix and gently scrapes out residual material from inside the uterus. Without this precaution, a woman is more susceptible to infections.

It is normal for a woman to feel depressed by the loss of the expected child, but it is usually safe for her to attempt to conceive soon afterward (six to eight weeks later) on the advice of her physician.

## Prevention

More and more information is becoming available about the effect of drugs and nutritional and environmental factors on pregnancy. It is advisable for a woman, at the beginning of her pregnancy, to obtain adequate prenatal care and the most up-to-date information on the substances and practices that may contribute to a miscarriage.

# Placenta previa

Placenta previa is an abnormal condition in which the fertilized egg, or zygote, travels to the lower portion of the uterus and attaches itself to a part of the uterine wall near or even over the uterine opening. As a result, the placenta (a temporary organ in the uterus, which develops during pregnancy to conduct nourishment and oxygen from the mother to the fetus) forms in such a way as to cover all or part of the uterine opening and thus interfere with normal delivery.

There are three types of placenta previa: (1) partial, in which only a portion of the cervix is covered; (2) complete, in which the cervix is completely covered; and (3) low-lying (or marginal), in which the placenta does not cover the cervix, but is close enough to it to potentially interfere with normal delivery.

Placenta previa occurs in one of every 100 to 500 pregnancies. It is more prevalent among women who have had two or more children than among those in their first pregnancy.

### Cause

The cause of placenta previa is unknown. Some authorities believe that placental implantation cannot take place on the same part of the uterine wall more than once. If a woman has had several pregnancies, the lower part of the uterus may be the only place left on which the placenta can become implanted.

### Symptoms

The major symptom of placenta previa is painless vaginal bleeding. Profuse bleeding may begin as early as the twenty-fourth week of pregnancy, with no apparent cause. The blood will be bright red, indicating that it is fresh. Bleeding

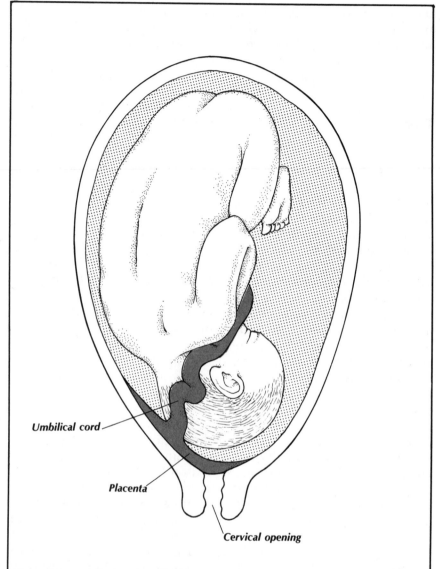

Umbilical cord

Placenta

Cervical opening

*The embryo usually becomes attached to the upper part of the uterine wall, but sometimes implantation takes place in a lower location. As the placenta grows, it can partially or completely cover the cervical opening, thus interfering with a normal delivery.*

occurs as the placenta separates from the wall of the uterus near the uterine opening. This bleeding occurs without any injury (from a fall, for example). In some cases, there is only spotting (light blood flow).

### Diagnosis

Any vaginal bleeding during pregnancy is abnormal and

should, therefore, be reported to the doctor immediately. An ultrasound scan of the woman's abdomen will then be performed. If placenta previa is present, it will be seen on an ultrasound scan.

### Treatment

There are two types of treatment: delayed and active. The

purpose of delayed treatment is to give the fetus time to mature. With active treatment, the fetus is delivered by cesarean section as soon as possible.

The degree of vaginal bleeding will usually dictate the type of treatment. If vaginal bleeding is slight, delayed treatment is generally chosen. If vaginal bleeding is heavy, a cesarean section will be performed immediately.

Bleeding from placenta previa may be extremely heavy, leading to severe blood loss by the mother. This bleeding stops only after the fetus and placenta have been delivered by cesarean section. Unless treatment is rapid, death of both the mother and the fetus may occur.

# Toxemia of pregnancy

Toxemia of pregnancy is a severe condition that sometimes occurs in the last stage of pregnancy and is characterized by high blood pressure; swelling of the extremities, especially the hands, feet, and ankles; and the presence of protein in the urine. If toxemia is allowed to worsen,

convulsions and coma may set in.

The term *toxemia of pregnancy* is actually a misnomer; formerly it was thought that the condition was caused by toxic (poisonous) substances in the blood. The illness is more accurately called preeclampsia before the convulsive stage and eclampsia afterward.

## Causes

The causes of toxemia of pregnancy are not clearly understood. It tends to be more common among mothers from lower socioeconomic groups. One theory is that dietary deficiencies may be at the root of some cases. Some types of toxemia may be the result of a deficiency of blood flow to the uterus.

## Symptoms

Toxemia is divided into three progressively more serious stages, each with its own characteristic symptoms. *Mild preeclampsia* is marked by edema (swelling due to fluid retention), hypertension (high blood pressure), and the presence of pro-

tein in the urine. The symptoms of *severe preeclampsia* may include headache, dizziness, fever, drowsiness, tachycardia (abnormally rapid heart rhythm), tinnitus (noise in the ears), double vision, nausea, vomiting, and scanty or absent urine production. In full-blown *eclampsia*, convulsions may be followed by severe hypotension (low blood pressure) and coma. The condition ultimately leads to death if not treated.

## Treatment

Toxemia cannot be completely cured until the pregnancy is over. Until then, treatment includes stimulation of kidney function, control of high blood pressure and convulsions, and, in severe cases, early delivery of the infant to ensure the survival of the mother.

## Prevention

There is no known preventive for toxemia of pregnancy. The first line of defense is the monitoring of all bodily functions in order to spot symptoms as they begin to appear.

# CARING FOR
# YOUR CHILD

Every parent knows the uneasy feeling that comes with the knowledge (or even the suspicion) that a child is sick. Part of the problem is that it can be very difficult to assess the seriousness of a childhood illness. How can you prepare yourself to make the best decisions about your child's health?

First, educate yourself. Carefully read this book so that you will know which symptoms to watch for and what to do about them. An informed parent is in the best possible position to deal with both the major and the minor crises of childhood.

Second, trust your instincts. As a parent, you know better than anyone else when your child is not acting or feeling right. Sometimes there are visible signs of illness, like diarrhea and a fever; at other times, a change in your child's behavior alerts you to a problem, even though there are no physical symptoms. If you feel that there is a problem or an emergency situation, act on it.

Third, ask questions. Don't worry that you will inconvenience the doctor or appear stupid if you are uncertain about a diagnosis or plan of treatment. It is the doctor's responsibility to make sure that you are fully informed about all matters that concern your child's health.

## WHEN TO CALL A DOCTOR

Here are some rules of thumb about the need for medical attention. Call your doctor if the following situations occur:
- *Fever* is higher than 101°F for more than 24 hours, or a child with a fever looks and acts extremely ill, is difficult to arouse, or is incoherent.
- *Common cold* lasts more than ten days or is accompanied by a fever higher than 101°F, a sore throat or puslike nasal discharge for longer than two days, or a persistent cough or wheezing.
- *Sore throat* is present for more than three days or is accompanied by a fever higher than 101°F.
- *Earache* lasts more than one hour, or a child with an earache looks very ill or has a temperature higher than 101°F.
- *Cough* is persistent or short, dry, and sharp or is accompanied by wheezing, difficulty in breathing, a fever of more than 101°F, or a cold that has lasted more than ten days.
- *Headaches* are frequent, and the child appears very ill.
- *Stomachache* pain has been constant for more than two hours or is accompanied by bloody stools or recurrent vomiting of green or yellow material.
- *Vomiting* is accompanied by fever, lasts more than 12 hours, or produces green or yellow material more than twice, or a vomiting child appears very ill or is difficult to arouse.
- *Diarrhea* is bloody, lasts more than one day, or is accompanied by vomiting, fever of more than 101°F, or absence of urination for eight hours.

Illness in babies may be a little harder to detect. Call the doctor when an infant:
- Refuses to nurse or take liquids.
- Urinates very little.
- Vomits repeatedly.
- Becomes extremely fretful or lethargic.
- Becomes hoarse, has difficulty in breathing, or has a crowing cry, especially if there is a fever.
- Becomes fretful and pulls on his ear.
- Has a marked increase in bowel movements.
- Has blood or mucus in his stools.
- Displays noticeable protrusion of the fontanelle (soft spot on the head).

Call your doctor if an existing condition is not improving or if you do not know what to do about certain symptoms. Although parents need to use common sense in calling the doctor, it is always better to err on the side of being overcautious. A doctor can often give directions and reassure you over the telephone.

Respiratory disorders account for almost half of all childhood illnesses. Fortunately, they are easy to diagnose, and the availability of antibiotics makes many respiratory infections fairly simple to cure.

Although children are helpless in the sense that they cannot provide for themselves, they are remarkably tough when it comes to recovering from illness and overcoming physical disorders. Their resilience sees them through a time when their undeveloped bodies make them vulnerable to mishaps and infections.

## MEDICATIONS

Treating a sick child with medication is an example of how parent and doctor must work together in the interests of the child's health. The doctor is responsible for making an accurate diagnosis of the child's condition and prescribing the appropriate drug. It then becomes the parent's responsibility to make sure that the drug is administered correctly.

It has been estimated that in 10 percent to 30 percent of cases in which medication apparently failed to work, the cause of the failure was improper administration of the medication. Whenever a doctor prescribes a medication for your child, make sure that you understand completely how much to give and how often to give it.

## How much medication to give

The quantity of medication the doctor prescribes for your child is determined by the child's weight and age. Thus, for a given medication, the dosage prescribed for a baby will be much different from that for an adolescent. Make sure that the child takes the complete dose—no more and no less. If the child vomits within 20 minutes of receiving a dose, you can assume that the medication was lost and can give another dose.

Do not use an ordinary kitchen teaspoon when measuring liquid medications; instead, use a specially marked measuring spoon for medication, which should be available from any pharmacist. If your child insists on taking medication from his "special" spoon, transfer the medication from the measuring spoon to the child's spoon after measuring.

## When to give medication

Medications vary in the amount of time it takes for them to be absorbed by the body. Some medications need to be given at very precisely regulated intervals. Therefore, make sure you fully understand the instructions on the label. For example, "four times a day" and "every six hours" do not mean the same thing; the former means that the child should have four doses at fairly equally spaced intervals during the waking hours,

whereas the latter means that each dose should be given six hours after the previous one, even if the child must be awakened to do so.

How long to give medication is also important. A common mistake is to assume that because a child acts as if he is well, he is well. The symptoms of an illness can subside long before the illness itself is over; in fact, the healing process may have barely begun. Stopping a child's medication too soon can cause a relapse and complications. For example, streptococcal infections require ten straight days of antibiotic treatment, and stopping too soon can allow the disease-causing organisms to flourish again. Therefore, such instructions as "Give for ten full days," "Continue for two weeks," and "Give until finished" should be followed exactly.

## How to give medication

Every parent needs to know how to give a child medication, and every child needs to understand that taking medicine is an unpleasant but unavoidable fact of life. A young child, approached in a reassuring and matter-of-fact manner, will usually accept medication without any trouble.

Liquid medicine can be given directly from the spoon (after careful measurement). An alternative method is to use a nonglass medicine dropper to squirt the liquid slowly into the child's mouth. Be careful not to direct the stream of liquid forcefully against the back of the throat and down the windpipe; instead, it should be released against the inside of the cheek.

If the medicine tastes unpleasant, you can give the child a

sweet treat afterward. (Some medications should not be diluted, however; check with your pharmacist.) The medicine can also be disguised in a little applesauce, ice cream, or juice. Make sure that the child takes the entire portion, however.

Do not give pills or capsules to a child under the age of five, because of the risk of choking. If the medication is not available in liquid form, a tablet may be mashed or the contents of a capsule emptied and mixed with a small quantity of juice or food. Always check with your pharmacist or physician first, though, to be certain that the medication will be effective if given in this way, and always make sure that the child takes the whole dose.

After the age of five or six, your child can probably swallow tablets or capsules whole. You can help the child learn how to do this by practicing when he needs a nonprescription remedy, such as acetaminophen. Show him how to put the pill on the back of his tongue and swallow it with a drink or with a spoonful of ice cream, applesauce, or jelly. You can also buy a special glass that delivers the pill into the mouth automatically with the first gulp of liquid. Whenever a child is taking a pill, watch to be sure that the medication goes down smoothly and that the child is in no danger of choking.

Don't encourage a child to take medication by saying that it is candy. Many cases of poisoning have occurred in children who took overdoses of medications that looked or tasted like candy. Many doctors discourage the use of children's vitamin pills that are sweet, brightly colored, or shaped like cartoon characters, believing that such products blur the distinction in the child's mind between candy and drugs.

# Apgar score

The Apgar score is a general evaluation of a baby's condition made soon after birth, to determine immediately whether the newborn needs emergency care. The Apgar scoring system was devised by the late Virginia Apgar, M.D., and the letters of her last name are an acronym for the factors being scored.

## Procedure

One minute and five minutes after an infant's birth, a delivery room nurse, anesthesiologist, or pediatrician rates five factors, using a scale of 0 to 2:

A (Appearance)—A score of 2 is given if the skin is completely pink; 1, if it is pink except for the hands and feet, which are bluish; 0, if the entire body is blue (indicating lack of oxygen).

P (Pulse)—A score of 2 is given for a pulse above 100; 1, for a rate of less than 100; 0, for no pulse.

G (Grimace, or reflex irritability)—A score of 2 is given if the baby cries vigorously when slapped lightly on the soles of the feet; 1, if the baby makes only a grimace or slight cry; 0, if he makes no response.

A (Activity)—An active infant is given a score of 2; an infant who makes some movement of the arms and legs, 1; a limp and motionless infant, 0.

R (Respiration)—Strong efforts to breathe, together with vigorous crying, score a 2; slow, irregular breathing, 1; no breathing, 0.

## Scores

Most babies score between 7 and 10 when tested one minute after birth. They are breathing well, crying, pinkish in color, active, and need no emergency measures.

Those babies who score from 4 to 6 usually need help immediately. The throat is suctioned to remove thick mucus, small blood clots, or bits of swallowed membrane (from the amniotic sac that enclosed the baby before birth). Oxygen is sometimes given to assist breathing and restore color.

The baby with an Apgar score of less than 4 is limp, pale or bluish, and perhaps without a heartbeat, and is in grave danger. The throat is suctioned, and the baby is placed on a mechanical respirator, which pumps air in and out of the lungs until the baby can breathe on his or her own.

A second Apgar score is determined five minutes after birth and recorded on the baby's chart beside the first score. The second score is a good measure of the baby's adaptation to the world outside the womb.

# Autism

Autism is a form of mental illness in children. The word *autism* comes from *auto*, the Greek word for self, and literally means self-absorption. The autistic child is wrapped up in his own inner thoughts, unable to communicate with or relate to other people.

## Causes

Although the cause of autism remains a mystery, several reasons for the disorder have been suggested. In some cases, an inborn mental defect may play a part, since many affected children do not smile and do not accept or respond to affectionate cuddling. In other instances, severe mental or physical trauma during childhood may have contributed to the disorder. The sex of the child may also be a factor; boys are four times as likely as girls to be autistic.

## Symptoms

Autism is a collection of symptoms of unknown cause that appear in the first 30 months of life. The autistic child is very withdrawn, unaffectionate, and uninterested in people, including parents, brothers, and sisters. The child behaves as if he were alone in the world. Accompanying this attitude is a speech and language disorder: the child may learn to speak late or not at all, and, if speech develops, it is odd and limited. One common characteristic is echolalia (repetition of the last phrase or word of everything another person says). Other marks of autism are a total resistance to change (even something so minor as rearrangement of furniture) and the repetition of some meaningless act, such as rocking, arm-flapping, or head-banging. Mental development is often uneven. Usually the child does best in learning nonverbal skills, and teaching methods that emphasize memorization and drill may be most useful. There are no established signs of nervous system defects, although half of all autistic children experience seizures before reaching their teens.

## Diagnosis

In diagnosing autism, the doctor must distinguish it from childhood schizophrenia, a mental illness that may also cause a child to be silent and withdrawn but that usually strikes later than does autism. The doctor must also make certain that deafness or severely impaired hearing is not present. The child is given neurologic and intelligence tests, to help determine the potential for training and education. A tranquilizer may be prescribed for emergency use to quiet violent outbursts.

## Treatment

An autistic child may have to be cared for in an institution or a specialized school. Day-care programs for autistic children are available in some cities, and the trend is to train parents to care for their children at home. The method of treatment most often used by professionals, and taught to parents, is known as behavior therapy. The main goals are to limit self-destructive or meaningless actions, to promote language development, and to make the child more social. In behavior therapy, the professional or parent works to develop a close relationship with the child, so that the child will want to imitate the adult. The adult also uses direct action (such as rewards and praise) to promote speech, play with other children, self-care skills (such as dressing and washing), and helpfulness. With such methods, some autistic children of average or near-average intelligence are able to develop into normal adults.

## Prevention

Unfortunately, because the cause is unknown, there are no preventive measures.

# Cerebral palsy

Cerebral palsy (CP) is a general term to describe various disorders of muscle control.

## Cause

Cerebral palsy is caused by brain or nerve damage that usually occurs before or around the time of birth. The damage may result when brain tissue becomes starved for oxygen for any reason. It may result from separation and bleeding of the placenta (the organ that anchors the fetus to the wall of the uterus and provides nourishment) in late pregnancy or from disorders caused by diabetes in the mother.

## Types

There are four major types of CP: spastic, athetoid, ataxic, and mixed. About 70 percent of cases of CP are the spastic type. Patients with spastic CP move stiffly and with great difficulty because their affected muscles are constantly tense and tight. One arm and one leg may be affected, or both arms or both legs. Affected extremities appear thin and wasted, are weak, and are likely to twist and jerk. Walking on the toes or with a scissors-like movement is typical. When all four limbs are affected, the mouth, tongue, and palate may also be affected, interfering with speech, eating, and drinking and causing constant drooling.

Athetoid, or dyskinetic, CP accounts for about 20 percent of cases. This disorder, which is caused by damage to the basal ganglia (a mass of nerve-cell bodies at the base of the brain), is characterized by continual slow, twisting movements of the fingers and hands during waking hours. Similar movements of the upper arms or legs and trunk may also occur. There may be sudden, jerky movements as well.

Ataxic CP results from damage to the cerebellum (a portion of the brain highly involved in muscular coordination) or the nerves leading from it. The characteristic signs of this type of CP are weakness, lack of balance and coordination, tremor, difficulty with fine or quick movements, and a clumsy way of walking, with feet wide apart.

Mixed CP occurs frequently. Often, spastic and athetoid types are combined. Ataxic and athetoid types are mixed less often.

## Symptoms

Possible signs of CP in a baby include twitching, convulsions, back-arching muscle spasms, partial paralysis of the face, and very late development of the ability to lift the head, sit, crawl, speak, stand, and walk. Any baby who may have suffered brain damage around the time of birth should be watched carefully for signs of CP (such a baby may have been born nearly lifeless or very small and premature, or may have suffered a severe infection soon after birth). Although it is difficult to diagnose any particular form of CP in the first two years of life, parents should report any suspicion promptly to their doctor.

After infancy, symptoms of cerebral palsy range from simple clumsiness or slight incoordination of muscles to multiple handicaps that prevent normal movement. Frequently, the brain damage that causes CP also causes mental retardation, epilepsy, hearing problems, visual defects, and learning and behavior disorders. However, some CP children are normal except for disordered muscle control.

### Diagnosis

Early diagnosis and treatment of CP are essential if a child is to develop as fully as possible. An important part of the diagnostic evaluation is to discover if there is any other reason for the symptoms. A wide range of medical diagnostic studies and psychological tests will be performed.

### Treatment

Treatment of a CP child may involve many different elements, such as speech therapy, physical therapy, special dental care, specially designed clothes, braces, corrective glasses, surgery, a hearing aid, special furniture, and special schooling. Occupational therapy can help the patient in self-care, including dressing and eating. About 25 percent of CP patients have convulsions, which usually can be controlled by anticonvulsant medicines. Ideally, a physician will work with a team of specialists in a hospital or other setting where treatments can be coordinated.

Because CP is a lifelong condition, parents need to learn as much as possible about caring for a CP child. The parents can learn how to continue therapy at home. Every effort must be made to help the child become self-reliant. Parents can often get valuable advice and support from other parents of CP children and from professionals at the local chapter of the United Cerebral Palsy Association. Therapy for CP children and adults is provided at rehabilitation centers sponsored by the National Easter Seal Society and by various other agencies.

### Prevention

Expectant mothers can guard against CP with good prenatal care emphasizing adequate diet, rest, and exercise. During labor and birth, the doctor can keep track of the baby's heartbeat with use of a fetal monitor and, if necessary, operate quickly to save the baby from brain damage caused by oxygen starvation. Expectant mothers with difficult pregnancies should try to have their babies delivered at a hospital with a newborn intensive care unit, directed by a certified neonatologist (a physician who specializes in the care of newborn babies). In such a unit, premature and ill babies can be watched closely and cared for by specially trained nurses and doctors using the latest methods.

# Child abuse

Child abuse encompasses all types of mistreatment—physical, emotional, and sexual—that can be inflicted on a child, particularly by a parent, guardian, or other family member. Closely related is child neglect, in which the parent or guardian chooses not to provide for the nutritional, emotional, physical, or health needs of a child.

### Causes

The principal cause of child abuse is emotional inadequacy of the parent or guardian. Most parents who abuse their children were themselves abused as children. They did not learn how to give or receive affection from their parents and thus find it hard to develop a good relationship with their own children. They often use the same harsh punishment methods—threats, ridicule, and physical violence—that were used on them as children, often because they do not know any other way of managing family problems.

Some parents who neglect their children are incompetent because of drug or alcohol abuse, medical or psychological disorders, or overwhelming socioeconomic problems. Parents who do not have a support system of close friends or relatives living nearby may feel isolated and overwhelmed by the constant demands of rearing children. Others who may abuse their children are young parents with their first child, parents of ill or premature babies who are separated from them shortly after birth, and parents who did not want a child in the first place. Such parents need special attention and support in order to get their families off to a good start.

### Symptoms

Physical symptoms of abuse (also known as the battered child syndrome) include old and new bruises; scars from cuts and burns; serious damage to the eyes, mouth, or internal organs; and x-ray evidence of bone fractures in various stages of healing. When parents cannot give reasonable explanations for the child's injuries, child abuse may be suspected.

Signs of emotional abuse are more difficult to detect. Babies who have been neglected emotionally may appear uninterested in people or even retarded. Another sign in babies is the condition known as failure to thrive, which is unexplained lack of growth even though no illness is present. Older children who are excessively well behaved and overly anxious to please adults, but who do not get along well with other children and are mistrustful may be victims of emotional abuse. At school, they may have trouble with teachers as well as with other children.

Sexual abuse by a parent or older sibling or other relative is often difficult to detect. There may be no physical symptoms, although venereal disease in a child is grounds for suspicion. The child may be too fearful or too embarrassed to reveal the situation to anyone outside the family.

### Outside intervention

When physicians suspect child abuse, they are required by law in most states to report it to a government social service agency or welfare department. However, punishment of the parents is not the goal of the law. Jailing a parent might injure the child as much as the original abuse if the parent is capable of being a good father or mother in the future. Removing the child from the family may be necessary to protect the youngster from future injury, but in most cases this is not done or the removal is only temporary.

The child may stay in the hospital for a few days while the case is studied and the parents are interviewed. In many communities, a team made up of a social worker, a pediatrician, a psychiatrist, and other specialists talk to the child and the parents and develop a long-term treatment plan. This often involves periodic visits by a social worker to the home and psychological help for one or both parents. Practical help, such as day care for small children and household help by a trained homemaker, can ease the burdens on an overworked mother. If there is a local chapter of Parents Anonymous, an organization of parents who formerly abused their children, this may be another source of emotional support.

### Prevention

Parents who are afraid that they might abuse their children should talk frankly to their family doctor or a social worker. Joining a support group of other parents may be a helpful way to share child-care ideas and experiences.

If a baby is born ill or prematurely and must stay in the hospital after the mother comes home, the parents should visit the baby every day and stay as close as possible so that the baby will not be a stranger when he comes home.

# Circumcision

Circumcision is the surgical removal of the foreskin, the retractable sleeve of skin covering the glans (the head of the penis). In some religions, the operation is performed as a religious ritual on the eighth day following birth. In hospitals, it is usually done on the day before a baby boy goes home. In any event, if it is to be done for nonmedical reasons, it should be done in infancy and not later, when it is a more serious operation and might harm the child psychologically.

During the five-minute operation, which is usually done without anesthesia, the foreskin is carefully cut away. Gauze coated with petroleum jelly is applied to the incision. In most cases, the incision heals rapidly, forming a dry scab that drops off after a few days. Although the incision should be kept as clean as possible (but not submerged in bathwater), no other special care is necessary. Other than a few drops of blood that might be produced if the diaper rubs against the cut, there is no bleeding in a normal baby.

### Pros and cons

Routine circumcision for newborns is a controversial issue. A decision about the procedure should be made by the parents after consideration of both sides of the question.

The operation has become standard in American hospitals in recent decades as a cleanliness measure. In a young boy, the foreskin completely covers the head of the penis and cannot be pulled back very far. If the penis is not kept clean, urine and other substances can cause irritation of the glans and perhaps lead to infection between the foreskin and the glans. However, normal care can prevent this problem. Even though the foreskin at first cannot be pulled back very far because of bands of tissue that bind it to the glans, it is necessary to wash only the part of the glans that can be uncovered comfortably at any one stage. The bands of tissue gradually dissolve, and by later childhood, the foreskin can be pulled back completely.

Some researchers believe that circumcision reduces the risk of cancer of the penis and cancer of the cervix (the neck of the uterus) in the sexual partner of the circumcised man and may help prevent venereal disease. However, there is insufficient evidence to support these views.

Very seldom is there a medical reason to perform a circumcision. It should never be done on the first day of life, or if the baby is ill or premature. Furthermore, it should be delayed indefinitely if there is any abnormality of the glans or penis, so that the foreskin can be used later as graft tissue to repair the defect. It should not be done if the mother was taking any medication that promotes bleeding, such as an anticoagulant or aspirin, during pregnancy or is taking such a medication while breast-feeding, nor should it be done if there is any family history of hemophilia or other bleeding disorders.

Risks of circumcision include local infection, which may lead to significant hemorrhage and mutilation. Many medical authorities feel that there is no absolute medical reason for routine circumcision of the newborn. Adequate hygiene offers the same advantages as routine circumcision without the risks of the operation.

Parents, therefore, should consider all factors—cultural, religious, and medical—before making a decision about circumcision.

# Cleft lip and cleft palate

Cleft lip and cleft palate, a defect in one of every 700 to 800 newborns, is characterized by a split running through all or part of the upper structure of the mouth. A cleft lip (or harelip) may be only a small notch near the center of the upper lip, or it may extend into the nostril. A cleft in the palate can be as minor as a split in the uvula (the little projection of tissue that hangs down in the back of the throat), or it may divide the entire soft palate (the muscular tissue that covers the roof of the mouth). In its most severe form, a cleft splits not only the soft palate but the entire hard palate (the bony roof of the mouth) and upper jaw, joining with a cleft lip. The cleft may even divide the palate into three parts, resulting in a split on either side of the nose and leaving the middle section of the upper jaw and gum dangling.

## Causes

The formation of a cleft lip occurs in the early stage of pregnancy, soon after the fourth week, when the baby's face

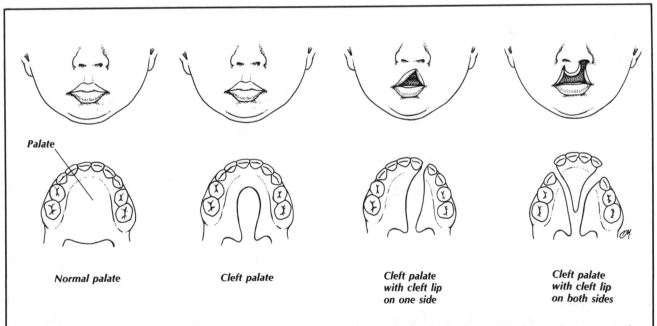

*Palate*

**Normal palate**

**Cleft palate**

**Cleft palate with cleft lip on one side**

**Cleft palate with cleft lip on both sides**

*A cleft palate is a division of the tissues that form the roof of the mouth. This condition does not deform the outward appearance of the face, but makes feeding difficult for the child. The division may also extend through the entire palate and one side of the upper jaw, resulting in a cleft palate with cleft lip. In the most severe form, a cleft palate with a cleft lip on both sides, the palate is divided into three parts, resulting in a split on either side of the nose and leaving a middle section of upper jaw and gum dangling.*

starts to form. Bulges of tissue on either side of the face grow toward the midline to form the nostrils and lips. At about the seventh week they normally meet and join; if they do not, a cleft lip is the result.

A failure of development in the eighth week of pregnancy causes cleft palate. The palate is formed from two plates of tissue, which originally are on either side of the developing tongue. As the head and neck grow, the tongue moves downward and the tissue plates move into position and fuse into one—unless there is a mistake or weakness, which results in cleft palate.

The underlying causes of cleft lip and cleft palate are not fully understood. There is an inherited tendency toward the defects. More than one-fourth of children with cleft lip also have a relative with a cleft. If parents without cleft defects have one child with a cleft, they have a 5 percent risk of having a second child with a cleft; if they have two children with clefts, there is a 12 percent risk of a cleft in future children. Perhaps some difference in the uterus, such as poor blood supply to the fetus, combines with an inherited weakness to produce the error of development. Certain chemicals or medications, too many vitamins or not enough, and viruses have been suggested as possible causes of cleft defects.

Cleft lip and cleft palate are often associated with other birth defects. Of every six children who have a cleft lip, with or without cleft palate, one will have one or more other birth defects. Almost 50 percent of children with cleft palate also have another defect, such as joined fingers or toes, malformed ears, spina bifida, heart disease, or clubfoot.

## Treatment

Treatment of a patient with a cleft lip or a cleft palate (or both) requires the services of a specialized team that includes a pediatrician, an orthodontist (a dentist who specializes in the prevention or correction of misalignment of the teeth), a speech therapist, a plastic surgeon, a psychologist, an audiologist (a specialist in communication disorders), and an otolaryngologist (a physician who specializes in the diagnosis and treatment of disorders of the ears, nose, and throat). Treatment may take place at a specialized clinic or hospital center or may be coordinated by a pediatrician who consults experts as needed.

Before any treatment can begin, however, steps must be taken to permit the child to eat. A cleft lip prevents normal sucking, and a cleft palate allows milk to run out of the nose, often causing choking and vomiting. Special feeding devices are used, such as a nipple with an enlarged flange to cover the cleft or a regular nipple with enlarged holes. A small syringe with a short rubber tube, like one used to baste a turkey, may be used to feed a child with a cleft lip, although sometimes such a child can be breast-fed. A few days after birth, an orthodontist skilled in cleft palate repair may be able to fashion an appliance that provides a temporary roof for the mouth, enabling regular feeding. At the same time, the appliance prevents the mouth from being distorted before the palate can be closed.

Some surgeons correct a cleft lip in the first few days of the child's life because it will make the baby more acceptable to his parents and make it easier to feed the baby by bottle. How-

ever, other surgeons delay the operation for two to eight months, so that surgery will not interfere with the growing bonds of affection between mother and baby (for one thing, the baby cannot breast-feed for six weeks after the operation) and to rule out other birth defects that might interfere with recovery.

Plastic surgery to correct cleft palate usually takes place in the second year of life. Some surgeons repair the soft palate first, when the child is between 6 and 18 months of age, and the hard palate much later—sometimes not until the age of five years. Although early surgery helps the child's emotional and speech development, some surgeons wait because they are concerned that early surgery may cause distortion of growth in the middle third of the face. While waiting, the child wears an appliance that acts as a roof over the mouth.

The problems created by cleft palate and cleft lip cannot be solved only by surgery. The services of an orthodontist are needed for youngsters with cleft palate, not only to make appliances but to straighten teeth that are poorly positioned. A speech therapist aids the child in developing speech, which is altered because of the missing or inadequate soft palate or artificial palate. A psychologist helps to treat emotional and social problems sometimes caused by being different in speech or appearance. An otolaryngologist should examine the child monthly for middle ear infections, which are common in young children with cleft palate. An audiologist helps those children who develop hearing loss because of middle ear infections. With proper care and encouragement and with modern plastic surgery, the average child with a cleft can make a good recovery.

# Clubfoot

Clubfoot, or talipes, is a common birth defect in which one or both feet are fixed in an awkward, twisted position. The foot resists efforts to stretch or turn it back. In talipes equinovarus, the most frequent form, the foot points down and turns in while the front of the foot curls toward the heel. If not corrected, the condition worsens and interferes with walking. The person seems to walk on the ankle and the outside or inside edge of the foot.

*Talipes equinovarus*

*Metatarsus varus*

The most common form of clubfoot is talipes equinovarus, in which the foot points down and turns in while the front of the foot curls toward the heel. Related to clubfoot is metatarsus varus ("pigeon toe"), in which the front of the foot turns inward.

## Causes

The cause of clubfoot is unknown. However, there seems to be an inherited tendency for development to be arrested around the ninth week of pregnancy, when the fetus' feet are being formed. Clubfoot may begin as a muscle abnormality. The Achilles tendon is shortened, the ankle and its muscles are deformed, and the heel bone is shortened and flattened to some extent.

## Treatment

Correction of clubfoot should begin as early as the first week after birth, when the bones, muscles, ligaments, and tendons are soft and pliable. The correction is usually done in stages, rather than all at once. In talipes equinovarus, the first stage is to uncurl the front of the foot away from the heel. The next is to turn the foot so that the sole faces outward. The third stage is to put the foot in a cast with the toes

pointing up. This may require surgery to lengthen the Achilles tendon and to free the ankle joint.

Correction generally takes place in a series of small, painless, gradual adjustments. Typically, the doctor flexes and stretches the foot by hand and then fixes it in a cast in a partially corrected position. After a week or so the cast is removed, the foot is manipulated into a better position, and a new cast is applied. Sometimes, instead of making a new cast each time, the doctor places wedges inside the existing cast to adjust the foot. The entire casting process may take three months.

Once the correction has been made, it must be followed up with exercises, devices that hold the feet in place at night while the baby is sleeping, and orthopedic shoes. A night splint (corrective shoes with soles joined by a flat metal bar that keeps the feet in exactly the right position) is often used.

Because clubfoot sometimes recurs, periodic checkups are necessary until the child becomes an adult. However, in most cases, the correction is completely successful, and the individual can walk and run normally.

If early treatment has not succeeded, or if a child is not treated until the age of nine or ten, more extensive surgery may be necessary. This is followed by several weeks with the foot in a cast. Satisfactory results are usually obtained. The foot is rather stiff, but this does not prevent the child from engaging in the most active sports.

Related to true clubfoot is a condition called metatarsus varus, in which the front of the foot turns inward. Also known as apparent clubfoot and pigeon toe, this is a milder deformity, which may not be diagnosed in the first several weeks. Unlike a true clubfoot, the apparent clubfoot can be moved easily into a correct position. It can usually be corrected by manipulation and exercise, without the need for casts or surgery.

# Colic

Colic means different things to different people, but the universal characteristic is crying—not just short periods of fussiness that can be stopped by changing or feeding or cuddling—but long periods of crying with no apparent cause that defy all attempts to stop them.

### Causes

It has long been assumed that colic arises from some gastrointestinal disorder. However, studies have shown no correlation between colic and poor weight gain or excessive vomiting, constipation, or diarrhea. Colicky babies are generally quite healthy, with no sign of nutritional problems. Nor does the problem appear to be hunger; the crying spells often begin after a feeding, not before one. It has been suggested that bottle-feeding is at fault, but breast-fed infants are just as likely to have colic. Lactose intolerance, food sensitivities, and allergies have also been suggested as causes.

Some babies with colic seem to have no such digestive symptoms—their crying seems to be related to general irritability, possibly because of immaturity of the nervous system or exceptional sensitivity to the environment. Other babies have a combination of the two types of colic.

### Symptoms

Colic most often begins when an infant is two to four weeks old. The baby will cry inconsolably for hours a day. These bouts of crying often occur as if on schedule (most often in the late afternoon or early evening). The colicky baby pulls his legs up, clenches his fists, screams, and turns red. He may nurse briefly but then stop to continue crying. His abdomen may be distended as if with gas, and he may even pass gas frequently. He generally has no other gastrointestinal symptoms; his bowel movements are normal, and he doesn't spit up any more than most babies. His sleep pattern is often disrupted—he may wake frequently (every two hours or so), cry fretfully, take one to two ounces of formula or a few minutes at the mother's breast, fall into a fitful sleep, and then waken to repeat the sequence.

### Diagnosis

Before assuming that your baby has colic, check for other possible causes of crying, such as pain from an open diaper pin or discomfort from being overheated, constipated, hungry, or wet. See whether your baby responds promptly to talking and cuddling—a baby in pain can be distracted, but only temporarily. Also check for signs of illness: colic is not associated with fever, diarrhea, vomiting, cough, a runny nose, or reddened eyes.

Your pediatrician will want to rule out more serious causes of crying before assuming that your baby has colic. Signs of illness, such as sores in the mouth or gastrointestinal or urinary tract problems, will be sought. Although conclusive scientific evidence for a dietary basis for colic is lacking, your doctor may want to investigate the possibility that something in the baby's diet (or in the mother's diet if she is breast-feeding) may be causing the condition.

### Treatment

If the colic seems to be due, at least in part, to an accumulation of gas in the abdomen, be careful not to overfeed the baby and be sure to burp him thoroughly after feedings. If you are bottle-feeding, check the nipple hole; if it is too large or too small, the baby may be swallowing more air than he should. A warm hot-water bottle on the abdominal area may relieve some discomfort. The baby may be most comfortable lying on his stomach.

If the colic seems to be due to irritability, it might be helpful to restrict visitors and to keep the home environment as peaceful as possible. Some researchers believe that overly sensitive babies may be upset by an atmosphere charged with too much noise, too much activity, and too much emotional stress.

Your physician will probably not recommend any medical treatment for colic. Colic usually ends two or three months after it begins, with no physical or emotional consequences.

# Congenital hypothyroidism

Congenital (present at birth) hypothyroidism is a condition that leads to defective physical and mental development because of a deficiency of thyroid hormone. If untreated, a person born with congenital hypothyroidism grows to a maximum height of three or four feet and has a large, flat, broad head; short forehead; puffy, wide-set eyes; broad, short, upturned nose; thick lips; large tongue protruding from a drooling mouth; narrow chest; potbelly; swayback; rough skin; dry hair; and severe mental retardation.

## Causes

Iodine is necessary for the body to produce thyroid hormone, and foods obtained from the ocean are the best source of iodine. Before the widespread use of iodized salt, hypothyroidism was much more common in inland areas, where foods naturally contain little iodine.

Congenital hypothyroidism can result from a defect in the development of a child before birth. The thyroid gland may be missing or underdeveloped, possibly because of a severe deficiency of iodine in the mother's diet during pregnancy. In rare cases, congenital hypothyroidism is caused by an inherited absence of a body chemical needed to produce thyroid hormone.

When hypothyroidism first appears in children over the age of two years, it is usually due to an inflammation of the thyroid gland resulting from an immune disorder. It can also be caused by certain diseases of the pituitary gland or hypothalamus.

## Symptoms

The first symptoms of untreated congenital hypothyroidism usually appear between the ages of three and six months or whenever the mother stops breast-feeding (breast milk contains tiny quantities of thyroid hormone). The baby is "too

good," in the sense that he seldom cries (when the baby does cry, it is a strange, hoarse cry), sleeps more than normal, is inactive, and thus is easy to care for. This behavior is a result of the baby's lack of thyroid hormone, which regulates the rate of body processes, and increasing mental retardation. The baby's movements are slow and awkward, and the child has feeding difficulties, is constipated, and develops jaundice. The stomach protrudes, and a hernia may develop at the navel.

These symptoms are followed by the appearance of the characteristic facial features: the thick tongue, which interferes with breathing; the wide-set eyes; the turned-up nose; and the dull expression, indicating mental deficiency. The baby's heart beats slowly, resulting in poor circulation and cold skin. The hair is dry and dull. The teeth come in late and decay easily.

The child in whom symptoms of hypothyroidism first appear after the age of two is typically short and fat, with short legs and arms and a head that appears too large. Sexual development in an older child may be delayed.

## Diagnosis

Early diagnosis is now much more common since all states began to require that every newborn be tested for thyroid hormone level.

Diagnosis of congenital hypothyroidism may require not only a blood test to determine thyroid hormone levels, but also a nuclear medicine study after the administration of radioactive iodine to evaluate thyroid function. Special x-ray studies may also be used to detect delayed development of the skeleton,

and an electrocardiogram may be ordered to reveal heartbeat patterns.

## Treatment

Treatment for congenital hypothyroidism is lifelong replacement of thyroid hormone with a synthetic substitute, ideally starting at birth. Those who begin to receive the hormone before the age of three months usually develop normally. Children born without a thyroid gland are more at risk than those whose thyroid gland works poorly; if not treated by three months of age, they will be mentally retarded even though their growth is corrected.

## Prevention

Pregnant women can help prevent congenital hypothyroidism in their offspring by eating a well-balanced diet that includes iodine-rich foods, such as fish and seafood, and by using iodized salt. At birth, every child's blood should be tested for thyroid hormone level.

# Croup

Croup is a condition marked by a hoarse, barking cough that sometimes follows a cold or fever in very young children, most commonly those under the age of two years. A croup attack may occur only once, or it may linger or reappear after it seems to have gone.

## Causes

Croup is usually caused by a viral infection of the larynx

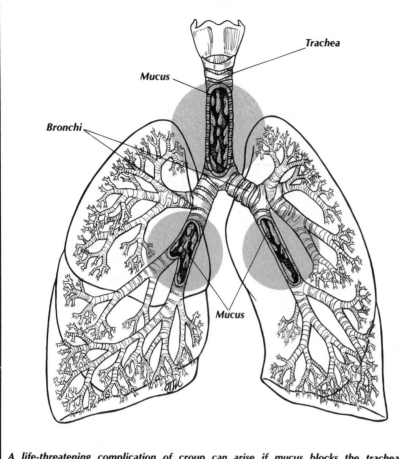

*A life-threatening complication of croup can arise if mucus blocks the trachea (windpipe) and the bronchi leading into the lungs, causing serious breathing difficulties.*

(voice box). The characteristic barking cough is produced when air forces its way through the child's swollen larynx. The air passageways in a child's throat are very narrow; when an infection causes swelling, little room is left for air to pass through, and breathing can be severely hampered. Also, the windpipe and the bronchi (the main breathing tubes that connect the windpipe and the lungs) may become blocked with mucus, further impairing breathing.

## Symptoms

The identifying symptoms of croup are a deep, barking cough and breathing difficulties, especially when inhaling. Sometimes a fever and hoarseness are also present. The child may gag while coughing, causing vomiting, which usually relieves the cough somewhat. The coughing attack often occurs in the evening and usually lasts less than an hour.

Symptoms that indicate a worsening condition include blue skin and lips, drooling, and extreme exhaustion. When the croaking sound continues while the child is inhaling, a condition called stridor has developed. If any of these symptoms occurs or if there are severe breathing difficulties, medical help should be obtained *immediately*.

## Diagnosis

The emphasis in diagnostic evaluation is on establishing that the difficulty in breathing is actually due to croup and not to epiglottitis, a life-threatening emergency condition in which the inflamed epiglottis (the lidlike structure covering the opening to the windpipe) rapidly becomes completely obstructed.

Choking on a foreign object may also resemble croup, since both conditions share the symptom of frantic efforts to breathe. An x-ray may be performed to rule out this possibility.

## Treatment

Croup can usually be treated at home. The first step is calming the child. The barking cough, especially when accompanied by difficulty in breathing, can frighten the child, and this fear can only aggravate the symptoms. Sometimes the child can be told to imagine a relaxing scene or can listen to a calming bedtime story; a relaxed child will respond much better to home remedies.

The goal is to relieve the cough by reducing the inflammation and swelling in the larynx. This can be accomplished by breathing in moist air from a humidifier or vaporizer, by leaning over a pan of hot water with a towel draped over the head, or by sitting in a steamy bathroom with a hot shower running. Moist air reduces the swelling and makes breathing easier. Of course, precautions should be taken to protect a young child from being scalded while taking part in these treatments, and the child should never be left alone.

Drinking extra fluids (not milk or orange juice) at room temperature is also recommended. Cough medicine will not help (and may even harm) a child with croup, nor is it advisable to put a spoon or any other object into the mouth in an attempt to aid the breathing. In a severe case, a physician may administer drugs to control the inflammation in the throat; also, antibiotics can sometimes control the infections connected with croup.

## Prevention

It is not known why some children develop croup after a cold or fever and others do not; therefore, there is really no way to prevent croup.

# Fontanelles

Fontanelles are the gaps between the bony plates of an infant's skull. The largest and most noticeable of these gaps is the ''soft spot'' on top of the head and toward the front. There is also a groove that runs like a center part toward the back of the head, where a much smaller soft spot is located. The fontanelles serve two purposes. During birth, they permit the head to adapt without injury to being squeezed as it passes through the birth canal. After birth, they permit the brain to grow. During the first two or three years of a child's life, the skull plates grow toward each other until they meet, covering the soft spots. However, the plates do not fully knit together until shortly before adolescence, when the brain stops growing.

The baby's soft spot is supported by a tough membrane and does not have to be treated more delicately than any other part of the head. It is normal for

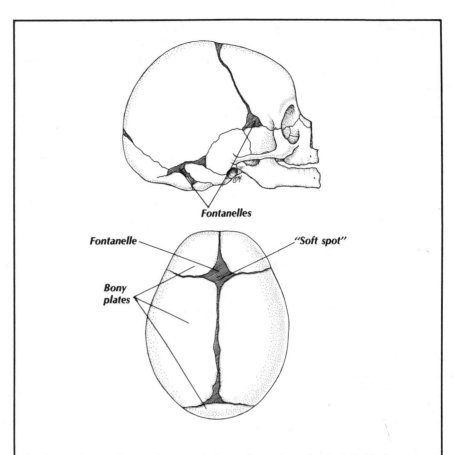

*Fontanelles*

*Fontanelle* — *''Soft spot''*

*Bony plates*

*The fontanelles are the gaps between the bony plates of an infant's skull. The largest and most noticeable of these gaps is the ''soft spot'' on top of the head toward the front. The fontanelles permit the head to adapt without injury to being squeezed during birth. After birth, they allow room for the brain to grow. Shortly before adolescence, the bony plates meet and knit together.*

it to be slightly depressed, to tense up when the baby cries, and to pulsate in rhythm with the heartbeat. (The pulsation is not that of an artery directly beneath the soft spot. Instead, it is caused by changes in the pressure of the cerebrospinal fluid, which surrounds and protects the brain and spinal cord.)

# Gilles de la Tourette's syndrome

Gilles de la Tourette's syndrome is a neuromuscular disorder marked by intense tics (twitchy, repetitive movements of certain muscles). It occurs most often in boys. It generally begins around the age of seven or eight years. At first the tics are simple: facial twisting, blinking, grimacing, shoulder shrugging, or twitching. Later the tics progress to vocal tics accompanied by psychological involvement.

## Causes

The causes of Gilles de la Tourette's syndrome are unknown. It is still disputed whether the disorder is of physical or psychological origin.

349

## Symptoms

The symptoms of Gilles de la Tourette's syndrome are at first limited to the muscles in the face, head, neck, and shoulders. Often, the first symptom is a characteristic breathing noise from the larynx (voice box), as if the patient were barking, wheezing, or gasping for air. As the tics spread to the shoulders and arms, there are shoulder shrugs and twitches, as well as twisting of the neck and arms. Vocal tics, such as grunting, snuffing, shouting, and barking sounds, then begin to develop. As the vocal symptoms worsen, the patient begins to exclaim in a loud voice words or phrases with obscene meanings or "swear words." Echolalia (repetition by the patient of words that have been said to him) is common. The patient will seem to fixate on a word or phrase and repeat it over and over with increasing speed. Often, too, the individual will spasmodically and automatically repeat or mimic the actions of those around him.

The symptoms of Gilles de la Tourette's syndrome tend to come and go, especially as the patient approaches puberty and adulthood. Tics that are very violent during waking hours often stop during sleep. Some tics are intensified by emotional upheavals. The tics of Gilles de la Tourette's syndrome, unlike those of most neuromuscular disorders, are often suppressed in school or social settings and expressed more often when the patient is alone or with family members. In some cases, the tics can be controlled voluntarily. The excessive swearing, however, occurs only in the presence of others; some patients attempt to cover it up by coughing, thus developing another tic. Often

symptoms decrease in adult life and disappear, only to return during a period of stress. Mental activity remains normal.

## Diagnosis

Diagnosing Gilles de la Tourette's syndrome is often difficult, since symptoms in the early stages often resemble common childhood tics seen in many young school-age children. Also, early- and middle-stage symptoms are difficult to distinguish from those of certain brain conditions. However, Gilles de la Tourette's syndrome can often be diagnosed with some assurance as the course of the illness unfolds.

## Treatment

Gilles de la Tourette's syndrome can be treated with medications, starting with small doses and increasing the dosage until the tics are controlled. Often a combination of drugs is used. Group psychotherapy can be helpful in some cases. In extreme cases, leukotomy (surgical interruption of white nerve fibers of the frontal lobe of the brain) is considered.

## Prevention

There are no known preventive measures.

# Hyaline membrane disease

Hyaline membrane disease (HMD) is a respiratory distress

syndrome that occurs in premature infants who do not have fully functioning lungs. It is the leading cause of illness and death in premature infants.

## Cause

The cause of HMD is the inability of the immature lungs to produce enough pulmonary surfactant, which is a chemical in the alveoli (the tiny air sacs in the lungs) that keeps them expanded. Without adequate surfactant, the alveoli tend to collapse when the infant exhales. As a result, the lungs do not expand completely, and the blood passing through them cannot obtain enough oxygen to sustain life.

## Symptoms

The symptoms of HMD are easily observable. The skin is bluish due to lack of oxygenation of the blood, as well as other symptoms of oxygen deprivation—irregular heartbeat; rapid, labored, and shallow breathing; flaring of the nostrils; grunting when breathing out; and edema (swelling of tissues due to fluid accumulation).

## Treatment

Treatment of HMD is aimed at maintaining adequate oxygen levels. Until the lungs can sufficiently oxygenate the blood, oxygen must be provided in such a way as to prevent damage to the infant. An oxygen face mask is often used to provide warmed, moisturized oxygen. In more severe cases, a ventilator is necessary to "breathe" for the infant.

Fluids, glucose (a form of sugar), and electrolytes (certain chemicals needed by the body) are provided intravenously.

Either the condition will clear up as the lungs develop and begin to produce surfactant in about three to five days, or the infant will not survive.

### Prevention

The best preventive measure is to guard against premature birth. Women should be carefully monitored during the last weeks of pregnancy for any signs of premature labor.

If the mother is diabetic, the fetal lungs may not be fully formed until the fortieth week of pregnancy, and HMD is possible until then.

# Hydrocephalus

Hydrocephalus (sometimes inaccurately referred to as "water on the brain") is an abnormal accumulation of cerebrospinal fluid within the cavities (hollow spaces) of the brain.

Normally, cerebrospinal fluid is secreted in the cavities of the brain and absorbed by a membrane that lines the cavities. If the membrane does not absorb the fluid or if the fluid is blocked, it builds up in the cavities. The fluid buildup causes the head to become enlarged and the brain to become compressed. This condition can lead to paralysis, blindness, mental retardation, inability to speak, and convulsions.

### Cause

Hydrocephalus is usually the result of a brain infection or a malformation in the fetus prior to birth. Although the baby's head

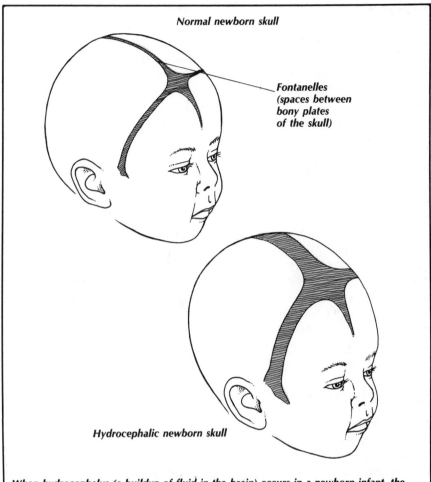

*Normal newborn skull*

**Fontanelles (spaces between bony plates of the skull)**

*Hydrocephalic newborn skull*

*When hydrocephalus (a buildup of fluid in the brain) occurs in a newborn infant, the loosely connected bony plates of the skull spread apart to accommodate the swelling.*

may not appear abnormally large at birth, it expands rapidly from month to month; if untreated, the child usually dies by the end of the second year. If the blockage is only partial, the child may live for a number of years or may even live a normal life span.

Although hydrocephalus is usually a congenital (present at birth) condition, it can occur later as a result of an infection or tumor.

### Symptoms

When hydrocephalus occurs in an infant, the loosely con-

nected bony skull plates pull apart to accommodate the swelling. As a result, the head becomes greatly enlarged. In addition to having an oversized head, the child with hydrocephalus may have an abnormally enlarged forehead and swollen or enlarged blood vessels in the scalp.

### Diagnosis

Diagnosis is accomplished through the use of x-rays and CT scans (special x-ray studies). If infection is suspected, samples of the blood and cerebrospinal fluid will be examined.

## Treatment

Surgery can make it possible, in some cases, to bypass the blockage or obstruction, causing the fluid buildup to escape through other exits. Often, the insertion of a small tube connecting a brain cavity with the abdomen or a major blood vessel will allow the fluid to drain. As the child grows, the tube may become blocked, again allowing pressure to build in the brain. If this happens, the tube must be replaced or the blockage removed. When surgery is successful, the probability of mental retardation is greatly reduced, and the prospects of normal physical and intellectual development are increased.

# Hyperkinesis

Hyperkinesis is a nervous disorder that usually affects children. The condition is characterized by very high levels of physical activity, consistently impulsive and immature behavior, and an extremely short attention span. Because of these behavioral patterns, the condition is also known as minimal brain dysfunction, attention deficit disorder, and, most commonly, hyperactivity.

Although hyperkinesis does no physical damage to the body, it can trigger long-lasting social, emotional, and educational problems. Because hyperkinetic children cannot sit still and concentrate for long periods, they may have trouble with schoolwork. They often appear to be immature, uncoordinated, and boisterous and may have trouble getting along with classmates, teachers, and parents; consequently, they often suffer from a poor self-image.

## Causes

The cause of hyperkinesis is not known, but several theories have been proposed in recent years. None of these theories has been proved or disproved.

The condition may be the result of a nervous system malfunction or a deficiency of neurotransmitters (chemicals in the brain that transmit impulses between the nerves). According to one theory, based on the supposition that the brain has two systems for responding to situations—one that prompts immediate action and one that encourages hesitation and consideration—the neurotransmitters that control the hesitation response are malfunctioning in the hyperkinetic child. In some cases, damage to a fetus during pregnancy or a complication of childbirth may have caused a neurologic defect.

Because the condition is four to five times more common in boys than in girls, some researchers believe that the tendency toward hyperkinesis may be inherited as a sex-linked hereditary trait. Support for a genetic basis for hyperkinesis comes from the finding that parents who were hyperkinetic as children tend to have hyperkinetic children.

It has also been suggested that the additives, preservatives, and colorings found in processed foods may have a toxic or allergic effect on some children.

## Symptoms

A variety of symptoms point to hyperkinesis. The hyperkinetic child is overly active, fidgety, restless, overly talkative or boisterous, impulsive, and seemingly uncoordinated. In school, this child has a very short attention span and seems to forget facts quickly, disrupts the classroom, does schoolwork hastily and incorrectly, skips or adds words when reading, laughs too loud and hard, and prefers to play with younger children.

## Diagnosis

There are no specific tests to diagnose hyperkinesis. The symptoms seem to be present in all children to some degree, and since hyperkinesis is rather vaguely defined, the symptoms displayed by an individual child should be carefully observed. The quantity, intensity, and duration of these symptoms may single out hyperkinetic children from others who are merely bored with school or who are having other behavior problems.

## Treatment

Although controversial, drug therapy has proved successful in treating hyperkinesis. Several stimulant drugs appear to have a calming effect on hyperkinetic children because they seem to affect the hesitation response. However, these drugs have been shown to have unpleasant side effects, such as stomach cramps, susceptibility to colds, nervous mannerisms, and stunted growth. Therefore, many children on this therapy are required by their doctors to take "drug holidays" to give their bodies a break from the side effects of the medication.

Special diets that are designed in an attempt to eliminate all food additives have been prescribed, in keeping with the theory that additives cause hyperkinesis. The findings from studies on this treatment have been either inconclusive or contradictory. However, many parents report dramatic changes in behavior after this treatment, although part of the change may be due to the extra attention paid to the child whose meals have to be specially prepared.

Parents can help to influence the child's actions by praising or rewarding good behavior and ignoring bad behavior.

# Immunization

Immunization is the means of producing immunity, or resistance by the body, to a specific disease. (For information about how immunizations work, see pages 83–84.) Immunization can provide protection against measles, mumps, rubella (German measles), polio, pertussis (whooping cough), diphtheria, and tetanus, all of which can cripple or kill.

Every child should receive injections of the combined diphtheria-tetanus-pertussis (DTP) vaccine at 2, 4, 6, and 18 months of age. The child should also receive a dose of the oral polio vaccine (OPV) at 2, 4, and 18 months of age. At 15 months, a child should receive the combined measles, mumps, and rubella (MMR) vaccine and a test for tuberculosis (TB). Some doctors are also recommending that a relatively new vaccine against *Hemophilus influenzae* type B (HiB) infection be given to children at about two years of age, especially if they are in day care, where they may have a greater risk of exposure to infection. Booster shots of DTP vaccine and OPV should be given around the time of school entry (when the child is four to six years old). A diphtheria-tetanus

toxoids (DT) booster shot should be given between 14 and 16 years of age.

## Immunization and testing schedule

| | |
|---|---|
| 2 months | DTP and OPV |
| 4 months | DTP and OPV |
| 6 months | DTP |
| 15 months | MMR and TB test |
| 18 months | DTP and OPV |
| 2 years | HiB |
| 4–6 years | DTP and OPV |
| 14–16 years | DT booster |

If the family does not have a family physician, immunizations can usually be obtained through the local public health department.

# Nephrotic syndrome

Nephrotic syndrome is a kidney disorder in which the glomeruli (tiny clumps of blood vessels, which filter the blood to produce urine) do not work properly. The defective glomeruli allow proteins, most notably albumin, to escape from the bloodstream and seep into the urine, while letting fluid that should be eliminated as waste accumulate within the tissues.

Nephrotic syndrome most often affects children, particularly those between the ages of one and six years. Boys are more likely than girls to be affected.

## Causes

Nephrotic syndrome is caused by other diseases that affect the kidneys. The syndrome in turn

creates vulnerability to other infections, including peritonitis (inflammation of the lining of the abdominal cavity).

## Symptoms

As a result of fluid accumulation, the body gradually swells (a condition called edema), becoming especially bloated around the face, abdomen, and ankles. The child may urinate very little (approximately one-fifth the normal amount).

To prevent complications, a doctor should be consulted as soon as either less frequent urination or unusual swelling in the face, abdomen, or ankles is noted.

## Diagnosis

If initial blood and urine tests point to nephrotic syndrome, the doctor will order more tests and possibly a kidney biopsy (removal of a tissue sample for microscopic examination).

## Treatment

The condition can be controlled with proper medical care, usually in a hospital, where medication (diuretics to eliminate excess fluid and steroids to control inflammation) and diet can be carefully supervised. Symptoms are likely to clear up after a few weeks, and the patient can finish recuperating at home, sometimes with no aftereffects.

# Osteomyelitis

Osteomyelitis is inflammation of the bone and bone marrow, usu-

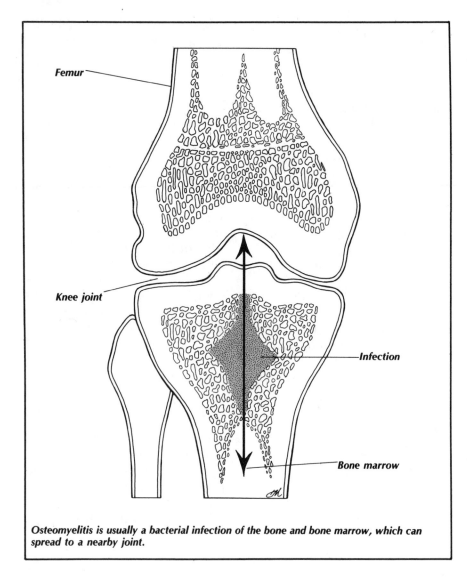

Femur

Knee joint

Infection

Bone marrow

*Osteomyelitis is usually a bacterial infection of the bone and bone marrow, which can spread to a nearby joint.*

joint or at the affected area, fever in the range of 102°F to 104°F, redness, and swelling.

### Diagnosis

Although a physician can often diagnose osteomyelitis from the symptoms, x-rays and blood tests confirm its presence.

### Treatment

The child with osteomyelitis may be hospitalized and given antibiotics in liquid, tablet, or intravenous form. It may be necessary to drain any pus and clean the area in a minor surgical procedure and then immobilize the limb in a splint. The child is released from the hospital once the healing begins, but may have to take antibiotics for six more weeks.

### Complications

Possible complications include septicemia (blood poisoning); destruction of the bone; spread of the infection to a nearby joint, possibly resulting in a permanent deformity; transference of the infection to the surface of the skin, where it erupts as an abscess; damage to the cartilage adjacent to the bone, which may retard bone growth; and suppurative (infectious) arthritis.

Chronic (long-term) osteomyelitis may be a delayed complication of acute (sudden-onset) osteomyelitis, especially if it results from a fracture or the presence of a foreign body in the wound, such as a bullet or a piece of metallic debris. The major sign of chronic osteomyelitis is a flare-up or reopening of

ally due to a bacterial infection. It is considered a childhood disease, occurring most often in boys between the ages of 5 and 14 years, but it also occurs in adults. Since the introduction of antibiotics, osteomyelitis has become rare in the United States, but it is still common in countries lacking good medical care and proper nutrition.

### Causes

Along with essential oxygen and nutrients, blood may also carry bacteria and other organisms, which tend to settle in the capillaries (tiny blood vessels) of the long bones of the arms and legs. Infectious agents can also reach the bones directly from adjacent infected tissue or through an open wound or fracture. Osteomyelitis usually affects only one area of the bone or bone marrow, but it can attack more than one bone at a time.

### Symptoms

Symptoms include pain and excruciating tenderness near a

an abscessed wound, with periodic pain and discharge of pus. X-rays show irregular bone and pieces of dead bone. Treatment for chronic osteomyelitis may require several operations to remove all the dead bone and other tissue, drain the abscess, and repair the bone structure when possible. Large doses of antibiotics may be necessary.

### Prevention

To prevent osteomyelitis, clean and disinfect all wounds thoroughly and, especially in children, apply a bandage to keep the area clean until it has healed. Chronic osteomyelitis can be prevented by immediate antibiotic treatment of acute osteomyelitis.

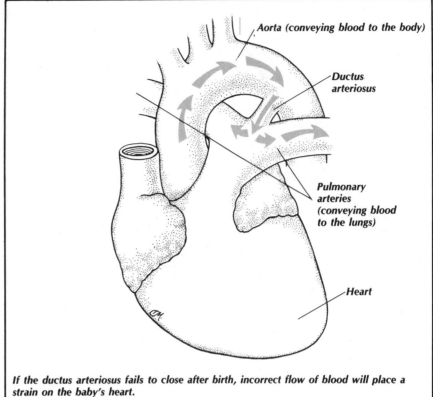

If the ductus arteriosus fails to close after birth, incorrect flow of blood will place a strain on the baby's heart.

# Patent ductus arteriosus

Patent ductus arteriosus is a congenital (present at birth) heart disorder in which the ductus arteriosus, an extra blood vessel present in the fetus that allows the blood to pass from the pulmonary artery (which conveys blood from the heart to the lungs) to the aorta (the main blood vessel that conveys blood from the heart to the rest of the body) fails to close after birth. This condition is most common in premature babies.

During the nine months of growth and development in the uterus, the fetus is immersed in amniotic fluid, and the lungs are not used. The blood bypasses the lungs through the ductus arteriosus, and the fetus receives oxygen from the placenta.

If the ductus arteriosus remains open after birth, some blood is rerouted from the aorta back through the lungs. As a result, less oxygen-rich blood can be supplied to the tissues throughout the body and the work of the left side of the heart (which pumps blood from the heart to the rest of the body) is increased.

### Cause

In most babies, the duct begins to close before birth and is completely closed by the age of three months. The reasons for this normal closure (and for failure to close) are poorly understood.

### Symptoms

Although obvious symptoms are rare, the affected infant may display shortness of breath or develop congestive heart failure.

### Treatment

Patent ductus arteriosus can be treated with medication if diagnosed very early. Various prenatal (before birth) tests have become available in recent years for diagnosis if the condition is suspected. After birth, the condition can be corrected by tying off the duct in a relatively simple surgical procedure.

# Phimosis

Phimosis is a constriction of the foreskin (the skin fold over the head of the penis), which prevents the foreskin from being drawn back over the glans (the head of the penis).

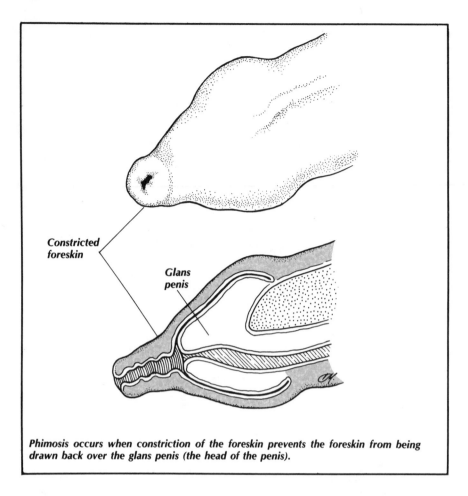

*Phimosis occurs when constriction of the foreskin prevents the foreskin from being drawn back over the glans penis (the head of the penis).*

# Pinworms

Pinworms (any of a variety of worms called oxyurids) are parasites that may infect the gastrointestinal tract and occasionally other sites, such as the female reproductive tract. These worms are tiny (about one-eighth to one-half inch in length).

## Cause

The usual cause of the infection is eating food contaminated with fertilized oxyurid eggs. Contamination results from contact with infected feces. Eggs can also survive on clothes and bedding for two or three weeks.

After being ingested (taken into the body), the eggs hatch and release their larvae (an immature form of the worm) into the upper portion of the small intestine. The larvae mature as they pass through the first part of the large intestine. After mating, the adult male worms die and the females migrate down the large intestine and lay their eggs around the anus. The eggs are transferred by the child's hands from the anus to the mouth, and the cycle continues. Pinworms can be transmitted to other children and adults in the same manner. Also, the hatched larvae can migrate back through the anus and into the bowel.

## Symptoms

Many children who have pinworms do not have obvious symptoms. Symptoms that may occur are itching and inflammation around the anus. Worms can also cause irritation, inflammation, and obstruction in the appendix. In girls and women, pinworms can work their way

## Causes

Phimosis is either congenital (present at birth) or acquired. The acquired form is usually due to an infection involving the penis that leaves adhesions (growths of tissue that adhere both to the inner aspect of the foreskin and to the glans itself). Phimosis also allows debris (dirt, dead cells, and normal fluid secretions) to accumulate between the foreskin and the glans, providing a breeding ground for bacteria.

## Symptoms

If infection becomes established, ulcers (open sores) may appear on the glans, and swelling of the lymph nodes in the groin may occur.

## Diagnosis

The condition will be apparent on physical examination of the child. If infection is present, cultures may be performed.

## Treatment

The definitive treatment for this condition is circumcision (the surgical removal of the foreskin). If, for some reason, circumcision must be delayed, there must be careful attention to keeping the area clean and dry and free from infection until the procedure can be performed.

into the vagina and urethra (the passageway from the bladder to the outside) and cause inflammation or infection in the reproductive system and the bladder.

### Diagnosis

Aside from noting the symptom of itching, diagnosis is made by identifying the eggs or worms through a microscope.

### Treatment

Treatment of pinworms is not difficult. Usually one dose of the drug pyrantel pamoate is sufficient. Other medications are also available. In addition, in group infections, all members should be treated simultaneously, and their bedclothes, towels, and underwear should be laundered at the same time. Also, the eggs around the anus should be removed by cleaning the anal area thoroughly at the time of treatment. Reinfection is common, and when symptoms develop, another course of treatment is necessary.

### Prevention

It is important to teach children clean eating habits, to encourage them to wash their hands frequently, and to be alert to other children who may be infected (as evidenced by scratching around the anus).

# Reye's syndrome

Reye's syndrome is a relatively rare condition in which encephalitis (inflammation of the brain) is associated with liver damage due to the collection of fatty deposits in that organ. It strikes children and adolescents (most commonly, children between the ages of 5 and 11 years), often while they are recovering from a viral infection, such as influenza or chicken pox. For some unknown reason, it occurs most often between December and March.

Reye's syndrome is a serious disease that requires *immediate* treatment. Brain damage, coma, or death can result if it is not diagnosed and treated quickly. It is fatal in about 25 percent of cases.

### Cause

The exact cause of Reye's syndrome is not known, but since it almost always follows a viral infection, scientists suspect that the virus combines with an unknown substance in the body to produce a toxin (poison).

### Symptoms

The symptoms of Reye's syndrome are sudden vomiting, abnormal sleepiness or hyperactivity, and confusion. Convulsions and coma may occur as the disease progresses.

### Diagnosis

Early diagnosis is crucial. Reye's syndrome is diagnosed by careful observation of the symptoms, testing of a sample of cerebrospinal fluid (the clear fluid of the central nervous system, which is produced in the brain), blood tests to determine the

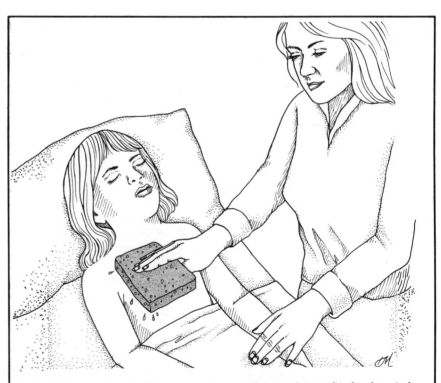

*Because of the association between aspirin use during and immediately after viral infections (particularly chicken pox and influenza) and Reye's syndrome, it is strongly recommended that an aspirin substitute, such as acetaminophen, be used instead to treat discomfort or fever. Sponge baths may also be helpful in reducing fever.*

presence of liver damage, and tests of the blood sugar level, which is often low in young children with this disease.

**Treatment**

There is no known cure for Reye's syndrome. Treatment consists in helping the child to weather the first few days of the illness, maintaining normal blood sugar levels, and reducing pressure on the swollen brain. Usually, if the child survives for three or four days, the symptoms will subside and recovery will follow.

If the blood sugar level is low, a normal concentration is restored with the intravenous administration of glucose (a form of sugar). Increased pressure on the brain from the swelling is also reduced with medication.

**Prevention**

An association has been established between aspirin use during and immediately after viral infections (particularly chicken pox and influenza) and Reye's syndrome. It is therefore strongly recommended that aspirin not be given to a child or adolescent with such an infection. A doctor can suggest an aspirin substitute, such as acetaminophen, if needed for discomfort or fever. Sponge baths may also be helpful in reducing fever.

# Scoliosis

Scoliosis is curvature of the spine. There is usually a main curve in one direction and an upper curve or lower curve, or both, to compensate for it in the opposite direction.

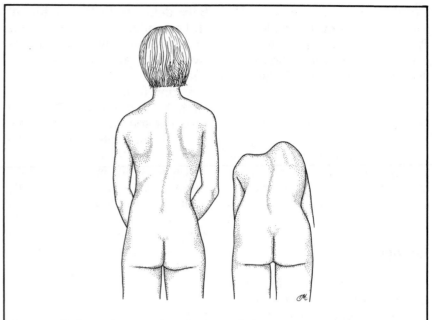

*Severe scoliosis can be seen when viewing a child from the back, and even mild scoliosis can be noticed when the child bends at the waist. Bending forward rotates the chest, making one side of the back more prominent.*

Before the age of three years, boys are more likely to be affected, developing an upper curve to the left and a lower curve to the right. Between the ages of four and ten years, boys and girls are affected in equal numbers, and the direction of curvature varies. Most prevalent is the adolescent form, usually affecting girls between the age of ten and the time their skeletons mature. Most often, the upper spinal area (behind the chest) curves to the right, with compensating curves to the left in the lower neck area and in the small of the back.

Severe, untreated scoliosis can cause diminished lung capacity, back pain, spinal arthritis, and disease of the cartilage disks between the vertebrae.

**Causes**

Scoliosis can result from unequal leg lengths, or it may be due to defective development of the vertebrae (the bones of the spine) while the fetus was growing in the uterus. Paralysis of the trunk muscles on one side of the body caused by polio, cerebral palsy, or muscular dystrophy; tilting of the pelvis due to hip disease; or deformities of the spine caused by rickets or rheumatism can also lead to scoliosis. Idiopathic scoliosis, the most common kind, has no known cause.

**Symptoms**

Parents should be alert for the signs of scoliosis. At first the child may appear to have an uneven hemline, unequal pant legs, or one hip higher than the other. To make a preliminary assessment, ask your child to stand up straight with his shirt off while you observe from the rear. Notice if one shoulder is higher than the other or if one shoulder blade sticks out. When the child's arms hang loosely at the sides, notice if one arm hangs farther away from the body than does the other. See if one hip appears higher or more prominent than the other. See if the child seems to tilt to one side. Finally, ask your child to bend forward, arms hanging in front and palms together at the level of the knees. A hump on the back at the ribs or near the waist may also be a sign of scoliosis.

### Diagnosis

If you have any suspicions, report them to your child's doctor, who will give the child a similar checkup and, if necessary, take x-rays or refer you to an orthopedic surgeon (bone specialist) to confirm the diagnosis.

### Treatment

Treatment of scoliosis may involve only exercises if the curvature is mild. Sit-ups, exercises to stretch the spine, and breathing exercises may strengthen the muscles of the trunk enough to correct the situation. Frequent x-rays and physical examinations may be needed to determine if the exercises are working.

More severe scoliosis may require the wearing of a special leather brace or a plastic pelvic girdle with one vertical brace in front and two in back, connected to a ring around the neck. In many cases, this must be worn 24 hours a day, except when the patient is bathing or exercising, until the child's skeleton has matured. It is adjustable for growth.

The use of specially designed electrical stimulation devices has met with some success.

The most severe scoliosis requires spinal-fusion surgery, in which certain vertebrae are fused together, with stabilization provided by metal rods, cable, or staples. Frequent checkups are needed after surgery to make sure that the correction is being maintained.

# Spina bifida

Spina bifida is a congenital (present at birth) defect of development, marked by defective closure of some of the vertebrae (the bones of the spine) that normally encase the spinal cord. If the meninges (the membranes that cover the brain and spinal cord) protrude as a sac through the gap in the spine, the condition is known as spina bifida cystica; if not, it is called spina bifida occulta. The severity of the defect can range all the way from a form with few visible symptoms to a completely open spine.

### Cause

The cause of spina bifida is unknown.

### Description

Spina bifida commonly affects the chest and lower back regions of the spine and extends for three to six segments of the spinal column. If there is a sac, it may collapse while the child is still in the uterus, but it fills with cerebrospinal fluid soon after birth. If the sac is not covered with skin, it can rupture, perhaps

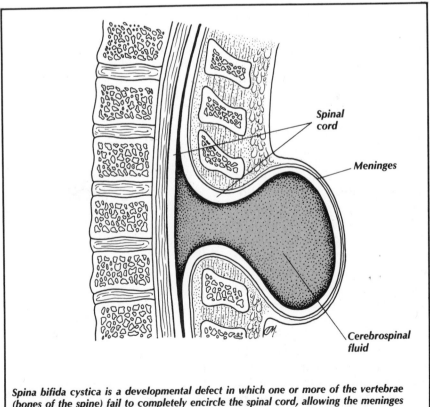

*Spina bifida cystica is a developmental defect in which one or more of the vertebrae (bones of the spine) fail to completely encircle the spinal cord, allowing the meninges (membranes surrounding the spinal cord) to protrude as a sac through the opening.*

leading to meningitis (inflammation of the meninges).

Spina bifida can be accompanied by varying degrees of paralysis, depending on the extent of involvement of the spinal cord and its nerve roots. The paralysis can lead to orthopedic problems, such as clubfoot and dislocated hip, and may also affect the sphincters (closure muscles) of the bladder and rectum, resulting in genitourinary disorders. Abnormal curvature of the spine can hinder surgical closure. Hydrocephalus (accumulation of cerebrospinal fluid within the skull) also accompanies many cases of spina bifida.

### Diagnosis

Diagnostic evaluation of the condition begins with x-rays of the spine, skull, hips, and lower extremities. Urine tests are also necessary. The need for further tests depends on the extent of the defect. Such tests may include a CT scan (a special x-ray study) and an evaluation of the cerebrospinal fluid.

### Treatment

Treatment requires an extensive evaluation of the child's condition by neurosurgeons, urologists, orthopedists, and pediatricians. In some cases, social service workers and psychiatrists will work with the parents. Closure of the defect ensures a better outcome. Long-term survival and quality of life depend on the type and extent of the spinal defect, other defects present, the infant's general health, and treatment resources. In addition to surgical closure of the spine, the infant may need other surgery to correct accompanying problems.

The most common complications are loss of kidney function, clubfoot, dislocation of the hip joints, scoliosis (curvature of the spine), pressure sores, and muscle weakness and spasm.

### Prevention

There is no known preventive for spina bifida. Prenatal (before birth) diagnosis through amniocentesis is growing progressively more accurate.

# Strabismus

Strabismus is commonly referred to as "squint-eye" or "cross-eye." Technically, the term refers to a deviation of one eye from being parallel with the other.

### Causes

In most cases, strabismus is congenital (present at birth), although it can result from later injury to one eye or impaired vision because of disease. The cause of congenital strabismus is unknown, but the effect is generally paralysis or malfunction of the tiny muscles that control the movement of the eyes.

### Symptoms

Symptoms include obviously crossed, wandering, or squinting eyes, although in some cases lack of parallelism of the eyes is so subtle that it can be detected only by special testing.

### Diagnosis

Complete evaluation of the eyes is essential to rule out more serious eye or nervous disorders and to determine how best to correct the strabismus. Such an evaluation is usually performed by an ophthalmologist (a physician who specializes in eye disorders).

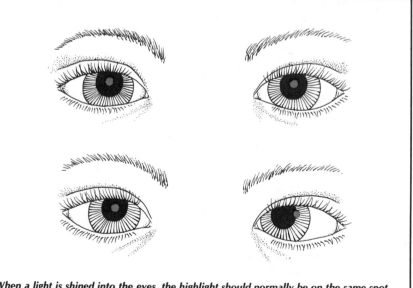

*When a light is shined into the eyes, the highlight should normally be on the same spot in each eye. The eyes shown above are properly aligned, while the eyes of a child with strabismus, shown below, are not parallel.*

## Treatment

If muscle imbalance alone is responsible, the strabismus can usually be treated easily with corrective glasses or contact lenses. Eye exercises are effective in many less severe cases. Surgical restoration of the muscle balance can be done in more extreme cases. Permanent visual loss can result if strabismus is not treated by the time the child is four to six years old.

# Sudden infant death syndrome (SIDS)

Sudden infant death syndrome (also called crib death) is the unexplained and sudden death of a baby—often a baby who was perfectly well when put to bed dies silently in his sleep. In the United States, SIDS is second only to accidents as a cause of death in infants from two weeks to one year of age, causing 8,000 to 10,000 deaths per year. Most deaths from SIDS occur in the third or fourth month of life, with higher death rates for boys, children of teenage mothers, infants from poor families, and babies who were premature. There are more such deaths in the winter than in the summer.

## Cause

It once was thought that SIDS is caused by smothering in the bedding, but this rarely occurs. It is also not attributable to clogging of the airways by vomited food, to bottle feeding, or to any other cause that parents could prevent. Some investigators believe that a combination of conditions is necessary to trigger SIDS, including a narrowed and inflamed airway, temporary airway obstruction, chronic oxygen deficiency, and irregular breathing, leading to a spasm of the trachea (windpipe) and death. Research continues.

## Counseling for parents

Parents who lose a child to SIDS are totally unprepared for the death and usually have overwhelming guilt feelings—that something they did or did not do caused the death of their child. An autopsy will usually prove that the death was not the parents' fault. Doctors and nurses who take the time to discuss the death fully with the parents can be very helpful. So can another parent who has lost a child to SIDS. There are now many local chapters of the National Sudden Infant Death Syndrome Foundation and the International Council for Infant Survival, both of which can be valuable sources of counseling and information.

# Undescended testes

Undescended testes is a condition in which one or both of the testes (male sex glands) do not descend into the scrotum (the sac between the legs that normally contains the testes), but remain in the abdomen, where they developed before birth.

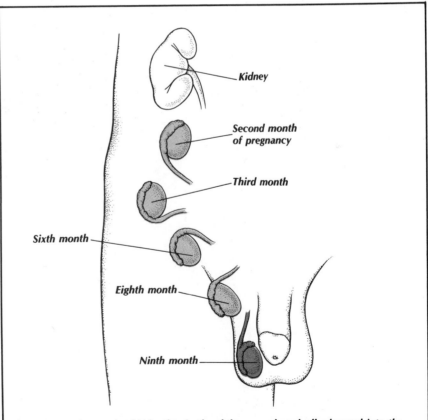

*The testes (male sex glands) develop in the abdomen and gradually descend into the scrotum before birth. Occasionally, this progression does not occur, and the boy is born with undescended testes.*

This condition is also called cryptorchidism or cryptorchism and is not uncommon.

If the testes do not descend, they often degenerate or atrophy (shrink), and thus do not secrete the male sex hormones that they ordinarily supply. This, in turn, can cause the elimination or suppression of the development during puberty of secondary male sex characteristics such as body hair, heavier musculature, deepening voice, and so forth. Damaged sperm, or insufficient production of them, can also result from undescended testes, especially if the situation is still present in adolescence or adulthood. If one testis is damaged but the other has descended and is normal, sexual development will be normal.

## Causes

The causes of this condition are not clearly understood. It is conjectured that a membrane in the abdomen gets in the way of normal testicular positioning. If only one testis is undescended, the problem is most likely mechanical in nature; if both are involved, the underlying cause may well be hormonal.

## Treatment

Treatment for this condition is controversial. In deciding on treatment, three important considerations must be kept in mind: the potential lack of fertility if the testes do not descend, the likelihood that they will descend without intervention, and the risk that the undescended testes will become cancerous. Hormone therapy is sometimes an effective treatment, but in many cases in which it has apparently been successful, some doctors think that the testes would probably have descended by themselves anyway. Surgery to bring the testes into the scrotum is usually successful if done before the age of five years. The physician can sometimes cause the testes to descend by manipulation of the tissues around them.

## Prevention

There is no known means of preventing undescended testes.

# EMOTIONAL AND MENTAL ILLNESS

Emotional and mental problems vary greatly in degree. Today, many mentally healthy people turn to psychotherapy for help in coping with an emotional crisis, such as the loss of a loved one or a divorce. At the other extreme are people who are so disturbed that they cannot take care of their basic needs.

All of us experience emotional ups and downs throughout our lives and are prone to feelings of anxiety, fear, guilt, or depression. It is when these feelings seriously interfere with the ability to work or to deal with home or social life that a problem exists.

### Warning signs

The borderline between "normal" and distorted actions and feelings is not scientifically exact. However, there are general warning signs of emotional or mental difficulties that indicate a need for professional help:

- Severe anxiety that is not attributable to reality
- Unreasonable fears of people, places, or events
- Prolonged depression or the inability to recover from a major crisis or loss
- Difficulty in getting along with other people or in holding a job
- Self-destructive behavior, such as compulsive drinking, gambling, or drug use
- Sexual dysfunction, such as impotence, frigidity, promiscuity, or perversion
- Sleeping difficulties, insomnia, or recurring nightmares
- Feelings of hopelessness or confusion or suicidal thoughts
- Inability to make simple decisions, moodiness, or feeling out of control
- In children, failure at school, disruptive behavior at school and home, senseless destructiveness, delinquency, or frequent physical complaints

Since some medical disorders (for example, having a low blood sugar level or an overactive thyroid gland) can produce physical symptoms that resemble those of an emotional problem (such as shakiness, which may result from anxiety), the first step in seeking treatment is to have a thorough physical examination. In addition to ruling out a physical problem, the doctor can make a referral to a competent therapist or mental health agency.

### Types of professional help

There are several different kinds of professional therapists qualified to treat emotional and mental difficulties:

- Psychiatrists are doctors with a medical degree plus three or more years of training in psychiatry. Psychiatrists are the only therapists qualified to prescribe drugs. Like other medical specialists, they must be licensed by the state in which they practice and certified by their specialty board.
- Clinical or psychiatric social workers are professionals with a master's or doctoral degree in mental health plus two years of internship in a clinical setting. They may be certified by the state in which they practice and are listed in the *National Registry of Health Care Providers in Clinical Social Work*.
- Clinical psychologists are therapists with a doctoral degree in psychology and one year of supervised clinical training. Psychologists are licensed by the state in which

they practice, certified by their specialty board, or listed in the *National Registry of Health Service Providers in Psychology*.

- Psychiatric nurses are nurses with a master's degree in psychiatry or mental health who are accredited by the American Nurses' Association Division on Psychiatric and Mental Health Nursing Practice.
- Psychoanalysts are psychiatrists or clinical psychologists with special psychoanalytic training. (However, a person with little or no training can use the title of psychoanalyst—be careful to check the person's credentials.) At present, psychoanalysts are licensed only in California, but others may be listed in the *National Registry of Psychoanalysts*.
- Pastoral counselors are members of the clergy with training or a degree in psychology or social work. They are certified by the American Association of Pastoral Counselors.

### Finding help

One of the biggest keys to success in therapy is finding a qualified professional with whom the person seeking treatment feels comfortable. Before making an initial appointment, ask the therapist about his or her credentials. During the first appointment, ask for an explanation of the methods or forms of therapy the therapist uses, for an estimate of how long treatment may last and how much it will cost, and for an opinion on the results that can be expected.

The patient seeking treatment should ask himself these questions: Do I feel comfortable talking to this therapist? Do I trust him or her? Do the proposed method of treatment and the expected results sound plausible? It may take more than one appointment or session with the therapist to answer these questions. If you have doubts, it is perfectly permissible to look for another therapist. It is also possible that the therapist will feel unqualified to work successfully with you and will refer you to another professional.

### Types of therapy

There are many kinds of therapy, but the most common are the following:
• Psychoanalysis—an intensive (four or five times a week for several years) program of sessions with a therapist with the aim of understanding and changing long-standing personality problems
• Individual psychotherapy—a series of one-on-one discussions with a therapist about problems, worries, emotional attitudes, and ways of coping with life
• Group therapy—a series of discussions with peers (under the guidance of a professional therapist), in which life experiences are shared and criticism, praise, and support may be offered
• Family therapy—sessions in which family members work with a therapist to arrive at better ways of interacting with one another
• Behavior modification—use of special techniques to break old habits that cause problems and to learn new ways of dealing with people
• Drug therapy—use of medication to modify brain chemistry, preferably reserved for the treatment of severe problems and complemented by some form of "talk" therapy

• Relaxation training—use of special biofeedback techniques to increase awareness and control of body processes so as to relieve physical conditions, such as tension headaches and high blood pressure

There is a lot of misinformation about the subject of emotional and mental illness, which is left over from the days when little was known about the workings of the mind and body. Some people still label those who have sought and received treatment for mental or emotional disorders as crazy, unpredictable, and dangerous. Such labels are not only unfair, but usually inaccurate; the number of persons with problems who pose any threat at all to others is very small.

Fortunately for all of us, emotional and mental illness is gradually becoming better understood and accepted as a condition that can be treated and frequently cured. Even more important, emotional health is being recognized as a goal that should and can be attained.

# Anorexia nervosa

Anorexia nervosa is an eating disorder that most often strikes young women. Anorexics suppress the urge to eat and continue to lose weight to the point of malnutrition and starvation. This disorder can be fatal, because an anorexic can literally starve herself to death.

The reasons for anorexic behavior are still unknown, but theories abound. One theory is that anorexics continue to starve themselves because they mistakenly believe that they are fat and need to diet. The result is not only an unattractively thin appearance but also abnormality

of menstrual periods (which very frequently cease when a certain percentage of body fat has been lost) and, most important, the destruction of healthy muscle and organ tissue, which the body uses as sources of energy when faced with starvation.

### Those at risk

Ninety-five percent of all anorexics are female; most are teenagers from upper- or upper-middle-class homes. It is estimated that about one in 200 young women of this age and social class has anorexia nervosa.

Anorexia seems to be a psychiatric disorder, since it often develops in young women with deep-seated problems, although the classic anorexic may not seem to be a "troubled" teenager. The young girl who has always been "perfect" and obedient, and who has tried to fulfill all the wishes of her parents, teachers, and friends may become anorexic because of an unconscious need to have total control over at least one area of her life.

Impending adulthood and all that it entails may scare the anorexic into dieting away those characteristics that are symbolic of her developing maturity—larger breasts, fuller hips and thighs, and the monthly cycle of menstrual periods.

Our culture's obsession with thinness as the ideal in beauty can also trigger in an adolescent girl a desire to diet down to her "perfect" weight; often a casual remark that a girl is slightly overweight can lead to a case of anorexia in a susceptible person.

In addition, people with jobs or hobbies that require strict weight control, such as athletes, ballerinas, and fashion models,

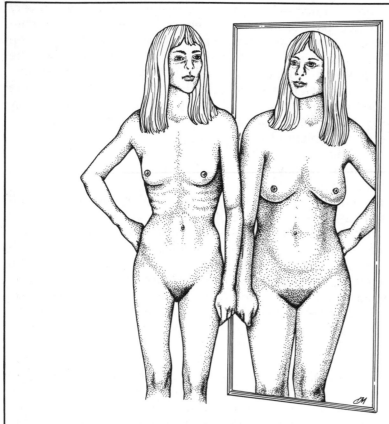

*A person with anorexia nervosa often has a distorted body image that makes her perceive herself as fat even when viewing her extremely thin body in a mirror.*

may find that simply watching their weight has become an obsession with dieting. In fact, the few males who develop this disorder often do so in an attempt to qualify for an athletic team.

### Symptoms

The most obvious symptom of anorexia nervosa is drastic weight loss to the point of extreme underweight, which can be accompanied by overly vigorous exercise that burns off the few calories that are consumed. Menstrual periods often stop completely, and a growth of fine, downy hair appears all over the body.

Anorexics cannot be convinced to eat by threats or reasoning. Many have a distorted body image that tells them they are fat even as they view their extremely thin bodies in a mirror. Despite the refusal to eat more than tiny amounts of particular foods, the anorexic may be obsessed with the idea of food and may prepare elaborate meals for others. She may also suffer from another eating disorder, bulimia, which is characterized by binge-eating, followed by self-induced vomiting and excessive use of laxatives.

### Diagnosis

Diagnostic evaluation of anorexia nervosa begins by ruling out the possibility that the extreme weight loss has been caused by a serious physical illness, such as cancer, an infectious disease, a disorder of the digestive organs, or inadequate absorption of vitamins and minerals. Anorexia can usually be diagnosed when the patient displays the classic symptoms before the age of 25 and has lost 25 percent of her body weight.

### Treatment

Anorexia is sometimes treated with hospitalization and forced feeding, but anorexics can usually be treated on an outpatient basis by a doctor, psychiatrist, or specialist in eating disorders. The anorexic's distorted body image as well as her eating habits must be changed in order for her to conquer this disorder. Most important, the underlying psychological problems must be resolved. Often, this means psychological therapy for both the anorexic and her family.

# Bulimia

Bulimia is abnormal and excessive eating, usually triggered by emotional factors. Victims of the disorder overeat far beyond the needs of their bodies. In extreme cases, they resemble alcoholics, employing food instead of drink as an escape from problems. They may even go on food binges and eat themselves into a stupor. They often feel guilty after overeating and force themselves to vomit; overuse of laxatives to purge the food from their bodies is also common.

### Causes

To a bulimic person, food provides a way to relieve stress.

Some experts think that excessive eating is an unconscious attempt to recapture the feelings of security experienced in childhood when food was received from the mother. Psychiatrists have speculated that overeating may also represent a hunger for affection that was denied in early childhood, when the child's attention was focused on the mouth and eating. It may be a substitute for affection, attention, or sexual contact that the person is not receiving. It may be an outlet for hostile feelings, since food is being destroyed by the acts of biting and chewing. Another possibility is that the person may unconsciously seek to become more important and safer by becoming physically larger through weight gain. Bulimia is sometimes found among mental patients, especially those who have regressed to infantile behavior.

Excessive eating may also result from hyperthyroidism (overactivity of the thyroid gland), a disorder in which great quantities of calories may be eaten without weight gain. In a very small percentage of cases, bulimia may be caused by damage to the appetite control center of the brain.

## Treatment

Attempts to cure bulimia have not been very successful and have frequently caused the patient to become even more distressed. However, it is generally agreed that a logical first step is to help the patient discover the emotional causes of the disorder. This may require individual or family counseling by a psychiatrist or clinical psychologist, who also tries to help the patient gain confidence and become

more sociable and self-reliant. New satisfactions are sought to replace those formerly found in overeating. Nutritional counseling by a registered dietitian and a sensible exercise program may be recommended.

# Delirium

Delirium is a confused mental state marked by disorganized or incoherent speech and hallucinations (imagined perceptions). Often, the person is unaware of time or place; is fearful, excited, and restless; and suffers from delusions. The heartbeat is rapid, the pupils of the eyes are dilated (enlarged), and sweating is common.

## Causes

Delirium can occur because of fever, disease, injury, poisoning, or mental disease. It may result from the sudden withdrawal of alcohol or another drug on which the individual has become dependent; from liver, kidney, or heart failure; or from deficiencies of certain B vitamins or thyroid hormone. It can also be caused by bruising of brain tissue or by pressure on brain tissue, which may be caused by inflammation, hemorrhage, a tumor, or an abscess.

## Symptoms

Delirium often develops rapidly and fluctuates in severity. The patient usually cannot remember what happened during the episode of delirium and does not recall past events well. Depending on its cause, delirium may last from hours to weeks.

## Treatment

Treating the underlying disease or condition is the first step in treating delirium. In the meantime, the patient should be cared for patiently and sympathetically in a quiet, relaxed environment. Every effort should be made to answer questions, remove fears, and keep the patient in touch with reality.

Partial or complete recovery depends on the nature, severity, and treatability of the underlying cause.

# Depression

Depression, the most common form of emotional disorder, is characterized by prolonged sadness, combined with other negative mood symptoms, such as indecisiveness, inability to concentrate, anxiety, apathy, loneliness, lowered self-esteem, self-blame, and loss of interest in others, in work, and in recreation.

## Temporary depression

Deep sadness or depression is a normal reaction of an emotionally healthy person to discouraging life events such as loss, separation, death of a family member, and disappointment. It is probably a protective reaction, enabling a person to withdraw from everyday concerns long enough to sort out his feelings and prepare for a new approach to life.

Temporary depression can also occur because of normal chemical changes in the body. Two examples are premenstrual depression and postpartum (after childbirth) depression—both of which are thought to be linked to female hormonal activity. In addition, alcohol and certain drugs, including oral contraceptives, reserpine (used to lower blood pressure), and some sedatives, may cause depression as a side effect in some people. Certain infections (including influenza, viral hepatitis, infectious mononucleosis, and tuberculosis) can depress a person's mood, as can deficiency of vitamin $B_{12}$, overproduction or underproduction of hormones by the outer layer of the adrenal gland, and various diseases of the nervous system.

Temporary depression can be eased by the support of family and friends or simply by the passage of time and by steps the person takes to change his life situation. Medication is not usually necessary, nor is any other treatment. However, a visit to a physician can provide valuable reassurance that the depression is not abnormal.

## Severe depression

Unlike temporary depression, which is sometimes called reactive depression because it is a reaction to a specific circumstance, severe depression does not have an obvious cause. Even if there is an apparent cause, the reaction is out of proportion, and it may continue for weeks or months.

The causes of severe depression are unclear. Loss of a parent at an early age or growing up in a cold, critical, unstable, or unfriendly family setting may make a person susceptible to depression. There is also an inherited tendency to suffer certain forms of depression.

## Symptoms

The symptoms of severe depression include crying spells, slowing of speech and thought processes, agitation, feelings of hopelessness and helplessness, withdrawal from usual activities, recurring thoughts of death and suicide, and irritability. (Some of these symptoms also occur in temporary depression, to a lesser degree.) Early awakening, insomnia, fatigue, loss of appetite, weight loss or gain, loss of sexual desire, and imagined pains are also common. Depressed patients with certain mental diseases may hear voices accusing them of unpardonable crimes, see visions of coffins or dead relatives, believe that others are watching or persecuting them, or suffer delusions that they are worthless, sinful, or ill with some incurable disease.

Sometimes periods of deep depression alternate with periods of elation, high hopes, grandiose ideas, and overactivity. This is known as manic-depressive disorder. When in the manic phase, the person is overwhelmingly confident and inexhaustible, racing from thought to thought. Eventually, however, the mood changes to bleakest despair.

## Diagnosis

Diagnosis of severe depression can be complicated. Some depression is masked—the person is "smiling on the outside, crying on the inside" and may not even be aware of his depressed mental state. Instead, the depression is expressed in symptoms, such as headaches and backaches, that have no physical cause. In addition, the person may seem to have lost all emotion, including the ability to take pleasure in anything.

The physician needs to rule out physical causes of depression, such as nutritional deficiencies and the side effects of certain medications. Drug abuse and alcoholism may be involved (however, they may be the result, rather than the cause, of the depression). Schizophrenia and other mental disorders must be considered.

## Treatment

With appropriate treatment, the symptoms of severe depression can often be reduced or eliminated. Hospitalization is not usually necessary, unless the patient is suicidal, in a stupor, agitated and out of touch with reality, or physically deteriorated as a result of the depression. Hospital treatment for the first three types of cases may involve treatment with antidepressant drugs or electroconvulsive therapy (for more information on electroconvulsive therapy, see page 369).

Most severe depression, however, can be managed with a combination of drugs and psychotherapy (counseling by a psychiatrist or psychologist, with office visits once or twice a week at the beginning of treatment and less often as improvement occurs). It is extremely important to find a professional who is not only knowledgeable but also reassuring and encouraging, and who is trusted by the patient. An extended course of psychotherapy is usually not called for unless there is a serious personality disorder. If depression is a result of a serious physical illness, individual reassurance and support groups may provide the most help.

Lithium carbonate is used to treat manic-depressive illness both in its extreme form and in its moderate form, known as cyclothymia. In the latter condition, the person alternates between brief periods (usually days) of gloom and elation.

Suicide is a major risk in depression and should be guarded against, especially when the person seems to be recovering from the depression but is still feeling "low," when anniversaries of landmarks in the person's life occur, and in the days preceding menstruation.

# Electroconvulsive therapy

Electroconvulsive therapy (ECT) is a procedure in which an electric current is passed through the brain to create a convulsion of the central nervous system, like an epileptic seizure, after which the patient is often in a clearer state of mind. Also referred to as electroshock therapy and shock treatment, ECT is used chiefly in cases of severe depression and manic-depressive illness. Occasionally, it is employed to arouse a schizophrenic patient from catatonia (an unresponsive state).

Prior to treatment, the patient is examined and given appropriate tests, which may include an electroencephalogram (brain-wave recording) to detect brain injury that might be related to the patient's condition. Such an injury would rule out the use of ECT.

Usually, ECT is given early in the morning, because the patient must not have had anything to eat or drink for eight hours before treatment. The patient is put to sleep with an anesthetic given intravenously. Electrodes are placed on one or both sides of the head, and electric current is administered. The seizure that results lasts from 5 to 20 seconds. Recovery is rapid; after

half an hour or an hour of drowsiness, most patients are alert and willing to talk. Some temporary memory loss is common, and headaches sometimes occur. However, the use of general anesthesia prevents the anxiety and spinal injuries that used to occur occasionally during ECT treatments. The incidence of serious complications of ECT has been reported to be less than one case in a thousand.

A usual course of ECT treatments is two or three times a week for three to four weeks. A faster method, in which the patient's heart rate is monitored with an electrocardiograph, employs repeated surges of electric current in one to three sessions.

# Hyperventilation

Hyperventilation is abnormally rapid and deep breathing, as a result of which large quantities of air are drawn into the lungs and abnormally large amounts of carbon dioxide are expelled.

## Causes

Although hyperventilation can result from a physical disorder that interferes with the exchange of oxygen and carbon dioxide in the lungs, most often hyperventilation is a physical response to stress, anxiety, and emotional upset. It begins slowly and builds up to the point at which symptoms appear and the person panics. The breathing then becomes even more rapid and difficult.

## Symptoms

The diminished level of carbon dioxide in the blood can

lead to buzzing in the ears; a tingling feeling in the fingers, toes, and lips; light-headedness; and fainting. It may also cause tightness in the chest and a feeling of suffocation. Episodes of hyperventilation may last longer than half an hour, and they may recur several times in a 24-hour period.

Symptoms of hyperventilation may be strikingly similar to those of heart disease and other serious illnesses. The individual experiencing these symptoms should, therefore, consult a doctor to rule out the existence of any of these conditions.

## Treatment

The symptoms of hyperventilation can often be relieved by having the person breathe into a paper bag. In this way, the needed carbon dioxide that has been exhaled into the bag can be inhaled again; as a result, the level of carbon dioxide in the blood is restored to normal, and the breathing rate is slowed.

# Hypochondria

Hypochondria is persistent, exaggerated worry—usually based on self-diagnosis—about one's health, especially in the absence of any real illness. The condition reflects an often morbid concern over any unusual physical or mental sensation or feeling. For example, to the hypochondriac, a headache indicates a brain tumor; a cough has to mean tuberculosis; and a mole is sure to be cancerous. Despite normal test results and reassurances to the contrary, the person is convinced that he either has a serious illness or will have one very soon.

## Symptoms

Frequently, the hypochondriac complains of pain or discomfort in the stomach, chest, head, or neck. Symptoms common among hypochondriacs include nausea, loss of appetite, vomiting, and belching. These symptoms become worse after the person has received expressions of sympathy and concern from family members or friends. The hypochondriac often makes repeated visits to the doctor or consults several doctors at the same time, without their knowledge, in order to obtain prescriptions for a variety of drugs.

## Treatment

Hypochondria is very difficult to treat. It has been estimated that only a small percentage of persons afflicted with this disorder recover completely. Psychotherapy is sometimes useful in such situations; in many cases, however, a more helpful approach is to encourage the individual to divert the energy spent on worrying about his health to more productive interests and activities.

# Mania

Mania is a term that refers to an abnormal elevation of mood, characterized by wild excitement, overactivity, and lack of concentration. It is also characterized by excessive irritability, hostility, and sometimes violence.

Mania is a component of the manic-depressive disorder, in which periods of mood elevation alternate with periods of depression, with periods of normalcy in between.

## Symptoms

Persons in a manic state are likely to go on spending sprees; start, but not finish, new projects; become sexually promiscuous; exhibit restlessness and distractibility; and chatter rapidly and often incoherently. In addition, their judgment is often impaired. Because persons in the manic state think they are functioning at their very best, they tend to overextend themselves, becoming involved in many activities without considering the consequences.

## Diagnosis

Mania must always be diagnosed by a doctor because apparently manic behavior may actually have a physical basis. Certain disease states can cause similar symptoms. Mood elevation can also be a side effect of some medications. Both possibilities must be ruled out (and treated, if necessary) before assuming that a purely psychiatric disorder is present.

## Treatment

Mania and manic-depressive disorder are usually treated with medication and psychotherapy. The medication most commonly used is lithium carbonate. The chief value of lithium is in preventing manic episodes. However, it may take several weeks for the effects of the drug to become apparent. Tests to monitor the level of lithium in the blood are essential, since excessive lithium can cause serious side effects. It is not known exactly how lithium works to combat mania, although it has been shown that lithium affects chem-

ical transmitters in the central nervous system.

# Paranoia

Paranoia is a personality disorder characterized by delusions of grandeur and suspicions of persecution.

## Causes

An internal conflict between the need for recognition and the compulsion to guard certain aspects of emotional life may be the root of paranoia. Unconscious sexual conflicts often play a role.

## Symptoms

Paranoid persons display unreasonable distrust and constant unfounded suspicion that others are out to do them harm; interpret innocent comments as personal attacks; develop grandiose or exaggerated estimations of their own worth, yet feel that others do not recognize their value; believe they are the center of attention because everyone else openly criticizes them; and strenuously defend their fears with reason and logic.

Paranoia differs from paranoid schizophrenia, a much more serious problem in which the individual not only has delusions of grandeur and a persecution complex, but also demonstrates deranged thought processes, hallucinations, and other signs of disturbed personality.

## Diagnosis

Almost everyone exhibits short-lived symptoms that suggest paranoia at some time, usually from excessive worry over an embarrassment or from disappointment. It is only when paranoid behavior persists or worsens and impairs the person's ability to function that concern is warranted. Like the symptoms of many other mental disorders, paranoid symptoms can have an underlying physical cause, such as a brain disease or a drug side effect. Diagnosis should always be made by a physician, who will first rule out (and treat) purely physical causes and then recommend appropriate therapy.

## Treatment

Paranoid persons can often be helped with psychotherapy and medication.

# Phobia

A phobia is a psychological disorder characterized by persistent, abnormal, excessive, or unfounded dread of something that is often not inherently dangerous or considered threatening by most people. A phobic reaction resembles acute or chronic anxiety, but rather than being a generalized response, it is linked to specific environmental stimuli, such as being alone or in an open space, seeing a spider, or hearing thunder.

Phobias affect fewer than 1 percent of the total population. They seem to occur more often in some families and more often in women than in men.

## Causes

Anxiety is a fearful reaction to the emergence of forbidden or unconscious drives. In most cases, the psychological mechanisms called projection and displacement focus anxiety on specific external objects, persons, or situations, which then come to represent the original cause of the anxiety. In shifting attention to a secondary symbol, a patient learns to use avoidance of the object or situation (spiders, heights, open places, and so on) to prevent rearousal of the painful anxiety. The "choice" of the phobic object is often at random; it may be the first object, location, or situation at hand when the original anxiety first appeared.

Phobias usually begin in early adulthood and follow a long course of alternate improvement and worsening of symptoms. The longer a patient has phobic symptoms, the less likely he or she is to achieve a complete recovery.

## Symptoms

The symptoms of a phobia depend on the phobic object. Often, the very thought or mention of the object induces anxiety in the patient. The more inescapable the exposure or contact becomes, the more anxiety mounts toward panic. As a result, the patient spends more and more time avoiding the phobic stimulus, and this avoidance often begins to restrict her daily activities (for example, she becomes unable to travel because of fear of flying).

## Common phobias

Agoraphobia (a fear of open, public places, such as stores, malls, parks, theaters, and stadiums, or of crowds and crowded situations) is the most common phobia, accounting for about 60 percent of all cases. This abnormal fear of being in open places greatly restricts the life of the victim, who in extreme cases will not leave home, except perhaps if accompanied by a close friend or relative. The first sign of the condition may be a panic attack when out in public, with feelings of anxiety and a sense of approaching doom, restlessness, breathlessness, and rapid or irregular heartbeat. Thereafter, the person may stay at home to avoid another panic attack. Often, the agoraphobic person experiences the phobia selectively—she can face the phobic situation fairly well in the company of someone close or trusted.

Another common phobia, claustrophobia, is an intense and unrealistic fear of being confined in an enclosed space, such as an elevator or a small room. Commonly, the claustrophobic person becomes anxious at even the thought of being "trapped" in a small room or passageway. If the person unexpectedly has to face the phobia, as when caught in a stuck elevator, real panic may result. Unlike some phobias, such as a fear of mice, snakes, or spiders, which the average person seldom sees, claustrophobia can cripple one's vocational and social life, since enclosed spaces are part of the everyday environment.

Some childhood phobias, such as fear of the dark or of animals, disappear with age. But adults, too, experience phobias of specific objects or situations, such as arachnephobia (fear of spiders), ophidiophobia (fear of snakes), acrophobia (fear of heights), and monophobia (fear of being alone). If the objects are easily avoided, like spiders and snakes, there is usually no great problem. However, fear of flying due to acrophobia may cause great inconvenience for a person whose work or social life involves frequent air travel, and monophobia may handicap a worker whose job requires long periods of isolation to complete a project.

The phobias of function, or social phobias, are those in which the presence of others causes the anxiety. Among them are erythrophobia (fear of blushing), haphephobia (fear of being touched), and phagophobia (fear of being seen eating, which makes the victim incapable of eating in the presence of others).

### Treatment

A type of psychotherapy called insight therapy may be helpful in less severe cases; patients learn to recognize the real, underlying object of anxiety and come to see the phobic object as merely symbolic of that other fear. More extreme cases often respond better to behavioral therapy, in which the patient is deconditioned to the phobic stimulus by being required to confront it. At the same time, the patient is encouraged to try various relaxation techniques to combat anxiety. In the most severe cases, a psychiatrist may use a technique called flooding, by which the patient is forced to experience prolonged phobic anxiety with a constant exposure to the dreaded object or situation.

Although drug therapy generally is less effective when used alone than when it is combined with psychotherapy, mild tranquilizers and antidepressants can often delay the onset of panic attacks or reduce their severity.

# Psychosomatic illness

Psychosomatic illnesses are a broad category of disorders in which psychological or emotional factors cause or contribute to physical symptoms. Psychosomatic illnesses are often considered to be imaginary. This is unjustified, since the patient is not pretending to be ill, and his symptoms are no less real than if there were a purely physical basis for his complaint. (There is a psychiatric disorder called Munchausen's syndrome, in which a person knowingly pretends to be ill or intentionally injures himself in order to become ill; however, this rare condition is quite different from psychosomatic illness.)

### Causes

It is known that psychological factors can contribute directly or indirectly to some physical disorders. For example, having a Type A personality (characterized by aggressiveness, competitiveness, preoccupation with deadlines and time constraints, and chronic impatience) has been associated with an increased risk of heart disease. In addition, there is evidence that stress can change the response of the body's immune system to disease.

Emotional stress may also be reflected in the appearance of physical symptoms, especially if a person has a hard time expressing his emotions. In some families, having pain due to physical illness is accepted and elicits a caring response, whereas expressing unhappiness and anger is not tolerated. For someone in such a family situation, a

physical symptom may be an unconscious expression of his emotional state.

It is also quite common for someone who is unhappy at home or at work to become preoccupied with everyday aches and pains. For that person, a genuine—albeit minor—illness may take on unwarranted importance because of his emotional state.

### Symptoms

Almost any type of symptom may be psychosomatic. In fact, it has been estimated that one-third of all complaints reported by patients to their doctors are at least partially psychosomatic. The most typical psychosomatic symptom is pain—for example, facial pain, headaches, generalized abdominal pain, and backache.

### Diagnosis

It is important not to dismiss a person's seemingly psychosomatic illness as being "all in his head." A physician should always give serious consideration to a patient's complaints, even when it may seem obvious that they are psychosomatic. There have been cases in which symptoms with a purely physical basis have been disregarded because of a suspicion that they were psychosomatic. It should also be remembered that psychosomatic factors can set the stage for a serious physical disorder, and that psychosomatic symptoms, although they may be exaggerated, may nonetheless reflect a physical illness.

A physician who takes the time to learn about the patient's life circumstances can often discover the stresses that may be contributing to an illness, even though the patient himself may be overlooking or denying the underlying emotional factors.

## Treatment

If, after a thorough examination, no physical cause can be discovered for a disorder, the best treatment the doctor can offer may be to listen sympathetically and to show concern. Some patients may demand more dramatic treatment methods and may go from doctor to doctor until they find someone who will prescribe the treatment they want. It is important to avoid risky or expensive procedures and testing, as well as unnecessary medication. Helping the patient to recognize that certain symptoms are caused or worsened by stress and to learn how to deal effectively with that stress can often be helpful.

# Schizophrenia

Schizophrenia is not a single mental disorder, but rather a group of mental disorders that are characterized by disturbances of thought processes, emotional response, and behavior. Among the characteristics common to most types of schizophrenia are extreme mental confusion, withdrawal from reality, delusions, hallucinations, extreme mood changes, and bizarre behavior.

## Causes

Most cases of schizophrenia are due to a combination of inherited and environmental factors. A genetic predisposition ap-

pears to be an important factor in schizophrenia. It has been estimated that approximately 10 percent of relatives of schizophrenics are schizophrenic themselves. Schizophrenia is not inherited, however. Even if the genetic predisposition is present, the occurrence of the illness is often related to stressful life events and the individual's ways of coping with them.

## Symptoms

Schizophrenia affects persons of all ages, although it commonly begins in late adolescence or early adult life. There is no specific personality type that can be singled out as predisposing to development of schizophrenia, but many schizophrenics show such traits as extreme sensitivity, shyness, lack of emotion, antisocial behavior, and paranoid attitudes early in life.

The onset of schizophrenia may be sudden or gradual. Some or all of the following symptoms will be present:
• Mental disturbances—progressive confusion of thought and speech; disruption of logical reasoning
• Emotional disorders—absent or inappropriate emotional responses; extremes of depression, excitability, anxiety, and elation
• Hallucinations—distorted or imaginary perceptions involving any of the senses, such as hearing voices or seeing things that are not there
• Delusions—mistaken notions that one is being persecuted, that one is more powerful or important than one is (called delusions of grandeur), or that one's thoughts are being broadcast to others or are being controlled by some outside agency

• Movement disorders—extreme hyperactivity; stupor and immobility; adoption of strange positions, facial expressions, mannerisms, and abnormal activity patterns, such as rocking and pacing
• Violent behavior—such as threats of violence and assassination attempts against authority figures and persons in the public eye
• Withdrawal from reality and social contact

## Diagnosis

As with other mental disorders, the physician will obtain a personal and medical history from (or about) the patient and will conduct a physical examination to rule out the possibility that some medical condition or drug reaction may be causing the symptoms of schizophrenia.

## Treatment

The chief treatment measures for schizophrenia include drug therapy, psychotherapy, counseling, social support, and rehabilitation. For a first illness or acute relapse, hospitalization is usually indicated in order to stabilize the patient's condition. However, hospitalization for more than a few months may be inadvisable; if the patient is able to function outside an institution, leading some semblance of a normal life may be therapeutic.

Schizophrenia is not necessarily a chronic condition. About 30 percent of patients recover completely, and most of the rest show marked improvement with appropriate treatment, although impaired emotional response and motivation may persist.

# Senility

Senility is the medical term applied to the gradual process of mental and physical deterioration that is sometimes associated with old age.

## Causes

The causes of senility are many—arteriosclerosis (hardening of the arteries) and other blood vessel diseases, heart and lung diseases (which decrease the amount of oxygen available to the brain and other body tissues), and diseases of the liver, the kidneys, and other organs. Senility is not linked to a single disease, nor is it inevitable. However, the years take their toll, and chronic disorders hasten senility. Lifelong harmful habits are also a cause of early senility; alcohol, tobacco, and drug abuse are among the worst offenders.

## Symptoms

Gradual loss of physical and mental vigor is the most common symptom of oncoming senility. A lack of interest in the surroundings or in activities once enjoyed is another symptom. Victims experience a loss of complex skills, such as the ability to do puzzles, math problems, or logic problems, or even to balance their checkbooks. If the onset of senility is relatively sudden, as it is with a condition called Alzheimer's disease, the victim will often be in a panic, as he feels his mental powers waning. Short-term memory is one of the first faculties to go, and many victims are painfully aware of their condition.

Physical senility is gradual, unless a chronic illness accelerates the process. The skin becomes dry and loses its resilience, the muscles lose their tone and become weak, the bones become brittle, and the organs gradually fail.

## Diagnosis

Do not assume that a relative is suffering from senility simply on the basis of confusion and apparent loss of mental skills. Depression and a number of physical conditions can cause similar symptoms. Such symptoms may also be related to the use of certain medications (or combinations of medications). Always consult a physician so that such conditions can be ruled out (and, in some cases, treated).

## Prevention

Although there is no way to stop the clock, there are many ways that one can continue leading a vigorous, active life. Getting regular exercise; avoiding toxic substances, such as tobacco, alcohol, drugs, and pollutants; and eating a balanced diet, with adequate amounts of vitamins and minerals, seem to have a positive effect at any age. Protection from debilitating disease and avoidance of injuries (such as broken bones) can also add years of activity to the lives of the elderly.

Mental senility can often be avoided simply by not "turning off" the mind on retirement. The mind begins to deteriorate quickly if it is not used, in much the same way that muscles shrink when they are not used.

# HEREDITY AND
# INHERITED DISEASES

To understand how some disorders can be passed from one generation to another, one must first understand the role played by the genes in determining the form and function of each cell in the body.

The genes are the basic units that determine the hereditary (inborn) characteristics of an organism. Genes, which are composed of molecules of deoxyribonucleic acid (DNA), can be thought of as chemical instructions. Each gene, by virtue of the particular structure of its DNA molecule, contains the code for a specific trait, determining both what a cell is and how it works (as if a computer program not only told the computer what to do but helped to form the machine itself).

Within each cell, thousands of genes are linked in a specific order, like beads on a necklace, to form structures called chromosomes, which are in effect continuous strands of DNA. It has been estimated that each cell contains about five feet of coiled DNA strands and that each strand is made of about 100,000 genes.

The particular composition of the genes and their arrangement on the chromosomes are what constitute the genetic blueprint for each individual. Cells that develop into liver tissue, rather than blood cells or nerve fibers, for example, do so because that is what their genetic coding dictates. In this way, the cells of the body are programmed to create a person with a certain color of eyes and hair, as well as the hundreds of thousands of other characteristics that make each human being unique.

### Sex cells

Each cell in the human body contains 46 chromosomes. The only exceptions are the sex cells—the ovum (egg) and the sperm—each of which contains only 23 chromosomes. When these sex cells unite in the fertilization of the ovum by a sperm, the result is a full complement of 46 chromosomes, with genes donated by both parents. Since each parent contributes only 23 chromosomes (half of the genetic coding that makes each parent a unique individual), the genetic makeup of their offspring is a blend of components of both parents' genetic material.

### Dominant and recessive traits

The traits that genes give rise to may be either dominant or recessive. A recessive gene is one that produces a certain trait only

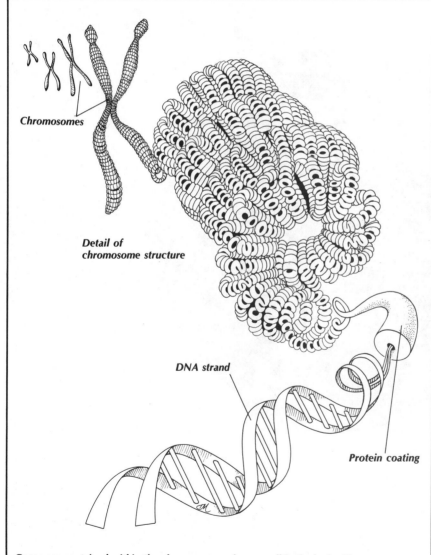

**Chromosomes**

**Detail of chromosome structure**

**DNA strand**

**Protein coating**

*Genes are contained within the chromosomes of every cell in the body. Chromosomes are threadlike coils that contain the genetic code for the cell. Chromosomes are composed of DNA, which has a spiral, ladderlike structure. The composition and arrangement of the DNA determine the genetic code of the cell.*

if its effects are not overridden by those of a dominant gene.

Eye color provides a relatively straightforward illustration of how inheritance of traits works. The gene for brown eyes is dominant; the gene for blue eyes is recessive. The child of a brown-eyed parent who has two brown-eye genes and a blue-eyed parent (who must have two blue-eye genes) will have brown eyes because the brown-eyed parent has only dominant brown-eye genes to contribute to the child's genetic makeup. However, if the brown-eyed parent has a dominant brown-eye gene and a recessive blue-eye gene, the child has a fifty-fifty chance of receiving a blue-eye gene from each parent and thereby having blue eyes. (Actually, inheritance does not always work with such textbook simplicity—sometimes the child of a brown-eyed parent and a blue-eyed parent will have green or hazel eyes.) The union of two blue-eyed persons, because it involves only recessive blue-eye genes, will always produce blue-eyed offspring. The offspring of two brown-eyed persons who each have a recessive blue-eye gene have a one-in-four chance of receiving a blue-eye gene from each parent and, as a result, having blue eyes. (This final combination illustrates how recessive genes can be present but unsuspected, allowing a trait to appear unexpectedly after skipping generations.)

## Mutation

Genes are normally transmitted unchanged from one generation to the next. Sometimes, however, mutations occur—that is, the structure of the gene itself is changed, perhaps due to the effect of a toxic substance, an in-

fection, or exposure to radiation. Offspring that receive a mutated gene will exhibit a characteristic that is not present in either parent.

The discovery of the structure of the DNA molecule opened a new era in medical research. Scientists in the new field of genetic engineering are exploring ways of artificially creating mutations in genes so that someday it may be possible to correct the errors in genetic coding that cause various disorders.

## Genetic counseling

As the medical profession has learned more about inherited diseases, it has been able to offer genetic counseling to couples concerned about the possibility of having a child with an inherited disease or abnormality. A genetic counselor or specialist in genetic disorders can estimate the likelihood that a couple's offspring will be afflicted with a problem due to an inherited trait or to the age of the parents. For some genetic disorders, tests can determine whether one or both parents are carriers or can detect whether a defect is present in a fetus. However, genetic counseling cannot guarantee the health of a child; it can only be a source of advice.

# Celiac disease

Celiac disease, or celiac sprue, is a chronic disorder of the small intestine caused by sensitivity to gluten, a protein found in wheat and rye and, to a lesser extent, in oats and barley. The disorder causes poor absorption by the intestine of fat, protein, carbohydrates, iron, water, and vitamins A, D, E, and K. Removal of glu-

ten from the diet normally brings improvement.

## Causes

The basic cause is probably an inherited defect found mostly in people of northwestern European ancestry. It affects one person in 300 in western Ireland, and approximately one in 5,000 in the United States. It is twice as likely to affect women as men.

One theory about celiac disease holds that the body reacts to gluten and its derivative gliadin as if they were viruses or bacteria. When food containing gluten reaches the portion of the small intestine called the jejunum, antibodies in the intestinal wall are stimulated. In the process, for some unknown reason, the intestinal villi (hairlike projections through which nutrients from the intestine are absorbed into the bloodstream) are destroyed. Destruction of the villi is almost total in the jejunum, less so in the rest of the small intestine. Poor absorption of food and water is the result. Another theory states that gluten and gliadin act directly on the intestinal wall as toxins (poisons). One or both of these theories may be correct.

## Symptoms

Symptoms of celiac disease may begin in infancy when the child starts eating wheat cereal or other foods containing gluten. The child does not thrive, suffers painful bloating in the abdomen, and passes pale, foul-smelling, bulky stools. Failure to absorb enough iron produces anemia (deficiency of oxygen-carrying red blood cells). Poor absorption of protein may cause edema (swelling of body tissues). There is little fat on the body. Growth may be stunted, signs of vitamin deficiency appear, and softening of bones may produce bone deformities and fractures. Sometimes the symptoms disappear in adolescence and reappear in adulthood.

Adults with celiac disease have many of the same symptoms, including bulky, foul-smelling stools; weight loss; vitamin deficiencies; edema; anemia; and bone pain. It can also cause burning, pricking, tickling, or tingling in the hands and feet; dry skin; eczema; acne; cessation of menstruation; mood changes; and irritability. The disease may appear for the first time as late as age 60.

### Diagnosis

The most definitive test for celiac disease is microscopic examination of a piece of tissue taken from the wall of the small intestine. The sample is taken with the aid of a flexible tube with a cutting instrument at the tip, which is inserted through the mouth into the intestine. The specimen from a celiac patient has almost no villi, and the surface is alternately flat and bumpy, with a disorganized network of blood vessels. Various blood tests taken after the patient has eaten specific substances reveal how well the intestine has absorbed these substances. In addition, blood tests may reveal low levels of protein, calcium, potassium, and sodium. Tests of the stools reveal excess fat.

### Treatment

The primary treatment of celiac disease is to remove all gluten from the diet, which is easier said than done. Hot dogs, ice cream, commercial soups and sauces, candy bars, and all kinds of baked goods can be sources of gluten (even small amounts of gluten must be avoided). Many doctors refer the patient to a dietitian for detailed lists of foods to avoid and for advice on following a healthful diet, which should be high in calories and protein and low in fat. Vitamin and mineral supplements are given as needed. In stubborn cases, a cortisone drug may be given, which will often result in improvement.

The outlook is good for most patients. Recovery is most dramatic in children. In severe cases, complete return to normal bowel function and normal absorption may take months or may never occur. For that reason, and to rule out other diseases of nutritional deficiency or poor absorption, it is best to see a doctor as soon as symptoms appear. This is one ailment that is almost completely treatable.

# Cystic fibrosis

Cystic fibrosis is a serious hereditary disease characterized by abnormal secretions that affect many parts of the body, but primarily the lungs, pancreas, and digestive tract.

### Cause

Cystic fibrosis is caused by an inherited defective gene. This gene is recessive, meaning that it must be inherited from both parents for the child to suffer from the disease. If the gene is received from only one parent, the child is a carrier but will not get the disease. About 5 percent of the white population in the United States are carriers; the incidence in the black and Oriental populations is much lower. Approximately one in every 400 marriages involves two carriers. A child of two carriers has a 25 percent chance of getting the disease, a 50 percent chance of being a carrier, and a 25 percent chance of being completely free of the defective gene.

The effect of the defective gene is to cause the exocrine glands to release abnormal mucus, sweat, and other secretions. (Exocrine glands are those that release their secretions through ducts, rather than directly into the bloodstream.) The most serious effects of cystic fibrosis occur when the mucous glands release thick, gummy mucus rather than the normal clear, free-flowing fluid. This thick mucus accumulates in the glands, causing swelling, forming cysts, and, most important, blocking various ducts throughout the body. One of the more serious complications of cystic fibrosis occurs when the mucus in the lungs, which normally sweeps bacteria and foreign particles from the lungs, becomes thick and sticky, accumulating in the airways and creating a breeding ground for infection, rather than preventing it. Consequent infections cause still more mucus to be produced, and the airways, already narrowed from the swelling, become even more clogged. Recurrent infections can lead to long-term breathing difficulties. Most deaths from cystic fibrosis are due to respiratory failure caused by obstruction of the airways and by persistent infections.

Also affected by this disorder is the pancreas, the organ that normally secretes digestive en-

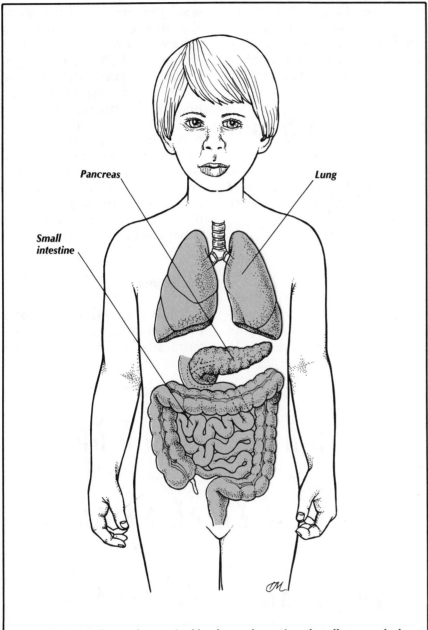

*Cystic fibrosis is a disease characterized by abnormal secretions that affect many body parts, particularly the lungs, the pancreas, and the intestinal tract. In the lungs, thick mucus hampers breathing and promotes infection. Thickened secretions can obstruct the ducts in the pancreas and block the passage of pancreatic digestive enzymes into the small intestine.*

zymes through a series of ducts into the small intestine. These ducts become blocked by abnormally thickened mucous secretions, preventing digestive enzymes from reaching the small intestine, where they are needed to digest fats.

Reproductive tract secretions are also thickened. In women, an overabundance of mucus in the cervix may block the passage of sperm, making it difficult to become pregnant. About 98 percent of male patients are sterile because the ducts through which the sperm normally travel are blocked by thickened mucus.

Heat exhaustion is another problem related to this disease, because of the large salt loss due to excessive sweating.

## Symptoms

The symptoms of cystic fibrosis may show up at birth or may not appear until adolescence. About 10 percent of babies with cystic fibrosis are born with a mucous plug in their intestinal tract, which must be corrected surgically.

Because the pancreas is prevented from releasing the enzymes necessary to digest fat, digestive problems are common, and stools are large and foul-smelling. Typically, children afflicted with the disease eat well but gain weight slowly and show signs of malnutrition because the fat in their food is excreted from the body without being used. In addition, the patient usually has excessively salty sweat, a chronic cough accompanied by mucous discharge, and rapid and difficult breathing, and frequently experiences fatigue and muscle cramps from salt loss. Sinusitis (inflammation of the air-filled cavities in the facial bones), nasal polyps (growths within the nose), and a barrel-shaped chest from overinflated lungs may also develop.

Because many of these symptoms are also indications of less serious disorders, cystic fibrosis often remains undiagnosed or undetected for some time while the disease progresses.

## Diagnosis

Diagnostic evaluation usually includes a physical examination, medical history, chest x-ray, and a sweat test. (Most cystic fibrosis patients have excessively salty sweat, although the salt level does not indicate the severity of the condition.) Tests of the stool and digestive juices can show how well the pancreas is functioning.

### Treatment

Although cystic fibrosis cannot be cured, its symptoms can be relieved to some extent. Dietary management is extremely important; patients are advised to reduce the fats in their diets, to eat nutritious foods with high amounts of essential minerals and vitamins, to take salt tablets, and to take pancreatic enzyme tablets to aid digestion of fats. The risk of respiratory infections can be reduced by means of antibiotics, aerosol mists, appropriate vaccinations, and postural drainage (in which the patient is positioned so that gravity can be used to help clear mucus from clogged lungs). Regular exercise may also be useful.

### Prevention

There is no means of preventing cystic fibrosis today. Researchers continue to look for a reason why the defective gene causes mucus to become abnormal, as well as for a way to identify carriers of the gene. One new test measures certain chemicals present in the amniotic fluid (the liquid that surrounds a fetus in the womb), so that an unborn baby with the gene can be identified. Meanwhile, scientific advances in this area have at least helped those with the disease to live more comfortably. Until the 1960s, few patients

lived beyond the age of 10, but today those with cystic fibrosis can live to age 25 or beyond because of medical advances in managing the condition.

# Down's syndrome

Down's syndrome is a congenital (present at birth) disorder characterized by some degree of mental retardation and a variety of physical abnormalities.

### Cause

Normally, each cell in the human body has 46 chromosomes; the cells in someone with Down's syndrome have 47. In ways that are as yet unknown, the presence of the extra chromosome causes all of the unusual characteristics of Down's syndrome. In 95 percent of cases, the condition is called trisomy 21 (because the extra chromosome is attached to the twenty-first pair of chromosomes), and the mistake in genetic coding is one that apparently could happen to anyone. In 5 percent of cases, the syndrome is caused by a defect that is believed to run in families.

### Symptoms

Down's syndrome is marked by a number of physical characteristics: somewhat slanted eyes

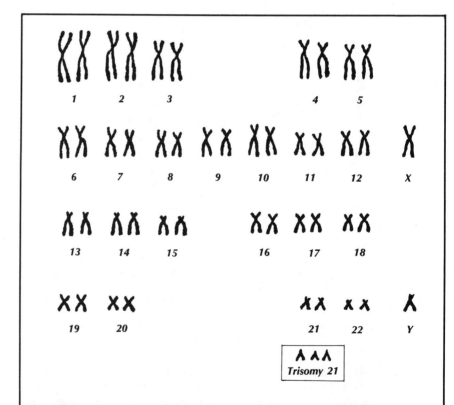

*The normal human cell contains 23 pairs of chromosomes, one of which is a pair of sex chromosomes (either two X chromosomes or one X and one Y chromosome), for a total of 46 chromosomes. In Down's syndrome (also called trisomy 21), however, there are three number 21 chromosomes, rather than two; the presence of this extra chromosome is responsible for the collection of symptoms that characterize Down's syndrome.*

in small sockets (which is why it used to be called mongolism); a small, short head, flattened in back and front; a nose flattened at the bridge; a thick tongue; short hands, feet, neck, trunk, arms, and legs; a single, rather than a double, crease across the top of the palm; flabby arms and legs with poor muscle tone; a wide gap between the first and second toes; and generally retarded physical development. A child with Down's syndrome may have a poorly functioning thyroid gland (which regulates metabolism, the rate at which the body uses energy) and pituitary gland (which regulates other glands, including those responsible for growth, maturation, and reproduction). About one third are born with heart defects, and both the skin and mucous membranes are especially susceptible to infection.

### Education

Characteristically slower than other children to walk, talk, and learn, youngsters with Down's syndrome benefit from "early intervention" programs designed to help them develop their abilities as much as possible. Such programs are frequently available from the time the mother and baby leave the hospital after the birth. A number of organizations exist to promote such programs and assist parents in developing their child's potential. The degree of retardation that accompanies Down's syndrome ranges from mild to severe (the average IQ is about 50), and the extent to which an individual will be affected is not predictable at birth. Some children with Down's syndrome can attend special education classes in public schools; others can at-

tend special schools for the mentally retarded. As adults, some may be able to live independently or semi-independently and work in the community. Depending on the degree of retardation that is present, others will require more supervised living arrangements and may be able to hold simple, routine jobs, perhaps in what is called a "sheltered workshop."

### Prevention

Prospective parents can reduce their chances of having a child with Down's syndrome by starting their families early. At age 20 a woman's risk of giving birth to a child with Down's syndrome is only one in 2,000 live births, but at age 35 the risk is one in 300, at age 40 it is one in 100, and at age 45 it is one in 40 live births. The age of the father also has some bearing on the risk, but not as much as the age of the mother. Diagnosis of Down's syndrome can be made between the twelfth and thirteenth weeks of pregnancy, by testing samples of amniotic fluid, which surrounds the developing fetus and contains cells shed by the fetus.

# Hemophilia

Hemophilia is a sex-linked hereditary bleeding disorder in which the clotting mechanism of the blood does not function properly. Blood normally contains several factors that enable clotting to occur. These are designated coagulation factors I through XIII. In the most common form of hemophilia—classic hemophilia, or hemophilia A—factor VIII is deficient. In this case, factors I through VII function adequately,

but the clotting process is interrupted by a lack of sufficient amounts of factor VIII. Hemophilia B is the other common form of hemophilia, although it occurs significantly less often than hemophilia A. Hemophilia B is caused by a deficiency of factor IX. Hemophilia B is also known as Christmas disease.

### Cause

Hemophilia is inherited as a sex-linked recessive trait—a woman can pass on the defective gene for the trait without being affected herself. The gene that causes the disorder appears on the X chromosome, which is the female sex chromosome. (Males have one X chromosome and one Y chromosome, while females have two X chromosomes.) If a woman has one defective X chromosome, the presence of her other, normal X chromosome ensures that she will not suffer from the disease herself. However, she can pass on her defective X chromosome to her sons, who will have the disease because they do not have a normal X chromosome to counteract the defect. If she passes the defective chromosome to her daughters, they, too, will be carriers but will not have the disease. A male hemophiliac passes his defective X chromosome to his daughters, making them carriers. However, he passes on only his normal Y chromosome to his sons, who therefore will not have the disease (unless their mother is a carrier). Although the condition appears almost exclusively in males, a woman can be a hemophiliac if her mother is a carrier and her father is a hemophiliac (in such a case, she inherits two defective X chromosomes).

### Symptoms

Although affected individuals are born with the disease, the onset of symptoms is variable. Milder cases may not be readily apparent. The symptoms of hemophilia usually appear during early childhood. When a cut in the skin occurs or an injury is suffered, the bleeding may be substantial and prolonged. In severe cases, spontaneous internal bleeding may occur without any obvious cause. Blood may appear in the urine due to internal bleeding. Pain is also a symptom when the bleeding occurs internally, between muscles and into joints. The course of the disease may result in irreversible damage to the joints, which, in turn, results in greater pain and in limitation of movement.

### Diagnosis

If a child has any of the symptoms of hemophilia, or if there is a family history of hemophilia, a physician should be consulted. The physician will order laboratory tests to establish the diagnosis. The most common test for hemophilia is determination of the partial thromboplastin time (PTT), which indicates how long it takes for the blood to clot. Additional laboratory tests may be ordered in certain cases.

### Treatment

Treatment of hemophilia has recently undergone dramatic changes. One important breakthrough has been the development of factor VIII replacement therapy. One factor VIII replacement, cryoprecipitate, is prepared from donated blood plasma (the fluid portion of blood,

which contains more factor VIII than whole blood does). The plasma of an individual donor is quickly frozen by a special process and then slowly thawed, so that the portion rich in factor VIII can be separated out. This portion can then be prepared later for intravenous administration. Cryoprecipitate has the disadvantage of having to be stored and prepared in a hospital. Also, since cryoprecipitate is produced from the plasma of a single donor, the amount of factor VIII present in a given preparation is variable.

Treatment of hemophilia A has been further advanced by the development of a process of rapid freezing and dehydration (removal of water) of plasma, called lyophilization. Freeze-dried concentrates are prepared and packaged so that they can be readily dissolved by a simple mixing procedure. (This process is similar in concept to the preparation and use of freeze-dried coffee.) This concentrate, which quickly stops bleeding, is particularly efficient for home use in comparison with cryoprecipitate.

There is a drawback, however, to the use of freeze-dried concentrate. Whereas the cryoprecipitate is prepared from the blood plasma of a single donor, the concentrate is prepared from the plasma of thousands of donors. The recipient of concentrate is therefore placed at increased risk of infection compared with a recipient of cryoprecipitate. Hepatitis (a serious infection of the liver), for example, may be transmitted in blood products, and the virus that causes acquired immune deficiency syndrome (AIDS) is carried in bodily fluids. Both of these diseases have developed in a number of hemophilia patients

who were treated with concentrate. (New blood-testing procedures have now reduced this risk.) Scientists are therefore continuing to investigate the relative risks and benefits of concentrate and cryoprecipitate for treatment of hemophilia A.

Treatment of hemophilia B involves the use of fresh or stored plasma. Concentrate is also available for hemophilia B and is known as prothrombin complex concentrate.

### Prevention

There is no preventive for hemophilia. Genetic testing can now identify carriers of hemophilia with considerable accuracy, however, allowing affected individuals to decide whether they wish to risk transmitting the disorder to their offspring.

# Huntington's chorea

Huntington's chorea is an inherited degenerative nerve disorder that seldom becomes apparent before early middle age. It is characterized by disorganized body movements (the word *chorea* comes from a Greek word meaning dance) and mental deterioration. It is thought that Huntington's chorea is the result of a disturbance in the part of the brain that automatically regulates voluntary movements.

### Cause

The condition is transmitted as a dominant genetic trait from a parent who has the disease. There is about a 50 percent chance of a child's inheriting the disease from an affected parent. Since the symptoms of Huntington's chorea usually do not appear until the victim is between 30 and 50 years of age, a person with a family history of Huntington's chorea lives through the years of adolescence and early adulthood in dread of reaching the middle years, when the symptoms may begin. Even more tragic, a person who is unaware of a family history of Huntington's chorea may have children before discovering that he has the disease.

### Symptoms

The first symptoms of mental deterioration are usually personality changes—obstinacy, moodiness, lack of interest in surroundings, and inappropriate behavior may be displayed. It should be noted, however, that all of these symptoms can also be due to psychological or other disorders that have nothing to do with Huntington's chorea.

These symptoms are accompanied by irregular, jerky movements that begin in the arms, the neck, and the face. They may start as "fidgeting" and gradually develop into facial grimaces, halting speech, irregular movements of the torso, and muscle contractions in the neck that cause the head to be held to one side.

In advanced cases, a wide stance will be adopted in an attempt to maintain balance. The gait will become prancing, as control of the legs deteriorates. As the disease progresses, the victims usually become paranoid, walking ability is lost altogether, swallowing becomes difficult, and dementia (loss of intellectual capabilities) increases.

### Treatment

No treatment has yet been found to control the symptoms or halt the disease. However, the body movements may be controlled somewhat by drugs, most notably haloperidol and chlorpromazine. There is no known treatment for the mental degeneration that accompanies the physical symptoms.

### Prevention

There is no preventive for Huntington's chorea, other than advising affected patients not to have children.

# Muscular dystrophy

Muscular dystrophy is the general term for a group of rare diseases in which the body's muscles weaken and waste away. Muscular dystrophy almost always strikes in childhood and is usually inherited. Duchenne muscular dystrophy, which is usually inherited through the mother, is the most common form of the disease.

The disease is progressive, that is, it becomes gradually worse once it takes hold. In severe forms of muscular dystrophy, the child must use a wheelchair to get around by the age of 11 or 12. Scoliosis (curvature of the spine) may also result from the disease. Severe cases may be fatal, often when the patient is a young adult. Pneumonia is sometimes a fatal complication because of weakening of the muscles involved in breathing.

Muscular dystrophy is sometimes confused with multiple sclerosis, which is a disease of the nervous system that can ultimately result in spasticity and paralysis. There is no deterioration of the nervous system in muscular dystrophy.

### Symptoms

Symptoms of muscular dystrophy vary. Muscles usually begin to weaken first in the hips, legs, and shoulders. A child of four or five who waddles from side to side, who has difficulty standing up properly, or who falls frequently should be examined by a physician. The child may also have difficulty in standing up straight or raising an arm high above the head.

Parents should not be overly concerned about the natural awkwardness that occasionally overtakes the older toddler. However, a child near five years of age who consistently has problems with muscular coordination should be checked.

### Diagnosis

The diagnosis of Duchenne muscular dystrophy is rarely made before the age of three. It is most commonly seen in boys; girls are rarely affected.

The physician may want to obtain a muscle biopsy specimen (a small tissue sample) to confirm a diagnosis of muscular dystrophy. The biopsy may be done on an outpatient basis in a hospital or in a physician's office.

### Treatment

There is no treatment for the disease, but an exercise program designed by a physical therapist may be helpful. The patient's diet should be regulated so that he does not become overweight; excess weight taxes the child's weakening muscles and hastens the course of the disease.

## Prevention

Because muscular dystrophy is an inherited disease, women in the family of an affected child should be tested to see if they are carriers (they can pass on the disease to their children). Such women should receive genetic counseling regarding any pregnancy.

# Phenylketonuria

Phenylketonuria (PKU) is a congenital (present at birth) disorder characterized by the presence of increased amounts of certain amino acids in the blood and urine. (Amino acids are the chemical building blocks of protein.) The condition is caused by the inability to convert phenylalanine (an amino acid essential for optimal growth in infants and for maintenance of nitrogen balance in adults) into tyrosine (another amino acid). Excess phenylalanine is normally eliminated from the body by conversion to tyrosine. In PKU, this mechanism does not work, permitting an accumulation of phenylalanine. The result is mental retardation in infants or young children if the disorder is untreated.

## Cause

Phenylketonuria is hereditary and is found in most population groups, although it is very rare in Jewish and black children. The incidence in the United States is about one in every 16,000 live births.

## Diagnosis

Early diagnosis of phenyl-ketonuria is essential because symptoms are usually not obvious in a newborn infant. Therefore, screening tests are now mandatory for all babies born in the United States and Canada. Sometimes infants with PKU will have nervous system disorders, very light coloring of the skin and hair, eczema (a skin disorder), and a musty odor. Older children may be extremely hyperactive. The light coloring is often an early clue to the disease; the infant's skin, hair, and even eyes will be lighter than those of other members of the family.

## Treatment

Treatment of this disorder within the first few days after birth is essential if mental retardation is to be prevented. Treatment consists of limiting the child's phenylalanine intake so that the essential amino acid requirement is satisfied without any excess. This can be done by feeding the infant special formulas with little or no phenylalanine. Milk is a protein food rich in phenylalanine, so it must be avoided. When it is time to introduce solid foods into the infant's diet, low-protein natural foods, such as fruits, vegetables, and certain cereals, are permitted.

If PKU is not diagnosed in the first few days of life, extreme hyperactivity, seizures, and mental retardation usually occur. Some physicians think that treatment and special diet must be continued throughout the child's life; others believe that it can be ended when brain development is virtually complete (around five years of age).

It is important to remember that, although untreated PKU can lead to retardation and other problems, early diagnosis and treatment can enable the child to develop normally and to lead a normal life.

# Sickle cell anemia

Sickle cell anemia is an inherited blood disorder, occurring almost exclusively in black persons, in which the normally round red blood cells are transformed into crescentic, or sickle-shaped, cells that are less able to transport needed oxygen. The disease is chronic, marked by fatigue, breathing difficulty on exertion, swollen joints, attacks of extreme illness, complications from other diseases, and shortened life. In the past, half of all victims died by the age of 20 and few survived past 40. With new technology and forms of treatment, the outlook is much better, but sickle cell anemia remains a chronic debilitating disease.

## Cause

The deformation of the red blood cells occurs because of the presence of defective hemoglobin (the iron-protein compound in the red blood cells that carries oxygen). It occurs when part or all of the body is not getting enough oxygen. Because of their hooked shapes, the blood cells tend to tangle together and pile up, temporarily clogging tiny blood vessels and slowing circulation. Tissue formerly nourished by the clogged blood vessels becomes starved for oxygen and may die. The anemia (deficiency of red blood cells) that results from the accelerated breakdown of defective red blood cells not only weakens the body, but increases oxygen deficiency, which results in more "sickling" of the cells.

The disease occurs in about one of every 330 black persons in the United States. About one in ten black persons in America is a carrier of the defective gene for sickle cell anemia but has no symptoms and is not affected by the disease. However, if one carrier marries another, the risk that their child will be afflicted by the disease is one in four. The risk that the child will also be a carrier is one in two. Both the carrier state and the active state of the disease can be established by a blood test.

*Sickle cell anemia is a blood disorder in which the normally round red blood cells are transformed into crescentic, or sickle-shaped, cells. The sickle-shaped cells tangle together and interfere with blood circulation.*

## Symptoms

In half the victims, symptoms of sickle cell anemia begin between the ages of six months and two years. Among the first signs is unusual swelling of the fingers and toes. The bones of the hands and feet thicken, and clumping of sickle cells may affect the bone marrow, where new blood cells are produced.

Youngsters are especially subject to "sickle cell crises," marked by severe pain in the abdomen, joints, bones, and muscles due to lack of oxygen. These crises may last from four days to several weeks, and commonly occur eight to ten times a year before the age of ten. They occur much less often in later years. Signs of a sickle cell crisis include paleness of the lips, tongue, and palms; lack of energy; sleepiness and difficulty in awakening; irritability; pain; and a temperature of 104°F (or one over 100°F that lasts for at least two days).

Thickening of the heart muscle; enlargement of the heart, liver, and spleen in children; heart murmurs; and gallstones are common. The heartbeat is usually rapid. Children with the disease are usually small for their age. Those who survive to adulthood may have narrow shoulders and hips, a barrel chest, a curved spine, long arms and legs, and an elongated skull.

## Treatment

At present there is no cure for the disease. Treatment includes giving painkillers, making the patient as comfortable as possible, and treating problems as they occur. These problems include severe anemia, which may require a blood transfusion, and frequent infections, which occur because of impairment of the immune system.

## Prevention

Avoiding cold, fatigue, and other stress may help to reduce the number of sickle cell crises.

Screening programs are available for those who wish to know whether they carry the gene for sickle cell anemia. Those who have the gene can obtain genetic counseling. There is no risk of disease in offspring if only one parent is a carrier, but each child will have a one in two chance of being a carrier.

# Tay-Sachs disease

Tay-Sachs disease is a hereditary metabolic disorder that chiefly afflicts infants of eastern European Jewish descent. This disease is fatal, usually by the age of four years. It is marked by retarded development, loss of vision, and paralysis.

## Cause

The disease is caused by a deficiency of a certain digestive enzyme (a substance that causes chemical changes without being altered itself). This deficiency results in the accumulation of fatty acids in the brain.

## Symptoms

The symptoms of Tay-Sachs disease in an infant are most often noted after four to six months of normal development. A previously well infant begins to lose motor coordination skills that had been attained and to exhibit loss of interest in his surroundings. As the condition becomes more advanced, seizures occur, and the head becomes considerably enlarged.

## Diagnosis

The physician may notice poor muscle tone and an exaggerated startle response to sound. A distinctive cherry-red spot may be seen in the retina of the eye. The diagnosis is confirmed with special blood tests.

Diagnosis of the disorder may be made before birth by amniocentesis, a procedure in which a small amount of amniotic fluid (the fluid in the sac surrounding the fetus in the uterus) is removed for laboratory examination.

## Treatment

There is no known treatment for Tay-Sachs disease other than supportive care.

## Prevention

There is a blood test available that will help identify carriers of the defective gene. (A carrier has the defective gene but does not have the disease.) This test is especially recommended for all Jews of reproductive age. If two carriers have children, each child conceived has a one in four chance of having the disease. It is, therefore, a good idea for carriers to seek genetic counseling before starting their families.

# CANCER

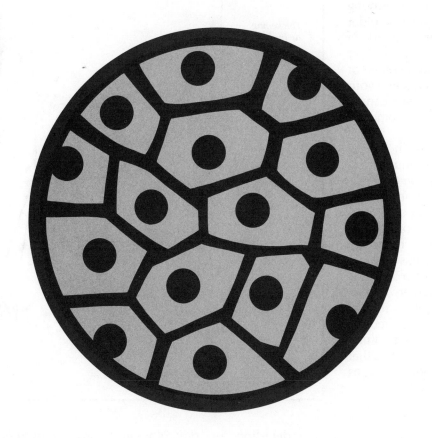

Cancer is the term used to describe a broad group of diseases in which certain body cells grow out of control.

## RISK FACTORS

Who is most likely to develop cancer? This question is very difficult, if not impossible, to answer. There are, however, certain risk factors that increase the possibility that you may develop cancer in your lifetime. Among these are age (as a rule, the older you are, the higher your risk of getting cancer), family history (for example, if your mother or sister had breast cancer, your risk of developing breast cancer is increased), and environmental and other factors.

The rapid increase in cancer rates during this century has been blamed largely on the environment. Polluted air and water, food additives and colorings, and changes in diet from "natural" to "processed" foods all have been implicated as possible causes. Cigarette smoking has been shown conclusively to be a cause of lung and other related cancers. If you wish to reduce your risk of getting cancer, think about changing those factors that are within your control, such as diet and tobacco use.

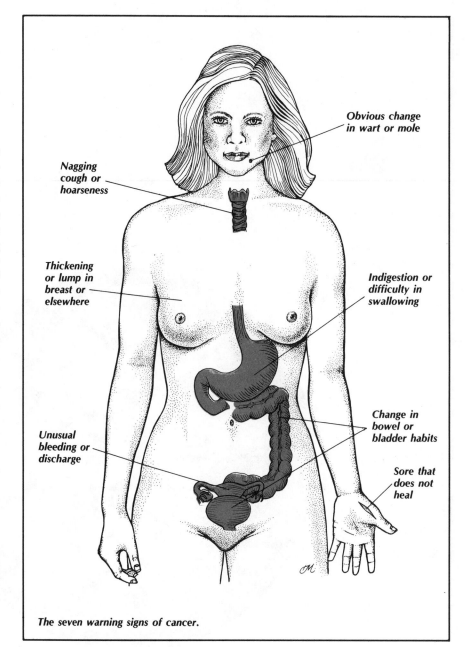

*Obvious change in wart or mole*

*Nagging cough or hoarseness*

*Thickening or lump in breast or elsewhere*

*Indigestion or difficulty in swallowing*

*Unusual bleeding or discharge*

*Change in bowel or bladder habits*

*Sore that does not heal*

*The seven warning signs of cancer.*

## WARNING SIGNS

Often a patient is the first to suspect cancer. This is why it is important to learn cancer's seven warning signs:

1. Change in bowel or bladder habits
2. A sore that does not heal
3. Unusual bleeding or discharge
4. Thickening or lump in the breast or elsewhere
5. Indigestion or difficulty in swallowing
6. Obvious change in a wart or mole
7. A nagging cough or hoarseness

The chances of cure are greatest if cancer is discovered at an early stage. If you are a woman, you should learn to perform breast self-examination to detect suspicious lumps as early as possible. If you are a man, many

physicians recommend self-examination for testicular cancer.

## CAUSES AND TYPES

Unlike normal cells, which grow and reproduce in the orderly manner dictated by the genetic coding in their chromosomes, cancer cells grow at an uncontrolled rate—taking over, causing the death of, or replacing

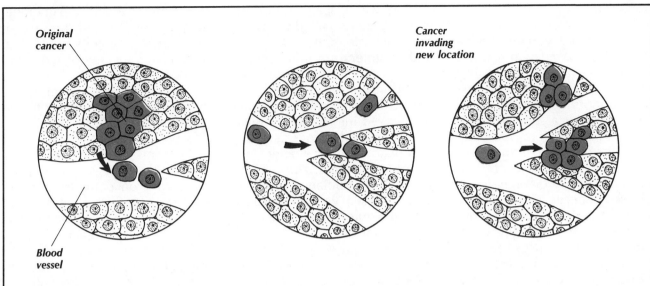

*Original cancer*

*Cancer invading new location*

*Blood vessel*

*The spread of cancer from its original site to other locations in the body is called metastasis. As cancer progresses, cells often travel through the circulatory system to start growth in other parts of the body.*

normal cells. As the disease progresses, cancer cells often travel through the circulatory system to start growth in other parts of the body; this process is called metastasis.

A tumor is an abnormal tissue growth. A tumor may be either malignant (cancerous) or benign (noncancerous). A benign tumor commonly grows within a capsule and does not invade surrounding tissue (although it can cause trouble by pressing on surrounding tissue) or spread throughout the body. Malignant tissues may grow out of control and quite often spread.

More than 200 types of cancer have been identified. There are three basic categories of cancer: carcinoma (cancer of the epithelial cells, which line organs and secrete mucus, among other functions), sarcoma (cancer of connective tissue, such as bone, fat, and muscle), and fluid cancers (for example, leukemia). Some cancers may fall into more than one category.

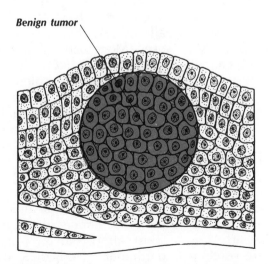

*Benign tumor*

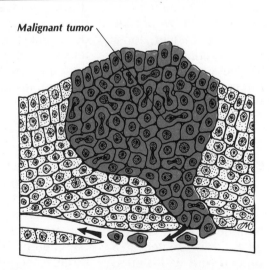

*Malignant tumor*

*A tumor may be either benign (noncancerous) or malignant (cancerous). A benign tumor commonly grows within a self-produced capsule and does not invade surrounding tissue or spread itself throughout the body (metastasize). A malignant tumor may grow out of control and metastasize.*

## DIAGNOSIS

If you suspect you may have cancer, *do not delay* in seeing a physician. Following a physical examination, if the doctor suspects abnormal growth, he or she may order a series of tests, including special x-ray examinations (for example, tomograms or CT scans, in which successive x-rays at slightly different levels are used to create a three-dimensional image of a structure), nuclear medicine scans (in which radioactive substances are used in the imaging process), ultrasound scanning (a technique that uses sound waves to create images of internal structures), cytologic tests (microscopic examination of cells), and various laboratory evaluations. The doctor may also order a biopsy (removal of a small tissue sample for microscopic examination) to determine the cell type of the suspected growth and whether it is benign or malignant.

Your physician may also refer you to a specialist with expertise in treating the type of cancer that you have. This may be an oncologist (cancer specialist), a cancer surgeon, a radiation oncologist (radiologist who uses radiation to treat cancer), or a hematologist (specialist in blood diseases). These physicians are specially trained to deal with the diagnosis and treatment of cancer.

## WHERE TO SEEK MEDICAL HELP

There are many places to get cancer treatment. Most cancers can be effectively treated at a well-equipped and well-staffed community hospital. There are, however, a number of large cancer centers throughout the country where specialized treatment programs (called protocols) are available. Often diagnosis and treatment are initiated at a special center and then continued in the community by an oncologist or a family physician. If you need information or referrals, cancer hotlines and the American Cancer Society are valuable resources. They or your personal physician should be able to assist you in getting a second opinion about your case, if you want one.

## TREATMENT

There are many ways of treating cancer. Many treatment protocols have been developed that are effective in certain types of disease. Cancer therapy often includes surgery to remove the cancer, to clear obstructions of vital passageways caused by the cancer, or to cut nerves sending pain messages to the brain; chemotherapy (use of powerful drugs to kill cancer cells); radiation therapy (use of radioactive materials in the form of energy beams or radioactive implants to destroy cancer cells); and immunotherapy (use of naturally occurring substances, such as interferon, to bolster the body's immune system). Combinations of therapies are often used.

### Surgery

Surgery is the most commonly used method of dealing with cancers that develop into tumors. If cancer is contained in one area, surgery can sometimes completely eliminate it. New surgical techniques are continually expanding the range of tumors that can be safely removed. Furthermore, if the surgeon is able to remove only a part of the tumor, the reduced tumor can often be successfully controlled with chemotherapy or radiation therapy.

More precise surgical techniques mean that surgery today is often less disfiguring than in the past. In addition, new developments in skin grafting make it possible to begin reconstructive work on patients—for instance, those with cancer of the head and neck—simultaneously with the cancer surgery.

Sometimes surgery is performed on a patient even though it is known that surgery will not cure the cancer. The removal of a tumor may simply make the patient more comfortable. In other cases, nerve pathways to the pain center in the brain may be cut. Certain noncancerous growths may be removed because they may develop into cancer or because they are exerting pressure on adjacent anatomic structures (which may lead to functional problems).

### Chemotherapy

Chemotherapy (the treatment of cancer with drugs) has gradually become much more widely used. More than 12 kinds of cancer can be effectively treated with chemotherapy alone. However, cancer drugs are most often used as an adjuvant (supplement) to primary treatment, such as surgery. Once surgery has reduced a cancerous growth, chemotherapy can often eliminate it. Chemotherapy has proved effective against some forms of cancer that formerly were almost always fatal, in particular, Hodgkin's disease (cancer of the lymph system), acute lymphocytic leukemia (a blood disease predominantly of children), and cancer of the testes (male sex glands).

Most cancer drugs attack any rapidly reproducing cells in the body, whether they are cancerous or not, producing some of the side effects of chemotherapy. Destruction of normal cells that reproduce frequently, such as those in the digestive tract, the hair follicles, and the bone marrow, can lead to nausea, hair loss, and lowered red blood cell count.

Usually, several drugs are administered in combination. If the cancer does not respond, or if resistance to a medication develops, another combination of drugs may be tried.

### Radiation therapy

Radiation destroys the ability of cells to divide. Cancer cells are far more susceptible to radiation than normal cells, although not all cancers respond to radiation. Like surgery, radiation therapy is usually a localized treatment, directed at a particular cancer site. Radiation treatment may also involve directly implanting into a tumor a radioactive object that destroys it from within. Radiation can be used before surgery to reduce a tumor to operable size, and frequently a patient receives radiation after surgery to destroy any cancer cells that might remain near the cancer site. Some tumors can be treated by radiation alone.

Radiation therapy is continually being refined. Drugs have been discovered that make cancer cells more sensitive to radiation. Different forms of radiation are being tested on resistant cancers. In addition, radiation today can be directed more precisely, and in stronger forms,

with little harm to surrounding tissue. However, there are still side effects, including loss of appetite, nausea, and temporary hair loss. It is not certain how dangerous it is to be treated with radiation, which is itself carcinogenic (capable of causing cancer); however, it is generally considered that a cancer in the body is far more threatening than the future effects of radiation therapy.

### Immunotherapy

The goal of immunotherapy is to enable the patient's body to produce substances that resist the growth of cancer. The basis of immunotherapy is the theory that cancer develops when, for some reason, the body fails to destroy abnormal cells. Immunotherapy for the treatment of cancer is still in the experimental stage.

### Unorthodox treatments

Sometimes, in desperation, a patient or his family will seek unorthodox methods of treatment, such as various forms of dietary therapy and the use of drugs of unproved value.

One such unorthodox treatment is the use of laetrile, an extract of apricot pits that some have proclaimed is a cure for cancer. This substance has been banned in the United States because it has been shown to be of no value against cancer in laboratory animals and has yet to be adequately tested in humans. Furthermore, laetrile has been shown to be poisonous.

The medical community is actively researching all known methods of treating cancer and carefully evaluating those that

look most promising. Many treatments are slow and often have severe side effects. Many quack cures offer—but do not deliver—rapid cure with fewer side effects. The harm done by quack practitioners is that they prevent a patient from seeking effective treatment until it is too late for any treatment to be of use. The best advice is to trust a physician to treat cancer and not waste time, money, and hope on an unproved "cure."

## PROGNOSTIC FACTORS

If you do develop cancer, a number of prognostic factors (factors that predict length of survival) are important. Most important are the stage and the type of the disease. The earlier the stage of the disease (that is, the earlier in its course it is diagnosed), the better the prognosis will be. The type of tumor is also important, since the various types respond differently to treatment. Furthermore, more than one type of cancer can occur within a specific organ. For example, all lung cancers do not involve the same kind of cell. Your age and overall physical condition are also important in determining your ability to win the fight against cancer.

Cancer should no longer be considered the dreaded scourge that it was 20 years ago. It is not always fatal and is, in many instances, curable. The keys to living today should be to avoid carcinogens (cancer-causing substances, such as tobacco and asbestos), to consult your physician regularly (and discuss possible risk factors), and to perform regularly the important self-examination procedures that your doctor suggests. Early detection is extremely important.

# Bladder cancer

This is the most common cancer of the urinary tract. It occurs most often between the ages of 50 and 70 and is the fourth leading cause of cancer death among men. Four times as many men as women are afflicted.

Bladder cancer has been connected with exposure to a number of carcinogens. This may be because the urinary tract comes into contact with so many foreign substances due to its excretory function. For many years it has been known that those who work with aniline dyes have a high incidence of cancer of the bladder. Bladder cancer is also associated with exposure to tar from tobacco smoke and with schistosomiasis (infestation with a tropical parasite).

Blood in the urine is usually the first symptom of bladder cancer. In addition, urination may be difficult, painful, and frequent. The appearance of blood in the urine may be intermittent, and if this symptom disappears, a doctor is sometimes not consulted. However, anyone with blood in the urine should consult a doctor, since in the early stages this disease is highly curable, and treatment is far more difficult later. If your doctor considers that the symptoms suggest bladder cancer, a cystoscopic examination may be ordered. With the patient under local or general anesthesia, a lighted, tubelike instrument called a cystoscope is passed into the urinary tract through the urethra (the passageway from the bladder to the outside), so that the interior of the bladder can be examined. This instrument can also be used to obtain a biopsy specimen (a small sample of tissue for laboratory analysis) of a suspicious growth.

Treatment of bladder cancer depends on how far advanced the disease is. A small tumor can sometimes be completely removed with a cystoscope. More advanced cases are treated with surgery or radiation or a combination of the two.

# Bone cancer

This rare form of cancer is most common in those between the ages of 5 and 20. Predisposing factors include bone diseases, bone fractures, and exposure to radiation.

Bone cancer usually develops first in the arms or legs. Pain, swelling, and brittleness of the bone may be its symptoms. It is often far advanced by the time it is discovered. The first tool in diagnosis is the x-ray, which may show whether the bone is cancerous and whether the disease has spread. If cancer is suspected, an orthopedic surgeon generally performs a biopsy. Bone cancer is usually treated with a combination of surgery, radiation, and chemotherapy.

# Brain cancer

Any tumor in the brain, whether cancerous or not, is very dangerous. Because the brain occupies an enclosed space within the skull, even a small tumor that weighs only a fifth of a pound can cause crowding sufficient to bring on death. Brain cancer is most often the result of metastasis from other cancer sites, particularly the breast, lung, and skin.

Symptoms of brain cancer are of two kinds. Increased pressure in the skull can cause seizures, headaches, nausea, forgetfulness, and personality changes.

However, symptoms may also arise in the part of the body controlled by the affected area in the brain. For instance, coordination, vision, or strength of limbs may be affected. In the past, brain tumors did not respond well to treatment, largely because diagnosis could not be made until late in the development of the disease. Recently, however, diagnostic techniques have improved. The CT scanner produces a three-dimensional image of the brain that can show the size and location of a tumor and can be used to monitor the progress of treatment. A new technique, magnetic resonance imaging, is also being used.

Surgery is the primary treatment for brain cancer. It is often not used, however, when cancer is present in multiple areas or when the tumor originated in another organ. Surgery in the brain is a delicate procedure; often, a tumor deep in the brain cannot be totally removed without risking impairment of body function. However, new techniques in brain surgery—sometimes with the use of a microscope—permit treatment of tumors once considered inoperable. Radiation therapy and chemotherapy are often used after surgery, although the sensitivity of brain tissue demands that these be administered cautiously. Steroid drugs may be given to reduce the dangerous swelling that a tumor can produce.

# Breast cancer

About one woman in 13 will develop breast cancer at some time in her life. It is the leading cause of cancer death in women and the leading cause of all deaths in women between the

*In the shower, examine each breast with the opposite hand while keeping the other hand overhead. Having wet, soapy skin may make it easier to feel lumps.*

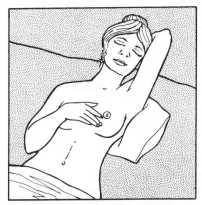

*Lie in bed with a pillow under one shoulder to elevate and flatten the breast. Examine each breast with the opposite hand, first with the arm on the same side as the breast under the head and then with that arm at the side.*

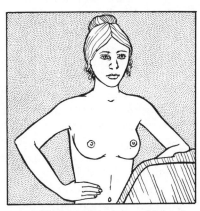

*Stand in front of a mirror, with hands resting on hips. Examine breasts for swelling, dimpling, bulges, and changes in skin.*

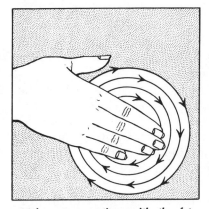

*Make rotary motions with the fat pads, not the tips, of the fingers, moving in concentric circles inward toward the nipple. Feel for knots, lumps, or indentations. Be sure to include the armpit area.*

*Standing in front of a mirror with arms extended overhead, examine breasts for changes. This position highlights bulges and indentations, which may indicate a lump.*

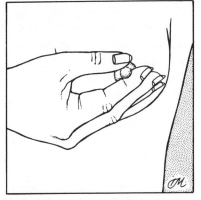

*Squeeze nipples gently to inspect for discharge. Report any suspicious findings to your doctor.*

ages of 40 and 44. The high-risk group includes women over 35, women who have never had children or who had a child for the first time after the age of 30, and women who began menstruation early or who experienced late menopause. Breast cancer also occurs more frequently in chemical workers, women with a family history of the disease, and women who have already had breast cancer.

Self-examination of the breasts can often lead to early detection. All women should perform these examinations monthly at the end of the menstrual period. About 90 percent of all breast tumors are discovered by self-examination. The recommended technique for breast self-examination is shown in the illustration in this section.

If a lump is discovered in a breast, the doctor will probably order an x-ray examination of the breast, known as a mammogram. The doctor may also take a biopsy specimen from the lump to test for the presence of cancer. If cancer is identified, surgery will probably be performed. Women with breast cancer often dread surgery because of the disfigurement that can result; however, surgery for a breast tumor is often less extensive today than in the past. At one time, all breast cancer patients received a radical mastectomy (removal of the breast, underlying chest muscles, and lymph nodes in the armpit). Now it is known that in many cases the removal of the breast, or even the tumor alone, may be equally effective. In addition, there are techniques for reconstruction of the breast after surgery and for rehabilitation of muscle tone in an arm that has been weakened by surgery. In some cases, radiation therapy

and chemotherapy will be used after surgery to destroy remaining cancer cells.

vanced forms of the disease are treated with radiation as well as surgery.

lower abdominal wall. A colostomy is covered with a bag to collect waste material.

# Cervical cancer

The cervix is the lower part of the uterus (womb), which extends into the vagina. Cancer of the cervix is the second most common cancer among American women. The death rate from this disease has decreased 50 percent over the last 50 years, largely as a result of early diagnosis. Early cervical cancer has no symptoms but can be detected by means of a Pap smear. A Pap smear is performed routinely in a doctor's office by scraping the surface of the cervix. The collected material is then tested for indications of cancer. Today, two out of three cases of cervical cancer are detected with this test before they display symptoms.

Cervical cancer has a higher incidence among black women and poor women. This cancer also occurs more frequently among women who were sexually active early with many partners and among those with genital herpes.

If a Pap smear indicates the possibility of cervical cancer, a biopsy of the affected area will probably be performed. Treatment depends on how far the disease has advanced; early forms are almost always curable by surgery. If a patient still hopes to bear children, and the cancer is in an early stage, this surgery can sometimes be put off until after children have been born. However, this is possible only if the disease does not seem to be progressing, and the cancer must be monitored carefully during this phase. The uterus should be removed eventually. More ad-

# Colon cancer

Every year about 40,000 Americans die of cancer of the colon and rectum. About half of all cases of cancer of the colon can be cured by surgery, and early detection can greatly improve this percentage. A simple test for occult (not visible to the naked eye) blood in the stool can indicate whether further tests should be made for the presence of this type of cancer. Everyone who is over 40 or who has chronic digestive problems should have this test regularly. Cure is twice as likely if the disease is discovered before symptoms occur.

Symptoms of cancer of the colon include a change in bowel movements, bleeding from the rectum, pencil-thin stools, and abdominal discomfort not eased by bowel movement. If you have any of these symptoms, your doctor will probably perform a rectal exam, inserting a finger into the rectum to search for unusual growths. If further examination is necessary, the doctor may introduce a sigmoidoscope (a lighted, tubelike instrument) into the colon through the anus. This instrument permits examination of the inside of the colon and can also be used to obtain a biopsy specimen of a suspicious growth. Sometimes a noncancerous growth called a polyp is removed with a similar instrument, because such a growth may become cancerous.

Surgery is the usual treatment for cancer of the colon. If the cancer is near or in the rectum, the surgeon may remove all of the rectum and create an artificial rectum, or colostomy, in the

# Leukemia

This is a disease that originates in the bone marrow, the site of blood cell production. The term *leukemia,* which is derived from Greek words that mean literally "white blood," refers to the fact that this disease is characterized by the presence of excessive numbers of white blood cells, especially immature and poorly functioning forms of these cells.

The symptoms of leukemia result from the impairment of normal blood cell functions. The primary role of white blood cells is fighting infection. Since many of the white blood cells present are immature, they function poorly and infections are common. Other blood cell types normally present in bone marrow (red blood cells, which carry oxygen throughout the body, and platelets, which are needed for blood clotting) may be crowded out by the cancerous leukemic cells. As a result, symptoms of deficiency of these cell types are often evident in leukemia patients. Symptoms include poor blood-clotting ability (due to a shortage of platelets) and tiredness resulting from anemia (due to decreased numbers of red blood cells). Other symptoms are easy bruising, bleeding from the gums, blood in the stools, fever, and frequent infections. The spleen and lymph nodes are usually enlarged.

A diagnosis of leukemia should be made by a cancer specialist. The doctor will probably insert a needle into the hipbone to withdraw a sample of the bone marrow, which will be tested for the presence of cancer.

Leukemia is often treated first with intensive chemotherapy to kill the cancer cells. The patient may appear to become even more ill during treatment because of the side effects of the cancer-fighting drugs. After this initial treatment phase, radiation and additional drugs may be administered. Bone marrow transplants are now often used.

Leukemia is the most common form of cancer in children. In recent years the outlook has improved dramatically for children with this disease. Twenty years ago, nearly all children who suffered from leukemia died. Today, the life spans of many are prolonged or normal.

# Liver cancer

Liver cancer usually results from the spread of cancer cells from another site in the body. However, cancer that originates in the liver can sometimes be traced to environmental carcinogens. It is known that anyone who has worked with vinyl chloride, a chemical used in plastics manufacture, has a higher risk of this disease. It also appears that cirrhosis of the liver (a disease in which normal liver cells are replaced by fibrous tissue) may cause an individual to be more susceptible to cancer of the liver.

Symptoms of liver cancer are difficult to identify. They may resemble the signs of a peptic ulcer—aching or burning pain in the upper abdomen, nausea, and vomiting. A swollen or hardened liver often indicates to the doctor the need for further diagnostic evaluation.

If this form of cancer is diagnosed early and is confined to the liver, it can be treated surgically, but most often the prognosis is not good.

# Lung cancer

Cigarette smoking is generally accepted as the major cause of lung cancer. Lung cancer is the leading cause of cancer death in men, and in recent years the incidence of lung cancer in women has been growing, probably as a result of the increase in the number of women who smoke. The incidence of lung cancer is also increasing among nonsmokers, possibly due to improved diagnostic techniques (many lung tumors were once diagnosed as tuberculosis) and to environmental pollution.

If you smoke and are over 45, or if you have a family history of lung cancer, you should be on the lookout for symptoms, since the early signs—a persistent cough or lingering respiratory discomfort—can be very mild. Later, coughing will increase, as will chest pain and shortness of breath, and blood may be found in the sputum (the material coughed up from the lungs).

A cancerous tumor in the lung is usually removed surgically. It is sometimes necessary to remove an entire lobe of the lung. Because lung cancers are usually not detected until they are well advanced, surgery alone may not be able to eliminate them, and radiation and chemotherapy may be used in combination with or in place of surgery.

In recent years, the deadliest form of lung cancer, small-cell carcinoma (also called oat-cell carcinoma), has yielded to a new drug therapy that has produced remission (absence of symptoms) in some patients.

# Lymphoma

This cancer attacks the lymphatic system, particularly the lymph nodes and the spleen. These organs manufacture lymphocytes (cells that protect the body against infection).

The first symptom of lymphoma is usually a swollen spleen or swollen lymph nodes in the neck, armpit, or groin (the juncture between the lower abdomen and the inner thigh). Fever and sweating are later symptoms. If these symptoms persist, a doctor should be consulted. If the doctor suspects cancer, a biopsy of the enlarged organ will probably be ordered.

There are two major forms of lymphoma: Hodgkin's disease and non-Hodgkin's lymphoma. In recent years, there have been dramatic strides in the treatment of Hodgkin's disease. In the early stages, radiation alone can be very effective. Later in the course of the disease, more extensive radiation or a combination of radiation and chemotherapy may be required. Treatment of non-Hodgkin's lymphoma is much the same as that of Hodgkin's disease. In the past, this form of lymphoma was usually discovered too late for treatment, but recent advances have made long periods of remission possible in many cases.

# Ovarian cancer

This is the most dangerous form of cancer of the female reproductive organs, because it is so difficult to diagnose in its early stages. Women over 50 have a higher incidence of the disease, as do childless women and those with a family history of ovarian cancer.

Symptoms may include pelvic discomfort, constipation, abdominal swelling, and irregular menstruation. Diagnosis is often not possible without an explor-

atory operation known as a laparotomy, during which a flexible, lighted, tubelike instrument is inserted through the abdominal wall for direct examination and sometimes treatment. Sometimes it is sufficient to remove only one ovary, but usually it is necessary to remove both ovaries and the uterus. Radiation therapy and chemotherapy may then be administered.

## Prostate cancer

After lung cancer, this is the most common cancer among men. Black Americans have a higher incidence of prostate cancer than any other group in the world. In general, it is more common in men over 55. Cancer of the prostate (the male sex gland that lies at the base of the bladder) can develop very slowly, often producing no symptoms until the disease is far advanced. Sometimes a routine examination discloses a lump in the prostate, which proves to be cancerous in about 50 percent of cases. Prostate examinations should be included in medical checkups of all men over 50.

When symptoms occur, they are usually the result of enlargement of the prostate, which causes difficult urination or blood in the urine. Prostate cancer often spreads to the bone, and patients may complain of bone pain before they show any other symptoms.

In the small percentage of cases in which prostate cancer is discovered before it has begun to spread, the cancer can be removed by surgery or radiation. When the disease has spread, usually only its symptoms are treated as they occur. Often a patient can live a long time with this form of treatment.

## Skin cancer

About 300,000 cases of skin cancer are discovered every year. Its incidence increases every year, particularly among women, perhaps because people currently are getting more exposure to sunlight. The ultraviolet rays of the sun are a major cause of skin cancer. Fair-skinned people have less melanin (a protective substance in the skin) than dark-skinned people do and are therefore more susceptible to the effects of these rays. Skin cancer can also result from prolonged exposure to certain chemicals, such as arsenic compounds. Burn scars and skin diseases sometimes develop into cancer.

Symptoms of skin cancer are a change in the surface of the skin, a wound that does not heal, and a sudden major change in a wart, mole, or birthmark. All such suspicious signs should be examined by a doctor.

Most skin cancers are highly treatable. Some can be removed in a doctor's office or an outpatient clinic. But since some forms of skin cancer can spread throughout the body, it is important that they be treated early. The most dangerous skin cancer, malignant melanoma, can metastasize through the lymph and vascular (blood vessel) systems. Melanomas usually develop from moles.

Skin cancer is an unusual form of cancer in that it can be prevented easily. Fair-skinned people and anyone with a family history of skin cancer should avoid exposure to the sun. Additionally, everyone who spends time in the sun should apply a protective sunscreen to exposed portions of the body. It is important that children, whose skin is more sensitive, be protected against the sun. The use of certain drugs, such as barbiturates, antibiotics, and birth control pills, can increase the sensitivity of the skin.

## Stomach cancer

The incidence of stomach cancer has decreased by 50 percent in the last 25 years. A change in diet may account for this. Stomach cancer is more common in men than in women and usually occurs between the ages of 50 and 70. The high-risk group includes those with a history of pernicious anemia or alcoholism and those who choose a diet rich in smoked, pickled, or salted foods.

The symptoms of stomach cancer are similar to those of peptic ulcer (heartburn and abdominal discomfort), which may make diagnosis more difficult. It may not be until the disease is well advanced that the identifying symptoms of bloody stools or vomit appear. A special x-ray study may be obtained after the patient swallows barium (a contrast substance that coats the lining of the stomach), which allows visualization of irregularities in the stomach (such as the presence of a tumor) on x-ray films. If a tumor is identified, a flexible, lighted, tubelike instrument called an endoscope may be inserted down the throat into the stomach to examine the tumor more closely and perhaps obtain a biopsy specimen of it.

Surgery is the most effective treatment of this disease, but only about 10 percent of victims survive more than five years after diagnosis. Surgery is most useful when the tumor has not begun to spread. It is sometimes necessary to remove all or part of the stomach. After such surgery, the patient will require a modified diet.

## Uterine cancer

This disease is most common in women over the age of 50. Especially susceptible are women who have never borne children, those who are obese or diabetic, and those who suffer from high blood pressure. Women who have taken the female hormone estrogen are probably at higher risk than those who have not.

Vaginal bleeding after menopause is the most common symptom of uterine cancer. If a Pap smear shows no abnormalities, a minor surgical procedure known as dilatation and curettage (D&C) may be performed. This involves scraping the interior walls of the uterus in order to examine the tissue for the presence of cancer. If cancer is identified, a hysterectomy (surgical removal of the uterus) is usually performed. (Often, the ovaries are removed as well.) Cancer of the uterus is harder to detect than that of the cervix; it is often discovered when it is too advanced for successful treatment.

## Vaginal cancer

Once confined to women over 50 years of age, vaginal cancer has begun to appear in women between the ages of 17 and 20. The mothers of most of these young women took artificial estrogens, particularly diethylstilbestrol (DES), during pregnancy to prevent miscarriage. A woman whose mother took artificial estrogens during pregnancy should have a Pap smear twice a year. Symptoms of vaginal cancer include vaginal pain and bleeding. The disease is usually treated with radiation.

# FACTS ABOUT MEDICAL TESTS

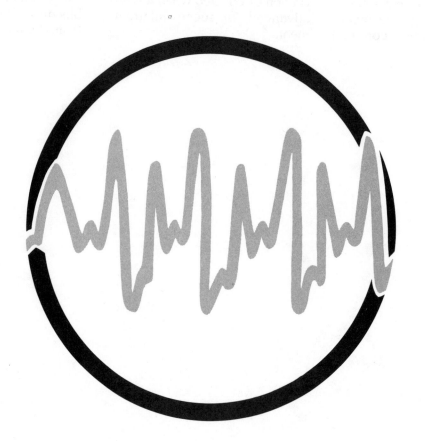

The basis of medical evaluation is a complete medical history and physical examination. Common health problems are primarily detected and diagnosed by means of the history and physical examination. Nevertheless, your doctor will also use a variety of diagnostic aids and tests to rule out a disease, to confirm a diagnosis, or to detect a disorder that is not apparent. Modern technology now enables medical professionals to inspect the structure of a cell, to see the inside of an organ, and to examine a detailed cross-sectional picture of the body. These tests provide essential information to aid your doctor in the diagnosis of illness and the selection of appropriate treatment.

This section is a guide to some of the more common medical tests and how they are performed.

# Common tests

## BLOOD TESTS

Although some blood tests can be done on a sample from a finger prick, most tests require a larger sample. The complete blood cell count (the most common of the blood tests) and blood chemistry screening tests are usually based on blood samples drawn by venipuncture (puncture of a vein by a hypodermic needle). The procedure is quick and relatively painless. The doctor who orders the blood tests will most often submit all the test orders together, so that more than one venipuncture is not needed.

Although some patients fear that a great volume of blood is being drawn in venipuncture, the usual laboratory tests do not ordinarily require more than 10 to 20 milliliters (two to four teaspoons). The total amount of blood circulating in the body of the average person is at least six quarts at any given time and is constantly being replenished. Therefore, fears about unusual blood loss from such testing are groundless.

## Complete blood cell count

A complete blood cell count (CBC) determines the number and types of blood cells in the blood. The CBC includes:
• Hematocrit—to measure how much of the blood is made up of red blood cells alone
• Hemoglobin test—to measure the amount of hemoglobin (the blood substance that carries oxygen to the body tissues) present in a given volume of red blood cells
• White blood cell count—to find out how many white blood cells are in the blood
• Differential count—to learn how many of the various types of white blood cells are present in the blood
• Platelet count—to determine the number of platelets (the blood elements that aid in clotting the blood) that are present

## Blood chemistry tests

Besides the complete blood cell count, there are other blood tests that together constitute what is known as a blood chemistry panel. These tests, which analyze many components and chemicals in the blood, can be done from a single sample of blood within minutes, using an automated blood chemistry machine.

Blood chemistry studies are performed routinely as screening tests for the detection of certain disorders, such as diabetes and kidney disease. They are also used as diagnostic tests when specific diseases, such as hepatitis, are suspected. Blood chemistry profiles are frequently used to determine the overall function of an organ, especially the liver (the usual profiles contain three or four indicators of liver function). These tests may not pinpoint a specific disease of the liver, but instead provide a general indication of whether the liver is functioning normally and whether specific diagnostic tests need to be performed. Many illnesses affect more than one organ; furthermore, failure in one organ may cause problems in another. It is here that blood chemistry profiles have great utility; using one sample, they give information about the function of several organs (particularly the liver and kidneys).

The following list briefly explains the purpose of some of the more common blood chemistry tests:
• Blood glucose—to aid in diagnosing diabetes mellitus (glucose is a form of sugar)
• Blood urea nitrogen (BUN)—to assess kidney function
• Creatinine—to assess kidney function
• Electrolytes—to check body fluid and salt balance (salts include sodium, potassium, and chloride)
• Uric acid—to aid in diagnosing gout
• Cholesterol or triglycerides—to measure fat levels in the blood
• Bilirubin—to assess liver function, to evaluate jaundice, and to help diagnose anemia
• Albumin—to assess general nutritional status and to get a general idea of liver function (albumin is a type of protein produced by the liver)

## URINALYSIS

A routine urinalysis is a microscopic examination and chemical analysis of the urine. If red or white blood cells can be seen under the microscope, bleeding or an infection is present somewhere along the urinary tract. Other microscopic elements, such as casts (formations of protein with or without cellular elements, which usually indicate disease in the kidneys) and crystals (of uric acid or calcium, for example) may also be seen. A chemical analysis can determine the presence of sugar, protein, or other substances that may indicate kidney or bladder diseases, as well as disorders unrelated to the urinary tract, such as diabetes mellitus and starvation. There is no risk to this test.

The patient is given a clean container and told to urinate directly into it. When a urine culture is indicated, a "midstream" specimen is usually requested, that is, a specimen obtained after the urinary tract opening has been properly cleansed and the initial spurt of urine has been passed. If you are to collect the specimen at home, you should also be provided with a clean container with a cap. If not, you should use a clean plastic or glass container. A container that has held food, perfume, chemicals, or cosmetics should not be used. Such containers may be difficult to empty and may still contain traces of the original contents, which would invalidate the test results.

## CHEST X-RAY

The most common standard x-ray examination is the chest x-ray, usually used to check for signs of lung diseases and abnor-

malities. Because the heart, parts of the aorta (the large artery that carries blood from the heart to much of the body), the ribs, the upper spine, the shoulders, the upper arm bones, and the collarbones are also seen, diseases other than those that affect the lungs, such as congestive heart failure (enlargement of the heart accompanied by fluid buildup in the lungs and their blood vessels), may be diagnosed and followed up with chest x-rays.

The patient undresses from the waist up. The usual chest x-ray is taken in two positions: with the patient standing sideways and with either his chest or his back resting against the cassette containing the x-ray film. The patient must be correctly positioned and must remain motionless if good x-ray pictures are to be obtained. The test is painless. The actual time of exposure to radiation is quite short; however, if the test is overused, there may be a risk of long-term effects of radiation exposure. Routine x-rays should be avoided by pregnant women; if such an examination is necessary, a lead shield can be used to protect the developing baby.

## ELECTROCARDIOGRAM

An electrocardiogram (ECG) is a visual record of the heart's electrical impulses, which control the rate and rhythm of beating and reflect many alterations in the heart muscle. This test, along with the history and physical examination, is used to diagnose a number of heart disorders, including previous and new myocardial infarctions (heart attacks), some congenital (present at birth) abnormalities of the heart, pericarditis (inflammation of the sac surrounding the heart),

and abnormal thickness of the muscle (such as is seen in long-term high blood pressure). There is no risk to this test, and it is totally painless.

Electrodes (small metal disks that are sensitive to the heart's impulses) are taped onto the body at various points on the chest, arms, and legs. The electrode cables are connected to the electrocardiograph, a machine that produces a visual record of the impulses. The ECG tracing for a normal heart consists of regularly occurring wave patterns, whereas that for an abnormal heart will show alterations in the rhythm or appearance of the wave patterns.

## STOOL BLOOD TEST

This test is used to detect tiny quantities of occult (hidden) blood in the stool (feces) that are not visible without a microscope. The presence of occult blood may signal bowel disease or bleeding somewhere along the digestive tract.

The test is usually done by the patient at home and mailed to a laboratory. The patient places a small sample of stool on specially coated paper that will reveal any blood when treated with a special developer. The test may have to be done several times, since the bleeding may be intermittent. The patient will be instructed to eat no red meat for at least three days before taking the stool specimen (the blood from meat, including cooked meat, may cause a falsely positive result on the test) and to take no aspirin-containing medications (aspirin may cause bleeding from the stomach).

This test is painless and has no risk. It is an excellent method of screening for colon cancer.

## THROAT CULTURE

This common procedure is used to determine the type of microorganisms causing infection in the throat. A sample of bacteria is obtained by rolling a cotton-tipped applicator around the swollen area. The test is painless but may cause gagging.

The cell samples are placed in a culture medium (a special mixture of chemicals and nutrients designed to support growth of bacteria), so that growth of microorganisms can be detected and measured. Special procedures are used to identify the specific types of bacteria. This procedure usually takes from 24 to 48 hours for definitive results.

Recently, "instant" throat cultures specifically for the detection of streptococcal infection have become available. The results are known within 15 minutes and are generally reliable.

# Special diagnostic tests

## ALLERGY TESTS

Tests to determine the existence of various allergies are as numerous and complex as the substances (called allergens) that cause the allergic responses. One of the most common allergy tests is the skin test. This procedure can be either a scratch skin test or an intracutaneous skin test. In the scratch test, suspected allergens are applied in small amounts to individual, tiny scratches on the skin, often several at a time and in a prescribed order. In the intracutaneous skin test, small quantities of the suspected allergens are injected into or under the skin. After a short period of time (about one half hour), the doctor notes which substances have caused a reaction. In both of these tests, a swollen, reddish bump at the site of the application is a positive reaction to that allergen. The skin scratches and injections can be uncomfortable while the procedures are being performed. In addition, there is the risk that an extremely sensitive individual may have an allergic reaction.

There is also a blood test to help identify allergens. The test, called a radioallergosorbent test (RAST), measures specific antibodies in the blood. Antibodies are substances formed by the immune system in response to foreign invaders, such as allergens. The test can be used for those people who should not have skin tests—persons with extremely sensitive skin, very young children, and persons suspected of being extremely sensitive to an injected allergen. However, the RAST may not be as sensitive as skin tests and is more expensive.

In the case of food allergies, diagnosis is often difficult. One method of identifying allergens is to have samples of suspected allergy-causing foods eaten in small quantities at times when there is nothing in the digestive system. Symptoms, if any, are noted. Adequate time is required between food samples so that each sample can clear the system before the next food is given. Someone with a history of severe reactions should not be tested in this fashion. Skin testing may be useful.

## BIOPSY

A biopsy is the removal of a small sample of tissue for examination under a microscope. This procedure is done to establish a precise diagnosis of abnormalities, including cancer. The tissue may be obtained by cutting, by aspirating (suctioning) with a needle, or by other methods, depending on the part of the body from which the sample is to be removed. For example, endoscopic biopsy is removal of tissue by instruments attached to or passed through an endoscope (a flexible, lighted, tubelike device) into a hollow organ, such as the colon.

The procedure varies with the type of biopsy to be performed. Some biopsies require hospitalization, especially if surgery is necessary to obtain a specimen from an internal organ. Other procedures, such as biopsy of small skin growths and needle aspiration of a breast lump, can be done in a doctor's office or an outpatient clinic. Many biopsies are done with some type of anesthesia, and there may be discomfort if a biopsy involves cutting or an invasive technique (one involving the insertion of an instrument or other device into the body). Also, there is some risk, which varies with the procedure being performed. The risks of outpatient biopsies are usually minimal, but complications, such as excessive bleeding, can occur.

## CARDIAC STRESS TEST

The cardiac stress test, also often called the treadmill test, is done basically to determine the reaction of the cardiovascular system (the heart and blood vessels) to physical exercise. Devices other than a treadmill, such as a bicycle, can also be used, depending on the situation. A stress test is done for many reasons—among them, to determine whether the cause of chest pain is a heart abnormality, to detect the presence of coronary artery disease, and to follow the progress of a patient in cardiac rehabilitation.

The patient is told to sleep well and eat lightly the night before the test and not to eat for at least three hours before the test. At the lab, the patient will put on exercise clothes and running shoes and will be questioned about his recent medical history and exercise habits.

For the test, electrodes for continuous electrocardiographic recording are attached so that the tester (usually a cardiologist) can monitor the heart rate and the response of the heart to graded exercise. A blood pressure cuff is also attached to one arm.

The patient then starts walking on the treadmill at a low work load. The work load (determined by the speed and incline of the treadmill) is gradually increased, usually at three-minute intervals, until the patient: (1) attains about 90 percent of the predicted maximum heart rate for his age (obtained from standardized tables); (2) experiences symptoms or electrocardiographic changes consistent with heart disease; or (3) cannot continue the test for some reason (for example, leg cramps or shortness of breath).

The time it takes to reach the target heart rate is related to the degree of cardiovascular fitness, but is not necessarily related to the presence or absence of heart disease. That is, an individual who attains his peak heart rate at only six minutes is less fit than someone who can exercise for 12 minutes on the treadmill before attaining peak heart rate. However, either individual may have changes or symptoms indicating heart disease.

At the individual's maximum performance level, the closer he comes to the predicted maximum heart rate, the more meaningful the test. For example, a negative ECG (indicating that there is no heart disease) would have greater diagnostic significance if it was obtained at a particular patient's age-predicted maximum heart rate of 180 beats per minute than if the patient had had to stop the test at a rate of 130 beats because of a leg cramp, fatigue, or some other noncardiovascular reason.

Stress tests may cause discomfort because of fatigue, tired muscles, and so forth. The main risk is bringing about a cardiac event, such as arrhythmia (abnormal heart rhythm) or a heart attack.

## CONTRAST EXAMINATIONS

Contrast media, known popularly as dyes, are materials that, when introduced into the body, alter radiopacity (the capacity to be "seen" on an x-ray examination of one part of the body in comparison with surrounding parts. The contrast materials are opaque, that is, they stop the passage of x-rays and are essential to visualize certain internal body organs, such as the stomach and intestines, which normally are not seen on x-ray examinations. When the contrast medium is introduced into the body, the radiologist performing the test often uses fluoroscopy (the projection of x-rays through the body onto a special screen) to observe the working of the internal body organs and then takes still x-ray films of the area being examined. Commonly performed contrast examinations include the upper gastrointestinal tract examination (upper GI

series), the lower gastrointestinal series (barium enema), the intravenous pyelogram (IVP, or kidney study), the gallbladder series, and the coronary angiogram (visualization of the heart and its blood vessels).

## Upper GI series

The upper GI series is a contrast examination of the esophagus, stomach, and duodenum (first part of the small intestine). This x-ray study is used to detect ulcers, cancer, and other abnormalities. The contrast medium used is barium sulfate, which is introduced by having the patient drink it after fasting overnight. The patient's stomach must be empty to accommodate the barium meal and also to avoid having food particles confuse the results. The radiologist observes the filling of the stomach on the fluoroscope as the patient drinks. The time required for the exam is about 30 minutes. In some instances, the doctor will order what is known as a small bowel follow-through, a series of x-rays taken to follow the movement of the barium through the small intestine. In this procedure, many films are taken at specified time intervals. This study may take hours. Patients can expect very light-colored stools after the test because of the presence of the barium sulfate. As with any x-ray examination, there may be a risk of effects from radiation exposure, but modern equipment and techniques have minimized this.

## Lower GI series

The lower GI series, or barium enema, is a contrast examination of the colon (large intestine), which is useful in detecting tumors, polyps (abnormal outgrowths of tissue from a mucous membrane), and other problems. For this examination, the colon must be cleared of all fecal matter. This is usually accomplished by taking a liquid diet for 24 to 48 hours, accompanied by laxatives and enemas. Nothing is then allowed by mouth until the examination has been completed. The time for the examination itself is usually about 30 minutes. The patient is given an enema consisting of a barium solution (which makes the colon opaque) introduced into the large intestine through a tube inserted into the anus; the solution must be retained until all the films have been obtained. When looking for polyps or when a detailed view of the lining of the colon is required, air is put into the colon to form a double contrast with the barium. This procedure is referred to as an "air-contrast barium enema" and is rapidly becoming more common than the plain lower GI series.

At the time of the examination, the radiologist observes the colon fluoroscopically as it fills with barium. X-ray films are made before, during, and after emptying of the barium-coated colon. Afterward, the patient is usually given a cleansing enema or a mild laxative to rid the colon of barium.

Although rare, obstruction of the colon by impacted (hardened) barium or perforation of the colon by the enema tube may occur. As with any x-ray study, there is a minimal risk from radiation exposure.

### Intravenous pyelogram (IVP)

This test is used to evaluate the size and functioning of the

kidneys and the urinary tract, as well as the presence of obstructions. In men, an enlarged prostate gland may also be noted. The test is done by injecting contrast material into a vein in the arm. The contrast material is then eliminated through the kidneys and urinary tract. X-ray films are made at specified time intervals to observe the rate of excretion, the concentration of the contrast medium inside the kidneys, and the outlines of the ureters (tubes from the kidneys to the bladder) and the bladder. Since fecal matter and gas in the intestinal tract obscure the observation of urinary tract structures, the lower bowel needs to be cleared for this examination. As with any x-ray study, there is a minimal risk from the effects of radiation exposure.

Patients with diabetes mellitus, kidney disease, or a history of previous reactions to x-ray contrast materials may be at risk of kidney damage or serious allergic reactions. These patients should inform the radiologist of such risk factors, because precautions can be taken to minimize the chance of complications.

### Gallbladder series

A gallbladder series, or oral cholecystogram, is performed to test gallbladder function and to detect gallstones. The oral cholecystogram allows correct diagnosis of gallbladder disease (including both poor function and gallstones) about 96 percent of the time.

For this examination, it is helpful to clear the intestinal tract of fecal matter and gas to allow for adequate viewing of the gallbladder. This is done by giving a special diet for the 24

hours before the examination and by administering enemas. Avoidance of cream, butter, and other fatty foods (fats stimulate the gallbladder, which must be at rest in order to concentrate the contrast material well) is also necessary.

Contrast medium in tablet form is given to the patient after dinner the day before the x-ray study begins. Usually, nothing is then given by mouth until the examination has been completed. If the gallbladder does not show up on the x-ray film (does not concentrate the contrast material), the dose of contrast is repeated the next day, and another film is taken. If the gallbladder still is not visible, this indicates that the gallbladder is diseased (assuming that the gastrointestinal tract and liver are processing the contrast material normally). In some x-ray departments, after the films of the contrast-filled gallbladder have been made, the patient is given a fatty meal to stimulate the gallbladder to empty, and another film is then obtained to evaluate this function. The time required for the actual examination is about one hour, excluding the time for the fatty meal.

There may be side effects, such as nausea, vomiting, and diarrhea. As with any x-ray study, there is a minimal risk from radiation exposure. There is also a risk (although uncommon) of an allergic reaction to the contrast material. Patients with diabetes and kidney disease should inform the radiologist so that precautions against kidney damage can be taken.

### Coronary angiography

Coronary angiography is required before most heart surgery

and for diagnosis of some heart diseases. In this procedure, the cardiologist introduces a tube called a catheter into the body, usually through a puncture in an artery in the groin or arm, and threads it through the vascular system until it reaches the heart. Through this catheter, an opaque contrast medium is injected, allowing moving pictures of the heart to be obtained. With this procedure, the cardiologist and the cardiovascular surgeon obtain crucial information, such as the location of defects in the walls and valves of the heart, the location and degree of narrowing of the coronary arteries (the arteries that supply blood to the heart muscle itself), and even the different pressures in the chambers (which reflect the overall functioning of the heart).

Nowadays, this procedure is commonly performed and carries a very low risk potential in the hands of experienced physicians. After the procedure, there is sometimes bleeding at the catheter introduction site, as well as mild discomfort there. During contrast injection, many patients complain of a ''hot flash'' or nausea. As with any x-ray study, there is a minimal risk of radiation exposure. Also, patients with diabetes, kidney disease, or a history of reaction to contrast materials may be at risk from the contrast material. Precautions can be taken to prevent complications if the physician performing the procedure is informed of these problems before the test. Possible risks should be discussed with the doctor.

## ELECTRO-ENCEPHALOGRAM

An electroencephalogram, or EEG, is a visual record of electri-

cal impulses discharged by brain cells. The EEG is used to detect abnormalities in the brain. The test is painless and without risk.

Electrodes (small metal disks) are placed at specified points on the surface of the head (in special circumstances, disks may be inserted through the nose into the throat, which may be uncomfortable) and then attached to the electroencephalograph, which is a machine that produces a visual tracing of the brain's electrical waves. If, for instance, the brain has been damaged or the patient has epilepsy, the waves produced by the electrical discharges form characteristic patterns. Tracings are taken when the patient is awake and calm; when he or she has been asked to hyperventilate (breathe rapidly) and has been stimulated with a flashing light, which may evoke changes characteristic of epileptic grand mal seizures; and when the patient is asleep. An EEG usually takes about one hour to complete.

Careful pretest preparation of the patient is essential for accurate results. On the day of the test, no coffee, tea, cola drinks, or other stimulants are permitted. Alcohol, which as a depressant would affect the accuracy of the EEG, must also be avoided. The physician ordering the test must be informed of any medications the patient is taking, as these can have profound effects on the EEG. After shampooing, no hair preparations should be used until after the tracing has been made. If sleep recording is planned, it is helpful if no naps are taken on the day of the test.

## ENDOSCOPY

Endoscopy is a method of directly viewing the inside of

hollow organs by inserting an endoscope (a flexible, lighted, tubelike instrument) into the organ. Five common endoscopic examinations are described here (in order, from the most frequently performed to the least frequently performed).

### Proctosigmoidoscopy

This is an examination of the rectum and colon for detection of cancers and other ailments of the lower 12 inches of the large intestine. In addition to cancer, the examination can reveal hemorrhoids (swollen veins), infected areas, anal fistulas (abnormal passageways), rectal polyps (abnormal growths), and abnormal narrowing of the intestine, among other problems.

The examination is frequently recommended as part of a complete checkup. It is a must for anyone with rectal bleeding or a change in bowel habits. The examination usually takes place on a tilting-top table with the patient in the knee-chest position (resting on the knees and chest, with the face turned to the side) or lying in a head-down position. After a manual examination (insertion of the physician's gloved finger into the anus), the doctor inserts a lubricated anoscope (an instrument that enlarges the anus and lower rectum to allow close inspection). Then a sigmoidoscope (a lighted, hollow instrument, also known as a proctoscope) is inserted through the anal canal into the large intestine. Formerly, sigmoidoscopes were rigid, but these have largely been replaced by flexible ones. The advantages of the flexible devices are that they cause less discomfort and generally allow more accurate visualization of a larger area.

Patients are advised to prepare for this examination by eating a light diet for 24 to 48 hours before the test and by emptying the lower intestinal tract with one or two enemas. If a barium x-ray of the colon is to follow the sigmoidoscopic examination, more detailed preparation, involving laxatives and a number of enemas, is undertaken.

There are few risks to a routine screening. Perforation of the colon is possible, but quite rare. There may be some discomfort or cramping during the examination, but there should be no actual pain.

## Gastroscopy

Gastroscopy is an examination of the interior of the esophagus, stomach, and duodenum (the first part of the small intestine). The test is performed to detect and examine ulcers or tumors and to determine the cause of gastrointestinal bleeding or any other known or suspected abnormalities. The response of an ulcer to treatment can also be followed up endoscopically rather than by x-ray studies. During this procedure, biopsy specimens (tissue samples) can be collected, and stomach contents can be suctioned out for examination.

The patient can have no solid food for the evening meal the night before the test is done. Water cannot be taken within eight hours before the test. Smoking is prohibited on the day of the test until the examination has been completed, since smoking stimulates secretion of digestive juices by the stomach. Any other stimulation, such as that triggered by alcohol, caffeine, or colas, should also be avoided.

In the procedure, the throat is first anesthetized with a spray or a gargle (or both). The patient is then given a sedative to induce relaxation. A gastroscope (a flexible, lighted, tubelike instrument) is then passed down the throat, through the esophagus, and into the stomach and duodenum.

There is little risk to this test. The patient may gag and experience a temporary sore throat afterward. On very rare occasions, the gastroscope may injure or perforate an organ, or the patient may vomit and inhale the contents of the stomach.

## Colonoscopy

This procedure is similar to proctosigmoidoscopy, but the entire colon (large intestine) is examined. The instrument used is a long, flexible, lighted, tubelike device. Usually, colonoscopy is performed to detect or remove polyps (small abnormal growths), to do a biopsy of tumors or suspicious areas, to look for sites of occult (hidden) or obvious bleeding, and to detect inflammatory bowel disease. The patient is asked to stay on a liquid diet for about 48 hours before the procedure. Laxatives and enemas are also given to cleanse the colon thoroughly. During the test, mild sedatives are given to aid in relaxation.

Some discomfort and cramping are common, but actual pain should not occur. The main risks are perforation and bleeding from the site of biopsy or growth removal; both are uncommon.

## Cystoscopy

Cystoscopy is the direct viewing of the interior of the urinary bladder and the urethra (the passageway from the bladder to the outside of the body). A flexible, lighted, tubelike instrument called a cystoscope is passed through the urethra into the bladder. The bladder and urethra are examined for cancer, polyps, and other abnormalities. If indicated, biopsy specimens can be collected for later examination.

Men generally enter the hospital for the procedure, and are usually given a sedative before the test and a spinal or general anesthetic during the procedure. Women frequently need only local anesthesia and often have the procedure done as outpatients. There is little risk involved in diagnostic cystoscopy, although there may be a slight chance of damage to the lining of the urethra, of perforation of the bladder, and of temporary retention of urine after the test.

Part of the prostate gland is viewed during this procedure in men, and an overgrown prostate gland can be "shaved down" through the cystoscope. This is referred to as a transurethral resection of the prostate and is considered a surgical procedure.

## Bronchoscopy

Bronchoscopy is the direct examination of the trachea (windpipe), larynx (voice box), and bronchi (the breathing tubes through which air travels from the trachea into the lungs). This examination can pinpoint the cause of an unexplained persistent cough, wheeze, or pneumonia. It is also used to investigate an unexplained abnormality on a chest x-ray or to diagnose a lung tumor. Bronchoscopy may also be used to obtain a tissue sample or to remove a small obstruction, such as a foreign body.

A lighted tube, either flexible or rigid, is inserted from the mouth or nose through the trachea into the bronchi. Some bronchoscopes are small enough in diameter to offer a view of even the smallest structures in the bronchial tree. A sedative and an anesthetic are used; the anesthetic may be in the form of a spray for the mouth and nose or a lubricating jelly to protect and anesthetize the tissues of the nose and throat. The patient fasts for at least eight hours prior to the test.

Patients with a history of heart disease and those over age 50 are frequently monitored with an electrocardiograph. There is a minor risk of damage to the teeth, throat, and bronchial structures, but damage to the respiratory tract is very rare. Bleeding from biopsy sites and areas of growth removal also occurs, but uncommonly. This procedure is almost always done in a hospital setting, on an outpatient basis.

## LUMBAR PUNCTURE

The lumbar puncture (also called a spinal tap) is a procedure used to withdraw a small amount of cerebrospinal fluid from an area (the subarachnoid space) surrounding the spinal cord. The cerebrospinal fluid is then examined microscopically and analyzed chemically to detect conditions that may exist in the central nervous system. These conditions include bleeding, infections, and other abnormalities of the brain and spinal cord. Often the appearance of the fluid, which is normally crystal clear, will suggest a preliminary diagnosis of a problem; if, for example, the fluid is cloudy, it may indicate the presence of an infection.

The patient usually lies on his side with the knees drawn up sufficiently to bow the back. After administration of a local anesthetic, the subarachnoid space (where the cerebrospinal fluid circulates) is entered with a special needle inserted through the skin and soft tissues and between two of the lower lumbar vertebrae (bones of the spinal column). The pressure of the cerebrospinal fluid in the central nervous system is measured with a manometer (an instrument for measuring the pressure of liquids and gases). Some fluid is then collected in a series of small, sterile test tubes for subsequent laboratory analysis.

Although patients are sometimes apprehensive about the lumbar puncture procedure, it is usually not painful. Headache after the tap is not uncommon. It seems that lying flat for an hour or so after the tap decreases the incidence of headache. Furthermore, if a headache should develop, lying flat seems to ease the pain.

There is a slight risk of nerve damage from the needle, but this is extremely rare. The site of the puncture is below the end of the spinal cord, so the cord itself cannot be injured in any way. Special precautions are necessary if the pressure in the central nervous system is elevated due to swelling of the brain or the presence of a tumor. Computed tomography or magnetic resonance imaging may be used to evaluate the brain before a spinal tap is performed. Although any procedure that invades the body carries a risk of infection, the incidence of infections following lumbar punctures is quite low.

## MAGNETIC RESONANCE IMAGING

Magnetic resonance imaging (MRI), sometimes referred to as nuclear magnetic resonance (NMR), is one of the newest and most versatile imaging techniques currently available. With it, physicians are able to distinguish the fine details of internal body structures.

The main component of an MRI facility is a massive cylindrical magnet, which weighs as much as one hundred tons. The patient is positioned at the center of the magnet, and a radio signal is transmitted through his body while a powerful magnetic field is simultaneously generated around him.

The magnetic field generated by such a huge magnet is extremely powerful—powerful enough to temporarily modify the position of the protons (charged particles in the center of each atom) in the patient's body. Under the influence of the magnet, these protons line up parallel to the magnetic field, in much the same way that a compass needle points toward the North Pole. The radio signal causes the protons to move out of alignment. When the radio signals are stopped, the protons once again align with the magnetic field, releasing energy in the process. This energy can be detected as tiny alterations in the magnetic field. The information can then be transmitted to a computer for analysis. The images generated by the computer are very thin cross-sectional "slices" through the body, which can show details unobtainable by any other means.

Physical effects from undergoing an MRI procedure are rare, but may include headache, nausea, and a warm, tingling sensation. No health risks from either the radio waves or the magnetic field have yet been reported.

## PHOTON ABSORPTIOMETRY

Due to increasing awareness of the risks associated with osteoporosis (a disease in which the bones become thinner and more easily breakable), a reliable means of determining the presence and degree of this disorder has been sought. Photon absorptiometry (also known as densitometry), a technique for measuring bone density, is being used increasingly for this purpose. Although this procedure is probably not harmful, its usefulness as a screening procedure is not yet fully known.

## PULMONARY FUNCTION TESTING

Pulmonary function testing (PFT) is a procedure for assessing how well the lungs are working. The results of this group of tests may reveal the existence of various diseases of the lungs, including asthma and emphysema. Diseases that cause restriction of lung movement can be diagnosed and differentiated from those that cause airway obstruction. Pulmonary function tests are also used to obtain baseline values when monitoring the course of a disease and the effects of therapy.

Routine PFT is done with a spirometer—long tubes resembling vacuum-cleaner hoses are connected to a device that measures the volume of air breathed in and out over a period of time and then displays that information on a graph. The patient breathes into the spirometer ac-

cording to instructions given during the test. The amount of air inhaled and exhaled and the rate of inhalation and exhalation are measured; sometimes specific exhaled gases are also measured. Some pulmonary function tests also require a blood sample from an artery to determine if the arterial blood (freshly oxygenated in the lungs) has adequate oxygen and a normal concentration of carbon dioxide.

The test is painless and without risk, with the possible exceptions of discomfort during, and complications after, an arterial puncture for the blood sample.

## RADIOISOTOPE SCANNING

Radioactive isotopes, or radioisotopes, are used primarily as a diagnostic tool to detect tumors, blood clots, and malfunctioning of organs in the body.

A radioisotope is a form of a chemical element in which the nucleus of each atom is unstable because it does not contain the usual number of neutrons. (The nucleus is the central portion of an atom, which is the smallest particle of an element.) Because the nucleus is unstable, it disintegrates and gives off electrically charged particles and energy (ionizing radiation).

Certain elements are concentrated in, or are used by, particular organs. For example, iodine, when given by mouth or injected, will travel to and be concentrated by the thyroid gland. Radioactive iodine, when administered to a patient, will also travel to the thyroid gland, where, because of its special properties, it will show up on x-ray films. A machine called a scanner is placed near the patient. It detects the radiation emitted by the radioactive iso-

tope as it travels to the organ being studied. The scanner converts the radiation into flashes of light that form an image on x-ray film or that are projected onto a special screen.

Using this technique, a physician can determine the position, shape, and size of an organ or the presence of a tumor. By looking at the rate at which the radioisotope is absorbed and eliminated, the doctor can also evaluate how the organ is functioning.

Radioisotopes are used mainly to study organs, such as the thyroid gland, brain, liver, spleen, and kidneys, which do not show up well on ordinary x-ray images. The most recent advance in radioisotope diagnosis has allowed doctors to observe the heart muscle. Although the procedure is still quite costly, it appears promising for victims of heart attack and other abnormalities. Some conditions that can be detected by using radioisotopes are tumors, blood clots, injuries, bone marrow disease, red blood cell irregularities, cirrhosis of the liver (a condition in which the tissues of the liver are scarred and otherwise damaged), hepatitis (inflammation of the liver), nonabsorption of vitamin $B_{12}$, and certain anemias.

There is no danger of radiation poisoning with this study. Because very small amounts of radiation can be detected and measured, only a minute amount of a radioisotope is required.

## TOMOGRAPHY

Tomography is a type of x-ray examination in which the shadows in front of and behind the part of the body being studied are blurred out on the x-ray picture. Successive exposures are made at different depths within the structure of the body part under study and from different angles. The effect is the same as that achieved when a microscope is adjusted back and forth and up and down while looking at a piece of tissue—it is possible to get a picture of a structure at different levels, each one pinpointed and sharply focused.

The combination of the tomographic x-ray technique and expanded computer capabilities led to the development of a highly sophisticated form of diagnostic imaging called computed tomography (also known as computerized axial tomography, CAT scanning, and CT scanning). With this special procedure, x-rays are not used to create images directly on film. Instead, the x-rays are detected by a scanner as they leave the body and that information is analyzed by a computer to construct a cross-sectional "map" of the body part under study.

The most widely known use of the CT scan has been in the detection of brain disorders. However, in recent years use of the technique has been extended to other parts of the body, so that, for example, cross-sectional images of organs in the abdomen, such as the liver and pancreas, can now be produced. These scans are quite sensitive and have greatly aided in the early detection of tumors. One of the breakthroughs that has made this possible is the development of equipment that can complete a scan in five seconds or less. Brain scanning does not require such speed, since the head can easily be immobilized. The abdominal area, however, is in constant movement, because of the action of the stomach, the intestines, and the diaphragm.

Consequently, the scan must be made fast enough to provide a clear image, in the same way that a fast shutter speed on an ordinary camera can "stop" the motion of the subject.

The test is painless, but there is a minimal risk of radiation exposure. Also, intravenous x-ray contrast medium is sometimes used to enhance the picture. Persons with kidney disease or diabetes may be at risk of kidney damage when contrast medium is used, and persons with a sensitivity to such dyes may suffer serious allergic reactions. These individuals should tell their radiologist of such risk factors so that adequate precautions can be taken to minimize the chance of complications. CT scanning is relatively expensive and therefore not done routinely.

### ULTRASONOGRAPHY

Ultrasonography (often called ultrasound) is a method of visualizing the structures of the body by recording the reflections of high-frequency sound waves off those structures. The procedure is painless and uses no radiation. Ultrasound, the sound range used in this diagnostic procedure, is a vibration beyond the range of human hearing.

The instrument used in ultrasonography is called a transducer. The transducer, placed over the area to be examined, directs ultrasonic waves at the tissue. The sounds returning from the internal structure are processed by machines that produce a multidimensional, detailed image of the structure. Formerly, only still pictures could be obtained; now, however, moving pictures in "real time" are possible—for example, in pregnancy, the fetus'

movements and beating heart can actually be visualized.

Sonography does not involve the use of contrast medium or invasive procedures (for example, injections, catheterization, and incisions). There is no known risk involved in sonography, although the long-term effects of sound waves have not been determined.

# Tests for women

### AMNIOCENTESIS

Amniocentesis is performed during pregnancy. A hollow needle is inserted through the abdominal and uterine walls into the amniotic sac surrounding the fetus in order to withdraw some amniotic fluid for testing. The analysis of amniotic fluid is useful in determining the condition of the fetus, since the amniotic fluid contains discarded fetal cells. Examination of these cells for chromosomal and chemical makeup can detect a large number of genetic defects and hereditary disorders. Testing certain chemicals in the fluid itself is done to determine fetal lung maturity and to detect certain fetal abnormalities, such as spina bifida. The fetal cells will also indicate the sex of the baby, which is important if a sex-linked hereditary disorder, such as hemophilia (a blood-clotting disease that occurs almost exclusively in males), is suspected. However, amniocentesis is never performed simply to satisfy curiosity about the sex of a baby.

The test is performed most often in women who are over the age of 35 or who have a family history of certain hereditary disorders. The incidence of chromosome abnormalities of the fetus increases rapidly after a woman reaches the age of 35. As each year passes, the chances of chromosome abnormalities increase.

The procedure is relatively painless, since a local anesthetic is used around the injection site. The test is usually done during the sixteenth to eighteenth week of pregnancy (before this time the test results are inconclusive). The final results are not available for three to four weeks; therefore, the waiting period can be the most difficult part of the test. However, approximately 95 percent of amniocentesis results are normal.

There is some risk to this test, which is why it is not routinely used. There is a risk of miscarriage, as well as a chance of striking the placenta or the fetus. However, this risk is minimized by the use of ultrasonography to reveal the position of both the fetus and the placenta before the needle is inserted. In addition, as with any invasive technique (that is, one that involves an incision, an injection, or the insertion of something into the body), there is a chance of infection. A patient experiencing pain, fever, or discharge from the puncture site or from the vagina should notify her doctor immediately.

## MAMMOGRAPHY

Mammography is a simple, generally painless examination of the breasts by means of a special x-ray machine that is designed to be used for soft tissues. This procedure is especially valuable for the detection of early breast cancers before they can be felt manually by the woman or her doctor. Mammography can frequently differentiate between malignant (cancerous) and nonmalignant (noncancerous) lumps and can provide information about fibrocystic breast disease.

Many medical experts recommend that a mammogram of the normal breasts be made when a woman is around the age of 35. This baseline study can then be used for comparison with subsequent mammograms to detect changes in the breasts. After the first mammogram, it is recommended that the test be repeated every one to two years, depending on individual risk factors, such as a family history of breast cancer. Most doctors suggest a mammogram every year for women past the age of 50, regardless of risk factors. However, a mammogram should not replace monthly breast self-examinations and regular breast examinations by a doctor; rather, the mammogram should be done in conjunction with these manual examinations.

Other related techniques for breast examination are xerography and thermography. Xerography is a form of mammography that records the image using a photoelectric process rather than standard x-ray film. Thermography is a diagnostic technique that uses no x-rays and thus can be repeated as often as desired. Thermography records differences in temperature among various parts of the breast. The basic premise of thermography is that rapidly growing cancer cells give off more heat than normal cells do. Thermography, however, is not as accurate as mammography and should be used only to augment information obtained from a physical examination and a mammogram.

There is some question about the risk of radiation exposure in mammography, especially for those women who receive a yearly mammogram. The radiation dosage has been reduced in modern testing, and many physicians feel that the benefits of early detection outweigh any risks. However, because of these risks, most doctors are conservative about the use of mammography. A woman should discuss the benefits and risks of this test procedure with a doctor who knows her medical history. As a general rule, mammography should not be performed on a pregnant woman.

## PAP TEST

The Pap test is a standard part of the gynecological examination for women. (Pap is an abbreviation of Papanicolaou, the name of the physician who developed the test.) Analysis of the specimen obtained is used to detect early cell changes that might indicate cancer or other abnormalities of the cervix (the neck of the uterus).

The Pap test involves scraping some cells from the surface of the area where the cervix opens into the vagina. The scraping is done with a small plastic spatula. The scrapings are smeared onto a glass slide for microscopic examination. The test is relatively painless, and there is virtually no risk.

The test results are categorized into five groups: Class I—no abnormal cells; Class II—atypical cells, usually caused by inflammation or infection; Class III—cells suspected of being cancerous; and Classes IV and V—cancer cells present. In some laboratories, a modification of this classification is used so that the report states that the smear is negative, doubtful, unsatisfactory, or positive.

A woman should have her first Pap test at about 18 years of age. It should be repeated every one to two years. Women over age 40 should have an annual test. Any woman with a history of cervical or uterine cancer or of abnormal Pap tests should have the test done every six months.

## PELVIC EXAMINATION

The pelvic examination is a manual and visual inspection of the female reproductive tract. It is done to detect disorders in the reproductive organs, including the vagina, cervix, uterus, and ovaries. A pelvic examination can also reveal pregnancy.

The patient lies on an examination table and places her heels in metal holders resembling the stirrups on a horse's saddle. The doctor inserts into the vagina a speculum, a special instrument that expands the vagina to permit visual examination of the vagina and cervix. A specimen for a Pap test may be obtained. After removing the speculum, the doctor inserts two gloved fingers into the vagina while simultaneously pressing lightly on the patient's abdomen; this procedure enables the doctor to detect abnormalities in the uterus and ovaries. Sometimes the doctor also inserts a finger into the rectum while pressing on the abdomen; this, too, enables the doctor to feel the uterus and ovaries.

A pelvic examination takes only a few minutes, is relatively painless, and entails virtually no risk.

# FACTS ABOUT PRESCRIPTION DRUGS

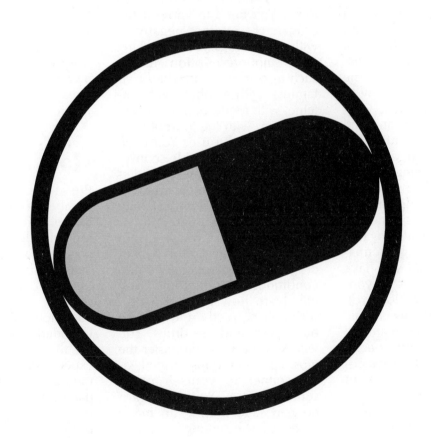

Because of the variety of drugs now available, both over the pharmacy counter and by prescription from a physician, a wide range of illnesses and disorders can be controlled, relieved, or even cured. We can control hypertension, eliminate the irritating effects of allergies and hay fever, relieve cold discomfort, cure a variety of stomach and intestinal disorders, control stress and insomnia, and end bacterial and fungal infections—all by taking a medication.

Along with the benefits of modern drug therapy, however, comes responsibility. There is a great deal that the informed patient ought to know about the medicine he is taking: how to take it, how often to take it, what its possible side effects are, and how it might react with other medications, foods, or alcohol.

The process of buying and taking a drug starts when your doctor writes out a prescription. The choice of drug is determined by many facts you have already told your doctor, including information about drugs that you have taken at various times in your life, any allergic reactions you might have suffered, any chronic conditions for which you are still taking medication, any special side effects that you have experienced with certain drugs or classes of drugs, and any chronic health problems you have. Based on this information, the doctor makes a decision about the right drug for your particular condition. The doctor's part of the process is now complete; your part is just beginning.

You need to know many facts before you take your first pill or swallow your first spoonful of medicine. You need to know how to administer the medicine. You need to understand the dos-

age schedule—how often to take the drug, how much each time, whether to schedule medication at night as well as in the daytime. You need to know something about common side effects in order to distinguish between those that are truly "minor side effects" and those that are signs of a serious drug reaction. You need to know whether you should continue the medicine after your symptoms have completely disappeared, or whether you should stop the medication when you no longer show symptoms. You need to know if the drug might interact negatively with other drugs you are taking (even nonprescription drugs, such as cold pills, aspirin, or vitamins), with alcohol, with caffeine, with foods, and, if you are a woman, with the form of birth control that you use. You need to know the possible consequences of overdosage or underdosage. In short, you need to assume responsibility for taking your prescription drugs.

As you read on, you will learn how some common types of drugs work to relieve certain conditions or symptoms. You will learn how to read a prescription correctly and how to buy, store, and use drugs. You will learn how to administer the most common forms of medication either to yourself or to someone else. You will learn how to save money, in many cases, by substituting a less expensive generic drug for a more expensive brand-name medication. Finally, you will learn to identify some common side effects of the most widely used prescription drugs and to recognize symptoms that will help you decide when your drug response is not a cause for concern and when it calls for prompt medical attention.

This chapter is not a substitute for informed advice from your doctor and pharmacist. You should keep these two persons informed at all times of your condition and of any reactions you are experiencing, as well as of other medication you take on a regular basis. You should also ask your doctor or pharmacist for the latest information about your medications; although every effort has been made to ensure that the information here is up-to-date, new developments occur rapidly in drug research. What this chapter can do is help you to work better with your pharmacist and your doctor by becoming a well-informed, aware patient who receives the maximum benefits from your medication and treatment.

# How drugs work

Prescription drugs fall into a number of groups according to the conditions for which they are prescribed. In the following pages we will provide you with a better understanding of the types of medications that are prescribed for different medical conditions. We will describe the intended actions of drugs and the therapeutic effects you can expect from the various types of medications. The generic drug names have been used here. If a brand-name product has been prescribed for you, read the label or ask your pharmacist its generic name.

## CARDIOVASCULAR DRUGS

### Antianginals

Since the heart is a muscle that must work continuously, it

requires a constant supply of nutrients and oxygen. The chest pain known as angina pectoris occurs when there is an insufficient supply of blood, and consequently of oxygen, to the heart. There are several types of antianginal drugs. These include vasodilators (which act by causing relaxation of blood vessels, thereby allowing more blood to flow through), such as nitroglycerin, papaverine, and isosorbide dinitrate; calcium-channel blockers (which are also vasodilators), such as diltiazem, nifedipine, and verapamil); and beta-blockers (which act by decreasing the work load of the heart), such as atenolol, metoprolol, nadolol, pindolol, propranolol, and timolol. All of these drugs act ultimately by increasing the amount of oxygen that reaches the heart muscle.

## Antiarrhythmics

If the heart does not beat rhythmically or smoothly (a condition called arrhythmia), it does not perform efficiently. This state of affairs can be dangerous and usually (but not in all cases) requires correction. Antiarrhythmic drugs, including disopyramide, procainamide, beta-blockers, and quinidine, prevent or alleviate some cardiac arrhythmias by altering nerve impulses within the heart. Phenytoin, most frequently used as an anticonvulsant in the treatment of epilepsy, can also act as an antiarrhythmic agent. The digitalis drugs, commonly used to strengthen heart contractions, are also helpful in treating arrhythmias. It is important to know that all of these drugs can actually also cause arrhythmias and must be carefully regulated by a physician.

## Antihypertensives

Hypertension, or high blood pressure, is a condition in which the pressure of the blood against the walls of the blood vessels is higher than what is considered normal. Hypertension is controllable. If a medication for high blood pressure has been prescribed, it is very important that you continue to take it regularly, even if you don't notice any symptoms of hypertension. If hypertension is controlled, other diseases can be prevented. Drugs that counteract or reduce high blood pressure may effectively prolong a hypertensive patient's life and reduce the risk of heart attack, stroke, and kidney failure.

Several different types of drugs have an antihypertensive effect (that is, they reduce blood pressure). Some drugs block nerve impulses that cause arteries to constrict (narrow); others slow the heart rate and decrease its force of contraction; still others reduce the amount of certain hormones in the blood that cause blood pressure to rise. Diuretics (drugs that reduce the volume of body fluids) are frequently prescribed for the treatment of hypertension as well.

## Diuretics

Diuretic drugs, such as chlorothiazide, chlorthalidone, furosemide, hydrochlorothiazide, methyclothiazide, and spironolactone, promote the loss of water and salt from the body (this is why they are sometimes called "water pills"). Because many antihypertensive drugs cause the body to retain sodium and water, they are often used concurrently with diuretics. Most diuretics act directly on the kidneys, but there are various types of diuretics, each with different actions. Thus, therapy for high blood pressure can be individualized for each patient's specific needs.

Thiazide diuretics are the most commonly prescribed water pills available today. They are generally well tolerated. Since patients do not develop a tolerance to their antihypertensive effect, they can be taken for prolonged periods. However, a major drawback to thiazide diuretics is that they often deplete the body of potassium. This depletion can be compensated for with a potassium supplement. Potassium-rich foods and liquids, such as bananas, apricots, and orange juice, can also be used to help correct a potassium deficiency. Salt substitutes are another source of potassium. (Too much potassium may also be dangerous, however. Do not make any change in your diet without first discussing the change with your doctor.)

Loop diuretics, such as furosemide, act more vigorously than thiazide diuretics. (The term "loop" refers to the loop-shaped structures in the kidneys on which these medications act.) Loop diuretics promote more water loss, but also deplete more potassium.

To remove excess water from the body but retain its store of potassium, manufacturers developed potassium-sparing diuretics, such as amiloride, spironolactone, and triamterene. Potassium-sparing diuretics have been combined with thiazide diuretics (for example, spironolactone and hydrochlorothiazide combination) to enhance the antihypertensive effect and reduce the loss of potassium; they are now among the most commonly used antihypertensive agents.

## Cardiac glycosides

Cardiac glycosides include drugs that are derived from digitalis (for example, digoxin and digitoxin). They affect the heart rate, but are not strictly antiarrhythmics. This type of drug can slow the rate of the heart but increases its force of contraction. Cardiac glycosides may be used to regulate the heart rhythm or to increase heart output in heart failure.

## Anticoagulants

Drugs that prevent blood from clotting are called anticoagulants. These drugs are commonly referred to as "blood thinners," but they do not actually thin the blood.

There are two categories of anticoagulants. The first category contains only one drug, heparin. Since heparin must be given by injection, its use is generally restricted to hospitalized patients.

The second category includes oral anticoagulants, principally derivatives of the drug warfarin. Warfarin can be used in the treatment of stroke, heart disease, and abnormal blood clotting. It is also used to prevent the enlargement of an existing clot, which could cause serious problems by embolizing (breaking off and moving to another part of the body). It acts by preventing the liver from manufacturing the proteins responsible for blood clot formation.

Persons taking warfarin must avoid using many other drugs (including aspirin) because their interaction with the anticoagulant could cause profuse bleeding. Patients taking warfarin should check with their pharmacist or physician before using any other medications, including over-the-counter products for coughs or colds. In addition, they must have blood samples checked frequently by their physician, to ensure that the drug is maintaining the correct degree of anticoagulation.

Drugs such as aspirin and dipyridamole are also, in a very broad sense, anticoagulants in that they inhibit the action of platelets, which aid in clot formation.

## Antihyperlipidemics

Antihyperlipidemic drugs are used to treat elevated serum levels of cholesterol and triglycerides (fats), which form plaques (deposits) on the walls of arteries. Some antihyperlipidemics, such as cholestyramine and colestipol, bind to bile acids in the gastrointestinal tract, thereby decreasing the body's retention of cholesterol. Clofibrate and probucol decrease the body's production of cholesterol. The efficacy of these drugs is in question; some researchers believe that following a special low-fat, high-fiber diet and a good exercise program may be just as beneficial in lowering cholesterol levels in many cases.

## Vasodilators

Vasodilating drugs cause the blood vessels to widen. Some of the antihypertensive agents, such as hydralazine and prazosin, lower blood pressure by dilating the arteries or veins. Other vasodilators are used in the treatment of stroke and diseases characterized by poor circulation. Ergoloid mesylates are used to reduce the severity of symptoms associated with senility.

## Beta-blockers

Beta-blocking drugs block the response of the heart and blood vessels to specific nerve stimulation, resulting in slower heart rate and reduced blood pressure. They are used in the treatment of angina, hypertension, arrhythmias, and migraine headaches. Propranolol and metoprolol are two examples of beta-blockers.

## Calcium-channel blockers

Calcium-channel blockers (diltiazem, nifedipine, verapamil) are primarily used for the prevention and treatment of angina pectoris. Verapamil is also useful in correcting certain arrhythmias and in lowering blood pressure. This group of drugs is thought to prevent angina and arrhythmias by blocking the effects of calcium on nerve transmission and blood vessel tone. This effect results in vasodilatation and greater oxygen delivery to the heart muscle.

Calcium-channel blockers have recently been found to be beneficial in the treatment of migraine headache and Raynaud's phenomenon (spasmodic constriction of small blood vessels, usually on exposure to cold, which causes color and temperature changes and pain in the fingers and toes).

## GASTROINTESTINAL DRUGS

## Antinauseants

Antinauseants reduce the urge to vomit. Perhaps the most effective antinauseant is a phenothiazine derivative such as prochlorperazine. This medication acts on the vomiting center in the brain. It is often administered rectally, and usually alleviates nausea and vomiting within a few minutes to an hour.

Antihistamines are also commonly used to prevent nausea and vomiting, especially when those symptoms are due to motion sickness. This type of medication may also work at the vomiting center in the brain.

## Anticholinergics

Anticholinergic drugs (for example, dicyclomine) slow the action of the bowel and reduce the amount of stomach acid. Because these drugs relax the intestinal muscles and relieve spasms, they are said to have an antispasmodic action. They are frequently used to relieve abdominal cramps. These drugs can cause dry mouth and blurred vision.

## Antiulcer medications

Antiulcer medications are prescribed to treat peptic ulcers. The antisecretory ulcer medications, cimetidine and ranitidine, work by suppressing the production of stomach acid. Another antiulcer drug, sucralfate, probably works by forming a chemical barrier (rather like a bandage) over an exposed ulcer, thereby protecting it from stomach acid. These medications provide sustained relief from ulcer pain and promote healing.

## Antidiarrheals

Diarrhea may be caused by many conditions, including influenza and ulcerative colitis, and can sometimes occur as a side effect of drug therapy. Nar-

cotics and anticholinergics are used in the treatment of diarrhea because they slow the action of the bowel. A medication such as diphenoxylate and atropine combination contains both a narcotic and an anticholinergic. These drugs can sometimes prolong certain infections, however; they should never be used without the advice of a physician.

## RESPIRATORY DRUGS

### Antitussives

Antitussives control coughs by acting on the cough center in the brain. There are numerous over-the-counter (nonprescription) antitussives available. Codeine is a narcotic antitussive that is an ingredient in many prescription cough medications.

### Expectorants

Expectorant drugs are used to change a nonproductive cough to a productive one (one that brings up phlegm). Expectorants are supposed to make mucus less viscous (thinner). (Drinking water or using a vaporizer or humidifier is probably as effective as using most expectorants, however.) Many cough preparations include an expectorant, such as ammonium chloride or potassium guaiacolsulfonate, in combination with other types of drugs (for example, an antitussive and an antihistamine).

### Decongestants

Decongestants constrict the blood vessels in the nose and sinuses to open up air passages. Decongestants can be taken

orally or as nose drops or spray. Oral decongestants act slowly, but they do not interfere with the production of mucus or the movement of the cilia (hairlike structures) in the respiratory tract. They can, however, increase blood pressure, so they should be used cautiously by patients with high blood pressure. Topical decongestants (nose drops or spray) provide almost immediate relief. At standard dosages, they do not usually increase blood pressure as much as oral decongestants, but they do slow the movement of the cilia.

People who use these products may develop a tolerance for them. (Tolerance can be described as a need for increasing dosages to achieve the same beneficial effect, accompanied by an increasing risk of side effects.) Therefore, these drugs should not be used for more than a few days at a time.

### Bronchodilators

Bronchodilators (agents that open the airways in the lungs) are used to stop wheezing and improve breathing. Theophylline and similar drugs are commonly used to relieve the symptoms of asthma and pulmonary emphysema.

### Antiallergy medications

Histamine is a body chemical that, when released in the body, typically causes swelling and itching. Antihistamines counteract these symptoms of allergy by blocking the effects of histamine. For mild respiratory allergies, such as hay fever, antihistamines can be used. Diphenhydramine and other antihistamines act relatively slowly. Severe allergic reactions sometimes necessitate the use of epinephrine, which is not an antihistamine but which acts on the circulatory system to prevent shock; in its injectable form, it acts very rapidly.

## CENTRAL NERVOUS SYSTEM DRUGS

### Sedatives

Medications used in the treatment of anxiety or insomnia selectively reduce activity in the central nervous system (brain and spinal cord). Drugs that have a sedating effect include barbiturates, chlordiazepoxide, clorazepate, diazepam, meprobamate, and oxazepam. Drugs to induce sleep (known as hypnotics) include flurazepam, temazepam, and triazolam.

### Tranquilizers

Tranquilizers calm the activity of certain areas of the brain but allow the rest to function normally; in other words, they act as a screening device to allow the transmission of some nerve impulses and to restrict others. The two types of tranquilizers are antipsychotics and antidepressants.

Antipsychotics are used to treat the symptoms of severe psychiatric disorders. The drugs most frequently used are the phenothiazines, such as chlorpromazine, thioridazine, and trifluoperazine. Haloperidol, a butyrophenone, has effects that are similar to those of chlorpromazine.

Antidepressants are used to treat mental depression. The most commonly used antidepressants are the tricyclic antidepressants, such as amitriptyline and amoxapine, and the monoamine oxidase (MAO) inhibitors, such as pargyline and phenelzine. Antidepressants must be used with caution, since they often produce dangerous side effects and can interact with other drugs in harmful ways. The MAO inhibitors must be used with particular care because they can interact with certain cheeses and other foods and beverages to greatly increase blood pressure.

### Anticonvulsants

Drugs such as phenytoin and phenobarbital can effectively control the occurrence of seizures in grand mal epilepsy. They act by selectively reducing electrical nerve discharges in the brain.

### Antiparkinsonism agents

Parkinson's disease is a progressive disorder that is due to a chemical imbalance in the brain. Victims of Parkinson's disease have uncontrollable tremors, develop a characteristic stoop, and eventually become unable to walk. Drugs such as benztropine, trihexyphenidyl, levodopa, and bromocriptine are used to alleviate the symptoms of the disease; they provide control, but not cure.

### Analgesics

Pain is not a disease, but a symptom. Drugs used to relieve pain are called analgesics. We do not fully understand how most analgesics work. Gener-

ally, analgesics fall into two categories: narcotic and nonnarcotic.

Narcotics are derived from the opium poppy. They act on the brain to cause deep analgesia and often drowsiness. Narcotics, particularly codeine, relieve coughing spasms; codeine is used in many cough syrups. Narcotics relieve pain and also give the patient a feeling of euphoria (well-being). They are also addictive. The pharmaceutical industry has attempted to produce nonaddictive synthetic narcotic derivatives, but has not yet been successful.

Of the many nonnarcotic pain relievers, salicylates (such as aspirin) are the most commonly used in the United States today. While aspirin does not require a prescription, many doctors recommend it to treat such diseases as arthritis. The aspirin substitute acetaminophen may be used in place of aspirin to relieve pain. It does not, however, reduce inflammation (such as that caused by arthritis).

A number of analgesic medications combine codeine or another narcotic with a nonnarcotic analgesic (such as aspirin or acetaminophen). These analgesics are not as potent as pure narcotics, but frequently they are as effective. Because these medications contain narcotics, they have the potential for abuse and must be used with caution.

### Anti-inflammatory drugs

Inflammation is the body's response to injury. It is characterized by swelling, pain, warmth, and redness. Aspirin is one of the most effective anti-inflammatory drugs, but other nonsteroidal anti-inflammatory drugs (NSAIDs), such as fenoprofen, ibuprofen, indometha-cin, naproxen, and tolmetin, may be more effective than aspirin in certain individuals. Steroids are also used to treat inflammatory diseases.

The tensing of sore muscles is commonly associated with inflammation. Skeletal muscle relaxants, such as orphenadrine and chlorzoxazone, may relieve inflammation and muscle spasm. Skeletal muscle relaxants are often given in combination with an anti-inflammatory drug, such as aspirin. Some doctors believe that aspirin and rest are better for alleviating the pain and inflammation of muscle strain than are skeletal muscle relaxants.

## TOPICAL DRUGS

Topical drugs are applied directly to the skin to treat skin disorders with minimal systemic (throughout the body) side effects. Antibiotic creams or ointments are used to treat skin infections, and adrenocorticosteroids are used to treat inflammatory skin conditions. Another common dermatologic (skin) problem is acne. Acne can be—and often is—treated with over-the-counter drugs, but sometimes prescription medication is necessary. Antibiotics such as tetracycline, erythromycin, and clindamycin are used orally or applied topically to slow the growth of the bacteria responsible for acne pustules. Keratolytics (agents that soften the skin and cause the outer cells to slough off) are also sometimes prescribed.

Some drugs applied to the skin do have prominent effects within the body. For example, nitroglycerin is absorbed into the bloodstream from ointment or patches placed on the skin. The absorbed nitroglycerin dilates blood vessels and prevents anginal pain. Other medications, such as antihypertensives and motion sickness preparations, are also available in patch form.

## DRUGS FOR THE EARS

For an ear infection, a physician usually prescribes an antibiotic and steroid combination in drop form. The antibiotic attacks the infecting bacteria, and the steroid reduces the inflammation and pain. A local anesthetic, such as benzocaine or lidocaine, may also be prescribed to relieve pain.

## DRUGS FOR THE EYES

Glaucoma is one of the major disorders of the eye, especially in people over 40 years of age. It is caused by increased pressure within the eyeball. Although glaucoma is sometimes treated surgically, the pressure in the eye can usually be reduced, and blindness prevented, through the use of eye drops. Two frequently used medications are epinephrine and pilocarpine.

Pilocarpine is a cholinergic drug. Cholinergic drugs act by stimulating the parasympathetic nerve endings. These are nerve endings that assist in the control of the heart, lungs, bowels, and eyes. When used in the eyes, pilocarpine causes constriction of the pupils, increasing the outflow of the fluid called aqueous humor and thereby reducing the pressure.

Epinephrine is an adrenergic agent. Drugs with adrenergic properties have actions similar to those of adrenaline. Adrenaline is a chemical that is secreted in the body when one must flee from danger, resist attack, or combat stress. Adrenaline increases the amount of sugar in the blood, accelerates the heartbeat, and dilates the pupils. The mechanism by which epinephrine lowers eye pressure is not completely understood, but it appears to involve both a decrease in production of aqueous humor and an increase in the outflow of this fluid from the anterior chamber of the eye.

Beta-blockers in drop form are also very effective antiglaucoma drugs. Antibiotics are used to treat bacterial eye infections. Steroids can also be used to treat noninfectious eye inflammations, as long as these medications are not used for too long a period of time.

Pharmacists carefully monitor requests for eye drop refills, particularly for drops that contain steroids, and may refuse to refill a prescription until you have revisited your doctor, because such drugs can cause further eye problems with long-term use.

## HORMONES

A hormone is a substance produced and secreted by a gland. Hormones stimulate and regulate body functions. Hormone drugs are given to mimic the effects of naturally produced hormones.

Hormone drugs are prescribed to treat various endocrine conditions, such as Addison's disease, Cushing's syndrome, and diabetes. Most often, they are used to replace hormones that are not being produced by the body in amounts sufficient to regulate specific functions. This category of medication also includes oral contraceptives and certain types of drugs that are used to combat inflammatory reactions.

## Thyroid drugs

Thyroid hormone was one of the first hormone drugs to be produced synthetically. Originally, thyroid preparations were made by drying and pulverizing the thyroid glands of animals and then forming them into tablets. Such preparations are still used in the treatment of patients who have reduced levels of thyroid hormone production. A synthetic thyroid hormone (levothyroxine) is also available.

## Antidiabetic drugs

Insulin, which is secreted by the pancreas, regulates the level of sugar in the blood, as well as metabolism of carbohydrates and fats. Glucagon stimulates the liver to produce glucose (a form of sugar). Both insulin and glucagon must be present in the right amounts to maintain proper blood sugar levels.

Treatment of diabetes (the condition in which the body is unable to produce or utilize insulin) may involve dietary adjustments alone or the administration of insulin or oral antidiabetic drugs combined with dietary adjustments. Glucagon is given only in emergencies (for example, insulin shock, when blood sugar levels must be raised quickly).

Oral antidiabetic drugs induce the pancreas to secrete more insulin by acting on small groups of cells within the pancreas that make and store insulin. Oral antidiabetic medications are prescribed for diabetic patients who are unable to regulate their blood sugar levels by diet modification alone. These drugs cannot be used by patients with insulin-dependent (juvenile-onset, or Type I) diabetes, who can control their blood sugar levels only with injections of insulin.

## Steroids

The pituitary gland secretes adrenocorticotropic hormone (ACTH), which directs the adrenal glands to produce adrenocorticosteroids. Oral steroid preparations (for example, methylprednisolone) can be used to treat inflammatory diseases, such as arthritis, or to treat poison ivy, hay fever, or insect bites. Steroids can also be applied to the skin to treat certain inflammatory skin conditions.

## Sex hormones

Although the adrenal glands secrete small amounts of sex hormones, these hormones are produced mainly by the sex glands.

Testosterone, or androgen, is the male hormone responsible for secondary sex characteristics, such as beard growth and enlargement of muscles. Testosterone reduces elimination of protein from the body, thereby producing an increase in muscle size. Athletes sometimes take drugs called anabolic steroids (chemicals similar to testosterone) for this effect, but such use of these drugs is dangerous. Anabolic steroids can adversely affect the heart, nervous system, and kidneys.

Estrogens are the female hormones responsible for secondary sex characteristics, such as development of the breasts, maintenance of the lining of the uterus, and enlargement of the hips at puberty. Progesterone, another female hormone, prepares the uterus for pregnancy.

Most oral contraceptives (birth control pills) combine estrogen and progesterone, but some contain only progesterone. The estrogen in birth control pills prevents egg production. Progesterone aids in preventing ovulation, alters the lining of the uterus, and thickens cervical mucus—processes that help to prevent conception and implantation of a fertilized egg. Oral contraceptives have many side effects, so their use should be discussed with a doctor.

Conjugated estrogens are used as replacement therapy to treat symptoms of menopause in women who are no longer producing sufficient amounts of estrogen. Medroxyprogesterone is used to treat uterine bleeding and menstrual problems. It prevents uterine bleeding by inducing and maintaining a lining in the uterus that resembles the lining produced during pregnancy. In addition, it suppresses the release of the pituitary gland hormone that initiates ovulation.

## ANTI–INFECTIVES

### Antibiotics

Antibiotics are used to treat a wide variety of bacterial infections. They are usually derived from molds or are produced synthetically. Antibiotics slow the growth of bacteria or actually cause their death by interfering with their production of necessary nutrients or by damaging their cell membranes. The body's natural defenses then have a much easier time in eliminating the infection.

When used properly, antibiotics are usually effective. To adequately treat an infection, antibiotics must be taken regularly for a specific period of time. If you do not take an antibiotic for the prescribed period, microorganisms are given the opportunity to continue growing, and your infection could recur. Aminoglycosides, cephalosporins, erythromycins, penicillins (including ampicillin and amoxicillin), and tetracyclines are some examples of antibiotics.

Antibiotics do not counteract viruses, such as those that cause the common cold. Their use in treating the common cold is, therefore, inappropriate.

### Antivirals

Antiviral drugs are used to combat viral infections. Amantadine is used to prevent or treat infections by influenza A virus. A drug called acyclovir is being used in the management of herpes. Although acyclovir does not cure herpes, it does reduce the reproduction of the herpes virus in initial outbreaks, lessen the number of recurring outbreaks, and speed the healing of herpes blisters. Another antiviral drug, zidovudine (formerly called azidothymidine, or AZT) is used in the treatment of the acquired immune deficiency syndrome (AIDS).

### Vaccines

A vaccine contains weakened or dead disease-causing microorganisms, which activate the body's immune system to produce a natural defense against a particular disease (such as polio or measles). A vaccine may be used to alleviate or treat an infectious disease, but most commonly it is used to prevent a specific disease.

### Other anti-infectives

Drugs called anthelmintics are used to treat worm infestations. Fungal infections are treated with antifungal agents (such as nystatin), which destroy and prevent the growth of fungi. A pediculicide is a drug used to treat head, body, and pubic lice infestations.

## PROSTAGLANDINS

Prostaglandins are fatty acids, similar in chemical structure to hormones, that occur naturally in the human body. The first of the prostaglandins to be isolated was from the human prostate gland, which is how the substances got their name. More than 16 prostaglandins in six groups have now been identified.

Prostaglandins regulate or trigger various activities in every organ system. For example, prostaglandins stimulate smooth muscle, affect heart rate, influence blood pressure, cause the uterus to contract, and initiate release of growth hormone by the pituitary gland.

Medical researchers have been experimenting with various preparations of synthetic prostaglandins for use in both diagnosis and treatment of disease. Because it was found that one prostaglandin stimulates contractions of the uterus in childbirth, a prostaglandin preparation was developed to help speed up some cases of difficult labor. Another prostaglandin has been used to reduce blood pressure in research subjects, but is not yet available as a prescription drug. Use of prostaglandins is being studied in the treatment of asthma, emphysema, shock, and the common cold. Researchers

have also used a prostaglandin to halt the progress of leukemia and melanoma (two types of cancer) in cells in laboratory experiments.

## ANTINEOPLASTICS

Antineoplastic drugs are used in the treatment of cancer. Most of the drugs in this category prevent the growth of rapidly dividing cells, such as cancer cells. Antineoplastics are usually extremely toxic and can cause serious side effects, but in most cases the benefits received from chemotherapy with antineoplastic drugs far outweigh the risks involved.

## VITAMIN AND MINERAL SUPPLEMENTS

Vitamins and minerals are chemical substances vital to the maintenance of normal body function. Some people have vitamin deficiencies, but most people obtain enough vitamins and minerals in their diet. People who have an inadequate or restricted diet, those with certain disorders or debilitating illnesses, and pregnant or breastfeeding women are among those who may benefit from taking supplemental vitamins and minerals. However, even these people should consult a doctor to see if a true vitamin deficiency exists.

# How to read and understand your prescription

Part of the process of becoming an informed patient is understanding as much as possible about the medications you are taking. This process starts in the doctor's office. Make sure that you understand what medication is prescribed for you, how often and how it should be taken, and for how long. Ask specifically if you should continue the medication once the symptoms subside. Some drugs, such as antibiotics, should be taken for a certain minimum period of time, even if all the symptoms have disappeared. Other drugs should be discontinued when the symptoms subside. Make sure, too, that you understand your dosage schedule, any precautions you need to take to prevent or reduce possible side effects, and how (if at all) you should alter your normal eating or drinking habits while you are taking the medication. You should also learn what side effects are to be expected, as well as which ones are within the "normal" range and which ones are signals that you need to consult your doctor again. Be sure that you know and understand all of these facts before you leave your doctor's office.

A more detailed, step-by-step review follows.

**Step 1:** Read your prescription.

You cannot be sure that your prescription has been filled correctly unless you can read it, so your first step is to read the prescription. There is nothing mysterious or secret about a prescription; the "indecipherable" notations are simply abbreviations of Latin or Greek words and phrases (holdovers from a time when doctors wrote in Latin). The following chart will help you understand the abbreviations—for example, "gtt" is an abbreviation for the Latin word *guttae*, meaning drops; "ut dict" is from the Latin *ut dictum*,

meaning as directed; and "bid" stands for the Latin *bis in die,* or twice daily.

Once you have familiarized yourself with this simple table, you will be able to check your prescription against the label on the drug container to make sure that the two coincide. The chart lists the most commonly used symbols and abbreviations that doctors use in writing prescriptions. Read it; then check your skills in Step 2.

**Step 2:** Try reading a sample prescription.

The sample prescription is for Darvon Compound-65 (appearing on the prescription as Darvon cpd-65). The prescription tells the pharmacist to give you 24 capsules (#24). It also directs you to take one capsule (cap i) every four hours (q̄4h) as needed (prn) for pain. In the space for refill information, the prescription indicates that you should receive up to five refills (5X). The prescription also says that the label on the drug container

should state the name of the drug (LABEL-yes). It also gives your name and address, your age, the date of the prescription, and the name of the physician. Many prescription blanks also give the doctor's office address and telephone number in case the pharmacist needs to call for clarification or verification.

**Step 3:** Talk with your pharmacist.

Once you have read the prescription, you may feel that you understand the instructions. But you may not understand them clearly enough. Using the sample Darvon prescription as an example, the prescription states that you can take one capsule every four hours as needed. What does "as needed" mean? Surely you shouldn't take a capsule each hour even if you feel you need one. How many capsules is your maximum for the day? You need to know your daily limit on this prescription.

As another example, suppose your prescription states that you

---

John D. Jones MD
Anytown, U.S.A.

DEA# 123456789                    PHONE# 123-4567

NAME *Your Name*                  AGE *25*
ADDRESS *Anytown, USA*            DATE *5/4/88*

℞     *Darvon cpd-65*
      *#24*
      *Sig: cap i q̄ 4h prn pain*

                                  *John D. Jones MD*
REFILLS *5X*
LABEL *yes*                                        MD

---

## COMMON ABBREVIATIONS AND SYMBOLS USED IN WRITING PRESCRIPTIONS

| Abbreviation | Meaning | Derivation and Notes |
|---|---|---|
| A$_2$ | both ears | *auris* (Latin) |
| aa | of each | *ana* (Greek) |
| ac | before meals | *ante cibum* (Latin) |
| AD | right ear | *auris dextra* (Latin) |
| AL | left ear | *auris laeva* (Latin) |
| AM | morning | *ante meridiem* (Latin) |
| AS | left ear | *auris sinistra* (Latin) |
| bid | twice a day | *bis in die* (Latin) |
| c̄ | with | *cum* (Latin) |
| cap | capsule | — |
| cc or cm$^3$ | cubic centimeter | 30 cc equals one ounce |
| disp | dispense | — |
| dtd# | give this number | *dentur tales doses* (Latin) |
| ea | each | — |
| ext | for external use | — |
| gt | drop | *gutta* (Latin) |
| gtt | drops | *guttae* (Latin) |
| h | hour | *hora* (Latin) |
| hs | bedtime | *hora somni* (Latin) |
| M ft | make | *misce fiat* (Latin) |
| mitt# | give this number | *mitte* (Latin) |
| ml | milliliter | 30 ml equals one ounce |
| O | pint | *octarius* (Latin) |
| O$_2$ | both eyes | *oculus* (Latin) |
| OD | right eye | *oculus dexter* (Latin) |
| OL | left eye | *oculus laevus* (Latin) |
| OS | left eye | *oculus sinister* (Latin) |
| OU | each eye | *oculus uterque* (Latin) |
| pc | after meals | *post cibum* (Latin) |
| PM | evening | *post meridiem* (Latin) |
| po | by mouth | *per os* (Latin) |
| prn | as needed | *pro re nata* (Latin) |
| q̄ | every | *quaque* (Latin) |
| qd | once a day | *quaque die* (Latin) |
| qid | four times a day | *quater in die* (Latin) |
| qod | every other day | — |
| s̄ | without | *sine* (Latin) |
| Sig | label as follows | *signa* (Latin) |
| sl | under the tongue | *sub lingua* (Latin) |
| SOB | shortness of breath | — |
| sol | solution | — |
| ss | half unit | *semis* (Latin) |
| stat | at once, first dose | *statim* (Latin) |
| susp | suspension | — |
| tab | tablet | — |
| tid | three times a day | *ter in die* (Latin) |
| top | apply topically | — |
| ung or ungt | ointment | *unguentum* (Latin) |
| UT | under the tongue | — |
| ut dict | as directed | *ut dictum* (Latin) |
| X | times | — |

should "take one tablet four times a day." Does that mean one tablet every six hours around the clock (which means getting up at night to take a tablet) or one tablet in the early morning, one at noon, one in the late afternoon or early evening, and one at bedtime? For other medications, it might mean one tablet every hour for the first four hours after arising in the morning. If you are confused about these instructions, be sure to ask the pharmacist while you are there in the pharmacy. He or she can always call the physician for clarification, if necessary.

**Step 4:** Check with your pharmacist about how to take this medication.

For some medications, it makes a difference whether you take the drug before a meal, after a meal, or along with it. *When* you take the drug can make an important difference; often, the effectiveness of the drug depends on exactly following the directions for its use. Your pharmacist can help you understand directions such as "take with fluid," "as directed," and "as needed." With some drugs you may take water, whereas with others you should take milk or fruit juice. Some diuretics, for example, should be taken with orange or other citrus juice or with tomato juice to decrease potassium loss, since these foods contain natural potassium. Also, be sure to check on the maximum number of doses per day if your prescription simply says "as needed."

**Step 5:** Ask about any foods, beverages, or other drugs that you should avoid.

This is a very important step, because some drugs may in-

teract in negative—even dangerous—ways with tobacco, alcohol, certain foods, or drugs you habitually take (even common nonprescription drugs like aspirin). Ask your pharmacist specifically about all these items, even if you have already discussed them with your doctor. You may have neglected to mention that you will be traveling and taking an antinausea medication, for example, or that you will be going to a dinner party where alcohol will be served, or that you take a certain medication for a chronic condition. Go over the list of items with your pharmacist just to make sure. Ask specifically about alcohol and about avoiding any foods. There are many drugs that interact dangerously with alcohol—don't become a "drug reaction" statistic. If you are taking oral contraceptives, be sure to mention the type you take and ask if you should continue to take it along with the new medication. If the pharmacist says no, check with your doctor about an alternative birth control method that can be used safely with the medication.

**Step 6:** Ask about activities that you should avoid or restrict.

Some drugs now contain warnings on the label that you should not drive or operate equipment or machinery because the drug causes drowsiness and slowed reactions. Even if your medication does not carry such a warning, ask anyway. Drowsiness is a common side effect and, in a driver, can be lethal. Also ask if you need to restrict travel or exposure to the sun. Some drugs, especially in combination with other drugs, cause photosensitivity (sensitivity to light—that is, to the sun), and you may suffer an uncomfortable rash and other side effects.

**Step 7:** Make sure that you know how long to continue the medication.

The length of time you need to take a medication varies with your condition and also with the drug itself. In some cases, it is advisable to stop the drug as soon as your symptoms disappear in order to minimize side effects or, in some cases, to avoid building up a tolerance to the drug. In other cases, you should continue taking the drug for a specified length of time regardless of whether you are free from symptoms. In some special cases, such as kidney infection, the treatment is long-term, and you'll need to take the medication for several weeks or months.

**Step 8:** Be certain that you are familiar with possible side effects.

This is probably the most important step of all. Your doctor will probably have already mentioned possible side effects to you, but check again with your pharmacist. What are the most common side effects of this drug? Write down the list if you have trouble remembering. Which can you expect and which are rare? Which side effects are not cause for concern and which ones are serious? For example, the drug phenylbutazone may cause a blood disorder, one of the first symptoms of which is a sore throat; thus, your pharmacist will urge you to check with your doctor if your throat becomes sore in the course of taking this medication. (This topic is discussed in more detail in the section on managing side effects.)

**Step 9:** Learn how to store your medication.

Finally, before you leave the drugstore or pharmacy, ask the pharmacist how to store the medication. This is important because many drugs can lose potency and therefore become ineffective if they are not stored correctly.

## STORING YOUR DRUGS

All medications should be kept in their original containers to protect them from heat and moisture, which may cause them to lose potency. To prevent confusion, do not mix different medications in one container. Also, some drugs lose their potency when stored with other medications. Never remove the label from the prescription vial. It contains your prescription number (for refills), the name of the medication, and directions for proper use.

You can safely store most prescription drugs at room temperature and out of direct sunlight. Even those drugs dispensed in colored bottles or containers that reflect light should be kept out of direct sunlight.

Some drugs require storage in the refrigerator; other medications should not be refrigerated. For example, some liquid cough suppressants thicken as they become cold, and will not pour from the bottle. Some people keep nitroglycerin tablets in the refrigerator because they mistakenly believe that the drug will be more stable if kept cold; however, nitroglycerin should not be stored in the refrigerator.

Even if the label on your medication states that it should be kept refrigerated, this does not mean that you can keep the drug in the freezer. If frozen and thawed, coated tablets may crack, and some liquid medications may separate into layers that cannot be remixed.

Many people keep prescription drugs and other medications in the bathroom medicine cabinet, but this is one of the worst places to keep drugs. Small children can easily climb onto the sink and reach drugs stored above it. Also, the temperature and humidity changes in the bathroom may adversely affect the stability of both prescription and nonprescription drugs.

## DEFINITIONS OF STORAGE TEMPERATURES

| | |
|---|---|
| **Excessive cold** | **Under 36°F (2°C)** |
| **Cold** | **Between 36° and 46°F (2° to 8°C)** |
| **Cool** | **Between 46° and 59°F (8° to 15°C)** |
| **Room temperature** | **Usually between 59° and 86°F (15° to 30°C)** |
| **Excessive heat** | **Above 104°F (40°C)** |

It is required by law that all prescription medications for oral use be dispensed in childproof containers. If you find the container difficult to open and if there are no small children in your home, you can request that your pharmacist dispense your medication in a nonchildproof container.

KEEP ALL DRUGS AWAY FROM CHILDREN, and do not keep unused prescription medications. Flush any leftover medication down the toilet or pour it down the sink, and wash and destroy the empty container.

Regularly clean out your medicine cabinet and discard all the drugs you are no longer using, as well as those for which the expiration date has passed (the expiration date is often listed on the prescription label). These drugs can be dangerous to your children. Also, you might be tempted to take them in the future if you experience similar symptoms; if those symptoms are not due to the same disease, you may complicate your condition by taking the wrong medication.

If a child accidentally swallows medication or receives too much of a prescribed medication, IMMEDIATELY CALL A POISON CONTROL CENTER OR THE NEAREST EMERGENCY ROOM for instructions and recommendations. These phone numbers should be written down in a readily accessible place. You should also keep a bottle of ipecac syrup (available without a prescription) for each child under five years of age in your home (in case the poison control center or emergency room recommends that you induce vomiting in the child). Do not administer ipecac syrup unless you have been instructed to do so by medical personnel.

# Buying drugs

Prescription drugs can be expensive. Therefore, you might want to ask your pharmacist about substituting a generic drug for a trade-name drug when filling your prescription, particularly if your drug therapy is a long-term affair.

A generic drug is one that is not protected by trademark registration. The generic name of a drug is often a shortened form of its chemical name. Any manufacturer can use this generic name (for example, many manufacturers make the drug called tetracycline).

Usually a manufacturer will use both a trade name (or brand name) and a generic name for a drug. A trade name is registered and reserved for the manufacturer who holds that trademark. Thus, to follow the previous example, only Lederle Laboratories can call their tetracycline Achromycin, and only Upjohn can use the name Panmycin for the same drug. (If you're uncertain about what the trade name is, it is usually capitalized in print and is accompanied by the registered symbol ®.)

It is not necessarily true that trade-name drugs are made by large manufacturers and generic drugs by small ones. Often a manufacturer will market large quantities of a certain drug under a trade name and then sell the base chemical to several other companies, some of which will sell the drug generically, while others will sell it under their own trade name.

The major difference between trade-name drugs and generic drugs is in cost. Generic drugs are often priced lower than trademarked equivalents because they are less widely advertised. You should be aware, however, that not all drugs are available generically. Furthermore, not every generic drug is significantly cheaper than, or equivalent to, the trademarked drug. You should seek your pharmacist's advice on these matters, since some trademarked drugs are superior to their generic equivalents, while others are not significantly different either in quality or in price. Remember, however, that although the Food and Drug Administration reports that there is no evidence of "serious differences" between

generic and trade-name drugs, private research has demonstrated differences in quality between certain brands.

If you do find an acceptable, safe generic equivalent for your drug, your cost saving can be significant. One hundred tablets of Inderal may cost $22 to $25, while the generic equivalent (propranolol) can be bought for about $18—a saving of $4 to $7. Motrin may cost $20 for 100 tablets, but its generic equivalent (ibuprofen) may cost as little as $12—a saving of $8 per prescription.

In most states, substitution laws allow pharmacists to fill prescriptions with the least expensive equivalent product. If such substitution is not yet legal in your state (contact your state pharmacy association to find out), you might ask your doctor to prescribe drugs by their generic names. However, you should be aware that there are sometimes differences, and your doctor may have a good reason for being specific.

Your pharmacist can also help you save money by recommending the use of over-the-counter (OTC) drugs. These are drugs that can be purchased without a prescription and consequently can be sold anywhere. There are no legal limitations on who can buy them.

In general, OTC drugs are safer to use than prescription drugs since they are not as strong as those that require a doctor's signature. Often, a pharmacist or a doctor can recommend an OTC drug that is less costly and less potent than a prescription medication but just as effective. For example, aspirin, which is inexpensive and widely available, is a highly effective anti-inflammatory drug that is commonly used in the treatment of

arthritis and other inflammatory diseases.

Patients with chronic conditions, such as heart disease, high blood pressure, and diabetes, may want to save money by purchasing medications in quantity. Generally, the price per dose decreases with the amount purchased. For example, a drug that costs 6 cents per tablet when bought in amounts of 25 or 30 tablets costs only 4 to 5 cents per tablet when bought in bottles of 100 or more. Many doctors will prescribe a one- to six-month supply of a drug that you take regularly.

If you have a history of drug reactions or allergies and are concerned about the side effects of a certain drug, you might ask the pharmacist to fill one half or one quarter of the prescription to see if the drug "agrees" with you. You may have to pay more per dose when you buy a small amount, but you will then have a chance to test the drug on yourself. Make sure that the pharmacist realizes that you took only part of the prescription so that you can get the rest if you need it. For many drugs, however, you must get another prescription once any part of the first has been filled.

## Administering medication correctly

You must use medication correctly to obtain its full benefit. If you administer drugs improperly, you may not receive their full therapeutic effects. Furthermore, improper administration can be dangerous. Some drugs become toxic if they are used incorrectly.

## LIQUIDS

Liquid medications are used in several different ways. Some are intended to be used externally on the skin; some are placed into the eye, ear, nose, or throat; still others may be taken internally. Before taking or using any liquid medication, look at the label to see if there are specific directions.

If a liquid product contains particles that settle to the bottom of the container, it must be shaken before you use the medication. If you don't shake it well each time, you may not get the correct amount of the active ingredient; as the amount of liquid remaining in the bottle becomes smaller, the drug becomes more concentrated, and you will get more of the active ingredient with each dose. The concentration may even reach toxic levels.

When opening the bottle, point it away from you. Some liquid medications build up pressure inside the bottle; the liquid could spurt out and stain your clothing. If the medication is intended for application to the skin, pour a small quantity onto a cotton pad or a piece of gauze. Do not use a large piece of cotton or gauze, as it will absorb the liquid and much will be wasted. Don't pour the medication into your cupped hand; you may spill some of it. If you're using it on only a small area, you can spread the medication with your finger or a cotton-tipped applicator. Never dip applicators or pieces of cotton or gauze into the bottle of liquid, since this might contaminate the rest of the medication.

Liquid medications that are to be swallowed must be measured accurately. When your doctor prescribes one teaspoonful of medication, he or she is thinking of a five-milliliter medical teaspoon. The teaspoons you have at home can hold anywhere from two to ten milliliters of liquid. If you use one of these to measure your medication, you may get too little or too much drug with each dose. Ask your pharmacist for a medical teaspoon or for one of the other plastic devices for accurately measuring liquid medications. Most of these cost only a few cents, and they are well worth their cost in ensuring accurate dosage. Such plastic measuring devices have another advantage. While many children balk at medication taken from a teaspoon, they often seem to enjoy taking it from a "special" spoon.

## CAPSULES, TABLETS, AND ORAL POWDERS

Many people find it hard to swallow a tablet or capsule. If tablets or capsules tend to catch in your throat, rinse your mouth with water, or at least wet your mouth, before taking one. Place the tablet or capsule on the back of your tongue, take a drink, and swallow. If it is too large, or still "sticks" in your throat, empty the capsule or crush the tablet into a spoon and mix it with applesauce, soup, or even chocolate syrup. BE SURE TO CHECK WITH YOUR PHARMACIST FIRST. Some tablets and capsules must be swallowed whole—your pharmacist can tell you which ones they are.

If you have trouble swallowing a tablet or capsule and do not wish to mix the medication with food, ask your doctor to prescribe a liquid drug preparation or a chewable tablet instead, if one is available.

Occasionally, medications come in oral powder form (for example, cholestyramine and colestipol). Such medications should be carefully mixed with a liquid or with applesauce before being swallowed. These medications should NOT be swallowed dry.

## EXAMPLES OF DRUGS THAT MUST BE SWALLOWED WHOLE

**aminophylline (sustained-release tablets)**
**cimetidine (tablets)**
**erythromycin (coated tablets, capsules)**
**isosorbide dinitrate (sustained-release tablets and capsules)**
**meprobamate (sustained-release capsules)**
**oxtriphylline (sustained-release tablets)**
**theophylline (sustained-release tablets and capsules)**

## EXAMPLES OF DRUGS THAT SHOULD BE USED QUICKLY (WITHIN 12 HOURS) IF CRUSHED OR OPENED

| | |
|---|---|
| amitriptyline | imipramine |
| chlorprom-azine | prochlorper-azine |
| doxepin | thioridazine |
| haloperidol | trifluoperazine |

## SUBLINGUAL TABLETS

Some drugs, such as nitroglycerin, are prepared as tablets that must be placed under the tongue. Such medications are more rapidly or more completely absorbed into the bloodstream from the lining of the mouth than they are from the stomach and intestines.

To take a sublingual tablet properly, place the tablet under your tongue, close your mouth, and hold the saliva in your mouth and under your tongue for as long as you can before swallowing (until the tablet has completely dissolved). If you have a bitter taste in your mouth after five minutes, the drug has not been completely absorbed. Wait at least five more minutes before drinking water. Drinking too soon may wash the medication into the stomach before it has been absorbed thoroughly. Do not smoke, eat, or chew gum while the medication is dissolving.

### EYE DROPS AND EYE OINTMENTS

Before administering eye drops or ointments, wash your hands. Then lie down or sit down, and tilt your head back. Using your thumb and forefinger, gently and carefully pull your lower eyelid down to form a pouch. If you're applying eye drops, lay your second finger alongside your nose and apply gentle pressure to your nose. This closes the duct that drains fluid from the surface of the eye into the nose and throat. If you don't close this duct, the drops may drain away too soon. Hold the dropper close to the eyelid WITHOUT TOUCHING IT. Place the prescribed number of drops into the pouch. Do not place the drops directly on the eyeball; you might blink and lose the medication. Close your eye and keep it shut for a few moments. Do not wash or wipe the dropper before replacing it in the bottle—you might contaminate the rest of the medication. Tightly close the bottle to keep out moisture.

To administer an eye ointment, squeeze a line of ointment one-quarter to one-half inch long into the pouch formed as described for administering eye drops, and close your eye. Roll your eye a few times to spread the ointment.

Be sure the drops or ointments you use are intended for use in the eye (all products manufactured for use in the eye must have been sterilized to prevent eye infections). Also, check the expiration date on the label or container of the medication. Do not use a drug product after the specified date, and never use any eye product that has changed color. If you find that the medication contains particles that weren't there when you bought it, do not use it.

### EAR DROPS

Ear drops must be administered so that they fill the ear canal. To administer ear drops properly, tilt your head to one side, turning the affected ear upward. Grasp the earlobe and gently pull it upward and back to straighten the ear canal. When administering ear drops to a child, GENTLY pull the child's earlobe downward and back. Fill the dropper and place the prescribed number of drops (usually a dropperful) into the ear, but be careful to avoid touching the sides or edge of the ear canal. The dropper can easily become contaminated by contact with the ear canal.

Keep the ear tilted upward for five to ten seconds while continuing to hold the earlobe. Then gently insert a small wad of clean cotton into the ear to ensure that the drops do not escape. Do not wash or wipe the dropper after use; replace it in the bottle and tightly close the bottle to keep out moisture.

Before administering the medication, you may warm the bottle of ear drops by rolling the bottle back and forth between your hands to bring the solution to body temperature. DO NOT place the bottle in boiling water. The ear drops may become so hot that they will cause pain when placed in the ear. Also, boiling water can loosen or peel off the label, and might even destroy the medication.

### NOSE DROPS AND SPRAYS

Before using nose drops or sprays, gently blow your nose if you can. To administer nose drops, fill the dropper, tilt your head back, and place the prescribed number of drops into your nose. To prevent contamination of the rest of the medicine when the dropper is returned to the container, do not touch the dropper to the nasal membranes. Keep your head tilted for five to ten seconds, and sniff gently two or three times.

Do not tilt your head back when using a nasal spray. Insert the sprayer into the nose, but try to avoid touching the inner nasal membranes. Sniff and squeeze the sprayer at the same time. Do not release your grip on the sprayer until you have withdrawn it from your nose (to prevent nasal mucus and bacteria from entering the plastic bottle and contaminating its contents). After you have sprayed the prescribed number of times in one or both nostrils, gently sniff two or three times.

Unless your doctor has told you otherwise, you should not use nose drops or sprays for more than two or three days at a time. If they have been prescribed for a longer period, do not administer nose drops or sprays from the same container for more than one week. Bacteria from your nose can easily enter the container and contaminate the solution. If you must take medication for more than a week, purchase a new container. NEVER allow anyone else to use your nose drops or spray.

## RECTAL SUPPOSITORIES

Rectal suppositories are used to deliver various types of medication. They may be used as a laxative, sleeping aid, or tranquilizer, or to relieve the itching, swelling, and pain of hemorrhoids. Regardless of the reason for their use, all rectal suppositories are inserted in the same way.

In extremely hot weather, a suppository may become too soft to handle properly. If this happens, place the suppository in the refrigerator, in a glass of cool water, or under running cold water until it becomes firm. A few minutes is usually sufficient. Before inserting a suppository, remove any aluminum wrappings. Rubber finger coverings or disposable rubber gloves may be worn when inserting a suppository, but they are not necessary unless your fingernails are extremely long and sharp.

To insert a suppository, lie on your left side with your right knee bent. Push the suppository, pointed end first, into the rectum as far as is comfortable. You may feel like defecating, but lie still for 20 to 30 minutes, until the urge has passed. If you cannot insert a suppository, or if the process is painful, you can coat the suppository with a thin layer of petroleum jelly or mineral oil to make insertion easier.

Manufacturers of many suppositories that are used in the treatment of hemorrhoids suggest that the suppositories be stored in the refrigerator. Be sure to ask your pharmacist if the suppositories you have purchased should be stored in the refrigerator.

## VAGINAL OINTMENTS AND CREAMS

Most vaginal products are packaged with complete instructions for use. If a woman is not sure how to administer vaginal medication, she should ask her pharmacist.

Before using any vaginal ointment or cream, read the directions. They will probably tell you to attach the applicator to the top of the tube and to squeeze the tube from the bottom until the applicator is completely filled. Then lie on your back with your knees drawn up. Hold the applicator horizontally or pointed slightly downward, and insert it into the vagina as far as it will go comfortably. Press the plunger down to empty the cream or ointment into the vagina. Withdraw the plunger and wash it in warm, soapy water. Rinse it thoroughly and allow it to dry completely. When the plunger is dry, return it to its package.

## VAGINAL TABLETS AND SUPPOSITORIES

Before using vaginal tablets or suppositories, carefully read the directions.

Remove any foil wrapping. Place the tablet or suppository in the applicator. Lie on your back with your knees drawn up. Hold the applicator horizontally or tilted slightly downward, and insert it into the vagina as far as it will go comfortably. Depress the plunger slowly to release the tablet or suppository into the vagina. Withdraw the applicator and wash it in warm, soapy water. Rinse it and let it dry completely. When the applicator is dry, return it to its package.

Unless your doctor has told you otherwise, do not douche for two to three weeks before or after you use vaginal tablets or suppositories. Be sure to ask your doctor for specific recommendations on douching.

## THROAT LOZENGES AND DISCS

Lozenges are made with crystalline sugar; discs are not. Both contain medication that is released in the mouth to soothe a sore throat, to reduce coughing, or to treat laryngitis. Neither should be chewed; they should be allowed to dissolve in the mouth. After the lozenge or disc has dissolved, try not to swallow or drink any fluids for a while.

## THROAT SPRAYS

To administer a throat spray, open your mouth wide and spray the medication as far back as possible. Try not to swallow—hold the spray in your mouth as long as you can, and do not drink any fluids for several minutes. This gives the medication a greater opportunity to work. Swallowing a throat spray is not harmful, but if you find that your throat spray upsets your stomach, don't swallow it; simply spit it out.

## TOPICAL OINTMENTS AND CREAMS

Most ointments and creams exert only local effects—that is, they affect only the area on which they are applied. Most creams and ointments are expensive (especially steroid products, such as betamethasone valerate, fluocinolone, fluocinonide, hydrocortisone, and triamcinolone), and should be applied to the skin as thinly as possible. A thin layer is as effective as (but less costly than) a thick layer, and some steroid-containing creams and ointments can cause toxic side effects if applied too heavily.

Before applying the medication, moisten the skin by immersing it in water or by dabbing the area with a clean, wet cloth. Blot the skin almost dry and apply the medication as directed. Gently massage it into the skin until it disappears. You should feel no greasiness after applying a cream. After an ointment has been applied, the skin will feel slightly greasy.

If your doctor has not indicated whether you should receive a cream or an ointment, ask your pharmacist for the one you prefer. Creams are greaseless and do not stain your clothing. Creams are best to use on the scalp or other hairy areas of the body. However, if your skin is dry, ask for an ointment. Ointments help keep the skin soft for a longer period of time.

If your doctor tells you to place a wrap on top of the skin after the cream or ointment has been applied, you may use a wrap of transparent plastic film like that used for wrapping food. A wrap holds the medication close to the skin and helps to keep the skin moist so that the drug can be absorbed. To use a wrap correctly, apply the cream or ointment as directed, and then wrap the area with a layer of transparent plastic film. Be careful to follow your doctor's

directions exactly. If you are told to leave the wrap in place for a certain length of time, do not leave it in place longer. If you keep a wrap on the skin too long, too much of the drug may be absorbed, which may lead to increased side effects. Do not use such a wrap without your doctor's approval.

## AEROSOL SPRAYS

Many topical (used on the surface of the skin) items are packaged as pressurized aerosol sprays. These sprays usually cost more than the cream or ointment form of the same medication. On the other hand, they are useful on very tender or hairy areas of the body, where it is difficult to apply a cream or ointment. Aerosols can provide a cooling effect on burns or rashes.

Before using an aerosol, shake the can to evenly disperse the particles of medication. Hold the container upright, four to six inches from the skin. Press the nozzle for a few seconds and then release it.

Never use an aerosol around the face or eyes. If your doctor tells you to use the spray on a part of your face, apply it to your hand and then rub it into the area. If you get it into your eyes or on a mucous membrane, it can be very painful; it may even damage the eyes.

Aerosol sprays may feel cold when they are applied. If this sensation bothers you, ask your pharmacist or doctor whether another form of the same product is available.

## TRANSDERMAL PATCHES

Transdermal patches allow controlled, continuous release of

medication. They are convenient and easy to use. For best results, apply the patch to a hairless or clean-shaven area of skin, avoiding scars and wounds. Choose a site (such as the chest or upper arm) that is not subject to excessive movement. It is all right to bathe or shower with a patch in place. In the event that the patch becomes displaced, discard and replace it. When replacing a patch, first apply the new unit and then remove the old one. This allows for uninterrupted drug therapy. Also, since you change the site each time, skin irritation is minimized.

If redness or irritation develops at the application site, consult your physician. Some people are sensitive to the materials used to make the patches.

## MEDICATIONS AND CHILDREN

There are some special considerations when administering medications to children, as well as some techniques for making the process easier for parent and child alike. These are discussed on pages 337–338.

A special concern with regard to medications is the danger that they can present to children. Poisoning due to medications— whether they are pills found in a visitor's purse, medications taken from a medicine chest to which the child has access, or overdoses of baby aspirin or vitamin or mineral supplements—is a common cause of death in children. It is important to teach children that drugs are not candy and to be vigilant about the risk of poisoning that any medication brought into your home can present to your child. Also, be sure to post the phone number of the local Poison Control Center next to every phone in your home in case of an overdose.

# Coping with side effects

Drugs have certain desirable effects—that's why they are taken. The desirable effects of a drug are known as the drug's activity or therapeutic effects. Drugs may, however, have undesirable effects as well. These side effects, or adverse reactions, can range from the relatively minor (such as a headache or an upset stomach) to the much more serious (such as heartbeat irregularity or a severe allergic reaction).

Even if you experience minor side effects, it is very important that you take your medication exactly as it was prescribed. You should take the full dose at the appropriate times throughout the day for the length of time prescribed by your doctor. Taking a lesser amount of medication to avoid side effects or because your condition appears to be improving is NOT appropriate. A smaller dose may not provide any benefit whatsoever; that is, half of the dose may not provide half of the therapeutic effects.

Some side effects are expected and unavoidable, but others may surprise the doctor as well as the patient. Unexpected reactions may be due to a person's individual response to the drug.

Side effects generally fall into one of two major groups—those that are obvious and those that cannot be detected without laboratory testing. Discussion between you and your doctor about your medication should not be restricted to easily recognized side effects; other, less obvious side effects may also be harmful.

If you know a particular side effect is expected from a particular drug, you can relax a little. Most expected side effects are temporary and need not cause alarm. You'll merely experience discomfort or inconvenience for a short time. For example, you may become drowsy after taking an antihistamine, or have a stuffy nose after taking reserpine or certain other drugs that lower blood pressure. Of course, if you find minor side effects especially bothersome, you should discuss them with your doctor, who may be able to prescribe another drug or at least reassure you that the benefits of the drug far outweigh its side effects. Sometimes side effects can be minimized or eliminated by changing your dosage schedule or taking the drug with meals. Consult your doctor or pharmacist before making such a change.

Many side effects, however, signal a serious, perhaps dangerous, problem. If these side effects appear, you should consult your doctor immediately. The following discussion should help you determine whether your side effects require attention from your physician.

## OBVIOUS SIDE EFFECTS

Some side effects are obvious to the patient; others can be discerned only through laboratory testing. We have divided our discussion according to the body parts affected by the side effects.

### Ears

Although a few drugs may cause loss of hearing if taken in large quantities, hearing loss is uncommon. Drugs that are used to treat problems of the ear may cause dizziness, and many drugs produce tinnitus (a sensation of ringing, buzzing, thumping, or hollowness in the ears). Discuss with your doctor any problem with your hearing or your ears if it persists.

### Eyes

Blurred vision is a common side effect of many drugs. For example, digoxin may cause you to see a halo around a lighted object (a television screen or a traffic light), and other drugs may cause night blindness. Chlordiazepoxide and clidinium combination may make it difficult to accurately judge distance while driving and may make the eyes sensitive to sunlight. While the effects caused by digoxin are danger signs of toxicity, those caused by chlordiazepoxide and clidinium combination are to be expected. In any case, if you have difficulty seeing while taking a drug, contact your doctor.

### Gastrointestinal system

The gastrointestinal system includes the mouth, esophagus, stomach, small and large intestines, and rectum. A side effect that affects the gastrointestinal system can be expected from almost any drug. Many drugs produce dry mouth, mouth sores, difficulty in swallowing, heartburn, nausea, vomiting, diarrhea, constipation, loss of appetite, or cramping. Other drugs cause bloating and gas, and some cause rectal itching.

Diarrhea can be expected after taking many drugs. Drugs can create localized reactions in intestinal tissue—usually a more rapid rate of contraction, which

## EXAMPLES OF DRUGS THAT MAY CAUSE DIARRHEA

| | |
|---|---|
| allopurinol | methyldopa |
| aminophylline | metronidazole |
| ampicillin | minocycline |
| cephalexin | oral antidia- |
| cimetidine | betics |
| digoxin | oral contra- |
| diphenhydra- | ceptives |
| mine | penicillins |
| disopyramide | prazosin |
| erythromycin | procainamide |
| haloperidol | propranolol |
| ibuprofen | spironolactone |
| imipramine | sulfa drugs |
| meprobamate | tetracycline |
| methyclothi- | |
| azide | |

leads to diarrhea. Diarrhea caused by most drugs is temporary and self-limiting; it should stop within three days. During this time, do not take any diarrhea remedy; drink liquids to replace the fluid you are losing. If the diarrhea lasts more than three days, you should call your doctor.

Diarrhea sometimes signals a problem. For example, some antibiotics can cause severe diarrhea. When diarrhea is severe, the intestine may become ulcerated and begin to bleed. If you have severe diarrhea (diarrhea that lasts for several days or stools that contain blood, pus, or mucus) while taking antibiotics, contact your doctor.

## EXAMPLES OF DRUGS THAT MAY BE ASSOCIATED WITH INCREASED INCIDENCE OF ULCERS

| | |
|---|---|
| fenoprofen | naproxen |
| ibuprofen | prednisone |
| indomethacin | sulindac |
| methylpred- | tolmetin |
| nisolone | |

As a side effect of drug use, constipation is less serious and more common than diarrhea. It occurs when a drug, such as chlorpromazine, slows the activity of the bowel. Constipation also occurs when drugs cause moisture to be absorbed from the bowel, resulting in a more solid stool. Some drugs, such as methyldopa, act on the nervous system to decrease nerve impulses to the intestine. Constipation produced by a drug can last several days. You may help relieve it by drinking eight to ten glasses of water a day (unless your doctor directs you to do otherwise). Do not take laxatives unless your doctor directs you to do so. If constipation continues for more than three days, call your doctor.

## EXAMPLES OF DRUGS THAT MAY CAUSE CONSTIPATION

| | |
|---|---|
| chlorprom- | metronidazole |
| azine | phenytoin |
| clonidine | prazosin |
| diazepam | prochlorper- |
| dicyclomine | azine |
| diphenhydra- | propranolol |
| mine | sulindac |
| haloperidol | thioridazine |
| methyldopa | trifluoperazine |

### Circulatory system

Drugs may speed up or slow down the heartbeat. If a drug slows the heartbeat, you may feel drowsy and tired, or even dizzy. If a drug accelerates the heartbeat, you probably will experience palpitations (a sensation of thumping in the chest). You may feel as though your heart is skipping a beat occasionally. If any of these symptoms occurs, consult your doctor, who may adjust your drug

dosage or prescribe other medication.

Some drugs cause edema (fluid retention)—fluid from the blood collects outside the blood vessels. Ordinarily, edema itself is not serious. However, if you are steadily gaining weight or have gained more than two pounds within a week, talk to your doctor.

Drugs may either increase or decrease blood pressure. When blood pressure decreases, you may feel drowsy or tired; you may become dizzy, or even faint, especially when you rise suddenly from a sitting or reclining position. If a medication makes you dizzy or lightheaded, sit or lie down for a while. To avoid light-headedness when you stand, contract and relax the muscles of your legs for a few moments before rising. Do this by pushing one foot against the floor while raising the other foot slightly, alternating feet so that you are "pumping" your legs in a pedaling motion. Get up slowly, and be especially careful on stairs. When blood pressure increases, you may feel

## EXAMPLES OF DRUGS THAT MAY CAUSE FLUID RETENTION*

| | |
|---|---|
| amitriptyline | oral contra- |
| chlordiaze- | ceptives |
| poxide | prednisone |
| conjugated | prochlorper- |
| estrogens | azine |
| disopyramide | sulfa drugs |
| fenoprofen | sulindac |
| hydralazine | thioridazine |
| ibuprofen | tolmetin |
| methylpred- | trifluoper- |
| nisolone | azine |
| naproxen | |

*Indicated by a weight gain of two or more pounds in a week.

dizzy, have a headache or blurred vision, hear a ringing or buzzing in your ears, or experience frequent nosebleeds. If you experience any of these symptoms, call your doctor.

### Nervous system

Drugs that act on the nervous system may cause drowsiness or stimulation. If a drug causes drowsiness, you may become dizzy or your coordination may become impaired. If a drug causes stimulation, you may become nervous or have insomnia or tremors. Neither drowsiness nor stimulation is cause for concern for most people. When you are drowsy, however, you should be careful around machinery and should avoid driving. Some drugs cause throbbing headaches, and others produce tingling in the fingers or toes. These symptoms should disappear in a few days to a week. If they do not, call your doctor.

### EXAMPLES OF DRUGS THAT MAY CAUSE DIZZINESS

| | |
|---|---|
| cephalexin | methyldopa |
| chlorothiazide | methylpred- |
| cimetidine | nisolone |
| dicyclomine | metronidazole |
| diphenhy- | nitroglycerin |
| dramine | oral contra- |
| disopyramide | ceptives |
| flurazepam | prazosin |
| imipramine | spironolactone |
| lorazepam | sulindac |
| meprobamate | |
| methyclothi- | |
| azide | |

### Respiratory system

Respiratory system side effects include stuffy nose, dry throat,

shortness of breath, and slowed breathing. A stuffy nose and dry throat usually disappear several days after starting a medication. If these side effects are bothersome, you may use nose drops (consult your doctor first) or throat lozenges or gargle with warm salt water to relieve them. Shortness of breath is a characteristic side effect of some drugs (for example, propranolol). If shortness of breath continues, check with your doctor. It may be a sign of a serious side effect, or you may simply be overexercising. Barbiturates (drugs that promote sleep) often slow breathing; if your breathing becomes labored, however, contact your doctor immediately.

### Skin

Skin reactions include rash, swelling, itching, and sweating. Itching, swelling, and rash frequently indicate a drug allergy. You should NOT continue to take a drug if you develop an allergy to it, but consult your doctor before stopping the drug.

Some drugs increase sweating; others decrease it. Drugs that decrease sweating may cause problems during exercise or hot weather, when your body needs to sweat to reduce body temperature.

If you have a minor skin reaction not diagnosed as an allergy, ask your pharmacist for a soothing cream. Your pharmacist may also suggest that you take frequent baths or dust the sensitive area with a suitable powder.

Another type of skin reaction is photosensitivity (also called phototoxicity or sun toxicity)—that is, unusual sensitivity to the sun. If, while taking a drug that can cause photosensitivity, you are exposed to the sun for even a

### EXAMPLES OF DRUGS THAT MAY CAUSE A MILD RASH

| | |
|---|---|
| allopurinol | imipramine |
| amitriptyline | indomethacin |
| ampicillin | lorazepam |
| chlordiaze- | methyclo- |
| poxide | thiazide |
| chlorothiazide | penicillins |
| cimetidine | prazosin |
| clonidine | procainamide |
| diazepam | prochlorper- |
| diphenhy- | azine |
| dramine | spironolactone |
| disopyramide | sulindac |
| haloperidol | trifluoperazine |
| hydrochloro- | |
| thiazide | |

brief period of time (10 or 15 minutes), you may receive a severe sunburn. You do not have to stay indoors while taking these drugs, but you should be fully clothed while outside, and you should not remain in the sun too long. You should also use a sunscreen while in the sun—ask your pharmacist to help you choose one. Since medications may remain in your bloodstream after you stop taking them, you should continue to follow these precautions for two days after treatment with these drugs has been completed.

### EXAMPLES OF DRUGS THAT MAY CAUSE PHOTOSENSITIVITY

| | |
|---|---|
| chlorothi- | hydrochloro- |
| azide | thiazide |
| chlorprom- | imipramine |
| azine | methyclothi- |
| chlorprop- | azide |
| amide | oral antidia- |
| diphenhy- | betics |
| dramine | prochlorper- |
| furosemide | azine |
| griseofulvin | sulfa drugs |
| haloperidol | tetracycline |

## MANAGEMENT OF SIDE EFFECTS

Consult your physician to determine whether the side effects you are experiencing are minor (relatively common and usually not serious) or major (signs that something is amiss in your drug therapy). If your side effects are minor, you may be able to compensate for them simply (see the table on the right for suggestions). However, consult your doctor if you find minor side effects persistent or particularly bothersome.

If you experience any major side effects, contact your doctor immediately. Your dosage may need adjustment, or you may have developed a sensitivity to the drug. Your doctor may want you to switch to an alternative medication to treat your disorder. Never stop taking a prescribed medication unless you first discuss it with your doctor.

## SUBTLE SIDE EFFECTS

Some side effects are difficult to detect. You may not notice any symptoms at all, or you may notice only slight ones. Therefore, your doctor may want you to have periodic blood tests or eye examinations to ensure that no subtle damage is occurring to any of your organ systems while you are taking certain medications.

### Effects on the blood

A great many drugs affect the blood and the circulatory system but do not produce noticeable symptoms for some time. Some drugs decrease the number of red blood cells—the cells responsible for carrying oxygen

## COMMON MINOR SIDE EFFECTS

| Side Effect | Management |
| --- | --- |
| Blurred vision | Avoid driving and operating machinery. |
| Constipation | Increase the fiber in your diet; drink plenty of fluids*; exercise.* |
| Decreased sweating | Avoid working or exercising in the sun. |
| Diarrhea | Drink plenty of fluids; if diarrhea is severe or bloody or lasts longer than three days, call your doctor. |
| Dizziness | Avoid operating machinery. |
| Drowsiness | Avoid operating machinery. |
| Dry mouth | Suck on hard candy or ice chips; chew gum. |
| Dry nose and throat | Use a humidifier or vaporizer. |
| Fluid retention | Avoid adding salt to foods; keep legs raised, if possible. |
| Headache | Remain quiet; take aspirin or acetaminophen.* |
| Insomnia | Take the last dose of the drug earlier in the day*; drink a glass of warm milk at bedtime; ask your doctor about an exercise program. |
| Itching | Call your doctor. |
| Nasal congestion | If necessary, use nose drops.* |
| Palpitations (mild) | Rest often; avoid tension; do not drink coffee, tea, or cola; stop smoking; call your doctor. |
| Upset stomach | Take the drug with milk or food.* |

*Consult your doctor first.

throughout the body. If you have too few red blood cells, you become anemic; you appear pale and feel tired, weak, and dizzy. Other drugs decrease the number of white blood cells—the cells responsible for combating bacteria. Having too few white blood cells increases susceptibility to infection and may prolong

## EXAMPLES OF DRUGS THAT MAY CAUSE BLOOD DISORDERS*

| | |
|---|---|
| allopurinol | oral contra- |
| amitriptyline | ceptives |
| chlorthalidone | steroids |
| cimetidine | sulfa drugs |
| furosemide | thioridazine |
| hydralazine | tolazamide |
| hydrochloro- | tolbutamide |
| thiazide | trifluoper- |
| imipramine | azine |

*Indicated by a sore throat that doesn't go away in one or two days.

illness. If a sore throat or a fever begins after you start taking a drug, you may have an infection and too few white blood cells to fight it. Call your doctor.

### Effects on the kidneys

If one of the side effects of a drug is to reduce the ability of the kidneys to remove chemicals and other substances from the blood, these substances begin to accumulate in body tissues. Over a period of time, this accumulation may cause vague symptoms, such as swelling, fluid retention, nausea, head-ache, and weakness. Obvious symptoms, especially pain, are rare.

### Effects on the liver

Drug-induced liver damage may result in fat accumulation within the liver. Since the liver is responsible for converting many drugs and body chemicals into compounds that can be elimi-nated by other organs of the body (kidneys, lungs, intestines), drug-induced liver damage can result in a buildup of these sub-stances. Because liver damage may be quite advanced before it produces any symptoms, peri-odic blood tests of liver function are recommended during ther-apy with certain drugs.

### DRUG USE DURING PREGNANCY AND BREAST-FEEDING

Because drugs can cross the placenta and can pass into breast milk, it is very important to tell your doctor if you are pregnant, planning to become pregnant, or breast-feeding an infant before taking any medications. For most drugs, complete informa-tion on safety during pregnancy and while breast-feeding is lack-ing. This is due not to negligence on the part of regulatory agen-cies or lack of concern, but rather to the fact that it would be unethical to conduct drug exper-iments on pregnant and nursing women. Thus, you should dis-cuss with your doctor the risks versus the benefits of taking any medication during pregnancy or while nursing.

# INDEX

toxic multinodular goiter, 276
toxic shock syndrome, 306–307
toxoplasmosis, 327
  and retinitis, 159
trachea, 163, 177
tracheostomy, 178
tracheotomy, 61
tranquilizer drugs, 416
transient ischemic attacks, 226–227
transurethral surgery, 285
traveler's diarrhea, 253–254
treadmill test. See cardiac stress
  test
triamterene, 413
triazolam, 416
trichinosis, 146
tricyclic antidepressants, 416
trifluoperazine, 416, 425, 430, 431,
  433
trigeminal neuralgia, 103–104
trihexyphenidyl, 416
trisomy 21, 380
TSH. See thyroid-stimulating hormone
  (TSH)
TSS. See toxic shock syndrome
tuberculosis, 189–190
  test for children, 83
tumor, 389
tunnel vision, 160
typhoid fever, 238
  immunization, 84
"typist's shoulder," 137

U
ulcer, 254–255
ulcerative colitis, 255–256
ultrasonography, 408
ultrasound. See ultrasonography
ultraviolet light therapy, 125
ultraviolet radiation, 127
umbilical cord, 329
umbilical hernia, 140
undescended testes, 361–362
upper GI series, 402
ureters, 258
urethra, 258, 281
urethritis, 68, 259
  nongonococcal, 316, 320–321
urinalysis, 400
urinary system, 258
urinary system disorders, 258–259
  bladder cancer, 392
  cystitis, 259–261
  cystocele, 288–289
  glomerulonephritis, 262–263
  incontinence, 263
  kidney failure, 263–264
  kidney stones, 264–265
  nongonococcal urethritis, 316,
    320–321
  proteinuria, 265–266
  pyelonephritis, 266
  rectocele, 305–306
  urethritis, 259
urine abnormalities, 258–259

urology, 38
urticaria. See hives
uterus, 287, 324. See also female
    reproductive system
  cancer of, 397
  fibroid tumors of, 295–296
  hysterectomy and, 296
  prolapse of the, 305

V
vaccination. See immunization
vaccines, 419
vagina, 287, 288. See also female
    reproductive system
vaginal disorders
  cancer, 397
  cystocele, 288–289
  vaginitis, 58, 59, 307–308
vaginismus, 292
vaginitis, 58, 59, 307–308
varicella zoster, 59
varicose veins, 227–228
vascular disorders. See heart and
    circulatory disorders
vasculitis, 80, 195
vas deferens, 281
vasectomy, 312
vasodilators, 413, 414
vasopressin, 269, 279
VD. See sexually transmitted
    diseases
veins, 192
vena cava, 192, 258
venereal diseases. See sexually
    transmitted diseases
venipuncture, 399
venous thrombosis, 189
ventricular fibrillation, 204,
    211–212
verapamil, 413, 414
vertebra(e), 130, 132
vertigo, 43–44
vibrios, 57
viral infections
  AIDS, 77–79
  aseptic meningitis, 61–62
  chicken pox, 59–60
  common cold, 165–166
  croup, 347–349
  encephalitis, 95–96
  enteroviral infections, 61–62
  Epstein-Barr virus infection, 67
  fever blisters, 118
  hand, foot, and mouth disease, 62
  hepatitis, 82, 242–243
  herpangina, 62
  herpes, 316–318
  influenza, 63, 64
  measles, 64–65
  meningitis, 100–101
  mononucleosis, 65–67
  mumps, 67–68
  myocarditis, 62
  paralytic disease, 62
  pericarditis, 62, 217

pleurodynia, 62
pneumonia, 186–188
poliomyelitis, 62
rabies, 106–107
respiratory disease, 62
Reye's syndrome and, 357, 358
rubella, 69–70
rubellalike rash, 62
shingles, 70–72, 103
subacute sclerosing
    panencephalitis, 65
warts, 127–128
virilization, 275
viruses, 55, 57
vision, 148–149, 153, 159
vital signs, 52–53
vitamin(s), 15–17, 18–21
vitamin A, 16, 18–19
  and night blindness, 159
vitamin and mineral supplements, 419
vitamin B complex, 16–17, 18–19
vitamin B$_1$. See thiamin
vitamin B$_2$, 16, 18–19
vitamin B$_6$, 16, 18–19
vitamin B$_{12}$, 16, 18–19
  and pernicious anemia, 194
vitamin C, 17, 18–19
  and common cold, 166
  and scurvy, 14
vitamin D, 17, 18–19
vitamin E, 17, 20–21
vitamin K, 17, 20–21
vitiligo, 270
vitreous humor, 148, 149
vomiting, 50–51
  during pregnancy, 325, 326. See
    also hyperemesis gravidarum

W
warfarin, 414
warts, 127–128
  genital, 314–315
"water on the brain." See
    hydrocephalus
white blood cells, 192. See also
    lymphocytes; phagocytes
whiteheads, 110
whooping cough (pertussis)
    immunization, 83
windpipe. See trachea
wrist, and carpal tunnel syndrome,
    92–94, 103

X
xerography, 409
xerophthalmia, 159

Y
yeast infection, 58, 59, 307
yellow fever immunization, 84

Z
zidovudine, 78, 419
zinc, 20–21, 23
zygote, 325